Developmental psychopathology

This important volume integrates interdisciplinary perspectives in the emerging field of developmental psychopathology. It elucidates the discipline's four central characteristics: (1) the use of classical developmental theory and research to inform issues of psychopathology, (2) the use of insights from atypical populations to increase understanding of normal developmental processes, (3) integration of methods and theories from various social science disciplines, and (4) derivation of implications for interventions and social policy.

Developmental Psychopathology describes a range of state-of-the-art research programs, providing multiple illustrations of integrated approaches in studying normal and abnormal development. As a textbook in developmental psychopathology, this volume will be invaluable to students and researchers working in child development, clinical psychology, psychiatry, and related disciplines.

Edward F. Zigler. Photograph by Michael Marsland, courtesy of Yale University, Office of Public Affairs.

Developmental psychopathology

Perspectives on adjustment, risk, and disorder

Edited by

SUNIYA S. LUTHAR
Columbia University

JACOB A. BURACK
McGill University

DANTE CICCHETTI
University of Rochester

JOHN R. WEISZ
University of California, Los Angeles

CAMBRIDGE
UNIVERSITY PRESS

PUBLISHED BY THE PRESS SYNDICATE OF THE UNIVERSITY OF
CAMBRIDGE
The Pitt Building, Trumpington Street, Cambridge, CB2 1RP, United Kingdom

CAMBRIDGE UNIVERSITY PRESS
The Edinburgh Building, Cambridge CB2 2RU, United Kingdom
40 West 20th Street, New York, NY 10011–4211, USA
10 Stamford Road, Oakleigh, Melbourne 3166, Australia

© Cambridge University Press 1997

First published 1997

Printed in the United States of America

Typeset in Times Roman

Library of Congress Cataloging-in-Publication Data
Developmental psychopathology : perspectives on adjustment, risk, and
    disorder / edited by Suniya S. Luthar . . . [et al.].
        p.   cm.
    Includes bibliographical references and index.
    ISBN 0–521–47142–7 (hbk.). – ISBN 0–521–47715–8 (pbk.)
    1. Developmental psychology.   2. Child psychopathology.
    3. Adolescent psychopathology.   4. Psychology, Pathological.
    I. Luthar, Suniya S.
    RJ499.D485   1997
    618.92'89 – dc20   96–26909
                                                            CIP

*A catalog record for this book is available from
the British Library*

ISBN 0–521–47142–7 hardback
ISBN 0–521–47715–8 paperback

Contents

Contributors

Nancy Apfel
Department of Psychology
Yale University
New Haven, CT

Thomas M. Achenbach
Department of Psychiatry
University of Vermont
Burlington, VT

Joseph P. Allen
Department of Psychology
University of Virginia
Charlottesville, VA

W. Todd Bartko
Center for Human Growth and
    Development
University of Michigan
Ann Arbor, MI

Marc H. Bornstein
National Institute of Child Health and
    Human Development
Bethesda, MD

Jacob A. Burack
Department of Educational Psychology
McGill University
Montreal, Quebec

Wanchai Chaiyasit
Child Mental Health Center
Bangkok, Thailand

Dante Cicchetti
Departments of Psychology,
    Psychiatry, and Pediatrics
Mt. Hope Family Center
University of Rochester
Rochester, NY

Donald J. Cohen
Child Study Center
Departments of Pediatrics, Psychology
    and Psychiatry
Yale University
New Haven, CT

Emory L. Cowen
Department of Psychology
University of Rochester
Rochester, NY

Gretta Cushing
Department of Psychiatry
Yale University
New Haven, CT

Samia Dawud-Noursi
Section on Social and Emotional
    Development
National Institute of Child Health and
    Human Development
Bethesda, MD

Kirby Deater-Deckard
Institute of Psychiatry
University of London
London, England

Dania Dialdin
Department of Psychology
Stanford University
Stanford, CA

Michael Drake
Department of Psychology
Stanford University
Stanford, CA

Karen L. Eastman
Department of Psychology
University of California
Los Angeles, CA

Marion Glick
Department of Psychology and Child
    Study Center
Yale University
New Haven, CT

E. Mavis Hetherington
University of Virginia
Charlottesville, VA

Robert M. Hodapp
Graduate School of Education and
    Information Studies
University of California
Los Angeles, CA

Phyllis A. Katz
Institute for Research on Social
    Problems
Boulder, CO

Alan E. Kazdin
Department of Psychology and Child
    Study Center
Yale University
New Haven, CT

Bonnie Klimes-Dougan
Laboratory of Developmental
    Psychology
National Institute of Mental Health
Bethesda, MD

Ami Klin
Child Study Center
Yale University
New Haven, CT

Jennifer A. Kofkin
Institute for Research on Social
    Problems
Boulder, CO

Gabriel P. Kuperminc
Department of Psychology
Yale University
New Haven, CT

Michael E. Lamb
Section on Social and Emotional
    Development
National Institute of Child Health and
    Human Development
Bethesda, MD

Mark R. Lepper
Department of Psychology
Stanford University
Stanford, CA

Suniya S. Luthar
Department of Human Development
Teachers College
Columbia University
New York, NY

Linda C. Mayes
Child Study Center and Department of
    Psychology
Yale University
New Haven, CT

Carolyn A. McCarty
Department of Psychology
University of California
Los Angeles, CA

Thomas J. McMahon
Department of Psychiatry
Yale University
New Haven, CT

Cynthia M. Moore
Department of Psychology
University of Virginia
Charlottesville, VA

Marian Radke-Yarrow
Laboratory of Developmental
    Psychology
National Institute of Mental Health
Bethesda, MD

Fred A. Rogosch
Mt. Hope Family Center
Department of Psychology
University of Rochester
Rochester, NY

Arnold J. Sameroff
Center for Human Growth and
    Development
University of Michigan
Ann Arbor, MI

Sandra Scarr
KinderCare
Montgomery, AL

Ronald Seifer
Department of Psychiatry
Brown University
East Providence, RI

Victoria Seitz
Child Study Center and Department of
    Psychology
Yale University
New Haven, CT

Sheena Sethi
Department of Psychology
Stanford University
Stanford, CA

Kathleen J. Sternberg
Section on Social and Emotional
    Development
National Institute of Child Health and
    Human Development
Bethesda, MD

Deborah Stipek
Graduate School of Education and
    Information Studies
University of California
Los Angeles, CA

Somsong Suwanlert
Child Mental Health Center
Bangkok, Thailand

Sheree L. Toth
Mt. Hope Family Center
Department of Psychology
University of Rochester
Rochester, NY

Penelope K. Trickett
Department of Psychology
University of Southern California
Los Angeles, CA

Fred R. Volkmar
Child Study Center
Departments of Pediatrics and
    Psychology
Yale University
New Haven, CT

John R. Weisz
Department of Psychology
University of California
Los Angeles, CA

William C. Work
Department of Psychology
State University of New York
Brockport, NY

Peter A. Wyman
Department of Psychology
Center for Community Study
University of Rochester
Rochester, NY

Foreword

Child development can be a passionate and intimate science. Nothing is closer to our own lived experiences and deepest concerns than the earliest relationships, the growth of mental life, the vicissitudes of falling in love, and the ways we modulate aggression. Nothing is more threatening than the abuse and neglect of children or more tragic than a child's physical and mental vulnerabilities, illnesses, and disorders. Often, the passion and intimacy of our field is concealed by the scholarly apparatus, but they are clearly present in the best work and teaching.

As the basic underpinning for clinical treatment and intervention, child development relates to all types of emotional and behavioral difficulties, and the roots of a child's troubles and disorders in biology, development, family, and community. These practical concerns give child development a particular urgency: authentic research can make lifesaving differences.

Child development is also a science that closely touches on sensitive political concerns. What parents do with and for their children, how nations and societies view their children's needs and rights, the value and roles of children and adolescents in their families and neighborhoods, and the resources provided for care and education are all deeply related to ideology. Societies prepare their children – implicitly and explicitly – for their adult roles as productive workers, parents, and citizens; societies also lead certain groups of children along quite disadvantaged paths, again more or less consciously and intentionally, depending on one's political point of view. A society's and a nation's commitments to children are deep expressions of history, culture, and politics, and the care of children and how they are equipped for adulthood are the bearers of these values from one epoch to the next.

To understand children as whole people is to appreciate both their minds and their bodies, their individuality in the context of their families, and the trajectories of their lives over the course of years and decades. Increasingly, we see development in even longer time frames of generations, and developmental psychopathology is now the multigenerational, life-course study of the biological and social transmission of the modes and forms of vulnerability and resilience.

While every child is biologically unique and lives in her own distinctive family and neighborhood, the scientific study of children and their families is the search for theories and concepts that clarify regularities and yet respect individuality and surprise. Child developmentalists enjoy continuities in development and yet acknowledge discontinuities, search for rules and general principles and yet delight in children's spontaneity and mysteries, hope for the best for children and yet remain with them when things are at their worst. Child development appreciates the multiple influences in a child's community, family, and biology that shape personality and abilities, and the forces that put them at risk. Nothing in development or in lives is simple, linear, easily predictable (except in retrospect); yet nothing should remain outside the domain of scrutiny. To understand children is to accept and delight in complexity and uncertainty, the role of accidents and good fortune, and the impact of trauma, as well as the remarkable capacity for self-righting.

For Edward Zigler, the scientific study of children has been a lifelong passion. As with other deeply committed thinkers and teachers, his career has been central to his entire being, the backbone of his life. He has thrown himself fully, heart and mind, into the major issues concerning research, practice, and policy in relation to children and families, without concern for his own welfare, health, or personal comfort. In this furnace of effort and belief, he has forged a new field bridging developmental psychopathology and children's social policy, and he has fostered several generations of leading scholars and advocates.

His research has been motivated by two deep, driving forces: the belief that the rigorous study of development can clarify the basic structures of the mind and the equally powerful belief that well-done science and hard data are the best guides for action on behalf of vulnerable children. He knows the power during a congressional debate of even one well-done study, or even a well-intentioned study on a critical issue. Ed's theoretical and methodological interests in the meaning of intelligence, the relations between cognition and personality, the importance of clear methodology in developmental research, the philosophy of science, and other academic topics define a life in scholarship. Nobody has read more broadly, deeply, and critically in child development, or has been more open to the intelligent ideas and good studies of others.

While epistemological and clinical motivations characterize Ed's life work as an investigator, the scientific pursuits have been deeply enriched by a third, and perhaps most highly charged motivation: his zeal for making a difference in this flawed world by small, incremental improvements. While Ed accepts no compromise in scholarship – as any student who has been on the wrong side of a methodological issue or statistical analysis can all too vividly recall – he has demonstrated a fantastic ability for compromise in relation to the politics of child development. He is a virtuoso in finding balance, in discovering an approach that can bring together opposing viewpoints (in which he might also have been a participant) in a shared concern for doing something useful.

Above all, in his distinctively crusty and yet surprisingly sentimental fashion, Ed's abiding concern has been for his students and for transmitting to younger scholars the tradition of child development research. I see in this commitment his most abiding ethnic identification, one that touches back into his earliest childhood and his cultural heritage that so highly values the intrinsic, ethical linkage between learning and teaching, the unique bond between student and rabbi in which souls are transformed.

From early in his career, Ed's work had a distinctive emphasis on bridging between clinic and laboratory, between theory and applications, between normal and atypical development. He has accepted all types of knowledge, derived from many different approaches, and he has championed the belief that serious research that addresses theoretical issues may also have important applications. When others avoided the problems of working with children with developmental disabilities, or saw this as peripheral to the mainstream of academic developmental psychology, Ed not only showed that such work can illuminate normal development but that it also could help improve the lives of children.

Starting as a clinician, he has maintained a clinician's interest in full people, rather than only mechanisms, and in research with a bottom line. He brought to his studies of mental retardation an intuitive understanding of the role of families and of context in children's competence, as well as a sensitivity to the children themselves as full people. Today, we take this orientation for granted. Yet, Ed was among the pioneers – and perhaps the most important figure in the entire field – who revealed that individuals with mental retardation were, first of all, children and adolescents who shared with other children an understandable course of development and whose behavior and thoughts were influenced by the same factors of loving concern and care of committed parents and other adults. He brought the study of mental retardation into the mainstream of the study of child development, with each being enriched by the other. His work on institutions, motivation, personality, and theory of development "humanized" individuals with retardation and placed the spotlight on their socialization and adaptive capacities as well as on their understandable psychological difficulties. This program of research and theorizing has been a continuing theme over the decades and has had a profound impact on all Ed's other work, including his interests in genetics, personality development, intervention, and social policy.

During the 1960s, developmental psychology achieved great intellectual vigor with new theories and methods; was well respected academically and attracted outstanding students and researchers; and, simultaneously, became vitally relevant to the study of social issues and the development of national policy concerning children. Ed's immersion in developmental psychology was multifaceted and responsive to the emergent opportunities. He was among that brilliant generation of academic psychologists who entered public life through their work on motivation and disadvantage, and he quickly became a leading figure and the champion of this cause. His contributions to Head Start are legendary: his vision, honed by science and clinical insights, shaped the entire course of this nation's policies concerning families, children, early intervention, and the role of schools. I consider it one of the privileges of my life to have been with him during these transitions – first as his student (1962–1966) when he was breaking new theoretic ground, then as his special assistant in the Office of Child Development in Washington (1970–1972) when he was shaping Head Start, and then as his younger colleague at Yale (1972 to the present) as he created the field of child social policy and showed how research, teaching, the study of social policy, and advocacy can be synergistic.

Had Ed pursued only one of his many lines of interest as a scholar, teacher, national leader, and policy analyst, he would have had a stellar and productive career. He somehow has managed to integrate all of these facets and more into one lifetime, and to continue to pursue a range of activities – studies, commissions, testimony, teaching, lecturing – with an endless source of energy and spunk.

There are deep paradoxes in Ed's life that add to his distinctive presence in our lives. First of all, he is remarkably private. In spite of his innumerable public presentations and lectures, his decades of teaching and mentoring, his thousands of informal meetings with parents, administrators, children, and colleagues, he is intensely private. His personal life and ambitions are marginal: His public beliefs and commitments are where he wishes the spotlight to focus. Second, at his core, he is remarkably untouched by acclaim. While he has received all the honors that the world can bestow on a scholar and public leader and he is very much at home in the world of academia, with hundreds of famous papers and books, he remains the tough, hardworking young man who has to make it on his own terms, battling adversities that would ground anyone else. Even when he is at the center of national power, he is a rebel. And thus there is particular joy when this seriously private scholar captures an important moment and his own role in some historic event in a charming, ethnic, self-depreciating observation: This capacity for bittersweet humor is a great source of resilience in a tough world.

To argue with Ed Zigler and be the victim of his sharply critical, immensely knowledgeable critiques has been a formative and formidable force in the lives of hundreds of students. They have benefited from the painful knowledge that they were being taken seriously, and being forced to develop their fullest potentials. To experience Ed's parental affections has been among life's goodness for many of the contributors to this volume, and untold hundreds of other students, colleagues, and friends. Those, like myself, who have experienced both the intellectual rigors and the enduring kindness have been blessed.

Donald J. Cohen, M.D.

Preface

Developmental psychopathology, a rapidly emerging scientific discipline, is characterized by attempts to understand psychopathology from within the framework of normative developmental psychology. Over the past two decades, this domain of inquiry has received increasing recognition as a distinct field. For example, three leading scientific journals published one or more special issues on this area during the 1980s, and more recently a journal entitled *Development and Psychopathology*, devoted exclusively to issues in this domain, was introduced.

Parameters of developmental psychopathology

Perhaps the most fundamental feature that defines the domain of developmental psychopathology – and that sets it apart from other areas such as developmental and clinical psychology – is its integrative nature, wherein principles from classical developmental theory are applied in investigating clinical and psychiatric phenomena (Cicchetti, 1984, 1990, 1993; Rutter, 1986; Rutter & Garmezy, 1983; Santostefano & Baker, 1972; Sroufe & Rutter, 1984; Zigler & Glick, 1986). This integration of perspectives is invaluable not only because it promotes our understanding of atypical development, but also because it illuminates theories of normative developmental processes (Burack, Chapter 7, this volume; Cicchetti, 1984; Hodapp & Burack, 1990; Sroufe, 1990). To illustrate, applications of developmental theories such as those of Piaget, Werner, and Erikson provide vital insights into the causes and the organization of different forms of maladaptation (Weisz & Zigler, 1979; Zigler & Glick, 1986). Conversely, studies of pathology, and those of resilience – the maintenance of positive adaptation despite adversity – each enhance our knowledge of normal development, particularly in the context of individual differences in development and in risk and protective processes associated with different types of outcomes (Luthar, 1993, 1995; Masten, Best, & Garmezy, 1990; Rutter, 1987).

Although developmental and clinical psychology constitute two fields that are integral to developmental psychopathology, the scope of this integrative discipline is by no means restricted to these areas. On the contrary, the attempt is to integrate theory and methodology from each of these domains with perspectives from other areas of scientific enquiry, such as epidemiology, biology, and sociology. Such multidomain, multicontextual measurement strategies are a prerequisite in moving toward the long-term goal of a more comprehensive understanding of the development of psychopathology.

A final feature of developmental psychopathology is that it strives to bridge the frequently wide span between empirical research and the application of knowledge to at-risk and clinical populations (Achenbach, Chapter 5, this volume; Zigler, 1980, in press). Investigators working within this tradition are able to design and implement intervention programs that are based in theory and are developmentally appropriate. For example, specific directions for preventive interventions have been obtained from data indicating associations between early developmental deviations and "full-blown" psychopathology in subsequent years (Cicchetti & Toth, 1992; Zigler, Taussig, & Black, 1992), and developmental research and theory have much to offer those who design interventions for behavioral and emotional dysfunction (Weisz, Chapter 1, this volume; Weisz & Weiss, 1989).

To summarize, then, four central or defining characteristics of the field of developmental psychopathology are (1) the use of classical developmental theory and research to inform issues of psychopathology, (2) the use of insights from at-risk or atypical populations to increase our understanding of normal developmental processes, (3) integration of developmental and clinical perspectives with those from other scientific disciplines, and (4) the derivation of implications for preventive and therapeutic interventions, and for social policy.

Dissemination and training

The freshness, vitality, and promise of the emerging field of developmental psychopathology conjointly highlight the value of concerted training efforts in this area. Given its integrative nature, this discipline fosters the development of unique research strategies that can yield rich contributions across diverse areas of inquiry. Since this is still an emerging scientific domain, there is a need for systematic training of current and future researchers in the tenets of developmental psychopathology, and in their application across different areas of risk and psychopathology (Achenbach, 1990; Cicchetti & Toth, 1991).

The teaching of any new and complex way of thinking is most effectively accomplished when the central principles are elucidated in diverse contexts; it is this premise that has shaped the design and development of essays in this volume. Current theoretical perspectives and state-of-the art research findings are presented across various domains of adjustment, risk, and disorder, with each presentation elucidating the major principles of developmental psychopathology. The integration of themes across chapters constitutes an important extension of previous efforts. Although the many scientific articles published in the past two decades have provided a beginning awareness about developmental psychopathology among professionals from other disciplines, these reports have varied in how completely they have clarified the different tenets of developmental psychopathology. For example, although the specific applications of developmental theory to studying pathology are generally fairly evident, lessons gleaned from research on atypical populations for developmental theory, as well as for applications in developing age-appropriate preventive interventions, are typically less clearly articulated.

In sum, the integrative approach adopted in this volume reflects an effort to foster the in-depth understanding of the tenets of developmental psychopathology within a scaffold of diverse state-of-the-art research efforts. This series of papers could facilitate comprehension of not only the broad potential contributions of developmental psychopathology, but also, more specifically, of ways in which this perspective might be applied within particular areas of research, thinking, or clinical practice.

Structure of this volume

Chapters in this volume are presented in four parts. The first focuses on individual differences and their implications for adaptation and maladjustment, including efforts to classify and alleviate maladjustment. The content of this part illustrates how core developmental theory and research may enrich our understanding of risk, dysfunction, and intervention in diverse psychosocial domains.

Parts II, III, and IV focus on specific areas of risk, and all chapters in these parts revolve around the four defining characteristics of developmental psychopathology: the application of developmental theories in studying atypical development, insights from vulnerable populations that aid understanding of normal development, interface across scientific disciplines, and implications of findings for interventions and social policy. Chapters in Part II focus on risks associated with specific forms of psychopathology such as mental retardation or depressive disorders. Part III covers risks associated with the "macrosystem" (e.g., culture), the "microsystem" (the family), and "ontogenic factors" (individual factors such as biology or temperament). The interplay among all these levels of risk is examined in Part IV, within the broad context of "exosystemic" (or community-level) risks associated with sociodemographic disadvantages.

The first chapter in each of the four parts provides an overview in which the emergence of the specific area is examined in relation to the expansion of developmental theory and research. The remaining chapters present descriptions of research programs led by contributing authors. Given the unifying framework within which all chapters in this volume are structured, collectively they richly illuminate the use of multidisciplinary, developmentally based approaches in understanding risk and psychopathology.

Dedication

This volume has been compiled as a tribute to a visionary in the field of developmental psychopathology, Edward Zigler, whose own research has been pioneering in the emphasis on studying the child as a whole person. Ed's work over the past three decades represents a primary impetus in the post-Piagetian emergence of an expanded approach to developmental psychology.

Chapters in this volume provide but a glimpse into the breadth of scholarly efforts that have been influenced by Ed's thinking. Notably underrepresented in this book, for example, are the many changes in social policy that Ed has pioneered, in the realms of Head Start, day care, and schools of the twenty-first century (Zigler, 1989; Zigler, Finn-Stevenson, & Marsland, 1995; Zigler & Lang, 1991; Zigler & Muenchow, 1991). Even given our restricted focus on empirical efforts in developmental psychopathology, this compilation of works is far from complete. To present the work of the many researchers whose research has been strongly influenced by Ed would require several such volumes.

Ed's contributions to the professional development of many is apparent in this and myriad other publications; what is less well known – except to those who have worked closely with him – is what an extraordinary human being he is. On the outside, Ed is an awe-inspiring, even intimidating figure. However, those well acquainted with him know that at a personal level, he is among the kindest, most gentle and compassionate of individuals. His loyalty to anyone he takes into his fold is unquestioning and unwavering. As an intellectual mentor, he pushes people to strive for their very best. Equally important, he shares with magnanimity and personal interest important events – marriages, births, jobs, and honors – and, with genuine concern and compassion, any crises that occur in the lives of his students and colleagues.

In a recent moment of reminiscences, Ed reflected about the major areas of his life's work – his research, his social policy initiatives, his time in Washington, and his role as an educator and mentor. In ending the conversation, he said, "D'you know, of all the things I've done in my career, the thing that's been most important to me – that I've felt most proud of – is mentoring my students? You young people, my students, have been so important to me throughout my life. I hope you know that."

We do, Ed. Here are reflections by some whose lives you have touched, on what you have meant to them.

> Although my specific research interests and Ed's have diverged over the years, it would be hard to overestimate the important influence that Ed has had, as a mentor and friend. Like Kurt Lewin in an earlier era, Ed Zigler has always been that most unusual of combinations – both a theoretician's theoretician and a practitioner's practitioner, in short, a practical theorist. His combination of hardheaded theory and rigorous experimental work with a deep humanistic concern and compassion

for the disadvantaged and the disenfranchised in our society will remain a model for generations to come. We owe him more than we can tell.

– Mark Lepper, Stanford University

Nearly two decades since receiving my degree I still find myself pausing mid-sentence in a lecture or conversation, suddenly realizing that Ed Zigler's words are coming out of my mouth. I hear myself cautioning graduate students, who can't wait to tell policy makers what to do, to learn first to be good scientists – to earn rather than demand their attention. I hear myself encouraging them to be advocates as well as observers of children, but to do so in a professionally and scientifically responsible way. I hear myself encouraging colleagues not to be shy about sharing what they know with policy makers and practitioners – maintaining that however limited or imperfect their knowledge might be, it is better than none at all. There are many other Ziglerisms that I find myself repeating, albeit less eloquently than Ed. When I am aware, I am reminded of how profoundly the man has influenced my own thinking – about science, about social policy, and about life. Ed is a model and an inspiration for his students and colleagues who, without his example, would be less able to persevere for the goals he has instilled.

– Deborah Stipek, University of California at Los Angeles

It is sobering to reflect on how the world might have been different if in carving out his career trajectory, Ed had heeded the advice of many well-wishers and relatives. His wife Bernice's Aunt Blumkin was concerned, for example, about how Ed would support Bernice once they were married. So she offered him a job at her furniture store in Kansas City. Ed replied to Aunt Blumkin, "What do I know about selling furniture?!!" To this she observed, "That doesn't matter, Eddie, because you got an ounce brains. I need someone with an ounce brains."

Aunt Blumkin – now over 100 years old – was extraordinarily successful with this philosophy, and she and her furniture company are still thriving. Ed, however, chose another course. He put his "ounce brains" – along with his integrity of character, tenacity of spirit, and vision of the future – into academia and social policy. His decision was a very fortunate one for those of us who have been his colleagues and students. He never did tell us, though, how Aunt Blumkin feels about his choice.

– Nancy Apfel and Vicki Seitz, Yale University

Ed Zigler holds a special place in my life – simultaneously a mentor and an example. In helping me develop from a (very green) postdoctoral student to an independent contributor, Ed has provided me opportunities, guidance, and encouragement on countless projects. At the same time, he has modeled how one deals with colleagues and students and how one handles success and setbacks (yes, even Ed has setbacks – he just works tenaciously to overcome them). He shows that through hard work and passion for a cause, one can succeed *and* make a contribution. Ed's contribution – to me, to others in the field, and to society at large – is almost beyond measure. Ed is truly an incredible person.

– Robert Hodapp, University of California at Los Angeles

And from the elders, your colleagues:

Over the years, Ed has wholeheartedly swung into action whenever the well-being of America's children was at stake. After the Johnson years, when Head Start was no longer a presidential priority, many soldiers of the War on Poverty left the field. Not Ed. Against the advice of some of his academic and scientific colleagues, he chose not only to join the battle, but also to lead it as director of both the Children's Bureau and the Agency for Children, Youth, and Families. It was about this time that Ed received the G. Stanley Hall Award of the American Psychological Society for excellence in research. As the presenter of the award on that occasion, I could not resist reminding the assembled researchers of his unwavering *dual* commitment by quoting Tom Paine: "The summer soldier and the sunshine patriot will, in this crisis, shrink from the service of their country." Not Ed; not once, during the four decades that he has fought on behalf of children and families in America.

— Urie Bronfenbrenner, Cornell University

For over thirty years, Ed Zigler has been a cherished colleague and dear friend. His contributions to child development theory and research, and to improving the lives of thousands of children and families in America, are immeasurable. Today and always, Ed has my deepest respect, regard, and personal affection.

— Norman Garmezy, University of Minnesota

Ed Zigler is a remarkable psychologist and a remarkable person. He has made powerful, career-long contributions both in the academic world, as teacher, conceptualizer, and scientist par excellence, and in the "real world," as leader and as steadfast contributor to the formulation of policies and implementation of programs for advancing the wellness of children and families. He embodies a unique blend of sound theory, sound research, and sound practices in his continuing efforts to further the socially vital goal of wholesome development in children. His constructive impact in this sphere has been nothing short of enormous. Behind all this is a no-frills, no-nonsense, honest, fair, up-front, and caring person who has, tenaciously and successfully, engaged the daunting challenge of enhancing children's development. We stand in awe of, and in debt to, Ed Zigler, for these extraordinary accomplishments.

— Emory Cowen, University of Rochester

Sentiments such as these are shared by scores of your students and colleagues, Ed. From all of us, and from the many children and families for whom your work and advocacy efforts have made such a significant difference, our deepest and most heartfelt appreciation. You have been an inspiration to us all.

Suniya S. Luthar
Jacob A. Burack
Dante Cicchetti
John R. Weisz

References

Achenbach, T. M. (1990). What is developmental about developmental psychopathology? In J. Rolf, A. S. Masten, D. Cicchetti, K. H. Nuechterlein, & S. Weintraub (Eds.), *Risk and protective factors in the development of psychopathology* (pp. 29–48). New York: Cambridge University Press.

Cicchetti, D. (1984). The emergence of developmental psychopathology. *Child Development, 55*, 1–7.

Cicchetti, D. (1990). An historical perspective on the discipline of developmental psychopathology. In J. Rolf, A. S. Masten, D. Cicchetti, K. H. Nuechterlein, & S. Weintraub (Eds.), *Risk and protective factors in the development of psychopathology* (pp. 2–28). New York: Cambridge University Press.

Cicchetti, D. (1993). Developmental psychopathology: Reactions, reflections, projections. *Developmental Review, 13*, 471–502.

Cicchetti, D., & Toth, S. L. (1991). The making of a developmental psychopathologist. In D. Cantor,

C. Spiker, & L. Lipsitt (Eds.), *Child behavior and development: Training for diversity* (pp. 34–72). Norwood, NJ: Ablex.

Cicchetti D., & Toth S. L. (Eds.). (1992). Special issue: Developmental approaches to prevention and intervention. *Development and Psychopathology, 4* (4), 489–728.

Hodapp, R. M., & Burack, J. A. (1990). What mental retardation teaches us about typical development: The examples of sequences, rates, and cross-domain relations. *Development and Psychopathology, 2,* 213–225.

Luthar, S. S. (1993). Annotation: Methodological and conceptual issues in research on childhood resilience. *Journal of Child Psychology and Psychiatry, 34,* 441–453.

Luthar, S. S. (1995). Social competence in the school setting: Prospective cross-domain associations among inner-city teens. *Child Development, 66,* 416–429.

Masten, A. S., Best, K. M., & Garmezy, N. (1990). Resilience and development: Contributions from the study of children who overcome adversity. *Development and Psychopathology, 2,* 425–444.

Rutter, M. (1986). Child psychiatry: The interface between clinical and developmental research. *Psychological Medicine, 16,* 151–169.

Rutter, M. (1987). Psychosocial resilience and protective mechanisms. *American Journal of Orthopsychiatry, 57,* 316–331.

Rutter, M., & Garmezy, N. (1983). Developmental psychopathology. In P. Mussen (Ed.), *Handbook of child psychology* (4th ed., pp. 775–911). New York: Wiley.

Santostefano, S., & Baker, A. H. (1972). The contribution of developmental psychology. In B. Wolman (Ed.), *Manual of child psychopathology* (pp. 1113–1153). New York: McGraw-Hill.

Sroufe, L. A. (1990). Considering normal and abnormal together: The essence of developmental psychopathology. *Development and Psychopathology, 2,* 335–347.

Sroufe, L. A., & Rutter, M. (1984). The domain of developmental psychopathology. *Child Development, 55,* 17–29.

Weisz, J. R., & Weiss, B. (1989). Cognitive mediators of the outcome of psychotherapy with children. In B. B. Lahey & A. E. Kazdin (Eds.), *Advances in clinical child psychology* (Vol. 18, pp. 27–52). New York: Plenum Press.

Weisz, J. R., & Zigler, E. (1979). Cognitive development in retarded and non-retarded persons: Piagetian tests of the similar-sequence hypothesis. *Psychological Bulletin, 86,* 831–851.

Zigler, E. (1980). Welcoming a new journal. *Journal of Applied Developmental Psychology, 1,* 1–6.

Zigler, E. (1989). Addressing the nation's child care crisis: The school of the twenty-first century. *American Journal of Orthopsychiatry, 59,* 484–491.

Zigler, E. (in press). Child development and social policy. *Child Development.*

Zigler, E. F., Finn-Stevenson, M., & Marsland, K. W. (1995). Child day care in the schools: The school of the 21st century. *Child Welfare, 74,* (6), 1301–1326.

Zigler, E., & Glick, M. (1986). *A developmental approach to adult psychopathology.* New York: Wiley.

Zigler, E. F., & Lang, M. E. (1991). *Child care choices: Balancing the needs of children, families, and society.* New York: Free Press.

Zigler, E. F., & Muenchow, S. (1992). *Head Start: The inside story of America's most successful educational experiment.* New York: Basic Books.

Zigler, E., Taussig, C., & Black, K. (1992). Early childhood intervention: A promising preventative for juvenile delinquency. *American Psychologist, 47,* 997–1006.

Part I

Individual differences: Implications for adaptation and maladjustment

1 Effects of interventions for child and adolescent psychological dysfunction: Relevance of context, developmental factors, and individual differences

John R. Weisz

A core principle of developmental psychopathology is that theory and research on individual differences in human development may be used to inform intervention for dysfunction. This informing function is variously illustrated in the collective works of Edward Zigler, to whom this volume is dedicated. Much of his career has been devoted to studies of individual differences that have important intervention implications, and to the development of major intervention programs. His studies of mental retardation (see Zigler & Balla, 1982; Zigler & Hodapp, 1986) have influenced interventions in special education programs and residential settings throughout this country and beyond. His research and theory bringing a developmental perspective to adult psychopathology (see Zigler & Glick, 1986) have influenced the ways countless mental health professionals construe and conduct their work. And his work on the development, and subsequent evaluation of Head Start (see Zigler & Muenchow, 1992) is certainly one of the most massive applications of developmental theory and research to social intervention in American history. In these and other ways, Ed Zigler has demonstrated that theory and research can be used to improve the lives of people at risk.

In the present chapter, this notion is applied to the study of interventions for children and adolescents with behavioral, emotional, and mental health problems. I review research findings on psychotherapy effects with young people, offering a critique of the field from a developmental perspective, and a number of suggestions for future work. The suggestions are aimed at making child psychotherapy research (1) more relevant to actual clinical practice, (2) more closely connected to core developmental research and theory, and (3) more sensitive to individual difference factors, such as those featured in this initial section of the book. Throughout this chapter, the term ''children'' will represent the age period from early childhood

The research program described in this chapter was supported through a Research Scientist Award (K05 MH01161) and research grants (R01 MH34210, R01 MH38450, R01 MH38240) from the National Institute of Mental Health, which I gratefully acknowledge. I also appreciate the important contributions made to this work by faculty and graduate student colleagues, clinic administrators and therapists, and the many children and parents who have participated in the research before, during, and after treatment.

3

through adolescence, except where we need to draw a distinction between children and adolescents.

Scope of the problem: Prevalence of child dysfunction and use of psychotherapy

Although there are vast individual differences in patterns of dysfunction, many children suffer from some significant behavioral, emotional, or mental health problem. Several epidemiologic studies in the late 1980s (all summarized by Costello, 1989) found that at least 17% of children and adolescents in the general population met criteria for at least one diagnosis in the official diagnostic manual of the time, the *Diagnostic and Statistical Manual of Mental Disorders,* 3rd edition (DSM-III; American Psychiatric Association, 1980); preliminary findings suggest that prevalence rates will be considerably higher for the most recent diagnostic manual. And, of course, many children who do not qualify for a formal diagnosis have very significant problems. Not all disturbed children receive psychotherapy, but many do. The most recent estimates available indicate that about 2.5 million American children receive treatment each year (Office of Technology Assessment, 1986), and that the annual cost in this country alone is more than $1.5 billion (Institute of Medicine, 1989). Just how effective is the treatment received by so many children at such great cost?

State of the field: Experimental evidence on child psychotherapy effects

Our answers to this question come primarily from clinical trials, outcome studies in which measures of behavioral and psychological functioning are used to compare a treatment group of children who received an intervention with a control group who did not. In addition to testing the significance of group differences posttreatment, investigators may also compute *effect size* (ES), an index of the magnitude and direction of treatment effects. For typical outcome studies, the ES is the posttreatment mean for the treated group on an outcome measure minus the mean for the control group, divided by the standard deviation (SD) of the outcome measure. Figure 1.1 is a guide to interpreting ES values. As the figure shows, ES values may be positive, indicating treatment benefit, or negative, indicating a detrimental treatment effect. Each ES corresponds to a percentile standing of the average treated child on the outcome measure(s) if that child were placed in the control group after treatment; for example, an ES of 0.50 would indicate that the average treated child scored better after treatment than 69% of the control group. Finally, note that Cohen's (1992) guidelines suggest that an ES of 0.20 should be considered a "small" effect, 0.50 a "medium" effect, and 0.80 a "large" effect.

Experimental findings on psychotherapy effects can be pooled in metaanalyses (see Mann, 1990; Smith, Glass, & Miller, 1980), using ES as the unit of analysis.

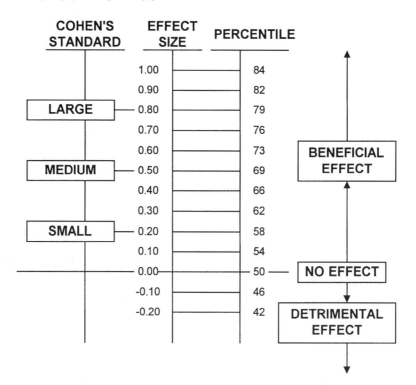

Figure 1.1. An aid to interpreting effect size (ES) statistics. Each ES value can be thought of as reflecting a corresponding percentile value (i.e., the percentile standing of the average treated child, after treatment, averaging across outcome measures, relative to the untreated group). *Source:* Weisz, J. R., Donenberg, G. R., Han, S. S., & Weiss, B. (1995). Bridging the gap between laboratory and clinic in child and adolescent psychotherapy. *Journal of Consulting and Clinical Psychology, 63,* 688–701. Copyright 1995 by the American Psychological Association. Reprinted with permission.

Typically, a single mean ES is computed for each study (or each treatment group) in the collection to be reviewed, by averaging across the various outcome measures. This makes it possible to compute an overall mean ES for the entire collection of studies, and to compare mean ES for studies differing in potentially important ways – for example, type of therapy employed, target problem being treated, age or gender of the children involved.

Findings of broad-based metaanalyses of child psychotherapy research

There have been four broad-based child therapy metaanalyses – that is, meta-analyses in which a variety of treated problems and types of intervention were included. Together, these four metaanalyses encompass more than 300 individual treatment outcome studies. Casey and Berman (1985) surveyed outcome studies published between 1952 and 1983, and focused on children aged 12 and younger.

Mean ES was 0.71 for the studies that included treatment-control comparisons; the average treated child scored better after treatment than 76% of control group children, averaging across outcome measures. Weisz, Weiss, Alicke, and Klotz (1987) reviewed outcome studies published between 1952 and 1983, and including children aged 4–18. The mean ES was 0.79; after treatment, the average treated child was at the 79th percentile of control group peers. Kazdin, Bass, Ayers, and Rodgers (1990) surveyed studies published between 1970 and 1988, including youngsters aged 4–18. For studies that compared treatment groups and *no-treatment control groups,* the mean ES was 0.88, indicating that the average treated child was better off after treatment than 81% of the no-treatment youngsters. For studies in the Kazdin et al. collection that involved treatment groups versus *active control groups,* the mean ES was 0.77, indicating that after treatment the average treated child was functioning better than 78% of the control group. Finally, a recent metaanalysis by Weisz, Weiss, Han, Granger, and Morton (1995), included studies published between 1967 and 1993, and involved children aged 2–18. Mean ES was 0.71, indicating that, after treatment, the average treated child was functioning better than 76% of control group children. (For more detailed descriptions of the procedures and findings of the various metaanalyses, see Weisz & Weiss, 1993.)

The evidence from these four broad-based metaanalyses shows rather consistent positive treatment effects; ES values ranged from 0.71 to 0.84 (estimated overall mean for Kazdin et al., 1990), near Cohen's (1992) threshold of 0.80 for a ''large'' effect. Figure 1.2 summarizes findings from the four child metaanalyses and compares them to findings from two often-cited metaanalyses with older groups – Smith and Glass's (1977) analysis of predominantly adult psychotherapy outcome studies, and Shapiro and Shapiro's (1982) analysis of exclusively adult psychotherapy outcome studies. The figure shows that mean effects found in child metaanalyses fall roughly within the range of the mean effects found in these two adult metaanalyses.

Beyond overall mean ES values, metaanalyses may also generate estimates of the impact of various factors of interest on treatment outcome. Such comparative estimates need to be carried out and interpreted with caution because of the confounding among factors that is common in metaanalyses. Some, but not all, of the confounding can be addressed via statistical control, and testing of interaction effects (see, e.g., Weisz et al., 1987; Weisz, Weiss, et al., 1995). In the two metaanalyses from our lab (Weisz et al., 1987; Weiss, Donenberg, Han, & Weiss 1995), studies involving behavioral treatments (e.g., behavioral contracting, modeling, cognitive-behavioral therapy) generated larger effects than studies using nonbehavior treatments (e.g., insight-oriented therapy, client-centered counseling). (The Casey-Berman [1985] metaanalyses showed the same effect, at $p = 0.06$; Kazdin et al. [1990] did not make this comparison.) By contrast, with minor exceptions (see Casey & Berman, 1985, pp. 392–393), metaanalyses have not found treatment outcomes to differ reliably for different types of treated problems (e.g., internalizing vs. externalizing). The relation between age and treatment outcome has been variable across metaanalyses. However, the metaanalysis of the most recent collection of studies (Weisz, Weiss, et al.,

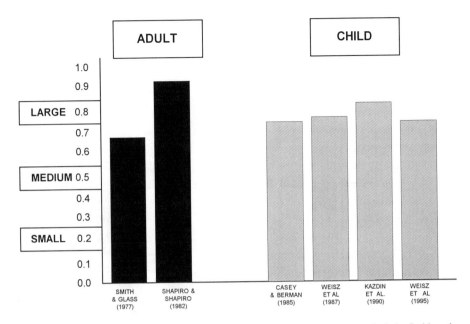

Figure 1.2. Mean effect sizes found in the predominantly adult metaanalysis by Smith and Glass (1977), in the exclusively adult metaanalysis by Shapiro and Shapiro (1982), and in four broad-based metaanalyses of psychotherapy outcome studies with children and adolescents. *Source:* Weisz, J. R., Donenberg, G. R., Han, S. S., & Weiss, B (1995). Bridging the gap between laboratory and clinic in child and adolescent psychotherapy. *Journal of Consulting and Clinical Psychology, 63,* 688–701. Copyright 1995 by the American Psychological Association. Reprinted with permission.

1995) found mean ES to be larger for adolescents than for children. That main effect was qualified by the age × gender interaction shown in Figure 1.3; mean ES for samples of predominantly or exclusively adolescent girls was twice as large as mean ES for adolescent boys and for children of both genders. Perhaps this recent collection of treatments fits the characteristics and needs of adolescent girls particularly well, but other interpretations are certainly possible.

Two other metaanalytic findings should be noted here. First, we have found in both our metaanalyses (Weisz et al., 1987; Weisz, Weiss, et al., 1995) that treatment effects immediately after treatment ends are strikingly similar to effects measured at follow-up assessments, which average about 6 months after treatment termination. This suggests that treatment benefits tend to be quite durable, at least within typical follow-up time frames.

A second finding (from Weisz, Weiss, et al., 1995) concerns specificity of treatment effects. Because children differ markedly from one another in the problems they present, and because various therapies differ from one another in the problems they are designed to address, it is useful to know whether these individual differences matter with respect to treatment outcome. Some (e.g., Frank, 1973) have

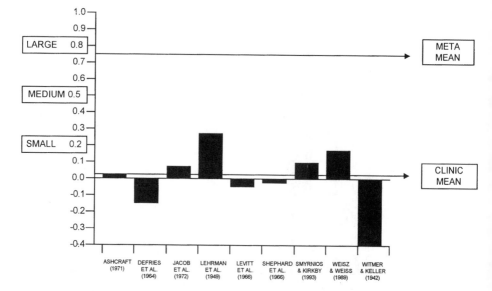

Figure 1.3. Estimated effect sizes for nine studies of clinic-based psychotherapy with children and adolescents. Horizontal arrows show mean effect size for four broad based metaanalyses of laboratory outcome studies (*top*), and averaging across the nine clinic-based studies (*bottom*). *Source:* Weisz, J. R., Donenberg, G. R., Han, S. S., & Weiss, B (1995). Bridging the gap between laboratory and clinic in child and adolescent psychotherapy. *Journal of Consulting and Clinical Psychology, 63*, 688–701. Copyright 1995 by the American Psychological Association. Reprinted with permission.

proposed that psychotherapy has general, "nonspecific" effects – for example, helping people with a variety of problems through such unfocused means as enhancing feelings of being understood or inducing expectations of relief. An alternative perspective is that therapies help in specific ways, having their most marked influence on the particular problems toward which they are directed. We sought to address this issue by assessing whether treatment effect sizes were larger for the specific problem domains targeted by a treatment than for other, more incidental domains. For example, we asked whether a treatment designed to reduce anxiety produced bigger changes in anxiety levels than in related but more peripheral problems such as depression. In comparisons like these, our analyses showed that effect sizes were about twice as large for the specific problems targeted in treatment as for related but untargeted problems. This suggests that psychotherapies for children are not just producing global good feelings that influence diverse outcomes equally; instead, the treatments appear to be rather precise and focused in their effects.

In sum, the evidence from metaanalyses, encompassing more than 300 studies, points to positive and durable effects of mental health interventions for a variety of child problems. In important ways, child psychotherapy research is thriving. However, even a healthy enterprise can be improved, and in this spirit I want to

Table 1.1. *Some common characteristics of research therapy and clinic therapy*

Research therapy	Clinic therapy
Recruited cases (less severe, study volunteers)	Clinic-referred cases (more severe, some coerced into treatment)
Homogeneous groups	Heterogeneous groups
Narrow or single-problem focus	Broad, multiproblem focus
Treatment in lab, school settings	Treatment in clinic, hospital settings
Researchers as therapists	Professional career therapists
Very small caseloads	Very large caseloads
Heavy pretherapy preparation for therapists	Little/light pretherapy preparation for therapists
Preplanned, highly structured treatment (manualized)	Flexible, adjustable treatment (no treatment manual)
Monitoring of therapist behavior	Little monitoring of therapist behavior
Behavioral methods (e.g., operant, respondent, modeling, CBT)	Nonbehavioral methods (e.g., psychodynamic, eclectic)

offer a three-part critique, with three sets of suggestions for improving research on child psychotherapy.

Critique: I. Limited attention to effectiveness in clinical contexts

One criticism of research in the field is that it has not focused sufficiently on the effectiveness of interventions with real clinical populations in real clinical settings. Most of the 300-plus studies included in the metaanalyses (particularly the recent and behavioral studies) appear to have involved children, interventions, and/or treatment conditions that are not very representative of conventional clinical practice. In many of these studies, (a) youngsters were recruited for treatment and were not actual clinic cases; (b) samples were selected for homogeneity, with therapy addressing one or two focal problems (e.g., a specific phobia); (c) therapists received concentrated pretherapy training in the specific intervention techniques they would use; and/or (d) the therapy involved primary or exclusive adherence to those specific techniques. In addition, (e) therapy was often highly structured, frequently guided by a manual and/or monitored for its adherence to a treatment plan.

These features of the experimental studies tend to coalesce around a genre that we refer to as *research therapy,* a genre that differs in a number of ways from conventional *clinic therapy.* Table 1.1 summarizes some of the most common differences between the two genres. Certainly no single feature listed in the table under research therapy is present in all laboratory outcome studies, nor is any single feature listed under clinic therapy present in all clinic-based treatment. However, differences between therapy in clinics and therapy in outcome studies are common enough that one might reasonably ask whether the positive outcomes that have been demonstrated in the research therapy studies, and summarized in the meta-analyses here, are representative of the outcomes achieved in actual clinical practice with children.

Evidence on the effects of clinic therapy

To address this question, we carried out an extensive search (described in Weisz, Donenberg, Han, & Weiss, 1995) for published outcome studies focused on what might fairly be called clinic therapy. We aimed for studies that involved treatment of clinic-referred (i.e., not recruited or "analog") youngsters; treatment in service-oriented clinics or clinical agencies, not in research settings (e.g., not a university lab or a school); therapy conducted by practicing clinicians (as opposed to, say, research assistants); and therapy done as a part of the regular service-related program of the clinic, not primarily for research. We required that the studies involve direct comparison between youngsters who received treatment and a control group who received none or a placebo condition.

The search taught us an important lesson: Clinic studies that meet the criteria outlined above are very rare. We had done one such study (Weisz & Weiss, 1989), but we found only eight others (spanning 50 years) that seemed to fit, and most of these had been published years ago. The studies all compared treatment and control groups, but via several different methodologies (for details, see Weiss, Donenberg, Han, & Weiss, 1995). To summarize findings of these nine studies for comparison with the metaanalytic evidence, we computed, for each of the nine studies, an ES or ES estimate (for reports that did not include the statistics needed for standard ES calculation, we used estimation procedures described by Smith et al., 1980, and Glass, McGaw, & Smith, 1981). As shown in Figure 1.4, the ES values ranged from -0.40 to $+0.29$, with the mean ES of the nine clinic studies (0.01) well below the mean ES of the four broad-band metaanalyses discussed earlier (0.77). This evidence obviously suggests that the outcomes of clinic therapy may be less positive than the outcomes of research therapy.

Next steps: Bridging the gap between laboratory and clinic

The agenda for future research on this issue needs to include at least three elements, in my view. First, we need a much richer base of information on the outcomes of treatment under representative clinical conditions. Carrying out research of this type is challenging, but certainly not impossible, as the nine studies shown in Figure 1.4 demonstrate (a discussion of the pros and cons of various methods is available in Weisz & Weiss, 1993). We certainly need to know more about psychotherapy effects in public clinics. And, to the best of my knowledge, there is currently no methodologically sound study of treatment effects in such common treatment con-

Figure 1.4. Mean effect size for samples of predominantly male and female children (11 years of age and younger) and adolescents (12 years and older). *Source:* Weisz, J. R., Weiss, B., Han, S. S., Granger, D. A., & Morton, T. (1995). Effects of psychotherapy with children and adolescents revisited: A meta-analysis of treatment outcome studies. *Psychological Bulletin, 117,* 450–468. Copyright 1995 by the American Psychological Association. Reprinted with permission.

figurations as individual and group private practice and HMOs. We need evidence on the child outcomes associated with these forms of practice if we are to know how outcomes across the range of today's clinic therapies compare with the outcomes achieved via laboratory interventions.

Second, we need research aimed at identifying factors that may account for the difference between the strong positive effects of therapy in laboratory studies and the thus-far weak effects of treatment in clinic settings. We have addressed this question in two studies (Weisz, Donenberg, Han, & Kauneckis, 1995; Weisz, Donenberg, Han, & Weiss, 1995). In both, we used our metaanalytic data sets to assess which, if any, of the factors that distinguish research therapy from clinic therapy (e.g., clinic vs. lab or school setting for therapy, analog sample vs. clinic-referred children) might account for substantial variance in treatment outcome. In our most recent look at this question, using our most compete sample (Weisz, Donenberg, Han, & Weiss, 1995), we examined eight factors that distinguish lab and clinic treatment, and we found that two were significantly related to treatment outcome: (1) Children receiving behavioral treatments fared better than those receiving nonbehavioral interventions, and (2) analog cases had better outcomes than children with problems serious enough to warrant clinic referral. The first finding suggests the possibility that effects of clinic treatment might be enhanced if more behavioral treatments were used in those settings; recent evidence does indicate that behavioral therapies are not the first choice of most practitioners (see Kazdin, Siegel, & Bass, 1990). The second finding suggests that even lab-tested treatment methods may be less successful in treating truly clinic-referred children than in treating the less disturbed children who are more often the subjects in lab studies.

Third, we need a new genre of treatment outcome research, research that involves taking empirically supported treatments out of the laboratories where they were developed and testing them in the crucible of clinical practice. Several investigators have taken steps in this direction – for example, by treating truly disturbed children in university-based lab clinics (see, e.g., Kendall, 1994; Lovaas, 1987). However, more complete efforts to incorporate lab-tested treatments into clinical practice, and to test their effects, may be needed before we can know just how exportable the experimentally derived treatment methods are, and what modifications will be needed to make them work with seriously disturbed children.

Critique: II. Limited attention to developmental factors

A second broad concern about current research on psychotherapy with children is that it has been conducted in relative isolation from developmental psychology. Despite heavy overlap in their populations of interest, and despite their common emphasis on the study of *change,* developmental psychology and child psycho-therapy have remained surprisingly separate, insular enterprises. The introductions to journal articles on the various child treatments are notable for the infrequency with which they cite empirical findings of developmental psychology as a basis for treatment programs. And the results sections are notable for relative inattention to developmental factors that may relate to treatment effects.

One contributor to this state of affairs may be the very success these relatively adevelopmental treatment efforts have had in generating beneficial effects. Such success might well undermine motivation to seek input from other subdisciplines. It seems likely, though, that treatment effects with children could be improved through closer ties to the study of development. In principle, treatment benefit should be enhanced to the extent that treatments are adjusted to fit the develop-mental characteristics of the treated individuals. Because outcome research provides the feedback needed to guide the development and refinement of treatment pro-cedures, we may also need to consider ways to attune such research to develop-mental questions, so as to stimulate clinical–developmental cross-pollenation.

Developmental factors relevant to design and evaluation of treatments

In developing an agenda for such outcome research, it may be useful to begin identifying developmental variables relevant to intervention outcomes with chil-dren. Here we consider a few examples.

Age as a summary variable. Most outcome researchers report the age of their samples, but the potential moderating effect of age is almost never assessed. Thus, we miss an important opportunity for first steps toward developmental outcome research. As noted already, metaanalyses have differed in their findings on the relation between mean sample age and outcome, but this pooled approach lacks precision. Age effects may differ by type of therapy, and each metaanalytic collection of studies differs from every other in its particular array of therapies. This limitation was addressed in a focused metaanalysis by Durlak, Fuhrman, and Lampman (1991); they included 64 treatment outcome studies, all involving cognitive-behavioral therapy (CBT). Durlak et al. hypothesized that effect sizes would be larger with adolescents than with preadolescent children, because adolescents are more likely to be functioning at a formal operational level, and thus to be ready to learn the cognitive skills involved in CBT – for example, the use of cognitive strategies to guide behavior. The hypothesis was supported. Durlak et al. found a mean effect size of 0.92 for adolescents (ages 11–13), but only 0.55 for ages 7–11, and only 0.57 for ages 5–7. This kind of metaanalysis deserves replication with forms of treatment other than CBT; more important, it suggests the potential importance of assessing the potential moderating role of age in each individual outcome study. Age is the one developmental variable to which all treatment researchers have ready access. However, it must also be noted that the age variable is, at best, a rough summary index of multiple, diverse developmental factors – cognitive, social, and contextual – each of which deserves attention in its own right. Examples follow.

Cognitions about the therapy process and its purpose. In most therapy with adults, we may assume that the individuals being treated understand the concept of psychotherapy and its purpose. Young children, by contrast, may have little grasp of the nature or purpose of therapy, and the concepts children at various developmental levels apply to the process are apt to be partly a function of their cognitive developmental level. There is room for a great deal of basic inquiry into how children construe psychotherapy, and outcome research could eventually profit from such inquiry. It seems likely that the ways children understand the process will influence their response to it, and their ultimate treatment outcome.

Ability to "decenter" and view self from the perspective of others. Piaget (e.g., 1929, 1962) wrote a good deal about development of "decentration," the ability to detach from one's own point of view and perceive objects or events from an alternate perspective. Although initial work on this theme dealt with visual perception, the notion was eventually extended to social contexts, encompassing the ability to recognize the cognitive perspective of others on activities, events, and even oneself. Limited ability to decenter, in this sense, may set limits on the impact of treatments (e.g., cognitive-behavioral, psychodynamic) that involve efforts to help children see events, conditions, and even themselves from the perspective of others.

Language ability. Developmental variations in children's ability to encode and decode language may set limits on the success of therapies that involve heavy reliance on language. Low-level encoding skills may limit children's ability to let the therapist know their thoughts and feelings, and thus limit the therapist's ability to plan intervention that is well tailored to the child's inner state. As a simple example, both cognitive-behavioral and psychodynamic treatments for anxiety may require that the young client describe his or her anxious state in terms of physiological arousal (e.g., "I feel tense, my heart pounds, and I have a knot in my stomach") and psychological state (e.g., "Feels like everyone is staring at me; I'm afraid if I make a mistake, they'll think I'm stupid, and I'll feel humiliated"). Children whose encoding facility is too limited to permit such descriptions may not be able to help therapists understand their anxious states well enough to tailor interventions with precision.

Limited ability to decode comments by the therapist designed to be helpful may limit how helpful those comments actually are. Prescriptive, manual-driven therapies that are language-rich and rigidly scripted may not provide sufficient flexibility for therapists to adjust the language to the young client's capacities. And, of course, lack of assessment of language skills may hamper our ability to detect language-related reasons for variations in treatment outcome.

Finally, considerable developmental theory and research, dating at least to the work of Piaget (1923/1955) and Vygotsky (1934/1962), points to developmental differences in the ability to use "private speech" or "inner speech" to guide or inhibit behavior (see also Kohlberg, Yaeger, & Hjertholm, 1968; Zivin, 1979). Piaget and Vygotsky offered rather different predictions about the shape of the developmental trend over time, and subsequent evidence has been equivocal and complexly linked to the specific type of inner speech involved (see, e.g., Meichenbaum & Goodman, 1979). However, it does seem clear that developmental differences in the use of language to guide behavior might well lead to differences in children's responsiveness to therapies in which language is used to promote self-control. An obvious example is CBT, in which children are taught to use "self-talk" to make themselves less impulsive, less anxious, less depressed, less aggressive, more prosocial, and/or more skilled at entering social groups. Use of such procedures assumes a well-developed connection between language and action, and this assumption may not be equally valid across developmental levels.

Comprehension of concepts or "lessons" of the treatment program. Closely related to language ability is another phenomenon that seems likely to vary with developmental level: comprehension of the conceptual content, the central principles of a therapy program. Many therapies for young people are, to some extent, educational programs. For example, some treatment programs for depression are aimed at teaching young people the basic components of depression, plus strategies for alleviating depressed mood; and some programs for anxiety try to teach children the building blocks of anxiety (e.g., fear, physiological arousal, habitual avoidance, relief that rewards the avoidance), plus specific techniques for promoting exposure to the feared situation. Are there developmental differences in children's acquisition of these concepts and skills, and might such differences influence treatment outcome? For most child therapies, so little evidence has been collected to address these questions that we simply cannot provide an empirically respectable answer.

Abstract reasoning. Developmental literature indicates that certain kinds of abstract thinking, including hypotheticodeductive reasoning, may emerge with the advent of formal operations, typically in adolescence. Yet many treatment programs for *preadolescent* children appear to involve considerable abstract reasoning. Consider, for example, social skills training programs in which children are encouraged to generate hypothetical stressful social situations, think of various ways that they might respond, envision ways that others in the situation might respond to their response, and imagine various possible outcomes of the successive interactions that might ensue. Consider also, the movement from concrete instances to abstract categories required by many cognitively oriented therapies. For instance, some therapies for depression involve efforts to teach young clients to recognize instances of depressogenic cognitive errors, such as *overgeneralization* and *catastrophizing,* and a number of other broad categories of cognition (see examples in Cicchetti, Rogosch, & Toth, Chapter 13, this volume). Outcome research could be used to guide treatment developers in the use of such procedures, by providing information on the extent to which clients at various developmental levels do, indeed, learn the skills involved.

Cognition-behavior connections. Developmental outcome research may also be used to examine one of the basic tenets of cognitive-behavioral intervention: the notion that cognitive changes will lead to behavior changes. This may not be a safe assumption for youth at all ages. In the metaanalysis of cognitive-behavioral treatment outcome studies by Durlak et al. (1991), cited earlier, the authors found that changes in cognitive processes and changes in behavior were essentially uncorrelated ($r = -.22$, NS). The finding reminds us that positive effects of treatment based on a particular model do not necessarily validate the model. This fact is especially important in the child treatment domain, given the extent to which child treatments have been downloaded from the adult psychotherapy literature. An important element of developmental outcome research will be the search for true mediators of therapeutic change among treated children at different developmental levels.

Developmental principles relevant to design and evaluation of treatments

This section concludes with a shift from developmental dimensions to ontogenetic principles that have implications for child therapy.

Werner's orthogenetic principle and Piaget's "organization." The early developmental theorist Heinz Werner (1957) proposed what he called the *orthogenetic principle,* the notion that "wherever development occurs it proceeds from a state of relative globality and lack of differentiation to a state of increasing differentiation, articulation, and hierarchic integration" (p. 126). One interpretation of this rather broadly worded principle is that the developing individual is continually assimilating new skills and information and fitting them into an increasingly well integrated system. This overlaps to some degree with Piaget's (1970) notion of *organization,* the process by which the developing system integrates cognitive building blocks into a working structure. In Piaget's view (supported by evidence), even memories of past experience can be reorganized to integrate that experience with newly developed cognitive structures. An implication for intervention researchers is that skills and information taught as part of a treatment program may be gradually integrated into the developing child's cognitive system, but that this process may not necessarily occur within the time frame of the typical child outcome study.

Such thinking, if taken seriously by intervention researchers, could radically alter both the goals they adopt and the outcome assessment methods they use. Instead of aiming at primary outcomes induced by their treatment programs alone and seen at the end of those 8 to 24-week programs, treatment planners might construe their interventions as perturbations designed to interact with ongoing developmental change, with the most profound outcomes likely to be evident months or years after the end of treatment. Extending outcome research well beyond traditional follow-up periods (which are rarely longer than 6–9 months) might permit detection of slow-blooming improvements in functioning, as the child's developing system makes ever better use of the lessons of therapy. The flip side of extended follow-up is an equally important prospect: detection of "treatment benefit fade" and its time course.

Context-boundedness of development. Perhaps the most challenging developmental principle to accommodate in treatment design and outcome research is this: Development is not a solitary pursuit in a sterile environment, but rather an ongoing transaction within a complex, multifaceted physical, and social tapestry. Numerous theorists and researchers (e.g., Bronfenbrenner, 1979; Masten, Best, & Garmezy, 1991) have emphasized the context-boundedness of development, and discussed implications for adaptation and dysfunction. It is clear that the psychosocial systems within which individuals develop may enhance or undermine mental health. Clearly, also, there are marked developmental differences in people's capacity to select their contexts; for very young children, the luck of the draw may be critical. All this means that contextual factors may moderate treatment outcome, and perhaps differentially so with development, with some social environments facilitating treatment gains and other environments having undermining effects (see, e.g., Luthar, 1995; Luthar, Chapter 20, this volume). This suggests that individuals in the child's social environment (e.g., parents, siblings, teachers, peers) should often be incorporated into the treatment process; but this is rarely a part of published treatment programs. It also suggests that the child's interactions with his or her social environment should often be tapped as a part of outcome assessment; this, too, is rarely a part of published outcome research. The ecological perspective would complicate life for treatment researchers, pushing beyond a narrow focus on child characteristics and toward a focus on potentiating and inhibiting forces in the social systems within which the child is growing up.

Critique: III. Limited attention to individual difference factors

A third concern about current child treatment research is that it may not be attentive enough to individual difference variables – variables that, though not developmental per se, have been shown to have important effects on the behavior and adjustment of children. The advent of manualized treatments, which increasingly define the field, reflects a press toward uniformity of intervention procedures across children. Although such uniformity offers important advantages (e.g., clear communication across researchers, faithful replication of procedures by new teams), it may also pose a risk: overlooking individual differences among children that can significantly influence treatment impact. To illustrate this point, we will focus on individual difference dimensions addressed in this first section of the book.

Problem profile

Achenbach (Chapter 5, this volume) describes the development and potential applications of his widely used problem checklist measures, which generate a summary profile of child problems, as reported by various informants. One part of the rich legacy of this landmark work is that child problems are cast within a multidimensional framework; each child has some position on multiple dimensions of psychopathology, and covariation is common, with many children showing relatively high standing on more than one problem dimension concurrently. In principle, the child's problem profile can be used as a basis for treatment planning. In practice, however, the technological level of most empirically validated child treatments is too primitive to take full advantage of such a multidimensional assessment. Typical current treatments focus on one particular diagnosis (e.g., depression), problem (e.g., aggression), or even narrowly defined behavior (e.g., out-of-seat), with relatively little attention given to nontargeted problems that may be a part of the child's full profile. Such nontargeted problems are part of the individual difference "noise" that may not be addressed, because treatment researchers are focused on the problem(s) that all in their sample have in common. Certainly, there are good reasons for such narrow focus in the early stages of treatment development. However, my guess is that the future of treatment research will involve

increasing attention to individual differences in problem profile, addressed via interlocking treatment manuals with branching options, designed to facilitate attention
to the most common kinds of problem covariation in the groups of interest.

Intrinsic versus extrinsic motivation

Lepper, Sethi, Dialdin, and Drake (Chapter 2, this volume) discuss the interplay of
intrinsic and extrinsic motivation, and they review evidence indicating that quality
of skill acquisition and performance may be undermined by low levels of intrinsic
motivation. Child therapy researchers might well bear this point in mind in designing their interventions, most of which appear to tacitly assume intrinsic motivation by the treated child. The assumption may be only variably true of children
in the typical treatment outcome study, which involves recruited analog subjects,
but it may be quite often untrue of truly clinic-referred children, the vast majority
of whom neither considered themselves disturbed nor sought treatment. In an ongoing study we are conducting with children referred to community mental health
clinics in Los Angeles, we ask both parents and children to rate how serious the
child's problems are and how important it is that the child get over his or her
problems soon. The ratings on both questions are strikingly lower for children than
for their parents. Often, motivation for a child's treatment is far from intrinsic, with
most of the "push" coming from parents, teachers, and other adults (e.g., the
therapist), and sometimes the process is downright coercive.

   Although the research described by Lepper et al. does not involve disturbed
children or mental health interventions, it may be relevant, nonetheless. Low levels
of intrinsic motivation for treatment may undermine the child's attentiveness, involvement, learning, and skill acquisition, not to mention the application of learning
and skills outside the therapy room when no one else is watching. Treatment programs might well profit from pretreatment assessment of children's motivation for
therapy, together with the techniques for addressing the problem at the outset. The
ideas of Lepper et al. could be a useful starting point for development of such
techniques.

Orientation toward learning: Therapy as teaching

In work nicely related to Lepper's, Stipek (Chapter 4, this volume) focuses on
orientation toward learning in schools. The evidence she reviews here suggests that
the degree to which children succeed in learning may be influenced by a package
of variables collectively labeled "motivation" but encompassing such components
as belief in one's ability to learn, orientation toward developing understanding and
mastering skills, and persistence in the face of difficulty. To see the immediate
relevance of this work to our present analysis we need only recognize that psychotherapy with children is actually a form of educational intervention, akin to

teaching in schools. Increasingly, manualized child psychotherapies involve teaching children (1) the nature of their particular problem (e.g., the physical and psychological components of an anxiety response), (2) techniques for recognizing the problem as it arises (e.g., signals that tell me I'm beginning to feel anxious), and (3) skills in problem solving and coping (e.g., deep breaths, making myself do what I fear). In principle, some of the same individual difference variables that are associated with success versus failure in school may well influence the degree to which children benefit from such educationally oriented therapies. The possibility deserves careful attention in treatment research.

Control-related beliefs

The chapters by Lepper et al. and Stipek touch on the theme of perceived control, a topic we and others have begun to study in relation to psychopathology and treatment (see, e.g., Bandura, 1986; Weisz, 1990; Weisz, Sweeney, Proffitt, & Carr, 1993). Early findings suggest that children's beliefs about their ability to exert control over events in their lives can significantly predict the degree of benefit they derive from psychotherapy (see Weisz, 1986; Weisz & Weiss, 1989; for related findings primarily with adults, see Bandura, 1986, chap. 9). Such findings suggest that there may be value to child therapy researchers in (1) targeting control beliefs as a focus of pretreatment assessment, (b) testing the degree to which such beliefs predict outcomes of their particular intervention, and (3) if the beliefs do predict outcomes, making those beliefs a target of the intervention, thus to enhance the impact of other treatment components.

Race, ethnicity, and gender

Some of the individual difference variables that are most salient in society are frequently overlooked in child therapy research. The work described by Katz and Kofkin (Chapter 3, this volume) reminds us that children's experiences in a variety of contexts are filtered through lenses of race, ethnicity, and gender, even when those factors are not explicitly noted or discussed. This must certainly be true in the area of psychotherapy (see, e.g., Sue, 1988), but the potential moderating roles of race, ethnicity, and gender are not often assessed in individual child outcome studies. Recent findings suggest that this may be a significant oversight. For example, metaanalytic findings shown earlier in Figure 1.3 suggest that adolescent girls may have benefited much more than other groups from the most recent wave of tested therapies; this highlights the need for gender (x age group) analyses at the level of individual studies of individual treatments. And Yeh, Takeuchi, and Sue (1994) found that Asian American children given treatments adjusted to their ethnicity had better outcomes than Asian American children who received "mainstream" interventions. Unfortunately, it would be difficult to assess, at present, whether child treatments adjusted to the ethnicity of their subjects usually generate better outcomes with minority youth than do treatments that are not thus adjusted. There are simply few studies in which ethnicity-related adjustments have been made to support a fair statistical test. My guess is that this state of affairs will change. The future of child intervention research seems likely to involve increased attention to the potential moderating roles of race, ethnicity, and gender, and to the possibility that benefit may be enhanced by attention to these factors in the design of treatment procedures.

Biological characteristics

Finally, the chapter by Scarr and Deater-Deckard (Chapter 6, this volume) reminds us that both intellectual and personality differences among children reflect, in part, genetic transmission. Genetic and other early biological influences (e.g., prenatal conditions, birth trauma) may set limits on the impact of mental health treatments, just as they set limits on the impact of educational and socioeconomic interventions. This fact must be weighed as treatment researchers set expectations for the outcomes of their work with youngsters so diverse as anxious, depressed, aggressive, and autistic children.

Biological predispositions also need to be considered in treatment design. For example, effective treatment for anxiety (e.g., Kendall, 1994) appears *not* to focus on eliminating the presumably constitutional pattern of physiological arousal (e.g., pounding heart, flushed face) that accompanies fearful states. Instead, the focus is on training youngsters to recognize their distinctive pattern of arousal and to confront the feared situations *in spite of* the arousal. As we learn more about biological givens associated with other kinds of child dysfunction, similar accommodations will need to be incorporated into the corresponding interventions. Learning what may not be changeable can narrow the search for responsive targets of intervention.

Summary and concluding comments

Our review of the state of mental health intervention research with children has suggested a substantial agenda for the future. This agenda involves extending our understanding of intervention effects beyond experimental laboratories and into clinical settings where more disturbed youngsters are found. The agenda also involves attending more fully to both developmental and other individual difference factors in an effort to improve the goodness of fit between treatments and child characteristics. The value of each of these ventures will be enhanced to the extent that outcome research is used as a feedback mechanism to guide the refinement of treatments. As Ed Zigler's career illustrates, we serve children best by asking tough questions about what does and does not work.

References

Achenbach, T. M., & Edelbrock, C. (1981). Behavioral problems and competencies reported by parents of normal and disturbed children aged four to sixteen. *Monographs of the Society for Research in Child Development, 46* (Serial No. 188).

American Psychiatric Association. (1980). *Diagnostic and statistical manual of mental disorders* (3rd ed.). Washington, DC.

Bandura, A. (1986). *Social foundations of thought and action: A social cognitive theory.* Englewood Cliffs, NJ: Prentice-Hall.

Bronfenbrenner, U. (1979). *The ecology of human development.* Cambridge, MA: Harvard University Press.

Casey, R. J., & Berman, J. S. (1985). The outcome of psychotherapy with children. *Psychological Bulletin, 98,* 388–400.

Cohen, J. (1992). A power primer. *Psychological Bulletin, 112,* 155–159.

Costello, E. J. (1989). Developments in child psychiatric epidemiology. *Journal of the American Academy of Child and Adolescent Psychiatry, 28,* 836–841.

Durlak, J. A., Fuhrman, T., & Lampman, C. (1991). Effectiveness of cognitive-behavior therapy for maladapting children: A meta-analysis. *Psychological Bulletin, 110,* 204–214.

Frank, J. D. (1973). *Persuasion and healing: A comparative study of psychotherapy.* Baltimore: Johns Hopkins University Press.

Glass, G. V., McGaw, B., & Smith, M. L. (1981). *Meta-analysis in social research.* Beverly Hills, CA: Sage.

Institute of Medicine. (1989). *Research on children and adolescents with mental, behavioral, and developmental disorders.* Washington, DC: National Academy Press.

Kazdin, A. E., Bass, D., Ayers, W. A., & Rodgers, A. (1990). Empirical and clinical focus of child and adolescent psychotherapy research. *Journal of Consulting and Clinical Psychology, 58,* 729–740.

Kazdin, A. E., Siegel, T. C., & Bass, D. (1990). Drawing on clinical practice to inform research on child and adolescent psychotherapy: Survey of practitioners. *Professional Psychology: Research and Practice, 21,* 189–198.

Kendall, P. C. (1994). Treating anxiety disorders in children: Results of a randomized clinical trial. *Journal of Consulting and Clinical Psychology, 62,* 100–110.

Kohlberg, L., Yaeger, J., & Hjertholm, E. (1968). The development of private speech: Four studies and a review of theories. *Child Development, 39,* 691–736.

Lovaas, O. I. (1987). Behavioral treatment and normal educational and intellectual functioning in young autistic children. *Journal of Consulting and Clinical Psychology, 55,* 3–9.

Luthar, S. S. (1995). Social competence in the school setting: Prospective cross-domain associations among inner-city teens. *Child Development, 66,* 416–429.

Mann, C. (1990). Meta-analysis in the breech. *Science, 249,* 476–480.

Masten, A., Best, K., & Garmezy, N. (1991). Resilience and development: Contributions from the study of children who overcome adversity. *Development and Psychopathology, 2,* 425–444.

Meichenbaum, D., & Goodman, S. (1979). Clinical use of private speech and critical questions about its study in natural settings. In G. Zivin (Ed.), *The development of self-regulation through private speech* (pp. 325–360). New York: Wiley.

Office of Technology Assessment. (1986). *Children's mental wealth: Problems and Services. A Background Paper.* (Publication no. OTA-BP-H-33). Washington, DC: U.S. Government Printing Office.

Piaget, J. (1955). *The language and thought of the child.* New York: Meridian. (Originally published, 1923)

Piaget, J. (1929). *The child's conception of the world.* Totowa, NJ: Littlefield, Adams.

Piaget, J. (1962). *Play, Dreams, and Imitation.* New York: Norton.

Piaget, J. (1970). Piaget's theory. In P. H. Mussen (Ed.), *Carmichael's manual of child psychology* (Vol. 1, pp. 703–732). New York: Wiley.

Shapiro, D. A., & Shapiro, D. (1982). Meta-analysis of comparative therapy outcome studies: A replication and refinement. *Psychological Bulletin, 92,* 581–604.

Smith, M. L., & Glass, G. V. (1977). Meta-analysis of psychotherapy outcome studies. *American Psychologist, 32,* 752–760.

Smith, M. L., Glass, G. V., & Miller, T. L. (1980). *Benefits of psychotherapy.* Baltimore: Johns Hopkins University Press.

Sue, S. (1988). Psychotherapeutic services for ethnic minorities: Two decades of research findings. *American Psychologist, 43,* 301–308.

Vygotsky, L. (1962). *Thought and language.* Cambridge, MA: MIT Press. (Originally published, 1934)

Weisz, J. R. (1986). Contingency and control beliefs as predictors of psychotherapy outcomes among children and adolescents. *Journal of Consulting and Clinical Psychology, 54,* 789–795.

Weisz, J. R. (1990). Development of control-related beliefs, goals, and styles in childhood and adolescence: A clinical perspective. In K. W. Schaie, J. Rodin, & C. Schooler, (Eds.), *Self-directedness and efficacy: Causes and effects throughout the life course* (pp. 103–145). New York: Erlbaum.

Weisz, J. R. (in progress). *Studying clinic-based child mental health care.* Ongoing research project, University of California at Los Angeles.

Weisz, J. R., Donenberg, G. R., Han, S. S., & Kauucckis, D. (1995). Child and adolescent psychotherapy outcomes in experiments versus clinics: Why the disparity? *Journal of Abnormal Child Psychology, 23,* 83–106.

Weisz, J. R., Donenberg, G. R., Han, S. S., & Weiss, B. (1995). Bridging the gap between laboratory and clinic in child and adolescent psychotherapy. *Journal of Consulting and Clinical Psychology, 63,* 688–701.

Weisz, J. R., Sweeney, L., Proffitt, V., & Carr, T. (1993). Control-related beliefs and self-reported depressive symptoms in late childhood. *Journal of Abnormal Psychology, 102,* 395–403.

Weisz, J. R., & Weiss, B. (1989). Cognitive mediators of the outcome of psychotherapy with children. In B. B. Lahey & A. E. Kazdin (Eds.), *Advances in clinical child psychology* (Vol. 18, pp. 27–52). New York: Plenum Press.

Weisz, J. R., & Weiss, B. (1993). *Effects of psychotherapy with children and adolescents.* Newbury Park, CA: Sage.

Weisz, J. R., Weiss, B., Alicke, M. D., & Klotz, M. L. (1987). Effectiveness of psychotherapy with children and adolescents: A meta-analysis for clinicians. *Journal of Consulting and Clinical Psychology, 55,* 542–549.

Weisz, J. R., Weiss, B., Han, S. S., Granger, D. A., & Morton, T. (1995). Effects of psychotherapy with children and adolescents revisited: A meta-analysis of treatment outcome studies. *Psychological Bulletin, 117,* 450–468.

Werner, H. (1957). The concept of development from a comparative and organismic point of view. In D. Harris (Ed.), *The concept of development.* Minneapolis: University of Minnesota Press.

Yeh, M., Takeuchi, D. T., & Sue, S. (1994). Asian-American children treated in the mental health system: A comparison of parallel and mainstream outpatient service centers. *Journal of Clinical Child Psychology, 23,* 5–12.

Zigler, E., & Balla, D. (Eds.). (1982). *Mental retardation: The developmental-difference controversy.* Hillsdale, NJ: Erlbaum.

Zigler, E., & Glick, M. (1986). *A developmental approach to adult psychopathology.* New York: Wiley.

Zigler, E., & Hodapp, R. M. (1986). *Understanding mental retardation.* New York: Cambridge University Press.

Zigler, E., & Muenchow, S. (1992). *Head Start: The inside story of America's most successful educational experiment.* New York: Basic Books.

Zivin, G. (Ed.). (1979). *The development of self-regulation through private speech.* New York: Wiley.

2 Intrinsic and extrinsic motivation: A developmental perspective

Mark R. Lepper, Sheena Sethi, Dania Dialdin, and Michael Drake

But to go to school on a summer morn
O, it drives all joy away;
Under a cruel eye outworn,
The little ones spend the day
In sighing and dismay.
              –William Blake

From Blake's plaintive lament in 1794 to the continuing complaints of current critics of our educational system two centuries later, schools have been repeatedly faulted by would-be reformers for their failure to motivate and interest students. The best two days of the school year, the old saying goes, are the first and the last. The evident joys of being reunited with friends and classmates in school are outweighed only, according to detractors, by the drudgery imposed by teachers on their captive student audiences. When the topic is boredom, schools are often discussed in the same breath as other "total institutions" such as prisons or asylums.

Such a vision of schools is, of course, a caricature. Yet, like most caricatures, it was derived from an exaggeration of actual salient features of the target. It is hard for thoughtful observers to spend much time in schools without being impressed by the appearance of boredom given off by many students (e.g., Dreeben, 1968; Jackson, 1968; Silberman, 1970). The telltale signs of fidgeting, inattention, and restlessness are often widespread among pupils. Few activities in school seem to command students' complete attention and interest.

Behind these everyday observations, however, lies at least a minor paradox – certainly, before school age, learning seems clearly and universally intrinsically motivating for children. Few of us have ever seen, or even heard of, a three- or four-year-old with a "motivational deficit." Instead, young children seem eager and excited about learning of all sorts, and the more typical parental complaints concern their children's apparently insatiable curiosity and boundless energy. Yet, by the time these same children have entered school, a sizable fraction are quickly labeled as having motivational difficulties of one sort or another in learning.

Preparation of this chapter was supported, in part, by Research Grant HD-25258 from the National Institute of Child Health and Human Development to Mark R. Lepper.

23

What happens? Are there actual developmental shifts in children's levels of intrinsic, or for that matter extrinsic, motivation? If so, what might account for those shifts? Are there things we, as a society, are doing wrong in the education of children? Are there things we might do differently, to help sustain or enhance children's interest in learning?

In the present chapter, we first review the existing literature and offer some new empirical evidence concerning developmental trends in intrinsic and extrinsic motivation. We then examine several possible explanations for these developmental findings and consider their implications for social and educational policy.

Intrinsic versus extrinsic motivation

Early history

In the early years of psychology, the field of motivation was rooted in the study of learning as conditioning. As late as 1960, the prototypic experimental paradigms for the study of motivational effects were Pavlov's classical conditioning model of the learning of involuntary associations and Watson's and Skinner's instrumental or operant conditioning model for the learning of contingencies between an organism's actions and outcomes. Both paradigms were derived from the study of lower animals or, later, of humans placed in deliberately simplified, artificial, and highly restricted learning environments that served to heighten the similarities between the process of de novo learning in people and in the rat or pigeon.

More important, in the present context, both paradigms involved the study of the learning of essentially capricious relationships between arbitrarily selected responses of the organism, arbitrary environmental stimuli, and arbitrary external rewards and punishments. A person might, thus, be asked to press a button/move a lever/state a preference, in the presence of a bell/light/tone/color, in order to obtain food/drink/money/social approval. Motivational theories of the time, in short, were focused deliberately and almost exclusively on *extrinsic* forms of motivation.

Around the beginning of the 1960s, however, a new perspective began to emerge. Theorists from a number of different fields began to react to the limitations of this dominant paradigm. Using the impoverished learning settings of the conditioning theorists as a foil, they began to examine forms of motivation that did not seem to fit the traditional extrinsic motivation model, but seemed instead to come from the organism itself, arising and persisting in the absence of external events that could be easily identified as the putative rewards or punishments motivating these actions.

Collectively, the phenomena of concern to these theorists came to be identified as *intrinsic* motivations (cf. Bruner, 1962, 1966; Hunt, 1961, 1965). They included several potentially distinct sources of motivation. Of these, the three most prominent were challenge, curiosity, and control.[1]

In perhaps the earliest influential contribution to this area, for example, Robert White (1959) made the case for a general motive he initially described as "effectance," and others later called mastery or competence motivation (e.g., Csikszentmihalyi, 1975; Harter, 1978). Drawing on a variety of observations of humans and animals actively exploring, studying, and manipulating their environments, even in the apparent absence of external rewards or punishments for doing so, White postulated that these organisms were intrinsically motivated to solve problems, to seek out and to master challenges posed by their surroundings. Activities that provided a challenge, some goal of uncertain but potential attainment – activities neither trivially easy nor impossibly difficult, but instead of some intermediate, optimal level of difficulty and uncertainty – would be sought out and kept at until they had been mastered and the organism could move on to some other challenge.

At this same time, a second class of intrinsic motivations, concerned with curiosity, uncertainty, incongruity, and discrepancy, became the focus of extensive theorizing by both Daniel Berlyne (1960, 1966) and J. McVicker Hunt (1961, 1965). Drawing once again on both animal and human findings (especially, in Hunt's case, the then new observations of Piaget on learning in young infants), these authors reviewed findings on the important attentional effects of a variety of informational parameters of environmental events, such as the novelty, complexity, variability, and incongruity of a stimulus. Here, the relevant metaphor was humans as information processors. People were hypothesized to derive motivation from activities and events that provide them with some optimal, hypothetically intermediate level of surprise, incongruity, or discrepancy from their current understanding and expectations.

Finally, during this same general period, other theorists such as Richard deCharms (1968) added a third, related form of intrinsic motivation, namely, a motive for control or self-determination (e.g., Condry, 1977; Deci, 1975, 1981; Nuttin, 1973). From this perspective, people were viewed as actors seeking to exercise and validate a sense of control over their external environments. As a result, they were theorized to prefer and to persist at activities that provide them with the opportunity to make choices, to control their own outcomes, and to determine their own fate. People will strive, in deCharms's early terminology, to see themselves as "origins" of their own purposeful actions rather than "pawns" of external environmental forces.[2]

Taken together, these various sources of intrinsic motivation were invoked to explain the large amount of effective learning and persistent activity that seems to take place in the absence of salient or powerful external contingencies. Because such factors could motivate learning both inside and outside of formal school settings, their cultivation quickly became a significant goal and ideal of many educational theorists (e.g., Bruner, 1962, 1966; Condry, 1977; Deci, 1975; Hunt, 1961, 1965; Lepper & Greene, 1978). Schools, it was suggested, should strive not only to train students' skills and to increase their knowledge; they should also strive to cultivate and foster feelings of intrinsic motivation in students that should sustain in them a desire to learn that will persist long after they have left school.

Undermining intrinsic motivation with extrinsic incentives

The contrast between intrinsic and extrinsic motivation that underlay much of the early theorizing in this area would soon receive even greater impetus from a series of studies that showed that the misuse of extrinsic incentives could actually undermine intrinsic interest. Indeed, within a very short period, the appearance of several independent studies examining this basic hypothesis served to suggest the power and the generality of this effect.

In the first of these studies, for example, Deci (1971) showed that Carnegie-Mellon undergraduates who had been offered money for solving a series of three-dimensional puzzles that they would otherwise have found of intrinsic interest spent less subsequent time with those same puzzles – in settings in which money was no longer available – than did subjects who had worked the same puzzles without receipt of any extrinsic financial rewards. At almost the same time, Kruglanski, Friedman, and Zeevi (1971) reported significant decreases on a wide variety of measures of task performance (e.g., creativity, memory, incidental learning), as well as on explicit ratings of interest in the activities themselves, among Israeli high school students offered the extrinsic incentive of a tour of the university for their task engagement, compared with other students offered no such extrinsic reward.

Finally, Lepper, Greene, and Nisbett (1973) demonstrated parallel effects with a sample of preschool children specifically selected on the basis of their demonstrated initial intrinsic interest in a new art activity put out by teachers in the children's regular classrooms. In this study, children who explicitly agreed to engage in the art activity in order to obtain a tangible "Good Player Award" showed only half as much subsequent interest in this activity, several weeks later and back in their regular classrooms (once again in the absence of any expectation of extrinsic rewards), as did children who had engaged in the same art activity without any promise of an external reward but who subsequently received the same award unexpectedly or children who had engaged in the activity without either the promise or receipt of any award.

Together these initial studies demonstrated considerable generality to this potential negative effect of the use of functionally superfluous extrinsic rewards on students' intrinsic motivation. Across very different subject populations, a variety of specific activities, and several types of extrinsic rewards, these various investigations had nonetheless produced comparable results. At the same time, as these early researchers had explicitly acknowledged, neither their theories nor their findings suggested that the use of extrinsic rewards would always, or even typically, produce such detrimental effects on intrinsic motivation. Hence, subsequent research was directed toward the specification of the precise conditions under which such negative effects, and those under which alternative positive effects, would appear.

This literature has been reviewed in some detail in a number of sources (e.g., Condry & Lepper, 1992; Deci & Ryan, 1985; Lepper, 1983a, 1988; Tang & Hall, 1995), roughly as follows. First, extrinsic rewards and punishments may have positive effects of several sorts. They may, for example, increase task engagement, which may in turn result in the acquisition of new skills or knowledge that could enhance the intrinsic value of the activity for the individual in the future. They may also provide the individual with important information signaling or emphasizing his or her competence at the activity, relative to some absolute or some social-comparative performance standard, again enhancing later intrinsic interest in it. Finally, of course, the receipt of extrinsic rewards or punishments may produce the expectation that the same activity will have comparable consequences in related future situations.

However, when these potential sources of beneficial effects are controlled or absent, as in each of the three original studies of this phenomenon, the offer of superfluous extrinsic incentives for engagement in activities of initial interest may produce a variety of negative effects on intrinsic motivation. The offer of superfluous but salient extrinsic incentives or constraints may, under these conditions, turn activities that were once seen primarily as "play" (i.e., things to be sought out and engaged in for their own sake) into tasks that are now viewed primarily as "work" (i.e., things to be engaged in only if one expects some continued external payoff).

Perhaps the most telling and informative illustration of this detrimental effect can be found in studies that examine what might be described as the minimal conditions under which extrinsic contingencies may influence intrinsic motivation. Lepper, Sagotsky, Dafoe, and Greene (1982), for example, studied the effects of the imposition of a purely nominal contingency on children's subsequent interest in activities presented either as "means" to some external end or as "ends" in themselves. In their study, two art activities of high – and equivalent – inherent initial interest were selected. In the experimental, means–end condition, students were asked to agree to engage in one of the two activities in order to "win" the chance to engage in the other. In a comparable control condition, students engaged in the same two activities for equivalent amounts of time, but without the imposition of any contingency between them. Two to three weeks later, students' subsequent intrinsic interest in both the activities was assessed in their regular classrooms, during "free play" periods in which no external constraints were present or anticipated. Compared with their counterparts in the control condition, children in the experimental condition showed decreased interest in whichever activity had been presented as a means, and increased interest in whichever activity had been presented as an end.

The effects illustrated in this literature, then, provide evidence of mechanisms –

both positive and negative – whereby the presentation of activities in the highly constrained and evaluative context of current schools might influence children's subsequent intrinsic motivation toward those activities. Perhaps, as some have argued (e.g., Condry & Chambers, 1978; Deci, 1975; Deci & Ryan, 1985; Holt, 1964), the ubiquity of grades, gold stars, report cards, and other aspects of formal evaluation in school may indeed undermine whatever intrinsic interest in the material taught that students may bring to the classroom. Perhaps, especially if used with care, those extrinsic incentives may, on the other hand, enhance feelings of competence or result in the acquisition of new skills that might enhance intrinsic interest. Without prejudging the outcome of these complex questions, this literature clearly highlights the potential significance of studies examining developmental trends in students' intrinsic motivation, particularly during the years when children are expected to be in school.

A final commentary on this literature is anecdotal, but especially relevant to these developmental concerns. Over the years, the senior author has had occasion to talk about these general findings to a number of groups of teachers and others involved in our educational system. In the process, a curious "finding" of its own emerged. When the results of this literature were described to audiences of educators who worked primarily with young children, the typical response was unadulterated approbation. These teachers clearly understood the phenomenon under discussion and thought that research documenting such effects was long overdue. By contrast, when these same findings were presented to educators who themselves worked more with older students, a second prototypic response began to appear. Although these teachers would often grant the importance of the phenomenon, they were quick to point out its lack of relevance to their own classroom situations. After all, they routinely indicated, students in their classes rarely displayed any intrinsic motivation whatsoever. There was simply nothing to be undermined. The older the students under discussion, in short, the less intrinsic motivation they were seen by their teachers to display in school.

Developmental findings

Is there, indeed, a developmental decrease in intrinsic motivation, at least in school, of the sort suggested by these teachers and by several generations of school critics? Let us turn now to the empirical evidence on this question.

Harter's scale and initial results

The first important developmental findings in this area were published in 1981 by Susan Harter, in a paper that also presented for the first time her Scale of Intrinsic versus Extrinsic Orientation in the Classroom. Since this scale represents the primary instrument through which developmental trends in intrinsic–extrinsic motivation have been assessed, it is worth examining its characteristics in some detail.

The aim of Harter's scale was to assess children's general levels of intrinsic versus extrinsic motivation along three related dimensions that could be derived from the earlier literature on intrinsic motivation and applied to the classroom context. The first of these dimensions involved a "preference for challenge" and difficult alternatives versus a "preference for easy work assigned." The second involved the undertaking of tasks out of "curiosity/interest" versus "pleasing the teacher/getting good grades." The third examined the dimension of "independent mastery" versus "dependence on the teacher" for guidance and assistance. Intrinsically motivated students, it was presumed, would be more likely to seek out challenging and interesting activities and assignments and would prefer to plan and face difficulties on their own. Extrinsically motivated children, by contrast, should prefer easy and assigned work, at which they would be sure to succeed and for which they could be sure to get credit; and they should be more likely to seek out help from the teacher in deciding what to do next or how to respond when difficulties arise.[3]

For each of these dimensions, then, Harter created half a dozen items, each contrasting a characteristically intrinsic versus a characteristically extrinsic alternative. For example, one item from the curiosity scale reads as follows: "Some kids work really hard to get good grades" (extrinsic choice) versus "Other kids work really hard because they like to learn new things" (intrinsic choice). A comparable item from the challenge scale reads: "Some kids like to go on to new work that's at a more difficult level" (intrinsic choice) versus "Other kids would rather stick to the assignments which are pretty easy to do" (extrinsic choice). For each of the items on the questionnaire, then, a child must first choose between an intrinsic and an extrinsic response, by indicating which of the two types of children he or she is more like. Once this choice has been made, the child is asked to indicate the strength of his or her convictions by indicating whether the chosen alternative is either "somewhat like me" or "a lot like me," as shown in the top panel of Figure 2.1. The net result is an overall 72-point scale of an individual's self-reported general intrinsic versus extrinsic motivational orientation, comprising three subscales of challenge, curiosity, and independence.

Among the many findings reported using this scale by Harter (1981), the most interesting were clearly the developmental trends that emerged when Harter administered this scale to a sample of 793 California public school children, ranging from third through ninth grade. The results were clear and striking: On each of the three component measures, and consequently on a composite measure as well, the data showed systematic and significant decreases in intrinsic motivational orientation (and/or significant increases in extrinsic motivational orientation, since the two are perfectly negatively correlated) with increases in age or grade level.

Figure 2.2 displays these results, summarized in a single composite measure of intrinsic motivation, from Harter's initial article – findings that were taken by many

Sample Item from Harter's (1981) Scale of Intrinsic vs. Extrinsic Motivational Orientation:

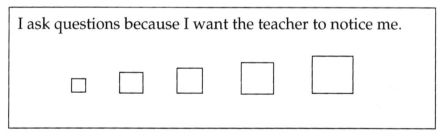

Sample Item Above Decomposed into Separate Scales for Intrinsic and Extrinsic Motivation:

Intrinsic Item:

I ask questions in class because I want to learn new things.

Extrinsic Item:

I ask questions because I want the teacher to notice me.

Figure 2.1. Scale of intrinsic versus extrinsic motivational orientation, from Harter (1981).

as a striking confirmation of the worst fears and strongest claims of educational critics concerned about student motivation in our schools. From the early elementary school years, when children reported themselves to be highly intrinsically motivated, to the later elementary and middle school years, there was a steady

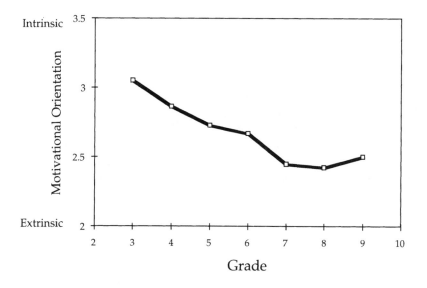

Figure 2.2. Overall intrinsic versus extrinsic motivation, by grade, from Harter (1981).

decrease in reported intrinsic motivation. The longer children remained in school, it seemed, the less intrinsically motivated they became.

Subsequent findings with Harter's scale

Such findings were greeted, quite appropriately, with great interest and concern, and several other investigators sought to replicate Harter's developmental results using her same scale. These follow-up studies, in general, provided further support for Harter's initial conclusions concerning a decline in intrinsic motivation during the elementary and middle school years, at least for middle-class populations.

Tzuriel (1989), for instance, used Harter's scale with a very large sample of 3,005 middle-class Israeli children, representing the same age/grade range as Harter's original sample. He found, like Harter, a large and significant decline in reported overall intrinsic motivational orientation from third through ninth grade, although specific separate scores for the three subscales are not reported. Similarly, Newman (1990) administered Harter's scale to 177 third-, fifth-, and seventh-grade students in Riverside, California. On both the preference for challenge and the independent mastery scales, he found significant decreases in intrinsic motivation with increasing age and grade. (Because the items making up Harter's curiosity/interest subscale did not show sufficient internal consistency in Newman's sample, data from this measure were not reported.)

For disadvantaged and academically problematic students, by contrast, there are significantly fewer data available, and the developmental trends are less clear. Dollinger and Seiters (1988) gave Harter's scale to a sample of 50 second- through seventh-grade children who had been referred to a university clinic because of academic and/or behavioral difficulties in school. In this sample, there were no significant relationships between age/grade and any of Harter's three motivational scales. Tzuriel (1989), however, found a curvilinear relationship between reported overall intrinsic motivation and age/grade among a large sample of 1,287 students taken from schools identified by the Israeli Ministry of Education as serving students from relatively more disadvantaged backgrounds. For these students, there was a decline in reported intrinsic motivational orientation from third through sixth grade, but this decline was followed by an increase on this same overall measure from sixth through ninth grade. Although neither of these findings has, as yet, been replicated, Zigler's (e.g., 1966, 1971) extensive work on outerdirectedness among institutionalized and retarded children would suggest the importance of further investigations with these sorts of populations.

Disentangling intrinsic and extrinsic motivation: New results

There is, of course, one potentially crucial methodological problem with interpreting any of the studies using Harter's scale as strong evidence of a decrease with age in students' intrinsic motivation in school: Perhaps rather than a decrease in intrinsic motivational orientation, the typical results discussed here reflect instead an increase in extrinsic motivational orientation. As children grow older and progress through school, this alternative interpretation might suggest, they learn to take increasingly seriously the extrinsic indicators of success or failure in school.

Because Harter's scale presumes that intrinsic and extrinsic motivation are negatively correlated, indeed that they are mutually exclusive, a child who scores high on one index will necessarily score correspondingly low on the other. Respondents are forced to indicate, for example, that they ask questions in class either "because they want to learn new things" or "because they want the teacher to notice them." Nowhere is it possible for students to report both being curious about a subject, but also interested in recognition from their teacher. This presumption that there must be a perfect negative correlation between a student's levels of intrinsic and extrinsic motivation places a very strong constraint on our ability to interpret clearly the developmental findings using this instrument.

In fact, there is no reason why these two constructs, intrinsic and extrinsic motivation, might not be independently assessed, as Harter herself has indicated (Harter, 1981). In fact, there are good theoretical reasons, even within the overjustification literature, to suggest that both extrinsic rewards that carry significant information about one's competence (like grades in school may do in many circumstances), as well as more purely social rewards (like teacher, or parental, attention), may not undermine intrinsic motivation (e.g., Condry, 1977; Deci & Ryan, 1985, 1991; Lepper, 1983a; Lepper & Hodell, 1989).

Indeed, it should be possible to examine separately students' levels of intrinsic and extrinsic motivation by using only a slight modification of Harter's own scale. If, instead of forcing children to choose to describe themselves as either intrinsically or extrinsically motivated, one were to ask children separately about each half of each of Harter's items, one could arrive at independent assessments of these two dimensions. Just as Sandra Bem's studies (1974, 1993) on sex roles and gender identity demonstrated the importance and utility of assessing masculinity and femininity as two separate dimensions, rather than the single bipolar dimension that had been characteristic of previous scales in this area, it seemed possible that disentangling measures of intrinsic and extrinsic motivation might pay theoretical dividends. At the very least, a developmental study that included independent measures of the two should help to clarify previous developmental findings obtained using bipolar scales.

Following this reasoning, the present authors undertook such a study. In it, 358 children from two large and ethnically diverse schools in San Jose, California, which served the third through eighth grades, were administered a modified version of Harter's scale designed to permit the independent assessment of reported intrinsic and extrinsic motivation. In our adaptation of Harter's scale, each original question from her scales of challenge, curiosity, and independence was divided into two separate questions, yielding both an intrinsic motivation and an extrinsic motivation item.

Thus, a question that had initially asked children to say whether they were more like "some kids [who] ask questions in class because they want to learn new things" or more like "other kids [who] ask questions because they want the teacher to notice them" would be converted into two items: "I ask questions in class because I want to learn new things" (intrinsic item) and "I ask questions in class because I want the teacher to notice me" (extrinsic item). The respondents were then asked to rate each such item on a five-point Likert scale, with one being "not at all like me" and five being "very much like me," as shown in the bottom panel of Figure 2.1. These choices were illustrated with a line of boxes of increasing size, and students were given explicit training on a number of pretest items, to be sure that they understood how to use the scales provided.

A first issue, then, is whether intrinsic motivation and extrinsic motivation toward one's schoolwork, if assessed independently, will in fact prove mutually exclusive. Our findings indicate that this is not, in fact, the case. Overall, the correlation between separate composite measures of intrinsic and extrinsic motivation proved slight, $r = -.14$ and, although statistically significant, $p < .01$, clearly accounted for only a tiny fraction of the variance. Across the three component measures of intrinsic and extrinsic motivation, moreover, there was clear inconsistency. On the one hand, the correlation between curiosity/interest versus desire for teacher ap-

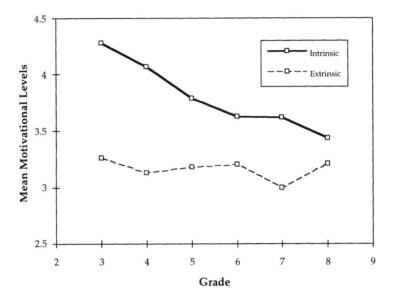

Figure 2.3. Overall intrinsic motivation and overall extrinsic motivation, by grade.

proval was actually positive, $r = .22$, $p < .001$; on the other, the correlation between a desire for challenge versus a desire for easy work was fairly strongly negative, $r = -.53$, $p < .0001$, whereas the correlation between independent mastery attempts versus dependence on teacher guidance proved negative, but quite slight, $r = -.16$, $p < .01$. This relative independence of the two scales was also apparent within each grade level.

Given the relative independence of these two forms of motivation, it is of particular interest to reexamine the separate developmental trends for measures of both intrinsic and extrinsic motivation. The relevant data for our composite measures of intrinsic and extrinsic motivation are presented in Figure 2.3, and the separate data for each of the subscales are presented in Figure 2.4. They tell an interesting story.

For intrinsic motivation, on the one hand, the findings seem quite clear. For the composite measure, we find a highly significant and monotonic decline in overall intrinsic motivation, $F = 12.35$, $p < .0001$, as children progress from third grade (M = 4.28, SD = .48) through eighth grade (M = 3.44, SD = .48). This overall gradual decline in intrinsic motivation was also found to be independently significant for each of the three component measures of preference for challenge, $F = 11.33$, $p < .001$, of curiosity/interest, $F = 14.22$, $p < .001$, and of independent mastery, $F = 4.27$, $p < .001$.

For extrinsic motivation, by contrast, there was no significant main effect of grade, $F = 1.43$, n.s. The average level of overall extrinsic motivation (M = 3.20, SD = .52) did not vary across grade level. Nor were there any significant developmental trends for either desire for easy work or dependence on teacher guidance.

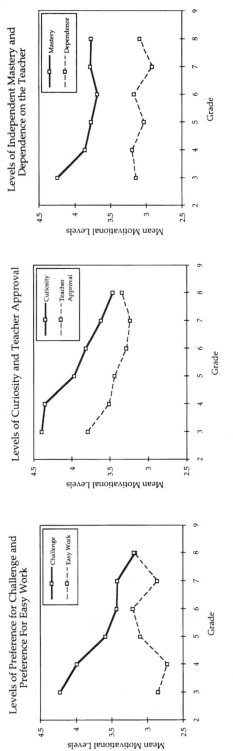

Figure 2.4. Intrinsic motivation and extrinsic motivation for the three component scales of challenge, curiosity, and mastery.

Only the component measure of desire for teacher approval showed any significant effect of grade, $F = 4.48$, $p < .001$. Moreover, the effect shown on this one component was a gradual decline, rather than an increase, in extrinsic motivation from third (M = 3.79, SD = .80) through eighth grade (M = 3.34, SD = .59).

These findings replicate and clarify Harter's original developmental results. Even when intrinsic motivation and extrinsic motivation are assessed separately, we continue to find a steady decline in reported intrinsic motivation with increased age and grade. At the same time, there is no evidence of a complementary increase in reported extrinsic motivation during this period. Instead, extrinsic motivation remains relatively constant or shows, if anything, a slight parallel decline.

Other developmental findings

These new findings give added weight to the argument that there is indeed an important developmental decline in students' intrinsic motivation in the classroom. Because even these most recent findings still share many particulars of methodology with other results obtained using Harter's scale, it may be important to note, as well, comparable findings from other studies using very different measures.

Epstein and McPartland (1976), for example, created measures to assess children's satisfaction with school, their commitment to classwork, and their attitudes toward their teachers. These measures were then administered to over 4,000 students in the 5th, 6th, 7th, 9th, and 12th grades. The authors report a steady decline in students' ratings, on a composite of these measures which the authors term "quality of school life," from 5th through 12th grade. Similarly, Haladyna and Thomas (1979) administered measures of children's attitudes toward school in general to a sample of nearly 3,000 students from grades 1 through 8 and reported a steady decrease in the positivity of students' attitudes toward school from the 1st through the 8th grade.

Using a very different methodology, Sansone and Morgan (1992) asked groups of kindergarten and first-graders, fifth- and sixth-graders, and college undergraduates to describe activities they found intrinsically motivating, both in and outside of school, and to indicate for each activity how much they enjoyed it and how much they would like to repeat the experience. With increases in age and grade, they found – for the school-based activities only – systematic decreases in reported intrinsic motivation, both in terms of their enjoyment of, and their willingness to repeat, the activity.

Still other studies have focused on differences in attitudes toward, and satisfaction with, school between children in the elementary and children in the middle-school years. Across a wide variety of measures and samples, as reviewed in detail by both Anderman and Maehr (1994) and Eccles and Midgley (1990), a dozen different authors have documented decreases in reported motivation, interest, or liking for school from the elementary-school to the middle-school years.

Finally, some further data regarding potential developmental changes in intrinsic motivation have also been reported by Adele Gottfried (1985) in her article describing the development of her Children's Academic Intrinsic Motivation Inventory – another self-report scale also designed to measure children's intrinsic motivation for school learning, but to do so separately for four different specific curriculum areas (namely, reading, math, social studies, and science) as well as in general. Perhaps because Gottfried's studies examined a narrower age distribution (i.e., fourth through seventh, or fifth through eighth grades), she reports relatively few significant developmental effects. Reported intrinsic interest in reading, however, does show reasonably large and significant declines with increases in age and grade in two of her three studies.[4]

Summary

On balance, the results of the many studies that have thus far examined developmental trends in intrinsic motivation provide fairly strong evidence that students' reports of their intrinsic motivation in school in general and their interest in the subjects taught there decrease with age and grade in school – at least in the range from third through ninth grade. By contrast, the only direct developmental data that we have concerned specifically with developmental trends in extrinsic motivation suggest little consistent change with age across this same grade range.

Developmental trends: A discussion

If we accept these conclusions, the next evident question is, What should we make of this pervasive decrease in intrinsic motivation? Is it "real"? Does it matter? If so, what causes it? And, if so, what might be done about it? A consideration of these questions will form the substance of the following discussion.

Is it real? Does it matter?

In view of these widespread developmental decreases in reported intrinsic motivation, a first obvious question is whether these decreases are "real" or merely apparent. That is, do these findings represent actual changes in general motivational patterns that might influence children's choices, activities, and learning across situations – as the authors of these studies would suggest? Or, do these apparent developmental effects reflect merely stylistic or linguistic changes specific to children's responses to explicit questions concerning their motivations – changes, for example, in students' willingness to describe themselves as really interested in their schoolwork, in the standards of comparison they use in answering such questions, or in their perceptions of the socially desirable answers? Are these, in short, differences that "make a difference"? Although the answer to these questions is not as well documented as one would like, several lines of evidence suggest that the reports children give on these questionnaire measures of intrinsic motivation do reflect some realistic differences in their motivational orientations.

A first line of evidence for the construct validity of these scales comes from studies that have compared students' self-reports with the reports of others who know them well. Here, the most common technique has been to compare students' self-reports of intrinsic versus extrinsic motivation with teachers' reports concerning the motivational orientations of those students, although this has been done using a number of somewhat different specific procedures. Harter (1981), for instance, asked the teachers of the students she surveyed to rate their pupils' motivation using an abbreviated version of the same scale the children had filled out about themselves. With this procedure, she found highly impressive correlations between teachers' ratings and students' self-reports, with r's ranging from .61 to .73.

Other investigators, using slightly different techniques, have found similar, though typically less striking, correlations. For instance, both Gottfried (1985, 1990) and the present authors found significant correlations between students' reports of their own levels of motivation in school and simple Likert-scale ratings of those students' motivational levels obtained from their classroom teachers. Similarly, Dollinger and Seiters (1988) found significant correlations between students' self-reports and measures of their general intrinsic motivational orientation computed from selected theoretically relevant items from their mothers' Q-Sort descriptions of them. Thus, the tendencies that students report about themselves on these measures also seem apparent to others who know these students well.

A second form of evidence concerning the validity of these scales takes a different tack, by examining the correlations between children's reports of their motivational orientations and various external and more ''objective'' indices of school performances that have been hypothesized to depend, in part, on those motivational orientations. Several studies, for instance, have reported significant positive correlations between intrinsic motivational orientation and performance on various standardized achievement tests (e.g., Boggiano, Shields, Barrett, Kellam, Thompson, Simons, & Katz, 1992; Gottfried, 1985, 1990); others have reported positive correlations between intrinsic motivational orientation and classroom grades (e.g., Gottfried, 1985). Still others working with academically problematic populations (e.g., Dollinger & Seiters, 1988) have reported negative correlations between intrinsic motivation and academic failure (i.e., having been retained in one or more grades).

Third, there are two findings that seek to speak to the issue of scale validity by examining specific, predicted behavioral correlates of reported intrinsic interest in school, but only for the specific subscale of preference for challenge. For this one scale, however, both Harter (1981) and Boggiano et al. (1992) report positive relationships between reported intrinsic motivation, in terms of a preference for more difficult and challenging work, and students' specific preferences when offered choices among different levels of difficulty of some particular activity (e.g., whether they would like to work on 3-, 4-, 5-, 6-, or 7-letter anagrams). Unfortunately, comparable investigations of the behavioral concomitants of differences in reported curiosity and independence have not yet been undertaken.[5]

Finally, there are a few findings concerning the relevance of these scales to children's emotional or behavioral problems. Thus, several studies have reported an association between an extrinsic motivational orientation and high levels of anxiety over academic performance (Deci & Ryan, 1985; Gottfried, 1985, 1990). Still other studies have suggested a link between children's extrinsic motivational orientation and their vulnerability to helplessness in the face of failure, and possibly even their susceptibility to depression (Boggiano, Main, & Katz, 1991; Boggiano et al., 1992).

Overall then, these several lines of evidence, though less complete than one would hope, do suggest that the reported declines in intrinsic motivation in school with increasing age and grade represent a more general phenomenon of some substantive theoretical and practical significance. If so, the obvious next question is what causes these developmental declines in intrinsic motivational orientation.

What causes it?

In thinking about the causes of this developmental decline, three initial considerations seem of paramount importance. First, this phenomenon appears to be specifically related to students' perceptions of their *schoolwork,* rather than to some more general orientation. In studies where children are asked comparable questions about nonschool activities (e.g., Sansone & Morgan, 1992), developmental declines are not seen. Nor, in the very few studies reporting explicit developmental data on specific behaviors presumed to be indicative of intrinsic motivation, has there been any evidence of developmental decreases in intrinsic motivation (cf. Harter, 1978).

Instead, and this is the second important point about this phenomenon, most of our developmental theories about intrinsic motivation, as well as a few scattered supportive findings, might have led one to expect, if anything, a precisely opposite developmental effect. Thus, a variety of theorists have postulated that many forms of intrinsic motivation may be produced or augmented by a process of progressive "internalization" of initially external incentives and constraints (e.g., Deci & Ryan, 1985, 1991; Harter, 1978; Maslow, 1954; Rigby, Deci, Patrick, & Ryan, 1992). Here, at least in principle, these types of intrinsic motivation would be seen as developmentally "higher" forms.

In similar fashion, one might also find support for this opposing view in the scattered findings involving developmental variables other than age. With the singular exception of the "disadvantaged" Israeli students studied by Tzuriel (1989), for example, students identified by independent diagnostic criteria as mentally retarded or academically problematic have been shown to display much less intrinsic and/or more extrinsic motivational orientations than their more "average" counterparts (Dollinger & Seiters, 1988; Harter, 1981). Indeed, in the most extensive and elegant study of this sort, Harter and Zigler (1974) showed normal children to display behavioral evidence of higher levels of curiosity, of desire for independent mastery, and of preference for challenge than either institutionalized or noninstitutionalized retarded children of a comparable mental age. Likewise, students who see themselves, and are seen by others, as less competent, rate themselves as less intrinsically and more extrinsically motivated than their more competent peers (e.g., Boggiano, et al., 1992).

The third point to be kept in mind in evaluating potential causes of the developmental decline in intrinsic motivation is rather more technical. Cross-sectional developmental trends of this sort could reflect either fairly broad-based and general effects across a population, or more localized effects in some smaller subset of that population. Perhaps the trends we have examined, in particular, might reflect a small but gradually increasing group of "motivational dropouts," who have disidentified with the goals and practices of school (cf. Steele, 1992).

Fortunately, there is a clear empirical test of this family of explanations: If the declines we have seen were the result of a progressive increase in the number of totally alienated students, there should be a corresponding gradual increase with age and grade in the variability of children's scores on these measures. This, however, is not the case. Indeed, in our own data, for instance, there are no changes in the variances with grade, and the trends are in the opposite direction on each of the scales. Similar results are also apparent in the standard deviations reported by grade for Harter's (1981) original scale of intrinsic versus extrinsic motivation, as well as for measures of general attitudes toward school reported by Epstein and McPartland (1976) and Haladyna and Thomas (1979). Thus, it would appear that the phenomenon involves more widespread and gradual changes.

What could it be, then, that happens as children grow and progress through school that produces these systematic decreases in their intrinsic interest in the work they undertake there? No doubt, there is no single answer to this question, and certainly there are no compelling data to help one choose among alternative possibilities. Nonetheless, let us examine some of the possible contributing factors.

One theoretically obvious possibility, stemming directly from previous literature in this area, is that the heavy use of extrinsic incentives and constraints in schools these days may result, over time, in the progressive undermining of children's intrinsic interest in the subjects they study in school. Of course, as we have already noted, the mere ubiquity of tests, grades, and other extrinsic contingencies does not by itself mean that intrinsic interest will be subverted, because grades and the like can have both informational components that could heighten intrinsic interest and controlling components that could decrease intrinsic interest (cf. Deci & Ryan, 1985; Kruglanski, 1978; Lepper & Greene, 1978).

However, observational studies by Deci and colleagues (e.g., Deci, Schwartz, Scheinman, & Ryan, 1981), Dweck and associates (e.g., Dweck, Davidson, Nelson,

& Enna, 1978), and others (e.g., Dreeben, 1968; Jackson, 1968; Silberman, 1970) have shown just how focused on control the contingencies of the typical classroom are. Winnett and Winkler's (1972) systematic analysis of the uses of extrinsic incentives in classrooms, for instance, shows a preponderance of attention paid to rewarding students for being "quiet," "still," and "docile." Moreover, several studies employing tests and grades in a seemingly "typical" fashion have indeed shown detrimental effects on intrinsic motivation and learning (e.g., Benware & Deci, 1984; Grolnick & Ryan, 1987; Harter, 1978; Rigby, Deci, Patrick, & Ryan, 1992).

A second potential contributing factor to the observed developmental decline in intrinsic motivation in school might be what Bruner (1962, 1966) first referred to as the "decontextualization" of learning that takes place in schools and appears to increase with increasing grade in school. At least in the typical school in our country, we deliberately seek to divorce the learning of academic skills from the natural contexts in which their inherent utility might be obvious to students. Instead, we usually try to teach subjects in their most abstract form, presumably because we believe that this sort of abstract presentation will result in more generalizable learning than learning of the same material in any particular concrete context. Inherent in this pedagogical practice is a sacrifice of potentially critical motivational appeal (e.g., Condry & Chambers, 1978; Ginsberg, 1977; Perkins, 1992). Indeed, more generally, one might argue that as children grow older, schools are likely to make fewer and fewer motivational "concessions," but become instead more likely to presume that students ought to be able and willing to learn material even when it is no longer "sugarcoated" for them.

Still another set of potentially significant contributing factors has been discussed in detail by Eccles and Midgley (1988, 1990). Focusing on the transition from elementary to middle school, they note that with increasing grades, schools tend to become more impersonal, more formal, more evaluative, and more competitive. These changes in the social context that schools provide for students, they argue, fit poorly the social-developmental needs of children. Just as students are entering adolesence and are seeking greater autonomy, the school environment in which they are situated is becoming more controlling and constrained.[6]

What can be done about it?

Most likely, all of these factors and perhaps others may contribute to the loss of intrinsic motivation that we see in schools – although there are no compelling comparative findings available to test any of these hypotheses directly. If these factors do play a significant part in the phenomenon of declining intrinsic interest, however, they might suggest several obvious possibilities for the redesign of class-rooms that might help to avoid this negative effect.

To the extent that the prevalence of highly controlling systems of extrinsic contingencies and constraints is indeed involved in the observed developmental decline in intrinsic motivation, the obvious implication would be to modify the way in which extrinsic incentives are employed in classrooms accordingly. Although there is not space here for an extended discussion, at least three complementary approaches for implementing such changes suggest themselves, ranging from the relatively microscopic to the relatively macroscopic.

At one extreme, a number of experimental studies have suggested that, at least in the laboratory, even small differences in the wording of otherwise identical extrinsic contingencies – to highlight either the student's own competence or the teacher's control over the student – can influence the likelihood that those contingencies will have positive or negative effects (e.g., Boggiano & Main, 1986; Boggiano, Main, & Katz, 1988; Pittman, Davey, Alafat, Wetherill, & Kramer, 1980; Ryan, 1982). Similarly, in the laboratory, small differences in the description of the goals of an activity to emphasize either how much one can learn or how well one can perform can similarly have large effects on students' motivation and learning (e.g., Dweck, 1986; Dweck & Leggett, 1988; Heyman & Dweck, 1992). In both cases, one might imagine programs designed to modify these specific aspects of teachers' classroom presentations of contingencies.

At a more general level of analysis, one might similarly imagine interventions based on studies of existing differences among teachers in their more general emphasis on autonomy versus control in the classroom, of the sort studied by Deci and associates (1981) and by Boggiano and colleagues (1992). Or, one might imagine programs designed to shift teachers' models concerning classroom performance from what Dweck (1986) has termed "entity-based" theories to "incremental" theories – that is, from theories that attribute performance primarily to stable characteristics of the student to theories that stress the malleability of students and their potential susceptibility to effective instruction. Finally, at the macroscopic extreme, one might imagine attempts to alter more centrally the characteristic structure of the classroom, such as to shift the typical focus from comparative assessment to the documentation of individual mastery, or to encourage more cooperation and less competition in the classroom (cf. Deci & Ryan, 1985; Nicholls, 1988).

In parallel fashion, to the extent that the standard practice of decontextualization of learning may be in part responsible for the decline in intrinsic motivation in school, one can imagine interventions targeting this practice for reform. And, once again, there is an array of possibilities for modifying current practices, ranging from the quite concrete to the relatively wide-ranging.

At a relatively specific level, a number of recent laboratory studies have demonstrated the potentially powerful beneficial effects of seemingly minor manipulations that place traditional abstract learning activities in some concrete, meaningful context for learners. Embedding educational problem-solving activities even in briefly described, but motivationally appealing, concrete situations, for example, has been shown not only to increase students' interest in these activities, but also to promote more effective learning and the use of more efficient and systematic problem-solving skills (e.g., Cordova & Lepper, in press; Lepper &

Cordova, 1992; Parker & Lepper, 1992). Moreover, all of these beneficial effects on motivation and learning can be shown to increase significantly if the concrete context is personalized on the basis of students' interests, backgrounds, or specific choices (e.g., Anand & Ross, 1987; Cordova & Lepper, 1996; Ross, 1983).

At a higher level, these same considerations underlie considerably more general calls for the increased use of what has been termed the "project approach" to schooling (e.g., Edwards, Gandini, & Forman, 1993; Katz & Chard, 1989) – an idea that dates back at least to John Dewey (1913, 1938). In this model, the goal is to integrate a variety of traditional curriculum goals into the pursuit of long-term projects selected on the basis of students' demonstrated interests. Whether the particular goal is to teach mathematics in the context of running a store or computing statistics for a school team, or to embed science education in the running of an amateur meterological station or language skills in the production of a classroom newsletter, such techniques share the aim of enhancing motivation and learning by situating instruction in meaningful and interesting concrete contexts.

Finally, to the extent that declines in intrinsic motivation may be due to the more general social characteristics of schools elaborated by Eccles and Midgely (1988, 1990), efforts at amelioration might take yet a different tack. Proposals for the integration into regular classrooms of techniques such as reciprocal teaching (e.g., Palincsar & Brown, 1984), cross-age or peer tutoring (e.g., Levin, Glass, & Meister, 1984), apprenticeship learning (e.g., J. Brown, Collins, & Duigood, 1989; Rogoff, 1990), and communities of collaborative learning (Aronson, Blaney, Stephan, Sikes, & Snapp, 1978; A. Brown, Campione, Reeve, Ferrara, & Palincsar, 1991; Campione, Brown, & Jay, 1992) all share the goals of promoting student autonomy and interest.

Intrinsic versus extrinsic motivation revisited

Implicit, but hardly hidden, in virtually all of the foregoing discussion is an important premise regarding the value, the importance, and the utility of intrinsic motivation for students. Indeed, as described in some detail, we believe that there are data that demonstrate a variety of beneficial consequences of high levels of intrinsic motivation. At the same time, because almost all of the relevant studies have tended to examine intrinsic motivational orientations only in contrast to extrinsic motivational orientations, one could argue that there is a second, less evident, implicit premise in these studies assigning less value or significance to students' extrinsic motivation. In this final section, we examine and question this latter seductive, but only rarely explicit (e.g., Kohn, 1993), extrapolation.

In defense of extrinsic motivation?

Success in school, and in much of life outside of school, we would argue, may require at least a modicum of both intrinsic and extrinsic motivation (cf. Heyman

& Dweck, 1992; Jackson, 1968; Lepper, 1983a; Nisan, 1992). The very existence of an institution we call "compulsory schooling" is itself a recognition of the fact that our society is unwilling to limit the content of what is taught in school to the set of tasks and topics that students happen to find (or, even, can be made to find) interesting and enjoyable – and appropriately so. The acquisition of many fundamental skills requires hard work and discipline. Mastery of new material will frequently necessitate persistence in the face of an array of initial difficulties and failures. Even ignoring society's demands, the accomplishment of any individual's personal long-term goals will typically require many short-term sacrifices.

This raises some very interesting, if completely unstudied, questions. If one suggests, as we have in this review, that it is possible to assess separate intrinsic and extrinsic motivational orientations that may be largely independent of one another, then one might ask what combination of the two might best predict achievement and other outcomes for different children. Indeed, in this particular sense, possible analogies to the classic literature on "internal" versus "external" locus of control (e.g., Lefcourt, 1973; Rotter, 1966), or Erikson's (1950) "psychosocial" conflicts, suggest themselves. Perhaps too exclusive a preoccupation with either intrinsic or extrinsic motivation may have deleterious effects – though presumably of predictably different sorts. A student driven only by intrinsic motivation might be expected to run quickly afoul of the ubiquitous rules and regulations by which schools govern their pupils, and in the end to be seen as unruly, unresponsive, or antisocial. A student driven solely by extrinsic motivation, on the other hand, might be expected to fit more easily into the school setting, but to suffer more from the effects of chronic performance anxiety, and perhaps depression.

At the very least, these sorts of speculations would seem to suggest the importance of empirical research explicitly designed to evaluate the adaptive value of different forms of student motivation. At the same time, even an exhaustive investigation of these factors would leave unstudied one final consideration of potentially crucial importance – namely the development of other forms of "internalized," but neither purely intrinsic, nor extrinsic, motivation.

Internalization: A missing link?

Although the contrast between intrinsic and extrinsic motivation highlights two distinctive and important forms of academic motivation, it fails to capture a third form of potentially equal importance. This third form involves the conceptually in-between case of initially imposed and purely extrinsic goals that, with socialization and development, come to be internalized and integrated into the individual's own value system (e.g., Lepper, 1983b; Rigby et al., 1992). We come to learn to do things not only because they are fun or likely to lead to some immediate payoff, but because we have come to believe that we "ought" to do them, either to facilitate our own long-term goals (i.e., because it would be "good for" us) or to follow the norms of the group or the situation in which we find ourselves (i.e., because it seems the "right" thing to do).

Surely these sorts of motives assume increasing importance as students progress through school, or at least that is our hypothesis. It is also the main result of one relevant developmental study that analyzed the reasons that children from 5 through 15 gave in response to open-ended questions about why they engaged in a variety of different activities (Chandler & Connell, 1987). More specifically, when children were asked about activities they had said they liked, they gave, at all ages, comparable and predominantly "intrinsic" reasons. When they were asked about activities they had said they disliked, on the other hand, significant developmental trends were apparent: Across this age range, "extrinsic" reasons (e.g., "I study hard to satisfy my parents") decreased, being replaced instead with "internalized" reasons (e.g., "I study hard because I want to get into a good college").

Certainly, such considerations illustrate the wisdom of the inclusion in future developmental studies of this third category of potential academic motivations. Perhaps they even suggest the importance of taking as an explicit goal of the process of schooling the development of such internalized motivations (Lepper, 1983a), as well as the cultivation of intrinsic interests. As Thomas Huxley put the case a century ago: "Perhaps the most valuable result of all education is the ability to make yourself do the thing you have to do, when it ought to be done, whether you like it or not; it is the first lesson that ought to be learned, and however early a man's training begins, it is probably the last lesson that he learns thoroughly."[7]

Notes

1 Many years later, we should note for the sake of completeness, Malone and Lepper (Lepper & Malone, 1987; Malone, 1981; Malone & Lepper, 1987) found it important to add yet a fourth general category – that of fantasy involvement – to the taxonomy of sources of intrinsic motivation. People derive inherent pleasure and motivation, they suggested, from participation in a world of fantasy and pretense, from identification with remote and/or fictitious characters and settings, and even, these days, through the vicarious experience of what has been called "virtual reality."

2 Although many theorists have viewed the desire for control in relatively unitary terms, others (e.g., Weisz, Rothbaum, & Blackburn, 1984) have suggested a distinction between "primary control" (i.e., striving to bring environmental events into line with one's wishes) and "secondary control" (i.e., striving to adjust oneself to environmental conditions – for example, by modifying one's own expectations, attributions, and interpretations of events – so as to control their impact, rather than the conditions themselves).

3 In addition to the three "motivational" dimensions considered here, Harter's (1981) full scale of intrinsic versus extrinsic motivational orientations also encompasses two "informational" dimensions regarding children's dependence on their teachers' judgments and on external criteria in defining success. However, across many studies, including Harter's original presentation, these informational dimensions have loaded on a second, separate "factor" in analyses and have displayed different correlates, consequences, and developmental trends than the motivational items of interest here (Dollinger & Seiters, 1988; Harter, 1981; Tzuriel, 1989).

4 In fairness, it should be noted that Gottfried (1985) also reported a significant increase in

intrinsic motivation toward social studies as children progressed from fourth through eighth grade. Other studies that have assessed attitudes toward specific school subjects, however, have not reproduced this latter finding. Haladyna and Thomas (1979), for instance, found decreases in reported attitudes toward social studies across this same age/grade range, while simultaneously replicating Gottfried's reported decrease in attitudes toward reading.

5 Newman (1990) does report, however, a positive relationship between scores on both Harter's (1981) challenge and independent mastery scales and third- and fifth-grade students' verbal reports of their willingness to seek help from their classroom teacher in mathematics.

6 In our view, there is evidence showing both the relatively steady decreases in intrinsic motivation that we have focused on here and the relatively larger decreases in intrinsic motivation associated more specifically with the transition from elementary to middle school. Details of this latter literature can be found in Anderman and Maeher (1994) and Eccles and Midgley (1990).

7 Despite the potential wisdom of Huxley's remarks, we should note that it is altogether too easy to take this position much too far. Just as John Watson (1924) once extrapolated from the possibility that children might be "spoiled" by their parents to grand pronouncements that mothers should avoid kissing or hugging their babies and should rely instead on head pats and handshakes to express approbation for a job especially well done, a surprising number of educators have expressed to us some version of the opinion that schools really "ought" to remain boring and unpleasant – in order to prepare children to get along in the tough and unpleasant world they will surely face when they graduate. Plainly, we would disagree.

References

Anand, P., & Ross, S. M. (1987). A computer-based strategy for personalizing verbal problems in teaching mathematics. *Educational Communication and Technology Journal, 35,* 151–162.

Anderman, E. M., & Maehr, M. L. (1994). Motivation and schooling in the middle grades. *Review of Educational Research, 64,* 287–309.

Aronson, E., Stephan, C., Sikes, J., Blaney, N., & Snapp, M. (1978). *The jigsaw classroom.* Beverly Hills, CA: Sage.

Bem, S. L. (1974). The measurement of psychological androgyny. *Journal of Clinical and Consulting Psychology, 42,* 155–162.

Bem, S. L. (1993). *The lenses of gender: Transforming the debate on sexual inequality.* New Haven: Yale University Press.

Benware, C., & Deci, E. L. (1984). Quality of learning with an active versus passive motivational set. *American Educational Research Journal, 21,* 755–765.

Berlyne, D. E. (1960). *Conflict, arousal, and curiosity.* New York: McGraw-Hill.

Berlyne, D. E. (1966). Curiosity and exploration. *Science, 153,* 25–33.

Boggiano, A. K., & Main, D. S. (1986). Enhancing children's interest in activities used as rewards: The bonus effect. *Journal of Personality and Social Psychology, 51,* 1116–1126.

Boggiano, A. K., Main, D. S., & Katz, P. (1988). Children's preference for challenge: The role of perceived competence and control. *Journal of Personality and Social Psychology, 54,* 916–924.

Boggiano, A. K., Shields, A., Barrett, M., Kellam, T., Thompson, E., Simons, J., & Katz, P. (1992). Helplessness deficits in students: The role of motivational orientation. *Motivation and Emotion, 16,* 271–296.

Brown, A. L., Campione, J. C., Reeve, R. A., Ferrara, R. A., & Palincsar, A. S. (1991). Interactive learning and individual understanding: The case of reading and mathematics. In L. T. Landsmann (Ed.), *Culture, schooling, and psychological development.* (pp. 136–170). Hillsdale, NJ: Erlbaum.

Brown, J. S., Collins, A., & Duguid, P. (1989). Situated cognition and the culture of learning. *Educational Researcher, 18,* 32–42.

Bruner, J. S. (1962). *On knowing: Essays for the left hand.* Cambridge, MA: Harvard University Press.

Bruner, J. S. (1966). *Toward a theory of instruction.* Cambridge, MA: Harvard University Press.

Campione, J. C., Brown, A. L., & Jay, M. (1992). Computers in a community of learners. In E. DeCorte & M. Linn (Eds.), *Computer-based learning environments and problem solving* (pp. 163–188). Berlin: Springer-Verlag.

Chandler, C. L., & Connell, J. P. (1987). Children's intrinsic, extrinsic, and internalized motivation: A developmental study of children's reasons for liked and disliked behaviours. *British Journal of Developmental Psychology, 5,* 357–365.

Condry, J. (1977). Enemies of exploration: Self-initiated versus other-initiated learning. *Journal of Personality and Social Psychology, 35,* 459–477.

Condry, J., & Chambers, J. (1978). Intrinsic motivation and the process of learning. In M. R. Lepper & D. Greene (Eds.), *The hidden costs of reward* (pp. 61–84). Hillsdale, NJ: Erlbaum.

Condry, J., & Lepper, M. R. (1992). Special issue: Intrinsic motivation and education. *Motivation and Emotion, 16* (3), 157–296.

Cordova, D. I., & Lepper, M. R. (in press). Intrinsic motivation and the process of learning: Beneficial effects of contextualization, personalization, and choice. *Journal of Educational Psychology.*

Cordova, D. I., & Lepper, M. R. (1996). The effects of intrinsic versus extrinsic incentives on the process of learning. Unpublished manuscript. Stanford University.

Csikszentmihalyi, M. (1975). *Beyond boredom and anxiety.* San Francisco: Jossey-Bass.

deCharms, R. (1968). *Personal causation.* New York: Academic Press.

Deci, E. L. (1971). Effects of externally mediated rewards on intrinsic motivation. *Journal of Personality and Social Psychology, 18,* 105–155.

Deci, E. L. (1975). *Intrinsic motivation.* New York: Plenum Press.

Deci, E. L. (1981). *The psychology of self-determination.* Lexington, MA: Heath.

Deci, E. L., & Ryan, R. M. (1985). *Intrinsic motivation and self-determination in human behavior.* New York: Plenum Press.

Deci, E. L., & Ryan, R. M. (1991). A motivational approach to self: Integration in personality. In R. Dienstbier (Ed.), *Nebraska symposium on motivation* (Vol. 38, pp. 237–288). Lincoln: University of Nebraska Press.

Deci, E. L., Schwartz, A. J., Sheinman, L., & Ryan, R. M. (1981). An instrument to assess adults' orientations toward control versus autonomy with children: Reflections on intrinsic motivation and perceived competence. *Journal of Educational Psychology, 73,* 642–650.

Dewey, J. (1913). *Interest and effort in education.* Boston: Houghton-Mifflin.

Dewey, J. (1938). *Experience and education.* New York: Macmillan.

Dollinger, S. J., & Seiters, J. A. (1988). Intrinsic motivation among clinic-referred children. *Bulletin of the Psychonomic Society, 26* (5), 449–451.

Dreeben, R. (1968). *On what is learned in school.* Reading, MA: Addison-Wesley.

Dweck, C. S. (1986). Motivational processes affecting learning. *American Psychologist, 41,* 1040–1048.

Dweck, C. S., Davidson, W., Nelson, S., & Enna, B. (1978). Sex differences in learned helplessness: II. The contingencies of evaluative feedback in the classroom and III. An experimental analysis. *Developmental Psychology, 14,* 268–276.

Dweck, C. S., & Leggett, E. L. (1988). A social-cognitive approach to motivation and personality. *Psychological Review, 95,* 256–273.

Eccles, J. S., & Midgley, C. (1988). Stage-environment fit: Developmentally appropriate classrooms for young adolescents. In R. E. Ames & C. Ames (Eds.), *Research on motivation in education* (Vol. 3, pp. 139–186). New York: Academic Press.

Eccles, J. S., & Midgley, C. (1990). Changes in academic motivation and self-perceptions during early adolescence. In R. Montemayor, G. R. Adams, & T. P. Gullotta (Eds.), *Advances in adolescent development: From childhood to adolescence* (Vol. 2, pp. 134–155). Newbury Park, CA: Sage.

Edwards, C., Gandini, L., & Forman, G. (1993). *The hundred languages of children: The Reggio Emilia approach to early childhood education.* Norwood, NJ: Ablex.

Epstein, J. L., & McPartland, J. M. (1976). The concept and measurement of quality of school life. *American Educational Research Journal, 13,* 15–30.

Erikson, E. H. (1950). *Childhood and society.* New York: Norton.

Ginsberg, H. (1977). *Children's arithmetic: The learning process.* New York: Van Nostrand.

Gottfried, A. E. (1985). Academic intrinsic motivation in elementary and junior high school students. *Journal of Educational Psychology, 77,* 631–645.

Gottfried, A. E. (1990). Academic intrinsic motivation in young elementary school children. *Journal of Educational Psychology, 82* (3), 525–538.

Grolnick, W. S., & Ryan, R. M. (1987). Autonomy in children's learning: An experimental and individual difference investigation. *Journal of Personality and Social Psychology, 52,* 890–898.

Haladyna, T., & Thomas, G. (1979). The attitudes of elementary school children toward school and subject matters. *Journal of Experimental Education, 48,* 18–23.

Harter, S. (1978). Pleasure derived from challenge and the effects of receiving grades on children's difficulty level choices. *Child Development, 49,* 788–799.

Harter, S. (1981). A new self-report scale of intrinsic versus extrinsic orientation in the classroom: Motivational and informational components. *Developmental Psychology, 17,* 300–312.

Harter, S., & Zigler, E. (1974). The assessment of effectance motivation in normal and retarded children. *Developmental Psychology, 10,* 169–180.

Heyman, G. D., & Dweck, C. S. (1992). Achievement goals and intrinsic motivation: Their relation and their role in adaptive motivation. *Motivation and Emotion, 16,* 231–247.

Holt, J. (1964). *How children fail.* New York: Holt, Rinehart, & Winston.

Hunt, J. McV. (1961). *Intelligence and experience.* New York: Ronald Press.

Hunt, J. McV. (1965). Intrinsic motivation and its role in psychological development. In D. Levine (Ed.), *Nebraska symposium on motivation* (Vol. 13, pp. 189–282). Lincoln: University of Nebraska Press.

Jackson, P. (1968). *Life in classrooms.* New York: Holt, Rinehart & Winston.

Katz, L. G., & Chard, S. C. (1989). *Engaging children's minds: The project approach.* Norwood, NJ: Ablex.

Kohn, A. (1993). *Punished by rewards: The trouble with gold stars, incentive plans, A's, praise, and other bribes.* New York: Houghton Mifflin.

Kruglanski, A. W. (1978). Endogenous attribution and intrinsic motivation. In M. R. Lepper & D. Greene (Eds.), *The hidden costs of reward* (pp. 85–108). Hillsdale, NJ: Erlbaum.

Kruglanski, A. W., Friedman, I., & Zeevi, G. (1971). The effects of extrinsic incentives on some qualitative aspects of task performance. *Journal of Personality, 39,* 606–617.

Lefcourt, H. J. (1973). The function of the illusions of control and freedom. *American Psychologist, 28,* 417–425.

Lepper, M. R. (1983a). Extrinsic reward and intrinsic motivation: Implications for the classroom. In J. M. Levine & M. C. Wang (Eds.), *Teacher and student perceptions: Implications for learning* (pp. 281–317). Hillsdale, NJ: Erlbaum.

Lepper, M. R. (1983b). Social control processes and the internalization of social values: An attributional perspective. In E. T. Higgins, D. N. Ruble, & W. W. Hartup (Eds.), *Developmental social cognition: A sociocultural perspective* (pp. 294–330). Cambridge: Cambridge University Press.

Lepper, M. R. (1988). Motivational considerations in the study of instruction. *Cognition and Instruction, 5,* 289–309.

Lepper, M. R., & Cordova, D. I. (1992). A desire to be taught: Instructional consequences of intrinsic motivation. *Motivation and Emotion, 16,* 187–208.

Lepper, M. R., & Greene, D. (Eds.). (1978). *The hidden costs of reward.* Hillsdale, NJ: Erlbaum.

Lepper, M. R., Greene, D., & Nisbett, R. E. (1973). Undermining children's intrinsic interest with extrinsic rewards: A test of the "overjustification" hypothesis. *Journal of Personality and Social Psychology, 28,* 129–137.

Lepper, M. R., & Hodell, M. (1989). Intrinsic motivation in the classroom. In C. Ames & R. Ames (Eds.), *Research on motivation in education* (Vol. 3, pp. 73–105). New York: Academic Press.

Lepper, M. R., & Malone, T. W. (1987). Intrinsic motivation and instructional effectiveness in computer-based education. In R. E. Snow & M. J. Farr (Eds.), *Aptitude, learning, and instruction: III. Conative and affective process analyses* (pp. 255–296). Hillsdale, NJ: Erlbaum.

Lepper, M. R., Sagotsky, G., Dafoe, J., & Greene, D. (1982). Consequences of superfluous social constraints: Effects of nominal contingencies on children's subsequent intrinsic interest. *Journal of Personality and Social Psychology, 42,* 51–65.

Levin, H. M., Glass, E., & Meister, G. (1984). A cost-effectiveness analysis of four educational interventions. IFG Project Report No. 84-A11. Stanford, CA: Institute for Research on Educational Finance and Government.

Maehr, M. L. (1976). Continuing motivation: An analysis of a seldom considered educational outcome. *Review of Educational Research, 46,* 443–462.

Malone, T. W. (1981). Toward a theory of intrinsically motivating instruction. *Cognitive Science, 4,* 333–369.

Malone, T. W., & Lepper, M. R. (1987). Making learning fun: A taxonomy of intrinsic motivations for learning. In R. E. Snow & M. J. Farr (Eds.), *Aptitude, learning, and instruction: III. Conative and affective process analyses* (pp. 223–253). Hillsdale, NJ: Erlbaum.

Maslow, A. H. (1954). *Motivation and personality.* New York: Harper.

Newman, R. S. (1990). Children's help-seeking in the classroom: The role of motivational factors and attitudes. *Journal of Educational Psychology, 82,* 71–80.

Nicholls, J. G. (1988). *Competence, accomplishment, and motivation: A perspective on development and education.* Cambridge, MA: Harvard University Press.

Nisan, M. (1992). Beyond intrinsic motivation: "Sense of the desirable" as a link between responsible and effective teaching. In F. K. Oser, A. Dick, & J. Patry (Eds.), *Effective and responsible teaching: The new synthesis* (pp. 126–138). San Francisco: Jossey-Bass.

Nuttin, J. R. (1973). Pleasure and reward in human motivation and learning. In D. E. Berlyne & K. B. Madsen (Eds.), *Pleasure, reward, preference* (pp. 243–274). New York: Academic Press.

Palincsar, A. S., & Brown, A. L. (1984). Reciprocal teaching of comprehension–fostering and monitoring activities. *Cognition and Instruction, 1,* 117–175.

Parker, L. E., & Lepper, M. R. (1992). Effects of fantasy contexts on children's learning and motivation: Making learning more fun. *Journal of Personality and Social Psychology, 62,* 625–633.

Perkins, D. (1992). *Smart schools: From educating memories to educating minds.* New York: Free Press.

Pittman, T. S., Davey, M. E., Alafat, K. A., Wetherill, K. V., & Kramer, N. A. (1980). Informational vs. controlling verbal rewards. *Personality and Social Psychology Bulletin, 6,* 228–233.

Rigby, C. S., Deci, E. L., Patrick, B. C., & Ryan, R. M. (1992). Beyond the intrinsic–extrinsic dichotomy: Self-determination in motivation and learning. *Motivation and Emotion, 16* (3), 165–185.

Rogoff, B. (1990). *Apprenticeship in thinking: Cognitive development in social context.* New York: Oxford University Press.

Ross, S. M. (1983). Increasing the meaningfulness of quantitative material by adapting context to student background. *Journal of Educational Psychology, 75,* 519–529.

Rotter, J. B. (1966). Generalized expectancies for internal versus external control of reinforcement. *Psychological Monographs, 80,* whole no. 609.

Ryan, R. M. (1982). Control and information in the intrapersonal sphere: An extension of cognitive evaluation theory. *Journal of Personality and Social Psychology, 43,* 450–461.

Sansone, C., & Morgan, C. (1992). Intrinsic motivation and education: Competence in context. *Motivation and Emotion, 16,* 249–270.

Silberman, C. (1970). *Crisis in the classroom.* New York: Random House.

Steele, C. M. (1992, April). Race and the schooling of Black Americans. *Atlantic Monthly,* 68–78.

Tang, S., & Hall, V. (1995). The overjustification effect: A meta-analysis. *Applied Cognitive Psychology, 9,* 365–404.

Tzuriel, D. (1989). Development of motivational and cognitive-informational orientations from third to ninth grades. *Journal of Applied Developmental Psychology, 10,* 107–121.

Watson, J. B. (1924). *Behaviorism.* Chicago: University of Chicago Press.

Weisz, J. R., Rothbaum, F. M., & Blackburn, T. F. (1984). Standing out and standing in: The psychology of control in America and Japan. *American Psychologist, 39,* 955–969.

White, R. W. (1959). Motivation reconsidered: The concept of competence. *Psychological Review, 66,* 297–333.

Winnett, R. A., & Winkler, R. C. (1972). Current behavior modification in the classroom: Be still, be quiet, be docile. *Journal of Applied Behavior Analysis, 5,* 499–504.

Zigler, E. (1966). Research on personality structure in the retardate. In N. R. Ellis (Ed.), *International review of research in mental retardation* (Vol. 1, pp. 77–108). New York: Academic Press.

Zigler, E. (1971). The retarded child as a whole person. In H. E. Adams & W. K. Boardman (Eds.), *Advances in experimental clinical psychology* (pp. 47–122). New York: Pergamon Press.

3   Race, gender, and young children

Phyllis A. Katz and Jennifer A. Kofkin

Race and gender are two important social categories that influence developmental trajectories very early in life. The salience of gender is evident in a newborn baby's first introduction to the world – "It's a boy" or "It's a girl." While references to race are usually less overt than references to gender, especially with regard to young children, race is equally influential, and may even gain some of its power from the silence that surrounds it. How children come to understand and develop a sense of identity based upon these categories constitutes one important aspect of their developing social competence (Zigler, 1966, 1979).

The primary aim of this chapter is to explore the nature of this early understanding, based upon the authors' longitudinal research that examined the development of both race and gender learning in young children. The first two portions of this chapter describe the methods and findings of this research project. The project is unusual in several respects: in its simultaneous investigation of gender and race concepts in the same sample; in the inclusion of families from two racial groups (Euro- and African American); and in the early age at which assessment began. It is more typical for research to focus on either race *or* gender, thus failing to account for the fact that individuals belong to multiple social categories. It is also relatively rare for investigators to use more than one racial group in studies of race and gender. Studies of gender learning, for example, typically employ white, middle-class children, and researchers may well have overgeneralized their results from this group. Finally, because children begin to acquire gender and race stereotypes early in life (e.g., even 2-year-olds can correctly categorize clothing and some tasks by gender [Weinraub et al., 1984]), we began the investigation when the children were six months old.

Following a brief description of the study, some of the findings will be presented. This presentation is organized around four important components of gender and

Because this project has not yet been completed, there is no one existing publication that fully describes the results. Some of the tasks have been presented or published (and these references are included, where relevant). Any questions concerning specific procedures can be addressed to the authors. We would like to thank the people who made this research, and this chapter, possible. This project was supported by NICHD Grant #22929. We would also like to thank the families participating in the studies and the testers, Marty Barrett and Sylvia Grove.

51

race development: *awareness, identity, preferences,* and *stereotypes.* It has been hypothesized that these four components constitute the early preschool portions of a developmental continuum of attitude development (Aboud, 1988; Katz, 1976, 1982), and one of the purposes of the longitudinal study was to corroborate this sequence. Awareness of group differences (race or gender) appears to be a necessary prerequisite for other stages and thus was expected to appear first. It was further predicted that rudimentary identity development would follow awareness, and developmentally precede children's expressions of gender- or race-related preferences. Knowledge and endorsement of group stereotypes was expected to be the most developmentally advanced stage of preschool attitude development.[1] Some developmental overlap among these components was also anticipated.

The final portion of the chapter examines the implications of our findings for understanding normative development and developmental psychopathology. This discussion explores how psychologists define normality and deviance, and how these definitions, in turn, affect our understanding of child development, especially the development of children in minority groups.[2] Fortuitously, the two authors of this chapter come from the somewhat different disciplines of developmental and community psychology. The developmental approach focuses on how children acquire information about social categories, and how their socialization processes may differ as a result of the categories to which they belong. The community approach is concerned not only with the child and the family, but also with the broader sociopolitical and cultural milieu. The concluding section will attempt to synthesize two perspectives.

Longitudinal study: Methods

Recruitment of study participants began in 1988 and was done in several ways. Records of new births were obtained through the Colorado Department of Health, advertisements were placed in local newspapers, requests for participation were made at childbirth education classes, and networking was used, especially through the cooperation of obstetrician-gynecologists.

During the first 3 years of their lives, children and their families were tested seven times (at 6, 9, 12, 18, 24, 30, and 36 months of age). These age points constitute the major focus of this chapter. The children and their families are still being assessed. Data collection for the 60-month age point has just been completed, and the final testing (at 72 months) is ongoing.

The original sample of children consisted of 104 African Americans (54 boys and 50 girls) and 109 Euro-Americans (53 boys and 56 girls). There was, of course, some attrition. At 36 months, 63% of the original African American families (N = 66) and 76% of the Euro-American families (N = 83) were still participating. Because attrition rates were higher in the African American sample during infancy, a cohort of 20 African American families was added to the longitudinal sample at the 12- and 18-month age points.

In order to make participation in this research as convenient as possible, testing occurred in the participants' homes. Same-race testers were used to increase family members' comfort in responding to the questions. Assessments lasted approximately 1 hour at 6 months and increased to approximately 2 hours by 36 months. Families were paid for participation at each testing session.

We attempted to match both racial groups in terms of socioeconomic status and have a wide representation of socioeconomic levels within each group, ranging from those on welfare to professionals. Nevertheless, the two groups do show the anticipated mean differences. In addition, there was, as previously noted, more attrition in the African American sample, in part because these families were more mobile. This illustrates the inevitable influence of social factors relating to group membership on the research process itself, a point that will be revisited in the final section.

Research findings

Awareness development

Prior to the past decade, it was believed that children became aware of gender and race cues at 3 or 4 years of age (e.g., Proshansky, 1966). With the introduction of newer, nonverbal measurement techniques, it now appears that children are considerably more precocious than previously thought.

A variety of techniques has been employed to measure awareness, including an infant's differential responses to people. In the gender area (which is much more extensively investigated than race) young infants respond to male and female adults differently. For example, they condition more readily to, and prefer higher-pitched as compared with low-pitched voices (e.g., Fernald & Kuhl, 1981; Poulin-Dubois, Serbin, Kenyon, & Derbyshire, 1994), suggesting a rudimentary awareness of some gender-related cues.

More recently, visual habituation techniques have been employed to assess awareness of categories in young infants. There are several variations of the habituation paradigm, but they all are based on the assumption that a *decrease* in an infant's attention span after repeated presentation of the same, or similar stimuli represents habituation, whereas a subsequent *increase* in attention to a novel stimulus indicates dishabituation (cf. L. G. Cohen & Younger, 1983; Fagan, 1976). As part of the longitudinal study, a visual habituation task was administered when the children were 6, 9, and 12 months of age in order to determine the ages at which infants responded in a categorical fashion to gender and race cues. Responding on a categorical basis entails more than visual discrimination of individual exemplars.

To demonstrate categorical knowledge, the child had to respond to different stimuli within the category on the basis of similarities (i.e., habituation), and perceive stimuli outside the category to be very distinctive from these within the category (dishabituation). In order to assess when these trends were present, we employed a habituation paradigm. In this section, we will first describe results with the children using visual habituation. We will then examine the role of several parental variables that influence awareness of race and gender categories during the first years of life.

For the gender habituation task, we employed a series of four different faces that were either all female or all male (same race as the subjects). The faces were presented until the habituation criterion was attained (i.e., looking times of the last three consecutive trials being 50% of the average looking time of the first three trials). After habituation, a fifth face that was of the same gender as the previous four was introduced (the posthabituation trial), followed by a face from the other gender category (the test stimulus). A comparable approach was used to assess the racial category. The child was habituated to a series of either four Euro- or African American faces (same gender as the subject), followed by a novel within-category face, and then a face from the previously unseen racial category. The particular faces used were counterbalanced across research participants. Age of the models used in the photographs was also varied so that infants viewed a series of pictures that depicted either children or adults. Because physical gender cues vary with age, gender habituation was expected to occur at an earlier age for adult faces as compared with child faces. No such difference was predicted for race habituation.

Results indicated that at 6 months of age, the overwhelming majority of the sample habituated to both male and female faces. Children exhibited dishabituation (looking times significantly different from previous three trials) to both the within-category face and the new category. Responses to the test stimuli (i.e., the other-gender face) were, however, significantly longer than were responses to novel faces within the same gender category.[3] This finding suggests that infants categorize faces on the basis of gender cues at 6 months of age. As anticipated, infants exhibited stronger discriminative responses to gender cues in adult faces than in children's faces, but this disparity diminished by 1 year of age.

Although previous researchers have documented gender habituation in infants, results in this study were more consistent across subjects than those reported by others (e.g., Cohen & Strauss, 1979; Fagan, 1976; Leinbach, 1991). Almost 90% of the 6-month-olds in this sample could distinguish gender categories, irrespective of whether the habituation series consisted of male or female faces. One additional finding of interest is that white children exhibited stronger dishabituation to gender cues (e.g., longer looking times to faces outside the habituated category) than did black children at 6 months of age, a difference that disappeared by the 12-month age point.

In contrast to gender, there has been much less research conducted on children's early perceptions of race-related cues. Only one study of face recognition varied the race of faces (Fagan & Singer, 1979) and found that 5- and 6-month old white infants did not distinguish or categorize race cues. Because of this, we anticipated that awareness of racial cues and categories would occur later than gender categorization – after the age of 6 months. This turned out not to be the case. As with gender, presentation of a face of an unseen race category elicited significantly more looking in 6-month olds than did a novel but same-race face. In fact, the disparity in looking times between in-category and out-category faces was greater for race than for gender cues. Racial group differences were found at 6 months of age on race dishabituation as well – but in the opposite direction to those found with gender dishabituation. African American infants exhibited stronger dishabituation to race cues than did Euro-American infants. As with gender, this difference disappeared at later ages.

Thus, our research indicates that nonverbal awareness of both gender and race categories in person perception consistently occurs in most children by 6 months of age, suggesting that initial awareness probably begins even earlier. There appears to be some differential sensitivity to these two types of cues by research participants in the two racial groups. Out-category faces elicited higher looking times for Euro-American infants whereas African American infants showed higher looking times to faces of a different race following habituation. Greater sensitivity to race cues by African American children has also been found in earlier studies with older preschool children. Using a discrimination learning paradigm, Katz and Seavy (1973) found that among 4-year-olds, black children learned shade cues more rapidly than did white children.

The finding that very young infants exhibit awareness of gender and race categories in human faces suggests that these categories are visually salient long before language development. Thus, there appears to be a lag time of about 2 years between early nonverbal awareness of race and gender, and the ability to deal with these categories using verbal labels. As will be described further in the next section, research participants did not perform tasks correctly on the basis of verbal gender labels until 30 months of age, and they were not very proficient with regard to verbal race labels even at 36 months.

It seems that during the time period between children's early awareness of race and gender cues and language development, parents talk freely about gender differences, but provide little assistance to their children in making sense of the racial differences the children see around them. Parental reticence in talking about race has been documented both in self-report measures and a videotaped parent–child interaction task.

In an observational task, administered when children were 12 and 18 months, parents were asked to talk with their children about pictures in a book. Half of these pictures depicted African American people, and half depicted Euro-Americans. In addition, gender and age were systematically varied within each racial group. At 12 months, fewer than 2% of the parents made any mention of race. At 18 months, the number increased to 6%. For the sake of comparison, parents almost always mentioned gender to their children during this task: 94% of parents made gender references at 12 months, and 99% did so at 18 months.

Parental silence on the topic of race was also evident in self-report measures that were administered when their children were 36 months old. Parents indicated whether they thought it was important to discuss racial differences with their children, whether they actually did so, and the reasons why they thought it was or was not important to talk about race.

Interestingly, there was a trend for more white parents (54%) than black parents (38%) to believe race discussions were important. Even parents who reported that it was important to discuss race, however, did not necessarily do so. Three questions assessed whether parents actually talked about race with their children. For example, in response to the question "Do you comment about race differences if you see them in books, in magazines, or on TV?" fewer than 20% of parents commented on racial differences in books, magazines, and on television, and fewer than 10% commented on differences they encountered in playgrounds and stores. There was no notable difference in the frequency with which African American and Euro-American parents commented on race differences. African American parents were, however, more likely than white parents (48% vs. 12%) to discuss their child's own racial identity.

The reasons for parental discourse (or lack of discourse) about race differ for black and white parents. At 36 months we asked parents *why* they believed it was or was not important to discuss racial differences with their children. Among parents who believed it was important to discuss race, white parents most often cited the need to answer their children's questions and to teach them about equality and appreciating differences. Black parents most often cited the need to make children aware of race differences and to prepare children for the real world, including anticipated encounters with prejudice.

Among white parents who believed it was *not* important to discuss race, the most common reasons given were that their children had not asked, or that they did not want to make racial differences salient to their children. Black parents who thought race discussion was not important were most likely to say that their children were too young, implying that discussion would be important in the future. The results from the earlier habituation/dishabituation tasks may call these various parental reasons into question. Although children may not ask about race differences or understand many of the social meanings of race, they do appear to be aware of race as a category by 6 months of age. Stevenson (1994) suggests that a variety of fears may prevent parents from discussing race with children, including the fear of having their comments misinterpreted or the fear of feeling helpless to counter the injustices children may encounter. Additional research is needed on how parents might discuss race productively so as to help their children to think about race in nonbiased ways. Spencer (1983) cautions that when direct discussion and instruction do not occur, traditional views and prevalent stereotypes remain unchallenged. Our research confirms what others have found (e.g., Aboud, 1988; Bigler & Liben,

1993; Katz, 1983) – preferences and biases that reflect societal valuing of whites over blacks appear by the preschool years. Findings to be presented in the following section with regard to children's early identity development also suggest that children may begin to learn societal values regarding race before the age of 3 years.

Identity development

Some theorists have argued that gender constitutes the core aspect of an individual's identity, whereas others have argued that race is the most central aspect of identity (e.g. Gonzalez & Cauce, 1995). Debate about the primacy of different social identities may be less productive than the recognition that both race and gender are important to a child's developing identity, although development with regard to each may proceed in different ways.

Both gender and race identity are complex constructs, and their development goes through many stages throughout the life span (cf. Katz, 1982; Phinney, 1990). One cannot say with certainty when a sense of identity begins. Part of the problem is methodological. Psychologists have designed nonverbal techniques (such as habituation) to assess visual discrimination and categorization in infants, but the measurement of identity has relied mainly on verbal techniques.[4]

The first readily measurable step in the process of identity development is the child's ability to use an appropriate verbal label. There is considerable variation in when this occurs, and precocity in gender labeling relates to many other aspects of gender-role development (cf. Fagot & Leinbach, 1985). Interestingly, there are no comparable studies of when children begin identifying themselves as part of a racial group, and what variables correlate with race labeling.

As part of the longitudinal project, we assessed young children's ability to use gender and race labels. At 24, 30, and 36 months, children were asked direct questions (e.g., "Are you a boy or a girl?") that assessed their ability to label gender and race in themselves and others. Children also used dolls and pictures (of themselves and of others) in response to category labels. For example, with regard to self, children were asked to choose which of several dolls that varied in race and gender looked like them. They were also asked to place a Polaroid picture of themselves in one of two boxes depicting photographs of either males or females (for gender) or photographs of African Americans or Euro-Americans (for race).

As previously noted, gender schemas were expected to develop prior to race schemas. This prediction was based, in part, on the observation that access to individuals of other races varies and may be minimal (especially for white children), whereas children are normally exposed to multiple exemplars of both males and females. While the expected disparity between gender and race schema development was not found with regard to early awareness, it did appear on the identity measures.

Many children were unresponsive to direct questions concerning identity at 24 months. Half of the children either did not answer at all, or gave an inappropriate response (e.g., "Are you a girl or a boy?" "No."). A third of the children could correctly label themselves as to gender, and 16% mislabeled themselves. With regard to race, only 16% could correctly self-label at 24 months.

The pattern changes considerably at 30 months. At this age, more children responded appropriately to verbal questions, and children were much more accurate in self-labeling: 70% of them now used the correct gender label for themselves. Children were still not accurate when labeling other children, however (only 28% labeled other children's gender correctly). As was true at the earlier age point, self-labeling based on race was much less accurate than for gender (41% responded correctly to race labels). In addition, at 30 months black and white children behave very differently when self-labeling based on race. White children responded accurately more often than did black children (61% versus 19% correct, respectively). Furthermore, over half of the African American children at this age did not respond to the race question. They were often silent (3-year-olds rarely say they don't know) and testers reported that they seemed to be very uncomfortable.

At 36 months, 89% of the children could correctly self-label as to gender, although they remained considerably less accurate when labeling others (only 36% correctly labeled their friends). With regard to race, only 56% accurately self-labeled. As was true for the earlier assessment, race differences were still present. Only 32% of black children accurately self-labeled based on race, compared with 77% for the Euro-American children.

If self-labeling constitutes a first step in gender and race identity development, it would appear that considerable development occurs between 2 and 3 years of age. The percentage of children capable of self-labeling clearly increases during this time period, and by 3 years of age, the overwhelming majority of children correctly use gender labels for themselves (although children remain surprisingly inaccurate with regard to labeling others). Many fewer children correctly use race labels, however, and white children show clearer developmental increases than do black children. In contrast to the direction of group differences regarding early awareness of race cues, it is the white 3-year-olds who were more accurate in racial self-labeling than their black counterparts. As will be discussed in the final section, cognitive factors do not adequately explain these race differences in identity development.

Play preferences

Once children are able to identify themselves and others on the basis of race and gender, they may begin to use these categories to make choices. One important domain in which race and gender may influence children's choices is in the selection of preferred playmates.

For many, visions of boys and girls of all colors playing together without regard to race or gender portends a better, more harmonious future. It seems, however, that race and gender continue to be strong determinants of children's friendship choices. Research consistently documents a same-sex bias in choosing friends from known classmates and from pictures of unfamiliar peers (Ramsey, 1987). Although biases have also been demonstrated with regard to race preferences, the direction of these biases vary. Some researchers have found that young children prefer same-race peers (Finkelstein & Haskins, 1983; Newman, Liss, & Sherman, 1983), although most report a preference for ethnic majority group members and a bias against dark skin colors (e.g., Jaffe, 1988; Porter, 1991; Spencer & Markstrom-Adams, 1990).

In the present study, children at 30 and 36 months were shown photographs of 16 children (4 black boys, 4 black girls, 4 white boys, and 4 white girls) and were asked to choose the child with whom they would most like to play. The pictures were selected from an initial pool of 50 pictures of Euro-American and African American children that were taken by a professional photographer. An effort was made to photograph children with a range of skin tones and hair colors. Of the 50 pictures, 16 were eliminated because either the models appeared to be biracial or because their facial features, facial expressions, hair styles, or clothing were more distinctive than the others. The remaining pictures were piloted with 12 children, both black and white, between the ages of 3 and 5 years. Photographs that children looked at for either very short or very long periods of time were eliminated in order to obtain a final set of 16 pictures. At the 60-month testing, children selected the peer with whom they most wanted to play from a set of 4 photographs (one child of each race and sex). Additionally, at all age points, parents reported the race and sex of the friend with whom their child actually played most often.

The playmate task revealed different developmental trends in race preferences for each racial group. At 30 months, all children demonstrated a same-race preference when choosing a playmate from photographs of unfamiliar peers. The majority of both black children (69%) and white children (65%) selected a same-race playmate. At 36 months, a significant shift occurred. The number of white children exhibiting a preference for same-race playmates increased (to 82%), while the number of black children preferring same-race playmates decreased dramatically (to 32%). Thus, by 36 months, the majority of both black and white children chose white playmates.[5] At 60 months, the race difference in same-race preferences persisted, although the effect was weaker. Almost two-thirds of all children selected a white playmate at 60 months.

A marked race difference also occurred in actual playmates. Averaging across the toddler and preschool ages, white children almost always played most often with a same-race friend (90%), whereas only 60% of the black children played with a same-race friend. Furthermore, the percentage of black children playing with same-race friends decreased over time; by 60 months only 39% of black children had a same-race friend.

With regard to the role of gender in playmate choices, there was a clear trend for same-gender preferences to increase over time. At 30 months, there were neither strong same-sex preferences nor gender differences in picture choices, although there was a race difference: Black children had stronger same-sex preferences, accounted for by the strong same-sex preferences shown by black girls. At 36 months, this race difference disappeared, but a gender difference for same-sex play-mates emerged: Girls exhibited same-sex preferences but boys did not. By 60 months, a same-sex preference was clearly in place: 86% of all children chose a same-sex playmate. A same-sex preference also occurred in terms of actual friend-ships; approximately two-thirds of children played most often with a same-sex playmate at all age points, according to parental report.

In summary, both race and gender appear to play important roles in children's playmate choices. When choosing a playmate from photographs of unfamiliar chil-dren, most respondents selected a same-race playmate at 30 months. At 36 months, however, preferences for same-race playmates increased among white children, but decreased sharply for black children. The overall preference for white playmates is less marked but still strong at 60 months. These findings may reflect differences in the social environments of the two racial groups. There is very little variability for white children in the race of both actual and hypothetical playmates, perhaps because of their limited cross-race exposure. Black children may be more willing to choose an other-race playmate because of their greater exposure to different races. Indeed, black children who chose a white playmate on the photograph task were more likely to have a nonblack friend than were black children who chose a black playmate. The race of actual friends cannot be the sole factor influencing hypothetical choices, however, as the developmental trends in these two indicators of playmate preferences were not completely comparable. For example, while the proportion of black children actually playing with a same-race friend dropped at each testing point, the proportion of black children choosing a black child on the photograph task did not decrease after 36 months.

Gender appears to be a strong determinant of playmate choices, as well. Between 30 and 60 months of age, children became increasingly likely to choose a same-sex playmate on the photograph task. A sex difference at 36 months suggests that this same-sex preference may emerge first for girls. Although there were race as well as sex differences along the way, by 60 months the overwhelming majority of all 5-year-olds chose a same-sex playmate.

The precocity of girls in demonstrating same-sex preferences was also evident in a second indicator: preferences for sex-stereotyped toys. At all age points, chil-dren were given an opportunity to play with toys that were either male-stereotyped (e.g., tool set or baseball outfit), female-stereotyped (e.g., kitchen set or princess outfit), or neutral (e.g., zoo animals or clown outfit). The data presented for this task reflect the proportion of time children spent with the male- and female-stereotyped toys during the first minute of play.

While some researchers have reported a general preference for same-sex toys at 18 months (Caldera, Huston, & O'Brien, 1989), this was true only for the girls in our sample. At 18 months, girls spent 34% of their time with the female toy and 16% with the male toy, whereas boys spent the same amount of time with each toy. By 30 months of age, the girls showed a slight increase (51% of their time was spent with the female toy and 32% with the male toy) but the boys still did not show a same-sex toy preference.

Consistent with previous research (e.g., Martin & Little, 1990; Turner, Gervai, & Hinde, 1993), both boys and girls demonstrated clear same-sex toy preferences by 36 months. Boys exhibited a sharp increase in time spent with same-sex toys between 30 and 36 months. At 3 years of age, boys spent 67% of their time playing with the male toy, and only 14% with the female toy. The corresponding figures for girls was 58% of play time with the female and 27% with the male toy. At 60 months of age, both girls and boys spent the vast majority of their time with the same-sex stereotyped toy (71% of the time for girls, 77% for boys). Thus, the data with regard to same-sex preferences suggest an "escalator effect." The rates of speed may differ for each, but boys and girls both wind up in the same place.

A final finding of interest is that girls demonstrated more sex-role flexibility in their choices than did boys. Although, as noted, girls had strong same-sex toy preferences, they were also more likely than boys to play with the *other-sex* toy at 36 months. This sex-difference was even more marked at 60 months. Whereas girls spent an average of 21% of their time playing with the male toy, boys spent only 3% of their time with the female toy.

Stereotype development

Stereotypes do not arise full-blown but, as our previous theoretical elaborations indicate, may well be a later stage of schema development. The longitudinal project examined the developmental sequence of the building blocks of an intergroup attitude or schema. As previously noted, awareness is the initial step. The child must be capable of distinguishing members of different groups, and must also have a concept of the groups (i.e., even though individual members of the group differ, children respond to them in similar ways). The next requisite skills are the ability to categorize oneself and others into the correct group on the basis of relevant perceptual cues, and the ability to use group labels correctly with regard to oneself and others. These components were discussed in the earlier section on identity. Schemas usually have affective components as well. Thus, we also investigated when children begin to prefer members of one group over another in play choices. This was discussed in the earlier section on preferences. This final results section examines when children show a tendency to associate positive attributes to their own group and/or negative characteristics to other groups.

As young children begin to develop schemas about race, the relative immaturity of their cognitive structures provides fertile ground for stereotypic thought (Aboud, 1988; Katz, 1976). For example, young children often use transductive reasoning and so view people who are alike on one characteristic (e.g., skin color), as alike in other ways (e.g., intelligence). In addition, young children are not yet able to perform multiple classification tasks. They may be unable, therefore, to see that the same person can belong to a group consisting of doctors and also to a group of women.

The notion that stereotyping may be in part due to young children's cognitive limitations is consistent with reports that children's racial and gender stereotyping increases through the preschool years, peaks in kindergarten or early elementary school, and then decreases around the age of 6 or 7 – the age when cognitive skills associated with concrete operations develop (Aboud, 1988; Bigler & Liben, 1992, 1993). An alternative theoretical view, however, is that stereotyping does not decrease, but rather children become increasingly sophisticated and can respond in socially desirable ways so that their biases become more difficult to detect (e.g., Katz, 1982; Martin & Little, 1990).

Even if stereotyping does decrease with age, one should not conclude that race and gender biases in young children are of no concern because they will outgrow them. Stereotyping and negative intergroup attitudes do not by any means disappear in childhood. In addition, it is important to examine the *content* of children's stereotypes. The biases children exhibit are not random, and may reflect both subtle and not so subtle messages about the relative desirability of belonging to one group as opposed to another. For example, white children rarely exhibit anything other than a prowhite bias (e.g., Aboud, 1988).

At 36 months, the Preschool Racial Attitude Measure (PRAM II: Williams, Best, Boswell, Mattson, & Graves, 1975) was used to assess race biases in 3-year-olds. In this measure, children are shown drawings of two characters, one black and one white, and indicate which person possesses either a positive trait (e.g., smart) or negative trait (e.g., dirty). Scores reflect whether children exhibit a prowhite bias, problack bias, or no bias. At 60 months, the Katz-Zalk measure (Zalk & Katz, 1976) was used to assess whether children attribute positive or negative behaviors (such as doing well on a test or stealing candy) to white or black children (and to boys or girls). Scores on the Katz-Zalk measure were computed so as to be comparable with the PRAM II scores. Both measures have been widely used with children and have reliabilities that are sufficiently stable for group research (e.g., Williams et al., 1975; Zalk & Katz, 1976).

At 36 months, approximately one-third of the children in our sample (31% of whites and 34% of blacks) demonstrated a same-race bias. Most children (53% of whites and 55% of blacks) responded in an unbiased fashion. The remaining children (15% of white children and 11% of black children) displayed an other-race bias. Between 36 and 60 months the percentage of black children exhibiting a same-race bias decreased. At 5 years of age, same-race bias was once again exhibited by approximately one-third of the white children (30%), but by only 13% of the black children. Thirty-six percent of the black children exhibited an other-race bias as compared with only 15% of white children. Again, approximately half the sample responded in an unbiased fashion.

Gender attitudes were also assessed with the Katz-Zalk measure at 60 months. On this task, both boys and girls attributed positive behaviors to protagonists of their own gender. The negative attributes, however, were associated with the male protagonist for both girls and boys. This is in accordance with findings obtained with young grade school children (e.g., Zalk & Katz, 1976).

In summary, there is a tendency for children who exhibit any race bias to favor their own race at 36 months, but both black and white children exhibit a white bias at 60 months. Black children's shift from a problack to a prowhite bias parallels their shift from a same-race to an other-race playmate preference between 30 and 36 months. In terms of gender attitudes, at 60 months children associated positive behaviors to same-sex children and negative behaviors were associated to male protagonists. Given the higher frequency of acting out behavior by boys (e.g., Silvern & Katz, 1986; Dodge, 1983), this latter finding may reflect the children's experiences.

Implications for the understanding of normative development and psychopathology

Research suggests that both race and gender relate to the form and frequency of psychological symptoms (Kavanaugh & Hops, 1994; Zahn-Waxler, 1993). For example, the overwhelming preponderance of grade school children whose behavior is labeled conduct disordered are boys (Rutter & Garmezy, 1983; Silvern & Katz, 1986). Members of ethnic minority groups are also more likely than Euro-Americans to have their behaviors labeled as conduct disordered (Allen & Majidi-Ahi, 1989). Interestingly, the sex difference in the incidence of conduct disorder appears to be less marked in African Americans as compared to Euro-Americans (Rutter & Garmezy, 1983), underscoring the need to consider membership in multiple social categories simultaneously.

Although the roots of such sex and race differences in psychological disturbances warrant specific investigation, normative developmental trends should also shed light on the origins of these differences. A hallmark of developmental psychopathology is its dual focus on normal and atypical development. The research findings presented in this chapter add to our understanding of how race and gender affect "normal" developmental trajectories and thus, should also elucidate the roles these factors play in the development of psychopathology.

The relation between normative and atypical development is complex, however, and this final section will consider four questions that are germane to how findings of race and gender differences are conceptualized and interpreted. Can normative development be seen as universal across racial and gender groups, or does development differ in important ways for members of these different groups? What factors underlie different developmental trajectories? How have psychologists (who have usually been members of majority groups) labeled (and may continue to label) behaviors displayed by minority group members as deviant rather than just different? Finally, what alternatives to such a deficit-oriented approach exist?

What constitutes normative developmental trajectories?

The longitudinal project began assessments when children were 6 months of age, included both Euro- and African American children, and focused on the development of both race and gender schemas. Thus, we can draw some conclusions about similarities and differences in developmental trajectories for both African American and Euro-American girls and boys, beginning at a very early age, as they learn about these two important social categories.

Our findings suggest that there are both similarities and differences in development. In many areas, the similarities transcend membership in specific social categories. Nevertheless, important differences do occur, and the ways in which these differences are conceptualized have important implications for our understanding of child development. This section summarizes both the similarities and differences in developmental trajectories obtained for each of the four components of race and gender development discussed already: awareness, identity, preferences, and stereotypes.

The perceptual and cognitive underpinnings of intergroup attitudes begin very early in life for children in all the groups we studied. By 6 months of age, most infants, regardless of their race or gender, were capable of perceptually categorizing people on the basis of gender and racial cues. Although both African American and Euro-American infants evidenced these abilities at early ages, group differences already existed at 6 months of age. Euro-American infants responded more to gender cues, whereas African American infants were more attuned to racial cues.

With regard to identity development, all children showed two similar developmental sequences in the use of group labels. First, the correct use of gender labels preceded their ability to use race labels. Second, the ability to self-label occurred prior to the ability to label others. There were, however, important group differences as well. Most notably, despite African American children's early attunement to race cues, they were less accurate than white children in race-labeling tasks.

Both similarities and differences also emerged in the preference tasks. Although both boys and girls converged in their strong same-sex preferences by 60 months, the developmental trajectories differed. Girls showed same-sex preferences earlier than boys, who demonstrated a dramatic increase in same-sex preferences at a later age point so that they eventually "caught up." In the toy preference task, the earlier same-sex preference exhibited by girls was counterbalanced by greater flexibility at five – they were more willing than boys to play with the "other sex" toy.

In terms of race preferences and attitudes, similarities between racial groups occurred early, and developmental pathways then diverged. When choosing playmates from photographs of children, both African American and Euro-American children initially demonstrated a same-race preference. At later age points, however, African American children showed a reversal and began to prefer white playmates. The early similarities between racial groups and the shift in African American preferences were paralleled in the racial attitude task. Initially, more children evidenced a same-race as compared with an other-race bias regardless of racial group membership, but between 3 and 5 years of age, African American children became more likely to exhibit a prowhite bias.

How can the differences be interpreted?

Some psychologists have suggested that the examination of racial group differences should be minimized because such differences are too often used to justify hierarchies in which one group is viewed as somehow better than the other (see Yee, Fairchild, Weizmann, & Wyatt, 1993). This willingness to assign hierarchies may be due, in part, to the belief that group differences reflect the qualities of individuals who comprise the social groups. It is also true, however, that various groups experience different social environments based on both their minority or majority status in the larger society, and on their particular cultural practices. Adequate understanding of the contribution of social context to the development of group differences may increase intergroup understanding and reduce the need to form hierarchies among people based on a single (majority-group-defined) continuum.

Our findings with regard to the developmental sequencing of gender and race schemas demonstrate the importance of social context and the interplay of social and cognitive factors. Our general hypothesis was that gender schemas would develop prior to race schemas. This was expected to be true because most children grow up in households where there is considerable exposure to people of both genders, but exposure to people of different races may vary. The predicted sequencing of gender and race schemas was not obtained on the habituation task administered during the first year,[6] but it was obtained on tasks administered at later ages. For example, the ability to self-label based on gender developmentally preceded this ability based on race.

Children's greater ease in handling gender as compared with race information, especially when performing tasks using verbal labels, may be due not only to children's frequent exposure to people of both genders, but also to the greater availability of information pertaining to gender in their environment. As noted at the outset, gender is often the first bit of information provided about a newborn baby, and gender references continue to occur with great frequency. The observational data from the picture-book task presented compelling evidence of parents' greater willingness to mention gender as compared with race. Almost all parents referred to gender quite freely, but only the rare parent ever mentioned race. Parental self-report measures corroborate this reticence to talk about race when the children were 3. Fewer than one-quarter of the parents (irrespective of racial group) commented on racial differences they encountered in stores or playgrounds or on television. Parents' greater willingness to talk about gender as compared with race undoubtedly contributes to children's acquisition of gender schemas prior to race schemas.

As with gender, race schema development is also based upon complex social factors, and race differences in developmental trajectories may again reflect differing social contexts. One way in which social environments differ for African American and Euro-American children is in racial heterogeneity. Euro-American children, as compared with ethnic minority children, are less likely to have interracial contact and also have less exposure to other races in the media (Huston et al., 1992). White children's relative lack of familiarity with other races (and perhaps their subsequent lack of comfort with those seen as unfamiliar) may explain some of the obtained race differences, such as white children's reluctance to choose other-race playmates.

The differential exposure of white and black children to other-race people does not completely explain our findings with regard to race schema development, however. If it did, African American children might be expected to develop race schemas before Euro-American children. This did not seem to be the case. Despite black children's greater awareness of racial cues in infancy, as preschoolers black children were less accurate than white children in their use of race labels, and were often silent in response to questions about such labels. Three factors suggest that these differences were not primarily cognitive. First, the African American children exhibited a marked change in their response pattern after 30 months (i.e., from accuracy to inaccuracy in label use). Second, the African American children did not show a similar disadvantage with regard to gender labeling. Finally, they evidenced no difficulty in performing a racial sorting task that did not require the use of a verbal label. It may be, then, that the use of race labels elicits more emotion for black children, perhaps because they are already picking up messages about group status differentials. These messages may come, in part, from television viewing.

An increasing body of work highlights the importance of television and other media in the formation of children's concepts about race and gender (Graves, 1989; Katz & Boswell, 1986). Although depictions of females and people of color have increased in recent years, the majority of protagonists children see are still predominantly white and male (Graves, 1989; Huston et al., 1992; Spencer, 1990). In addition, the depictions of minority group members that do occur are often filtered through the vision of majority group members and emerge as stereotypes (Huston et al., 1992). Gaines and Reed (1995) note how these differences in portrayals might translate into confusion for young black children: "a great deal of what it means to be Black is based on the assumptions, attitudes, and expectancies of White

Americans. When an African American child first discovers his or her Blackness, it is often the discovery of socially constructed 'Blackness.' Certainly this discovery happens at such a young age that it is unlikely that the child will have a fully formed personality or a self-developed identity by which to define his or her Blackness'' (p. 99).

Abundant and affirming information about people who constitute the majority group (i.e., "norm") is readily available to members of both majority and minority groups. Moreover, majority group members throughout their lives are more likely to encounter fellow majority group members in positions of power. Whether going to a doctor, appearing in court, or testifying before Congress, the people to whom one appeals will most likely be of majority status. These differences in social contexts may make the development of race schemas less complex and time-consuming for majority children as compared with minority children (Katz, 1983). In general, children in majority groups experience a "fit" between their home and other environments (Eccles, 1993; Harrison, Wilson, Pine, Chan, & Buriel, 1990), whereas minority group members need to become bicultural – familiar with and able to function in both their home culture and the majority culture (Harrison et al., 1990; Phinney, 1990). Ignorance of the "other" is a luxury that minority group members cannot afford (Miller, 1986).

The majority group as the norm?

For the white parents in our sample, discussing race with their children entailed discussing others, that is, nonwhite people. White families seemed not to think of themselves as having a racial identity and so did not perceive a need for discussions of their child's own racial identity. This finding may illustrate that tendency of individuals in a majority group to view their own group as a standard, or norm, against which others may be compared. This same tendency can be seen in psychologists' attempts to understand what constitutes psychopathology and normality.

Definitions of normality differ along a number of dimensions (see Albee, Canetto, & Sefa-Dedah, 1991). The one aspect common to all definitions, however, is the notion of a norm (defined either statistically or otherwise). Behavioral deviations from the norm that are societally devalued indicate pathology. Importantly, it is not the deviation, per se, that determines what is pathological, but the evaluation of it by significant decision makers. There are vast cross-cultural and sociohistorical differences in the evaluation of particular deviations. In our society, for example, people who see and hear things that others do not are regarded as pathological; other cultures have often interpreted such "hallucinatory" behavior as powerful gifts of the gods or as some special type of wisdom. Perhaps more to the point, during the time of slavery in the South, slaves who tried to escape were considered to be exhibiting a form of pathology. With historical hindsight, we now praise Harriet Tubman and others who valued the liberation of slaves.

Decision makers with the power to label people as deviant must exercise particular care when interpreting behaviors of minority group members. These individuals are often numerical minorities, and also belong to groups that may be devalued. When these clients or research participants are found to deviate from prevailing norms, it becomes all too easy to label their behavior as pathological. Several psychologists have noted the potential of psychology to perpetuate existing injustices based on gender, race, or other social categories (Chesler, 1989; Prilleltensky, 1989; Szasz, 1991; Weisstein, 1971). As L. Brown (1992) asserts, "A theory of psychopathology that uncritically embraces the current social status quo as the hallmark of normalcy risks becoming a tool in the hands of those who would justify continued oppression" (p. 225).

Clearly we hold assumptions, often implicit, about which behaviors constitute the standard against which to assess pathology, and these assumptions determine how we interpret research findings. The debate about race preferences illustrates this point particularly well. Since the landmark doll studies of Clark and Clark more than five decades ago (e.g., Clark & Clark, 1939), the topic of white preferences in black children has generated considerable research and discussion. The earlier notion that white preference indicates low self-esteem in black children exemplifies the use of majority group behavior as the standard. Such interpretations have since been challenged (Cross, 1985; Spencer, 1984), and the possibility that white children may be deviant in that they suffer from elevated esteem (e.g., feelings of superiority and entitlement) has been raised (Jones, 1993).

Jones's (1993) recommendation that we begin to question the legitimacy of our assumed norms when considering race bias is echoed in recent feminist reappraisals of traditional theories of psychopathology (e.g., L. Brown & Ballou, 1992; Pantony and Caplan, 1991). Women, ethnic minorities, and members of other previously absent (and still underrepresented) groups in psychological research have challenged the approach of first identifying how a minority group differs from the majority norm, then explaining this difference in terms of some deficit in the minority group (Moore, 1985; Ryan, 1971). The historical shift in the interpretation of findings with regard to children's sex-stereotyped preferences illustrates the ways in which changing ideas about gender affect assumptions underlying research.

In the past 20 years, there has been a drastic shift in the ways in which departures from prescribed sex roles are conceptualized. Recently, researchers have stressed the *advantages* associated with sex-role flexibility and androgyny (e.g., Bem, 1975; Lott, 1978; Katz, 1986; Katz, Boggiano, & Silvern, 1993), whereas in earlier studies, non–sex-typed patterns were typically viewed as deviant or pathological (e.g., Rosenberg, Sutton-Smith, & Morgan, 1961). For example, D. Brown (1957) interpreted the finding that girls were less sex-typed than boys as indicative of girls' inadequate resolution of the Oedipal conflict and weaker superego development. Perhaps the fact that girls rather than boys have been the ones to evidence greater sex-role flexibility contributed to the willingness of researchers to view departures from prescribed sex roles as pathological (i.e., deviating from the "norm"). Contributing to the change in conceptualization was the increase in the number of female psychologists.

It is incumbent on those charged with assessing normality and psychopathology to be cognizant of the shortage of accurate information about minority groups, as well as the tendency (not always conscious) to label minority or low-status groups as deviant. Failure to attend to these two possible sources of bias may lead to questionable assumptions and interpretations, as well as to ineffective treatment strategies (e.g., Kagawa-Singer, Katz, Taylor, & Vanderryn, 1996).

An alternative model of psychological health?

Increased awareness of different "normative" trajectories for members of minority groups is an important step, but it does not resolve the question of whether normative behaviors are necessarily preferable. Although psychology has begun to move somewhat beyond the deficit model, assessments of normality and abnormality from a qualitative perspective continue to emphasize the absence of psychopathology. Alternatively, we might ask the question, What constitutes a healthy individual? Consideration of *optimal* as opposed to *normative* development may allow for a view of psychological health and pathology that transcends some of the problems inherent in the still prevalent deficit-oriented approach.

In this time of increasing diversity in American society, it becomes even more evident that definitions of mental health need to include the presence of nonoppressive attitudes and relationships. It should be recalled that Zigler's primary goal in planning Head Start was to enhance children's social competence (Zigler, 1979), and that one of the most significant components of this construct is learning how to get along with others. Racism and sexism in our society interfere with the mature development and social competence of all Americans. A focus on mental health and social competence changes the interpretations of research findings, as well. Take, for example, the finding that African American children make same-race friendship choices less often the Euro-Americans. While it might be argued by some that this reflects black children's weaker group identity, an equally tenable argument is that black children's greater interest in playing with people from other racial groups is healthy and should be the standard (or "norm") for *all* children. Analogously, as we begin to question whether white preference in white children indicates healthy self-acceptance or cross-race rejection (perhaps due in part to a lack of exposure to other races), we might also raise questions as to the desirability and implications of the well-documented, and perhaps too well accepted increase in children's same-sex play preferences. Why do children become less and less willing to play with other-sex children, and is this really healthy for them, and for society more generally?

In assessing the relation between various behaviors and positive mental health, it is necessary to incorporate a perspective that extends beyond the individual. Some behavior deemed pathological from a majority person's perspective may represent adaptation in a different social context. For example, in a milieu characterized by violence, the illegal act of owning a gun may be the only alternative that some high school students see for staying alive past adolescence. Is this pathological or adaptive? And if pathology is involved, does it lie within the student or society? Certainly, the health of a person and the health of his or her social context are inextricably linked, and questions of how to define and create healthy communities warrant further consideration and study (see Iscoe, 1974). To foster optimal development in children, effects of the *broad* social context must be considered, including social, economic, and political factors that occur beyond the level of the individual or the family (e.g., Bronfenbrenner, 1979; Ogbu, 1981).

The presence of a chapter on race and gender in this book should not imply the desirability, or even possibility of cordoning off discussions of race and gender from discussions of development and psychopathology. A careful analysis of the roles of race and gender in all psychological research will enrich our understanding of human behavior. Researchers (like the parents in our study) may be reluctant to enter into discussions about race and gender, and the analysis of these variables often occurs or is presented as either an afterthought (e.g., Scarr, 1988) or as an attempt to control for "nuisance" variables (Spencer, 1990). A more complete understanding of human behavior will require us to consider, in a conscious and critical way, the impact of race, gender, and other important social categories not only on study participants and clients, but also on ourselves as researchers and clinicians.

Notes

1 Space limitations preclude discussion of the developmental sequence proposed. It has not received prior empirical support in the race schema area because of the absence of longitudinal studies that begin in infancy. In general, however, the results of the project described are in accordance with this sequence, for both race and gender. Operationalizations of these four constructs have varied somewhat from study to study, and differ according to the child's verbal capacity. Specific measurement techniques used in our longitudinal project are discussed herein.

2 The terms "minority" and "majority" should be seen as reflecting social power as well as relative numbers, and so females should also be viewed as constituting a minority group.

3 Photographs of actual people were used, so we were not able to ascertain what specific gender cues were used by the children. Some investigators have suggested that hair length is the most significant cue (Fagot & Leinbach, 1988), but children and adults are still able to distinguish gender of faces when hair length is kept constant (although they do make more errors). Perception of gender is complex and seems to involve multiple cues (cf. Bruce et al., 1993).

4 While Michael Lewis (1979) has employed nonverbal mirror techniques to test self-recognition in infants, this procedure does not yield information concerning the dimensions the infant is using. Psychoanalytic writers (e.g., Melanie Klein, 1950) have talked about identity development in terms of the infant's differentiation from the caretaker, but this has not been operationalized.

5 Although a wide variety of photographs was used and every attempt was made to make photographs comparable across race and gender groups, we cannot rule out the possibility that factors such as perceived physical attractiveness, expression, and the like may have affected choices.

6 The hypothesis was, however, correct for the white subsample, reflecting, perhaps, the researchers' own biases and greater familiarity with white people's experiences.

References

Aboud, F. (1988). *Children and prejudice.* New York: Basil Blackwell.

Albee, G. W., Canetto, S. S., & Sefa-Dedah, A. (1991). Naming a syndrome is the first step. *Canadian Psychology, 32* (2), 154–160.

Allen, L., & Majidi-Ahi, S. (1989). Black American children. In J. T. Gibbs, L. N. Huang, & Associates. *Children of color: Psychological interventions with minority youth,* 148–178. San Francisco: Jossey-Bass.

Bem, S. L. (1975). Sex role adaptability: One consequence of psychological androgyny. *Journal of Personality and Social Psychology, 31* (4), 634–643.

Bigler, R. S., & Liben, L. S. (1992). Cognitive mechanisms in children's gender stereotyping: Theoretical and educational implications of a cognitive-based intervention. *Child Development. 63* (6), 1351–1363.

Bigler, R. S., & Liben, L. S. (1993). A cognitive-developmental approach to racial stereotyping and reconstructive memory in Euro-American children. *Child Development, 64,* 1507–1518.

Bronfenbrenner, U. (1979). *The Experimental Ecology of Human Development.* Cambridge, MA: Harvard University Press.

Brown, D. G. (1957). Masculinity-femininity development in children. *Journal of Consulting Psychology, 21,* 197–202.

Brown, L. S. (1992). A feminist critique of the personality disorders. In L. S. Brown & M. Ballou (Eds.), *Personality and psychopathology: Feminist reappraisals,* 206–228. New York: Guilford Press.

Brown, L. S., & Ballou, M. (1992). *Personality and psychopathology: Feminist reappraisals.* New York: Gilford Press.

Bruce, V., Burton, A. M., Hanna, E., Healey, P., Mason, O., Coombes, A., Fright, R., & Linney, A. (1993). Sex discrimination: How do we tell the difference between male and female faces? *Perception, 22,* 131–152.

Caldera, Y. M., Huston, A. C., & O'Brien, M. (1989). Social interactions and play patterns of parents and toddlers with feminine, masculine, and neutral toys. *Child Development, 60,* 70–76.

Chesler, P. (1989). *Women and madness,* 2nd ed. San Diego: Harcourt Brace Jovanovich.

Clark, K. B., & Clark, M. P. (1939). The development of consciousness of self and the emergence of racial identity in Negro preschool children. *Journal of Social Psychology, 10,* 591–599.

Cohen, L. B., & Strauss, M. S. (1979). Concept acquisition in the human infant. *Child Development, 50,* 419–424.

Cohen, L. G., & Younger, B. A. (1983). Perceptual categorization in the infant. Paper presented at the Symposium of the Sean Piaget Society, Philadelphia, May 1981.

Cross, W. E. (1985). Black identity: Rediscovering the distinction between personal identity and reference group orientation. In M. B. Spencer, G. K. Brokins, & W. A. Allen (Eds.), *Beginnings: The social and affective development of black children,* 155–172. Hillsdale, NJ: Erlbaum.

Dodge, K. A. (1983). Behavioral antecedents of peer social status. *Child Development, 54,* 1386–1399.

Eccles, J. S. (1993). School and family effects on the ontogeny of children's interests, self-perceptions, and activity choices. In *Developmental perspectives on motivation:* Volume 40 of the *Nebraska symposium on motivation,* 145–208. Lincoln: University of Nebraska Press.

Fagan, J. F., III (1976). Infants' recognition of invariant features of faces. *Child Development, 47,* 627–638.

Fagan, J. F., III, & Singer, L. T. (1979). The role of simple feature differences in infants' recognition of faces. *Infant Behavior and Development, 2,* 39–45.

Fagot, B. I., & Leinbach, M. D. (1985). Gender identity: Some thoughts on an old concept. *Journal of the American Academy of Child Psychiatry, 24,* 684–688.

Fagot, B. I., & Leinbach, M. D. (1988, October). *Gender role development in young children.* Paper presented at the symposium entitled Gender Roles through the Life Span. Ball State University, Muncie, IN.

Fernald, A., & Kuhl, P. K. (1981, April). *Fundamental frequency as an acoustic determinant of infant preference for motherese speech.* Paper presented at the meeting of the Society for Research in Child Development, Boston, MA.

Finkelstein, N. W., & Haskins, R. (1983). Kindergarten children prefer same-color peers. *Child Development, 54,* 502–508.

Gaines, S. O., & Reed, E. S. (1995). Prejudice: From Allport to Dubois. *American Psychologist, 50* (2), 96–103.

Gonzales, N. A., & Cauce, A. M. (1995). Ethnic identity and multicultural competence: Dilemmas and challenges for minority youth. In W. D. Hawley & A. W. Jackson (Eds.), *Toward a common destiny: Improving race and ethnic relations in America,* 131–162. San Francisco, CA: Jossey-Bass.

Graves, S. G. (1989, April). *Who's watching what, when? The impact of media on African-American children.* Paper presented at biennial conference of the Society for Research in Child Development, Kansas City, MO.

Harrison, A. O., Wilson, M. N., Pine, C. J., Chan, S. Q., & Buriel, R. (1990). Family ecologies of ethnic minority children. *Child Development, 61,* 347–363.

Huston, A. C., Donnerstein, E., Fairchild, H., Feshbach, N. D., Katz, P. A., Murray, J. P., Rubinstein, E. A., Wilcox, B. L., & Zuckerman, D. (1992). *Big world, small screen: The role of television in American Society.* Lincoln: University of Nebraska Press.

Iscoe, I. (1974). Community psychology and the competent community. *American Psychologist, 29,* 607–613.

Jaffe, E. D. (1988). Ethnic preferences of pre-school children. *Early Child Development and Care, 39,* 83–94.

Jones, J. M. (1993, August 20). *Racism and civil rights: Right problem. Wrong solution.* Invited address to Society for Psychological Study of Social Issues, 101st Annual Convention, American Psychological Association. Toronto.

Kagawa-Singer, M., Katz, P. A., Taylor, D., & Vanderryn, J. (1996, June). *Health issues for minority adolescents.* Lincoln: University of Nebraska Press.

Katz, P. A. (1976). The acquisition of racial attitudes in children. In P. A. Katz (Ed.), *Towards the elimination of racism,* 213–241. New York: Plenum.

Katz, P. A. (1982). A review of current research in children's racial attitude acquisition. In L. Katz (Ed.), *Current topics in early childhood education,* 17–54. Norwood, NJ: Ablex.

Katz, P. A. (1983). Developmental foundations of gender and racial attitudes. In R. L. Leahy (Ed.), *The child's construction of social inequality,* 41–78. New York: Academic Press.

Katz, P. A. (1986). Gender identity: Development and consequences. In R. D. Ashmore & F. K. Del Boca (Eds.), *The social psychology of female–male relations,* 21–67. New York: Academic Press.

Katz, P. A., Boggiano, A. K., & Silvern, L. (1993). Theories of female personality. In F. Denmark & M. Paludi (Eds.), *Handbook of the psychology of women,* 247–280. Westport, CT: Greenwood.

Katz, P. A., & Boswell, S. (1986). Flexibility and traditionality in children's gender roles. *Genetic, Social, and General Psychology Monographs, 112* (1), 103–147.

Katz, P. A., & Seavy, C., (1973). Labels and children's perception of faces. *Child Development, 44,* 770–775.

Kavanaugh, K., & Hops, H. (1994). Good girls? Bad boys? Gender and development or contexts for diagnosis and treatment. *Advances in Clinical Child Psychology, 16,* 45–79.

Klein, M. (1950). *The psycho-analysis of children.* London: Hogarth Press.

Leinbach, M. D. (1991, April). *The beginnings of gender: What's happening before age two?* Paper presented at the Society for Research in Child Development symposium on Development of Stereotypes in Infants, San Francisco, CA.

Lewis, M. (1979). Origins of early sex-role development. *Sex Roles, 5* (2), 135–153.

Lott, B. (1978). Behavioral concordance with sex-role ideology related to play areas, creativity, and parental sex-typing of children. *Journal of Personality and Social Psychology, 36,* 1087–1106.

Martin, C. L., & Little, J. K. (1990). The relation of gender understanding to children's sex-typed preferences and gender stereotypes. *Child Development, 61,* 1427–1439.

Miller, J. B. (1986). *Toward a new psychology of women,* 2nd ed. Boston: Beacon Press.

Moore, E. G. J. (1985). Ethnicity as a variable in child development. In M. B. Spencer, G. D. Brookins, & W. R. Allen (Eds.), *Beginnings: The social and affective development of black children,* 101–115. Hillsdale, NJ: Erlbaum.

Newman, M. A., Liss, M. B., & Sherman, F. (1983). Ethnic awareness in children: Not a unitary concept. *Journal of Genetic Psychology, 143,* 103–112.

Ogbu, J. U. (1981). Origins of human competence: A cultural-ecological perspective. *Child Development, 52,* 413–429.

Pantony, K., & Caplan, P. J. (1991). Delusional dominating personality disorder: A modest proposal for identifying some consequences of rigid masculine socialization. *Canadian Psychology, 32* (2), 120–133.

Phinney, J. (1990). Ethnic identity in adolescents and adults: Review of research. *Psychological Bulletin, 108,* 499–514.

Porter, C. P. (1991). Social reasons for skin tone preferences of black school-age children. *American Journal of Orthopsychiatry, 61* (1), 149–154.

Poulin-Dubois, D., Serbin, L. A., Kenyon, B., & Derbyshire, A. (1994). Infants' intermodal knowledge about gender. *Developmental Psychology, 30* (3), 436–442.

Prilleltensky, I. (1989). Psychology and the status quo. *American Psychologist, 44* (5), 795–802.

Proshansky, H. (1966). The development of intergroup attitudes. In I. W. Hoffman & M. L. Hoffman (Eds.), *Review of child development research,* vol. 2, 311–731. New York: Russell Sage Foundation.

Ramsey, P. G. (1987). Young children's thinking about ethnic differences. In J. S. Phinney & M. Rotherman (Eds.), *Children's ethnic socialization.* Newbury Park, CA: Sage.

Rosenberg, B. G., Sutton-Smith, B., & Morgan, E. (1961). The use of opposite-sex scales as a measure of psychosexual deviancy. *Journal of Consulting Psychology, 25,* 221–225.

Rutter, M., & Garmezy, N. (1983). Developmental psychopathology. In E. M. Hetherington (volume Ed.), *Handbook of child psychology,* Vol. 4, 775–911. New York: Wiley.

Ryan, W. (1971). *Blaming the victim.* New York: Vintage Books.

Scarr, S. (1988). Race and gender as psychological variables: Social and ethical issues. *American Psychologist, 43* (1), 56–59.

Silvern, L. E., & Katz, P. A. (1986). Gender roles and adjustment in elementary school children: A multidimensional approach. *Sex Roles, 14,* 181–202.

Spencer, M. B. (1983). Children's cultural values and parental child rearing strategies. *Developmental Review, 3,* 351–370.

Spencer, M. B. (1984). Black children's race awareness, racial attitudes and self-concept: A reinterpretation. *Journal of Child Psychology and Psychiatry, 25* (3), 433–441.

Spencer, M. B. (1990). Development of minority children: An introduction. *Child Development, 61,* 267–269.

Spencer, M. B., & Markstrom-Adams, C. (1990). Identity processes among racial and ethnic minority children in America. *Child Development, 61,* 290–310.

Stevenson, H. C., Jr. (1994). Racial socialization in African American families: The art of balancing intolerance and survival. *Family Journal: Counseling and Therapy for Couples and Families, 2* (3), 190–198.

Szasz, T. S. (1991). The myth of mental illness. In *Ideology and insanity: Essays on the psychiatric dehumanization of man,* 12–24. Syracuse: Syracuse University Press.

Turner, P. J., Gervai, J., & Hinde, R. A. (1993). Gender-typing in young children: Preferences, behavior, and cultural differences. *British Journal of Developmental Psychology, 11,* 323–342.

Weinraub, M., Clemens, L. P., Sockloff, A., Ethridge, T., Gracely, E., & Myers, B. (1984). The development of sex role stereotypes in the third year: Relationships to gender labeling, gender identity, sex-typed toy preferences, and family characteristics. *Child Development, 55,* 1493–1503.

Weisstein, N. (1971). Psychology constructs the female, or the fantasy life of the male psychologist. In Michelle Hoffnung Garskof (Ed.), *Roles women play: Toward women's liberation*, 68–83. Belmont, CA: Brooks/Cole Publishing.

Williams, J. E., Best, D. L., Boswell, D. A., Mattson, L. A., & Graves, D. J. (1975). Preschool racial attitude measure II. *Educational and Psychological Measurement, 35*, 3–18.

Yee, A. H., Fairchild, H. H., Weizmann, F., Wyatt, G. E. (1993). Addressing psychology's problems with race. *American Psychologist, 48* (11), 1132–1140.

Zahn-Waxler, C. (1993). Warriors and worriers: Gender and psychopathology. *Development and Psychopathology, 5* (1–2), 79–89.

Zalk, S. R., & Katz, P. A. (1976). The Katz-Zalk Projective Prejudice Test: Measure of racial attitudes in children. *Catalog of Selected Documents in Psychology, 6*, 7–38.

Zigler, E. (1966). Mental retardation: Current issues and approaches. In L. W. Hoffman & M. L. Hoffman (Eds.), *Review of child development research*, Vol. 2, 107–168. New York: Russell Sage Foundation.

Zigler, E. (1979). Project Head Start: Success or failure? In E. Zigler & J. Valentine (Eds.), *Project Head Start: A legacy of the War on Poverty*, 495–507. New York: Free Press.

4   Success in school – for a head start in life

Deborah Stipek

There are few variables more consistently or more strongly predictive of poor social outcomes and mental health than school failure. Youth who fail in school are more likely to drop out of school without a high school diploma (Eggert, Thompson, Herting, & Nicholas, 1994; Finn, 1989), get pregnant as teenagers (Brooks-Gunn, Guo, & Furstenberg, 1993), engage in delinquent acts (Grande, 1988), take drugs and abuse alcohol (Grande, 1988), be unemployed, and become dependent on public support (Fetler, 1989). School failure is also associated with low self-esteem (Finn, 1989), alcoholism (Rhodes & Jasinski, 1990), depression and suicide ideation (Eggert et al., 1994). Although most of the research is correlational, the associations between school failure and these negative mental health and social outcomes are often found even when socioeconomic status and other related variables are held constant.

In this chapter I examine ways in which research from two social science disciplines, developmental psychology and educational psychology, can be used to address this important societal problem. The research evidence related to success and failure in school will be supplemented with some of my own observations in school settings, plus "craft knowledge" that experienced teachers have shared with me.

I begin the chapter with a brief commentary on the linkages between children's previous experience of success or failure and aspects of their motivation for academic success. This is followed by a review of evidence in five broad areas of educational practice and experience that are relevant to children's success in school: (1) children's access to success experiences, (2) teachers' expectations, (3) children's self-confidence related to learning, (4) their goals in educational settings, and (5) the teacher's communication of personal regard for children. For each of these areas I describe evidence relevant to short-term and long-term student outcomes, and I offer recommendations for achieving maximum benefit. I conclude the chapter with a summary of the major issues raised, and I comment on implications for future interventions and policies.

Failure as a process

Children do not begin school feeling or acting like failures. To the contrary, my own and others' research indicates that most children, including those from the most disadvantaged backgrounds, begin school with enthusiasm and interest in school tasks (Stipek, 1984; Stipek, Feiler, Daniels, & Milburn, 1995).

But by the third grade emotional problems and maladaptive behaviors among children who are low achievers become clearly evident. Students who perform poorly in school often exhibit behavior problems, poor relationships with peers, and emotional withdrawal (Hartup, 1983; Berndt & Ladd, 1989). Fear of academic failure and ridicule in school is commonly cited by children manifesting some form of school phobia (Ollendick & King, 1990).

The debilitating effects of repeated failure on the behavior of children with mental retardation, documented in Zigler's ground-breaking work decades ago (Gruen & Zigler, 1968; Harter & Zigler, 1974; Yando & Zigler, 1971; see Zigler & Hodapp, 1986, for a review), are seen readily in nonretarded children as well. Some children who experience heavy doses of failure develop counteracademic values. A common complaint I hear from teachers, especially in economically disadvantaged neighborhoods, is that subgroups or even all of their students devalue school achievement, sometimes purposely failing to do schoolwork to maintain peer approval. (See Luthar, 1995, for empirical evidence.) Most likely this alienation is a consequence of failure as much as a cause.

Indeed, it would take an extraordinarily resilient child to persevere in a setting in which failure is an everyday experience. Although destructive in the long term – to children and to society – deciding that school success is not important may be an effective strategy for surviving such circumstances in the short term. But the alienation and maladaptive behavior that are common among older children might be avoided if earlier experiences were more positive.

Is school success for all children a realistic goal? What about the many factors over which schools have no control, that undermine the work of even the most expert teachers? Many children live in circumstances that provide little support, or even opportunity, for schoolwork. Many are surrounded by drugs and violence, or come to school hungry or traumatized by events in their home or neighborhood. Some children may be so disadvantaged that they cannot fully benefit from even the best educational program.

Notwithstanding these real and tragic constraints, changes in schools, even now, could diminish greatly the number of children who fail to achieve in school, and thus in life, and reduce the social costs associated with widespread school failure. The research evidence I summarize in this chapter suggests that this goal is within our grasp. Much is known about instructional practices that foster success in children. There is much more to be learned, but our knowledge base currently extends far beyond what is practiced in most American classrooms. Considerable progress could be made toward our goal of eliminating failure if classroom practices reflected the current knowledge base, however incomplete it might be.

This chapter focuses on practices affecting motivation. Motivation is what suffers most among children who experience failure at school, and it is critical for learning to occur.

What is a "motivated" student?

Whereas in the past educational theorists and practitioners defined motivation primarily in terms of behavior, recent motivation researchers have taken a very different approach. Currently, in addition to overt behaviors such as approach and persistence, studies assess beliefs, expectations, goals, and emotions (see Atkinson, 1964; Lepper, Sethi, Dialdin, & Drake, Chapter 2, this volume; Stipek, 1993, in press, Weiner, 1992); the nature of the strategies individuals use to complete tasks (e.g., Ames & Archer, 1988; Meece, Blumenfeld, & Hoyle, 1988); and what they think about while accomplishing a task (e.g., Peterson & Swing, 1982). Consistent with current multidimensional and cognitive as well as behavioral formulations, we define motivated learners in this chapter as individuals who are *willingly* engaged in the learning process, self-confident in their ability to learn and to complete school tasks, persistent in the face of difficulty, oriented toward developing understanding and mastering skills, enthusiastic and optimistic about learning, and proud of accomplishments.

Because motivation is a package of highly interrelated variables, practices that support one component of motivation tend to support others. For example, children who believe they are academically competent usually enjoy learning more and take more pride in their achievements than children who doubt their competence. Children who believe they are competent and who enjoy learning typically engage in constructive learning-related behaviors. Interventions aimed at increasing motivation and learning need to consider the entire package – not just a piece.

We turn now to research findings that suggest particular instructional strategies for improving all of these various aspects of children's motivation to learn. Widespread implementation of these strategies should increase substantially the number of students who succeed in school.

Research on effective practices

Making success accessible

One way to make success more accessible is to lower standards. This is common practice but it has no value for children or society. When standards are low the "floor" often becomes the "ceiling." Teachers accept the minimum standard as their goal and plan curriculum and instruction accordingly; children are never asked to go beyond the low standard despite their capacity to do so. Children see through it; most know that they could have reached a higher standard and they take little pride in achieving the success the low standard allows.

But given the inevitable wide range of academic performance we see in schools, how can all children succeed without lowering the standards of success? Won't there always be students who cannot keep up with their agemates?

I maintain that even wide individual differences in performance need not produce feelings of failure, discouragement, and alienation. Eliminating such negative motivational outcomes, however, requires a fundamental change in how "success" is defined.

By the definition most prominent in American classrooms, success in school is impossible for all children, regardless of how hard they work or what standard of performance they achieve. Consider the practice of grading on a curve. While this practice is less common now, more relaxed variations of the curve standard are commonplace. Other frequently used practices (e.g., displaying only the best work on the bulletin board) also limit the availability of success. Since only some children can get the higher grades and their work displayed on the bulletin board, other children *have* to fail. Simply providing information on an individual student's performance, without making overt comparisons, can be demoralizing for some children. Even if the bottom score on a math test, for example, represents a fairly high level of mastery (e.g., 74%), the child who received the worst score is likely to feel like a failure.

Children who have poor support for learning at home, or who are not proficient in English, or who learn slowly are likely to lose in an academic competition, even when they are eager to learn and willing to work. Some so-called low-achievers are actually achieving very well, relative to their capacities and other factors limiting the pace at which they can master the curriculum. But because they are lower achievers than their classmates, success is completely beyond their reach. Theory and abundant research make the consequences easy to predict; when children are not rewarded for a behavior (or, in this case, even punished), the behavior ceases. As effort ceases, so does academic progress, thus beginning a vicious cycle.

The motivation of relatively high-achieving students, as well as that of lower-achieving students, can be undermined by competitively based standards for success. Success by a relative standard is achieved by some students with little effort. Fast learners often become bored, complacent, and lazy – exerting only the minimal amount of effort required to come out close to the top. Their own progress in learning is therefore limited by their classmates' level of performance, not by their own capacities. If success usually comes easily, fast learners also fail to develop an ability to tolerate frustration or deal constructively with initial difficulty. When they do encounter significant challenges, their self-confidence and their ability to cope fade quickly.

Recent research suggests alternatives to competitive evaluation and recognition practices. Research cited here suggests the value of defining success in a way that makes it accessible to all children if they work hard.

Ames and her colleagues have compared competitive criteria, in which success is defined as performing better than classmates, to individual or mastery criteria, in which success is defined as personal improvement or meeting a predetermined standard (reviewed in Ames, 1986). Their research has shown, first, that criteria for success influence students' perceptions of the cause of success and failure (their attributions). Children emphasize ability more when interpreting their performance in competitive contexts, and effort more in situations in which success is determined by group performance, personal improvement, or meeting a preestablished standard (Ames, 1978, 1981; Ames & Ames, 1978, 1981). Failure attributed to low ability is of special concern; children who see ability as relatively stable and not under their control have no reason to try.

A study by Ames and Ames (1981) demonstrated that criteria for success also affect how children evaluate themselves. Children were given an opportunity to establish a personal performance history on a task (success or failure), and then introduced to one of two types of criteria for success: competitive (involving comparison with another child) or individualistic (based on self-improvement). When subsequently asked a series of questions, children's self-reward and feelings of satisfaction in the competitive situation were based on whether they won or lost, and not on the quality of their own performance. Children in the individualistic condition focused on their personal history with the task (whether they improved).

Covington and Omelich (1984) show additional benefits to a mastery standard for success. They found that undergraduate psychology students who were graded using a mastery standard (in which grades were determined by what score the student attained) perceived the grading system to be fairer and more responsive to effort than students who were graded using a competitive, norm-referenced standard. The students in the mastery condition also aspired to a higher grade and had more self-confidence about being able to achieve a high grade.

The research reviewed here does not mean that competition should be entirely banned from the classroom. I have seen teachers use competition in creative and beneficial ways to motivate students. *The competition must be designed, however, so that every child has some chance of winning.* This can be done by adapting the task – such as giving spelling words that are appropriate for each student's level of proficiency in a spelling bee, or varying the difficulty of problems in a game designed to make practicing the multiplication tables fun. Grouping children into heterogeneous and fairly well matched skill-level teams gives every child a chance to be on a winning team, and also has been shown to enhance substantially children's learning (see Slavin, 1983, 1984).

The evidence reviewed suggests that effort, progress, and mastery are more productive criteria for success than competition; all children have a realistic chance of experiencing success by the first three criteria, *if they try.* (See also Bloom, 1981.) A few children may not because they are for some reason unwilling to exert effort. But if success is genuinely within every child's grasp, most will reach for it.

Conveying high expectation

In an elementary school I visited, a teacher informed me that some of her students were prenatally exposed to drugs and most came from a violent neighborhood and dysfunctional families who didn't care about school. In the classroom the teacher seemed to be marking time. Her instruction was prescribed by the textbook and her children spent most of their time doing worksheets. She expected little and therefore taught little. Some children may have felt successful, even though their actual mastery was far below their capabilities. Or perhaps the whole class accepted their teacher's judgment – that their status in society as academic failures was inevitable.

I have also seen classrooms in which energetic teachers expected every child to master the curriculum. These teachers show little sympathy and sometimes appear a bit gruff. They encourage effort and persistence and if a child who is trying is having difficulty they adjust tasks and try different teaching strategies. They face many of the same challenges the other teacher described to me – but they expect their children to learn and they create a climate in which no child is *allowed* to fail.

Many studies have explored how teachers' expectations affect student outcomes. For example, researchers have identified ways in which teachers' expectations are associated with the social-emotional climate they provide students, as well as their instructional program. The evidence is not entirely consistent, and many studies find considerable variability in the degree to which teachers treat high and low achievers differently. But many studies have found that relatively low achieving students, and students for whom the teachers had low expectations (usually the same students), on average experienced a more negative social-emotional climate, often conveyed in subtle ways (e.g., facial expressions, tone of voice; see Babad, Bernieri, & Rosenthal, 1991). Teachers have been found to smile less often at low-expectancy students and be generally less friendly (e.g., less likely to engage in nonacademic conversation), to give them less challenging and less varied assignments, to call on them less often and to give them less time to respond to questions and less follow-up (e.g., clues, rephrased questions, elaborations). (See Good, 1987, for a review.)

Relatively low achieving students are also often placed in stable "ability" groups or tracks in which they are given less effective (e.g., more drill and practice) instruction as well as less input altogether (Borko & Eisenhart, 1986; Hart, 1982; Hiebert, 1983; McDermott, 1987). Weinstein (1976) found that the reading group to which students were assigned contributed 25% to the prediction of midyear achievement over and above the students' initial readiness scores, presumably because of differences in the quality of instruction across groups.

Weinstein and her colleagues have done a series of studies demonstrating that students as young as first-graders are well aware of the different treatment that relatively high and low performing students receive from teachers (Weinstein, 1985; Weinstein & Middlestadt, 1979). For example, students in many (but not all) of the classrooms they studied claimed that their teachers granted special privileges, provided more autonomy, gave more opportunity to take classroom responsibilities, interacted more informally, and trusted the higher-achieving students more than the lower-achieving students.

To plan appropriate instruction teachers need to make judgments about whether a student is likely to complete a particular task or is ready to learn a particular concept. But these judgments should be based on knowledge about children's specific skills, understanding, and learning styles. The problems arise when teachers make global judgments about a child's capacity to learn, or erroneous judgments based on stereotypes (e.g., boys have more trouble than girls learning to read; economically disadvantaged children learn more slowly than middle-class children) or irrelevant data (e.g., a sibling's performance). Average group differences are irrelevant when planning instruction for any particular child. All that is relevant is *that* child's skills and dispositions at the time an instructional decision is made.

In general children in classrooms in which the teacher expects all children to master the curriculum achieve at a higher level than children who began with similar skills but are in classrooms, like the first described, in which the teacher does not hold uniformly high expectations (Edmonds, 1979; Rutter, Maughan, Mortimore, Duston, & Smith, 1979). To be sure, teachers' expectations are significantly affected by the skills and motivation of the students assigned to their class. But whatever the qualities of their students, teachers who continue to expect each and every student in a class to succeed (albeit perhaps at different rates) will, on average, be more successful in achieving that goal than teachers who designate some or all students as difficult or impossible to teach.

To foster success in all children teachers need to convey to children, explicitly and implicitly, that they are expected to learn and master the curriculum and they need to consider only relevant information (e.g., current skills and learning styles) in planning their instructional program. Even past test scores and previous teachers' evaluations must be used cautiously because children can make dramatic changes in a relatively short period of time. Careful day-to-day observations and frequent, systematic assessments done by the teacher are the most reliable sources of information for structuring learning opportunities. Good classroom assessment is essential for teachers to be able to make the countless, day-to-day, sometimes moment-to-moment, decisions they need to make about a child's instruction.

Although adaptations in instruction need to be made to meet the needs of children with different skills and learning styles, teachers need to provide all children with the same opportunities for instruction that is challenging, personally meaningful, and requires critical thinking. The specific skill taught or tasks given may vary, but the principles of good instruction apply to all children.

Building self-confidence

Conveying high expectations for children's learning in school is necessary, but it is not sufficient. Children also need opportunities to develop and demonstrate their competencies. If they do not have these opportunities, they develop low perceptions of their competence and expect to fail in school despite their efforts. (See Stipek, 1993, in press.)

Attention to perceptions of competence is important in part because there is good evidence that they affect learning and educational choices. Marsh, for example, has demonstrated that perceptions of academic competence predict future performance (Marsh, 1990), subsequent course work selections (Marsh, 1989, 1990), and subsequent educational aspirations and even university attendance (Marsh, 1991) over and above previous, and in some cases concurrent, achievement.

There is also evidence suggesting that self-confidence in one's ability to succeed is one of the most important factors in children's interest and enthusiasm about learning (Deci & Ryan, 1985). Mac Iver, Stipek, and Daniels (1991) provide support for a causal relationship between perceptions of competence and interest in schoolwork. They assessed junior and senior high school students' perceptions of their competence and intrinsic interest in a course at the beginning and at the end of the semester. Analyses revealed that interest changed in the direction that perceived competence changed. Students whose perception of competence increased during the semester rated the subject as more interesting at the end of the semester than at the beginning, and students whose perception of competence decreased rated the subject as less interesting at the end of the semester. In brief, research strongly suggests that intervention efforts that are successful in increasing perceptions of academic competence should pay considerable dividends.

Many strategies currently used to help children develop self-confidence ignore their actual academic performance. In "add-on" or "pull-out" programs children are taken out of their classroom or go to after-school programs where they are told how wonderful they are and given strategies for reminding themselves that they are wonderful. Then they return to their classroom where they often continue to get low grades or be ignored or put down by their teacher and peers.

A strategy that some teachers practice in the classroom – heaping on praise, regardless of actual performance – has no more value. The teachers are well meaning; they are trying to build children's self-confidence. But research has demonstrated that by the middle elementary grades, children see through gratuitous praise, and such a strategy is more likely to undermine than to build confidence. Barker and Graham (1987), for example, found that children rated a hypothetical child praised by a teacher as lower in ability than a child who achieved the same score but was criticized. Another study reported that the amount of praise children received in their classroom was unrelated to their perceptions of their ability in mathematics; indeed, boys who typically were not praised believed that their teachers had high expectations for them (Parsons, Kaczala, & Meece, 1982).

Being sympathetic is another strategy that teachers use to alleviate the negative effects of failure on children. While well intentioned, like indiscriminate praise, such affective displays have been shown to undermine children's confidence in their abilities and their expectations for success. Graham (1984), for example, reports that among children who failed an experimental task, those to whom the experimenter expressed sympathy were more likely to attribute their failure to a lack of ability and had lower expectations for future success than those to whom the experimenter expressed mild anger.

Children who are in the most need of building self-confidence are the most likely to be targets of these subtle teacher behaviors (e.g., sympathy, indiscriminate praise). Graham (1990) suggests that minority children may be particularly vulnerable. But such well-meaning efforts to increase students' self-confidence can actually lower children's judgments of their ability to do well in school, and thus decrease the probability that they will, in fact, succeed.

The evidence strongly suggests that instruction that facilitates academic gains is critical for children to maintain self-confidence and motivation to learn. Correlational studies, for example, reveal strong associations between achievement and children's beliefs about their academic competencies, and suggest that perceived competencies are, to a significant degree, a *consequence* of academic performance (Marsh, 1992, 1994).

The first and most important step toward motivating children to learn, therefore, is to make sure they are learning. This, of course, requires good instruction. It is difficult for children to make gains in academic competence when instructions are unclear, students' understanding is not checked regularly, or adaptations are not made to ensure that instruction builds upon children's current understanding and skills.

The selection of tasks for students to complete has particularly profound effects on their perceptions of their ability to succeed. Not surprisingly, impossibly difficult tasks engender low expectations for success and a belief that no amount of effort will pay off. Children cannot maintain self-confidence in the face of tasks that they lack the prerequisite skills to complete. Their common responses – to give up quickly, guess, or copy a classmate's papers – make good sense; these are adaptive reactions, given that no amount of serious effort will give them a positive result.

Easy tasks are useful for practicing newly developed skills and building self-confidence in children who have a long history of failure, as Bybee and Zigler (1992) recently found in a study of children with mental retardation. But in the long run, easy tasks do not contribute to positive judgments of competence, pride, or satisfaction (Atkinson, 1964), and they produce little learning. Moderately difficult tasks – tasks that require some effort and persistence, but can be completed – engender a sense of developing competence and excitement.

Ensuring moderately difficult tasks for all students in a class with a broad distribution of skill levels is a real challenge for the teacher, requiring a great deal of training in how to assess, on an ongoing basis, children's skills and understanding. But teachers can be assisted in developing these skills. I have seen teachers use many creative strategies for meeting diverse needs in the same classroom – such as grouping students in flexible, skill-based groups. If skill-based groups are designed for children to work on a narrowly defined set of skills (e.g., subtraction) rather than based on general ability in the subject area, and flexible (i.e., children move in and out of groups as they master new skills), they are not likely to stigmatize and undermine the motivation of slower learners. Even whole-class or large-group instruction can allow for different levels of processing and engagement, and tasks given to all students can build in the potential of different levels of breadth and depth. The introduction of technology into classrooms should assist teachers in providing more individualization in tasks.

Teachers often resist adjusting tasks to children's skill levels on the grounds that it will damage the self-esteem of the children who receive the easier tasks. Their concern is valid, but I suspect that giving students tasks adapted to their skill level does not do as much damage as asking them to complete tasks that are too difficult for them. Moreover, much of the damage that could be done by differentiating tasks can be avoided by creating a social climate in which children are acknowledged and rewarded equally for improving and for achieving goals appropriate to their relative skill level.

Another strategy that helps maintain students' self-confidence as learners is providing diverse opportunities for children to demonstrate mastery. Rosenholtz and Simpson's (1984a, 1984b) research has shown that the degree to which tasks are differentiated across students and over time affects students' judgments about their own ability as well as the way they conceptualize ability. Less differentiation results in a more narrow definition of "schoolwork" and greater consensus about who is generally able and who is not, as well as a perception of ability as stratified and measurable.

If the nature of tasks varies from day to day, and if children are allowed to demonstrate their understanding in variable formats, more children can experience success. Thus, for example, mathematics assignments may involve computations, word problems, projects, or conversations. Children may demonstrate their understanding of a mathematical concept by doing correct computations, drawing diagrams, presenting problem-solving strategies verbally to other students, or writing out an explanation of their strategy. In addition to giving children with different kinds of talents more opportunities to excel, such variability provides children with different learning styles more opportunities to develop mastery.

Focusing children's attention on learning

Students' goals and the quality of their engagement have been examined primarily in the context of a recent distinction made between learning goals (referred to by some researchers as mastery or task goals) and performance goals (also referred to as ego goals). (See Ames, 1992; Blumenfeld, 1992; Meece, 1991; Nicholls, 1983.) Learning goals concern developing skills and understanding or achieving a sense of mastery. Students who are more concerned about developing skills and completing a task than about getting a good grade or public recognition have learning goals. Students with performance goals are more concerned about appearances – about looking smart or avoiding looking incompetent (rather than *being* competent). Looking smart is usually defined as performing better than others and sometimes can be achieved without much learning. A central feature of performance goals is a need for public recognition for superior performance. Thus, a student who works primarily for good grades or teacher praise has performance goals.

Dweck (1986) proposes that learning goals and performance goals have very different implications for the quality of students' motivation, including how they behave in achievement settings and how they interpret performance outcomes (see also Dweck & Leggett, 1988; Elliott & Dweck, 1988; Nicholls, Cobb, Wood, Yackel, & Patashnick, 1990). According to Dweck, students with learning goals – regardless of whether they perceive themselves as high or low in ability relative to others – seek challenging tasks that provide opportunities to develop new competencies (Ames & Archer, 1988; Elliott & Dweck, 1988). When they encounter difficulty, they assume that their current strategy is inappropriate and needs to be changed, or that they are not trying hard enough (Ames & Archer, 1988; Nicholls et al. 1990). For students with learning goals, judgments of competence are based on the amount of effort expended and on whether real learning or mastery was achieved (Jagacinski & Nicholls, 1987).

Dweck suggests that because students with performance goals are not focused on their own developing competencies, they judge their competence in terms of their performance relative to others or by external feedback. Those who are confident in their ability choose moderately difficult tasks – in order to display their competence. Because they are confident that they will succeed, they use effective strategies when they encounter difficulty, as do students with learning goals. But because their goal is to *look* competent (as opposed to *be* competent), they may use shortcuts that achieve their immediate goal but do not actually foster learning (see also Nicholls, 1983; Covington, 1992).

Dweck (1986; Elliott & Dweck, 1988) and others propose that students who lack self-confidence are more negatively affected by performance goals. According to Covington (1992; Covington & Beery, 1976) they choose easy tasks to avoid displaying incompetence. When they encounter difficulty, they engage in self-defeating strategies to avoid the public perception of being low in ability – such as procrastinating, making excuses, working halfheartedly, setting unrealistic goals, or cheating. Eventually some give up the game of trying to avoid looking stupid, accept what they believe is their ultimate fate, and quit trying altogether.

Covington and Beery (1976; see also Covington, 1992, chap. 4) explain that performance-oriented children who lack confidence face a serious dilemma; if they try and fail, their failure will provide unambiguous evidence of their low ability. If they do not try, they will have an explanation, aside from low ability, for their failure, but they may be punished. This is why Covington and Omelich (1979) refer to effort for these children as a ''double-edged sword.''

Mastery versus performance goals also have implications for students' problem-solving strategies. Studies have found, for example, that mastery goals are associated with reviewing material not understood, asking questions, making connections between current problems and past problems, planning, organizing material, and setting goals (Ames & Archer, 1988; Meece, Blumenfeld, & Hoyle, 1988; Nolen, 1988). Performance goals are associated with attention on the self, and especially on external evaluations of the self, and more use of superficial strategies (copying, guessing, skipping questions). In addition to promoting active problem solving, a task orientation has been shown to enhance pleasure and emotional involvement in the work at hand (Ames & Archer, 1988; Duda & Nicholls, 1992).

Research has pointed to a number of ways to promote learning goals in classrooms. (See Stipek, in press, for a review.) Two sets of principles have already been discussed; success and evaluation need to be defined in terms of personal improvement, meeting personalized goals, or achieving a level of mastery that is within each child's grasp, and tasks need to be moderately challenging. To focus on learning and developing competencies, children need to believe that they *can* learn, that effort and persistence will, in fact, result in their achieving their goals. If success and evaluation are defined in terms of relative performance, not only will some children necessarily fail, but many (those who fail consistently or who have developed an image of themselves as "failures") will be burdened with the dilemma described by Covington and Beery (1976).

Errors need to be treated as a normal part of learning that can actually be useful in figuring out what a child's misconceptions are and what needs to be done to increase mastery. Ironically, this is true in most spheres of life – for example, learning to cook, to play tennis, to fix cars – but not in most classrooms. Being afraid to make a mistake undermines children's ability to focus on and to explore and experiment with different strategies for learning and completing tasks. If the teacher's emphasis is on getting it right (rather than learning or understanding), the students' will be too.

External evaluation needs to be provided, but it should be substantive; it should provide information to children that they can use to guide further efforts. Constant reminders of external evaluation foster a performance orientation. Children will see getting a good grade (or avoiding a bad one) as the reason for their effort and they will focus their attention on the external evaluation rather than on what they are learning and what strategies they need to use to increase their mastery.

Focusing students' attention on learning and mastery rather than on external evaluation has the added value of increasing students' self-confidence in success. Every child can learn and master increasingly complex material. Consequently, every child can enjoy feelings of competence and success.

Unconditional regard

Children who are faring poorly in academics are burdened with more than the frustration and humiliation of their failure. They are often treated less well by their teachers and peers – not just as learners, but as people. Many children who fail in school have almost exclusively negative interactions with the teacher. They are often in trouble – for not completing assignments or not paying attention, or for goofing off or acting out. They deserve being sanctioned, but the classroom becomes a very unpleasant place for children who have mostly discipline-related interactions with their teachers.

Peers too can be cruel, partly because the poor achievers are also often the trouble-makers. Peers often exclude them from play and birthday parties, resist being placed in work groups with them, and even make fun of their academic problems. It is not surprising that many children's perception of themselves as being academically incompetent evolves into a perception of themselves as being unworthy human beings.

Only recently have researchers begun to examine the effect of children's relationships with teachers and their peers on motivation. Connell and Wellborn (1991) claim that "relatedness" is one of three basic human needs, along with feelings of competence and autonomy. Relatedness, in their framework, encompasses the need to feel securely connected to individuals in the social context and the "need to experience oneself as worthy and capable of love and respect" (p. 51). Their research has shown that students' feelings of relatedness to their teacher and classmates are strong predictors of their cognitive, behavioral, and emotional engagement in classroom activities.

Skinner and Belmont (1993) assessed teachers' perceptions of their involvement with their students with a measure that included items about their affection (how much they liked, appreciated, and enjoyed the student), their attunement (understanding, sympathy, and knowledge about the student), and dependability (availability in case of need). Using similar items, students rated their own involvement with their teacher. Teachers' ratings of their involvement with students in the fall strongly predicted students' self-perceptions (relatedness to the teacher, feelings of autonomy) assessed in the spring, which in turn predicted students' engagement in classroom activities.

This is a new area of research, but findings so far suggest the value of a social context that is accepting and supportive – where each student is valued regardless of his or her academic skills or performance relative to others. Such an environment should go a long way toward diminishing the negative consequences of relatively poor performance; in a caring, supportive social context, being a slow learner or having difficulties with schoolwork doesn't get translated into feelings of being unvalued or unworthy as a person.

Conveying acceptance of a child as a person, however, does not require indiscriminant praise, sympathy, or acceptance of all behavior. To the contrary, teachers convey their commitment to and respect for students by expecting and demanding (albeit in a gentle and supportive manner) appropriate behavior and a high level of effort. There are no simple recipes for balancing respect and high standards, but this is an important goal because children who feel devalued by teachers or who are not called upon to meet appropriately high standards of behavior and performance are not likely to give their best effort in school.

Summary

The research-based recommendations for educational practice discussed here are not easy to implement, in part because they have to be taken as a package. (See

Stipek, 1993, in press, for further details on the practical implications of research on motivation for classroom practice.) Teachers cannot implement one recommendation (e.g., deemphasizing external reasons for engaging in school tasks) without considering other issues (e.g., whether tasks are appropriately challenging and interesting to children). Adding to the complexity of the teacher's task, as mentioned already, is the need to balance some goals (e.g., valuing and respecting children) with others (e.g., holding students accountable for their behavior). There are also developmental issues teachers need to consider. For example, younger children may need more constant attention and encouragement than older children. And then there are the motivational orientations children bring to the classroom that need to be factored into planning. For example, children who are used to doing well in school without much effort are often frustrated and upset when they are initially presented with challenging work.

If we expect teachers to help children succeed, we must be prepared to provide them with the tools *they* need for success in this important but complicated task.

Schools for success

Most of the teachers I have met care deeply about their students and want to teach them better. But many feel overwhelmed by the obstacles (e.g., poverty, violence, lack of resources and parent support, students who do not speak their language). Most lack the knowledge and skills required to provide an instructional program that ensures success for students with such significant and diverse needs. Many teachers experience the same feelings of frustration, failure, and hopelessness that their students feel.

The same strategies that research suggests will increase student success applies also to teachers. Teachers need a supportive environment in which experimentation is encouraged and mistakes are considered useful guides for further instructional planning. Accountability is as important for teachers as it is for students, but too much emphasis on outcomes and external evaluation engenders strong performance concerns in teachers, as it does for students; it creates anxiety and stifles experimentation. Teachers also benefit from an environment in which there are high expectations for teacher effectiveness as well as student learning.

Teachers require professional development opportunities and support for their efforts to improve their teaching and their students' learning. They need a great deal of subject-matter knowledge, as well as knowledge about how children make meaning of the learning process; they need skills in assessing children's understanding and assistance in providing some degree of individualization in the context of a large group of students.

Most teachers have little chance of implementing the effective teaching and motivational practices identified by researchers and experts. Access to new knowledge and examples of good practices are limited. Teachers are typically paid only for the time school is in session, and although creative strategies (e.g, time banking) and teacher workdays are being used by some schools, paid out-of-classroom time remains minimal at best. Most teachers have no time during their work day to plan instruction, reflect on what they are doing, read, observe other teachers, or share problems and ideas with colleagues. Until opportunities to learn and time for planning, reflection, observation, and dialogue are considered central components of a teacher's job, we will see little improvement in the education we provide children in this country. Until teachers are given the support *they* need to succeed, many children will continue to fail.

The current political climate, which focuses more on accountability than on developing policies that will assist teachers in achieving high standards, could have more harmful than positive effects on student learning. Teachers in this nation face greater challenges than ever before. More attention needs to be given to the professionalism and the professional development of teachers if we are to make any progress in closing the gap between what we know about good teaching and what is practiced. Sustained attention in this direction could eventually result in schools in which teachers are more successful in assisting children to succeed – in the classroom and in their lives.

References

Ames, C. (1978). Children's achievement attributions and self-reinforcement: Effects of self-concept and competitive reward structure. *Journal of Educational Psychology, 70,* 345–355.

Ames, C. (1981). Competitive versus cooperative reward structure: The influence of individual and group performance factors on achievement attributions and affect. *American Educational Research Journal, 18,* 273–288.

Ames, C. (1986). Conceptions of motivation within competitive and noncompetitive goal structures. In R. Schwarzer (Ed.), *Self-related cognitions in anxiety and motivation* (pp. 229–245). Hillsdale, NJ: Erlbaum.

Ames, C. (1992). Classrooms: Goals, structures, and student motivation. *Journal of Educational Psychology, 84,* 261–271.

Ames, C., & Ames, R. (1978). Thrill of victory and agony of defeat: Children's self and interpersonal evaluations in competitive and non-competitive learning environments. *Journal of Research and Development in Education, 12,* 79–81.

Ames, C., & Ames, R. (1981). Competitive versus individualistic goal structures: The salience of past performance information for causal attributions and affect. *Journal of Educational Psychology, 73,* 411–418.

Ames, C., & Archer, J. (1988). Achievement goals in the classroom: Students' learning strategies and motivation processes. *Journal of Educational Psychology, 80,* 260–267.

Atkinson, J. (1964). *An introduction to motivation.* Princeton, NJ: Van Nostrand.

Babad, E., Bernieri, F., & Rosenthal, R. (1991). Students as judges of teachers' verbal and nonverbal behavior. *American Educational Research Journal, 28,* 211–234.

Barker, G., & Graham, S. (1987). Developmental study of praise and blame as attributional cues. *Journal of Educational Psychology, 79,* 62–66.

Berndt, T., & Ladd, G. (Eds.). (1989). *Peer relationships in child development.* New York: Wiley.

Bloom, B. (1981). *All our children learning.* New York: McGraw-Hill.

Blumenfeld, P. (1992). Classroom learning and motivation: Clarifying and expanding goal theory. *Journal of Educational Psychology, 84,* 272–281.

Borko, H., & Eisenhart, M. (1986). Students' conceptions of reading and their reading experiences in school. *Elementary School Journal, 86,* 589–611.

Brooks-Gunn, J., Guo, G., & Furstenberg, F. (1993). Who drops out of and who continues beyond high school? A 20-year follow-up of black and urban youth. *Journal of Research on Adolescence, 3,* 271–294.

Bybee, J., & Zigler, E. (1992). Is outerdirectedness employed in a harmful or beneficial manner by students with and without mental retardation? *American Journal on Mental Retardation, 96,* 512–521.

Connell, J., & Wellborn, J. (1991). Competence, autonomy, and relatedness: A motivational analysis of self-system processes. In M. Gunnar & A. Sroufe (Eds.), *Self processes and development: The Minnesota symposia on child development* (Vol. 23, pp. 43–77). Hillsdale, NJ: Erlbaum.

Covington, M. (1992). *Making the grade: A self-worth perspective on motivation and school reform.* Cambridge: Cambridge University Press.

Covington, M., & Beery, R. (1976). *Self-worth and school learning.* New York: Holt, Rinehart & Winston.

Covington, M., & Omelich, C. (1979). Effort: The double-edged sword in school achievement. *Journal of Educational Psychology, 71,* 169–182.

Covington, M., & Omelich, C. (1984). Task-oriented versus competitive learning structures: Motivational and performance consequences. *Journal of Educational Psychology, 7,* 1038–1050.

Deci, E., & Ryan, R. (1985). *Intrinsic motivation and self-determination in human behavior.* New York: Plenum Press.

Duda, J., & Nicholls, J. (1992). Dimensions of achievement motivation in schoolwork and sport. *Journal of Educational Psychology, 84,* 290–299.

Dweck, C. S. (1986). Motivational processes affecting learning. *American Psychologist, 41,* 1040–1048.

Dweck, C. S., & Leggett, E. L. (1988). A social-cognitive approach to motivation and personality. *Psychological Review, 95,* 256–273.

Edmonds, R. (1979). Effective schools for the urban poor. *Educational Leadership, 37,* 15–18.

Eggert, L., Thompson, E., Herting, J., & Nicholas, L. (1994). Prevention research program: Reconnecting at-risk youth. *Issues in Mental Health Nursing, 15,* 107–135.

Elliot, E., & Dweck, C. (1988). Goals: An approach to motivation and achievement. *Journal of Personality and Social Psychology, 54,* 5–12.

Fetler, M. (1989). School dropout rates, academic performance, size, and poverty: Correlates of educational reform. *Educational Evaluation and Policy Analysis, 7,* 109–116.

Finn, J. (1989). Withdrawing from school. *Review of Educational Research, 59,* 117–142.

Good, T. (1987). Teacher expectations. In D. Berliner & B. Rosenshine (Eds.), *Talks to teachers* (pp. 159–200). New York: Random House.

Graham, S. (1984). Communicating sympathy and anger to black and white children: The cognitive (attributional) consequences of affective cues. *Journal of Personality and Social Psychology, 47,* 14–28.

Graham, S. (1990). Communicating low ability in the classroom: Bad things good teachers sometimes do. In S. Graham & V. Folkes (Eds.), *Attribution theory: Applications to achievement, mental health, and interpersonal conflict* (pp. 17–36). Hillsdale, NJ: Erlbaum.

Grande, C. (1988). Delinquency: The learning disabled student's reaction to academic school failure? *Adolescence, 89,* 209–219.

Gruen, G., & Zigler, E. (1968). Expectancy of success and the probability learning of middle-class, lower-class, and retarded children. *Journal of Abnormal Psychology, 73,* 343–352.

Hart, S. (1982). Analyzing the social organization for reading in one elementary school. In G. Spindler (Ed.), *Doing the ethnography of schooling* (pp. 410–438). New York: Holt, Rinehart, & Winston.

Harter, S., & Zigler, E. (1974). The assessment of effectance motivation in normal and retarded children. *Developmental Psychology, 10,* 169–180.

Hartup, W. (1983). Peer relations. In P. Mussen (Ed.), *Handbook of child psychology,* Vol. 4: *Socialization, personality and social development* (pp. 103–196). New York: Wiley.

Hiebert, E. (1983). An examination of ability grouping in reading instruction. *Reading Research Quarterly, 18,* 231–255.

Jagacinski, C., & Nicholls, J. (1987). Competence and affect in task involvement and ego involvement: The impact of social comparison information. *Journal of Educational Psychology, 79,* 107–114.

Luthar, S. (1995). Social competence in the school setting: Prospective cross-domain associations among inner-city teens. *Child Development, 66,* 416–429.

Mac Iver, D., Stipek, D., & Daniels, D. (1991). Explaining within-semester changes in student effort in junior high school and senior high school courses. *Journal of Educational Psychology, 83,* 201–211.

Marsh, H. (1989). Sex differences in the development of verbal and mathematics constructs: The High School and Beyond study. *American Educational Research Journal, 26,* 191–225.

Marsh, H. (1990). Causal ordering of academic self-concept and academic achievement: A multiwave, longitudinal panel analysis. *Journal of Educational Psychology, 82,* 646–656.

Marsh, H. (1991). Failure of high-ability high schools to deliver academic benefits commensurate with their students' ability levels. *American Educational Research Journal, 28,* 445–480.

Marsh, H. (1992). Content specificity of relations between academic achievement and academic self-concept. *Journal of Educational Psychology, 84,* 35–42.

Marsh, H. (1994). Using the National Longitudinal Study of 1988 to evaluate theoretical models of self-concept: The self-description questionnaire. *Journal of Educational Psychology, 86,* 439–456.

McDermott, R. (1987). The explanation of minority school failure, again. *Anthropology and Education Quarterly, 18,* 361–364.

Meece, J. (1991). The classroom context and students' motivational goals. In M. Maehr & P. Pintrich (Eds.), *Advances in motivation and achievement* (Vol. 7, pp. 261–285). Greenwich, CT: JAI Press.

Meece, J., Blumenfeld, P., & Hoyle, R. (1988). Students' goal orientations and cognitive engagement in classroom activities. *Journal of Educational Psychology, 80,* 514–523.

National Council of Teachers of Mathematics. (1991). *Professional standards for teaching mathematics.* Reston, VA.

Nicholls, J. (1983). Conception of ability and achievement motivation: A theory and its implications for education. In S. Paris, G. Olson, & H. Stevenson (Eds.), *Learning and motivation in the classroom* (pp. 211–237). Hillsdale, NJ: Erlbaum.

Nicholls, J., Cobb, P., Wood, T., Yackel, E., & Patashnick, M. (1990). Assessing students' theories of success in mathematics: Individual and classroom differences. *Journal for Research in Mathematics Education, 21,* 109–122.

Nolen, S. (1988). Reasons for studying: Motivational orientations and study strategies. *Cognition and Instruction, 5,* 269–287.

Ollendick, T., & King, N. (1990). School phobia and separation anxiety. In H. Leitenberg (Ed.), *Handbook of social and evaluation anxiety* (pp. 179–214). New York: Plenum Press.

Parsons, J., Kaczala, C., & Meece, J. (1982). Socialization of achievement attitudes and beliefs: Classroom influences. *Child Development, 53,* 322–339.

Peterson, P., & Swing, S. (1982). Beyond time on task: Students' reports of their thought processes during classroom instruction. *Elementary School Journal, 21,* 487–515.

Rhodes, S., & Jasinski, D. (1990). Learning disabilities in alcohol-dependent adults: A preliminary study. *Journal of Learning Disabilities, 23,* 551–556.

Rosenholtz, S., & Simpson, C. (1984a). Classroom organization and student stratification. *Elementary School Journal, 85,* 21–38.

Rosenholtz, S., & Simpson, C. (1984b). The formation of ability conceptions: Developmental trend or social construction? *Review of Educational Research, 54,* 31–63.

Rutter, M., Maughan, B., Mortimore, P., Duston, P., & Smith, O. (1979). *Fifteen thousand hours.* Cambridge, MA: Harvard University Press.

Skinner, E., & Belmont, M. (1993). Motivation in the classroom: Reciprocal effects of teacher behavior and student engagement across the school year. *Journal of Educational Psychology, 85,* 571–581.

Slavin, R. (1983). *Cooperative learning.* New York: Longman.

Slavin, R. (1984). Students motivating students to excel: Cooperative incentives, cooperative tasks, and student achievement. *Elementary School Journal, 84,* 53–63.

Stipek, D. (1984). Young children's performance expectations: Logical analysis or wishful thinking?

In J. Nicholls (Ed.), *Advances in motivation and achievement,* Vol. 3: *The development of achievement motivation* (pp. 33–56). Greenwich, CT: JAI Press.

Stipek, D. (1993). *Motivation to learn: From theory to practice.* Needham Heights, MA: Allyn & Bacon.

Stipek, D. (in press). Motivation and instruction. In D. Berliner & R. Calfee (Eds.), *Handbook of educational psychology.* New York: Macmillan.

Stipek, D., Feiler, R., Daniels, D., & Milburn, S. (1995). Effects of different instructional approaches on young children's achievement and motivation. *Child Development, 66,* 209–223.

Weiner, B. (1992). *Human motivation: Metaphors, theories, and research.* Newbury Park, CA: Sage.

Weinstein, R. (1976). Reading group membership in first grade: Teacher behaviors and pupil experience over time. *Journal of Educational Psychology, 68,* 103–116.

Weinstein, R. (1985). Student meditation of classroom expectancy effects. In J. Dusek (Ed.), *Teacher expectancies* (pp. 329–350). Hillsdale, NJ: Erlbaum.

Weinstein, R., & Middlestadt, S. (1979). Student perceptions of teacher interactions with male high and low achievers. *Journal of Educational Psychology, 71,* 421–431.

Yando, R., & Zigler, E. (1971). Outerdirectedness in the problem-solving of institutionalized and non-institutionalized normal and retarded children. *Developmental Psychology, 5,* 290–299.

Zigler, E., & Hodapp, B. (1986). *Understanding mental retardation.* New York: Cambridge University Press.

5   What is normal? What is abnormal? Developmental perspectives on behavioral and emotional problems

Thomas M. Achenbach

Although he might not recognize them in my current work, Ed Zigler's ideas shaped my own in at least four ways. Beginning when I was a sophomore in the first course that Ed taught at Yale, I learned the following basic points from him:

1. To view pathological behavior on a continuum with normal behavior, as exemplified by particular behaviors among retarded children that could be better understood as normal outcomes of the children's developmental and experiential histories than as inherently pathological symptoms of mental retardation (e.g., Zigler, 1963).
2. To apply developmental perspectives to understanding mental retardation and psychopathology (Zigler, 1965).
3. To recognize that taxonomy is a fundamental problem in the study of psychopathology (Zigler & Phillips, 1961).
4. To use research-based knowledge to help people, especially children (Zigler & Valentine, 1979).

The normal–abnormal continuum in psychopathology

The normal–abnormal continuum in psychopathology is a concept that has implications for understanding human functioning in all developmental periods. It is especially pertinent to understanding psychopathology during periods of massive developmental change, such as from early childhood to young adulthood.

To be useful, the concept need not assume that *all* pathological functioning is on a continuum with normal functioning. It is quite possible, for example, that some pathological functioning is qualitatively different and has categorically different determinants than normal functioning. To determine what is abnormal in the sense of being maladaptively deviant, however, we need to know what is normal in the sense of typifying people who are adapting reasonably well. We also need to know the long-term consequences of particular adaptational patterns. Certain patterns that seem adaptive during one period may be maladaptive if they persist too long or if they impede the development of more advanced patterns. For ex-

This work was supported in part by research grants 94-1458-92 from the W. T. Grant Foundation and MH40305 from the National Institute of Mental Health.

ample, high school sports heroes may appear supercompetent in their teens but become abject failures in their 20s, if they do not develop new adaptive behaviors.

Methods for distinguishing the normal from the abnormal are especially needed for judging which children should receive special help for behavioral and emotional problems and what sort of help to provide. Unlike adults, children seldom identify themselves as having behavioral/emotional problems that warrant special help. Furthermore, children may be judged normal by people who see them in one context, such as school, but abnormal by people who see them in another context, such as home. Because behavior and emotions vary so much over the course of development, from one context to another, and between different interaction partners, efforts to distinguish the normal from the abnormal face a variety of challenges.

The purpose of this chapter is to describe an empirically based approach to distinguishing between the normal and abnormal. This approach entails a series of interlocking research tasks for acquiring knowledge about developmental aspects of psychopathology. The knowledge thus acquired can then be used for understanding and coping with maladaptive variations in development.

An empirically based approach to distinguishing between the normal and abnormal

In the absence of infallible a priori criteria for distinguishing between the normal and abnormal, we can turn to an empirically based bootstrapping strategy. That is, we can "lift ourselves by our own bootstraps" through an iterative process of progressively testing and refining various fallible criteria for judging the normal versus abnormal within particular developmental periods. Research tasks to be accomplished in this process can be conceptualized in terms of psychometrics, epidemiology, taxonomy, developmental changes, and cross-informant issues, as outlined in the following sections.

Psychometrics

A fundamental task is to obtain standardized data on the problems of subjects who are independently judged to be normal versus demographically similar subjects who are judged to be deviant in maladaptive ways. The problems and other characteristics of the groups chosen to represent the normal versus deviant can then be compared to identify those that discriminate between the groups. This task raises psychometric challenges, such as the following:

1. The assessment procedures need to be reliable and valid.
2. The normal and deviant criterion samples need to be representative of the larger populations to which findings are to be generalized.
3. The normal and deviant samples should be matched for demographic variables, such as age, gender, ethnicity, and socioeconomic status (SES), that might have

associations with the target problems, over and above the associations with the criterion variable of normal versus deviant status.

4. The sampling of problems should be broad enough to permit comparisons of the degree to which various problems discriminate between the normal and deviant criterion groups and to determine whether the discriminative power of particular items varies with other characteristics of the subjects, such as age, gender, ethnicity, and SES.

5. To test for cross-situational variations, problems should be sampled in multiple contexts, as reported by multiple informants.

6. Samples should be large enough to afford high statistical power for detecting a wide range of associations with multiple subject variables and for reliably quantifying the magnitude of the associations.

7. The problems should be assessed in quantitative form to maximize power for detecting their associations with each other and with other variables. If findings indicate that problems are more validly categorized as present versus absent, categorization can be imposed on quantitative scores. The reverse is not true, however, as data obtained only in categorical, present versus absent form cannot be subsequently rescored either quantitatively or in terms of different categorical cutpoints.

The importance of measurement. The foregoing challenges reflect the fundamental importance of *measurement* in efforts to identify characteristics that can help us distinguish between the normal and abnormal. Whether particular aspects of the normal versus abnormal are better understood in quantitative or categorical terms, we need to recognize that rigorous assessment of behavioral and emotional problems is essentially a measurement process. This means that we must know how to measure human behavior and must cope with the errors that affect all measurement. To be useful, measurement of behavioral/emotional problems must be reliable, valid, and statistically analyzable.

Measurement of behavioral/emotional problems is complicated by the fact that such problems do not "hold still" to be measured by purely mechanical procedures. Instead, the presence of behavioral/emotional problems must be judged from samples of behavior occurring in particular contexts. Judgments of behavioral/emotional problems are apt to be influenced by characteristics of the subjects such as age and gender, as well as by the judges' personal standards for reporting the subjects' behavior. As a consequence, no single measurement can provide an adequate picture of behavioral/emotional problems. It is therefore necessary to take account of multiple sources of variation relevant to decisions about the normal versus abnormal, as outlined in the following sections.

Epidemiological perspectives

Ability, achievement, and personality tests have long employed normative samples to provide standard scores against which to judge the performance of individuals who take the tests. Ideally, the normative samples should be randomly chosen from the population to which individuals are compared. In practice, the normative samples often fall short of being truly random, as ability and achievement tests are often "normed" on subjects from a few schools chosen for their cooperativeness (e.g., Wechsler, 1991, 1992). Similarly, personality tests are often "normed" on "convenience samples" that happen to be readily accessible or live within a limited geographical area (e.g., Williams, Butcher, Ben-Porath, & Graham, 1992).

As the study of distributions of diseases in populations, *epidemiology* plays a role in medicine that is somewhat analogous to the role of normative research in psychometrics. A major difference between epidemiological and normative psychometric research, however, is that epidemiology typically starts with fixed rules for defining diseases and then tabulates the obtained distributions of diseases defined according to these rules. Normative psychometric research, by contrast, uses obtained distributions of scores to distinguish the normal, in the sense of the typical, from the abnormal, in the sense of the rare or statistically deviant.

In distinguishing between normal and abnormal levels of behavioral/emotional problems, aspects of both the epidemiological and psychometric approaches can be helpful. Most people manifest some degree of behavioral/emotional problems throughout their lives. It is therefore unlikely that the mere presence of particular problems can be used to define behavioral/emotional disorders in a uniform fashion for people of all ages. On the other hand, there may be degrees or aggregations of problems that are clearly maladaptive regardless of their overall distribution in normative samples. If we obtain the distributions of particular problems and aggregations of problems in samples chosen to represent the healthy portion of the population versus the unhealthy portion, cutpoints on these distributions can be selected to discriminate between scores obtained by healthy versus unhealthy subjects.

Failure to consider distributions of particular problems in healthy versus unhealthy criterion groups can lead to incorrect assumptions about pathognomicity. For example, "always on the go" was included as a criterion for Attention Deficit Disorder with Hyperactivity in the third edition of the American Psychiatric Association's (1980) *Diagnostic and Statistical Manual of Mental Disorders* (DSM-III). However, a comparison between national samples of children referred for mental health services and demographically matched nonreferred children showed that the *nonreferred* children obtained significantly *higher* scores in parents' ratings of this item than did *referred* children (Achenbach, Howell, Quay, & Conners, 1991). The higher scores for nonreferred children suggest that this item reflects positive adaptive characteristics, rather than the pathological hyperactivity that the architects of DSM-III had in mind. Despite the epidemiological finding that this item was not pathognomic, the fourth edition of the DSM (DSM-IV; American Psychiatric Association, 1994) includes "often on the go" as a criterial feature of what DSM-IV calls Attention Deficit/Hyperactivity Disorder (ADHD).

To provide broader perspectives on the prevalence and distributions of problems in a particular culture and clues to possible etiological factors, it is helpful to compare epidemiological data obtained by similar standardized procedures across multiple cultures. It is also helpful to compare epidemiological data obtained in the same culture at multiple points in time. Such data can indicate whether the rates of particular problems are much higher or lower in some cultures than others (e.g., Verhulst & Achenbach, 1995) and whether the rates are changing in a particular culture over time (e.g., Achenbach & Howell, 1993). Cross-cultural and secular comparisons can also be used to test the generalizability and stability of assessment procedures.

Taxonomic tasks

In the absence of a priori criteria for childhood disorders, psychometric and epidemiological studies are needed to provide a basis for determining which problems are good candidates for defining and operationalizing disorders. Although labels such as ADHD, Oppositional Defiant Disorder (ODD), and Conduct Disorder (CD) are widely used, neither the nosological categories designated by these labels nor the specific criteria used to define them were derived directly from actual samples of disturbed children. Instead, nosological categories for child psychopathology have been chosen by committees of experts who then formulated the criteria for deciding whether particular individuals qualify for particular disorders (e.g., American Psychiatric Association, 1994). This approach can be described as working from the "top down," because it starts with decisions about what disorders exist and then works downward to decisions about how to define the disorders in terms of diagnostic criteria.

The third and fourth editions of the DSM provide explicit rules for applying particular diagnoses. For example, according to DSM-IV, a child qualifies for the diagnosis of ODD if at least four out of a possible eight criterial behaviors, such as "often loses temper," have been present over at least 6 months (American Psychiatric Association, 1994, pp. 93–94). Although requirements such as manifesting four out of eight criterial behaviors over at least 6 months are explicit, they do not constitute operational definitions, because no assessment operations are specified for determining the presence versus absence of the criterial behaviors. Instead, the diagnostician must make a yes or no decision about whether the child has often lost his or her temper and has manifested any of the other seven criterial behaviors over at least 6 months. In making this decision, the diagnostician would typically need reports from others such as parents. However, the DSM does not specify procedures for obtaining standardized reports, who they should be obtained from, how the diagnostician judges them, or how the diagnostician is to resolve discrepancies among different sources of data. It is also unclear whether at least four of the eight criterial behaviors must occur simultaneously over at least 6 months and how their occurrence over a specific 6-month interval would be verified.

In effect, the "top down" approach deals with the taxonomic task of determining what disorders exist and the assessment task of determining who manifests each disorder by stating definitional criteria for diagnostic categories. By contrast, an empirically based approach works from the "ground up" to develop assessment and taxonomic procedures in a bootstrapping fashion. That is, the empirically based approach starts with assessment procedures that are tested in various ways to identify problems that discriminate between criterion groups of subjects who are regarded as relatively normal versus maladaptively deviant according to other criteria, such as referral for mental health services.

After satisfactory assessment procedures and candidate problem items have been developed, the empirically based approach employs multivariate analyses of the problem items to identify sets of problems that tend to co-occur. Factor analytic and cluster analytic methodologies are often used to derive sets of co-occurring items. These empirically derived sets of items can be viewed as syndromes in the generic sense of things that go together (from the Greek root of *syndrome*, "the act of running together"). In this sense of the word syndrome, empirically derived syndromes do not imply any particular assumptions about the nature or causes of disorders. Instead, they provide starting points for operationally defining hypothesized disorders whose correlates can then be tested.

If particular syndromes of problems have important correlates and can discriminate significantly between criterion groups of normal and deviant subjects, they can become foci for research on the cause, course, and most effective intervention for each syndrome. Differences among syndromes and their correlates can also provide a basis for developing theories of psychopathology. The empirically based approach thus addresses assessment and taxonomy as primary tasks to be accomplished rather than as faits accomplis. When satisfactory taxa have been derived, the assessment procedures that are used to define the taxa operationally can be applied to new cases in order both to obtain standardized descriptions of the new cases and to determine the degree to which each new case matches the previously derived taxa.

Developmental changes

Consider for a moment the typical behavior of a 2-year-old child, a 10-year-old, a 16-year-old, and a 21-year-old. It is obvious that behavior regarded as normal at some of these ages would be abnormal at other ages.

Changes in prevalence. Developmental changes make it imperative to obtain data on healthy and unhealthy criterion groups for each developmental period in order to take account of changes in what is pathognomic. Problems such as fears, for example, may be equally prevalent in referred and nonreferred 3-year-olds but significantly more prevalent in referred than nonreferred 7-year-olds. Conversely, the *absence* of certain competencies may be pathognomic in 7-year-olds, but not in 3-year-olds. To judge the functioning of an individual, we thus need to compare assessment data for that individual with similar data for representative samples of peers assessed at the same developmental period. Normative-developmental data of this sort provide essential guidelines for determining what is normal versus abnormal within each developmental period.

Changes in patterns. In addition to developmental changes in the prevalence and pathognomicity of particular problems and competencies, *patterns* of problems and competencies may vary over the course of development in ways that require different standards for judging what is normal versus abnormal. For example, multivariate analyses of problems among 4- to 18-year-olds have yielded a clear-cut syndrome designated as "attention problems," which comprises attentional problems and overactivity (Achenbach, 1991a). However, similar analyses have not detected a counterpart syndrome at ages 2 and 3 (Achenbach, 1992). Multivariate analyses of problems for ages 19 to 28 have yielded a syndrome designated as Irresponsible that overlaps the Attention Problems syndrome found at ages 4 to 18. The irresponsible syndrome lacks problems of overactivity that are included in the preadult Attention Problems syndrome, but it includes additional problems such as the following: irresponsible; fired from a job; feels he or she cannot succeed; lacks initiative; has trouble making decisions; and too dependent. Some of these problems, such as being fired from a job, would be less relevant to judging adaptive functioning in the preadult than the adult years.

Developmental continuities. Longitudinal research has shown that scores on the young-adult Irresponsible syndrome are strongly predicted by scores on the Attention Problems syndrome in adolescence, which, in turn, are strongly predicted by scores on the same syndrome in childhood (Achenbach, Howell, McConaughy, & Stanger, 1995a, 1995b). These findings indicate developmental continuity in a pattern of problems that becomes detectible in early childhood but that changes somewhat in early adulthood. Changes in the phenotypic manifestations of what may be the same underlying disorder are called "heterotypy," whereas continuity in phenotypes is called "homotypy" (Kagan, 1969).

The possibility that childhood attention deficit disorders continue into adulthood is widely publicized (e.g., Cowley & Ramo, 1993; Shaffer, 1994). Yet, the prevailing procedures for diagnosing such disorders impose categorical distinctions between preadult and adult disorders, rather than allowing for continuity between them. For example, structured interviews designed to diagnose adults according to DSM criteria have not included the criterial features of disorders that are attributed to children and adolescents, such as ADHD. Even if such disorders continue into adulthood in precisely the same form as defined by the DSM criteria for preadult disorders (i.e., they are homotypic), they would not be detected by diagnostic procedures that do not assess their criterial features.

The neglect of possible heterotypic and homotypic continuities between child/adolescent and adult disorders is illustrated by the National Comorbidity Study, in which the Composite International Diagnostic Interview (CIDI; Wittchen et al., 1991) was administered to 15- to 54-year-old subjects (Kessler et al., 1994). Despite the inclusion of hundreds of adolescents, the CIDI did not provide criteria for such common preadult disorders as ADHD, ODD, or CD. Thus, because only the criteria for adult disorders were assessed, disorders that are prevalent at least through age 18 (and perhaps beyond these ages) could not be detected. Nor could adult versions of preadult problem patterns be found if they did not correspond to the CIDI criteria.

To determine whether syndromal patterns change or remain the same across developmental periods, the empirically based approach applies multivariate analyses to the problems reported for subjects within each developmental period. Certain syndromes, such as one designated as Aggressive Behavior, have been found from ages 2 through early adulthood (Achenbach, 1991a, 1992; Achenbach et al., 1995b). Other syndromes, such as the Attention Problems syndrome, have been found only in certain developmental periods, but they have heterotypic counterparts in other developmental periods, such as the Irresponsible syndrome among young adults.

Long-term developmental relations between syndromes can be ascertained only by means of longitudinal research. Several longitudinal studies are currently assessing psychopathology among young adults who were assessed via empirically based methods in earlier developmental periods (e.g., Achenbach et al., 1995b; Ferdinand, Verhulst, & Wiznitzer, 1995; Rheinherz, 1995). Such studies make it possible to track developmental relations between preadult and adult problem patterns more precisely than do studies that impose predefined diagnostic criteria without regard to developmental sequences and changes.

Cross-informant issues

Children's behavior often differs from one context to another, such as the home versus the school. Their behavior may also differ from one interaction partner to another even within a particular context, such as from their mother to their father within the home. In the assessment of adults, the adult subject is typically the main source of data about psychopathology. Although even adult subjects may not be adequate sources of data about their own psychopathology, it is obvious that assessment of children requires data from sources beside the children themselves.

Direct observations in settings such as the school, home, and clinic can contribute to assessment of children. Nevertheless, we also need reports from people who interact with the children across longer periods and different conditions than are accessible to trained observers. Reports by informants are constrained by their own standards of judgment and by the particular conditions under which they see children. However, this is also true of reports by trained observers, who have access only to limited samples of behavior, using particular data collection procedures, and under conditions where the observer's presence may affect the behavior. Fire setting, suicidal behavior, stealing, bedtime rituals, and sleep problems, for example, are unlikely to occur under the watchful eyes of trained observers. Although adolescents are more capable of providing information about their own psychopathology than are younger children, comprehensive assessment still requires reports from others, such as parents and teachers, who may impart information and judgments not apt to emanate from adolescents themselves.

Cross-informant discrepancies. Because different informants have different standards of judgment and access to different samples of subjects' behavior, it should not be surprising if cross-informant agreement is less than perfect. Metaanalyses of numerous studies have yielded a mean Pearson correlation of .60 between reports by pairs of informants who play similar roles with respect to the subjects, such as mothers and fathers, pairs of teachers, pairs of mental health workers, and pairs of observers (Achenbach, McConaughy, & Howell, 1987). Between informants who play different roles vis-à-vis the subjects, such as parents versus teachers, the mean correlation was .28. And between the subjects themselves and other informants, including parents, teachers, and mental health workers, the mean correlation was .22. Although all the mean cross-informant correlations were statistically significant, their modest size indicates that no one informant can substitute for all others.

Some authors have equated low cross-informant correlations with poor reliability (Gould & Shaffer, 1985) or lack of validity (Garrison & Earls, 1985). However, many of the assessment procedures included in the metaanalyses have demonstrated good test–retest reliability, as well as good validity with respect to external criteria (Brown & Achenbach, 1996). Different informants may thus reliably and validly provide different pictures of a child's functioning. It is therefore wrong to equate low cross-informant correlations with poor reliability or lack of validity.

If we are forced to judge psychopathology and its criterial features as categorically present versus absent, the discrepancies among informants' reports pose formidable obstacles. For example, consider the following DSM-IV criteria for ODD: "often loses temper," "often argues with adults," and "often deliberately annoys people;" or the following criteria for ADHD: "often fidgets with hands or feet or squirms in seat," "often talks excessively," and "often has difficulty awaiting turn" (American Psychiatric Association, 1994). Even though these criteria all refer to observable behavior, it would not be unusual for discrepancies to occur between parent, teacher, self, observer, and clinician reports of whether a particular child meets these criteria. Criteria for other disorders, such as "low self-esteem" for dysthymia and "muscle tension" for generalized anxiety disorder, are even more vulnerable to discrepancies among informants' reports.

Coping with cross-informant discrepancies in DSM criteria. One proposal for coping with discrepancies in reports of DSM criteria is the "or" rule (Bird, Gould, & Staghezza, 1992). According to this rule, if any informant reports a criterial feature, then that criterion is considered to be met (i.e., if the feature is reported by informant A *or* informant B *or* informant C, etc.). Thus, if only a parent reports that a child "often talks excessively," while only a teacher reports that the child "often has difficulty awaiting turn," then both these criteria for ADHD would be met. However, there are apt to be wide variations among informants' opportunities for observing each criterial feature, their thresholds for reporting it to be present, and its base rate for being manifested in their presence. Thus, a teacher's report that a 6-year-old boy "often fidgets" or "often has difficulty awaiting turn" may have much different discriminative value than yes-or-no reports of such behavior by a parent, clinician, observer, or the boy himself. Furthermore, the discriminative value of yes-or-no reports by each type of informant may vary according to the age and gender of the subject. For example, a teacher's report that a 6-year-old boy often fidgets may have much less value for discriminating that boy from his peers than does a teacher's report that a 12-year-old girl often fidgets. Although the "or" rule may be better than no rule for coping with discrepancies in categorical diagnostic data, it is vulnerable to many well-known problems in the measurement of human functioning. If we consider alternatives to the DSM model for psychopathology, other ways for dealing with cross-informant discrepancies become feasible, as outlined in the following sections.

Cross-informant taxonomic constructs. The DSM approach posits fixed criteria for each disorder, independently of specific assessment procedures and sources of data. That is, each criterial feature is viewed as an intrinsic part of the definition of a disorder, whether the assessment data come from parents, teachers, observers, self-reports, or clinical interviews. Based on whatever data are available, the diagnostician must judge whether each feature is truly present or absent in order to determine whether the subject has a particular disorder. This conception can be called "naive realism," because it implies that we truly know what features intrinsically define each disorder and whether the features are present in a particular case independently of the effects of our assessment procedures. Naive realism also equates abnormality with the features that are assumed to be intrinsic to disorders.

By contrast, the empirically based approach views the defining features of disorders as representing taxonomic constructs that are based on particular assessment procedures. Our concepts of disorders are thus recognized as being shaped by particular assessment procedures. In other words, *what* we know is affected by *how* we know it. Furthermore, the determination of which features are present in a particular case is a relativistic process. That is, the assessment procedures and sources of data affect the detection of each feature. Because feature detection is relativistic, we should not necessarily draw identical conclusions from a report of a particular feature by a particular informant for children of all ages and both genders. Data from different procedures and sources may also have different implications for conclusions about the features that characterize a case. For example, parents' intake reports, teachers' questionnaire reports, and interview self-reports might lead to different conclusions about whether a 7-year-old girl versus a 17-year-old boy has a conduct disorder. Definitions of disorders and of abnormality should thus take account of the relativistic nature of all assessment processes.

To take account of the relativistic nature of assessment in defining taxonomic constructs, the empirically based approach has derived syndromes separately from parent, teacher, and self-reports of problems for children of each gender in different age ranges (Achenbach, 1991a). Cross-informant syndrome constructs were then derived by first identifying those problems that were present in the different versions of a syndrome for a majority of the gender/age groups scored by a particular type of informant, such as parents. This procedure yielded *core syndromes* consisting of sets of problems that characterize children of both genders and different ages, as seen by a particular type of informant. For example, problems such as arguing, cruelty, fighting, and disobedience at home were found to co-occur in a syndrome designated as Aggressive Behavior that was derived from parents' ratings of both genders across ages 4 to 18 on the Child Behavior Checklist (CBCL; Achenbach, 1991b).

Next, to identify sets of co-occurring problems that were similarly evident in ratings by different informants, we compared the core syndromes derived from parent, teacher, and self-ratings. The teacher ratings were obtained with the Teacher's Report Form (TRF), while the self-ratings were obtained with the Youth Self-Report (YSR), both of which are parallel instruments to the CBCL. When we compared the core Aggressive Behavior syndromes from CBCL, TRF, and YSR ratings, we found that arguing, cruelty, and fighting were present in versions of the syndrome derived from multiple types of informants. We therefore retained these three items as part of the cross-informant Aggressive Behavior syndrome to be scored by all informants. However, because we found "disobedient at home" only in the CBCL version of the Aggressive Behavior syndrome, we retained it only for an instrument-specific scale for scoring the Aggressive Behavior syndrome from parents' ratings on the CBCL.

Eight cross-informant syndromes were derived by these procedures, as illustrated in Figure 5.1. The syndromes were given the following labels: *Aggressive Behavior, Anxious/Depressed, Attention Problems, Delinquent Behavior, Somatic Complaints, Social Problems, Thought Problems,* and *Withdrawn.* This taxonomic structure of syndromes has been supported by confirmatory factor analyses of several thousand clinically referred Dutch children, as assessed with the CBCL, TRF, and YSR (DeGroot, Koot, & Verhulst, 1994, 1996).

In addition to the eight syndromes that were found in ratings by different types of informants, a syndrome designated as Sex Problems was found in CBCL ratings of 4- to 11-year-olds of both genders, while a syndrome designated as Self-Destructive/Identity Problems was found in YSR ratings by adolescent boys. The empirically based approach takes account of variations in assessment data by including syndromes such as these that are found only in ratings of particular groups of subjects by particular types of informants. For the cross-informant syndromes

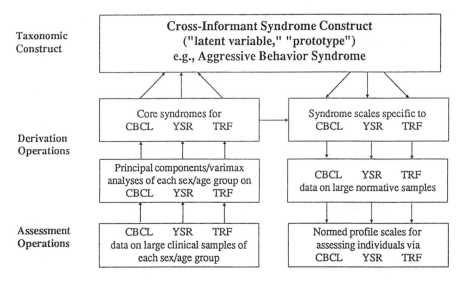

Figure 5.1. Relations between derivation of syndromes, formation of cross-informant syndrome constructs, and construction of scales (from Achenbach, 1991a).

that reflect sets of co-occurring problems common to both genders, different ages, and different types of informants, the empirically based approach takes account of assessment variations by permitting informant differences in items, such as inclusion of "disobedient at home" in the CBCL scale for Aggressive Behavior. It also provides separate norms for children grouped by gender and age, as rated by each type of informant. Distinctions between the normal and abnormal are thus based on distributions of scores from relevant samples. Even when clinical cut points are imposed on these distributions, borderline clinical ranges are flagged to distinguish intermediate scores from those that are more clearly in the normal versus clinical ranges.

Integration of cross-informant data. The foregoing section dealt with the derivation of eight cross-informant syndrome constructs that embody similarities in the patterns of problems identified in parent, teacher, and self-ratings. Even though the similarities are sufficient to warrant cross-informant constructs, there are differences in some of the problem items that are used to assess the constructs from the perspectives of different informants. As indicated earlier, "disobedient at home" was included in the Aggressive Behavior syndrome derived from the CBCL, but not from the YSR (although the item is included on the YSR), nor from the TRF, which does not include this item, because teachers would seldom have relevant information. Because "disobedient at home" loaded so consistently and strongly on the CBCL Aggressive Behavior syndrome, it was retained for the CBCL version of this scale and is included in the scale scores for normative samples of children rated by their parents. Other items that are specific to particular contexts and informants are also included in syndrome scales scored for those informants. For example, "disrupts class," which is included only on the TRF, loaded consistently and strongly on the TRF version of the Aggressive Behavior syndrome. It was therefore retained for the TRF Aggressive Behavior syndrome scale, even though it is not on the CBCL or YSR scales for this syndrome.

The small variations between the items used to operationalize a particular syndromal construct from parent, teacher, and self-ratings might contribute to discrepancies between syndrome scores obtained for the same child from different informants. On the other hand, the differences in items might strengthen the assessment of a construct in the context to which those items are specific, such as "disobedient at home" as judged by parents and "disrupts class" as judged by teachers. In fact, we have found cross-informant correlations between syndrome scores that included the instrument-specific items to be at least as high as correlations that included only the items that were the same for all informants. This may not always be the case, but the value of the informant-specific items for strengthening the syndrome scales that are actually scored from each informant argues for their retention in most applications.

Even if all informants rate the same items, discrepancies often arise from variations in children's behavior between different contexts, such as home versus school, variations in the way the children interact with different informants within a particular context, such as with mother versus father, and variations between informants' personal standards for judging the children's functioning.

Data from multiple informants can be combined in a variety of ways. To facilitate the display and integration of data, a computer program is available for entering competence and problem scores obtained from up to five informants, including parent, teacher, and self-reports for each child (Achenbach, 1993). Syndrome scale scores are computed from ratings by each informant. The computer program prints out profiles of T scores and percentiles that are based on nationally representative samples of nonreferred children, separately for each gender within particular age ranges, as scored by each type of informant.

To provide visual comparisons of cross-informant scores, the raw scores for each item and the T scores for cross-informant scales are displayed side by side. Q correlations are displayed for the item and scale scores obtained from each pair of informants. (Q correlations are between scores on multiple items drawn from just two sources, such as syndrome scales scored by a child's mother and father or any other pair of informants.) To provide benchmarks for judging how well particular pairs of informants agree, Q correlations are also displayed for large reference samples of the same combinations of informants, such as mothers versus fathers, parents versus teachers, parents versus youths, and youths versus teachers. In addition, the program computes intraclass correlations (ICCs) between the child's profile of syndrome scores, as scored from each informant, and profile types that have been derived from cluster analyses of thousands of clinically referred children.

Users can thus view agreement among informants at the level of item scores, syndrome scale scores, and profile patterns. Figure 5.2 illustrates a printout of cross-informant syndrome scores, Q correlations, and ICCs for 14-year-old Roberta.

If scores have been computed for each syndrome scale for a sample of children, the multisource data can be combined in several ways. One way is by averaging the scores obtained by each child from each rater on each syndrome. The norm-based T scores provide standard metrics that indicate each score's magnitude relative to the national normative sample. Because the T scores convert the informant-specific raw scale scores to a standard metric, they are appropriate for averaging ratings of the same child by different informants. However, when a substantial sample of children is available (e.g., N ≥ 100), more precise standardization of scores across informants can be achieved by converting the distribution of raw scores on a syndrome to standard scores within the sample, separately for each type of informant.

For example, if scores for 100 children are available from their mothers, fathers, teachers, and the children themselves, the distribution of mothers' scores on the CBCL Aggressive Behavior syndrome can be converted to standard scores. The mean and standard deviation can be chosen to suit the user, such as z scores with a mean of 0 and standard deviation of 1, or T scores with a mean of 50 and standard deviation of 10. The same can be done separately for the fathers' scores, teachers' scores on the TRF, and self-report scores on the YSR. To compute a global multisource score on a syndrome such as Aggressive Behavior, the sample-based standard scores are then averaged across all the informants for each child.

In research on one or more of the cross-informant syndromes, averaging of multisource data is likely to provide more reliable and valid measures of each syndrome than if only a single source of data is used. Averaging of standard scores across whatever informants are available also makes it possible to retain subjects for whom data from one informant are missing, because their average standard score can still be based on the available informants.

In addition to the averaging of unweighted standard scores, multisource scores can be employed in multivariate analyses that selectively weight the scores from each source in order to maximize their collective association with other variables. For example, if multisource scores on the Aggressive Behavior syndrome are used to compare the effects of different interventions for aggression, the scores from each source can be treated as dependent variables in a multivariate analysis of variance (MANOVA). Other approaches to weighting the syndrome scores from different informants include multiple regression and discriminant analyses.

A different approach to combining multisource syndrome scores is to classify individuals as deviant versus nondeviant according to clinical cut points on each syndrome, as scored from each informant. If the focus is on only one syndrome, users can select a criterion for classifying children as deviant versus nondeviant according to the number of different sources that indicate deviance on that syndrome. For example, if data from three sources are available (e.g., one parent, one

T Scores for 8 Syndrome Scales Common to CBCL, YSR and TRF

Scale	Mo.CBCL.1	Fa.CBCL.2	Slf.YSR.3	Tch.TRF.4	Tch.TRF.5
1. Withdrawn	84++	81++	82++	80++	68+
2. Somatic Complaints	56	56	56	50	57
3. Anxious/Depressed	77++	77++	76++	73++	70+
4. Social Problems	64	64	68+	69+	69+
5. Thought Problems	67+	70+	70+	65	58
6. Attention Problems	81++	81++	67+	68+	66
7. Delinquent Behavior	50	59	50	53	60
8. Aggressive Behavior	57	63	53	51	53

+Borderline Clinical Range
++Clinical Range

	Mo.CBCL.1	Fa.CBCL.2	Slf.YSR.3	Tch.TRF.4	Tch.TRF.5
Internalizing	77++	76++	73++	76++	73++
Externalizing	55	63+	52	51	55
Total Problems	72++	74++	68++	65++	65++

- -

Q Correlations Between 8 Scale Scores from Different Informants

For Reference Samples

For this Subject		25th %ile	Mean	75th %ile	Agreement between
Mo.CBCL.1 x Fa.CBCL.2 =	.97	.35	.58	.89	Mother and Father is above average.
Mo.CBCL.1 x Slf.YSR.3 =	.90	-.11	.26	.60	Mother and Youth is above average.
Mo.CBCL.1 x Tch.TRF.4 =	.89	-.14	.23	.60	Mother and Teacher is above average.
Mo.CBCL.1 x Tch.TRF.5 =	.70	-.14	.23	.60	Mother and Teacher is above average.
Fa.CBCL.2 x Slf.YSR.3 =	.82	-.11	.26	.60	Father and Youth is above average.
Fa.CBCL.2 x Tch.TRF.4 =	.86	-.14	.23	.60	Father and Teacher is above average.
Fa.CBCL.2 x Tch.TRF.5 =	.64	-.14	.23	.60	Father and Teacher is above average.
Slf.YSR.3 x Tch.TRF.4 =	.96	-.15	.17	.50	Youth and Teacher is above average.
Slf.YSR.3 x Tch.TRF.5 =	.75	-.15	.17	.50	Youth and Teacher is above average.
Tch.TRF.4 x Tch.TRF.5 =	.85				There is no reference sample for this combination

- -

Intraclass Correlations (ICCs) with Cross-Informant Profile Types from Different Informants

Cross-Informant Profile Types

ICC from	WITHDR	SOMAT	SOCIAL	DEL-AGG
Mo.CBCL.1	.161	-.064	.132	-.490
Fa.CBCL.2	.012	-.268	.174	-.528
Slf.YSR.3	.209	-.435	.420	-.542
Tch.TRF.4	.629**	.152	.312	-.586
Tch.TRF.5	.674**	.249	.230	-.675

** Significant ICC with profile type

Figure 5.2. Cross-informant syndrome *T* scores and *Q* correlations for 14-year-old Roberta.

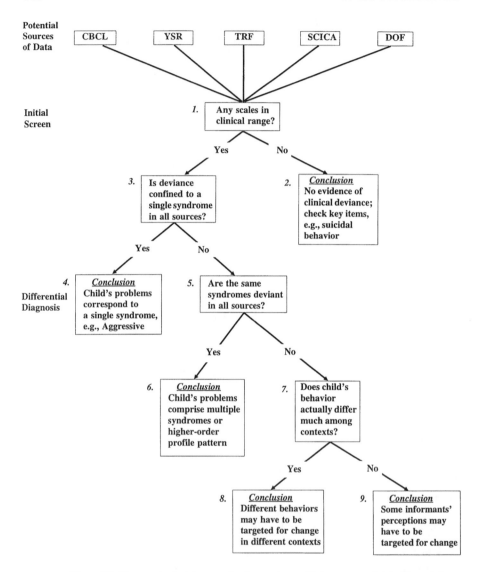

Figure 5.3. Taxonomic decision tree for integrating multiple sources of data (from Achenbach, 1993).

teacher, and a self-report), a user may decide to classify children as deviant on a particular syndrome if they obtain deviant scores from at least 2 of the 3 raters.

If users wish to classify children according to deviance on multiple syndromes, a sequence of decisions can be outlined, as illustrated by the *taxonomic decision tree* shown in Figure 5.3. Multiple sources of syndrome data are listed across the top of the tree. These sources can include self-report data, plus data from one or more parents and teachers. In addition, other types of syndrome data can be included, such as data obtained from interviews (e.g., Semistructured Clinical Interview for Children and Adolescents, or SCICA; McConaughy & Achenbach, 1994). Data can also be included from direct observations (e.g., Direct Observation Form, or DOF; see Achenbach, 1991b).

The taxonomic decision tree is designed to use multisource data in making a series of binary decisions. Each binary decision determines whether a case has reached an endpoint in the decision tree or whether it moves down to the next decision point. For example, the first question (Box 1, near the top of Figure 5.3) asks whether any of the child's syndrome scale scores are in the clinical range. If the answer is no, the child is concluded to show no evidence of clinical deviance and is placed in Box 2. Nevertheless, individual problem items should be examined to identify any that are of concern, such as suicidal behavior, even if no scale scores are in the clinical range.

On the other hand, if the answer to the first question was yes, the child would move to Box 3, where the next question is posed. This decision-making strategy can be applied to research samples as well as to individual children about whom clinical decisions must be made.

Practical applications

The preceding sections have presented research tasks to be accomplished in improving the empirical basis for distinguishing between the normal and abnormal. My formulation of these tasks was influenced by the first three facets of Ed Zigler's thinking that I mentioned at the beginning of the chapter. I now turn to the fourth facet of Ed Zigler's thinking that I mentioned – his emphasis on using research-based knowledge to help people, especially children (Zigler & Valentine, 1979).

Although my research with Ed focused mainly on mental retardation, I have since focused on behavioral and emotional problems. Just as Ed dispelled mythology about the purported rigidity of the retarded mind (Zigler, 1963), research on behavioral/emotional problems needs to dispel unfounded myths about the nature and cause of these problems. For example, until fairly recently, infantile autism and childhood schizophrenia were blamed on parents who "wish (that) their child should not exist" (Bettelheim, 1967, p. 125) and who "inadvertently hated one another and used the child emotionally" (Wolman, 1970, p. vii). Milder disorders were also assumed to be caused primarily by parental behavior and attitudes, often unconscious. Although parental behaviors may indeed affect children's functioning, theories about the causes of problems have too often taken precedence over documentation of what the problems are and empirical tests of their determinants.

The emergence of behavioral approaches in the 1960s and 1970s brought a new emphasis on documentation and determinants of specific behaviors, unlike the previously dominant psychodynamic, family systems, and biological theories of children's problems. However, the behavioral emphasis on the situational specificity of behavior may have been a "two-edged sword," as Kazdin (1979) called it. That is, if we view behavioral problems only in terms of a specific situation, we cannot draw conclusions about behavior across situations. Nor can we effectively assess covariation among behaviors that may comprise syndromes or other higher-order groupings (Kazdin, 1985).

The research tasks outlined earlier have yielded tools that provide a common data language for a broad range of workers who seek to help troubled children. Regardless of the workers' particular specialties or theoretical preferences, they need standardized descriptive data about each case in order to communicate about the case, to link the case to other cases about which knowledge has previously been gained, and to provide a baseline against which to measure change. For judging what is normal versus abnormal, it is equally important that norms be used to determine how the standardized data for a particular child compare with those for reference samples of peers of the same sex and age, as assessed by the same type of informant.

Because each informant sees a child from a different perspective, standardized data from all informants should be compared to identify specific areas of agreement and disagreement. This can be done by using the cross-informant computer program and taxonomic decision tree described earlier. It can also be done by visually comparing the profiles of syndrome scores obtained from all informants. If there are major discrepancies between particular informants and if the Q correlations between them are much lower than for the reference samples displayed by the cross-informant computer program, then the reasons for the discrepancies should be explored. For example, if a large discrepancy is found between syndrome scores from a child's mother and father or between two teachers, the discrepancies may indicate important variations in the child's behavior with different interaction partners. Discrepancies may also reveal that one informant perceives a child's behavior very differently from other informants or perhaps that one informant evokes different behavior than do other informants. Interviewing the informants may reveal the reasons for the discrepancies, which may validly reflect important facets of the child's functioning or may reflect characteristics of certain informants that should be targeted for change. In some cases, direct observations of the child's behavior in relation to different informants, such as in the classrooms of two teachers whose reports are discrepant, can be used to check the basis for the discrepancies.

Because the empirically based approach views behavior and judgments of abnormality in quantitative terms, users seldom need to make forced choices about whether a child is normal versus abnormal. Instead, by quantifying multiple sources of data, the empirically based approach provides mosaic-like pictures of children's functioning in different contexts. Some children's behavior may be very consistent across contexts. For other children, a mosaic that highlights variations may provide a more accurate picture. In either case, we can help children more effectively if we take account of both the cross-informant similarities and differences than if we seek a single "gold standard" conclusion about whether a child is normal or abnormal.

The value of multiple quantitative sources of data is not restricted to initial assessments. On the contrary, the empirically based approach can aid all stages of services to troubled children by providing a useful conceptual frame of reference, plus practical assessment and taxonomic procedures that are applicable under diverse conditions at low cost. Figure 5.4 illustrates a schematic model for applying empirically based assessment and taxonomy to helping troubled children.

As indicated in Box I of Figure 5.4, empirically based assessment procedures can be used at intake into a variety of services, including mental health, special educational, medical, and forensic. In conjunction with other assessment data, scores on empirically based syndromes can then be used to decide whether the reported problems indicate deviance from normative samples of peers and, if so, in what areas (Box II). If it is decided that help is needed, the cross-informant comparisons, plus previous research findings on correlates of the child's profile pattern, can be used to design an intervention plan. The empirically based assessment procedures can later be readministered to monitor changes (Box III) and outcomes (Box IV). Follow-up readministrations of the empirically based procedures can be used to determine whether improvements are maintained and whether further help is needed (Box V).

The overall strategy depicted in Figure 5.4 can, of course, be modified according to the specific needs of children seen under various conditions. To facilitate applications of research-based knowledge to helping children, a bibliography is available that lists over 1,700 published reports of the use of the empirically based procedures, grouped according to some 200 topics and including translations in 51 languages (Brown & Achenbach, 1996).

Summary and conclusions

This chapter presented an empirically based approach to distinguishing between the normal and abnormal in behavioral/emotional problems from early childhood to adulthood. The overall approach was influenced by the following facets of Ed Zigler's work: viewing pathological behavior in relation to normal functioning; using developmental perspectives to understand psychopathology; recognizing the key role of taxonomy in the study of psychopathology; and applying research-based knowledge to helping people, especially children.

To improve our ways of distinguishing between the normal and abnormal, a bootstrapping strategy was outlined that is conceptualized in terms of psychometrics, epidemiology, taxonomy, developmental changes, and cross-informant issues. This strategy has yielded a family of empirically based assessment procedures from which taxonomic constructs have been derived, including cross-informant syndromes and profile types that are scorable from parent, teacher, and self-ratings.

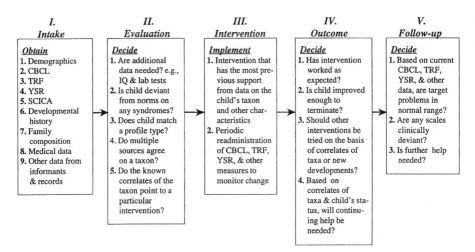

Figure 5.4. Schematic model for applying empirically based assessment and taxonomy to helping troubled children (from Achenbach, 1993).

The empirically based procedures provide standardized descriptions of problems and competencies for use by diverse workers under diverse conditions. Normative data enable users to judge how a child's scores compare with those of reference groups of peers, as rated by similar types of informants. Because behavioral/emotional problems are assessed quantitatively and are judged in relation to distributions of scores for large reference samples, there is no need for forced choices about whether a child is normal versus abnormal. Instead, the empirically based approach provides mosaic-like pictures of functioning in different contexts. Cross-situational consistencies and differences can thus be explicitly documented and appropriately targeted for interventions and for evaluation of change. Although it was originally prompted by the need for better assessment and understanding of childhood disorders, the empirically based approach has also been extended to young adulthood, where it has identified problem patterns that are strongly predicted by preadult syndromes.

References

Achenbach, T. M. (1991a). *Integrative guide for the 1991 CBCL/4–18, YSR, and TRF profiles*. Burlington: University of Vermont, Department of Psychiatry.

Achenbach, T. M. (1991b). *Manual for the Child Behavior Checklist/4–18 and 1991 Profile*. Burlington: University of Vermont, Department of Psychiatry.

Achenbach, T. M. (1992). *Manual for the Child Behavior Checklist/2–3 and 1992 Profile*. Burlington: University of Vermont, Department of Psychiatry.

Achenbach, T. M. (1993). *Empirically based taxonomy: How to use syndromes and profile types derived from the CBCL/4–18, TRF, and YSR*. Burlington: University of Vermont, Department of Psychiatry.

Achenbach, T. M., & Howell, C. T. (1993). Are American children's problems getting worse? A 13-year comparison. *Journal of the American Academy of Child and Adolescent Psychiatry, 32,* 1145–1154.

Achenbach, T. M., Howell, C. T., McConaughy, S. H., & Stanger, C. (1995a). Six-year predictors of problems in a national sample of children and youth: I. Cross-informant syndromes. *Journal of the American Academy of Child and Adolescent Psychiatry, 34,* 336–347.

Achenbach, T. M., Howell, C. T., McConaughy, S. H., & Stanger, C. (1995b). Six-year predictors of problems in a national sample: III. Transitions to young adult syndromes. *Journal of the American Academy of Child and Adolescent Psychiatry, 34,* 658–669.

Achenbach, T. M., Howell, C. T., Quay, H. C., & Conners, C. K. (1991). National survey of problems and competencies among 4-to 16-year-olds: Parents' reports for normative and clinical samples. *Monographs of the Society for Research in Child Development, 56* (3, Serial No. 225).

Achenbach, T. M., McConaughy, S. H., & Howell, C. T. (1987). Child/adolescent behavioral and emotional problems: Implications of cross-informant correlations for situational specificity. *Psychological Bulletin, 101,* 213–232.

Achenbach, T. M., & Zigler, E. (1963). Social competence and self-image disparity in psychiatric and nonpsychiatric patients. *Journal of Abnormal and Social Psychology, 67,* 197–205.

American Psychiatric Association (1980). *Diagnostic and statistical manual of mental disorders* (3rd ed.). Washington, D.C.

American Psychiatric Association (1987). *Diagnostic and statistical manual of mental disorders* (3rd rev. ed.). Washington, D.C.

American Psychiatric Association (1994). *Diagnostic and statistical manual of mental disorders* (4th ed.). Washington, D.C.

Arnold, J., & Jacobowitz, D. (1993). *The Cross-Informant Program for the CBCL/4–18, YSR, and TRF.* Burlington: University of Vermont, Department of Psychiatry.

Bettelheim, B. (1967). *The empty fortress.* New York: Free Press.

Bird, H. R., Gould, M. S., & Staghezza, B. (1992). Aggregating data from multiple informants in child psychiatry epidemiological research. *Journal of the the American Academy of Child and Adolescent Psychiatry, 31,* 78–85.

Brown, J. S., & Achenbach, T. M. (1996). *Bibliography of published studies using the Child Behavior Checklist and related materials: 1996 edition.* Burlington: University of Vermont, Department of Psychiatry.

Cowley, G., & Ramo, J. C. (1993, July 26). The not-young and the restless. *Newsweek,* 48–49.

De Groot, A., Koot, H. M., & Verhulst, F. C. (1994). The cross-cultural generalizability of the CBCL cross-informant syndromes. *Psychological Assessment, 6,* 225–230.

De Groot, A., Koot, H. M., & Verhulst, F. C. (1996). Cross-cultural generalizability of the Youth Self-Report and Teacher's Report Form cross-informant syndromes. *Journal of Abnormal Child Psychology.*

Ferdinand, R. F., Verhulst, F. C., & Wiznitzer, M. (1995). Continuity and change of self-reported problem behaviors from adolescence into young adulthood. *Journal of the American Academy of Child and Adolescent Psychiatry, 34,* 680–690.

Garrison, W. T., & Earls, F. (1985). The Child Behavior Checklist as a screening instrument for young children. *Journal of the American Academy of Child Psychiatry, 24,* 76–80.

Gould, M. S., & Shaffer, D. (1985, October). *Correspondence of adolescent and parental reports in a child psychiatry clinic.* Paper presented at the meeting of the American Academy of Child Psychiatry, San Antonio, TX.

Kagan, J. (1969). The three faces of continuity in human development. In D. A. Goslin (Ed.), *Handbook of socialization theory and research* (pp. 983–1002). Chicago: Rand McNally.

Kazdin, A. E. (1979). Situational specificity: The two-edged sword of behavioral assessment. *Behavioral Assessment, 1,* 57–75.

Kazdin, A. E. (1985). Selection of target behaviors: The relationship of the treatment focus to clinical dysfunction. *Behavioral Assessment, 7,* 33–47.

Kessler, R. C., McGonagle, K. A., Zhao, S., Nelson, C. B., Hughes, M., Eshleman, S., Wittchen,

H. U., & Kendler, K. S. (1994). Lifetime and 12-month prevalence of DSM-III-R psychiatric disorders among persons in the United States. *Archives of General Psychiatry, 51,* 8–19.

McConaughy, S. H., & Achenbach, T. M. (1994). *Manual for the Semistructured Clinical Interview for Children and Adolescents.* Burlington: University of Vermont, Department of Psychiatry.

Reinherz, H. Z. (1995). *Entering adulthood: A longitudinal community study.* Boston: Simmons College, School of Social Work.

Shaffer, D. (1994). Attention deficit hyperactivity disorder in adults. *American Journal of Psychiatry, 151,* 633–638.

Stevenson, H., & Zigler, E. (1961). Learning, motivation, and perception. In R. Wilcox (Ed.), *Strategies for behavioral research in mental retardation* (pp. 98–117). Madison: University of Wisconsin Press.

Verhulst, F. C., & Achenbach, T. M. (1995). Empirically based assessment and taxonomy of psychopathology: Cross-cultural applications. *European Child and Adolescent Psychiatry, 4,* 61–76.

Wechsler, D. C. (1991). *Wechsler Intelligence Scale for Children–Third edition.* San Antonio, TX: Psychological Corporation.

Wechsler, D. C. (1992). *Wechsler Individual Achievement Test.* San Antonio, TX: Psychological Corporation.

Williams, C. L., Butcher, J. N., Ben-Porath, Y. S., & Graham, J. R. (1992). *MMPI-A Content Scales: Assessing psychopathology in adolescents.* Minneapolis: University of Minnesota Press.

Wittchen, H. U., Robins, L. N., Cottler, L. B., Sartorius, N., Burke, J. D., Regier, D., & participants in the Multicentre WHO/ADAMHA Field Trials. (1991). Cross-cultural feasibility, reliability and sources of variance of the Composite International Diagnostic Interview (CIDI). *British Journal of Psychiatry, 159,* 645–653.

Wolman, B. B. (1970). *Children without childhood.* New York: Grune & Stratton.

Zigler, E. (1963). Rigidity and social reinforcement effects in the performance of institutionalized and noninstitutionalized normal and retarded children. *Journal of Personality, 31,* 258–269.

Zigler, E. (1965). Understanding mental retardation within the framework of normal development. *Journal of Pediatrics, 67,* 1047.

Zigler, E., & Phillips, L. (1961). Psychiatric diagnosis: A critique. *Journal of Abnormal and Social Psychology, 63,* 607–618.

Zigler, E., & Valentine, J. (Eds.). (1979). *Project Head Start: A legacy of the War on Poverty.* New York: Free Press.

6 Family effects on individual differences in development

Sandra Scarr and Kirby Deater-Deckard

Do parents have *any* effects on their children? This is an absurd question, of course, for a mammalian species with prolonged dependency. Human offspring die without careful parental nurturance from birth to maturity. Given that parents are sufficiently nurturant to insure their offsprings' survival, parents are also the major agents of socialization for most children in the world. Children must be socialized, or else they will not be normal human beings. Parents, complemented by relatives and other adults, afford children opportunities and support for both species-normal and culturally appropriate development.

A sensible question is, "Do parents have *differential* effects on their children?" This question about individual differences among parents and children is often confused with the nonsensical, species question. Parents transmit the culture, as it is filtered through their own location in the social structure and their own personal characteristics to children who are also individually different in their interests and abilities to learn what parents attempt to teach. As we will show, it is not at all clear that parents have *differential* effects on their children by using one style of rearing (e.g., authoritarian versus authoritative) or discipline (e.g., physical punishment or reasoning) than another (Harris, in press; Maccoby, 1992; Scarr & Ricciuti, 1991), particularly with respect to individual differences in intelligence and social adjustment. Parents, policy makers, and developmental researchers are all vitally concerned with family effects on children's outcomes. In this chapter, we examine theories and research on these questions.

How do parents affect their children's development? Everyone acknowledges parents' genetic contribution to their offspring (50% each). To the extent that behavioral characteristics are genetically variable, parents transmit behavioral resemblances to their children genetically, unless the children are adopted. Genetic parents also provide their children's rearing environments, unless the children are given up for adoption. In the ordinary biological family, parents transmit their influences via both genetic and environmental pathways, which are necessarily correlated.

By now, the overwhelming evidence is that individual differences in intellectual characteristics are genetically variable. Genetic differences in IQ in Euro-

115

American and European populations account for 60% to 80% of IQ differences (see Scarr, 1993). The expression of genetic variation in intelligence may be more restricted in minority and disadvantaged populations, but the evidence is that even for these populations the heritability of intellectual differences is in the 40% to 70% range (see Scarr, 1981). Indeed, both intelligence and academic achievement have been found to have moderate to high heritability (Behrman, Taubman, & Wales, 1978; Scarr & Yee, 1980; Taubman, 1976; Thompson, Detterman, & Plomin, 1993; Vogler & Fulker, 1983) and to be related to social class differences.

Social class differences in intelligence and academic achievement are predicted to arise from different distributions of intellectual and personality characteristics among adults in lower to higher strata in the social structure. Because these characteristics are partly heritable, the children in lower social class groups will, on average, have lesser abilities and other associated characteristics than will children born of parents at the top of the social structure (Herrnstein, 1973; Herrnstein & Murray, 1994; Lichtenstein, Pedersen, & McClearn, 1992).

However, children will have smaller average differences in intelligence and academic achievement by social class than do their parents, for two reasons: first, because variation in these characteristics is not totally heritable; and, second, because parents have migrated to their present positions based on their own individual characteristics, whereas children have not; on average, offspring will be less extreme genetically than their parents, resulting in regression of offspring toward the population mean. Thus, average differences among parents are predicted by behavior genetic theory to be greater than average differences among children born to different social class groups. *Social mobility* between generations is predicted to reestablish class differences from generation to generation, with upward mobility for the more intelligent, well-adjusted, and motivated offspring of lower social class groups and downward mobility for the offspring of upper class groups who lack these characteristics.

Personality differences among parents and children are moderately heritable, whether measured by self-report, psychometric tests (e.g., Loehlin, 1992), or observations of social behaviors in family interactions (e.g., Hetherington, Reiss, & Plomin, 1994). The Big Five personality dimensions (extroversion, agreeableness, conscientiousness, emotional instability, and openness to experience) yield remarkably consistent estimates of genetic and environmental effects. The heritability of all five personality traits explains 50% of the reliably measured variation, and the effect of being reared in the same family accounts for about 6% of the variation. The remaining personality variation is due to measurement error (about 10%) and to the effects of nonshared environments – those experiences that are unique to each person (summarized in Loehlin, 1992). As will be reviewed in a later section, personality variation studied in observations yields similar genetic and nonshared environmental results (Hetherington et al., 1994).

Do parents treat their children differently, and does it matter?

Research on normal and maladaptive development has focused predominantly on variability in environments between families. Covariation between parental behavior and child behavior is usually interpreted as an environmental effect of socialization practices by different parents on their children. Unfortunately, this approach leaves genes and environments hopelessly confounded (Plomin, 1994; Rowe, 1994), rendering the findings from these studies uninterpretable (Scarr, 1992).

Genetics creeps into socialization studies

Socialization studies, many of which are described by Baumrind (1993), have confounded genetic transmission of parental characteristics to children with socialization practices, because these are studies of biological families. Moreover, it is not at all clear how to measure family "environments" without including genetic differences among parents and offspring (Plomin & Neiderhiser, 1992). Whatever modest degree of similarity in intelligence, personality, and interests exists among biological family members is not primarily due to growing up or living in the same household (Hoffman, 1991; Loehlin, 1992; Plomin & Daniels, 1987).

More and more socialization researchers recognize the ubiquitous influence of genetic individual differences in intelligence and personality on the "socialization" variables they study and the need to take genetic variability into account. The need to incorporate environmental measures in behavior genetic studies has been recognized (e.g., Plomin, 1994; Scarr, 1993), but the need to include genetically informative designs in socialization studies is less often mentioned. The omission of genetically informative families in socialization studies has produced only uninterpretable results. With only these data, there is no way to test competing theories about sources of individual differences (Scarr & Grajek, 1982; Scarr, Weber, Weinberg, & Wittig, 1981).

Socialization theory has been moot on possible effects of genetic variability on intellectual development, and it ignores the confounding of genetic and environmental variability reported for the most common measures of family "environment" (Chipuer, Plomin, Pederson, McClearn, & Nesselroade, 1993; Plomin & Bergeman, 1991; Plomin & Daniels, 1987; Plomin, Loehlin, & DeFries, 1985; Plomin, McClearn, Peterson, Nesselroade, & Bergeman, 1989; Rowe, 1981, 1983, 1994).

Additional data about genetic effects on other aspects of children's rearing environments are also revealing. Peer relationships and the choice of peers have been shown to be genetically variable (Plomin, 1994; Rowe, 1981, 1983). Perhaps this result is not surprising, because children do choose their peers, whereas they cannot choose their family members. Whereas genotype–environment correlations in biologically related families may be of the passive type, peer relations may show the active and reactive types (Plomin, 1994). Adolescents' ratings of positive peer and teacher relationships were moderately heritable (.31 and .38), but parents' ratings of their adolescents' popularity with peers and the delinquent, drug abusing, or college-bound orientation of peers showed more heritability than parent ratings of the family environment. For separate mother and father ratings, the heritabilities of peer popularity were .62 and .73; for peer college orientation, .73 and .85; for peer delinquency, .70 and .49; and for peer substance abuse, .72 and .74 (Plomin, 1994, table 3.5, p. 86). Effects of shared environments on adolescents' peer relationships, based on the correlations of genetically unrelated siblings in the same family, were small to moderate (.00–.42, median = .13).

Plomin (1994, p. 80) summarized the research on genetic and environmental effects on self-report and observations measures of the family "environment."

> Genetic effects are not just limited to children's perceptions of their family environment. Parents' perceptions of their parenting implicate genetic contributions even in child-based genetic designs (i.e., twins are the children in the family). In child-based genetic designs, genetic effects can be detected only to the extent that parents' perceptions of their parenting reflect genetically influenced characteristics of their children.
> Finally, evidence of genetic effects emerges from four observational studies of parenting and sibling behavior using child-based genetic designs. The results from these observations studies suggest that the genetic contribution to measures of the family environment is not limited to subjective processes involved in questionnaires. Genetic effects appear to be not just in the eye of the beholder but also in the behavior of the individual. (pp. 79–80)

The implication of this rather recent research for studies of family environmental effects on children's personality and intellectual development is profound. In socialization studies, ubiquitous correlations between parent characteristics and features of the parent-provided home with child development have been erroneously explained as a causal effect of home environments on children. In fact, observations from behavior genetic studies, which vary genetic and environmental relatedness of participants, have shown that the correlation between parental and home characteristics and children's development is not explained primarily by the home environment but by genetic resemblance among family members. When only biologically related families have been studied, this genetic effect of parents on children (and siblings on each other) has been misinterpreted, with important misinferences for developmental theory and for intervention efforts to change some parents' child-rearing practices.

Genetically informative designs

Genetically informative designs test the degree to which individual variability results from genetic variability, environments shared by family members, and nonshared environments that differ between siblings in the same family.

The adoption design provides a direct estimate of the magnitude of family rearing effects (c^2), because *all* similarities between genetically unrelated, adopted siblings *must* arise from being reared in the same family (although selective placement of children may create some intellectual similarity). Adoption designs compare siblings who share no genes by common descent, and yet are reared in the same family. The shared environmental component (c^2) is simply the correlation between siblings on the trait of interest. Because the children do not share any genetic variance, all similarity arising between them must be due to common, nongenetic factors.

Some developmentalists seem to misunderstand the importance of the adoption design to test theories about hypothesized socialization effects. Although behavioral genetic studies cannot identify specific mechanisms by which family environments could have effects on children's outcomes, they do estimate the magnitude of *all* effects of being reared in different families. If the c^2 estimate is close to zero, as it is for intellectual and personality outcomes, that means that there is no phenomenon to be explained.

The logically parallel design, MZ twins reared in different homes (MZAs), gives a direct estimate of genetic variance (h^2), because separated identical twins share all of their genes but none of their rearing environments (although correlations in the characteristics in their rearing families can be controlled for). Calculating correlations between adopted siblings provides a direct estimate of the magnitude of between family effects (c^2). Correlations between identical twins reared apart provide direct estimates of the magnitude of genetic variation (h^2) on the trait. Thus, adopted siblings and identical twins apart directly estimate two important sources of individual differences in a population. Nonshared environments are the residual variance, which also includes measurement error. When reliable measures are employed, nonshared environmental effects can be accurately estimated by correcting for error.

Sibling similarities

The actual degree of personality and IQ similarity between biological siblings is quite modest, unless they are identical twins (Scarr & Grajek, 1982). The average personality correlation between full siblings is about .14 (Loehlin, 1992). The average IQ correlation between siblings is about .40. The IQ difference between ordinary siblings averages 12 IQ points, whereas randomly paired members of the population differ on average by 17 points (the standard deviation of IQ tests is 15; Jensen, 1980; Plomin & DeFries, 1980).

Nonetheless, degree of siblings' similarity in intelligence and personality follows genetic relatedness, not whether they were reared by the same parents (environmental relatedness). More generally, identical twins are very similar on all behavioral measures, much more similar than fraternal twins or siblings in the same family. Identical twins reared in different homes are nearly as similar in intelligence and personality as identical pairs reared in the same home, whereas adopted children reared in the same home hardly resemble each other at all (Loehlin, 1993; Plomin, 1994; Scarr & Weinberg, 1978; Scarr, 1992, 1993).

Differential parenting

As they grow older, children are predicted to have an increasing role in determining parental behaviors (Scarr & McCartney, 1983), a trend that is revealed in the Colorado Adoption Project's comparisons of parental behaviors toward biological and adoptive siblings (Dunn, Plomin, & Nettles, 1985; Dunn, Plomin, & Daniels, 1986; Dunn & Plomin, 1986). Not surprisingly, mothers changed their treatment of siblings from 12 to 36 months in response to the child's developmental status. Mothers behaved similarly with both siblings at 12, 24, and 36 months, with the exception of differential controlling behavior when the siblings were 24 months old. However, once the adoptive and nonadoptive children were older, differential maternal control and warmth were correlated with differential behavior problems between the siblings (Dunn and McGuire, 1993). Siblings who received more maternal control and less warmth were higher in anxiety and depression, and the elders of sibling pairs were higher in antisocial behaviors. In a recent family study of school-age siblings (McHale, Crouter, McGuire, & Updegraff, 1995), parental (mother–father) congruence in differential treatment was statistically significant, lending support to a "child effects" model. In most cases (55% for warmth/affection, 63% for discipline/control), mothers and fathers favored the same child, and the opposite treatment pattern was nearly nonexistent. Other studies have shown that parental warmth is more "child specific" than control (Deater-Deckard, in press; Rowe, 1981, 1983).

Comparisons of parental treatment of two children at different ages confound age differences with individual differences between the siblings. However, studies of twins have shown that more similar treatment of MZs is related to actual genetic relatedness, not to parents' perceptions of zygocity (Carter-Saltzman & Scarr, 1977; Lytton, 1977, 1990; Scarr, 1968). Parents, who were mistaken about their twins' zygocity, nonetheless behaved more or less similarly toward their children according to the twins' actual genetic resemblance, not according to the parents' perception of their zygocity. Lytton (1977) found that individual differences among older children's characteristics and behaviors evoked differences in parental rearing techniques, and that parents did not deliberately treat their children differently.

Genetic effects on environments

Because family members report *perceptions* of the family environment, and because individual differences in social perception are partly genetic, measures of family "environments" such as the Family Environment Scales (Moos & Moos, 1981) and the HOME scales (Caldwell & Bradley, 1984) are partly heritable (Anderson, Hetherington, Reiss, & Plomin, under review; Bouchard & McGue, 1990; Deal, Halverson, & Wampler, 1994; Jang, 1993; Plomin, 1994; Plomin & Bergeman, 1991; Plomin & Neiderhiser, 1992; Plomin et al., 1985; Plomin, McClearn, Pedersen, Nesselroade, & Bergeman, 1988, 1989; Plomin, Reiss, Hetherington & Howe, 1994; Rowe, 1981, 1983).

By comparing the similarities in perceptions of the family environment among families with genetically identical twins, first-degree relatives, and adopted relatives, behavior genetic analyses show that genetic similarities affect the similarity of perceptions of relationships in the family on major dimensions of parenting and on intellectual stimulation in the home.

Most striking is the finding that, as adults, identical twins reared apart (MZAs) perceived their rearing families to have been as similar as those of fraternal twins reared together, even though the MZAs were reporting on *different* families! The MZAs were not as similar as the MZs reared together but considerably more similar than DZs reared apart. Thus, the heritability estimates for various FES scales for the adult twins' rearing environments ranged from .15 to .35 (Plomin et al., 1988). When reporting on rearing practices with their own children, the adult MZAs were as similar as adult MZTs (those pairs reared together), and both MZ groups reported more similar child-rearing practices than DZ twins (Plomin et al., 1989).

Heritabilities of the FES scales for adult twins rating their offspring families ranged from .12 to .40 (median = .26). Both parents' and offspring perceptions, measured when the offspring were adolescents to older adults, showed that 25% to 50% of the variability in measures of perceived family environments were due to genetic variability.

In summary, there is considerable evidence that popular measures of family ''environments'' such as the HOME scale and the Family Environment Scales are confounded by genetic differences among parents and children (Bouchard & McGue, 1990; Jang, 1993; Plomin, 1994; Plomin & Bergeman, 1991; Plomin & Neiderhiser, 1992; Plomin et al., 1985; Plomin et al., 1988, 1989; Reiss et al., 1994; Rowe, 1981, 1983). By comparing the similarities in perceptions of the family environment among families with genetically identical twins, first-degree relatives, and adopted relatives, behavior genetic analyses show that genetic similarities affect the similarity of perceptions of relationships in the family on major dimensions of parenting (warmth and control) and on intellectual stimulation in the home.

Not in the eye of the beholder: Genetic effects in observations

Perhaps, one could dismiss results of self-reports and ratings as *perceptions* of the family environment that show merely that genetic differences affect people's perceptions of relationships and emotional climates in their homes. Fortunately, there

are four observational studies of parent–child interactions that provide similar evidence of genetic effects on family environments. In the largest study ever done of
genetic contributions to family environments, Hetherington, Reiss, and Plomin
(1994; also reported in Plomin, 1994) found large effects for genetic differences
(52–64% of the variance) and nonshared environments (25–37%) in adolescents'
positivity and negativity in interactions with family members, scored from videotaped observations. By contrast, the shared environment (all of the sibling and twin
pairs in this study were reared in the same homes) accounted for 0–23% of the
variance in adolescents' interactions. Still, parental positivity and negativity in interactions with their adolescent children showed more shared environmental effect
(34–63%) and lesser effects of genetic differences among the children (0–38%)
and nonshared environments (19–34%).

The results from these observational studies suggest that the genetic contribution
to measures of the family environment is not limited to subjective processes involved in questionnaires. Genetic effects are not just in the eye of the beholder but
also in the behavior of the individual. Parent behaviors reflect intellectual and other
personal differences among people, and the proportion of genetic variance in those
characteristics has been repeatedly found to be 50% to 70%, with much of the
remaining nongenetic variance due to individual experiences. Parenting child-
rearing styles, such as Baumrind's *authoritative, authoritarian, permissive,* and
uninvolved classification are certainly genetically variable. Parental styles *are,* after
all, parental behaviors, for which there is a great deal of evidence for heritability.

Gene–environment correlations

Scarr and McCartney (1983) predicted that heritability would increase from early
childhood to adolescence and adulthood, because people increasingly make their
own environments with active genotype–environment correlations. Influences of
passive genotype–environment correlations, which arise because parents both transmit genes and provide their children's environments, were predicted to decline, as
older children moved increasingly outside the family home. Two lines of evidence
support that theoretical prediction.

First, to test the theory, McCartney, Harris, and Bernieri (1990) conducted a
metaanalysis of twin studies on IQ and personality to evaluate the effects of subjects' age on heritability estimates. If active genotype–environment correlations
increased with age, and passive correlations decline, then heritability of intelligence
and personality will increase with age. McCartney et al. found a correlation of .36
between increasing age and increasing heritabilities for IQ and .30 for personality
measures, indicating that indeed genetic differences become more and more important to explain individual differences in personality and intelligence as children
can select and make their own environments. They also found evidence for declin-

ing effects of shared environments, in keeping with the theory (Scarr, 1992; Scarr & McCartney, 1983).

Second, estimates of common environment effects (or effects of being reared in different families) were much higher from adoption than from twin studies; inconsistencies needed to be resolved. Studies of young adoptees found the genetically unrelated children's IQ scores correlated .24 on average with their adoptive parents and .34 with unrelated siblings. Although biological relatives had correlations in the .40 to .55 range, heritability estimates based on adopted children were much lower (.4 to .6) than those based on twins reared together and apart. Further, the correlations of unrelated siblings *is* a direct estimate of the magnitude of shared environmental effects, which were found to be negligible in twin studies but accounted for about 25% of the variation in adoption studies.

The mystery of inconsistent results is solved by examining Scarr and Weinberg's (1978, 1983) study of older adolescent and young adult adoptees that found IQ correlations of −.03 for older, unrelated sibling pairs and adoptive parent–child correlations of <.10. Shared environmental effects for young adults match the null to small effects estimated from twin studies; with biological siblings' IQ correlations at .35, and biological parent–child correlations at .40, heritability estimates for WAIS IQ in the older samples approached those of the twin studies (.76 and .70).

Results of the Minnesota Adolescent Adoption Study have been replicated by three other adoption studies of older adolescents and adults, adopted in infancy (Loehlin, in press; Kent, 1985; Teasdale & Owen, 1985). Two adoption studies have reported longitudinal data from childhood to adulthood. The Texas Adoption Project (Loehlin, in press) found that genetically unrelated siblings' IQ correlations declined from .17 at age 8 years to −.02 at the average age of 18 years. The Minnesota Transracial Adoption Study (Scarr, Weinberg, & Waldman, 1993), which included adoptive families with at least one child of African American origin, found adopted siblings' IQ correlations decline from .34 to .13. Although .13 was significantly different from 0, the IQ correlation of the transracial adoptees at age 18 years was also significantly lower than their IQ correlation at the average age of 7 years.

The theory of genotype–environment correlations has received strong support from twin and adoption studies of personality and intelligence. Young children are more influenced by differences among their home environments than are older children and adolescents. This is logical, as young children's experiences are largely provided by their parents, whereas older children and adolescents receive more influence from those friends with whom they spend time, doing some activities and ignoring other opportunities. Adopted siblings become less and less similar to each other the longer they live together! Their lack of genetic resemblance means that they do not seek similar environments, such as peers, hobbies, and academic interests. For biological siblings, their genetic correlation leads them to have correlated experiences; identical twins, of course, select and experience the most similar environments, because of their own similar characteristics.

Competing theories about family effects

Social environmental theories, which include both opportunity and socialization hypotheses, can be contrasted with behavior genetic theory to explain observations about family effects on individual differences in development.

Behavior genetic theory is focused on both genetic and environmental causes of individual variation. Behavior genetics is not the study of species invariants or of gene action pathways that affect behaviors. Rather, behavior genetics emphasizes *sources of variation in populations.* It makes predictions about parental influences on children from both genetic and environmental transmission (Rowe, 1994; Segal, 1993).

By contrast, what we refer to here as *opportunity* hypotheses focus on differences in development that are hypothesized to arise from *differences in opportunities to learn* that are afforded by different social classes and from differences in the support that poor families offer to their children, compared with what middle-class families can offer; in this view, social classes are environmentally different rearing environments.

Socialization hypotheses propose that differences in intellectual development arise from differences in parenting practices (Darling & Steinberg, 1993; Steinberg, Dornbusch, & Brown, 1992). The opportunity hypothesis is compatible with the socialization hypothesis, because parents in different social classes are said to behave differently (Kohn, Naoi, Schoenbach, & Schooler, 1990). Kohn's theory of these differences in socialization bridges the theoretical gap between social-class-as-opportunity and social-class-as-socialization by asserting that parents at different locations in the social structure value different outcomes for their children and socialize them for different roles in the society. Marjoribanks (1987) proposed that social status and socialization concepts should be kept separate, because social status groups do not provide homogeneous family environments.

Opportunity theory has consistently claimed that social class differences in intelligence and academic achievement result from difference in opportunities to acquire the knowledge and skills valued by the middle class. Behavior genetic research offers strong evidence that differences in intelligence by social class arise, in large part, from genetic variability and not from differences in opportunities to learn, *but only in families that are not abusive, neglectful, or culturally different.*

The unpalatable finding, generated by behavior genetic theory from the observation of parent–child IQ correlations in adoptive and biologically related families, is that individuals from different social class groups, on average, do not have equal intellectual potential (Herrnstein, 1973; Herrnstein & Murray, 1994; Scarr & Weinberg, 1978, 1994; Weinberg, Scarr, & Waldman, 1992). Because between-family environmental effects have been shown to be small, social class differences must be heritable to some extent. Such a conclusion about social class differences should not be confused with findings of ethnic group differences in achievement and IQ scores; this crucial distinction is described in more detail later.

Implications of theory for developmental research

The implication of recent research for studies of family environmental effects on children's intellectual development is profound. Similarity in intelligence and other aspects of individuality (e.g., personality) among biological family members does *not* arise from growing up or living in the same household (Plomin & Daniels, 1987; Scarr & Grajek, 1982; Scarr & Ricciuti, 1991).

Differences in socialization history have negligible effects on development of intelligence or personality past childhood in European and North American populations who are not specially deprived of opportunities to acquire developmentally appropriate experiences (Bouchard et al., in press; Scarr, 1992, 1993). The implication of these results is that any redistribution of existing environments considered favorable to those in environments considered unfavorable can have only limited effects on intellectual or personality development, because environments experienced by these samples are largely functionally equivalent.

Even socialization researchers say that they do not expect that living in the same family makes siblings or parents and children similar to each other (Baumrind, 1993; Bronfenbrenner & Ceci, 1994; Hoffman, 1991), because each person perceives and reacts to the family environment in different ways (for the theory, see Scarr & McCartney, 1983). The observed family correlations are not in dispute, but the causal mechanisms by which family members do and do not resemble each other remain hotly contested.

Parenting style as context

Noting the many inconsistencies in results of socialization research, particularly for ethnic groups other than Euro-Americans, Darling and Steinberg (1993, p. 487) reinterpreted the theoretical meaning of parenting style. Parenting style is most usefully considered, they argued, as a constellation of attitudes of the parent toward the child that alters the efficacy of parenting practices and changes the child's openness to socialization.

In the revised model of socialization effects, specific parenting practices, such as parents' school involvement and encouragement (Steinberg et al., 1992), are hypothesized to have direct effects on adolescent outcomes, which they illustrated with academic achievement. Parenting style, the emotional climate, is hypothesized to have only indirect effects on child outcomes via two paths: Parents demonstrate their attitudes toward the child, affecting the child's willingness to be socialized, and parenting style augments or depreciates the effects of specific parenting practices. Parental goals and values are also hypothesized to have indirect effects.

Ethnic differences in achievement

To illustrate the model, Darling and Steinberg (1993) offer an explanation of ethnic differences in academic achievement. Perhaps, they suggest, the association between parental authoritativeness and academic achievement is much stronger among European American and Hispanic American adolescents than among Asian American and African Americans because parental goals differ. Perhaps, "authoritative parenting is as effective in socializing children across all cultural contexts, but the goals toward which children are socialized, and thus parents' practices, vary across these very same ecologies (Baumrind, 1971)" (Darling & Steinberg, 1993, p. 494).

The same questionnaire data described in the foregoing section were divided by ethnicity into samples of black, Asian, Hispanic, and white families (Dornbusch, Ritter, Leiderman, Roberts, & Fraleigh, 1987). Socialization theory was to be tested *within* each group to assess the generality of socialization hypotheses about authoritative parenting producing socially competent children, whose academic achievement is one manifestation (Steinberg, Elmen, & Mounts, 1989). Parental social status on 4,047 families was defined by education, categorized into six levels from less than high school graduation to professional or graduate degree. With ethnic groups combined, parental education was found to correlate $-.21$ with authoritarian rearing style, $-.13$ with permissive style, and $+.11$ with authoritative style. Unfortunately the zero order correlations were not provided by ethnic group, but regression equations by ethnicity suggest that correlations between parenting style and parental education were quite different.

On average, Asian, black, and Hispanic parents were reported by their adolescents to use *more authoritarian* parenting than white parents (one-third to one-half standard deviation more). Asian and Hispanic parents were also reported to be significantly *less authoritative* than white and black parents, who did not differ in authoritativeness. Although no means were given for school achievement, it is evident from regressions that adolescents' school achievement varied enormously by ethnicity: Compared with the results for whites, the coefficients to predict school grades were for blacks, $-.21$; Hispanics, $-.12$; and Asians, $+.47$. One problem for socialization theory is that authoritative parenting style is supposed to predict higher achievement, which was contradicted in this study because Asian adolescents had the highest achievement scores but their parents had the lowest authoritative scores. Only one parenting-style coefficient was predictive in the Asian group (higher authoritarian parenting predicted lower grades), and no parenting-style variable predicted achievement differences among either blacks or Hispanics. Because the sample of whites was larger than the other groups, even small coefficients for parenting variables were statistically reliable, although, with the exception of authoritarian parenting ($-.26$), parenting styles had negligible associations with school grades. Note that the only statistically reliable coefficient for authoritative parenting, the heart of the theory, was .05 for whites. In other ethnic groups, coefficients for authoritative parenting varied from $-.07$ for Asians to .12 for Hispanics.

Close inspection of the results suggests that the prediction of school grades is modest in any ethnic sample ($R^2 = .08–.16$), and that gender predicted a great deal of the explained variance for Hispanics and blacks, whereas parental education was more important among Asians and whites. Authoritarian parenting had negative coefficients in three of the four groups and positive in one; authoritative parenting was positive in two groups and negative or zero in two.

In a further discussion of results from this study (Steinberg et al., 1992), socialization theory was put to a further test: "This (parental style) literature indicates that adolescent competence, virtually however indexed, is higher among youngsters raised in *authoritative* homes – homes in which parents are responsive and demanding – than in other familial environments. Presumably, better performance in school is just one of many possible manifestations of psychosocial competence" (p. 724).

The paradox of higher school performance and lower parental authoritativeness

"Can ethnic differences in school performance be explained by use of authoritative parenting?" the authors asked (Steinberg et al., 1992, p. 725). The "paradox" of higher school performance and lower authoritativeness among Asian students suggested to them that the ecology of adolescents' lives needed to be considered. The four ethnic samples were further subdivided by socioeconomic status (working and below versus middle and above), family structure (intact, nonintact), yielding 16 groups. Within each cell, families were categorized as authoritative (above median for entire sample in authoritative style) or nonauthoritative (below median in authoritativeness). As in the earlier report, Asian students were least likely to come from an authoritative home. In contrast to the earlier report, the authors concluded (Steinberg et al., 1992, p. 725):

> Within African-American and Asian groups, youngsters whose parents were authoritative did not perform better than youngsters whose parents were nonauthoritative. Virtually regardless of their parents' practices, Asian-American students in our sample were receiving higher grades in school than other students, and the African-American students were receiving lower grades than other students. Indeed, we found that African-American students' school performance was even unrelated to their parents' level of education (Dornbusch, Ritter & Steinberg, in press) – a finding that is quite surprising, given the strong association between parental social class and scholastic success reported in the sociological literature on status attainment.

To explain why parenting practices had no effects on black and Asian students' school performance, they turned to potentially modifying influences of peer groups, hypothesizing that minority adolescents are more influenced by peers than whites. Further, they proposed that authoritative parenting is associated with affiliation with peers who earn good grades. Because of ethnically segregated peer associations, Asian students reared by authoritative parents are more likely to belong to a high-achieving, Asian peer group, whereas black students who lack authoritative parents will affiliate with low-achieving black peers.

There is just one problem with this explanation: "Surprisingly, among African-American and Asian-American students, we found no relation between parenting practices and peer crowd membership. In other words, authoritatively raised minority youngsters do not necessarily belong to peer groups that encourage academic success" (p. 728). The lack of clear results was attributed to the complex ecology of family life.

A more parsimonious explanation of results from both studies is that *parenting style is not associated with differences in adolescents' school achievement.* In the analysis reported for the entire sample (Steinberg et al., 1992) authoritative parenting accounted for less than 1% of the variation in school achievement. When the same sample was divided by ethnicity, results suggested that the highest achieving ethnic group has the least authoritative parents, and peers did not mediate parental influences because peer influences were unrelated to parenting styles – perhaps not surprising, given that adolescents choose their peers, and peer selection has been shown to be genetically variable (Plomin, 1994; Rowe, 1981, 1983).

The most prudent conclusions are that (1) the socialization model does not fit data from socialization studies, even those by the same research group, (2) authoritative parenting is unrelated to ethnic groups' differences in academic achievement, (3) authoritative parenting does not work the same way in all ethnic groups, and (4) there is little evidence that authoritative parenting is related to academic achievement or social competence in any group.

Relationships between genetic variability and achievement depend on opportunities to achieve

There is another explanation from behavior genetic theory for the "surprising" result that parental educational level was not related to academic achievement among African Americans (Fischbein, 1980; Scarr-Salapatek, 1971; Scarr, 1981). Arbitrary environmental barriers (segregation, racial discrimination) have prevented social mobility among African Americans by criteria of individual intellectual and academic achievement; therefore, there is less genetic variance, on average, between socioeconomic groups, and more genetic variability within socioeconomic groups, in the African American community, than among Euro-Americans. A theory of active genotype–environment correlations (Scarr & McCartney, 1983) depends on people having varied environments from which to choose and construct experiences. The theory does not apply, therefore, to people with few choices or few opportunities for experiences that match their genotypes. This is particularly true for children reared in very disadvantaged circumstances and for adults with little or no choice about work and leisure activities.

In another article, Dornbusch, Ritter, and Steinberg (1991) presented an additional observation about African Americans from the same study of achievement variation: Achievement differences among African American youth were not related to parent educational levels, but to the percentage of other African Americans living in the neighborhood. Living in a predominantly minority community, they suggested, can swamp family effects on academic achievement. In this report, community socioeconomic status was the only reliable predictor of variation in African American adolescents' school achievement (beta = .23), whereas among whites, parent education (.26), community socioeconomic status (.14), gender (.25), and two parent family (.11) were all significant predictors.[1]

Historical differences in social mobility could also explain these differences. African Americans living in predominantly Euro-American communities in the San Francisco Bay area are likely to be upwardly mobile adults, whose own achievements reflect their intelligence and educational level, so that their children's intelligence and achievements are better predicted by the parents' values. By contrast, African Americans living in predominantly black areas are more likely not to have been socially mobile for reasons that are *uncorrelated* with their individual intelligence or academic achievements (i.e., racial discrimination); thus, parents' achievements do not predict their children's achievements, if their children have opportunities for developing intelligence and academic skills according to their own abilities. For instance, lower social class communities that are predominantly black are more likely to contain a mix of adults with realized and unrealized abilities and achievement levels, compared with variation among African Americans in predominantly white, middle-class communities. Thus, children's levels of ability and achievement will be predicted by parental values for minority children living in predominant white areas but not well predicted in predominantly black communities.

Recall that Asian American parents' educational levels also did not correlate with their (high-scoring) children's academic achievements; oddly, neighborhood ecology was not offered as an explanation for this phenomenon (Dornbusch et al. 1991), presumably because predominantly Asian American communities cannot be accused of hindering adolescent achievement. Behavior genetic theory, however, does predict that Asian parents' educational levels will be less correlated with their children's intelligence and academic achievements than white parents', because many Asian parents, especially immigrants, have lacked educational opportunities. Therefore, years of schooling do not reflect genetic variability in intelligence among Asian American parents so much as opportunity differences to get schooling according to their abilities. Thus, the same lack of correlation between African American *and* Asian American parents' educational levels and their children's academic achievements is unlikely to result from neighborhood characteristics, which are different in the two communities.

Rather, the lack of parent–child educational achievement correlation can be explained by the same behavior genetic theoretical principle: Educational level is a poorer indicator of parental abilities among *both* Asian American and African American parents than among white parents, and thus a poorer predictor of children's abilities and achievements than is the case among whites.

Opportunities and heritability

When equal opportunities to schooling are available to parent generations in ethnic minorities, then parent–child correlations in academic achievements are predicted by behavior genetic theory to increase, which means that the heritability of educational achievements will rise among African American and Asian Americans, as opportunities for education are more readily available (Fischbein, 1980; Scarr-Salapatek, 1971).

This hypothesis can, of course, be tested empirically. In some countries where educational opportunities have become more equal over time, the prediction of rising heritabilities for academic achievement has been supported. Higher heritabilities of academic achievement were found with more equal educational opportunities in Norway (Sundet, Tambs, Magnus, & Berg, 1988), Denmark (Teasdale & Owen, 1985), Sweden (Fischbein, 1980; Pedersen, Plomin, Nesselroade, & McClearn, 1992; Thompson, Detterman, & Plomin, 1993), and the United States (Scarr-Salapatek, 1971; Scarr, 1981). The heritability of educational achievements rose with more equal opportunities, whether the opportunity differences had been experienced by social class, gender, or ethnicity. More equal opportunities reduce arbitrary environment differences, thereby highlighting genetic variability.

Challenge to policy makers

Policy makers should be aware that the reinterpretation of opportunity and socialization theories, in light of behavior genetic theory and research, explains why educational interventions most often have small effects on children's intellectual and educational development. Unless children are being reared in abusive or neglectful homes or with extremely limited opportunities, and unless minority children are isolated from the mainstream culture, they probably have sufficient opportunities and emotional support to acquire skills and knowledge, without intervention. Children whose families do not provide emotional support and learning opportunities, of course, can be significantly benefited by interventions to provide those essentials. Early intervention programs have health, nutritional, and other benefits for most poor children, but raising IQ and insuring acquisition of academic skills are not the primary outcomes.

Limits on intervention effects

The reasons that many interventions have disappointing results are genetic individual differences and genotype–environment correlations: Poorly educated, low-income parents are not a random sample of the population for intelligence, mental health, or other achievement-related characteristics (Herrnstein & Murray, 1994). Such parents are likely to have below-average IQ scores, which are transmitted genetically to their children. Offspring of lower IQ parents score, on average, below children from higher IQ parents.

Naturally occurring differences in environments between high-and low-income families reflect differences in parents' and children's abilities and achievements, which are best described as genotype–environment correlations. Thus, predictions of the effects of interventions, based on observed differences between poor and nonpoor families, are unrealistic, because they ignore genetic transmission and correlations of environments with parents' and children's abilities.

A compelling example

A very detailed longitudinal study of low-income, working-class, and professional-class families (Hart & Risley, 1995) illustrates these points. Predictably, preschool children from low-income families did not develop language or cognitive skills at the same rate as working-class children, who lagged behind children from professional families. Voluminous samples of adult speech to children showed that professional parents used *three times* as much language in everyday interactions with their children as do low-income parents. Working-class parents' language use was twice as frequent as that of poor parents. Needless to say, more parental language was associated with children's better language and cognitive development.

What can be inferred from these naturally occurring correlations between parents' behaviors and children's outcomes? Based on the correlations, the authors (Hart & Risley, 1995) calculated the potential payoffs of planned interventions to improve the language and cognitive performance of low-income children: *Even if parental language use were the effective difference, and if poor parents could be taught to behave like professional parents,* there would not be enough waking hours in a child's life to bring the language and cognitive levels of poor children to the levels naturally achieved by professional-class children. The authors concluded that to bring poor children to levels naturally achieved by working-class children would require 43 hours of programmed language intervention per week! Hart and Risley recognize that genetic differences may play a role in the enormous differences in language and cognitive development among poor, working-class, and professional-class children and that interventions of this magnitude are not feasible.

When to intervene

More intelligent parents provide more stimulating rearing environments, which are correlated with their children's abilities, and more intelligent children naturally evoke and select more intellectually stimulating environments than less able children. Intervention programs that merely recreate environments that intelligent parents provide for their children, and deliver them to less able children, cannot have the magnitude of effects that naturally occurring correlations would seem to predict. These unpopular, even unpalatable, conclusions follow from the recognition of genetic variability in abilities and achievements and genotype–environment correlations, but they *should not* deter us from providing good environments for children who do not currently have them.

All children benefit from supportive environments with varied opportunities to learn. Adoptive studies show that most nonminority children in North American and Western European nations currently have environments that meet those criteria. Supportive environments with varied opportunities to learn do not produce the same intellectual and academic outcomes for all children who experience them, because children's intellectual potentials are genetically variable, and children produce their own experiences from the environments to which they are exposed. Merely redistributing environments that *appear* to be better, because they are correlated with better outcomes, to children whose environments *appear* to be worse will have only small effects on the current distributions of abilities and achievements. Novel interventions can, of course, have unpredictable results.

Conclusion

All children need supportive environments that nurture their development to enable them to be the best and happiest people they can become. Beyond loving support, children need opportunities to develop their own individual abilities, talents, and personalities. The range and variety of opportunities are important, because below some threshold there are insufficient opportunities for normal development to occur. Parenting effects are nonlinear (Scarr, 1993; Deater-Deckard & Dodge, in press); among families where parents provide adequate opportunities for learning, genetic variability predominates; however, when parents are abusive or neglectful, genetically based potential can not be expressed.

Venturing advice to policy makers, we believe the most beneficial policies assure that all children have supportive environments with plentiful opportunities to learn and to feel appreciated as individuals. Individual differences in intellect and achievement among children who grow up in supportive environments arise primarily from genetic variability and correlated experiences that people make for themselves. However, we do not claim that differences in environments cannot influence differences among individuals in deficient and unsupportive situations; some families do not afford their children support and opportunities, so that the larger society must make these available. Children must have opportunities and support for their development to be optimal; every child deserves varied learning opportunities and emotional support for development (Zigler & Berman, 1983; Zigler, Taussig, & Black, 1992). When parents do not or cannot provide these essential ingredients, others must step in and do so.

Note

1 When the African American group was divided into those who live in predominantly or substantially white communities versus predominantly African American communities (Dornbusch, Ritter, & Steinberg, 1991, table 9), the correlations between parental education and adolescent school achievement were still not statistically different from zero in any community, but they had positive signs, rather than negative ones, for blacks living in predominantly white communities. The authors concluded that parental education showed consistently positive relations to adolescent achievement only in the white group.

References

Anderson, E. R., Hetherington, E. M., Reiss, D., & Plomin, R. (under review). Parent's nonshared treatment of siblings and the development of social competence during adolescence.

Baumrind, D. (1971). Current patterns of parental authority. *Developmental Psychology Monographs, 4*, 1–103.

Baumrind, D. (1993). The average expectable environment is not good enough: A response to Scarr. *Child Development, 64*, 1299–1317.

Berhman, J., Taubman, P., & Wales, T. (1978). Controlling for the effects of genetics and family environment in equations for schooling and labor market success. In P. Taubman (Ed.), *Kinometrics: The determinants of economic success within and between families.* New York: North Holland-Elsevier.

Bouchard, T. J., Jr., Lykken, D. T., Tellegen, A., & McGue, M. (in press). Genes, drives, environment and experience: EPD theory – revised. In C. Benbow & D. Lubinski (Eds.), *From psychometrics to giftedness: Essays in honor of Julian Stanley.* Baltimore: Johns Hopkins University Press.

Bouchard, T. J., Jr., & McGue, M. (1990). Genetic and rearing environmental influences on adult personality: An analysis of adopted twins reared apart. *Journal of Personality, 58*, 263–292.

Bronfenbrenner, U., & Ceci, S. (1994). Nature-nurture reconceptualized in developmental perspective: A bioecological model. *Psychological Bulletin, 101*, 568–586.

Caldwell, B. M., & Bradley, R. H. (1984). *Home observation for the measurement of the environment.* Little Rock: University of Arkansas Press.

Carter-Saltzman. L., & Scarr, S. (1977). MZ or DZ? Only your blood grouping laboratory knows for sure. *Behavior Genetics, 7*, 273–280.

Chipuer, H. M., Plomin, R., Pederson, N. L., McClearn, G. E., & Nesselroade, J. R. (1993). Genetic influence on family environment: The role of personality. *Developmental Psychology, 29*, 110–118.

Darling, N., & Steinberg. L. (1993). Parenting style as context: An integrative model. *Psychological Bulletin, 113*, 487–496.

Deal, J. E., Halverson, C. F., Jr., & Wampler, K. S. (1994). Sibling similarity as an individual difference variable: Within-family measures of shared environment. In E. M. Hetherington, D. Reiss, & R. Plomin (Eds.), *Separate social worlds of siblings: The impact of nonshared environment on development* (pp. 205–218). Hillsdale, NJ: Erlbaum.

Deater-Deckard, K. (in press). Within-family variability in parental negativity and control. *Journal of Applied Developmental Psychology.*

Deater-Deckard, K., & Dodge, K. A. (in press). Externalizing behavior problems and discipline revisited: Nonlinear effects and variation by culture, context, and gender. *Psychological Inquiry.*

Dornbusch, S. M., Ritter, P. L., Leiderman, P. H., Roberts, D. F., & Fraleigh, M. J. (1987). The relation of parenting style to adolescent performance. *Child Development, 58,* 1244–1257.

Dornbusch, S., Ritter, P., & Steinberg, L. (1991). Community influences on the relations of family statuses to adolescent school performance: Differences between African-American and non-Hispanic whites. *American Journal of Education, 99,* 543–567.

Dunn, J., & McGuire, S. (1993). Young children's nonshared experiences: A summary of studies in Cambridge and Colorado. In M. Hetherington, D. Reiss, & R. Plomin (Eds.), *Separate social worlds of siblings: The impact of nonshared environment on development* (pp. 111–128). Hillsdale, NJ: Erlbaum.

Dunn, J., & Plomin, R. (1986). Determinants of maternal behavior towards 3-year-old siblings. *British Journal of Developmental Psychology, 4,* 127–137.

Dunn, J., Plomin, R., & Daniels, D. (1986). Consistency and change in mothers' behavior toward young siblings. *Child Development, 57,* 348–356.

Dunn, J., Plomin, R., & Nettles, M. (1985). Consistency of mothers' behavior toward infant siblings. *Developmental Psychology, 21,* 1188–1195.

Fischbein, S. (1980). IQ and social class. *Intelligence, 4,* 51–63.

Harris, J. R. (in press). Where is the child's environment? A group socialization theory of development. *Psychological Review.*

Hart, B., & Risley, T. R. (1995). *Meaningful differences in the everyday experience of young American children.* Baltimore: Paul H. Brookes.

Herrnstein, R. (1973). *IQ in the meritocracy.* Boston: Atlantic Monthly Press.

Herrnstein, R., & Murray, C. (1994). *The bell curve.* New York: Free Press.

Hetherington, E. M., Reiss, D., & Plomin, R. (Eds.). (1994). *Separate social worlds of siblings: The impact of nonshared environment on development.* Hillsdale, NJ: Erlbaum.

Hoffman, L. W. (1991). The influence of family environments on personality: Accounting for sibling differences. *Psychological Bulletin, 110,* 187–203.

Horn, J., Loehlin, J. C., & Willerman, L. (1980). Genetic variation in development: The Texas Adoption Project. *Behavior Genetics, 13,* 212–225.

Jang, K. L. (1993). *A behavioral genetic analysis of personality, personality disorder, the environment, and the search for sources of nonshared environmental influences.* Unpublished doctoral dissertation, University of Western Ontario, London, Ontario.

Jensen, A. R. (1980). *Bias in mental testing.* San Francisco: Freeman.

Kent, J. (1985). *Genetic and environmental contributions to cognitive abilities as assessed by a telephone test battery.* Unpublished doctoral dissertation, University of Colorado, Boulder.

Kohn, M. L., Naoi, A., Schoenbach, S., Schooler, C., et al. (1990). Position in the class structure and psychological functioning in the United States, Japan, and Poland. *American Journal of Sociology, 95,* 964–1008.

Lichtenstein, P., Pederson, N. L., & McClearn, G. E. (1992). Genetic and environmental predictors of socioeconomic status. *Behavior Genetics, 22,* 731–732.

Loehlin, J. C. (1992). *Genes and environments in personality development.* Newbury Park, CA: Sage.

Loehlin, J. C. (1993). *Genetics and personality.* Thousand Oaks, CA: Sage.

Loehlin, J. C. (in press). Heredity, environment, and IQ in the Texas Adoption Project. In R. J. Sternberg & E. Grigorenko (Eds.), *Intelligence: Heredity and environment.* New York: Cambridge University Press.

Lytton, H. (1977). Do parents create, or respond to, differences in twins? *Developmental Psychology, 13,* 456–459.

Lytton, H. (1990). Child and parent effects on boys' conduct disorder: A reinterpretation. *Developmental Psychology, 26,* 683–697.

Maccoby, E. E. (1992). The role of parents in the socialization of children: An historical overview. *Developmental Psychology, 28,* 1006–1017.

Marjoribanks, K. (1987). Ability and attitude correlates of academic achievement: Family-group differences. *Journal of Educational Psychology, 79,* 171–178.

McCartney, K., Harris, M. J., & Bernieri, F. (1990). Growing up and growing apart: A developmental meta-analysis of twin studies. *Psychological Bulletin, 107,* 226–237.

McHale, S., Crouter, S., McGuire, S., & Updegraff, K. (1995). Congruence between mothers' and fathers' differential treatment of siblings: Links with family relations and children' well-being. *Child Development, 66,* 116–128.

Moos, R. H., & Moos, B. S. (1981). *Family Environment Scales manual.* Palo Alto, CA: Consulting Psychologists Press.

Pedersen, N. L., Plomin, R., Nesselroade, J. R., & McClearn, G. E. (1992). A quantitative genetic analysis of cognitive abilities during the second half of the lifespan. *Psychological Science, 3,* 346–353.

Plomin, R. (1994). *Genetics and experience: The interplay between nature and nurture.* Thousand Oaks, CA: Sage.

Plomin, R., & Bergeman, C. S. (1991). The nature of nurture: Perspective and prospective. In R. Plomin & G. E. McClearn (Eds.), *Nature, nurture, and psychology* (pp. 457–493). Washington, DC: American Psychological Association.

Plomin, R., & Daniels, D. (1987). Why are children in the same family so different from one another? *Behavioral and Brain Sciences, 10,* 1–60.

Plomin, R., & DeFries, J. (1980). Genetics and intelligence: Recent data. *Intelligence, 4,* 15–24.

Plomin, R., Loehlin, J. C., & DeFries, J. C. (1985). Genetic and environmental components of "environmental" influences. *Developmental Psychology, 21,* 391–402.

Plomin, R., McClearn, G. E., Pederson, N. L., Nesselroade, J. R., & Bergeman, C. S. (1988). Genetic influence on childhood family environment perceived retrospectively from the last half of the lifespan. *Developmental Psychology, 24,* 738–745.

Plomin, R., McClearn, G. E., Pederson, N. L., Nesselroade, J. R., & Bergeman, C. S. (1989). Genetic influences on adults' ratings of their current environment. *Journal of Marriage and the Family, 51,* 791–803.

Plomin, R., & Neiderhiser, J. M. (1992). Genetics and experience. *Current Directions in Psychological Science, 1,* 160–164.

Plomin, R., Reiss, D., Hetherington, E. M., & Howe, G. W. (1994). Nature and nurture: Genetic contributions to measures of the family environment. *Developmental Psychology, 30,* 32–43.

Reiss, D., Plomin, R., Hetherington, M., Howe, G., Rovine, M., Tryon, A., & Hagan, M. (1994). The separate worlds of teenage siblings: An introduction to the study of the nonshared environment and adolescent project. In M. Hetherington, D. Reiss, & R. Plomin (Eds.), *Separate social worlds of siblings: Impact of the nonshared environment on development* (pp. 1–32). Hillsdale, NJ: Erlbaum.

Rowe, D. C. (1981). Environmental and genetic influences on dimensions of perceived parenting: A twin study. *Developmental Psychology, 17,* 203–208.

Rowe, D. C. (1983). A biometrical analysis of perceptions of family environment: A study of twin and singleton sibling kinships. *Child Development, 54,* 416–423.

Rowe, D. (1994). *The limits of family influence.* New York: Guilford.

Scarr, S. (1968). Environmental bias in twin studies. *Eugenics Quarterly, 15,* 34–40.

Scarr, S. (1981). *Race, social class and individual differences in IQ: New studies of old issues.* Hillsdale, NJ: Erlbaum.

Scarr, S. (1992). Developmental theories for the 1990's: Development and individual differences. *Child Development, 63,* 1–19.

Scarr, S. (1993). Biological and cultural diversity: The legacy of Darwin for development. *Child Development, 64,* 1333–1353.

Scarr, S., & Grajek, S. (1982). Similarities and differences among siblings. In M. E. Lamb & B. Sutton-Smith (Eds.), *Sibling relationships.* Hillsdale, NJ: Erlbaum.

Scarr, S., & McCartney, K. (1983). How people make their own environments: A Theory of genotype-> environment effects. *Child Development, 54,* 424–435.

Scarr, S., & Ricciuti, A. (1991). What effects *do* parents have on their children. In L. Okagaki & J. Sternberg, (Eds.), *Directors of development: Influences on the development of children's thinking* (pp. 3–23). Hillsdale, NJ: Erlbaum.

Scarr, S., Weber, P. L., Weinberg, R. A., & Wittig, M. A. (1981). Personality resemblance among adolescents and their parents in biologically related and adoptive families. *Journal of Personality and Social Psychology, 40,* 885–898.

Scarr, S., & Weinberg, R. A. (1978). The influence of "family background" on intellectual attainment. *American Sociological Review, 43,* 674–692.

Scarr, S., & Weinberg, R. A. (1983). The Minnesota adoption studies: Genetic differences and malleability. *Child Development, 54,* 260–267.

Scarr, S., & Weinberg, R. A. (1994). Educational and occupational achievements of brothers and sisters in adoptive and biologically related families. *Behavior Genetics, 24* (4), 301–325.

Scarr, S., Weinberg, R. A., & Waldman, I. D. (1993). IQ correlations in transracial adoptive families. *Intelligence, 17,* 541–555.

Scarr, S., & Yee, D. (1980). Heritability and educational policy: Genetic and environmental effects on IQ, aptitude, and achievement. *Educational Psychologist, 15,* 1–22.

Scarr-Salapatek, S. (1971). Race, social class and IQ. *Science, 174,* 1285–1295.

Segal, N. L. (1993). Twin, sibling, and adoption methods: Tests of evolutionary hypotheses. *American Psychologist, 48,* 943–956.

Steinberg, L., Dornbusch, S. M., & Brown, B. B. (1992). Ethnic differences in adolescent achievement. *American Psychologist, 47,* 723–729.

Steinberg, L., Elmen, J. D., & Mounts, N. S. (1989). Authoritative parenting, psychosocial maturity, and academic success among adolescents. *Child Development, 60,* 1424–1436.

Sundet, J. M., Tambs, K., Magnus, P., & Berg, K. (1988). On the question of secular trends in the heritability of intelligence: A study of Norwegian twins. *Intelligence, 12,* 47–59.

Taubman, P. (1976). The determinants of earnings: Genetics, family, and other environment. A study of white, male twins. *American Economic Review, 66,* 858–870.

Teasdale, T. W., & Owen, D. R. (1985). Heredity and familial environment in intelligence and educational level – a sibling study. *Nature, 309,* 620–622.

Thompson, L. A., Detterman, D. K., & Plomin, R. (1993). Cognitive abilities and scholastic achievement: Genetic overlap but environmental differences. *Psychological Science, 3,* 158–165.

Vogler, G. P., & Fulker, D. W. (1983). Familial resemblance for educational attainment. *Behavior Genetics, 13* (4), 341–354.

Weinberg, R. A., Scarr, S., & Waldman, I. D. (1992). The Minnesota transracial adoption study: A follow-up of IQ test performance at adolescence. *Intelligence, 16,* 117–135.

Zigler, E., & Berman, W. (1983). Discerning the future of early childhood intervention. *American Psychologist, 38,* 894–906.

Zigler, E., Taussig, C., & Black, K. (1992). Early childhood intervention: A promising preventative for juvenile delinquency. *American Psychologist, 47,* 997–1006.

Part II

Atypical populations: Lessons on developmental processes

7　The study of atypical and typical populations in developmental psychopathology: The quest for a common science

Jacob A. Burack

Imagine a mythic community whose existence is largely dependent on water. The elders study and examine water from the lake around which they live and are confident in their understanding of its characteristics and uses. Some time afterward, friendly neighbors introduce fire to the community. In their experimentation, the elders are surprised to observe that water exposed to the fire becomes increasingly hot, then bubbles, until an apparently different substance (which we know as steam) eventually rises from it. Intrigued (and somewhat frightened) by this discovery, a subcommittee of elders sets out to study the characteristics of this new matter.

Some time later, aberrant forces of nature lead to temperatures that are considerably colder than ever before experienced. One morning, a particularly brave (or thirsty) couple emerges from their newly fire-heated cave. To their dismay, they find that the water in the lake is gone and there is a solid and very cold substance (which we know as ice) that is relatively clear in color. After being summoned with much urgency from the depths of their warm caves, the elders appoint a subcommittee to study this newly discovered substance.

As the years pass, water, steam, and ice continue to be studied separately by the community's scientists. Then one young but daring newcomer to the group of elders suggests that ice and steam appear to simply be forms of water that have changed properties due to variations in environmental conditions (i.e., temperature) and, therefore, all are essentially the same substance. Although the traditionalists continue to think of water, steam, and ice as distinct, the newcomer and some like-minded others view them simply as different forms of the same substance. They

I am indebted to Ed Zigler, Bill Kessen, Eugene Galanter, Gary Schwartz, Sheldon Wagner, Bob Hodapp, and Ethan Gorenstein, all of whom personally influenced me greatly in my thinking about the issues discussed in this chapter. I hope that I have not done a disservice to any of them. I thank Suniya Luthar for helping me to think through many of the issues. I thank Suniya, Dante Cicchetti, and John Weisz for their helpful, encouraging, and thoughtful insights throughout the project. I thank Orah Burack, Jeff Derevensky, Nurit Yirmiya, Grace Iarocci, and Beth Randolph for their comments on various drafts. And I thank Julie Brennan for her assistance in preparing the manuscript. My work on this paper and on the entire volume was supported by a New Researcher Award from the Social Sciences and Humanities Research Council of Canada.

learn about the relationship between temperature and water in its typical, steam, and frozen forms. They find that these changing states are affected by other factors, most notably the purity and volume of the water. More important, they realize that they can predict, depending on certain environmental conditions (the temperature) and properties of the water (volume and purity level), when water will change or regain its form. These revelations further their knowledge of basic properties of water, steam, and ice. Eventually, they use this information to optimize the utility of water, in all its forms for developing their community.

The story of developmental psychopathology

What is the relevance of the fanciful story of water, steam, and ice to the study of developmental psychopathology? One, it is a not too subtle allegory of the basic tenet of this discipline – the merger of typical and atypical development. Two, as in the analogy, the field of developmental psychopathology was largely influenced by the scholarly works of a young maverick. In this case, Edward Zigler challenged the traditional boundaries of the disciplines of development and psychopathology by integrating theory and methodology of the two. Zigler and a few contemporaries, notably Michael Rutter and Norman Garmezy (other innovative elders), initiated large-scale developmental studies of atypical populations and were largely responsible for the advent of developmental psychopathology and its eventual formal incorporation into academic psychology (Cicchetti, 1984, 1989a, 1989b, 1989c).

These two issues reflect the primary purposes of this chapter. The first is to demonstrate the unique value of developmental psychopathology both as an independent discipline and as a contributor to its primary originating sources, developmental psychology and psychopathology (for discussions of contributions from other fields, see Cicchetti, 1984; Sroufe & Rutter, 1984). I will examine: (1) the historical precedents for the merger of development and psychopathology; (2) reasons for the traditional divide between the two and why it was maintained so long; (3) changes in these disciplines, particularly in developmental psychology, that facilitated and shaped the emergence of developmental psychopathology; (4) contributions of the fledgling discipline to understanding its parent disciplines; and (5) relevant conceptual and methodological issues specific to developmental psychopathology. The second purpose is to highlight a few of the many theoretical and methodological contributions of Edward Zigler, whose work and innovations are seminal to the emergence and continued growth of the discipline of developmental psychopathology.

At the outset, I clarify the use of certain terms. In discussing development and developmental theory, I refer to the notions of traditional organismic development as depicted by Piaget and Werner (e.g., Overton & Reese, 1973; Reese & Overton, 1970), and not to the empirical study of children (for distinctions, see Kessen, 1983, 1984). The persons studied within the framework of developmental psychopathology are referred to as atypical rather than psychopathological. They manifest or are at risk for compromised development due to some inter- or intraorganismic factor, and do not necessarily suffer from psychopathology of any kind (see Cicchetti, 1989a; Sroufe & Rutter, 1984). In addressing problems in development, the terms delay and impairment are typically used jointly in order to encompass disparate perspectives (for a discussion of delay and deviance, see Burack, 1992). Unless specified otherwise, the term environment is used in the most general sense to include the communal, social, and/or biological components. These issues will all be delineated in greater detail.

Typicality and atypicality: The idée fixe

Reciprocally informative relationship between the regularly occurring common state and a less common atypical one is an integral aspect of scientific study. Information from the regular state provides the context and standards for recognizing and understanding differences from the norm. Conversely, data from atypical states are informative about the extent to which the laws and principles derived from the usual situation are universally maintained even in the extreme. In a recent example from physics, scientists discovered how to bring atoms to a standstill with a process that entails initially trapping the atoms and then freezing them to within billionths degrees of absolute freezing on the Kelvin scale. Examining atoms in this rare and unusual state should provide new insights into the nature of atoms and physical states as we know them. Conversely, it is only with the current understanding of atoms that this breakthrough in an atypical atom state could be achieved.

The specific value of studying human atypicalities is similarly well acknowledged in the medical and related sciences. For example, in the neurosciences, the study of persons with brain lesions and trauma are central to the discipline (e.g., Kingstone, Grabowecky, Mangun, & Gazzaniga, in press). Behavioral evidence from these persons is used to identify the parts of the typical brain that are responsible for specific aspects of functioning, and the ways in which the various parts interact with and compensate for each other. Concordantly, basic knowledge, theories, and methodologies in this field are central to identifying the specific deficits of persons with brain injury and to developing appropriate treatment programs. Similar examples can be found in genetics, neurology, anatomy, and essentially all medically related fields.

The historical story

Although evidently a mundane aspect of scientific theory in other disciplines, the theoretical relationship between common processes and those which are somehow atypical was revelatory to many working in the areas of development and psychopathology (Cicchetti, 1984). Thus, developmental psychopathology, the merger of the two, only recently emerged as a formal discipline within academic psychology (for discussions regarding the formalization of the field, see Cicchetti, 1984, 1989a, 1989b, 1989c). Yet, the underlying idea is not necessarily a new one to the relevant fields (Cicchetti, 1993). Rather, it is one that was prominent in applied psychology throughout the 20th century. A particularly compelling example is the development of intelligence testing, a universally recognized hallmark of psychology in this century. At the turn of the century, early tests of general intellectual functioning were designed by Binet and colleagues (Binet & Henri, 1895; Binet & Simon, 1905) to identify school-aged children with mental retardation or who would otherwise be unable to benefit from traditional school curricula. Despite many inherent problems, this type of test continues to be used as a primary index of both typical and atypical development.

The relationship between typical and atypical development was even more central to the historically important writings of psychoanalysts and a few other clinical theoreticians who examined psychopathology within large systemic views of development (Enns & Burack, in press). For example, Sigmund Freud used information from sessions with his patients, most of whom suffered from some type of neurosis, to generate a model of development. Subsequently, he used this model of development to study and treat other types of psychopathology. The developmental influence on psychopathology was explicit as Freud stressed that adult disorders were the outcome of both internal and interpersonal conflicts in childhood.

Similarly, Heinz Werner, both a clinician and a developmental theorist, demonstrated parallels between the developmental differences among children of different ages and those among adults with different psychiatric disorders. Just as developmental principles are relevant to understanding behavioral changes associated with increasing age in children, so is it informative for understanding distinctive behaviors associated with different psychiatric disorders. Accordingly, Werner (1957) argued that differences in cognitive functioning among persons with different types of psychopathology allow for a developmental ordering that corresponds with the developmental progression of typical children.

Werner's legacy is best exemplified by the work of his student and colleague, Edward Zigler. Zigler applied basic cognitive developmental principles of sequences, structures, and rates as the contexts for understanding persons as diverse as those with mental retardation and psychiatric disorders (e.g., Zigler, 1967, 1969; Zigler & Glick, 1984; Zigler & Hodapp, 1986). Conversely, the data from these groups provide evidence concerning the notions of universality and invariance within general development. Zigler emphasized that development continues throughout the life-span, regardless of the incidence or onset of disorder, and that the understanding of its numerous components is informative to clinically relevant tasks, including differentiating diagnostic subtypes and assessing adaptive behavior and prognosis. Zigler envisioned all the manifestations of psychopathology as inherently linked to general developmental processes. Thus, he championed developmental theory as a single framework for understanding all persons, regardless of specific problem.

Why has it taken so long? Contemplating the schism between development and psychopathology

The examples of Binet, Freud, Werner, and Zigler are evidence that the underlying notion of developmental psychopathology originated well before the 1980s (also, see Hodapp, Chapter 9, this volume). However, these examples of integrative writings and frameworks remained the exceptions. Despite its historical roots, this discipline was not formalized until Cicchetti (1984) united various workers in the field. At that time, he articulated the essential battle cry, that "we can learn more about the general functioning of an organism by studying its pathology, and, likewise, more about its pathology by studying its normal condition" (Cicchetti, 1984, p. 1).

The question then is why did it take so long for this inevitable merger of development and psychopathology within academic psychology. A likely answer is that the schism between development and psychopathology is a significant one between two sciences with different world views and little common ground.

The academic outsiders

At the most basic level, there was no common ground for the disciplines of development and psychopathology since they evolved independently, both primarily outside the domain of academic psychology. Neither is inherently compatible with mainstream academic psychology, with its roots in the methodologically rigorous frameworks of the 19th-century, German-based scientist/philosopher models of experimental psychology (e.g., Herman Ebbinghaus; Gustav Fechner; Hermann von Helmholtz; Ernst Heinrich Weber; Wilhelm Wundt; and later Edward Bradford Titchener in the United States) and the American-based schools of functionalism (e.g., James Rowland Angell; William James) and behaviorism (e.g., John B. Watson) (for a review, see Boring, 1929; and for excerpts from original writings, see Dennis, 1948; Herrnstein & Boring, 1966).

The exclusion of the study of persons with psychopathology from mainstream academic psychology dates back at least to Wundt and the other German experimentalists who were interested in building a science of the "normal human" experience of the objective world (Herrnstein & Boring, 1966). The task of understanding typical experiences is difficult enough, without the added complexities inherent in understanding the deviations. Thus, aberrancies are largely ignored or relegated to the status of statistical anomalies or outliers. Conversely, psychopathology is, almost by definition, focused on the abnormalities of human functioning and experience. Its empirical value was generally disparaged due to its inherent association with clinical psychology, a discipline that was found lacking with regard to every aspect of the scientific endeavor, from theory to methodology to instrumentation (e.g., Esper, 1964; Meehl, 1960; Zilboorg, 1941). Eventually, the experimental study of psychopathology found at least a tenuous place in mainstream academic psychology, although the rift between clinical and academic psychology remains.

Similarly, traditional development was excluded from mainstream academic psychology because of its inherent complexities and often questioned scientific merits. The types of intricate evolving relationships described by developmental theorists (e.g., Piaget, 1970; Werner, 1957) are not easily tested with experimental rigor (Zigler, 1963). Experimentalists questioned the scientific utility of the methods of observation used by Piaget and colleagues. Accordingly, the admittance of developmental psychology into mainstream psychology became possible only when the emphasis on developmental theory was abandoned in favor of an experimental science of children (Kessen, 1983, 1984).

The pragmatic divide. The reasons for the divide between development and psychopathology are the same that are implicated in their exclusion from mainstream academic psychology. The endeavor to understand an ever evolving complex organism is incompatible with the study of specific individual or group differences. Accordingly, the scientific pursuits were discordant in the most basic ways – with regard to specific issues and questions, levels of analyses, and methodologies.

In developmental theory, questions revolve around the typical progression of innate changes throughout childhood and even adulthood. Analyses are primarily based on behavioral differences, at various ages, that are used as indices of common developmental change. Strictly speaking, the study of human development entails within-group studies (or groups of studies) of relatively uniform and consistent changes during the life-span. In contrast, the science of psychopathology involves comparisons among any number of atypical and typical groups. Thus, analyses are generally between-group comparisons in which the focus is on unique behavioral, emotional, intellectual, or physiological phenomena at a given moment and/or as a specific outcome of some potentiating environmental factor. Even within-group comparisons are focused on some aspect of difference between subgroups. These basic differences between the disciplines of developmental theory and psychopathology are indicative of the primary source of schism between the two – they are grounded in conflicting, and largely irreconcilable, world views.

The constructivist versus deconstructivist divide and differences in world views

The traditional developmental theory of Piaget and Werner is best described within the framework of an organismic world view in which the organism is a dynamic and organized whole that develops according to universal laws and processes (Altman & Rogoff, 1987; Overton & Reese, 1973; Reese & Overton, 1970). Subsequent theories of development that better incorporate environmental factors are viewed within the realm of a transactional view in which the organism and environment are intertwined such that they continuously transact at multiple levels

(Altman & Rogoff, 1987; Sameroff, 1990). Both are seen as constructivist approaches since they are frameworks for inclusion, growth, and organized systems. Conversely, experimental psychopathology is largely a deconstructivist enterprise that is consistent with the trait and mechanistic world views. It is focused on aspects of functioning unique to persons with specific disorders or living in certain environments. With these differences, the merger of development and psychopathology was realized only after each of the disciplines, but particularly the former, was taken far from its conceptual origins.

Traditional and expanded developmental theories: Constructivist models and limitations. Traditional developmental theory (e.g., Piaget, 1970; Werner, 1957) is inherently a constructivist framework on several levels (for a discussion, see Bronfenbrenner, Kessel, Kessen, & White, 1986). First, at its grandest level, the theory is oriented to building an understanding of general notions of development that are applicable to animals as well as to humans, to societies as well as to individuals, and to ideas as well as to living things. Second, it is holistic as developmental inquiry is directed at understanding principles of organization and the evolving structural relationships among the parts and whole (Reese & Overton, 1970). Consistent with the orthogenetic principle, developmental organization is seen as proceeding from a state of relative globality to those that are increasingly differentiated and hierarchically integrated (Werner, 1957). Third, development involves coherent, invariant, and orderly growth to an increasingly adaptive end point. The processes and changes in structure are cohesive and meaningful such that development can be seen within the context of a teleological relationship or universal directionality (Flavell, 1982; Overton & Reese, 1973). And, fourth, it entails an organism that actively engages the environment in the growth process (Overton, 1976; Piaget, 1970).

With increasing attention in the 1960s, 1970s, and 1980s to individual, environmental, and cultural differences, the organismic world view as the primary framework of developmental psychology came under attack. Ironically, it was too big for the consideration of variations in development and too narrow for understanding the entire picture of development. The ''bigness'' is indicative of the difficulties in studying the complexities of the organismic structure, whereas the narrowness reflected the emphasis on internal development at the expense of extraorganismic factors. At both extremes, a primary concern was that there was insufficient consideration of individual and group differences. (These criticisms led to emergent traditions aimed at incorporating individual differences, and even psychopathology, within the realm of developmental psychology [Enns & Burack, in press].)

As the focus changed to more specific aspects of extra- and intraorganismic components of development, developmental psychology became increasingly fragmented (Bronfenbrenner et al., 1986). The nature of the field's theoretical questions and, subsequently, the empirical paradigms changed significantly. Piagetian-type qualitative analyses of cognitive processes, functions, and structures were abandoned in favor of models and analyses that were more characteristic of a mechanistic world view and that allowed for quantitative assessments of the effects of numerous extracognitive factors (e.g., social, emotional, and personality) (Altman & Rogoff, 1987; Overton & Reese, 1973; Reese & Overton, 1970). Despite its organismic holistic roots, the study of developmental psychology was transformed largely into a deconstructivist endeavor as the foci of research became increasingly compartmentalized and fragmented (Kessen, 1984). Decentralized positions were prominent, and criticisms of traditional development theory were based on work such as Gardner's (1983) multiple intelligence framework of intelligence, Chomsky's (1980) notion of the nativism of language, and Fodor's (1982) independent modules of cognition.

This transformation within the field represented so marked a change in orientation and conceptualization that the most prominent of developmental theorists declared that the "king (Piaget) was dead" (Kessen, 1984) and considered whether the age of development had come to an end (e.g., Bronfenbrenner et al., 1986; Frye, 1991; Kessen, 1984). Urie Bronfenbrenner argued that the fragmented deconstructivist position is a "cop out" for those unwilling to search for underlying complex relationships among the various aspects of development. However, his prominent colleagues Bill Kessen and Sheldon White despaired that the understanding of the developing human organism was too fragmented to ever be reconstituted into a single whole (Bronfenbrenner et al., 1986).

The abandonment of primary developmental principles led to the growth of theoretical schools in which the adherents attempted to maintain a traditional framework while incorporating issues of individual differences and the environment. For example, neo-Piagetians integrated traditional cognitive developmental notions with other less monolithic frameworks such as those of information processing (e.g., Case, 1985, 1992) and behaviorism (e.g., Fischer, 1980). Similarly, complexities of environments were increasingly considered by Bronfenbrenner (1979) and others who stressed the understanding of the various layers of social systems in which children develop and interrelate. With this increasing interest in individual and environmental differences, post-Piagetians were more willing than their predecessors to consider the role of psychopathology, impaired functioning, and deleterious environments and behaviors.

Development and the transactional framework. This evolving emphasis on environment and individual differences also led to a broadened developmental psychology and even more complex constructivist frameworks. These incorporated social, biological, and environmental factors, and the complex transactional relationships among them. They were appropriate to assess the impact on development of issues as diverse as gender, parenting history, physiological integrity, emotions, temperament, and communal, cultural, and societal background. Thus, a transactional world view was adopted as it allowed for a hierarchically organized framework for conceptualizing the evolving multiplicities of interrelationships among the many aspects of the individual's genotype, phenotype, and environment (Sameroff, 1990; Sameroff, Seifer, & Bartko, Chapter 22, this volume).

The transactional view was hailed by many as it allowed developmentalists to maintain the structural, holistic aspects of the organismic approach, while improving upon it by providing for the inclusion of individual differences and environmental considerations. More than previous frameworks, it allowed for the study of the "whole child," as well as of the whole environment and even community and society. The significance of this approach was originally articulated in a landmark review by Sameroff and Chandler (1975), who challenged common conceptions of direct links between various pre-, neo-, and postnatal problems and later negative outcomes. They demonstrated that most children considered to be at risk for developmental problems, except those who suffer from severe biological insult or as the victims of extreme maltreatment, are relatively resilient and develop typically if raised in reasonably intact environments. In doing so, Sameroff and Chandler (1975) highlighted the inherent problems associated with the simple cause – effect relationships of typical at-risk studies, and argued for the need to assess secondary and tertiary variables as moderating and intervening variables.

Unfortunately, as with the organismic view, the transactional world view is more valuable conceptually than it is methodologically practical. The complexities inherent in this ultimately constructivist framework, with so many continuously interacting interrelated components, limits systematic and empirically rigorous work. Thus, researchers working within this framework, including Sameroff and Chandler (1975), generally utilize complex cause–effect models in which the specific relationships are related to or mediated by other, usually extraorganismic, factors. With increasing sophistication in statistical knowledge and computer technology, however, empirical work within transactional frameworks may ultimately be a viable enterprise. In the meantime, transactional models are conceptually useful guides for the study of the complex relationships of typical and atypical intra- and extraorganismic factors in development.

The science of psychopathology: An example of a deconstructivist science. In contrast to the study of development, that of psychopathology is essentially a deconstructivist enterprise. Researchers of psychopathology typically attempt to identify one or a few problems that they consider to be central traits of a disorder or markers of some deleterious situation – as behavioral manifestations, inter- or intraorganismic causes of certain characteristic behaviors, outcomes of biological etiology, factors in the maintenance and/or prognosis of the disorder, or the consequences of some precipitating disorder or situation (for recent discussions of the nature of psychopathology, see Gorenstein, 1992; Lilienfeld & Marino, 1995; and Wakefield, 1992). The focus is on the discrete–particular disorders, situations, behaviors, and components and/or processes of functioning. People are classified accordingly into distinct populations or groups. Even among the developmental, nonbehaviorist approaches, variant forms of the trait and/or mechanistic cause–effect models are most common. Traditional psychoanalysts discuss personality types that persist throughout the life-span, and view aspects of parent–child relationships during early childhood as direct precursors of specific disorders or problems later in life. Similarly, the classically developmental-based longitudinal at-risk research is centered around the continuity through the life-span of disorder-specific traits and/or cause–outcome relationships between certain risk-potentiating variables and corresponding outcomes.

The deconstructive nature permeates all aspects of the discipline and is even evident in the bounding of psychopathology research. The choice of the specific foci of research about an identified group varies considerably as researchers differ with regard to backgrounds and theoretical orientations and interests. They come from numerous disciplines including psychology, psychiatry, genetics, neurology, biochemistry, and related areas. Even within psychology and psychiatry, there is considerable variation in theoretical backgrounds and research interests. As no common theoretical link is applied consistently to these different frameworks and approaches, the study of even a single population entails a wide range of relatively independent empirical viewpoints and methodologies. The links among researchers studying different groups are even more tenuous. Thus, researchers of psychopathology share a general interest in atypical functioning and some methodologies, but little else.

The emerging discipline, and its precursors

With these basic differences in foci, methodologies, and world views, the emergence of a discipline that bridges development and psychopathology represents a potentially important advance for each of these fields as well as for related areas. Researchers of this new area draw from the unique histories, knowledge, paradigms, and applications of the parent disciplines while adding to each with contributions from the other. As is the case with other mergers, this bridging is beneficial only to the extent that it contributes to scientific understanding not available when the two disciplines are maintained independently.

Contributions of developmental psychology to understanding atypical populations

Within a developmental framework, the study of atypical populations is considered an integral, but not sole, aspect of the continuing development of the affected individuals within their environments. The psychopathological phenomena are not viewed simply as anomalies, discordant with typical human experience at a given moment in time in a person's life, but as the natural sequelae of certain developmental paths. These paths are forged through the ongoing relationships among multidimensional aspects of typical and atypical behavioral, biological, and environmental factors throughout the life-span (see Achenbach, Chapter 5, this volume;

Sameroff, Seifer, & Bartko, Chapter 22 this volume). As Sroufe and Rutter (1984) articulated in a defining statement of purpose, developmental psychopathology, "is the study of the origins and course of the individual patterns of behavioral maladaptation, whatever the age of onset, whatever the causes, whatever the transformations in behavioral manifestations, and however complex the course of the developmental pattern may be" (p. 18).

For example, within a traditional psychopathology framework, the study of the effects of the Holocaust would primarily entail the examination of specific aspects of functioning among survivors of that tragedy, usually in comparison to other specified groups. However, with the added perspective of development, the interest is on factors that impact development prior to, during, and following the Holocaust and how they might affect behavior, functioning, and emotional well-being both during and after the years of the Holocaust. The relevant issues might include parenting, community support, beliefs and values, nutritional and stimulation levels, and the extent and duration of exposure to life-threatening situations. Throughout, issues such as age, and the intensity, frequency, and/or duration of the problematic situation are important to understanding the nature and severity of potential problems as well as the possibility of maintaining an adaptive life-style during and after the Holocaust.

Examples for understanding persons with disorders. The continua of typical and atypical development was emphasized by Zigler in his work both with persons with mental retardation and psychiatric disorders (for reviews, see Glick, Chapter 11, this volume; Hodapp, Chapter 9, this volume). For example, in explaining deficient performance by persons with mental retardation on certain cognitive tasks, Zigler highlighted the impact of a lifetime of experiences as a person with intellectual handicap on the development of personality and motivational characteristics (e.g., Bennet-Gates & Zigler, in press; Zigler & Hodapp, 1986). The types of characteristics described by Zigler and colleagues are found in everyone, but are particularly exacerbated among those who experience histories of failure, come from low SES areas, suffer(ed) social deprivation, and/or have histories of institutionalization.

To illustrate this point, Bybee & Zigler (1992) found that children with and without mental retardation matched for mental age (MA) similarly looked to an adult experimenter for cues on a complex/novel task. On a simple task, however, only the children with mental retardation relied on an outerdirected search for cues, a strategy typical of lower MA children. Bybee and Zigler (1992, in press) concluded that persons of all ages, abilities, and backgrounds search the environment for cues in situations that are ambiguous, with which they are unfamiliar, or that they do not understand. In contrast, persons with mental retardation and others who experience failure are overdependent on otherwise adaptive outerdirected strategies in circumstances in which they are evidently capable of acting appropriately. These findings are consistent with Zigler's notion that the same developmental factors are similarly relevant to both typical and atypical persons, although their specific manifestations might be affected by certain characteristics and/or life circumstances.

Zigler similarly discusses developmental continuities in his work with persons with psychiatric disorders (Burack & Zigler, 1989; Zigler & Glick, 1984, 1986). He argues against the notions that the onset of a psychiatric problem represents either a developmental regression or a cessation of development, and that psychopathology occurs outside of general development. To Zigler and colleagues, development is always ongoing and all aspects of psychopathology, including age of onset, type and manifestation of disorder, specific symptomatology, and prognosis, are part of the developmental growth of affected individuals (e.g., Burack & Zigler, 1989; Zigler & Glick, 1984, 1986).

Analogous to the survivors of the Holocaust, those with psychiatric problems are considered within the context of their unique developmental histories prior to onset of the disorder, and their continuing development during the disorder's manifestation and remission. In extending Werner's work, Zigler and colleagues (Zigler & Glick, 1986; Zigler, Levine, & Zigler, 1976) ordered developmentally the various psychiatric problems. Persons with nonparanoid schizophrenia are considered to be developmentally lower than those with either paranoid schizophrenia or affective disorders. These differences are reflected in the ages of first hospitalization and levels of social competence that are considered indices of developmental level (Burack & Zigler, 1989; Zigler & Phillips, 1961). Even manifestations of symptoms such as hallucinations and delusions, which are common to all these groups, are considered with regard to developmental complexity and sophistication (Zigler & Glick, 1986; Zigler & Levine, 1983).

An example of understanding an at-risk population. The increased awareness of the complex interplay of organism and environment is depicted in Kaufman and Zigler's (1989) challenge to the myth that adults who were victims of child maltreatment generally become maltreating parents. Evidence for this commonly accepted "truth" came primarily from traditional retrospective cause–effect models of research. Using a prospective transactional framework to assess available data, Kaufman and Zigler (1989) demonstrated that most victims of childhood maltreatment are quite capable of good parenting skills, especially with strong family and community support. Thus, as is the case with persons who never experience maltreatment, effective parenting is dependent on a wide range of transacting environmental and personal factors. This important alternative view of the sequelae of maltreatment exemplifies the conceptual value of the transactional approach to understanding developmental outcome among a group of persons with an atypical experiential history.

Lessons from atypical populations to understanding development

The study of persons with psychopathology also extends basic knowledge of developmental psychology. It provides information about the limits and potential sources of deviations of basic developmental processes and mechanisms (Hodapp & Burack, 1990). Within the expanded approach (Cicchetti & Pogge-Hesse, 1982; Hodapp, Burack, & Zigler, 1990), persons with atypical behaviors, impaired levels of functioning, and/or problematic environmental histories are "experiments of nature" (Bronfenbrenner, 1979). Information about them is helpful for understanding basic developmental principles, the universality of processes, and the organization of the developing organism in conditions that cannot be created due to ethical or practical reasons.

Insights from extreme or unusual situations in understanding basic principles is a fundamental tenet of science. In contemporary times, the primary impetus for space exploration is the opportunity to examine the extent to which scientific principles observed and devised on earth are applicable in environments that are distant and not immediately replicable. Analogously, children from impoverished, abusive, and/or neglectful homes or with histories of acting out behaviors provide developmentalists with insight into situations where social development might be most compromised. The populations of persons with brain injuries/lesions, mental retardation, and other aspects of brain dysfunction provide information regarding the essential nature of cognitive development in situations in which it is most jeopardized. For all aspects of development, the lessons for understanding mechanisms, processes, and general developmental theory are integrally linked to the information from specific populations (Hodapp & Burack, 1990).

Lessons for social development. Writers, philosophers, physicians, psychologists, and lay persons have all long been intrigued by the extent to which persons are able to develop according to societal expectations despite "growing up" outside of human environs or in appallingly abusive or neglectful situations. This fascination permeates mythic and popular literature as evidenced by the legend of Remus and Romulus, the many versions of the Tarzan story, and the popularity in literature of 19th-century children growing up outside the mainstream society (e.g., Twain's Huck Finn, Dickens's Oliver and friends, and Kipling's Jungle Boy). Not surprisingly, then, there is a commensurate interest in the development of real children who experienced these types of situations, such as Victor, the Wild Boy of Aveyron (Lane, 1976), and little Genie who was confined to a closet for several years during her childhood (Curtiss, 1977). As might be expected, the development of the fictional characters was generally more successful than that of the real-life ones.

Unfortunately, examples of particularly problematic social environments are not confined to a few isolated circumstances or to myths, and are numerous and diverse in contemporary reality. In many developing countries, there are insufficient means to feed or educate children, and in Western countries both large cities and rural areas are plagued by poverty and high levels of violent crimes. Rates of marital discord are high throughout Western society, and increasing numbers of children are being raised in single-parent households with little community support. The study of the variability of outcomes of children in these conditions is informative about the roles and relationships of various aspects of social development.

The outcome of children and adolescents growing up in inner cities is an example of a naturally occurring societal concern. It is studied primarily to understand better the affected youths and to initiate intervention programming, but is also informative to understanding general development. In initial analyses, there was apparent consensus that youths from these environments are at considerable risk for later problems, but that there are those who can be considered resilient as they seem to perform well in school and are viewed positively by peers and adults (e.g., Luthar & Zigler, 1991; Masten, Best, & Garmezy, 1990). In reexamining these issues, however, Luthar (1995) found that the children with the highest initial levels of interpersonal and emotional adjustment are most likely to have failing grades and show disruptive behaviors later in the school year. This counterintuitive evidence, that adaptation in one area may jeopardize functioning in another, reflects the intricacies of the relationships among various aspects of development. It highlights the need to differentiate between examples of generalized adaptation and those that are more limited (Luthar, 1995). In a more general sense, Luthar's work exemplifies the need to rethink developmental theories in order to integrate the deviations or abnormalities that can occur with considerable variations in ecological settings.

Lessons for cognitive development. By studying those persons in which cognitive development is most impaired or delayed, developmentalists gain unique insights into basic issues such as those of rate, sequences, and cross-domain structural relationships (Hodapp & Burack, 1990). For example, support for the universality of the sequences of cognitive development, regardless of rate, is evident in the finding that typical sequences of development are also evident among persons with all types of mental retardation and related biological insults, with the possible exception of persons with epilepsy (Weisz & Zigler, 1979; Weisz, Yeates, Zigler, 1982; also see Hodapp, 1990). Although slowed rate is not associated with differences in sequences within domain (Zigler, 1967, 1969), it allows for a unique ''slow motion'' look at the intricacies of developmental organization (Cicchetti & Sroufe, 1978; Wagner, Ganiban, & Cicchetti, 1990).

By definition, there is a discrepancy between chronological age (CA) and level of developmental functioning (loosely measured in terms of MA) among persons with mental retardation. Evans, Hodapp, and Zigler (1995) examined the discrepancy between CA and MA as related to choice of leisure activities among children and adolescents with mental retardation attending a special school. They found that MA was more predictive of leisure-time behaviors both for children and adolescents, albeit to a somewhat lesser extent in the older group. Concordantly, at the other end of the IQ continuum, Luthar, Zigler, and Goldstein (1992) found that gifted children's behavior was more indicative of MA than CA. Although not necessarily generalizable, these findings provide convergent evidence, from two disparate populations, of the primary of the rate of cognitive development rather than that of simple chronological aging.

In addition to the generally slowed rate, there is considerable cross-domain variation in rate across individuals and specific etiological groups of persons with mental retardation (Burack, 1990; Hodapp & Burack, 1990). These widely disparate profiles of strengths and weaknesses among persons with different etiologies of mental retardation were deemed problematic for the conservative approach to developmental psychology in which the structure of development was considered to be tightly integrated. Accordingly, Cicchetti and colleagues (e.g., Cicchetti & Pogge-Hesse, 1982; Cicchetti & Sroufe, 1978) articulated a liberal approach to development in which the examples of uneven patterns of development are indicative of the extent to which the developmental links among the various components of development can be stretched, but still maintained within an organized and systematic developmental framework. For example, unevenness in development among persons with certain etiological types of mental retardation allows researchers to assess whether cross-domain relationships of functioning that are evident in typical development are essential or happenstance (Cicchetti & Pogge-Hesse, 1982; Hodapp & Burack, 1990; Hodapp & Zigler, 1995; Rutter, 1989). This liberal approach marks an important extension of traditional developmental theory as it provides a more flexible framework within which to incorporate individual as well as group differences.

Lessons for developmental theory. Although developmental psychopathology represents a considerable extension of mainstream development, researchers in this area are among the most passionate defenders of traditional developmental theory. The notion of a coherent structural approach, albeit different than that envisioned by Piaget, is essential to their task of providing a hierarchic and integrative theoretical framework with which to study the spectrum of atypicalities. In contrast, many mainstream developmentalists and cognitivists cite examples of atypical groups and individual differences as reflecting the inadequacies of developmental theory for the study of human behavior (e.g., Bronfenbrenner et al., 1986; Kessen, 1962, 1984). These skeptics refer to intraindividual variability and individual and group differences as compelling evidence for a disassociation and separability of the areas of functioning (Cicchetti & Wagner, 1990; Kaplan, 1967).

As the debate regarding the integrity of organized development continues, the realm of atypical populations is increasingly the battlefield on which the issues are contested. Theory of mind (ToM) research among persons with autism is a provocative example. ToM refers to the abilities to understand that other persons have beliefs, desires, and intentions different than one's own. Among nonautistic children of average intelligence, ToM typically emerges at approximately 4 years. In initial work, ToM delays/deficits were cited uniquely among persons with autism (Baron-Cohen, 1989; Baron-Cohen, Leslie, & Frith, 1985, 1986). Their performance on ToM tasks was inferior to that of MA-matched nonautistic persons with mental retardation and of average intelligence. The delays/deficits were so pronounced that it appeared that the majority of persons with autism might never develop even the most basic aspects of ToM, although impairments were not evident in many related areas of functioning (Baron-Cohen, 1993; Leslie, 1991). This evidence among persons with autism of pronounced deficits/delays in one area but not in another is cited as primary support for the notion of a ToM module that unfolds independently of other components of cognitive functioning (e.g., Baron-Cohen, 1993; Leslie, 1991; Leslie & Thaiss, 1992).

However, other data from persons with autism and other developmental disorders are also used to challenge these notions of developmental modularity. The claim that ToM deficits are unique to persons with autism is questioned as these deficits are also found among persons with Down syndrome (Zelazo, Burack, Benedetto, & Frye, 1996) and other types of mental retardation (Yirmiya, Salmonica-Levy, Shulman, & Pilowsky, in press). More important, the specificity of the ToM deficits is challenged as there is considerable evidence that the development of ToM functioning is integrally related to more general aspects of cognitive functioning among persons with Down syndrome (e.g., Zelazo, Jacques, Burack, & Frye, 1996) and autism (Zelazo et al., 1996), as well as among children of average intelligence (Frye, Zelazo, & Palfai, 1995; Zelazo & Frye, in press). These findings are incongruent with the notion of a module of ToM development and consistent with traditional viewpoints of organized development, albeit within a more liberal framework.

Bounding the realm of atypical groups

Issues related to understanding specific atypical populations are primary contributions from the parent discipline of psychopathology to its descendant developmental psychopathology. But which groups are included within the rubric of atypical populations and what does the label entail?

As discussed by Sroufe and Rutter (1984) in their early formulation of developmental psychopathology, the discipline is relevant to persons from across the life-span who differ considerably with regard to type of, severity of, and proneness to deviant/delayed development. They experience any one or a number of developmental problems including those that are behavioral, intellectual, traditionally psychiatric, and/or emotional, or are exposed to risk due to physiological, genetic, environmental, social, and/or experiential anomalies. The source of the problem may be dated to any point or aspect of the person's history: for example, earlier generations in which ancestors were the focus of discrimination or moved to poverty-stricken areas; familial genetic patterns or personal anomalies in genetic structure; parental behaviors prior to, during, and/or following pregnancy; pre-, peri-, or postnatal complications or physical trauma; onset of identifiable disorder or problem behaviors at any age; and traumatic change(s) in family, community, or environment. The identified markers may be the sequelae of earlier problems, indices of current problems, or potentiating factors for problems later on. Thus, persons with any type of problem that might be related to developmental growth are appropriate for study.

In this broadened context, it is evident that the notion of psychopathology per se does not adequately describe the entire range of persons that fall within the realm. That construct may be suitable for the subgroup of persons with problems defined as psychopathological by current diagnostic criteria. However, it is not applicable to the other, larger, groups of persons who suffer from some type of nonpsychopathological disabilities such as mental retardation, sensory deficit, neurological impairment, or physical disability; or who are simply at developmental risk, but do not, and may never, manifest any symptoms of psychopathology or developmental compromise. In the study of at-risk populations, the emphasis is on understanding protective factors and resilience, the ability to overcome problematic situations (see Luthar, Chapter 20, this volume). In many cases, only a small percentage of persons at risk, albeit often a larger one than in the typical population, show any deleterious outcome of the risk-potentiating factor. Thus, children who experience maltreatment typically do not show psychopathology, but are of considerable interest due to the consideration of the effects of maltreatment on development and of the factors related to both positive and negative outcomes.

To extend further the notion of atypicality in this context, it may refer to any characteristic feature that can be distinguished and identified as potentially detrimental to development. Thus, this may include characteristics as diverse as left-handedness, femininity/masculinity, irritability, athletic incompetence, membership in a nonmajority culture or religion, low socioeconomic status, attendance at boarding school, or physical unattractiveness. In each of these cases, there is nothing inherently "wrong" with the individual. Yet, the pervasiveness of the characteristic/situation may result either in some aspect of functioning or social interaction that is unusual and potentially deleterious, thereby leading to compromised development. In sum, persons of any group are of interest within this discipline if there is any reason – physiological, cultural, societal, cognitive, social, and/or emotional – that their development has, is, will be, or might be negatively affected.

The issues of group and group comparisons: Methodological considerations

Although the emphasis on group identification and differentiation is inconsistent with the traditional developmental premise that basic developmental processes are common to all persons, it is central to developmental psychopathology. Exact specifications about groups and subgroups allow for the identification of unique patterns of development, specific markers of current deviance/delays, and distinct indicators of later problems. Accordingly, researchers must identify precisely one or more target groups/subgroups and one or more comparison groups/subgroups. The role of the nontarget subjects is as comparisons as they provide a standard with which to judge the development of the target persons. However, they are often inappropriately referred to as control rather than comparison subjects. The former term is, of course, relevant in clinical studies that include intervention and control conditions, each with subjects chosen randomly from the same population, but not in studies where persons from different populations are compared on the same conditions (Enns & Burack, in press).

In the case of behavioral research, the usual story is that members of the target population behave (or will behave) in a certain manner and this may be similar to or dissimilar from the comparison population(s). The efficacy of these comparison analyses is contingent upon (1) the precise classification and homogeneity of subject groups; (2) the choice and use of comparison populations; and (3) the matching of persons in the target and comparison groups (Enns & Burack, in press).

Defining the groups. Precise definitions of the subject groups and of their environments are essential to telling a specific story. Conclusions regarding specific group characteristics are only meaningful to the extent that the subjects are homogeneous with regard to relevant defining criteria. Comparisons across studies are informative only with precise delineation of criteria for subject inclusion. In cases of high concordance, there is greater reliability across studies, and where concordance is low, exact specifications at least alerts readers to a likely source of differences among studies. In particular, specifics need to be provided about the exact diagnostic or classification systems utilized for both the target and comparison subjects; the severity, duration, and extent of the disability or problematic environment; demographic variables; and the precise levels of functioning/age.

Unfortunately, findings are often confounded and/or obscured by a lack of precision in defining target group membership. In mental retardation research, this problem was so extensive that it became a primary impetus for Zigler's original articulation of the developmental approach to mental retardation (Zigler, 1967; 1969). He and his colleagues (e.g., Zigler, 1967, 1969; Zigler & Balla, 1982; Zigler & Hodapp, 1986) demonstrated that empirical work was typically clouded by heterogenous groupings of both persons with familial retardation and those with organic etiologies. Although not the first to make the distinction between the two groups, Zigler and colleagues formalized it as a necessary research strategy consistent with developmental theory (for a review, see Burack, 1990).

Zigler long argued that the development of persons with (nonorganic) familial mental retardation is the same as that of persons of average intelligence except that it occurs at a slower rate and with a lower asymptote (Zigler, 1967, 1969; Zigler & Hodapp, 1986). Thus, mental retardation per se is not related to specific cognitive deficits beyond the general developmental delay (for discussions, see Mundy & Kasari, 1990; Weiss, Weisz, & Bromfield, 1986; Weisz & Yeates, 1981; Weisz et al., 1982). Accordingly, he and his colleagues asserted that there should be no differences on cognitive performance between persons with familial retardation and MA-matched persons of average intelligence. However, differences are likely among persons with organic retardation since they suffer physiological damage (Burack, 1990; Zigler & Balla, 1982).

Subsequently, Burack, Hodapp, & Zigler (1988, 1990) extended this distinction between familial and organic mental retardation and argued for the differentiation among the several hundred etiological types of organic mental retardation, each of which has its own characteristic pattern of development. With increasingly sophisticated research technologies, there is growing awareness of the need to distinguish even among various subtypes of specific disorders, such as the trisomy 21, translocated, and mosaic subtypes of Down syndrome (Burack et al., 1988). In addition to its value for work with persons with mental retardation, this type of specificity in delineating among groups and subgroups is relevant to all populations that are studied in developmental psychopathology. It is relevant to within- and between-group differences and to distinguishing among the entire gamut of developmental problems, risk-potentiating factors, and protective characteristics.

Although precise grouping is always methodologically preferable, it has three primary drawbacks (Burack, 1990). First, precise classifications and diagnoses are often difficult. This may be due to insufficiently sophisticated technologies for accurately detecting abnormalities; to imprecise/unreliable systems for classifying behavioral, neurological, environmental, and/or biological problems; or to the lack of community interest and resources. Second, stricter inclusion criteria result in fewer eligible subjects (Burack, 1990). This is particularly problematic for the study of specific groups of atypical persons who are often few in number, difficult to identify, and hard to recruit. Third, precise groupings preclude generalizations to other populations. Each of these drawbacks is associated with a narrowed scope of the empirical implications. Thus, series of studies may be needed to construct a larger picture of the phenomenon across the various subgroups. It is useful to study several subgroups to determine which features are common to the larger population and which are unique to certain subgroups.

Choosing and matching the comparison groups. The choice of comparison group depends largely on the main story line (for a review of issues related to comparison strategies, see Wagner, Ganiban, & Cicchetti, 1990). If the intent is to determine whether the development or behavior of a target group is "normal," then the target group would be compared with the typical population. However, if the primary questions revolve around the uniqueness of certain aspects of the target group, then the comparison is between the target group and other atypical groups that are as similar as possible, except with regard to the specified characteristic(s). For example, persons with Down syndrome are compared with other persons with mental retardation to ensure that the specific deficit is related to Down syndrome and not to their generally lower IQ. With the heterogeneity of persons with mental retardation, however, there is a considerable chance that the story will be confounded by within-group differences in the comparison group. A more precise comparison is that of persons with Down syndrome and those with another syndrome such as fragile X or Williams syndrome. The larger the number of specific comparison groups, the greater certainty of statements regarding the uniqueness of characteristics to the target group.

With the continuing expansion of the domain of developmental psychopathology, there is an awareness of the potentially confounding effects of a multiplicity of group characteristics. Group differences with regard to any aspect of specific functioning, physiology, family life, the environment, community, or culture are often sources of empirical uncertainty. As specific atypical groups often vary among themselves as well as from the typical population on one or more of these variables, appropriate matching is both necessary but difficult. Often, more than one comparison group is needed in order to adequately establish a relationship between a specific disorder and a certain behavior level or pattern.

Particularly compelling examples of these difficulties in identifying appropriate comparison groups are evidenced in the work on the development of children of substance abusers (Luthar, Cushing, & McMahon, Chapter 19, this volume; Mayes & Bornstein, Chapter 8, this volume). These children are often subjected to direct physiological risks associated with in-utero exposure to alcohol and/or drugs, and to continued exposure after birth to maternal psychiatric problems, poor parenting related to continuing substance use, low socioeconomic status, and little community support. With this complex picture of interrelated physiological and environmental factors, it is impossible to isolate a group of persons who are similar on all counts except for the issue of interest, for example, in-utero cocaine exposure or parental abuse of alcohol.

Issues of matching by developmental level. Typically, a primary goal of matching in developmental psychopathology research involves equating groups by level of development and/or functioning. Little is learned when persons functioning at lower levels perform worse than those at higher levels. Thus, simple matching by CA is usually not sufficient in studies of persons with disorders. Although apparently obvious, developmentalists' insistence on MA-matching in studies comparing persons with mental retardation and those with average intelligence is a seminal contribution to the field of mental retardation (Zigler, 1967, 1969). Similar arguments were forwarded for studies of persons with schizophrenia (Chapman & Chapman, 1973), and autism (Burack, 1994; Frith & Baron-Cohen, 1987).

However, the choice of the measure of level of functioning (MA) is problematic. General measures of MA based on standardized IQ tests are typically used for this task, although several problems are cited. For example, the tests, the value of which are generally decried by skeptics, are of especially questionable utility with persons with many different types of impairment (e.g., sensory, motor, emotional, social, communication, or intellectual), from nonmajority cultures and backgrounds, or with behavior problems/styles that may impede task performance. Also, measures of general functioning are often, and particularly, inappropriate for atypical groups with specific profiles of strengths and weaknesses across domains, a common characteristic among atypical populations. The generalized measure may over- or undervalue levels of functioning in areas specifically related to the task at hand. For example, among persons with autism who typically score lower on verbal as compared with general MA, a general score will overestimate their ability for a language-based task. Accordingly, when persons with autism are assessed on tasks of language-related abilities, matching might best be accomplished with a measure of language functioning.

Issues of development and age

The developmental concern of age or level of functioning is primary to developmental psychopathology. Each age/developmental level is characterized by specific salient developmental issues and histories that are often quite different from those at other levels (Sroufe & Rutter, 1984). Therefore, the current and long-term effects of specific problems or encounters with environmental risk factors are largely determined by the person's age at that time. Problems that have disastrous effects at one point in development may be less relevant, or even inconsequential, at another (see Robbins & Rutter, 1990).

In all cases, developmental level at time of identification is instructional to predicting the sequelae of the problem since a defect/delay in a specific area of behavior may be manifested in several different ways throughout development (e.g., Kazdin, Chapter 12, this volume). For example, the long-term or cumulative effects of an early cognitive processing problem or inadequate environment may lead to profound deficiencies/delays in any number of domains of functioning, including those not obviously related to the original problems. Similarly, problems in other areas may be precursors to later deficiencies/delays in cognitive functioning or antecedents to deleterious family relationships (Sroufe & Rutter, 1984). Zigler's theoretical link between the lifetime history of failure experiences and subsequently impaired performance on cognitive tasks among persons with mental retardation is an example of this type of relationship (e.g., Zigler & Burack, 1989). Within the ever evolving complex web of interrelated internal and external components of the organism and its environment, significant deviations from the norm are likely to have far-reaching and enduring consequences, which eventually permeate the entire developing system.

Assessments at different ages/levels of functioning are central to creating a comprehensive picture of development for specific aspects of functioning. This is necessary since certain problems are apparent at an early age/level of functioning but not later on. In other cases, development appears typical at young ages when all that is required are simple tasks indicative of lower developmental levels, but is deficient with the more sophisticated and complicated tasks that reflect higher developmental levels. Thus, understanding the unique relationship between specific problems/disorders and relevant aspects of development entails longitudinal and/or series of cross-sectional studies in which functioning is considered at various ages/developmental levels.

Notions of delay and deficit. The joint contributions of, and differences between, development and psychopathology are particularly relevant to interpreting group differences. Within a typical psychopathology framework, the differences are the primary foci. They are viewed as indicative of some intraorganismic deviance, impairment, psychopathology, or at-risk status due to some extra- or intraorganismic factor. This is in contrast to the developmental perspective in which the onus is to explain behaviors or environments within a developmental framework, rather than as unique to specific groups.

One way in which specific areas of differences in functioning can be understood within a developmental framework is as a delay. Delays are identified by a level of functioning that is lower than that expected by CA or MA, but still related to them in some consistent and systematic way (Burack, 1992). In cases of general developmental delay, levels of functioning across domains are lower than among same-CA peers of average functioning, but commensurate with same-MA persons. However, in the common examples of specific developmental delay, a certain aspect of functioning is lower than predicted by either CA or general MA. Rather than labeling this phenomenon an example of deviance/impairment, the task is to identify a meaningful relationship between it and apparently related domains of functioning (Hodapp & Zigler, 1995).

In the case of developmental delays evident early in life, the tasks are often eventually attained. This is particularly common among basic processes of cognitive or social development that may be problematic in infancy and early childhood but are so basic that they are achieved by everyone who attains minimal levels of functioning. For example, in the case of theory of mind deficiencies among persons with autism, a developmental delay is indicated at least for some aspects of ToM that are not acquired at the expected general MA level, but are finally attained by those who ultimately reach concordant levels of functioning in related areas of cognitive development (Zelazo et al., 1996). Similarly, attentional problems among low-functioning persons with autism (Burack, 1994) may not be evident among their high-functioning peers (Burack et al., 1996) on a task in which developmental changes are evidenced in early childhood.

A deficit, rather than a delay, is only identified when a certain aspect of functioning is never acquired or, at least, not with the same quality. Often this is evident with regard to aspects of functioning that only become pervasive or significantly more sophisticated later in development and, therefore, may never be attained by certain persons. Yet, even in this case, the search for developmental sources of the deficit and the connections among precursors and concordant areas of functioning may elucidate the integral relationship between the apparent deficit and other components and processes of the developing organism. This quest to understand compromised development within the domain of developmental theory is central to the primary tasks of developmental psychopathology – the better understanding of both typical development and persons with atypicalities.

Summary

When I first began studying with Ed Zigler, he and colleagues were working on two books that would be published in the same year. One was on mental retardation (Zigler & Hodapp, 1986) and the other on adult psychiatric disorders (Zigler & Glick, 1986). Both volumes were enlightening and impressive with regard to the care and precision in presenting both developmental theory and information about the relevant disorders. But I was intrigued and, to be honest, somewhat skeptical in that both were based on the same developmental theory and even included some of the same figures. Armed with an undergraduate background in experimental psychology and some experimental psychopathology research, I couldn't understand how the same framework could be applied to such different populations. It seemed yet another case of researchers trying to capitalize on one idea by applying it to as many different situations as possible. Years later, as I think back, I realize that is the theoretical and ethical elegance of Ed's work. He worked with one idea, development. It applied to all people, regardless of backgrounds, problems, or stations in life. By extending the prevailing notions of development, Ed provided us a common lens with which to see persons who beforehand were only viewed with regard to their differences or atypicalities. Clearly, development is an evolving concept that still requires considerable expansion, but, as Ed has shown, it provides researchers and care providers an essential context for understanding and working with all persons.

References

Altman, I., & Rogoff, B. (1987). World views in psychology: Trait, interactional, organismic, and transactional perspectives. In D. Stokols & I. Altman (Eds.), *Handbook of environmental psychology* (pp. 7–40). New York: Wiley.

Baron-Cohen, S. (1989). The autistic child's theory of mind: A case of specific developmental delay. *Journal of Child Psychology and Psychiatry, 30,* 285–297.

Baron-Cohen, S. (1993). From attention-goal psychology to belief-desire psychology: The development of a theory of mind, and its dysfunction. In S. Baron-Cohen, H. Tager-Flusberg, & D. J. Cohen, *Understanding other minds: Perspectives from autism* (pp. 59–82). New York: Oxford University Press.

Baron-Cohen, S., Leslie, A. M., & Frith, U. (1985). Does the autistic child have a "theory of mind"? *Cognition, 21,* 37–46.

Baron-Cohen, S., Leslie, A. M., & Frith, U. (1986). Mechanical, behavioural, and intentional understanding of picture stories in autistic children. *British Journal of Developmental Psychology, 4,* 113–125.

Bennet-Gates, D., & Zigler, E. (in press). Resolving the developmental-difference debate: An evaluation of the triarchic and systems theory models. In J. A. Burack, R. M. Hodapp, & E. Zigler (Eds.), *Handbook of mental retardation and development.* New York: Cambridge University Press.

Binet, A., & Henri, V. (1895/1966). La psychologie individuelle. *L'Année Psychologie, 2,* 411–465.

Translated in R. J. Bernstein & E. G. Boring (Eds.), *A source book in the history of psychology* (pp. 428–433). Cambridge, MA: Harvard University Press.

Binet, A., & Simon, T. (1905). Sur la nécéssité d'établir un diagnostic scientifique des états inférieurs de l'intelligence. *L'Année Psychologie, 11,* 163–190.

Boring, E. G. (1929). *A history of experimental psychology.* New York: Appleton-Century.

Bronfenbrenner, U. (1979). *The ecology of human development: Experiments by nature and design* (chapter 2). Cambridge, MA: Harvard University Press.

Bronfenbrenner, U., Kessel, F., Kessen, W., & White, S. (1986). Toward a critical social history of developmental psychology. *American Psychologist, 41,* 1218–1230.

Burack, J. A. (1990). Differentiating mental retardation: The two-group approach and beyond. In R. M. Hodapp, J. A. Burack, & E. Zigler (Eds.), *Issues in the developmental approach to mental retardation* (pp. 27–48). New York: Cambridge University Press.

Burack, J. A. (1992). Debate and argument: Clarifying developmental issues in the study of autism. *Journal of Child Psychology and Psychiatry, 33,* 617–622.

Burack, J. A. (1994). Selective attention deficits in persons with autism: Preliminary evidence for an inefficient attentional lens. *Journal of Abnormal Psychology, 103,* 535–543.

Burack, J. A., Hodapp, R. M., & Zigler, E. (1988). Issues in the classification of mental retardation: Differentiating among organic etiologies. *Journal of Child Psychology and Psychiatry, 29,* 765–779.

Burack, J. A., Hodapp, R. M., & Zigler, E. (1990). Technical note: Toward a more precise understanding of mental retardation. *Journal of Child Psychology and Psychiatry, 31,* 471–475.

Burack, J. A., Iarroci, G., Mottron, L., Stauder, J., Robaey, P., & Brennan, J. M. (1996, August). *Visual filtering in persons with autism: A developmental perspective.* Paper presented at the XXVI International Congress of Psychology, Montreal, Canada.

Burack, J. A., & Zigler, E. (1989). Age at first hospitalization and premorbid social competence in schizophrenia and affective disorder. *American Journal of Orthopsychiatry, 59,* 188–196.

Bybee, J., & Zigler, E. (1992). Is outerdirectedness employed in a harmful or beneficial manner by normal and mentally retarded children? *American Journal on Mental Retardation, 96,* 512–521.

Bybee, J., & Zigler, E. (in press). Outerdirectedness in individuals with and without mental retardation: A review. In J. A. Burack, R. M. Hodapp, & E. Zigler (Eds.), *Handbook of mental retardation and development.* New York: Cambridge University Press.

Case, R. (1985). *Intellectual development: Birth to adulthood.* Orlando, FL: Academic Press.

Case, R. (1992). Neo-Piagetian theories of intellectual development. In H. Beilin & P. B. Pufall (Eds.), *Piaget's theory: Prospects and possibilities.* Hillsdale, NJ: Erlbaum.

Chapman, L. J., & Chapman, J. P. (1973). *Disordered thoughts in schizophrenia.* New York: Appleton-Century-Crofts.

Chomsky, N. (1980). On cognitive structures and their development. In M. Piatelli Palmarini (Ed.), *Language and learning: The debate between Jean Piaget and Noam Chomsky.* Cambridge, MA: Harvard University Press.

Cicchetti, D. (1984). The emergence of developmental psychopathology. *Child Development, 55,* 1–7.

Cicchetti, D. (1989a). A historical perspective on the discipline of developmental psychopathology. In J. Rolf, A. Masten, D. Cicchetti, K. H. Nuechterlein, & S. Weintraub (Eds.), *Risk and protective factors in the development of psychopathology* (pp. 2–28). Cambridge: Cambridge University Press.

Cicchetti, D. (1989b). Developmental psychopathology: Some thoughts on its evolution. *Development and Psychopathology, 1,* 1–4.

Cicchetti, D. (1989c). *The emergence of a discipline: Rochester symposium on developmental psychopathology.* Hillsdale, NJ: Erlbaum.

Cicchetti, D. (1993). Developmental psychopathology: Reactions, reflections, projections. *Developmental Review, 13,* 471–502.

Cicchetti, D., & Pogge-Hesse, P. (1982). Possible contributions of the study of organically retarded persons to developmental theory. In E. Zigler & D. Balla (Eds.), *Mental retardation: The developmental-difference controversy* (pp. 277–318). Hillsdale, NJ: Erlbaum.

Cicchetti, D., & Sroufe, L. A. (1978). An organizational view of affect: Illustration from the study of

Down's syndrome infants. In M. Lewis & L. Rosenblum (Eds.), *The development of affect* (pp. 309–350). New York: Plenum Press.

Cicchetti, D., & Wagner, S. (1990). Alternative assessment strategies for the evaluation of infants and toddlers: An organizational perspective. In S. J. Meisels & J. P. Shonkoff (Eds.), *Handbook of early childhood intervention* (pp. 246–277). New York: Cambridge University Press.

Curtiss, S. (1977). *Genie: A psycholinguistic study of a modern day "Wild-Child."* New York: Academic Press.

Dennis, W. (Ed.). (1948). *Readings in the history of psychology.* New York: Appleton-Century-Crofts.

Enns, J. T., & Burack, J. A. (in press). Attention and developmental psychopathology: The merging of disciplines. In J. A. Burack & J. T. Enns (Eds.), *Development, attention, and psychopathology.* New York: Guilford.

Esper, E. A. (1964). *A history of psychology.* Philadelphia: Saunders.

Evans, D. W., Hodapp, R. M., & Zigler, E. (1995). Mental and chronological age as predictors of age-appropriate leisure activity in children with mental retardation. *Mental Retardation, 33,* 120–127.

Fischer, K. W. (1980). A theory of cognitive development: The control and construction of hierarchies of skills. *Psychological Review, 87,* 477–531.

Flavell, J. (1982). Structures, stages, and sequences in cognitive development. In W. A. Collins (Ed.), *The concept of development: The Minnesota symposia on child psychology* (pp. 1–28). Hillsdale, NJ: Erlbaum.

Fodor, J. (1982). *The modularity of mind.* Cambridge, MA: MIT Press.

Frith, U., & Baron-Cohen, S. (1987). Perception in autistic children. In D. J. Cohen & A. Donnellan (Eds.), *Handbook of autism and pervasive developmental disorders* (pp. 85–102). Silver Spring, MD: Winston.

Frye, D. (1991). The end of development. In F. S. Kessel, M. H. Bornstein, & A. J. Sameroff (Eds.), *Contemporary constructions of the child: Essays in honor of William Kessen.* Hillsdale, NJ: Erlbaum.

Frye, D., Zelazo, P. D., & Palfai, T. (1995). Theory of mind and rule-based reasoning. *Cognitive Development, 10,* 483–527.

Gardner, H. (1983). *Frames of mind: The theory of multiple intelligence.* New York: Basic Books.

Gorenstein, E. E. (1992). *The science of mental illness.* New York: Academic Press.

Herrnstein, R. J., & Boring, E. G. (1966). *A source book in the history of psychology.* Cambridge, MA: Harvard University Press.

Hodapp, R. M. (1990). One road too many? Issues in the similar-sequence hypothesis. In R. M. Hodapp, J. A. Burack, & E. Zigler (Eds.), *Issues in the developmental approach to mental retardation* (pp. 49–70). New York: Cambridge University Press.

Hodapp, R. M., & Burack, J. A. (1990). What mental retardation teaches us about typical development: The examples of sequences, rates, and cross-domain relations. *Development and Psychopathology, 2,* 213–225.

Hodapp, R. M., Burack, J. A., & Zigler, E. (1990). The developmental perspective in the field of mental retardation. In R. M. Hodapp, J. A. Burack, & E. Zigler (Eds.), *Issues in the developmental approach to mental retardation* (pp. 3–26). New York: Cambridge University Press.

Hodapp, R. M., & Zigler, E. (1995). Past, present, and future issues in the developmental approach to mental retardation and developmental disabilities. In D. Cicchetti & D. J. Cohen (Eds.), *Manual of developmental psychopathology* (pp. 299–331). New York: Wiley.

Kaplan, B. (1967). Meditations on genesis. *Human Development, 10,* 65–87.

Kaufman, J., & Zigler, E. (1989). The intergenerational transmission of child abuse. In D. Cicchetti & V. Carlson (Eds.), *Child maltreatment: Theory and research on the causes and consequences of child abuse and neglect* (pp. 129–150). Cambridge: Cambridge University Press.

Kessen, W. (1962). Stage and structure in the study of young children. In W. Kessen & C. Kuhlman (Eds.), Thought in the young child. *Monographs of the Society for Research in Child Development, 27,* 53–70.

Kessen, W. (1983). The child and other cultural inventions. In F. S. Kessel & A. W. Siegel (Eds.), *The child and other cultural inventions* (pp. 26–39). New York: Praeger.

Kessen, W. (1984). Introduction: The end of the age of development. In R. Sternberg (Ed.), *Mechanisms of cognitive development* (pp. 1–17). San Francisco: Freeman.

Kingstone, A., Grabowecky, M., Mangun, G. R., & Gazzaniga, M. S. (in press). Paying attention to the brain. In J. A. Burack & J. T. Enns (Eds.), *Attention, development, and psychopathology*. New York: Guilford.

Lane, H. (1976). *The wild boy of Aveyron*. Cambridge, MA: Harvard University Press.

Leslie, A. M. (1991). The theory of mind impairment in autism: Evidence for a modular mechanism of development? In A. Whiten (Ed.), *Natural theories of mind*. Oxford: Blackwell.

Leslie, A. M., & Thaiss, L. (1992). Domain specificity in conceptual development: Neuropsychological evidence from autism. *Cognition, 43,* 225–251.

Lilienfield, S. O., & Marino, L. (1995). Mental disorder as a Roschian concept: A critique of Wakefield's "harmful dysfunction" analysis. *Journal of Abnormal Psychology, 104* (3), 411–420.

Luthar, S. S. (1995). Social competence in the school setting: Prospective cross-domain associations among inner-city teens. *Child Development, 66,* 416–429.

Luthar, S. S., & Zigler, E. (1991). Vulnerability and competence: A review of research on resilience in childhood. *American Journal of Orthopsychiatry, 61,* 6–22.

Luthar, S. S., Zigler, E., & Goldstein, D. (1992). Psychosocial adjustment among intellectually gifted adolescents: The role of cognitive-developmental and experiential factors. *Journal of Child Psychology and Psychiatry, 33,* 361–373.

Masten, A. S., Best, K. M., & Garmezy, N. (1990). Resilience and development: Contributions from the study of children who overcome adversity. *Development and Psychopathology, 2,* 425–444.

Meehl, P. E. (1960). The cognitive activity of the clinician. *American Psychologist, 15,* 19–27.

Mundy, P., & Kasari, C. (1990). The similar-structure hypothesis and differential rate of development in mental retardation. In R. M. Hodapp, J. A. Burack, & E. Zigler (Eds.), *Issues in the developmental approach to mental retardation* (pp. 71–92). New York: Cambridge University Press.

Overton, W. (1976). The active organism in structuralism. *Human Development, 19,* 71–86.

Overton, W., & Reese, H. (1973). Models of development: Methodological implications. In J. Nesselroad & H. Reese (Eds.), *Life span developmental psychology* (pp. 65–86). New York: Academic Press.

Piaget, J. (1970). Piaget's theory. In P. Mussen (Ed.), *Carmichael's manual of child psychology* (3rd ed., pp. 703–732). New York: Wiley.

Reese, H., & Overton, W. (1970). Models of development and theories of development. In L. R. Goulet & P. Baltes (Eds.), *Life span developmental psychology: Research and theory* 115–145. New York: Academic Press.

Robbins, L., & Rutter, M. (Eds.) (1990). *Straight and devious pathways from childhood to adulthood.* New York: Cambridge University Press.

Rutter, M. (1989). Pathways from childhood to adult life. *Journal of Child Psychology and Psychiatry, 30,* 23–51.

Sameroff, A. J. (1990). Neo-environmental perspectives on developmental theory. In R. M. Hodapp, J. A. Burack, & E. Zigler (Eds.), *Issues in the developmental approach to mental retardation* (pp. 93–113). New York: Cambridge University Press.

Sameroff, A. J., & Chandler, M. (1975). Reproductive risk and the continuum of caretaker casualty. In F. D. Horowitz, M. Hetherington, S. Scarr-Salapatek, & G. Siegel (Eds.), *Review of child development research* (Vol. 4, pp. 187–244). Chicago: University of Chicago Press.

Sroufe, L. A., & Rutter, M. (1984). The domain of developmental psychopathology. *Child Development, 55,* 17–29.

Wagner, S., Ganiban, J. M., & Cicchetti, D. (1990). Attention, memory, and perception in infants with Down syndrome: A review and commentary. In D. Cicchetti & M. Beeghly (Eds.), *Children with Down syndrome: A development perspective* (pp. 147–179). New York: Cambridge University Press.

Wakefield, J. C. (1992). The concept of mental disorder: On the boundary between biological facts and social values. *American Psychologist, 47,* 373–388.

Weiss, B., Weisz, J. R., & Bromfield, R. (1986). Performance of retarded and nonretarded persons on information processing tasks: Further tests of the similar structure hypothesis. *Psychological Bulletin, 100,* 157–175.

Weisz, J. R., & Yeates, K. (1981). Cognitive development in retarded and nonretarded development: Piagetian tests of the similar-structure hypothesis. *Psychological Bulletin, 90,* 153–178.

Weisz, J. R., Yeates, K., & Zigler, E. (1982). Piagetian evidence and the developmental-difference controversy. In E. Zigler & D. Balla (Eds.), *Mental retardation: The developmental-difference controversy* (pp. 213–276). Hillsdale, NJ: Erlbaum.

Weisz, J. R., & Zigler, E. (1979). Cognitive development in retarded and nonretarded persons: Piagetian tests of the similar sequence hypothesis. *Psychological Bulletin, 86,* 831–851.

Werner, H. (1957). The concept of development from a comparative and organismic point of view. In D. Harris (Ed.), *The concept of development.* Minneapolis: University of Minnesota Press.

Yirmiya, N., Salmonica-Levy, D., Shulman, C., & Pilowsky, T. (in press). Theory of mind abilities in individuals with autism, Down syndrome, and mental retardation of unknown etiology: The role of age and intelligence. *Journal of Child Psychology and Psychiatry.*

Zelazo, P. D., Burack, J., Benedetto, E., & Frye, D. (1996). Theory of mind and rule use in individuals with Down's syndrome: A test of the uniqueness and specificity claims. *Journal of Child Psychology and Psychiatry, 37,* 479–484.

Zelazo, P. D., & Frye, D. (in press). Cognitive complexity and control: A theory of the development of deliberate reasoning and intentional action. In M. Stamenov (Ed.), *Language structure, discourse, and access to consciousness.* Philadelphia: John Benjamins.

Zelazo, P. D., Jacques, S., Burack, J., & Frye, D. (1996). *The relationship between theory of mind and rule use.* Paper presented at the XIVth Biennial ISSBD Conference, Quebec City, Canada.

Zigler, E. (1963). Metatheoretical issues in developmental psychology. In M. Marx (Ed.), *Theories in contemporary psychology* (pp. 341–369). New York: Macmillan.

Zigler, E. (1967). Familial retardation: A continuing dilemma. *Science, 155,* 292–298.

Zigler, E. (1969). Developmental versus difference theories of mental retardation and the problem of motivation. *American Journal of Mental Deficiency, 73,* 536–556.

Zigler, E., & Balla, D. (Eds.). (1982). *Mental retardation: The developmental-difference controversy.* Hillsdale, NJ: Erlbaum.

Zigler, E., & Burack, J. A. (1989). Personality development and the dually diagnosed person. *Research in Developmental Disabilities, 10,* 225–240.

Zigler, E., & Glick, M. (1984). Paranoid schizophrenia: An unorthodox view. *American Journal of Orthopsychiatry, 54,* 43–71.

Zigler, E., & Glick, M. (1986). *A developmental approach to adult psychopathology.* New York: Wiley.

Zigler, E., & Hodapp, R. M. (1986). *Understanding mental retardation.* New York: Cambridge University Press.

Zigler, E., & Levine, J. (1983). Hallucinations versus delusions: A developmental approach. *Journal of Nervous and Mental Disease, 171,* 141–146.

Zigler, E., Levine, J., & Zigler, B. (1976). The relation between premorbid competence and paranoid-nonparanoid status in schizophrenia: A methodological and theoretical critique. *Psychological Bulletin, 83,* 303–313.

Zigler, E., & Phillips, L. (1961). Social competence and outcome in psychiatric disorder. *Journal of Abnormal and Social Psychology, 63,* 264–271.

Zilboorg, G. (1941). *A history of medical psychology.* New York: Norton.

8   The development of children exposed to cocaine

Linda C. Mayes and Marc H. Bornstein

> The growing incidence of such major social problems as poverty, homelessness, violence, crime, and substance abuse make it difficult for parents to create a decent life for themselves, much less protect their offspring from harm and plan for their children's future.
>
> – Zigler, 1995, p. ix

The problem of prenatal cocaine exposure is one well suited to the analysis of five central tenets in developmental psychopathology (Zigler & Glick, 1986; see, too, Cicchetti, 1993; Sroufe & Rutter, 1984). These tenets include (1) examining transactions between biological or genetic factors and external environmental conditions as related to patterns of disordered behavior; (2) focusing on individual patterns of adaptation and maladaptation; (3) allowing that individuals may shift back and forth between normal and abnormal modes of functioning as a consequence of differing developmental stressors and environmental conditions; (4) utilizing naturally occurring events or "experiments of nature" to understand the expected developmental ontogeny of specific functions; and (5) employing the conceptual frames and methods of multiple disciplines to study any one mode of function, adaptation, or behavior.

For children exposed to cocaine prenatally or postnatally, the outcome is not one of static impairment or dysfunction, but rather reflects a dynamic transaction between biologic conditions (resulting from prenatal cocaine exposure in the intrauterine environment) on fetal brain development and postnatal environments also shaped by ongoing parental substance abuse (e.g., Mayes & Bornstein, 1995, in press a). Prenatal cocaine exposure does not appear to exert a singular effect on any one developmental function, nor does any single effect appear to express itself in all infants (e.g., Mayes, Bornstein, Chawarska, & Granger, 1995). Some prenatally cocaine exposed infants and young children may develop adaptively and along essentially normal trajectories in their first years of life, a clinical observation that raises important questions about both what constitute detrimental prenatal levels of exposure and what the postnatal environmental conditions that mediate pos-

This chapter summarizes selected aspects of our collaborative research and portions of the text have appeared in our previous scientific publications cited in the references. We thank D. Cohen and R. Schottenfeld for their support of our studies of prenatal cocaine exposure.

itive versus negative effects of prenatal cocaine exposure may be. For the child and parent, prenatal cocaine exposure presents risks for multiple other problems, such as involvement in violence and crime, homelessness, poor school performance as well as early dropout, and multigenerational drug abuse, problems that trap both parent and child in poverty and discord (Aber & Zigler, 1981; Kaufman & Zigler, 1989). These factors influence children's level of adaptation at any given point in time and may contribute to shifts between adaptive and maladaptive patterns of response over the course of development (Luthar & Zigler, 1991).

Prenatal cocaine exposure also offers an "experiment of nature" in that the developing fetal brain is exposed to an agent that may have potentially teratogenic effects on specific developmental capacities. In the case of prenatal cocaine exposure, as well as adult substance abuse, capacities that are potentially affected involve the regulation of states of attention and arousal, which in turn may affect information processing, learning, and social relatedness (Bornstein, Mayes, & Tamis-LeMonda, 1996; Mayes & Bornstein, 1995 in press a, in press b) and are sensitive to environmental disruption and discord. Finally, studies of cocaine exposure require a multidisciplinary approach that draws at least on the following fields: neurobiological models of brain development, neuropharmacological data on the effects of cocaine at the level of the neurotransmitter, behavioral teratology, pediatrics, developmental psychology, psychiatry and the treatment of substance abuse, child psychiatry, sociology, and social policy. Understanding the methods for studying prenatal cocaine exposure and the implications of findings in this field calls for the integration of data from each of these disciplines, from animal as well as human models, and from individual or small group studies as well as population surveys.

Historical and social context of cocaine abuse

Viewed at close range, the contemporary world of cocaine abuse is all encompassing in its origins and outcomes (Mayes & Bornstein, in press b). It cuts across gender and socioeconomic class (and did so in the late 19th as it does in the late 20th century; Musto, 1973). It involves individuals who come to cocaine abuse after extraordinarily traumatic life events, who began abuse as a way of being with peers, who started their abuse in early adolescence and have known little else since, and who use cocaine as a means of remediating what they perceive to be personal deficits. The cocaine abusing adult may continue to attend school or work regularly and maintain productivity in a profession, or may be a high school dropout, unemployed, and homeless. The addict may have sustained years of heavy use with little visible effect or be seriously physically disabled and psychologically ill after only a few years of use (Khalsa, Anglin, Paredes, Potegan, & Potter, 1993). The addicted adult may have tried repeatedly to stop use or adamantly refuse to acknowledge any degree of dependence or accept any intervention. In short, there is no single pattern to cocaine abuse, but in the past decade two larger trends relevant to this essay have raised cause for concern.

The first is the increasing use of cocaine and other substances of abuse among women living in impoverished inner city neighborhoods (Amaro, Zuckerman, & Cabral, 1989; Zuckerman, Frank, Hingson, & Amaro, 1989). Some major cities in the United States report that up to 50% of women receiving prenatal care at inner-city hospital clinics have used cocaine regularly during their pregnancy and for several years before (Amaro, Fried, Cabral, & Zuckerman, 1990; Osterloh & Lee, 1989); and the majority of urban areas across the United States report a persistently high (10% to 20%) incidence of cocaine abuse among women of childbearing age (Chasnoff, Landress, & Barrett, 1990; Frank et al., 1988). The second related trend is the increasing number of children born to cocaine-using women and/or growing up with substance abusing parents (Scherling, 1994). No one estimate is certain, but currently perhaps more than 350,000 children in the United States are born each year to mothers who have used cocaine with or without other substances (such as alcohol, marijuana, or tobacco) throughout their pregnancy (Besharov, 1990; Gomby & Shiono, 1991). These twin trends have, in turn, led to two expanding areas of research, the first focusing on the effects of prenatal cocaine exposure on children's development (e.g., Mayes & Bornstein, in press b), and the second on studies of the characteristics of women who abuse substances and the effects of that substance abuse on their ability to parent (e.g., Mayes, 1995).

The more extensive study and concern about the effects of cocaine abuse on children and on maternal and family functioning are special themes of contemporary focus in light of the so-called crack/cocaine epidemic. This chapter reviews the effects of cocaine on infant and child development; we begin with a summary of available data on developmental outcomes in children exposed prenatally to cocaine. How cocaine abuse affects parental functioning is the second area reviewed. We conclude with a summary of prominent pathways through which the effects of prenatal cocaine exposure on basic neurodevelopmental functions may be mediated.

The potential effect of prenatal cocaine exposure on developing brain is a central question that guides studies of prenatal cocaine exposure. However, other factors, including notably the general postnatal environment and parental characteristics, also exert both direct effects on developing brain as well as on the developmental and behavioral domains regarded as the markers of direct central nervous system effects. Investigators seeking to understand the influences of prenatal cocaine exposure on children's psychological development face the dilemma that cocaine affects development through multiple pathways and that rarely, if ever, is it possible to speak of a "pure" cocaine effect or of a singular and identifiable effect on one aspect of brain development. Further, no one pathway of cocaine exposure on development appears to be primary – each pathway contributes variance to the relation between prenatal or continuing exposure and the child's developmental status – and so adequate study of the cocaine-exposed child must also involve studies of parenting and the child's general environment. In other words, because cocaine is a teratologic agent with profound effects on the child's immediate parental and global social environment, as well as the child's prenatal development, studies of the outcome of prenatally cocaine-exposed infants necessarily involve multivariate, multitime biologic-environment transaction models (Bergeman & Plomin, 1989).

Throughout the sections that follow, the different potential pathways of cocaine effect on fetal development will be referenced to an overall model shown in Figure 8.1. This model indicates how the direct biologically related effect of cocaine on brain development may be mediated and shaped by environmental conditions and by postnatal experiences. It is important to note also that Figure 8.1 presents an inclusive, multivariate, but nonetheless theoretical model that is specifically focused on the developmental domain of arousal regulation. The specific focus on arousal regulation is guided by the available data from both studies of animals and human infants (see next two sections), and, even in these areas, there are not a sufficient number of studies to permit estimates of the range the effects sizes reported. Moreover, with the exception of data from animal models regarding the effects of prenatal cocaine exposure on brain development and findings regarding infants in the first 2 years of life (see next section), there are few data available to address all of the pathways included in the figure. In particular, much more research is needed to address the effects of cocaine use on the child's parenting environment and on the effect of continued parental postnatal use on children's development. To date, the principal focus of the majority of studies has been on prenatal cocaine exposure; thus, the section on postnatal effects draws largely from other literature on the effects of dysfunctional parenting and chaotic environments on outcome.

Prenatal cocaine exposure and child outcome

Cocaine and brain development

Cocaine influences brain development directly through effects on developing neurotransmitter systems critical to neuronal differentiation and brain structure formation and indirectly through effects on blood flow to developing fetal brain (see reviews by Mayes, 1994; Mayes & Bornstein, 1995 in press a, in press b). Cocaine is a central nervous system stimulant that acts through the monoaminergic neurotransmitter systems including dopamine, norepinephrine, and serotonin (5-HT) (Gawin & Ellinwood, 1988; Wise, 1984). The primary central nervous system action of cocaine occurs at the level of neurotransmitter release, reuptake, and recognition at the synaptic junction. Cocaine blocks the reuptake of dopamine, norepinephrine, and 5-HT at the level of the synapse (Swann, 1990), a process that is primarily responsible for inactivation of neurotransmitters. Blocking reuptake leaves more dopamine, norepinephrine, and 5-HT available within the synaptic space (and, thus, in the peripheral blood as well) and results in enhanced activity

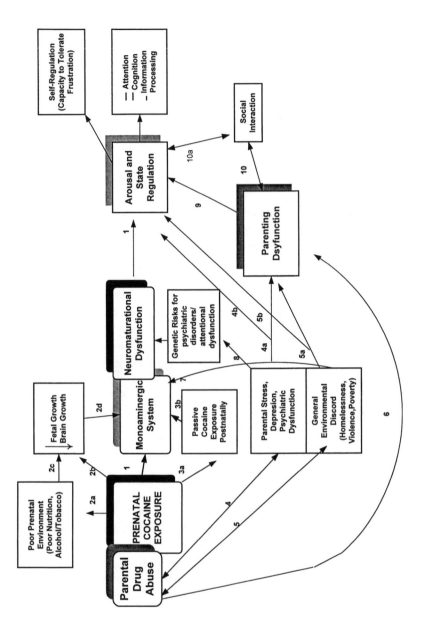

Figure 8.1: Conceptual model for study of cocaine exposure in infants and children

of these agents in the central nervous system (Goeders & Smith, 1983) with associated physiologic reactions (e.g., tachycardia and vasoconstriction with hypertension) and behaviors (e.g., euphoria and increased motor activity) (see Richie & Greene, 1985).

Areas of the brain regulated by the monoaminergic neurotransmitter systems are involved in a number of basic neuropsychological functions including arousal and attention modulation and the regulation of anxiety and other emotional states (Mayes, 1994). In fetal brain development, monoaminergic neurotransmitters are also critical to the definition of brain structure and neuronal formation through their effects on cell proliferation, neural outgrowth, and synaptogenesis (Lauder, 1988; Mattson, 1988). Thus, because cocaine alters the metabolism of monoaminergic neurotransmitters, cocaine exposure in early brain development may influence the formation and remodeling of monoaminergic-rich brain structures (Figure 8.1, Path 1). Additionally, cocaine may change the actual ontogeny of monoaminergic neurotransmitter systems and thus alter monoaminergic-dependent brain growth and differentiation monoaminergic-rich areas (Akbari & Azmitia, 1992; Akbari et al., 1992; Dow-Edwards, 1989; Dow-Edwards, Freed, & Milhorat, 1988).

Prenatal cocaine exposure also alters blood flow to the developing fetal brain through norepinephrine-related decreased uteroplacental blood flow, severe uteroplacental insufficiency (acute and chronic), maternal hypertension, and fetal vasoconstriction (Moore, Sorg, Miller, Key, & Resnik, 1986; Woods, Plessinger, & Clark, 1987). Reduction in placental blood flow in turn results in a relative state of fetal hypoxia, which may generally compromise brain growth instead of, or in addition to, specifically affecting monoaminergic systems. Various congenital malformations (e.g., limb reductions, renal anomalies) seen among infants who were prenatally exposed to cocaine have been linked to the effects of cocaine on fetal vascular tone at critical times in morphogenesis (Bingol, Fuchs, Diaz, Stone, & Gromisch, 1987; Hoyme et al., 1990; Zuckerman & Frank, 1992). Similarly, the effect of cocaine use on placental blood flow probably contributes to the relation between cocaine and fetal growth – low birth weight and microcephaly – observed by several investigators (Fulroth, Phillips, & Durand, 1989; Hadeed & Siegel, 1989; MacGregor, Keith, Chasnoff, et al., 1987; Mayes, Granger, Frank, Bornstein, & Schottenfeld, 1993; Oro & Dixon, 1987; Ryan, Ehrlich, & Finnegan, 1987). Chronic cocaine users also frequently report marked appetite reduction (Scherling, 1994), thus compromising fetal nutrition, as well as regular use of other drugs, including alcohol, tobacco, and opiates (Amaro et al., 1989; Frank et al., 1988). Both alcohol and tobacco adversely affect fetal growth, and there are potentially direct effects of alcohol exposure on developing fetal brain (Day, 1992; Streissguth, 1992). Combinations of poor nutrition, uteroplacental insufficiency, and polydrug use during pregnancy further contribute to an overall poorer state of maternal health and increased risk for fetal growth retardation and impaired fetal outcome (Figure 8.1, Paths 2a, 2b, 2c, and 2d).

Developmental outcomes in prenatally cocaine-exposed children

Behavioral and cognitive outcome measures beyond the neonatal period in studies of children exposed to cocaine prenatally have, for the most part, utilized general measures of developmental competency (Mayes, 1996), such as the Bayley Scales of Infant Development (BSID; Bayley, 1969, 1993). In early reports of infants exposed to cocaine as well as combinations of heroin, methadone, and marijuana, cocaine exposure was predictively linked to moderate to severe developmental delays across diverse developmental domains (see Mayes, 1992). Subsequent studies have reported mild to no impairments in overall developmental functioning in cocaine-exposed children compared to non–cocaine-exposed groups (Mayes, 1994; Scherling, 1994; Zuckerman & Frank, 1992). Chasnoff and colleagues reported on the developmental profiles of a group of cocaine/alcohol-exposed 24-month-olds followed from birth compared with the performance of non–cocaine-, but marijuana- and/or alcohol-, exposed children (Chasnoff, Griffith, Freier, & Murray, 1992). Mothers of infants in the non–cocaine-using comparison groups were similar to the cocaine-using mothers in terms of socioeconomic status, age, marital status, and tobacco use during pregnancy but, importantly, both groups were drug-exposed. On repeated developmental assessments using the BSID at 3, 6, 12, 18, and 24 months, there were no mean differences across groups in either the mental or motor domains.

These investigators cautioned, however, that a higher percentage of cocaine-exposed infants scored two standard deviations below the mean on standard scores of mental development (Chasnoff et al., 1992). Also, there was a high rate of attrition from the original cohort, but whether the attrition biases the sample toward families of lower risk is not clear. Cocaine-exposed children from this cohort followed through age 3 years continued to show no differences from non–cocaine-exposed controls on overall performance on the Stanford-Binet, although the cocaine-exposed group scored significantly lower on verbal reasoning (Griffith, Azuma, & Chasnoff, 1994), a finding, even though not yet replicated by other investigators, that may have implications for later learning. Other researchers have reported similar failures to find deficits on general measures of developmental competency in cocaine-exposed children in the first, second, and third years of life (e.g., Anisfeld et al., 1991; Arendt, Singer, & Minnes, 1993; Billman, Nemeth, Heimler, & Sasidharan, 1991). Findings such as these have resulted in the re-evaluation of early concerns about global developmental delay in prenatally cocaine-exposed children.

However, studies of more specific developmental functions suggest that cocaine-exposed infants and young children may exhibit impairments in attention and state or arousal regulation (Mayes & Bornstein, 1995 in press a, in press b). For example, it has been reported that, despite no apparent differences on either motor or mental indices on the BSID, cocaine-exposed 24-month-olds appear to have more difficulty attending to several objects at the same time, and they fail more often in structuring an approach to a nonfamiliar task in the context of developmental assessments (cited in Hawley & Disney, 1992).

In the few studies to examine more specific neurodevelopmental functions, such as attention or state and arousal regulation, differences between cocaine-exposed and non–cocaine-exposed infants have been reported in startle responsivity, neonatal orientation, motor and state regulatory capacities, habituation, recognition memory, and reactivity to novelty. In the newborn period, the habituation response, as usually measured by the Neonatal Behavioral Assessment Scales (NBAS; Brazelton, 1984), reflects the infants' reactivity or arousal response to the presentation of novel stimuli. After the neonatal period, habituation and the complementary processes of novelty responsiveness and recognition memory provide information about the organization of looking behavior and attention (Bornstein, 1985a). When a stimulus is presented continuously or repeatedly, the infant's attention to the stimulus declines, a decrement referred to as habituation. If a novel stimulus is presented subsequently, the infant reorients and attends to the novel information showing novelty responsiveness. The habituation process and related novelty responsiveness represent early forms of some type of information processing and encoding by the child (Bornstein, 1985a; Bornstein & Mayes, 1992; Colombo & Mitchell, 1990; Lewis, Goldberg, & Campbell, 1969; Lewis & Brooks-Gunn, 1981). Habituation measures discriminate among samples of infants differing in risk status (reviewed in Bornstein, 1985a; Mayes & Bornstein, in press).

Attention indexed by habituation also involves arousal and arousal regulation (Mayes & Bornstein, 1995, in press b), and the development of attention is directly linked to the development of control of states of sleep and wakefulness (see Thoman & Ingersoll, 1989). Sustained attention to a novel stimulus entails not only the active intake of information but also requires more tonic alteration in state or arousal. A deficit in the modulation of arousal or in the activation of states of arousal will influence attentional processes and habituation performance (Pribram & McGuiness, 1975; Ruff, 1988). Links between the dopaminergic system and arousal regulation as well as attentional mechanisms that are indexed by the habituation process (B. Coles & Robbins, 1989) make it plausible to hypothesize that prenatal cocaine exposure could affect the infant's reactivity or regulation of arousal to novel stimulation as well as early habituation performance and the processes generally related to habituation, such as novelty responsiveness.

Several studies have examined state regulatory and habituation processes in newborns and infants 3 to 12 months of age. Anday, Cohen, Kelley, and Leitner (1989) observed that cocaine-exposed newborns showed increased startle response to reflex-eliciting stimuli as well as to specific auditory stimuli. In the neonatal period, findings of neurobehavioral impairments including increased irritability, poor state control, and impaired orientation as measured by the NBAS (Brazelton, 1973) have also been reported but are inconsistent among investigative groups (C. Coles, Platzman, Smith, James, & Falek, 1992; Chasnoff, Griffith, Freier, & Murray, 1989;

Eisen et al., 1990; Mayes et al., 1993). Chasnoff and colleagues (1989) found impairments of orientation, motor, and state regulatory behaviors on the NBAS. Eisen and colleagues (1990), studying neonates who were urine-screen positive only for cocaine at birth and whose mothers denied opiate use, and Mayes et al. (1993) found significant deficits in cocaine-exposed infants in habituation performance as assessed by the NBAS.

After the newborn period, Struthers and Hansen (1992) reported impaired recognition memory among cocaine- or amphetamine-exposed infants compared to non–drug-exposed infants between 7 and 8 months of age. Similarly, Alessandri, Sullivan, Imaizumi, and Lewis (1993) reported impaired contingent learning well into the second half of the first year of life in cocaine-exposed infants. Mayes, Bornstein, Chawarska, and Granger (1995) found that, compared to a non–drug-exposed group, infants exposed prenatally to cocaine were significantly more likely to fail to begin a habituation procedure and significantly more likely to react with irritability early in the procedure. Cocaine-exposed infants show more irritability and crying, that is, state changes indicative of an overaroused state, with the presentations of novel stimuli (Mayes, Bornstein, Chawarska, Haynes, & Granger, 1995). However, during habituation procedures the majority of cocaine-exposed infants showed a habituation response, and among those who did there were no significant differences between cocaine- and non–cocaine-exposed infants in habituation performance or in recovery to a novel stimulus (Mayes, Bornstein, Chawarska, & Granger, 1995). In summary, available findings suggest that the neurodevelopmental effects of prenatal cocaine exposure may be expressed primarily in the general area of arousal regulation experienced in novel or stimulating situations. Impaired arousal regulation in turn influences attention and reactivity and the child's response to both nonsocial and social situations (Mayes, Bornstein, Chawarska, Haynes, & Granger, 1995).

The parenting environment of cocaine-exposed children

The biologically or genetically based developmental trajectory of capacities for the regulation of states of arousal and attention is also sensitive to environmental influences and parental input (Figure 8.1, Paths 4a, 4b, 5a, 5b, 6, 7, 8, and 9; Gable & Isabella, 1992; Hofer, 1994). Thus, the relation of prenatal cocaine exposure to impairments in such basic functions may also be moderated by the child's parenting environment. The comprehensive evaluation of parenting behaviors among cocaine-abusing adults is a relatively neglected area of research (Mayes, 1995): It is not clear whether cocaine-abusing parents have impaired relationships with their children that differ from impairments found in other dysfunctional or disadvantaged families not affected by substance abuse, and, if they do, are the patterns of parenting impairment uniquely related to the effects of cocaine on adult psychological functioning.

Observations of parenting behaviors based on animal models of cocaine exposure suggest that cocaine use during pregnancy alters mothers' behaviors when caring for their own infants and that such alterations in turn influence the behavior of the offspring. For example, in the rat, cocaine-treated mothers were significantly more aggressive to intruders when protecting their young than either non–cocaine-treated mothers or cocaine- or non–cocaine-treated foster mothers (Heyser, Molina, & Spear, 1992). Infant behavior was also altered in that, regardless of the prenatal exposure conditions, infants reared by cocaine-treated mothers were more quickly aggressive to challenge (Goodwin et al., 1992). Animal models for parenting behavior in substance-abusing conditions are only recently being developed. They may find value in suggesting hypotheses for interactive effects between pre- and postnatal exposure conditions on both infant outcomes and parenting behaviors (Mayes, 1995) but should be evaluated with caution as they are not a direct model for more complicated parenting relations among humans.

Parenting functions among substance-abusing human adults have been examined primarily with indirect measures, such as surveys of the incidence of child abuse and of the home environment to assess the adequacy of the child's physical care. That parents who are actively abusing cocaine and other substances have problems caring for their children is indicated in part by the increased incidence of physical abuse and neglect in such families (Black & Mayer, 1980), and by the proportionately higher than national average numbers of children from substance-abusing families who come to foster care or other types of placements (Lawson & Wilson, 1980; Rogosch, Cicchetti, Shields, & Toth, 1995). A case–control study of all consecutive emergency room or hospital evaluations of injuries thought to be secondary to abuse showed that children who were physically abused were significantly more likely to come from households with cocaine-abusing adults as parents (Wasserman & Leventhal, 1993).

Other commonly used measures of parenting among substance-abusing adults include questionnaires that assess the level of stress or competency parents experience in caring for their children (e.g., Abidin, 1983), the adult's own experience of being parented (e.g., Bernardi, Jones, & Tennant, 1989), or the parent's perceptions of his or her role (Wellisch & Steinberg, 1980). On measures such as these, substance-abusing mothers report a broad range of difficulties in parenting including reliance on a more disciplinarian, threatening style of parenting and negative reinforcement (Bauman & Dougherty, 1983). However, self-report instruments are often distorted or inaccurate when completed by substance-abusing adults and do not address the question of whether active cocaine abuse limits or distorts mothers' immediate interactions with their children.

Direct observations of interactions between substance-abusing parents and their children have utilized measures of children's and mothers' responses to brief separations and of interactions between mothers and infants. Studies of separation paradigms and attachment patterns among the children of substance-abusing adults suggest an increased incidence of disrupted or disturbed relationships between parents and children and higher rates of disorganized attachment behaviors (group D;

Main & Solomon, 1986; Rodning, Beckwith, & Howard, 1989, 1991). Drug-exposed children reared in foster care may be less likely to be insecurely attached than those living with their biological mothers (Rodning et al., 1989), although these differences in attachment patterns by rearing conditions are not consistent (Rodning et al., 1991). Failure to find a difference between prenatally exposed infants in foster care and those in the care of their biological mothers reflects in part the fact that children in foster care have often been in their biological parents' care for months to years and have also experienced the disruptions of more than one foster placement. Indeed, the child's caregiving situation at the time of the attachment assessment does not necessarily reflect the situation even a month earlier. (Even defining who is the primary caregiver is a difficult problem in studies of substance-abusing parents and reflects a difficult dilemma in all studies of parenting of cocaine-exposed children because, in many substance-abusing families, a child may be in the care of many different adults in the course of a day or week.) Moreover, disordered attachment patterns may not be specific to substance abuse but may be more reflective of the overall increased disorganization, stress, abuse, and exposure to violence among drug-using families (Carlson, Cicchetti, Barnett, & Braunwald, 1989; O'Connor, Sigman, & Brill, 1987).

Direct observational measures of child and parent together have been employed less often with substance-abusing families and have mainly included measures of parental involvement and intrusiveness (e.g., for heroin/methadone-using families, Bernstein, Jeremy, Hans, & Marcus, 1984, and Bernstein, Jeremy, & Marcus, 1986; for cocaine-using adults, K. Burns, Chethik, Burns, & Clark, 1991; Gottwald & Thurman, 1994). Gottwald and Thurman (1994) reported that cocaine-using mothers spent significantly more time disengaged from their 12- to 48-hour-old newborns than did non–drug-using mothers. Bernstein and colleagues (1984) reported that mothers participating in a methadone-maintenance program in comparison to a non–opiate-addicted group reacted less often and less contingently to their 4-month-olds' communicative bids and tried less often to elicit or encourage communicative play with their infants. Similar impairments in maternal responsiveness were reported by Burns and colleagues (1991) in a group of five polydrug using mothers, two of whom used cocaine primarily, with no comparison group. These mothers infrequently responded to their infants' cues. Far more work is needed using direct observational measures of interactions between cocaine-using parents and their children.

Apparently dysfunctional parenting behavior may also relate to impairments in the infant (Figure 8.1, Path 9; Lewis & Rosenblum, 1974). Diverse infant characteristics and infant behaviors, related to the effects of prenatal drug exposure (as with fetal alcohol effects or narcotic withdrawal or the more general contributions of prenatal drug exposure to prematurity and intrauterine growth retardation; Zuckerman, Frank, Hingson, & Amaro, 1989), may render the infant more difficult to care for. Only recently have investigators of parenting among substance-abusing mothers begun to employ interactive models that examine how variations in infant characteristics also influence maternal behaviors (Griffith & Freier, 1992). For example, in a study of maternal alcohol use, mother–infant interaction, and infant cognitive development, O'Connor, Sigman, and Kasari (1992, 1993) reported that maternal prenatal alcohol use was associated with impaired infant affective regulation, which in turn influenced mother–infant interaction and subsequent infant cognitive outcome. Postnatal maternal alcohol consumption did not relate to maternal interactive characteristics.

More detailed studies of specific alterations in parenting associated with substance abuse are needed not only because developmental trajectories for domains such as attention and arousal regulation in infants are influenced by parental interactions (Figure 8.1, Path 10) but also to guide the design of more effective interventions for substance-abusing parents (Bornstein, 1985b; Bornstein & Lamb, 1992; Bornstein & Tamis-LeMonda, 1990; Tamis-LeMonda & Bornstein, 1989). Infant attention, exploration, and use of language are influenced by maternal activity, including such behaviors as responding and directing the infant's attention to the environment, naming and pointing, or elaborating on child play. Although attention and reactivity reflect neuropsychological functions that are biologically based, these functions are sensitive to parental level of environmental organization, responsiveness, and adaptability. Problems in the regulation of arousal in infants may also contribute to infants' being more difficult to care for, which further influences the potentially compromised cocaine-abusing adult's ability to respond to and support that particular infant's needs (Figure 8.1, Path 10 and 10a). Finally, because of the debilitating effects of chronic cocaine abuse on overall adult psychological health, parental responsiveness and adaptation may deteriorate over time (Mayes, Feldman, Bornstein, Haynes, Schottenfeld, & Granger, in press) or fluctuate depending on the severity of the cocaine abuse and intoxication (Figure 8.1, Path 10).

Transactional pathways of postnatal cocaine effects on child development

As outlined in the preceding sections, several transactional pathways partially explain the effects of cocaine on specific functions in children such as attention and reactivity or arousal regulation, areas for which the most suggestive data exist regarding prenatal cocaine effects on development. In this section, we make explicit four possible pathways of *postnatal* cocaine-related developmental effects. They are additional to prenatal direct effects of cocaine on developing monoaminergic neurotransmitter systems in fetal brain (Figure 8.1, Path 1), on overall fetal brain and physical growth through placental vasoconstriction (Figure 8.1, Path 2b), and to the relation between cocaine addiction and parenting dysfunction that may be expressed in the immediate neonatal period (Figure 8.1, Paths 9 and 10). Each of these pathways may express itself on attention and arousal regulation and have its effect shaped by the infant's difficulties in these areas. Thus, these pathways are bidirectional and interactive. Each pathway also carries considerable risk or is a marker for parents' continued involvement with drugs and impaired parenting function. They may increase the child's likelihood of later involvement in substance abuse, poor school performance and early dropout, and chronic entrapment in poverty, unemployment, and social isolation. It is important to note that, in contrast to studies of the effects of prenatal cocaine exposure on fetal growth and brain development, the pathways we outline next have received much less investigative attention.

The first of these pathways for the effect of cocaine on development is through the child's continued postnatal cocaine exposure via passive absorption of crack smoke (Figure 8.1, Path 3b; Kjarasch, Glotzer, Vinci, Wietman, & Sargent, 1991). Brain development continues through at least the first 12 months postnatally with extensive synaptic remodeling, pruning, and actual structural refinement, and monoaminergic neurotransmitter systems are involved in aspects of postnatal brain growth (Goldman-Rakic, 1987). Because of the effect of cocaine on monoaminergic neurotransmitter levels and receptor sensitivity, passive postnatal exposure to cocaine may affect the crucial brain processes of synaptic remodeling, loss, and formation.

The second pathway relates to issues that bring adults to cocaine abuse (Figure 8.1, Path 4). For many substance-abusing adults, psychiatric disorders, such as depression or even attention deficit disorder, appear to predate substance abuse per se and, at least for some, may represent a significant factor in the adult's initial experimentation with cocaine or other substances (Khantzian, 1985; Khantzian & Khantzian, 1984; Woods, Eyler, Behnke, & Conlon, 1991). This circumstance will have two consequences: (1) Drug-abusing parents will suffer other psychiatric symptoms and associated psychological and social disorders; and (2) drug-abusing parents may pass to their offspring an increased genetic risk for these psychiatric conditions.

The association between active substance abuse and major psychopathology has been noted by several investigators. Among substance-abusing adults, the incidence of major depression, recurrent and early psychiatric hospitalizations, and, for men, conduct problems often resulting in criminal prosecution is higher than that of the general population (Mirin, Weiss, Griffin, & Michael, 1991; Rounsaville et al., 1991). Substance abusers' parents and siblings also experience a high rate of psychiatric disorders such as depression and antisocial personality disorder, which are comorbid with substance abuse (Mirin et al., 1991; Rounsaville et al., 1991). This comorbidity appears to be a general conveyance of risk and an elevation in the incidence of several disorders (Luthar, Anton, Merikangas, & Rounsaville, 1992; Merikangas, Rounsaville, & Prusoff, 1992). Parental death or desertion, marital discord, divorce, substance abuse, and high rates of physical and sexual abuse have also been identified as characteristics of the families of origin of substance abusers (Aber & Zigler, 1981; Chambers, Hinesby, & Moldestad, 1970; Raynes, Climent,

Patch, & Ervin, 1974; Zigler, 1995). Rounsaville and colleagues (1982) reported that disruptive events such as family violence, hospitalizations, or unexpected separations were common historical incidents in the early experiences of substance abusers (see, too, Kaufman & Zigler, 1989).

This comorbidity of substance abuse with other psychiatric conditions will have implications as well for the genetic transmission of disorders in the second-generation offspring of these families (Figure 8.1, Path 8; Pauls, 1991). In particular, both affective disorders and impairments in attention regulation may be at least partially genetically transmitted from the substance-abusing adult to offspring. Thus, if not directly related to cocaine exposure itself, maternal cocaine addiction may serve as a marker for genetic loading for such disorders in the newborn.

Impairments in parenting by a cocaine-abusing adult may reflect preexisting psychological and psychiatric conditions that contributed to the individual's addiction (Figure 8.1, Path 4a). An extensive literature describes the early effects of maternal postpartum depression on maternal responsiveness and sensitivity to the infant and, in turn, on the infant's active engagement (Field, 1995). The substance-abusing adult's depression may be worsened by poor social supports, the repeated stress of violence and poverty, and the often poor physical health associated with her addiction (see Zigler, Hodapp, & Edison, 1990). Severe depression may also make it more difficult for an adult to decrease or desist from cocaine use. Thus, the adult becomes more dysfunctional because of depression and worsening drug abuse resulting in dysfunctional parenting.

The third pathway of postnatal effects of cocaine on developmental outcome relates to the effects of chronic cocaine use on specific neuropsychological domains that are crucial for certain aspects of parenting (Figure 8.1, Path 6; Bauman & Dougherty, 1983; Mayes, 1995). All substances of abuse alter the individual's state of consciousness, memory, affect regulation, and impulse control in varying degree and may become so addictive that the adult's primary goal is to supply his or her addiction to the exclusion of other activities and other people in her or his life. These types of alterations will markedly influence the adult's capacity, for example, to sustain critical interactions with an infant or young child at any given moment (Bornstein, 1995). Neuropsychological impairments in memory, verbal fluency, attention, persistence, and task orientation associated with chronic cocaine abuse might be expected to influence certain parenting behaviors such as the capacity to sustain an interaction (Ardila, Rosselli, & Strumwasser, 1991; Berry et al., 1993; Manschreck et al., 1990; O'Malley, Adamse, Heaton, & Gawin, 1992). Parenting infants and older children relies extensively on remembering previous experiences – familiar routines that support the child's emerging regulation of states and later anticipation of mother's responsiveness. Both are rooted in part in parental consistency. Similarly, the neuropsychological effects of prolonged addiction on memory, persistence, and concentration may also impede an adult's response to drug-treatment interventions and contribute to an intractable addiction involving multiple drugs in addition to cocaine (e.g., alcohol, marijuana, and tobacco). This circumstance also precludes attributing developmental effects on child or parent to cocaine alone.

A fourth potential pathway of postnatal cocaine exposure on children relates to the global amount of family discord, virtual homelessness, poverty, and, on a more basic level, chronic uncertainty, despair, and fear in both adults and children that characterize the cocaine-using world (Figure 8.1, Paths 5 and 5a). Abuse of cocaine often involves the user directly or indirectly in criminal activities such as prostitution, theft, or actual drug dealing (Boyd & Mieczkowski, 1990) and exposes the user as well as her or his children to personal and property violence. Because of these activities, cocaine-abusing adults are more likely to be arrested and incarcerated repeatedly, exposing their children to multiple episodes of parental separation and placements usually with different foster families or with other (often substance-abusing) neighbors or relatives (Lawson & Wilson, 1980). The levels and types of violence that the children of cocaine-abusing mothers are exposed to range from verbal abuse between adults to physical fights with deadly weapons. Children through age 5 to 6 years have also seen and participated in scenes well beyond their psychological capacities either to understand or cope.

Acute and chronic trauma affect brain development and psychological function (Figure 8.1, Path 7). Children developing amid drug-associated violence, poverty, discord, neglect, and uncertainty may experience a level of acute and ongoing stress and trauma of potentially sufficient intensity and chronicity so as to alter the development of centrally regulated, basic psychophysiological functions. Moreover, many of these children may experience impairments in the capacity to regulate states of arousal in response to novel or highly stimulating situations and are thus exposed to conditions that further stress dysfunctional regulatory systems (Figure 8.1, Path 5b). In instances of severely overwhelming, and perhaps chronically stressful trauma, stress-related neurotransmitters potentially contribute to increased central nervous system sensitivity to stimulating and novel events and altered arousal regulatory mechanisms (Pittman, 1988). Compromise secondary to traumatic events may further impede children's already impaired ability to respond to ongoing discord and chaos in the world around them.

Conclusions

Comprehensive study of the developmental effects of prenatal and postnatal exposure to cocaine calls for a developmental psychopathologic approach that emphasizes interactions among biologic, genetic, and environmental conditions. Investigators need to examine interactions among many conditions of risk due to prenatal exposure to a potential teratogen and various environmental disruptions ascribable also to the effects of cocaine abuse. Cocaine exposure affects the child and family through multiple bidirectional and interactive pathways. Cocaine exposure may directly affect fetal and postnatal brain development and adult neuropsychological functions requisite to adequate parenting. Moreover, the cocaine-associated environment is characterized by increased parental psychopathology, abuse and violence, and poverty and homelessness, each of which threatens the child's cognitive and social development and traps parent and child in a deteriorating cycle of chronic substance abuse, poor health, and social isolation. It is an experiment of nature in which individuals may be more or less adapted at any point in time depending on transactions between environmental stressors and level of developmental functioning.

Despite the complexities of these multilayered interactions, the problem of childhood cocaine exposure submits to modeling of biologic–environment interaction. The following represent only some potentially fruitful and much needed lines of investigation in this area: (1) studies of reactivity, arousal, and attention regulation and the stability of such capacities from infancy into the second and third year of life; (2) studies of language and communication with attention to early communicative precursors; (3) direct observations of parent–child interaction with emphasis on parental responsive and structuring activities. Closer investigations of basic functions such as attention and the regulation of arousal that underlie broader developmental competencies, and the interaction of such functions with the parental environment, will provide a more adequate profile of the specific and nonspecific problem areas for cocaine-exposed children who reach school age.

Finally, multidisciplinary approaches to understanding the effects of cocaine exposure on young children's development are requisite to guiding interventions with these innocents. Whether the intervention needs of children from substance-abusing families are different from those of children of similar high-risk but non–drug-using environments is not clear. But the same integrative models applied to the research questions that allow for interactions between multiple domains of effect might apply equally well to interventions for children from drug-using homes. As with the investigative questions, intervening on only one level (e.g., early stimulation but no services for families or vice versa) will likely not be adequate. Cocaine-exposed children represent a population at both biologic and environmental risks for developmental impairments, and they require interventions that address both biologic and environmental factors, and the interactions between these conditions.

The problem of prenatal cocaine exposure raises significant issues for the field of developmental psychopathology. It illustrates well the value and application of interactive models, requires a multidisciplinary focus, emphasizes adaptation as well as maladaptation, and provides by comparisons and contrasts information about the normal ontogeny of basic developmental functions.

References

Aber, J. L., & Zigler, E. (1981). Developmental considerations in the definition of child maltreatment. *New Directions for Child Development, 11,* 1–29.

Abidin, R. R. (1983). *The Parenting Stress Index – manual.* Virginia: Pediatric Psychology Press.

Ainsworth, M. D. S., Blehar, M. C., Waters, E., & Wall, S. (1978). *Patterns of attachment: A psychological study of the strange situation.* Hillsdale, NJ: Erlbaum.

Akbari, H. M., & Azmitia, E. C. (1992). Increased tyrosine hydroxylase immunoreactivity in the rat cortex following prenatal cocaine exposure. *Developmental Brain Research, 66,* 277–281.

Akbari, H. M., Kramer, H. K., Whitakerasmitia, P. M., Spear, L. P., et al. (1992). Prenatal cocaine exposure disrupts the development of the serotonergic system. *Brain Research, 572,* (1–2) 57–63.

Alessandri, S. M., Sullivan, M. W., Imaizumi, S., & Lewis, M. (1993). Learning and emotional responsivity in cocaine-exposed infants. *Developmental Psychology, 29,* 939–997.

Amaro, H., Fried, L. E., Cabral, H., & Zuckerman, B. (1990). Violence during pregnancy and substance abuse. *American Journal of Public Health, 80,* 575–579.

Amaro, H., Zuckerman, B., & Cabral, H. (1989). Drug use among adolescent mothers: Profile of risk. *Pediatrics, 84,* 144–151.

Anday, E. K., Cohen, M. E., Kelley, N. E., & Leitner, D. S. (1989). Effects of in utero cocaine exposure on startle and its modification. *Developmental Pharmacology and Therapeutics, 12,* 137–145.

Anisfeld, E., Cunningham, N., Ferrari, L., Melendez, M., et al. (1991). Infant development after prenatal cocaine exposure. Abstract. *Society for Research in Child Development,* p. 153.

Ardila, A., Rosselli, M., & Strumwasser, S. (1991). Neuropsychological deficits in chronic cocaine abusers. *International Journal of Neuroscience, 57,* 73–79.

Arendt, R., Singer, L., & Minnes, S. (1993). Development of cocaine exposed infants. Abstract. *Society for Research in Child Development,* p. 236.

Bauman, P. S., & Dougherty, F. E. (1983). Drug-addicted mothers' parenting and their children's development. *International Journal of the Addictions, 18,* 291–302.

Bayley, N. (1969). *Manual for the Bayley Scales of Infant Development.* New York: Psychological Corporation.

Bayley, N. (1993). *Bayley Scales of Infant Development – revised edition.* New York: Psychological Corporation.

Bergeman, C. S., & Plomin, R. (1989). Genotype–environment interaction. In M. H. Bornstein & J. S. Bruner (Eds.), *Interaction in human development* (pp. 157–171). Hillsdale, NJ: Erlbaum.

Bernardi, E., Jones, J., & Tennant, C. (1989). Quality of parenting in alcoholics and narcotic addicts. *British Journal of Psychiatry, 154,* 677–682.

Bernstein, V., Jeremy, R. J., Hans, S., & Marcus, J. (1984). A longitudinal study of offspring born to methadone-maintained women: II. Dyadic interaction and infant behavior at four months. *American Journal of Drug and Alcohol Abuse, 10,* 161–193.

Bernstein, V., Jeremy, R. J., & Marcus, J. (1986). Mother–infant interaction in multiproblem families: Finding those at risk. *Journal of the American Academy of Child Psychiatry, 25,* 631–640.

Berry, J., Van, G. W. G., Herzberg, D. S., Hinkin, C. E., Boone, K., Steinman, L., & Wilkins, J. N. (1993). Neuropsychological deficits in abstinent cocaine abusers: Preliminary findings after two weeks of abstinence. *Drug and Alcohol Dependence, 32,* 231–237.

Besharov, D. J. (1990). Crack children in foster care. *Children Today, 19* (4), 21–25, 35.

Billman, D., Nemeth, P., Heimler, R., & Sasidharan, P. (1991). Prenatal cocaine exposure: Advanced Bayley Psychomotor Scores. *Clinical Research, 39,* 697A.

Bingol, N., Fuchs, M., Diaz, V., Stone, R. K., & Gromisch, D. S. (1987). Teratogenicity of cocaine in humans. *Journal of Pediatrics, 110,* 93–96.

Black, R., & Mayer, J. (1980). Parents with special problems: Alcoholism and opiate addiction. *Child Abuse and Neglect, 4,* 45–54.

Bornstein, M. H. (1985a). Habituation as a measure of visual information processing in human infants: Summary, systemization, and synthesis. In G. Gottlieb & N. Krasnegor (Eds.), *Development of audition and vision during the first year of postnatal life: A methodological overview* (pp. 253–295). Norwood, NJ: Ablex.

Bornstein, M. H. (1985b). How infant and mother jointly contribute to developing cognitive competence in the child. *Proceedings of the National Academy of Science* (U.S.A.), *89,* 7470–7473.

Bornstein, M. H. (1995). Parenting infants: In M. H. Bornstein (Ed.), *Handbook of parenting* (Vol. 1, pp. 3–39). Hillsdale, NJ: Erlbaum.

Bornstein, M. H., & Lamb, M. E. (1992). *Development in infancy: An introduction* (3d ed.). New York: McGraw-Hill.

Bornstein, M. H., & Mayes, L. C. (1992). Taking measure of the infant mind. In F. Kessell, M. H. Bornstein, & A. Sameroff (Eds.), *Contemporary constructions of the child: Essays in honor of William Kessen* (pp. 45–56). Hillsdale, NJ: Erlbaum.

Bornstein, M. H., Mayes, L. C., & Tamis-LeMonda, C. S. (1996). Habituation, information processing, mental development, and the threat of cocaine exposure in infancy. In P. G. Hepper & Kendal-Reed (Eds.), *Perinatal Sensory Development: Psychology and Psychobiology.* Cambridge: Cambridge University Press.

Bornstein, M. H., & Tamis-LeMonda, C. S. (1990). Activities and interactions of mothers and their firstborn infants in the first six months of life: Covariation, stability, continuity, correspondence, and prediction. *Child Development, 61,* 1206–1217.

Boyd, C. J., & Mieczkowski, T. (1990). Drug use, health, family, and social support in "crack" cocaine users. *Addictive Behaviors, 15,* 481–485.

Brazelton, T. B. (1984). *Neonatal Behavior Assessment Scale,* 2nd ed. Clinics in developmental medicine, no. 88. Philadelphia: Lippincott.

Burns, K., Chethik, L., Burns, W. J., & Clark, R. (1991). Dyadic disturbances in cocaine-abusing mothers and their infants. *Journal of Clinical Psychology, 47,* 316–319.

Burns, W. J., & Burns, K. A. (1988). Parenting dysfunction in chemically dependent women. In I. Chasnoff (Ed.), *Drugs, alcohol, pregnancy, and parenting* (pp. 159–171). London: Kluwer Academic Publishers.

Byck, R. (1974). *Cocaine papers: Sigmund Freud.* New York: Stonehill.

Carlson, V., Cicchetti, D., Barnett, D., & Braumwald, K. (1989). Disorganized/disoriented attachment relationships in maltreated infants. *Developmental Psychology, 25,* 525–531.

Chambers, C. D., Hinesby, R. K., & Moldestad, M. (1970). Narcotic addiction in females: A race comparison. *International Journal of the Addictions, 5,* 257–278.

Chasnoff, I. J., Griffith, D. R., Freier, C., & Murray, J. (1992). Cocaine/polydrug use in pregnancy: Two-year follow-up. *Pediatrics, 89,* 284–289.

Chasnoff, I. J., Griffith, D. R., MacGregor, S., Dirkes, K., & Burns, K. (1989). Temporal patterns of cocaine use in pregnancy. *Journal of the American Medical Association, 261,* 1741–1744.

Chasnoff, I. J., Landress, H. J., & Barrett, M. E. (1990). Prevalence of illicit drugs or alcohol abuse during pregnancy and discrepancies in mandatory reporting in Pinellas County, Florida. *New England Journal of Medicine, 322,* 102–106.

Cicchetti, D. (1993). Developmental psychopathology: Reactions, reflections, projections. *Developmental Review, 13,* 471–502.

Coles, B. J., & Robbins, T. W. (1989). Effects of 6-hydroxydopamine lesions of the nucleus accumbens septi on performance of a 5-choice serial reaction time task in rats: Implications for theories of selective attention and arousal. *Behavioral Brain Research, 33,* 165–179.

Coles, C. D., Platzman, K. A., Smith, I., James, M. E., & Falek, A. (1992). Effects of cocaine and alcohol use in pregnancy on neonatal growth and neurobehavioral status. *Neurotoxicology and Teratology, 14*(1), 23–33.

Colombo, J., & Mitchell, D. W. (1990). Individual differences in early visual attention. In J. Colombo & J. Fagen (Eds.), *Individual differences in infancy: Reliability, stability, and prediction* (pp. 193–227). Hillsdale, NJ: Erlbaum.

Courtwright, D. T. (1982). *Dark paradise.* Cambridge, MA: Harvard University Press.

Day, N. L. (1992). Effects of prenatal alcohol exposure. In I. S. Zagon & T. A. Slotkin (Eds.), *Maternal substance abuse and the developing nervous system* (pp. 27–44). Boston: Academic Press.

Dow-Edwards, D. L. (1988). Developmental effects of cocaine. *NIDA Research Monograph, 88,* 290–303.

Dow-Edwards, D. (1989). Long-term neurochemical and neurobehavioral consequences of cocaine use during pregnancy. *Annals of the New York Academy of Science, 562,* 280–289.

Dow-Edwards, D., Freed, L. A., & Milhorat, T. H. (1988). Stimulation of brain metabolism by perinatal cocaine exposure. *Brain Research, 470,* 137–141.

Eisen, L. N., Field, T. M., Bandstra, E. S., et al. (1990). Perinatal cocaine effects on neonatal stress behavior and performance on the Brazelton Scale. *Pediatrics, 88,* 477–480.

Field, T. M. (1995). Psychologically depressed parents. In M. H. Bornstein (Ed.), *Handbook of parenting,* Vol. 4: *Status and social conditions of parenting.* (pp. 85–99) Hillsdale, NJ: Erlbaum.

Frank, D. A., Zuckerman, B. S., Amaro, H., Aboagye, K., et al. (1988). Cocaine use during pregnancy: Prevalence and correlates. *Pediatrics, 82,* 888–895.

Fulroth, R., Phillips, B., & Durand, D. J. (1989). Perinatal outcome of infants exposed to cocaine and/or heroin in utero. *American Journal of Diseases of Children, 143,* 905–910.

Gable, S., & Isabella, R. A. (1992). Maternal contributions to infant regulation of arousal. *Infant Behavior and Development, 15,* 95–107.

Gawin, F. H., & Ellinwood, F. H. (1988). Cocaine and other stimulants. *New England Journal of Medicine, 318,* 1173–1182.

Goeders, N. E., & Smith, J. E. (1983). Cortical dopaminergic involvement in cocaine reinforcement. *Science, 221,* 773–775.

Goldman-Rakic, P. S. (1987). Development of cortical circuitry and cognitive function. *Child Development, 58,* 601–622.

Gomby, D. S., & Shiono, P. H. (1991). Estimating the number of substance-exposed infants. *Future of Children, 1* (1), 17–25. (Available from Center for the Future of Children, David & Lucille Packard Foundation, Los Alto, CA.)

Goodwin, G. A., Heyser, C. J., Moody, C. A., et al. (1992). A fostering study of the effects of prenatal cocaine exposure: II. Offspring behavioral measures. *Neurotoxicology and Teratology, 14,* 423–432.

Gottwald, S. R., & Thurman, S. K. (1994). The effects of prenatal cocaine exposure on mother–infant interaction and infant arousal in the newborn period. *Topics in Early Childhood Special Education, 14,* 217–231.

Griffith, D. R., Azuma, S. D., & Chasnoff, I. J. (1994). Three-year outcome of children exposed prenatally to drugs. *Journal of the American Academy of Child Psychiatry, 33,* 20–27.

Griffith, D. R., & Freier, C. (1992). Methodological issues in the assessment of the mother–child interactions of substance-abusing women and their children. *NIDA Research Monograph, 117,* 228–247.

Hadeed, A. J., & Siegel, S. R. (1989). Maternal cocaine use during pregnancy: Effect on the newborn infant. *Pediatrics, 84,* 205–210.

Hawley, T. L., & Disney, E. R. (1992). Crack's children: The consequences of maternal cocaine abuse. *Social Policy Report of the Society for Research in Child Development, 6* (4), 1–22.

Heyser, C. J., Molina, V. A., & Spear, L. P. (1992). A fostering study of the effects of prenatal cocaine exposure: I. Maternal behaviors. *Neurotoxicology and Teratology, 14,* 415–421.

Hofer, M. A. (1994). Hidden regulators in attachment, separation and loss. In N. Fox (Ed.), *The development of emotion regulation* (pp. 192–207). *Monographs of the Society for Research in Child Development, 59* (2–3, Serial No. 240).

Hoyme, H. E., Jones, K. L., & Dixon, S. D., et al. (1990). Prenatal cocaine exposure and fetal vascular disruption. *Pediatrics, 85,* 743–747.

Kagan, S., Powell, D., Weissbourd, B., & Zigler, E. (Eds.). (1987). *America's family support programs: Perspectives and prospects.* New Haven: Yale University Press.

Kauffman, J., & Zigler, E. (1989). The intergenerational transmission of child abuse. In D. Cicchetti & V. Carlson (Eds.), *Child maltreatment: Theory and research on the causes and consequences of child abuse and neglect* (pp. 129–150). New York: Cambridge University Press.

Khalsa, M. E., Anglin, M. D., Paredes, A., Potepan, P., Potter, C. (1993). Pretreatment natural history of cocaine addiction: Preliminary 1-year follow-up results. *NIDA Research Monograph, 135,* 218–236.

Khantzian, E. J. (1983). An extreme case of cocaine dependence and marked improvement with methylphenidate treatment. *American Journal of Psychiatry, 140,* 784–785.

Khantzian, E. J. (1985). The self-medication hypothesis of addictive disorders: Focus on heroin and cocaine dependence. *American Journal of Psychiatry, 142,* 1259–1264.

Khantzian, E. J., & Khantzian, N. J. (1984). Cocaine addiction: Is there a psychological predisposition. *Psychiatric Annals, 14,* 753–759.

Kjarasch, S. J., Glotzer D., Vinci, R., Wietzman, M., & Sargent, T. (1991). Unsuspected cocaine exposure in children. *American Journal of Diseases of Children, 145,* 204–206.

Lauder, J. M. (1988). Neurotransmitters as morphogens. *Progress in Brain Research, 73,* 365–387.

Lawson, M., & Wilson, G. (1980). Parenting among women addicted to narcotics. *Child Welfare, 59,* 67–79.

Lewis, M., & Brooks-Gunn, J. (1981). Visual attention at three months as a predictor of cognitive functioning at two years of age. *Intelligence, 5,* 131–140.

Lewis, M., Goldberg, S., & Campbell, H. (1969). A developmental study of information processing within the first three years of life: Response decrement to a redundant signal. *Monographs of the Society for Research in Child Development, 39* (9, Serial No. 133).

Lewis, M., & Rosenblum, L. A. (1974). *The effect of the infant on the caregiver.* New York: Wiley.

Luthar, S., Anton, S. F., Merikangas, K. R., & Rounsaville, B. J. (1992). Vulnerability to substance abuse and psychopathology among siblings of opioid abusers. *Journal of Nervous and Mental Disorders, 180,* 153–161.

Luthar, S., & Zigler, E. (1991). Vulnerability and competence: A review of research on resilience in childhood. *American Journal of Orthopsychiatry, 61,* 6–22.

MacGregor, S. N., Keith, L. G., Chasnoff, I. J., et al. (1987). Cocaine use during pregnancy: Adverse perinatal outcome. *American Journal of Obstetrics and Gynecology, 157,* 686–690.

Main, M., & Solomon, J. (1986). Discovery of an insecure-disorganized/disoriented attachment pattern. In T. B. Brazelton & M. Yogman (Eds.), *Affective development in Infancy.* Norwood, NJ: Ablex.

Manschreck, T., Schneyer, M., Weisstein, C., Laughery, J., Rosenthal, J., Celada, T., & Berner, J. (1990). Freebase cocaine and memory. *Comprehensive Psychiatry, 31,* 369–375.

Mattson, M. P. (1988). Neurotransmitters in the regulation of neuronal cytoarchitecture. *Brain Research Reviews, 13,* 179–212.

Mayes, L. C. (1992). The effects of prenatal cocaine exposure on young children's development. *Annals of the American Academy of Political and Social Science,* p. 521.

Mayes, L. C. (1994). Neurobiology of prenatal cocaine exposure: Effect on developing monoaminergic systems. *Infant Mental Health, 15,* 134–145.

Mayes, L. C. (1995). Substance abuse and parenting. In M. H. Bornstein (Ed.), *The handbook of parenting* (pp. 101–125). Mahwah, NJ: Erlbaum.

Mayes, L. C. (1996). Exposure to cocaine: Behavioral outcomes in preschool aged children. In C. L. Witherington, V. L. Smeriglio, & L. Finnegan (Eds.), *Behaviors of drug-exposed offspring.* (Vol. 164, pp. 211–229). NIDA Technical Symposium. Washington, DC: U.S. Dept. Health and Human Services.

Mayes, L. C., & Bornstein, M. (1995). Developmental dilemmas for cocaine abusing parents and their children. In M. Lewis & M. Bendersky (Eds.), *Cocaine mother and cocaine babies: The role of toxins in development.* (pp. 251–272). Hillsdale, NJ: Erlbaum.

Mayes, L. C., & Bornstein, M. (in press a). Attention regulation in infants born at risk: Preterm and prenatally cocaine exposed infants. In J. Burak & J. Enns (Eds.), *Development, attention, and psychopathology.* New York: Guilford.

Mayes, L. C., & Bornstein, M. (in press b). The context of development for young children from cocaine-abusing families. In P. Kato & T. Mann (Eds.), *Health psychology of special populations.* New York: Plenum.

Mayes, L. C., Bornstein, M. H., Chawarska, K., & Granger, R. H. (1995). Information processing and developmental assessments in three month olds exposed prenatally to cocaine. *Pediatrics, 95,* 539–545.

Mayes, L. C., Bornstein, M. H., Chawarska, K., Haynes, O. M., & Granger, R. H. (1996). Regulation of arousal in three-month-old infants exposed prenatally to cocaine and other drugs. *Development and Psychopathology, 8,* 29–42.

Mayes, L. C., Feldman, R., Bornstein, M. H., Haynes, O. M., Schottenfeld, R., Granger, R. H. (in press). Interactions between cocaine using mothers and their 3- and 6-month-old infants. *Infant Behavior and Development.* Child Study Center.

Mayes, L. C., Granger, R. H., Bornstein, M. H., & Zuckerman, B. (1992). The problem of intrauterine cocaine exposure. *Journal of the American Medical Association, 267,* 406–408.

Mayes, L. C., Granger, R. H., Frank, M. A., Bornstein, M., & Schottenfeld, R. (1993). Neurobehavioral profiles of infants exposed to cocaine prenatally. *Pediatrics, 91,* 778–783.

Merikangas, K. R., Rounsaville, B. J., & Prusoff, B. A. (1992). Familial factors in vulnerability to substance abuse. In M. Glantz & R. Pickens (Eds.), *Vulnerability to drug abuse* (pp. 75–98). Washington, DC: American Psychiatric Association Press.

Mirin, S. M., Weiss, R. D., Griffin, M. L., & Michael, J. L. (1991). Psychopathology in drug abusers and their families. *Comprehensive Psychiatry, 32,* 36–51.

Moore, T. R., Sorg, J., Miller, L., Key, T. & Resnik, R. (1986). Hemodynamic effects of intravenous cocaine on the pregnant ewe and fetus. *American Journal of Obstetrics and Gynecology, 155,* 883–888.

Musto, D. (1973). *The American disease: Origins of narcotic control.* New Haven: Yale University Press.

O'Connor, M. J., Sigman, N., & Brill, N. (1987). Disorganization of attachment in relation to maternal alcohol consumption. *Journal of Consulting and Clinical Psychology, 55,* 831–836.

O'Connor, M. J., Sigman, N., & Kasari, C. (1992). Attachment behavior of infants exposed prenatally to alcohol: Medicating effects of infant affect and mother–infant interaction. *Development and Psychopathology, 4,* 243–256.

O'Connor, M. J., Sigman, M., & Kasari, C. (1993). Maternal alcohol use and infant cognition. *Infant Behavior and Development, 16,* 177–193.

O'Malley, S., Adamse, M., Heaton, R. K., & Gawin, F. H. (1992). Neuropsychological impairments in chronic cocaine abusers. *American Journal of Drug and Alcohol Abuse, 18,* 131–144.

Oro, A. S., & Dixon, S. D. (1987). Perinatal cocaine and methamphetamine exposure: Maternal and neonatal correlates. *Journal of Pediatrics, 111,* 571–578.

Osterloh, J. D., & Lee, B. I. (1989). Urine drug screening in mothers and newborns. *American Journal of Diseases of Children, 143,* 791–793.

Pauls, D. (1991). Genetic influences on child psychiatric conditions. In M. Lewis (Ed.), *Child and adolescent psychiatry: A comprehensive textbook* (pp. 351–363). Baltimore: Williams and Wilkins.

Pittman, R. K. (1988). Post-traumatic stress disorder, conditioning, and network theory. *Psychiatric Annals, 18,* 182–189.

Pribram, K. H., & McGuiness, D. (1975). Arousal, activation, and effort in the control of attention. *Psychological Review, 82,* 116–149.

Raynes, A. E., Climent, C., Patch, V. D., & Ervin, F. (1974). Factors related to imprisonment in female heroin addicts. *International Journal of the Addictions, 9,* 145–150.

Richie, J. M., & Greene, N. M. (1985). Local anesthetics. In A. G. Gilman, L. S. Goodman, T. N. Rall, & F. Murad (Eds.), *The pharmacologic basis of therapeutics* (7th ed., pp. 309–310). New York: Macmillan.

Rodning, C., Beckwith, L., & Howard, J. (1989). Characteristics of attachment organization and play organization in prenatally drug-exposed toddlers. *Development and Psychopathology, 1,* 277–289.

Rodning, C., Beckwith, L., & Howard, J. (1991). Quality of attachment and home environments in children prenatally exposed to PCP and cocaine. *Development and Psychopathology, 3,* 351–366.

Rogosch, F. A., Cicchetti, D., Shields, A., & Toth, S. L. (1995). Parenting dysfunction in child maltreatment. In M. H. Bornstein (Ed.), *Handbook of parenting* (Vol. 4, 127–159). Hillsdale, NJ: Erlbaum.

Rothbart, M. K., & Posner, M. I. (1985). Temperament and the development of self regulation. In H. Hartlage & C. E. Telzrow (Eds.), *Neuropsychology of individual differences: A developmental perspective* (pp. 93–123). New York: Plenum.

Rounsaville, B. J., Kosten, T. R., Weissman, M. M., Prusoff, B., Pauls, D., Foley, S., & Merikangas, K. (1991). Psychiatric disorders in the relatives of probands with opiate addicts. *Archives of General Psychiatry, 48,* 33–42.

Rounsaville, B. J., Weissman, M. M., Wilber, C. H., et al. (1982). Pathways of opiate addiction: An evaluation of differing antecedents. *British Journal of Psychiatry, 44,* 437–466.

Ruff, H. A. (1988). The measurement of attention in high-risk infants. In P. M. Vietze & H. G. Vaughan (Eds.), *Early identification of infants with developmental disabilities* (pp. 282–296). New York: Grune and Stratton.

Ryan, L., Ehrlich S., & Finnegan, L. (1987). Cocaine abuse in pregnancy: Effects on the fetus and newborn. *Neurotoxicology and Teratology, 9,* 295–299.

Scherling, D. (1994). Prenatal cocaine exposure and childhood psychopathology. *American Journal of Orthopsychiatry, 64,* 9–19.

Sroufe, L. A., & Rutter, M. (1984). The domain of developmental psychopathology. *Child Development, 55,* 17–29.

Streissguth, A. P. (1992). Fetal alcohol syndrome and fetal alcohol effects: A clinical perspective on later developmental consequences. In I. S. Zagon & T. A. Slotkin (Eds.), *Maternal substance abuse and the developing nervous system* (pp. 5–26). Boston: Academic Press.

Struthers, J. M., & Hansen, R. L. (1992). Visual recognition memory in drug-exposed infants. *Journal of Developmental and Behavioral Pediatrics, 13,* 108–111.

Swann, A. C. (1990). Cocaine: Synaptic effects and adaptations. In N. D. Volkow & A. C. Swann (Eds.), *Cocaine in the brain* (pp. 58–94). New Brunswick, NJ: Rutgers University Press.

Tamis-LeMonda, C. S., & Bornstein, M. H. (1989). Habituation and maternal encouragement of attention in infancy as predictors of toddler language, play, and representational competence. *Child Development, 60,* 738–751.

Thoman, E. B., & Ingersoll, E. W. (1989). The human nature of the youngest humans: Prematurely born babies. *Seminars in Perinatology, 13,* 482–494.

Wasserman, D. R., & Levanthal, J. M. (1993). Maltreatment of children born to cocaine-abusing mothers. *American Journal of Diseases of Children, 147,* 1324–1328.

Wellisch, D. K., & Steinberg, M. R. (1980). Parenting attitudes of addict mothers. *International Journal of Addictions, 15,* 809–819.

Wise, R. A. (1984). Neural mechanisms of the reinforcing action of cocaine. *National Institute of Drug Abuse Research Monograph, 50,* 15–33.

Woods, J. R., Plessinger, M. A., & Clark, K. E. (1987). Effect of cocaine on uterine blood flow and fetal oxygenation. *Journal of the American Medical Association, 257,* 957–961.

Woods, N. S., Eyler, F. D., Behnke, M., & Conlon, M. (1991, April). *Cocaine use during pregnancy: Maternal depressive symptoms and neonatal neurobehavior over the first month.* Paper presented at the Society for Research in Child Development, Seattle, WA.

Zigler, E. (1970). Social class and the socialization process. *Review of Educational Research, 40,* 87–110.

Zigler, E. (1976, February). Controlling child abuse: An effort doomed to failure? In W. A. Collins (Ed.), *Newsletter of the Division on Developmental Psychology, American Psychological Association,* (pp. 17–30).

Zigler, E. (1992). Head Start's future: The challenge for research. In *New directions in child and family research: Shaping Head Start in the 90's* (pp. 15–16). Conference proceedings presented by the Administration on Children, Youth and Families, the Administration for Children and Families, Department of Health and Human Services.

Zigler, E. (1995). Forward. In M. H. Bornstein (Ed.), *Handbook of parenting* (Vol. 1, pp. ix–x). Mahwah, NJ: Erlbaum.

Zigler, E., & Balla, D. (Eds.). (1982). *Mental retardation: The developmental difference controversy.* Hillsdale, NJ: Erlbaum.

Zigler, E., & Freedman, J. (1990). Psychological-developmental implications of current patterns of early child care. In S. S. Chehrazi (Ed.), *Psychosocial issues in day care* (pp. 3–20). Washington, DC: American Psychiatric Press.

Zigler, E., & Glick, M. (1986). *A developmental approach to adult psychopathology.* New York: Wiley.

Zigler, E., & Gordon, E. W. (Eds.) (1982). *Day care: Scientific and social policy issues.* Boston: Auburn House.

Zigler, E., & Hall, N. (1989). Physical child abuse in America: Past, present and future. In D. Cicchetti & V. Carlson (Eds.), *Child maltreatment: Theory and research on the causes and consequences of child abuse and neglect* (pp. 38–75). New York: Cambridge University Press.

Zigler, E., & Hodapp, R. M. (1986). *Understanding mental retardation.* New York: Cambridge University Press.

Zigler, E., Hodapp, R. M., & Edison, M. (1990). From theory to practice in the care and education of retarded individuals. *American Journal of Mental Retardation, 95,* 112.

Zuckerman, B., Amaro, J., Bauchner, H., & Cabral, H. (1989). Depressive symptoms during pregnancy: Relationships to poor health behaviors. *American Journal of Obstetrics and Gynecology, 160,* 1107–1111.

Zuckerman, B., & Frank, D. A. (1992). Prenatal cocaine and marijuana exposure: Research and clinical implications. In I. S. Zagon & T. A. Slotkin (Eds.), *Maternal substance abuse and the developing nervous system* (pp. 125–154). Boston: Academic Press.

Zuckerman, B., Frank, D. A., Hingson, R., & Amaro, H. (1989). Effects of maternal marijuana and cocaine use on fetal growth. *New England Journal of Medicine, 320,* 762–768.

9 Developmental approaches to children with disabilities: New perspectives, populations, prospects

Robert M. Hodapp

In 1974, Thomas Achenbach declared that *Developmental Psychopathology* "is a book about a field that hardly exists" (p. 3). Such a view has generally held sway. Most researchers date developmental psychopathology's origins to the 1970s and early 1980s, and are amazed at just how quickly this "hardly existing" field has advanced. But the idea that developmental psychopathology began over the past 20 years is not precisely accurate. If one considers the joining of typical and atypical development as an integral component of developmental psychopathology, then at least portions of the field predate modern times by many decades. Over 50 years ago, Werner, Piaget, and Vygotsky all applied their developmental views to children with disabilities. More recently, Edward Zigler formulated the "developmental approach to mental retardation" in the late 1960s. Thus, not all aspects of developmental psychopathology date only to the 1970s and 1980s.

This disabilities wing of the developmental psychopathology house is also more than just an historical relic. As this chapter illustrates, developmental approaches to children with disabilities are advancing in several interrelated directions. First, such approaches have recently expanded their very sense of "development," such that family and ecological perspectives are now commonplace for children with disabilities. Second, these wider approaches have been applied to children with different types of retardation and, increasingly, to children with other disabilities such as deafness and blindness. Third, recent disability studies tell us much about the operation of typical developmental processes. As a result, we now know much more about development in both typical and disabled populations.

This chapter provides a short description of the past, present, and future issues in developmental approaches to children with disabilities. After briefly overviewing the early precursors of developmental approaches, the chapter reviews Zigler's developmental approach to mental retardation, the best-known developmental approach in the developmental disabilities field. The bulk of the chapter then explores new issues in developmental perspectives, new populations, and new prospects.

189

Early workers

The works of Heinz Werner, Jean Piaget, and Lev Vygotsky might, in retrospect, be considered the prehistory of developmental approaches to children with disabilities. Each contributed important ideas to what have now become more fully fledged, integrated developmental approaches, but none inaugurated a formal developmental approach to these children.

Heinz Werner is the first major developmentalist to consider children with mental retardation. Before his more well known Clark University days, Werner worked from 1937 to 1943 as a research psychologist at the MacGregor Laboratories of the Wayne County Training School outside of Detroit. There, along with his colleague Alfred Strauss, Werner published approximately 30 studies on children with retardation (for a review, see Witkin, 1964).

Several themes characterize this work. First, Werner originated the distinction between "process and achievement" (Werner, 1937), the idea that the child's underlying mental processes were not necessarily equivalent to the child's achievement, or behavior. This realization amply demonstrated itself in children with mental retardation. In one study, children were given the job of arranging a multipiece puzzle. Werner and Strauss (1939) noted that, in contrast to nonretarded children, the children with mental retardation "merely put the parts together quite mechanically, taking care only that the edges of the different pieces agreed perfectly with one another" (p. 39). By adopting this strategy, children with mental retardation could sometimes perform selected behaviors as well as their nonretarded peers.

Yet in terms of the processes themselves, Werner generally viewed children with mental retardation as less developed, showing less "differentiation and hierarchic integration" (Werner, 1957) than did same-aged nonretarded children. In conceptualizing these children as developing normally but at slower rates than do nonretarded children, Werner was the first important Western developmental theorist to apply theories of normal, nonretarded development to children with mental retardation.

Werner's final contribution concerned a distinction between organic and familial mental retardation. Although such a distinction has often been made from the late 1800s until today (Burack, 1990), Werner (1941) felt that only those children showing no specific cause of their retardation – those who were "endogenous" in their retardation – necessarily showed "normal" (albeit slower) developments. Other children, specifically those whose retardation was due to external or "exogenous" causes (such as Down syndrome, anoxia at birth, or other organic etiologies), were not considered to follow the usual developmental progressions. This distinction was to enter more explicitly into Zigler's developmental formulation in the 1960s.

Although Heinz Werner may have initiated the idea of a general developmental approach, Jean Piaget allowed for the approach's elaboration. Beginning in the

1920s, Piaget proposed a series of hierarchically organized stages with numerous specific, detailed sequences by which development occurred. Developmentally oriented workers could then determine whether these sequences also held for children with retardation. In subsequent studies, Piagetian sequences were examined in children with mental retardation during the 1930s (Lane & Kinder, 1939), 1940s (Prothro, 1943), and 1950s (Woodward, 1959, 1963).

Most important, though, was the work of Piaget's colleague Barbel Inhelder. In her studies of children with mental retardation of various etiologies, Inhelder (1943/1968) noted both similarities and differences between these children and children without retardation. Like nonretarded children, children with mental retardation also appeared to develop along similar sequences in various Piagetian domains. Yet in other ways, children with mental retardation differed markedly from those without. Inhelder (1943/1968) pointed to regressions, incomplete developments, and oscillations in children's responses between higher- and lower-level answers. Inhelder thus highlighted that children with retardation show more fits and starts, more tentative, more fragile developments than do nonretarded children. Such work previews more contemporary studies on regressions in children with Down syndrome by Dunst (1990), and Wishart and Duffy (1990).

If Werner began and Piaget-Inhelder made specific the developmental analyses of children with mental retardation, Lev Vygotsky previews analyses that have yet to be done. Like Werner, Vygotsky worked with children with disabilities early in his career, from about 1924 to 1930 (van der Veer & Valsiner, 1991). His disability work centered around three major ideas: developmental analyses, mediation, and sociogenesis (Wertsch, 1985).

Like Werner and Piaget, Vygtosky was a "big picture" developmentalist who focused on many aspects of development. He was therefore acutely interested in how development occurs in children with disabilities. His focus was on how the child's entire personality structure is reorganized in relation to a particular disability (Reiber & Carton, 1993). His writings presaged ideas of compensation that exist throughout the wider field of developmental psychopathology.

Vygtosky also decried any static or atheoretical system of classification. He railed against IQ tests as estimates solely of current – but not future – development and against static classification systems of childhood personality or psychopathology. To Vygotsky, any such system "is powerless to solve questions of origin, development, and growth" (Reiber & Carton, 1993, p. 154).

A centerpiece of such developmental analyses involves mediation. Vygotsky conceptualized mediation in two ways: the adult mediating the child's development and the child mediating his or her own development. In the first, more social sense, mediation involves mother–child interactions and other individual or societal contacts that aid the developing child. Concerning children with disabilities, Vygotsky was particularly interested in how special education should be performed and whether these children should be in contact primarily with others like themselves or with the wider society. His goal, always, was for children with disabilities to become fully functioning, fully contributing members of their societies. In contrast to Werner or Piaget, Vygotsky's mediational views contributed to current debates concerning mainstreaming, normalization, and how best to educate children with disabilities (Hodapp, in press).

Another sense of mediation involved children mediating themselves through symbol systems such as language – hence Vygotsky's fascination with blind and deaf children. He was an especially strong proponent of Braille, which he felt has "done more for the blind than thousands of do gooders" (Reiber & Carton, 1993, p. 100). He also advocated a more natural, interactive form of oral education for children who are deaf, although he was more ambivalent about sign training (Hodapp, in press). In short, Vygotsky applied his two senses of mediation to children with different disabilities.

The third major theme in Vygotsky's work involved sociogenesis, or the idea that higher developments occur as a result of interactions with adults. Such views led to Vygotsky's (1978) Zone of Proximal Development, probably his best-known idea to most Western psychologists. Even early on Vygotsky applied this "zone" to children with mental retardation (van der Veer & Valsiner, 1991). His idea was to use the "width" of the zone – the time between the child's successful behaviors with and without adult help – to predict future development in individual children with mental retardation. To Vygotsky, two children with mental retardation can have identical levels of current functioning (i.e., mental ages) but very different prognoses. If with adult help one child is able to perform higher-level behaviors than the other, that first child has a wider zone and therefore a better prognosis. Gradually over the past two decades, such applications of Vygotsky's work have begun to be attempted (e.g., Budoff, 1974; Brown & Ferrara, 1985).

We see, then, that Werner, Piaget, and Vygotsky all contributed ideas to later developmental analyses. None, however, performed the sustained research needed to bring about a formal developmental approach to children with mental retardation or other developmental disabilities. This distinction is reserved to the scholar to whom this book is dedicated, Edward Zigler.

Zigler's developmental approach to mental retardation

Influenced by developmentalists such as Werner and Piaget and by movements within the mental retardation field (Zigler, 1984), Edward Zigler initiated a formal "developmental approach to mental retardation" in the late 1960s. Detailed here are the approach's three main contents and those individuals to whom the approach was originally applied.

Contents of the approach

Similar sequence hypothesis. The similar sequence hypothesis is the idea that children with retardation develop – in order – through the usual or normal developmental sequences. This hypothesis originally related to Piagetian stages, but might also apply to other cognitive or linguistic domains. In essence, Zigler (1967, 1969) surmised that, if children with retardation were "developing normally," then they should traverse, in order, Piagetian or other universal developmental sequences (Weisz & Zigler, 1979).

Similar structure hypothesis. With the similar structure hypothesis, Zigler stated that, when matched to nonretarded children on overall levels of mental functioning (e.g., on mental age), children with retardation should show similar levels of functioning on other tasks. In contrast to those mental retardation researchers who claim that all of mental retardation is due to some specific "defect" or "deficit" in functioning, the similar structure hypothesis holds that children with mental retardation do not show any particular area of deficit. Instead, these children show global, across-the-board delays in functioning. In addition to countering the deficit position, this view was also in line with Piagetian ideas that development in diverse areas is unified and organized, forming a single "structure d'ensemble." The idea, for children with or without mental retardation, is that a child's levels of functioning in one area were similar to levels in other areas (Weisz & Yeates, 1981; Weisz, Yeates, & Zigler, 1982).

Motivation-personality functioning. In contrast to the first two aspects of Zigler's developmental approach, the focus on motivational and personality features is not as clearly a "hypothesis" per se. Instead, this focus illustrates Zigler's (1971) long-standing interest in "extracognitive" factors that affect behavior. In essence, Zigler stated that children with retardation react as do nonretarded children to their life experiences. But the experiences of children with retardation differ from those of nonretarded children. Different living and educational settings and different success and failure experiences characterize the histories of these children. As a result, these children may show different responses.

Such responses fall under several broad categories. The *positive reaction tendency,* or dependency, refers to the ways that children with retardation are overly dependent on strange adults, particularly when these children come from inadequate homes or institutions in which they receive little love and attention. *Negative reaction tendency* involves the opposite tendency, an initial fear of strange adults. *Outerdirectedness* is the tendency to look outside oneself for answers to difficult problems. Given the child with mental retardation's history of failing difficult tasks, these children more often look to others for solutions to problems, imitate, and in other ways do not rely on their own, internally generated solutions. *Expectancy of success* refers to the degree to which one expects to succeed in any new task. Again due to their history of failure experiences, children with retardation are less likely to attempt or receive pleasure from solving difficult tasks. *Self-image* refers to the ways one sees oneself. Due to a less complex cognitive system, the self-image of persons with retardation has fewer domains than found in same-aged nonretarded persons.

Zigler and his colleagues have examined each of these constructs in numerous studies over the past 30 years (for reviews, see Zigler & Burack, 1989; Zigler & Hodapp, 1986). Across all of these studies, a major point persists: Children with retardation are "whole persons," more than cognitive or language-using beings. These individuals are affected both by their levels of development and by the environments in which they have been raised. Thus, such issues as whether the child has experienced a caring, loving home environment or a more impersonal institutional existence, or has succeeded or failed in intellectual endeavors, will all affect that child's personality and motivation to succeed. Along with the focus on developmental sequences and structures, Zigler's motivation-personality ideas have been considered a "lasting legacy" of his developmental approach (Weisz, 1982).

Applications

As originally proposed, Zigler's developmental ideas did not pertain to all children with mental retardation. Following Werner (1941), Lewis (1933), and others, Zigler (1967) differentiated between two types of mental retardation: familial and organic. Familial retardation involves those children for whom there appears to be no obvious cause of their mental retardation. For reasons that probably involve both genetics and environments, these children form the lower end of the normal distribution of intelligence. It is not that the retardation of these children has no cause, simply that their lower IQs are due to the same (undefined) causes that lead to higher or lower IQs throughout the normal distribution of IQ. This type of retardation, which accounts for approximately half of all persons with retardation (Zigler & Hodapp, 1986), remains controversial concerning its definition, cause, and, to some researchers, even its very existence.

A second group shows one or more clear organic causes for mental retardation. The retardation of these individuals may be due to any pre-, peri-, or postnatal causes. Children with Down syndrome, fragile X syndrome, prematurity, anoxia, or any of a host of other disorders fall into this group. The group is also now thought to include approximately half of all persons with retardation.

In Zigler's original formulation, he clearly stated that developmental hypotheses involving sequences and structures concerned the first, or familial, group. His reasoning was that children with familial mental retardation are essentially normal. They are within the normal or Gaussian curve of intelligence and their IQs, like those of nonretarded children, are due to the same complicated mixture of genetic and environmental factors. These children should therefore develop, in order, through the usual sequences of development (the similar sequence hypothesis) and should show no specific intellectual strengths or weaknesses when matched to nonretarded children of comparable mental ages (the similar structure hypothesis).

But for children with one of the many organic forms of mental retardation, Zigler hedged his bets. Like Werner before him, Zigler did not know whether different organic insults would cause children to change their developmental sequences or structures. He noted that "If the etiology of the phenotypic intelligence (as measured by an IQ) of two groups differs, it is far from logical to assert that the course of development is the same, or that even similar contents in their behaviors are mediated by exactly the same cognitive process" (Zigler, 1969, p. 553).

In evaluating Zigler's developmental approach to mental retardation, we see its importance to developmental work, both old and new. Its enduring strengths are obvious: Even though Werner, Piaget, and Vygotsky contributed to developmental thinking, none formally established a developmental approach to children with disabilities. When reading these early workers, one is struck by how issues such as sequences and structures are implied but never explicitly described. By writing about, defending, and even modifying this approach over a 25-year period, Zigler has made the developmental approach among the field's most important theoretical perspectives (Baumeister, 1987).

Though a product of the late 1960s, Zigler's developmental approach has also led to later developmental work. The original approach centered on specific aspects of the individual child's development, but this approach has been enlarged over the years. Later workers, often in collaboration with Zigler himself, have examined issues such as families, mother–child interactions, or wider ecologies of children with mental retardation (e.g., Burack, Hodapp, & Zigler, in press; Hodapp, Burack, & Zigler, 1990). Similarly, these wider, more expanded developmental approaches would later be applied to children with Down syndrome (Cicchetti & Beeghly, 1990), fragile X syndrome (Dykens & Leckman, 1990), and other organic forms of mental retardation. Like any thinker's ideas, Zigler's original developmental approach to mental retardation relates to its historical moment and context. Yet, to this day, it is Zigler's developmental approach that has been expanded and applied to a wider range of children with disabilities.

New perspectives, populations, and prospects

Zigler's original developmental approach has been extended in three ways. First, the approach itself has been expanded, such that "developmental approaches" differ today from 20 years ago. Second, new populations have come under the developmentalist's microscope. Third, recent developmental knowledge has led to new prospects – examinations and interventions not previously considered possible.

New perspectives: Expanding our sense of what constitutes "developmental" approaches

As currently conceptualized, developmental approaches to mental retardation consist of many areas. These include sequences, structures, rates, developmental transitions, mother–child interactions, families, and motivation-personality functioning (Hodapp & Zigler, 1995). Although a complete review is beyond the scope of this chapter, two issues – structures and families – illustrate recent expansions of Zigler's original developmental approach. One issue (structures) has changed from the way it was originally proposed, whereas the other (families) has arisen from recent understandings of what development is and how it operates.

Structurization of development: From the similar structure hypothesis to modularity. In Zigler's original developmental approach, children with retardation (or at least those with familial retardation) were considered to have no specific areas of deficit when matched on overall functioning to nonretarded children. In recent years, however, this "horizontally organized" perspective has given way to a view that a child's level of functioning may differ across distinct domains. Originally suggested by Gardner (1983) and Fodor (1983), many developmentalists now question whether development is "all of a piece," noting instead that a child's levels in one area can often differ considerably from functioning in other areas.

Such thinking has also been prominent among developmental researchers in mental retardation. Indeed, children with mental retardation have provided many intriguing cases of divergent developments. For example, Genie, the "wild child" locked in a closet for the first 12 years of life, showed a later (i.e., after age 12) development of pragmatic and vocabulary abilities, even as she seemed unable to develop the most rudimentary of grammatical skills (Curtiss, 1977). Conversely, Laura, another young woman with retardation, showed remarkably intact grammatical abilities, even as her vocabulary and overall intelligence were very low (Yamada, 1990).

More recently, Bellugi, Wang, and Jernigan (1994) have studied children with Williams syndrome, a rare genetic disorder in which children are highly verbal in spite of their low IQs and display particular difficulties in various visuospatial abilities. These children demonstrate syntactic, vocabulary, pragmatic, and even storytelling skills that are years above their overall levels of mental age. Compare, for example, two descriptions of a picture-book story, the first by a child with Down syndrome, the second by a child with Williams syndrome who is of the same age, MA, and IQ:

> He looks in the bowl. He . . . sleep. Then the frog got away. He looked in the bowl . . . and it empty.

> Once upon a time there was this boy who had a dog and a frog. And it was nighttime. And there was a . . . bowl. And the boy and the dog looked in the . . . looked in the bowl. Then, it was nighttime and time for the boy to go to bed. But, as the boy and the dog were sleeping the frog climbed out. And, when it was morning [whispers] "The frog was gone." (From Reilly, Klima, & Bellugi, 1991, p. 377)

Clearly, particular linguistic skills are shown by the child with Williams syndrome (although possibly not by all children with this disorder; Udwin & Yule, 1990). These children produce long and complicated sentences, and also employ linkages, time clauses ("And then . . ."), and the extralinguistic devices (whispering, sound effects) that help build interest. The stories of identical-level children with Down syndrome are not nearly so advanced.

The field has thus moved from a view that favors a single, unified sense of development to a concept of independent or semiindependent developmental domains. Further, much of this work relates to linguistic – often grammatical – development in children with disabilities (e.g., Tager-Flusberg, 1994). Future years will reveal exactly how different domains do – or do not – go together at various points during development in both typically developing and disabled populations.

Development of children with retardation as seen within the family unit. The changes that characterize the similar structure hypothesis involve a rethinking of "classic" issues of horizontal stages that developmental thinkers have struggled with from the time of Piaget on. Other issues, however, are of more recent vintage. Specifically, families and additional "other-than-child" environments were missing from the original developmental approach of the late 1960s. Such additions stem largely from Bronfenbrenner's (1979) focus on the ecology of children's development, and the resultant flurry of family and ecological work performed with nonretarded children beginning in the early 1980s.

In mental retardation as well, children with retardation are now conceptualized as developing within the family unit. Three general themes characterize this new work (Hodapp, 1995). The first involves the *changing models* that have been used to conceptualize parental and familial reactions to raising the child with retardation. Before the 1980s, parents and families of children with retardation were examined with what might be called "pathology-based" models. For example, parents of children with retardation were thought to "mourn" – as in a death – the loss of their idealized perfect child, and such mourning was considered to be either stage-dependent (Blacher, 1984; Solnit & Stark, 1961) or recurrent (Olshansky, 1962). Siblings were examined for their degrees of "role tension" and depression, and couples and families as a whole were primarily examined for the negative consequences of the child with disabilities. Nowadays, the child with mental retardation is conceptualized as a stressor in the family system (Crnic, Friedrich, & Greenberg, 1983). Like any stressor, the child's effects may be either positive or negative. The child – and the many issues relating to the child's care and upbring – can either strengthen or weaken parents, siblings, the marital couple, and the family as a whole.

In addition, various stress-coping models help make this perspective specific. Minnes (1989) and others have adapted McCubbin and Patterson's (1983) "Double ABCX" model of family functioning to understand the effects of the child with retardation on the family unit. Within this model, the effects of the "crisis" (or X) of raising the child with retardation is a product of the characteristics of the child (A), the family's internal and external resources (B), and the family's perceptions of the child (C). Each of these factors can also change over time; thus, the "double" in the Double ABCX model.

Although the Double ABCX model is very general, it does lead to the second theme of recent family work, an emphasis on *individual differences* among families. All families of children with mental retardation are not alike. Some do very well in raising their child with retardation, whereas others are adversely affected. In a series of studies examining families of children with retardation, Mink, Nihira, and Meyers (1983, 1984) have shown that families can be characterized along several general family "types." For example, some families are "cohesive and harmonious," whereas others are "low disclosure and unharmonious." Such different family styles would seem to affect the child with mental retardation, other family members, and the family as a whole.

A third theme concerns the influence of *child characteristics.* Just as families themselves are not all alike, so too do children with disabilities differ one from another. For example, some studies (not all) show that parents experience more stress during "critical points" in the child's development, when the child begins puberty or reaches early adulthood (Wikler, 1986). Families may also have more difficulties dealing with more impaired children (Minnes, 1989). Even the child's particular type of mental retardation may lead to specific problems for families. For example, faced with parenting children with Prader-Willi syndrome, a genetic disorder often characterized by a variety of behavioral problems, parents experience more stress as the child shows greater amounts of overeating, hoarding, skin-picking, and other "Prader-Willi problems" (Hodapp, Dykens, & Masino, 1997). Conversely, compared with groups of families of children with mixed etiologies, families of children with Down syndrome are more likely to be cohesive and harmonious (Mink et al., 1984) and to feel less stressed and more supported (Seltzer, Krauss, & Tsunematsu, 1993). Although the exact mechanisms leading to different family characteristics remain unknown, it is clear that the age, severity, and type of retardation may all affect the stress and coping of families of children with mental retardation.

New populations: Within and beyond mental retardation

Just as the developmental approach itself is expanding, so too has that approach been applied to new populations. Such extended applications go in two directions: toward examinations of subgroups within mental retardation, and toward children (and their families) with other disabilities.

Expanded applications within mental retardation. Beginning with Zigler's "two group approach" – the distinction between familial and organic forms of retardation – developmental workers have been cognizant of the etiology of the child's retardation. Like Werner before him, Zigler (1969) originally applied his ideas about sequences and structures only to children with familial retardation. These ideas appeared to work reasonably well. Summarizing numerous studies of Piagetian tasks, Weisz and Zigler (1979) found that, with very few exceptions, children with familial mental retardation do indeed traverse Piagetian sequences in the usual, predicted order. Similarly, at least for Piagetian tasks, such children seemed to have no specific deficits compared with mental-age-matched nonretarded children (Weisz & Yeates, 1981); these children may, however, be deficient compared with non-retarded children on a few specific tasks of information processing (Weiss, Weisz, & Bromfield, 1986; see Mundy & Kasari, 1990, and Weisz, 1990, for explanations).

In the early 1980s, however, several workers began applying Zigler's similar sequence and structure ideas to children with organic forms of mental retardation. Comparing their approach with Zigler's, Cicchetti and Pogge-Hesse (1982) described Zigler's original approach as a "conservative" application, in that it applied only to children showing no obvious cause of their retardation. They proposed instead a more "liberal" developmental approach that could be applied to children with Down syndrome and other organic causes of mental retardation. Cicchetti and his colleagues subsequently examined children with Down syndrome in terms of their sensorimotor sequences and structures (Cicchetti & Mans-Wagener, 1987), links between affect and cognition (Cicchetti & Sroufe, 1976, 1978), and the development of symbolic play and its relations to early language development (Beeghly & Cicchetti, 1987).

As the 1980s progressed, this more liberal developmental approach was formally applied to children with various forms of mental retardation. Burack, Hodapp, and Zigler (1988) explicitly called for a differentiation of the organic group, so that the many different organic forms of retardation could be examined separately. A good example of this approach relates to fragile X syndrome, the second most common genetic disorder of retardation (Dykens, Hodapp, & Leckman, 1994). In a series of studies, these children have been shown to be deficient in sequential, or bit-by-bit, processing (Dykens, Hodapp, & Leckman, 1987), to slow in their development in the early teen years (Dykens, Hodapp, & Leckman, 1989; Hodapp et al., 1990), and to show a specific profile of adaptive and maladaptive behaviors (Dykens et al., 1989). Many of these characteristics – for example, the weakness in sequential processing – do not characterize other organic groups such as Down syndrome (Hodapp et al., 1992).

And yet, although the call has been made to examine separately behavioral development in different organic forms of retardation, such an approach has only begun to be followed. With the exception of Down syndrome and, to some extent, fragile X syndrome, few etiologies of mental retardation have been the focus of in-depth developmental studies. Hodapp and Dykens (1994) attribute this lack of study to what they call the "two cultures" of behavioral research in mental retardation. These two cultures include biomedical workers – for example, geneticists, pediatricians, and psychiatrists – who are interested in etiology but are less sophisticated in behavioral studies, and behavior workers, including psychologists (of various subdisciplines), family researchers, and special educators, who are more sophisticated in behavioral research but who have historically been less interested in separating research groups by etiology. These two cultures must work together if we are ever to understand development in children with different forms of mental retardation.

Expanded applications to other disabled populations. Just as the expanded developmental approach has been applied to different organic groups within the retarded population, so too is that approach increasingly being applied to children with other disabilities. Although from Vygotsky on some developmentalists have been interested in children with deafness and blindness, only recently have developmentally oriented workers begun to examine development in children with these two disability conditions (Hodapp, in press).

The most exciting research so far has concerned deaf children's acquisition of sign language. In work beginning in the mid-1970s, Klima and Bellugi (1979) showed that sign language is indeed a fully fledged human language. Developmentally oriented workers have subsequently found that deaf children show a "similar sequence" in early grammatical and semantic development.

But such parallels to development in hearing children may occur even before formal language. Petitto and Marentette (1991) have recently discovered that deaf infants of deaf parents "babble" in sign from 10 to 14 months. Although both hearing and deaf infants demonstrate gestures such as holding out their hands to be picked up, deaf infants much more often produce complex hand movements found in signed letters or numbers, and repeat again and again these signlike gestures. Further, such manual babbling becomes increasingly complex with age, leading to what in hearing infants is called "jargon babbling," or meaningless babbling sequences that have intonation patterns similar to sentences. Petitto and Marentette (1991) conclude that infants possess an innate predisposition to babbling; such babbling – be it vocal or manual – provides "the mechanism by which infants discover the map between the structure of language and the means for producing this structure" (p. 251).

At later ages, deaf infants produce one-sign sentences at slightly earlier ages than the one-word utterances of hearing children. Yet these one-sign sentences express many of the same words as are found in the one-word sentences of hearing children ("Mommy," "Daddy," "milk," etc.; Newport & Meier, 1985). Two-word sentences next occur that relate semantic relations such as existence ("that ball"), action ("eat sandwich"), and state ("chair broken"); such relations develop in the same order in deaf children learning sign as in young children acquiring spoken language (Newport & Ashbrook, 1977). As such, young deaf children may develop early language along "similar sequences" to hearing children.

It also seems that signing deaf mothers provide input that mirrors the input of mothers of hearing children. Masataka (1992) examined the linguistic input of Japanese deaf mothers using sign with their 8- to 11-month-old deaf infants as compared with these mothers' signing with other deaf adults. In interacting with their infants, mothers "use signs at a relatively slower tempo and are more likely to repeat the same sign, and movements used to make the signs are exaggerated"

(p. 459). Similar to the behaviors of mothers with their hearing children, deaf mothers produce their own version of "motherese" in conversations with their language-learning infants.

Yet some interactional differences do occur because of the visual nature of sign language. Hearing mothers of deaf children, like mothers of hearing children, often provide linguistic input while they and their children jointly attend to a picture book or other object (Swisher, 1992). As a result of the mother's communicating while the child is attending to the object, these deaf children miss some of the mother's signs. In contrast, deaf mothers of deaf children let the child look at the object, wait until the child looks to the mother, and then sign their comments. Deaf mothers are thus optimally responsive to their young deaf children, but in a way that differs from the usual behaviors of hearing mothers with hearing children.

Although less often studied, blind children too are beginning to be the subject of modern developmental work (see Warren, 1994, for a review). Here the striking issue involves compensation. Not possessing the ability to visually "check" the face, direction of gaze, and physical movements of the adult interactor, blind children appear to more often use language to maintain the topic of their conversations (Mills, 1988). Parents, too, must learn to "read" their blind children – hence Fraiberg's (1977) seminal work on how mothers need to learn how to "hand-watch" to understand the emotional state of their infants. These findings are reminiscent of Vygotsky's views of how particular disabilities change the child's entire personality structure and of how adults need to find "roundabout ways" to reach children with disabilities (Reiber & Carton, 1993). To date, however, these differences – on the part of either the child or the adult interactor – remain generally unexplored.

New prospects using developmental approaches

Having briefly surveyed some past and present issues, we now turn to three future prospects using developmental approaches.

Better understandings of children with disabilities. Through modern developmental studies of children with disabilities, we have begun to know about the development of children with more disability conditions than ever before. We know, for example, how children with different disorders develop through various sequences and even which disability conditions show certain "nondevelopmental" patterns. Witness, for example, the blind child's use of language (and not nonlinguistic cues) to maintain the focus of conversation. In short, developmental approaches provide the yardstick by which usual orderings, rates, and patterns can be observed, as well as when compensations are used.

In the same way, future family work will better describe exactly which aspects of the child, parents, and family lead to different family outcomes. Given the recent emphasis on family functioning in both academic and policy circles (e.g., the Individualized Family Service Plan of PL 99-457, the federal early education initiative), it is critical to understand how families of these children operate, and how they can best be supported.

These advances have begun to occur by moving beyond examinations of "all children with retardation" or "all children with disabilities." Modern work has thus started focusing on development of children with particular genetic disorders in mental retardation, or on language development in deaf children of deaf parents. Only by more detailed, circumscribed studies will we increase our knowledge about development within each specific disorder or etiology.

Better, more focused interventions. Along with increases in developmental knowledge have arisen concomitant insights into how interventions are performed. Again, more specific information leads to more specific interventions. Thus, parents and teachers of children with fragile X syndrome have increasingly presented information in gestalt-like ways, capitalizing on these children's strengths (Hodapp & Dykens, 1991). The recent adoption of the LOGOS and other "whole word" reading programs follows from this insight (Sharfenaker, Hickman, & Braden, 1991).

Such insights are not limited to children with mental retardation. Using Swisher's (1992) finding of the importance of sequential and not simultaneous "input signing" to deaf children, educators are tailoring their programs to the visual nature of sign language. Such attempts, which have already been tried informally, should help these children to develop. More specialized, and effective, intervention programs should result.

Better understandings of "typical" developmental processes. Although this chapter applies developmental ideas to children with disabilities, one can also turn the equation around, focusing on children with disabilities to tell us about normal developmental processes. Such work capitalizes on the idea of the "experiment of nature," the use of any naturally occurring condition – be it organismic or environmental – to inform us about the typical or "usual" processes of development.

Although disabled development has provided many experiments of nature (Hodapp & Burack, 1990), a few deserve special notice. Most notably, research on Williams syndrome is demonstrating that language and thought need not always be so closely related. In effect, these children seem to display "language in the (relative) absence of thought," and discrepancies – mainly in strikingly high or low grammatical abilities – are also shown by the cases of Genie and Laura. From all these examples we know that horizontal structures of development may not exist; even if such structures do occur, they are likely to exist only at specific points in development, or to show only smaller "packets" of organization. Such conclusions are arising partly from studies of children with disabilities.

Similarly, deaf children may indicate that language is amodal, and not so tied to speech as was originally thought (Lenneberg, 1967). In contrast to earlier views, Petitto and Marentette's work argues that language is not necessarily related to speech per se. Instead, such findings suggest that the human brain is predisposed to learn any human language, whether that language be verbal, visual, or other. The young human needs only some input, in any modality, to begin to develop in language.

Conclusion

In considering developmental approaches to children with disabilities, we see a perspective that has a distinguished, living history as well as a productive future. Grounded in the ideas of great developmentalists such as Werner, Piaget, and Vygotsky, researchers have examined children with disabilities from the widest possible developmental perspectives. With Zigler's developmental approach, such ideas became formalized and applied to children with mental retardation. Since that time, Zigler's approach has been used as the gateway to new perspectives, populations, and prospects. The perspective has expanded to include new views of old topics (e.g., structures), as well as to encompass additional, heretofore unexplored topics (families, ecologies). Within and outside of mental retardation, new populations have been the subject of this expanded developmental approach. These extensions and applications, in turn, have led to new prospects for developmental approaches.

Although these new perspectives, populations, and prospects show the excitement inherent in developmental approaches, in many ways developmental perspectives have barely scratched the surface. Right now, for example, little is known about development in most types of retardation and in many different disabilities. Knowledge about family and other ecologies is even less advanced. In essence, then, while developmental approaches to children with disabilities predate Achenbach's "hardly existing" field of developmental psychopathology, much more remains to be learned.

References

Achenbach, T. (1974). *Developmental psychopathology.* New York: Ronald Press.
Baumeister, A. (1987). Mental retardation: Some concepts and dilemmas. *American Psychologist, 42,* 796–800.
Beeghly, M., & Cicchetti, D. (1987). An organizational approach to symbolic development in children with Down syndrome. *New Directions for Child Development, 36,* 5–29.
Bellugi, U., Wang, P., & Jerrigan, T. (1994). Williams syndrome: An unusual neuropsychological profile. In S. H. Broman & J. Grafman (Eds.), *Atypical cognitive deficits in developmental disorders* (pp. 23–56). Hillsdale, NJ: Erlbaum.
Blacher, J. (1984). Sequential stages of parental adjustment to the birth of a child with handicaps: Fact or artifact? *Mental Retardation, 22,* 55–68.
Bronfenbrenner, U. (1979). *The ecology of human development.* Cambridge, MA: Harvard University Press.
Brown, A. L., & Ferrara, R. (1985). Diagnosing zones of proximal development. In J. V. Wertsch (Ed.), *Culture, communication, and cognition: Vygotskian perspectives* (pp. 273–305). New York: Cambridge University Press.

204   R. M. HODAPP

Budoff, M. (1974). *Learning potential and educability among the educable mentally retarded.* Cambridge, MA: Research Institute for Educational Problems.

Burack, J. A. (1990). Differentiating mental retardation: The two-group approach and beyond. In R. M. Hodapp, J. A. Burack, & E. Zigler (Eds.), *Issues in the developmental approach to mental retardation* (pp. 27–48). New York: Cambridge University Press.

Burack, J. A., Hodapp, R. M., & Zigler, E. (1988). Issues in the classification of mental retardation: Differentiating among organic etiologies. *Journal of Child Psychology and Psychiatry, 29,* 765–779.

Burack, J. A., Hodapp, R. M., & Zigler, E. (Eds.). (in press). *Handbook of mental retardation and development.* New York: Cambridge University Press.

Cicchetti, D., & Beeghly, M. (Eds.). (1990). *Children with Down syndrome: A developmental approach.* New York: Cambridge University Press.

Cicchetti, D., & Mans-Wagener, L. (1987). Sequences, stages, and structures in the organization of cognitive development in infants with Down syndrome. In I. Uzgiris & J. McV. Hunt (Eds.), *Infant performance and experience: New findings with the Ordinal Scales* (pp. 281–310). Urbana, IL: University of Illinois Press.

Cicchetti, D., & Pogge-Hesse, P. (1982). Possible contributions of the study of organically retarded persons to developmental theory. In E. Zigler & D. Balla (Eds.), *Mental retardation: The developmental-difference controversy* (pp. 277–318). Hillsdale, NJ: Erlbaum.

Cicchetti, D., & Sroufe, L. A. (1976). The relationship between affective and cognitive development in Down syndrome infants. *Child Development, 47,* 920–929.

Cicchetti, D., & Sroufe, L. A. (1978). An organizational view of affect: Illustration from the study of Down's syndrome infants. In M. Lewis & L. Rosenblum (Eds.), *The developmental of affect.* (pp. 309–350). New York: Plenum.

Crnic, K., Friedrich, W., & Greenberg, M. (1983). Adaptation of families with mentally retarded children: A model of stress, coping, and family ecology. *American Journal of Mental Deficiency, 88,* 125–138.

Curtiss, S. (1977). *Genie: A psycholinguistic study of a modern-day "wild child."* New York: Academic Press.

Dunst, C. J. (1990). Sensorimotor development of infants with Down syndrome. In D. Cicchetti & M. Beeghly (Eds.), *Children with Down syndrome: A developmental approach* (pp. 180–230). New York: Cambridge University Press.

Dykens, E. M., Hodapp, R. M., & Leckman, J. F. (1987). Strengths and weaknesses in the intellectual functioning of males with fragile X syndrome. *American Journal of Mental Deficiency, 92,* 234–236.

Dykens, E. M., Hodapp, R. M., & Leckman, J. F. (1989). Adaptive and maladaptive functioning of institutionalized and noninstitutionalized fragile X males. *Journal of the American Academy of Child and Adolescent Psychiatry, 28,* 422–426.

Dykens, E. M., Hodapp, R. M., Leckman, J. F. (1994). *Behavior and development in fragile X syndrome.* Newbury Park, CA: Sage.

Dykens, E. M., Hodapp, R. M., Ort, S., Finucane, B., Shapiro, L., & Leckman, J. F. (1989). The trajectory of cognitive development in males with fragile X syndrome. *Journal of the American Academy of Child and Adolescent Psychiatry, 28,* 422–426.

Dykens, E. M., & Leckman, J. F. (1990). Developmental issues in fragile X syndrome. In R. M. Hodapp, J. A. Burack, & E. Zigler (Eds.), *Issues in the developmental approach to mental retardation* (pp. 226–245). New York: Cambridge University Press.

Fodor, J. (1983). *Modularity of mind: An essay on faculty psychology.* Cambridge, MA: MIT Press.

Fraiberg, S. (1977). *Insights from the blind.* New York: Basic Books.

Gardner, H. (1983). *Frames of mind.* New York: Basic Books.

Hodapp, R. M. (1995). Parenting children with Down syndrome and other types of mental retardation. In M. Bornstein (Ed.), *Handbook of parenting,* Vol. 1: *How children influence parents.* (pp. 233–253). Hillsdale, NJ: Erlbaum.

Hodapp, R. M. (in press). *Development and disabilities: Intellectual, sensory, and motor impairments.* New York: Cambridge University Press.

Hodapp, R. M., & Burack, J. A. (1990). What mental retardation tells us about typical development: The examples of sequences, rates, and cross-domain relations. *Developmental Psychopathology, 2,* 213–225.

Hodapp, R. M., Burack, J. A., & Zigler, E. (Eds.). (1990). *Issues in the developmental approach to mental retardation.* New York: Cambridge University Press.

Hodapp, R. M., & Dykens, E. M. (1991). Toward an etiology-specific strategy of early intervention with handicapped children. In K. Marfo (Ed.), *Early intervention in transition: Current perspectives on programs for handicapped children* (pp. 41–60). New York: Praeger Publishers.

Hodapp, R. M., & Dykens, E. M. (1994). Mental retardation's two cultures of behavioral research. *American Journal on Mental Retardation, 98,* 675–687.

Hodapp, R. M., Dykens, E. M., Hagerman, R., Schreiner, R., Lachiewicz, A., & Leckman, J. F. (1990). Developmental implications of changing trajectories of IQ in males with fragile X syndrome. *Journal of the American Academy of Child and Adolescent Psychiatry, 29,* 214–219.

Hodapp, R. M., Dykens, E. M., & Masino, L. L. (1997). Families of children with Prader-Willi syndrome: Stress-support and relations to child characteristics. *Journal of Autism and Developmental Disorders, 27,* 11–24.

Hodapp, R. M., Leckman, J. F., Dykens, E. M., Sparrow, S. S., Zelinsky, D. G., & Ort, S. I. (1992). K-ABC profiles in children with fragile X syndrome, Down syndrome, and nonspecific mental retardation. *American Journal on Mental Retardation, 97,* 39–46.

Hodapp, R. M., & Zigler, E. (1995). Past, present, and future issues in the developmental approach to mental retardation and developmental disabilities. In D. Cicchetti & D. J. Cohen (Eds.), *Manual of developmental psychopathology Vol. 2: Risk, disorder, and adaptation* (pp. 299–331). New York: Wiley.

Inhelder, B. (1943/1968). *The diagnosis of reasoning in the mentally retarded.* New York: John Day Company.

Klima, E., & Bellugi, U. (1979). *The signs of language.* Cambridge, MA: Harvard University Press.

Lane, E. B., & Kinder, E. F. (1939). Relativism in the thinking of subnormal subjects as measured by certain of Piaget's tests. *Journal of Genetic Psychology, 54,* 107–118.

Lenneberg, E. (1967). *Biological foundations of language.* New York: Wiley.

Lewis, E. O. (1933). Types of mental retardation and their social significance. *Journal of Mental Science, 79,* 298–304.

Masataka, N. (1992). Motherese in a signed language. *Infant Behavior and Development, 15,* 453–460.

McCubbin, H., & Patterson, J. (1983). Family transitions: Adaptation to stress. In H. McCubbin & C. Figley (Eds.), *Stress and the family* (Vol. 1). New York: Brunner/Mazel.

Mills, A. (1988). Visual handicap. In D. Bishop & K. Mogford (Eds.), *Language development in exceptional circumstances* (pp. 150–164). Edinburgh: Churchill Livingstone.

Mink, I., Nihira, K., & Meyers, C. E. (1983). Taxonomy of family life styles: I. Homes with TMR children. *American Journal of Mental Deficiency, 87,* 484–497.

Mink, I., Nihira, K., & Meyers, C. E. (1984). Taxonomy of family life styles: II. Homes with slow-learning children. *American Journal of Mental Deficiency, 89,* 111–123.

Minnes, P. M. (1989). Family stress associated with a developmentally handicapped child. *International Review of Research in Child Development, 15,* 195–226.

Mundy, P., & Kasari, C. (1990). The similar structure hypothesis and differential rate of development in mental retardation. In R. M. Hodapp, J. A. Burack, & E. Zigler (Eds.), *Issues in the developmental approach to mental retardation* (pp. 71–92). New York: Cambridge University Press.

Newport, E. L., & Ashbrook, E. F. (1977). The emergence of semantic relations in American Sign Language. *Papers and Reports in Child Language Development, 13,* 16–21.

Newport, E. L., & Meier, R. P. (1985). The acquisition of American Sign Language. In D. Slobin (Ed.), *The cross-linguistic study of language* (pp. 881–938). Hillsdale, NJ: Erlbaum.

Olshansky, S. (1962, April). Chronic sorrow: A response to having a mentally defective child. *Social Casework, 43,* 190–193.

Petitto, L. A., & Marentette, P. F. (1991). Babbling in the manual mode: Evidence for the ontogeny of language. *Science, 251,* 1493–1496.

Prothro, E. T. (1943). Egocentricity and abstraction in children and in adult aments. *American Journal of Psychology, 56,* 66–77.

Reilly, J. S., Klima, E., & Bellugi, U. (1990). Once more with feeling: Affect and language in atypical populations. *Development and Psychopathology, 2,* 367–391.

Rieber, R. W., & Carton, A. S. (Eds.). (1993). *The fundamentals of defectology,* Vol. 2: *The collected works of L. S. Vygotsky* (J. Knox & C. B. Stephens, trans.). New York: Plenum.

Seltzer, M., Krauss, M., & Tsunematsu, N. (1993). Adults with Down syndrome and their aging mothers: Diagnostic group differences. *American Journal on Mental Retardation, 97,* 496–508.

Sharfenaker, S., Hickman, L., & Braden, M. (1991). An integrated approach to intervention. In R. J. Hagerman & A. C. Silverman (Eds.), *Fragile X syndrome* (pp. 327–372). Baltimore: Johns Hopkins Press.

Solnit, A., & Stark, M. (1961). Mourning and the birth of a defective child. *Psychoanalytic Study of the Child, 16,* 523–537.

Swisher, M. V. (1992). The role of parents in developing visual turn-taking in their young deaf children. *American Annals of the Deaf, 137,* 92–100.

Tager-Flusberg, H. (Ed.). (1994). *Constraints on language acquisition: Studies of atypical children.* Hillsdale, NJ: Erlbaum.

Udwin, O., & Yule, W. (1990). Expressive language of children with Williams syndrome. *American Journal of Medical Genetics* (Supplement), *6,* 108–114.

van der Veer, R., & Valsiner, J. (1991). *Understanding Vygotsky: A quest for synthesis.* Oxford: Blackwell.

Vygotsky, L. S. (1978). *Mind in society.* Cambridge, MA: Harvard University Press.

Warren, D. B. (1994). *Blindness and children: An individual differences approach.* New York: Cambridge University Press.

Weiss, B., Weisz, J. R., & Bromfield, R. (1986). Performance of retarded and nonretarded persons on information-processing tasks: Further tests of the similar structure hypothesis. *Psychological Bulletin, 100,* 157–175.

Weisz, J. R. (1982). Learned helplessness and the retarded child. In E. Zigler & D. Balla (Eds.), *Mental retardation: The developmental-difference controversy* (pp. 27–40). Hillsdale, NJ: Erlbaum.

Weisz, J. R. (1990). Cultural-familial mental retardation: A developmental perspective on cognitive performance and "helpless" behavior. In R. M. Hodapp, J. A. Burack, & E. Zigler (Eds.), *Issues in the developmental approach to mental retardation* (pp. 137–168). New York: Cambridge University Press.

Weisz, J. R., & Yeates, K. (1981). Cognitive development in retarded and nonretarded persons: Piagetian tests of the similar structure hypothesis. *Psychological Bulletin, 90,* 153–178.

Weisz, J. R., Yeates, K., & Zigler, E. (1982). Piagetian evidence and the developmental-difference controversy. In E. Zigler & D. Balla (Eds.), *Mental retardation: The developmental-difference controversy* (pp. 213–276). Hillsdale, NJ: Erlbaum.

Weisz, J., & Zigler, E. (1979). Cognitive development in retarded and nonretarded persons: Piagetian tests of the similar sequence hypothesis. *Psychological Bulletin, 86,* 831–851.

Werner, H. (1937). Process and achievement: A basic problem of education and developmental psychology. *Harvard Educational Review, 7,* 353–368.

Werner, H. (1941). Psychological processes investigating deficiencies in learning. *American Journal of Mental Deficiency, 46,* 233–235.

Werner, H. (1957). The concept of development from a comparative and organismic point of view. In D. Harris (Ed.), *The concept of development* (pp. 125–148). Minneapolis: University of Minnesota Press.

Werner, H., & Strauss, A. (1939). Problems and methods of functional analysis in mentally deficient children. *Journal of Abnormal and Social Psychology, 34,* 37–62.

Wertsch, J. V. (1985). *Vygotsky and the social formation of mind.* Cambridge, MA: Harvard University Press.

Wikler, L. (1986). Periodic stresses of families of older mentally retarded children: An exploratory study. *American Journal of Mental Deficiency, 90,* 703–706.

Wishart, J. G., & Duffy, L. (1990). Instability of performance on cognitive tests in infants and young children with Down's syndrome. *British Journal of Educational Psychology, 60,* 10–22.

Witkin, H. (1964). Heinz Werner: 1890–1964. *Child Development, 30,* 307–328.

Woodward, M. (1959). The behavior of idiots interpreted by Piaget's theory of sensorimotor development. *British Journal of Educational Psychology, 29,* 60–71.

Woodward, M. (1963). The application of Piaget's theory of research in mental deficiency. In N. R. Ellis (Ed.), *Handbook of mental deficiency* (pp. 297–324). New York: McGraw-Hill.

Yamada, J. E. (1990). *Laura: A case for the modularity of language.* Cambridge, MA: MIT Press.

Zigler, E. (1967). Familial mental retardation: A continuing dilemma. *Science, 155,* 292–298.

Zigler, E. (1969). Developmental versus difference theories of retardation and the problem of motivation. *American Journal of Mental Deficiency, 73,* 536–556.

Zigler, E. (1971). The retarded child as a whole person. In H. E. Adams & W. K. Boardman (Eds.), *Advances in experimental clinical psychology* (pp. 47–121). Oxford: Pergamon.

Zigler, E. (1984). A developmental theory on mental retardation. In B. Blatt & R. Morris (Eds.), *Perspectives in special education: Personal orientations* (pp. 173–209). Santa Monica, CA: Scott, Foresman.

Zigler, E., & Burack, J. A. (1989). Personality development in the dually diagnosed person. *Research in Developmental Disabilities, 10,* 225–240.

Zigler, E., & Hodapp, R. M. (1986). *Understanding mental retardation.* New York: Cambridge University Press.

10   The pervasive developmental disorders: Nosology and profiles of development

Ami Klin and Fred R. Volkmar

Among the various seminal contributions to the field of mental retardation made by Ed Zigler over the years, two general ideas, the syndrome-specific approach to developmental disabilities (Zigler, 1967; Hodapp, Burack, & Zigler, 1990) and the consideration of the disabled individual as a "whole person" (Zigler & Hodapp, 1986), have recently engendered a great deal of attention and research in the field of autism and related disorders. The first idea is associated with the need to investigate the different developmental paths followed by individuals with early and severe social disabilities. This idea has energized clinical research programs intended to delineate in ever increasing detail and complexity new phenomenological (if not yet etiological) subgroups. The second idea is associated with the need to separate the disability from the individual affected by it, thus appreciating the complexity of each socially disabled person's psychological makeup and the vast heterogeneity characterizing the individuals grouped under broad diagnostic categories. This approach prompted the investigation of the interactions between empirical clusters of strengths and deficits on the one hand, and the demands of the social environment on the other hand, furthering our understanding of profiles of adjustment and their implication for the disabled individual's day-to-day life.

In this chapter, the syndrome-specific approach will be illustrated through a review of the new nosology of the pervasive developmental disorders: broad and amorphous categories are slowly evolving into empirically derived and more homogeneous subgroups, with increasingly greater importance ascribed to processes and pathways of development. The "individual as a whole person" approach will be illustrated through a discussion of recent investigations that have delineated two profiles of adjustment observed in individuals with "higher-functioning" autism (HFA) and in individuals with Asperger syndrome (AS). Although the profiles of individuals with HFA and AS resemble phenomenologically, they appear to evolve out of different constitutional endowment and to follow different adaptation pathways.

Syndrome specificity: A new nosology of the pervasive developmental disorders

Although the recent history of early and severe social disabilities dates from Kanner's (1943) description of "infantile autism," many important accounts had preceded it, documenting the puzzling deviance observed in some children in respect to their interaction with others as well as their numerous and conspicuous behavioral peculiarities. Langdon Down's (Scheerer, Rothmann, & Goldstein, 1945) descriptions of "idiot savants" with the emphasis on the curious juxtaposition of mental handicap and isolated prodigious skills, De Sanctis's concept of *dementia praecocissima* which attempted to extend into early childhood Kraeplin's accounts of conditions characterized by social and cognitive deterioration and stereotypic behavior, and Earl's (1934) report on mute children who exhibited a profound social aloofness and marked engagement in repetitive and purposeless movements, to name only a few, were all insightful attempts to capture the phenomenology of autism. None of these accounts, however, survived the test of time.

The absence of a discipline characterizing children's normative development led to simple extensions of psychopathological concepts derived from the work with psychotic adults. As such, these descriptions could contribute little more than an acknowledgment of the general clinical phenomena and the mistaken notion that, because of their severity, such conditions were simply the early precursors or equivalents of adult schizophrenia (Volkmar & Cohen, 1988). Devoid of a developmental perspective, there were no promising research leads or treatment interventions that could be derived and explored. Most of these diagnostic concepts are now of only historical value (Klin & Volkmar, 1997).

A notable exception to the absence of a developmental perspective in the description of childhood disorders can be found in the early work of Melanie Klein (1930/1975), whose clinical descriptions and object-relations theory prepared the ground for later psychoanalytic conceptualizations of autism (e.g., Mahler, 1952). However, the priority given to theory and the rigidity of its framework, combined with poor results of long-term psychoanalytic treatment and the emergence of empirical research contradicting its assumptions, resulted in the virtual abandonment of the psychoanalytic approach to early social disorders, at least in the English-speaking countries.

In contrast to these various approaches, Kanner's "infantile autism" reflected a clinical attitude that emphasized phenomenological description devoid of theoretical preconceptions, and that strived to incorporate the findings of the new discipline of child development, as exemplified in the work of Gesell (see D. Cohen, Volkmar, Anderson, & Klin, 1993, for a discussion). Free from the fetters of dogmatic theorizing and empowered by a burgeoning understanding of children's normative skills, Kanner's new approach represented not only a landmark accomplishment but also a paradigmatic shift that has shaped the new nosology of childhood disorders in general, and of social disabilities in particular. His concept of autism and its clinical features proved remarkably enduring, surviving almost intact to the present day.

Although the nosological status of Kanner's autism was never in question, the various other concepts and descriptions depicting variants of this condition never obtained a degree of consensual agreement among clinicians. As a result, when autism was first made official in the third edition of the *Diagnostic and Statistical Manual of the American Psychiatric Association* (DSM-III; APA, 1980), an overarching category of pervasive developmental disorders (PDD) was created with a view to differentiate conditions in which specific developmental processes are affected (e.g., language, motor skills) and conditions in which virtually no developmental process is spared (e.g., autism and autistic-like conditions). However, within the PDD class, DSM-III, as well as its revision, DSM-III-R (APA, 1987), included only autism and a "subthreshold" category (termed "atypical PDD" in DSM-III and "PDD – not otherwise specified," or PDD-NOS in DSM-III-R). The latter category was intended to encompass all variants of autism that did not fulfill criteria for Kanner's syndrome as summarized by Rutter (1978). An additional condition – childhood onset PDD, which differed from autism mainly in terms of its later onset – was dropped in DSM-III-R (APA, 1987) in view of the dearth of reported cases (Volkmar & Cohen, 1988).

The subthreshold or residual category of PDD-NOS, which by definition had no specific defining criteria in excess of a general autistic-like denotation, posed a challenge to clinicians' communication and hindered research on such conditions (as there were no defining criteria to characterize the experimental samples). In fact, this category added little more than a demarcation of uncharted territory of clinical complexity. And yet, children diagnosed with PDD-NOS appeared to correspond to the majority of children presenting with a pervasive developmental disorder (Klin, Mayes, Volkmar, & Cohen, 1995).

More recently, a renewed interest in variants of autism have resulted in the revival of several different diagnostic concepts. As a result of that, the 10th edition of the *International Classification of Diseases* (ICD-10; WHO, 1992), and DSM-IV (APA, 1994) now include various other syndromes under the overarching class of PDD. In contrast to previous nosologic systems, however, DSM-IV represents the result of a large clinical trial including over 1,000 children with autism and related conditions originating from 19 clinical centers worldwide (Volkmar et al., 1994). Categories were included on the basis of empirical analyses; great attention was given to developmental processes and onset of psychopathology. And yet, despite the various additions – Rett syndrome, child disintegrative disorder, and Asperger syndrome, the so-called residual category – PDD-NOS continues to be the commonest diagnosis among the PDDs. This emphasizes the need for increased attention and investigation into this undefined category.

The history of the autistic-like conditions has been, therefore, one of increased empiricism, of increased attention to developmental processes, and of unrelenting progress toward syndrome-specific understanding. This new nosology mirrors the progress made in the field of mental retardation (Hodapp and Dykens, 1991), although the two efforts are not equivalent. While mental retardation research can make use of genetic syndromes associated with mental retardation in order to accomplish subgrouping based on etiology, autism research can only, at this point, achieve subgrouping based on phenomenology and syndrome-specific developmental pathways. The achievement of a more homogeneous and detailed subclassification remains, however, the sine qua non of an improved understanding of these conditions' etiology and pathogenesis.

Autism

Kanner's (1943) original description of infantile autism contained detailed clinical descriptions of 11 children he had seen over a period of a few years whose most striking feature was a fundamental lack of the usual interest in other people, which had a very early onset. It is now recognized that this condition is often associated with mental retardation and a host of medical conditions (Volkmar & Cohen, 1988). Although the evidence in favor of some neurobiologic process or processes underlying the pathogenesis of the disorder is impressive, precise etiologic mechanisms have yet to be defined. The validity of autism as a diagnostic category has been suggested by various lines of evidence, including the age of onset of the condition, its clinical features, and associated neurobiologic findings (Kolvin, 1971; Rutter, 1978).

In his original description, Kanner emphasized the importance of a disturbance in social relatedness as the hallmark of the condition. Subsequent definitions have typically also included this feature as a central aspect of the disorder, along with delayed and deviant communicative development, a variety of unusual behaviors, and very early onset (Rutter & Schopler, 1992). Particularly in younger children with autism, social development is quantitatively and qualitatively different from that observed in both normally developing children and in children with mental retardation of comparable mental age (Klin & Volkmar, 1997). Quantitatively, social skills are typically at a much lower level than expected given the child's overall cognitive level (Volkmar et al., 1987), a phenomenon that has long been an important and defining criteria of the social disability exhibited by individuals with autism (Rutter, 1978). For example, a study directly comparing children with autism and children with mental retardation individually matched for chronological and mental age in regard to social behaviors normatively acquired in the first 9 months of life revealed that the two groups of children could be empirically differentiated based on the lack of these early social behaviors in the autistic group (Klin, Volkmar, & Sparrow, 1992).

Qualitatively, the deviant behaviors observed in autism are typically not found in children with other developmental disabilities regardless of developmental level. In normative development, there are a host of perceptual, affective, and neuroregulatory mechanisms that predispose and insure the young infants' engagement in social interaction from very early in their lives (Tronick, 1980; J. Cohn & Tronick, 1987). Against the background of normative development, the social deficits of autistic children are striking, appearing to be present from birth, or at least from the first few months of life (Rutter, 1974). In stark contrast to what happens with normally developing infants, the human face appears to hold little interest or have little salience for the autistic child (Volkmar, 1987). Typical forms of early non-verbal interchange are deviant, so that usually very early emerging forms of inter-subjectivity and communicative behavior are absent (Klin & Volkmar, 1993). Children with autism may not seek physical comfort from parents and may be difficult to hold (Ornitz, Guthrie, & Farley, 1977).

It is important to note, however, that the severity of the autistic social deviance is closely related to overall developmental level. For example, a range of social interactional styles has been described in autistic children. These styles range from aloof to passive and to eccentric (Wing & Atwood, 1987). These styles are strongly related to developmental level, the younger and more mentally retarded child more likely to be in the aloof extreme whereas the older and more cognitively advanced child more likely to be in the passive or "active but odd" or eccentric end of the spectrum (Volkmar, Cohen, Bregman, Hooles, & Stevenson, 1989).

Children with autism also exhibit profound problems with communication in all its various aspects (Paul, 1987). Many individuals with autism never talk communica-tively, and those who do have speech that is remarkably deviant in many ways, in-cluding echolalia, extreme literalness, poor intonational patterns, and limited pragmatic skills. Even those more cognitively advanced individuals with autism (i.e., with intelligence within the normal or above normal range) have major problems with the subtleties of communication, for example, with integration of affective cues, the nonliteral content (e.g., figurative language, irony) and suprasegmental aspects (e.g., intonation, stress) of speech and language (Klin & Volkmar, 1997).

Individuals with autism also exhibit a variety of unusual behaviors, which are usually subsumed under terms such as "resistance to change" or "insistence on sameness": These include difficulties with changes in routine (e.g., in the route taken to school) and transitions (e.g., from one activity to another), the development of stereotyped (i.e., purposeless and repetitive) behaviors (e.g., flapping hands, rocking, twirling), which appear to be a source of pleasure to the individual. There is often a preferential interest in the inanimate environment; for example, the child who does not respond to a parent's departure may become highly attached to a specific book or unusual object (e.g., a string). In contrast to normally developing toddlers, autistic children often have a particular interest in nonfunctional aspects of objects, and play may take the form of repeated ordering or reordering of toys, lining them up, or exploring unusual aspects of the play materials such as their smell or texture (Volkmar, 1987).

Nonautistic PDDs

Similarly to autism, which involves severe disturbance in multiple different areas of development, there are other disorders that have recently been included under the PDD class but which remain to be further validated and understood (Klin &

Volkmar, 1995). These conditions are of interest for various reasons, including the identification of potential neuropathological mechanisms. The effort to identify subgroups within the PDD class may provide more specific directives for biological and psychological research, thus reducing the common phenomenological heterogeneity found in study samples and advancing syndrome-specific knowledge (Volkmar et al., 1994).

Childhood disintegrative disorder. In 1908, Theodore Heller, a Viennese educator, reported six cases of children who had developed normally until 3 to 4 years of age and then exhibited marked developmental and behavioral deterioration with only minimal subsequent recover. He named this condition "dementia infantilis"; the name of the condition changed subsequently to Heller's syndrome and has been recently incorporated in DSM-IV (APA, 1994) as childhood disintegrative disorder. This is probably an extremely rare disorder, as only about 100 cases have been reported in the world literature (Volkmar, 1994). Generally, early development is entirely normal and the child progresses to the point of speaking in sentences prior to the onset of a profound developmental regression. Once established, the condition is behaviorally similar to autism, although the prognosis is even worse (Volkmar & Cohen, 1989). In some instances the condition has been reported in association with a specific disease process, for example, a progressive neurological condition (Corbett, 1987). As a result, the disorder was not included in DSM-III (APA, 1980) or DSM-III-R (APA, 1987) on the presumption that these cases invariably reflected some other degenerative medical condition. However, it is clear that such a medical condition is observed and documented only in a minority of cases (Volkmar, 1994).

Rett syndrome. Andreas Rett (1966) described a condition now commonly referred to as Rett syndrome. He had observed two girls in a waiting room who exhibited remarkably similar patterns of deviant behavior and course of development. Rett was later able to identify a series of 22 cases. Although autistic-like behaviors are observed, particularly during the preschool years, this syndrome differs from autism in several ways: It has been reported only in females, the more "autistic-like" phase is relatively brief, and it is associated with characteristic stereotyped motor behaviors (resembling hand "washing" or "wringing" movements) and abnormalities in gait or trunk movement. Breath-holding spells and seizures are common and associated mental retardation is even more severe than in autism. The early history is remarkable for initially normal early growth and development, followed (usually in the first months of life) by developmental regression and deceleration of head growth and loss of purposeful hand movements. The apparently normal period of development is much shorter than that observed in childhood disintegrative disorder (Tsai, 1994). Despite the insidious regression in development and other neurological findings, the pathophysiology of the condition remains unknown (Trevathan & Naidu, 1988).

Asperger syndrome. In the year following Kanner's (1943) report, Hans Asperger (1944/1991), a Viennese physician, described a group of individuals who, despite adequate intellectual skills, exhibited social and behavioral peculiarities that made it difficult for them to participate in group activities and develop friendships (e.g., problems with social interaction and communication, and circumscribed and idiosyncratic patterns of interest). However, Asperger's description differed from Kanner's in that speech was less commonly delayed, motor deficits were more common, the onset appeared to be somewhat later, and all of the initial cases occurred in boys. Asperger also suggested that similar problems could be observed in family members, particularly fathers. Unaware of Kanner's work, Asperger coined the term "autistic psychopathy" to characterize the condition as a personality disorder (Asperger 1944/1991).

This condition was essentially unknown in the English literature for many years. An influential review and series of case reports by Wing (1981) increased interest in the condition, and, since then, both the usage of the term in clinical practice and number of case reports have been steadily increasing (Klin, 1994). The commonly described clinical features of the syndrome include paucity of empathy; naive, inappropriate, one-sided social interaction, little ability to form friendships and consequent social isolation; pedantic and monotonic speech; poor nonverbal communication; intense absorption in circumscribed topics such as the weather, facts about television stations, railway tables or maps, which are learned in rote fashion and reflect poor understanding, conveying the impression of eccentricity; and clumsy and ill-coordinated movements and odd posture (Wing, 1981).

Although Asperger originally reported the condition only in boys, reports of girls with the syndrome have now appeared. Nevertheless, males are significantly more likely to be affected (Szatmari, Tuff, Finlayson, & Bartolucci, 1989; Wing, 1991). Although most individuals with the condition function within the average range of intelligence, some have been reported to be mildly retarded (Wing, 1981). The apparent onset of the condition, or at least its recognition, is probably somewhat later than autism; this may primarily reflect the more preserved language and cognitive abilities (Klin & Volkmar, 1996). Asperger syndrome tends to be highly stable (Asperger, 1979), and the higher intellectual skills observed suggest a better outcome than is typically observed in autism (Tantam, 1991). Specific learning problems and marked discrepancies between various intellectual skills may be present (Ozonoff, Rogers, & Pennington, 1991; Klin, Volkmar, Sparrow, Cicchetti, & Rourke, 1995).

Atypical PDD/PDD-NOS. The term PDD-NOS was used in DSM-III-R (APA, 1987) to replace the earlier term "atypical PDD"; this latter concept had unintentionally, although probably correctly, been suggestive of Rank's earlier diagnostic notion of "atypical personality development" (Rank & MacNaughton, 1950), a term also used to describe children with some, but not all, features of autism. Such children exhibit patterns of unusual sensitivities, difficulties in social interaction, and other problems suggestive of autism without meeting full criteria for autistic disorder (Volkmar et al., 1994).

The term PDD-NOS is problematic in several respects. The category is poorly defined since the definition is essentially a negative one, and although the condition is probably much more common than strictly defined autism (Klin, Mayes, Volkmar, & Cohen, 1995), research on PDD-NOS has been uncommon. The lack of an explicit definition also means that the concept is used rather inconsistently: For example, some investigators equate it with Asperger syndrome whereas others view it as on some underlying spectrum with autism, both in terms of developmental functioning and severity of symptomatology. More commonly the term PDD-NOS has been used for children with better cognitive and communicative skills, and some degree of relatedness. The most common reasons for referral in such cases include concerns of parents about the child's emotional and social development, rather than, as in autism, the failure to develop language.

Over the years, children currently captured by the term PDD-NOS have been characterized by numerous diagnostic labels that have been used to provide a taxonomic location and convey the nature of their social and emotional difficulties in relating. While informal descriptions included terms such as eccentric, odd, overanxious, aloof, and "weird," formal designations included terms such as borderline, schizotypal, schizoidal disorders, atypical development, childhood psychosis, symbiotic states, and others (Klin, Mayes, Volkmar, & Cohen, 1995). No term, however, has been fully satisfactory or broadly accepted, and while clinicians have had the sense of a category of such children, there are as yet no clearly defined diagnostic criteria that could guide systematic studies, including those on the basic validity or utility of such a grouping.

There have been several attempts to delineate subgroups within the larger PDD-NOS category, involving terms such as multiplex developmental disorder (Cohen, Paul, & Volkmar, 1986), childhood onset schizophrenia (McKenna, Gordon, Lenane, & Rappoport, 1994), and others. No taxonomy of conditions related to children currently assigned by default to the PDD-NOS category is, as yet, operationally defined or broadly accepted. Devoid of pathognomonic symptomatology such as the profound social disability in autism, or profound regression as in childhood disintegrative disorder, it becomes very difficult for investigators to agree on specific clusters of symptoms and deficits that define specific disorders. Given the vast variability in phenomenology, the need for careful studies of profiles of development and adjustment, including quantification of deficits and deviance, is in no area of childhood disorders more essential than in this rather amorphous PDD-NOS category. Future efforts must account for the fact that the pervasive impact inflicted by early disturbances of basic developmental processes, specifically socialization skills and the emergence of a consolidated sense of self, is likely to have a broad range of effects on multiple aspects of development with varied manifestations (Cicchetti & Cohen, 1995).

Developmental profiles in autism and related conditions: The developmental-difference controversy

Zigler's (1967) developmental approach to mental retardation has integrated developmental issues with personality and motivational factors as well as with etiologies (see Hodapp & Zigler, 1995, for a discussion). Within this approach a major focus of work has been the notions that the development of persons with mental retardation follows the same sequence as in the normative population (the similar sequence hypothesis), and that development across domains will be relatively even (the similar structure hypothesis) (Zigler, 1969). There is evidence to suggest that the similar sequence hypothesis applies for both familially and organically retarded individuals (Cicchetti & Pogge-Hesse, 1982; Weisz & Zigler, 1979) but that the similar structure hypothesis applies only to familially retarded persons (Weisz & Yeates, 1981).

The applicability of this framework to the development of individuals with autism and related disorders has been questioned for several reasons. Various reports have suggested that the development of such children is characterized by unusual lags and spurts (Fish, Shapiro, Halpern, & Wile, 1965), developmental regressions (Harper & Williams, 1975; Hoshino et al., 1987), and unevenness across domains of functioning (Volkmar et al., 1987; Snow, Hertzig, & Shapiro, 1987; Loveland & Kelley, 1988).

Burack and Volkmar (1992) compared sequences and structures of development in groups of autistic and nonautistic but developmentally disabled children. They noted that autistic children were more likely to have exhibited regression in communicative skills but other differences in developmental sequences were minimal within a given line of development. However, the autistic children showed significantly greater disparity between developmental domains. Similar findings have been reported by Prizant and Wetherby (1997) and others (see Volkmar, Burack, & Cohen, in press, for a discussion). Recent attention has been focused on aspects of different developmental profiles as a method of subtyping conditions with the pervasive developmental disorder class; in this emerging area of work the issues related to the developmental distinctions between higher-functioning autism and Asperger syndrome have been central.

Developmental profiles in "higher-functioning" autism and Asperger syndrome

As noted previously, two rather similar conditions are included in the higher-functioning (i.e., more cognitively advanced) end of the spectrum of the PDDs, namely autism unaccompanied by mental retardation or high-functioning autism and Asperger syndrome. Although the phenomenological similarities between these two conditions have prompted the argument that differences reported refer more to degree rather than nature of the social disability, some recent research developments question this belief, opening the possibility for the exploration of two, possibly distinct, pathogenic courses and consequent profiles of adjustment. More specifically, these recent developments have suggested that the final common pathway bringing together HFA and AS may actually originate from different developmental profiles, which may in turn correspond to different etiologies. The hypothesis in question traces autism to a constitutional inability to react differentially to social stimuli, expressed developmentally in a lack of interest in, and limited capacity to attach to, others, whereas AS is traced to a specific cluster of neurological deficits affecting the ability to process nonverbal stimuli, expressed developmentally in terms of an inability to interact competently with others despite a keen interest in, and motivation to interact with, other people. This hypothesis signifies an attempt to reconceptualize the phenomenology of HFA and AS in terms of pathways of adjustment resulting from the interaction between different constitutional disabilities and the demands posed by the social environment. The explication of this hypothesis is preceded by a more detailed description of the lines of convergence and divergence between HFA and AS.

HFA and AS: Convergence and divergence

Although AS may be differentiated from other pervasive developmental disorders on the basis of developmental/intellectual level (i.e., the vast majority of individuals with autism, Rett syndrome, and childhood disintegrative disorder are mentally retarded), and on the basis of severity of the social and, to a lesser extent, communicative deficits (e.g., individuals with AS appear to be more affected than individuals for whom the diagnosis of PDD-NOS seems more appropriate) (Volkmar & Cohen, 1991), its validity apart from HFA remains controversial (Rutter, 1985; Klin & Volkmar, 1996; Wing, 1991). Disagreements about the validity of the category and the absence until recently of "official" definitions of AS have meant that the concept is often used inconsistently by clinicians, who may employ it to refer to autistic persons with higher levels of intelligence, adults with autism, or even as a broader term for all "atypical" children who do not fulfill criteria for autism (Volkmar et al., 1994).

There is little disagreement over the fact that AS is on a phenomenological continuum with autism, particularly in relation to the problems in the areas of social and communication functioning (Rutter, 1989). What is less clear is whether the condition is qualitatively different from, rather than just a milder form of, autism unaccompanied by mental retardation (Volkmar & Cohen, 1991). There are several lines of divergence between the two syndromes, although most of these have not yet been definitively established (Klin, 1994).

Individuals with AS are often socially isolated but are not as unaware of the presence of others as persons with autism, even though their approaches may be inappropriate and peculiar. For example, they may engage the interlocutor, usually an adult, in one-sided conversation characterized by long-winded, pedantic speech, about a favorite and often unusual and narrow topic. Also, although individuals with AS are often self-described "loners," they may express a great interest in making friendships and meeting people. These wishes are invariably thwarted by their awkward approaches and insensitivity to other person's feelings, intentions, and nonliteral and implied communications (e.g., signs of boredom, haste to leave, and need for privacy) (Tantam, 1991). Chronically frustrated by their repeated failures to engage others and make friends, some of these individuals develop symptoms of a mood disorder. In regard to the emotional aspects of social trans-actions, individuals with AS may react inappropriately to, or fail to interpret the valence of, the context of the affective interaction, often conveying a sense of insensitivity, formality or disregard to the other person's emotional expressions. That notwithstanding, they may be able to correctly describe, in a cognitive and often formalistic fashion, other people's emotions, expected intentions, and social conventions, but are unable to act upon this knowledge in an intuitive and spon-taneous fashion, losing, therefore, the tempo of the interaction (Klin, 1994). Such poor intuition and lack of spontaneous adaptation are accompanied by marked reliance on formalistic rules of behavior and rigid social conventions (Wing, 1981). This presentation is largely responsible for the impression of social naiveté and behavioral rigidity that is so forcefully conveyed by these individuals.

The communicative functioning of individuals with AS differs from that of in-dividuals with HFA in that delays and deviance in formal language are much less typically observed. Nevertheless, at least three aspects of these individual's com-munication are of clinical interest. First, though inflection and intonation may not be as rigid and monotonic as in autism, speech may be marked by poor prosody. For example, there may be a constricted range of intonation patterns which are used with little regard to the communicative functioning of the utterance (assertions of fact, humorous remarks, etc.) (Klin, Sparrow, Volkmar, Cicchetti, & Rourke, 1995). Second, speech may often be tangential and circumstantial, conveying a sense of looseness of associations and incoherence (Asperger, 1944/1991). Even though in a few cases this symptom may be an indicator of a possible thought disorder (Dykens, Volkmar, & Glick, 1991), it is often the case that the lack of contingency in speech is a result of the one-sided, egocentric conversational style (the unrelenting monologues about, e.g., the names, codes, and attributes of innu-merable television stations in the country), failure to provide the background for comments and clearly demarcate changes in topic, and failure to suppress the vocal output accompanying internal thoughts. The third aspect typifying the communi-cation patterns of individuals with AS concerns the marked verbosity observed, which some authors (Tantam, 1991; Wing, 1981) see as one of the most prominent differential features of the disorder. The child or adult may talk incessantly, usually about a favorite subject, often in complete disregard to whether the listener might be interested, engaged, or attempting to interject a comment or change the subject of conversation. Despite such long-winded monologues, the individual may never come to a point or conclusion. Attempts by the interlocutor to elaborate on issues of content or logic, or to shift the interchange to related topics are often not successful.

Although these peculiarities in language use are less commonly reported in persons with autism, they have been difficult to substantiate empirically, given the paucity of good measures of the pragmatic and prosodic aspects of speech. Hence they cannot as yet be used for the purpose of differential diagnosis.

Two other areas of symptomatology are sometimes reported to differentiate AS from HFA. The first involves the delay of motor milestones and presence of "motor clumsiness," whereas the second involves an all-encompassing absorption with a circumscribed interest. These two symptoms, and particularly "clumsiness," are commonly mentioned in reports of AS (Ghaziuddin, Tsai, & Ghaziuddin, 1992a), and are in accordance with Asperger's (1944/1991) original description. Individuals with AS may have a history of delayed acquisition of motor skills such as pedaling a bike, catching a ball, opening jars, or climbing "monkey-bars" and are often visibly awkward, exhibiting rigid gait patterns, odd posture, poor manipulative skills, and significant deficits in visual–motor coordination. Although this presentation contrasts with the pattern of motor development in autistic children, for whom motor skills are often a relative strength (Volkmar et al., 1987), it is similar in some respects to what is observed in older autistic individuals (DeMyer, 1976). Nevertheless, the commonality in later life may result from different underlying factors, for example, psychomotor deficits in the case of AS and poor body image and sense of self in the case of autism. Hence the importance of describing this symptom in developmental terms (Ghaziuddin, Tsai, & Ghaziuddin, 1992b). The second area of symptomatology refers to an "isolated special skill, often related to abnormal preoccupations." Even though this formulation could encompass a wide range of "splinter skills" evidenced in individuals with PDD, from proficiency at assembling puzzles, drawing, and musical abilities, to amassing vast amounts of factual knowledge about unusual subjects such as meteorology. Manipulative, visual-spatial, and musical skills, as well as "savant talents" are more commonly described in autism, whereas the amassing of factual information about an all-absorbing, circumscribed topic appears to be more typical in AS (Klin & Volkmar, 1996).

A final area of divergence between AS and HFA regards the patterns of onset of the two conditions. By definition, the diagnosis of AS can only be made if there is a lack of clinically significant delay or deviance in regard to cognitive and language development, at least in respect to formal aspects of language (in contrast to language use) in the first 3 years of life. This contrasts with the patterns of onset in autism in which delays and deviance and language development are commonly observed (APA, 1994).

The lack of an operationally defined, and until recently, consensually agreed definition of AS has impeded progress in research intended to validate this condition. More important, the lack of markers independent of the phenomenological description has complicated the interpretation and comparability of available research findings, as these investigations have been characterized by a great deal of circularity (Klin, 1994). In order to validate the syndrome, particularly vis-à-vis HFA, there are two conditions that need to be established: (1) explicit, stringent, and operationally defined, consensual categorical descriptions of both AS and HFA need to be employed; and (2) factors external to the definition of the syndrome – for example, neurobiological, family genetic, or neuropsychological data – need to be explored in order to justify the utility of the diagnostic assignments as well as to investigate their external validity. In the past year, the first condition has been at least partially met with the formalization of AS in DSM-IV and ICD-10 (Volkmar et al., 1994). The second condition is currently being explored by some researchers through the use of a neuropsychological model of AS (Klin & Volkmar, 1996). This model relates to Rourke's (1989) concept of nonverbal learning disabilities syndrome (NLD).

Neuropsychological profiles in HFA and AS

The NLD profile is characterized by a cluster of deficits affecting the nonverbal aspects of the child's visual-spatial, social, and communicative functioning (Rourke, 1989). The neuropsychological characteristics of individuals exhibiting this condition include deficits in tactile perception, psychomotor coordination, visual-spatial organization, nonverbal problem solving, and appreciation of incongruities and humor. NLD individuals also exhibit well-developed rote verbal capacities and verbal memory skills, difficulty in adapting to novel and complex situations and overreliance on rote behaviors in such situations, relative deficits in mechanical arithmetic as compared with proficiencies in single-word reading, poor pragmatics and prosody in speech, and significant deficits in social perception, social judgment, and social interaction skills. There are marked deficits in the appreciation of subtle and even fairly obvious nonverbal aspects of communication, which often result in other persons' social disdain and rejection. As a result, NLD individuals show a marked tendency toward social withdrawal and are at risk for development of serious mood disorders.

When a study (Klin, Volkmar, Sparrow, Cicchetti, & Rourke, 1995) of 40 individuals with AS and HFA examined their neuropsychological functioning in 22 areas defining the concept of NLD, the two groups differed in 11 areas, 9 of which were independent from the psychiatric diagnostic assignment. There was a high level of concordance between AS (but not HFA) and NLD, suggesting that NLD could be seen as an adequate neuropsychological marker of AS. Interestingly, such neuropsychological differences between AS and HFA were captured in the groups' verbal–performance IQ discrepancy, with verbal IQ (VIQ) being universally higher than performance IQ (PIQ) for individuals with AS, whereas no differential was found for individuals with HFA, a finding that is supported by results of the DSM-IV autism/PDD field trial (Volkmar et al., 1994) and recent neuropsychological research of autism unaccompanied by mental retardation (Minshew, 1992). From a developmental viewpoint, these findings could suggest two different pathogenic courses and consequent profiles of adjustment in HFA and AS. Let us consider these models of HFA and AS.

Autism is typically marked by a profound lack of interest in social stimuli from very early in life (Klin & Volkmar, 1993), expressed in the lack of acquisition of basic social skills such as reacting differentially to speech sounds (Klin, 1991), appreciating the salience of faces (Volkmar, 1987), and developing the typical patterns of attachment normatively seen in babies (Klin et al., 1992). The developmental path that follows takes place alongside and with little interaction with the social realm, with emotional, cognitive, language, and play skills unfolding in a manner that is both rigid and lacking in symbolic content; a sense of self is diminished as a result of a poor conception of others, their feelings and motivations (Klin, 1989). In other words, a constitutional lack of mechanisms of sociability, yet to be fully understood (Brothers, 1989), sets the limitations on social adjustment irrespective of cognitive endowment.

In contrast, AS is marked by a cluster of neuropsychological deficits (as well as assets) (Klin, Volkmar, Sparrow, Cicchetti, & Rourke, 1995) that limit the child's ability to make full use of intact sociability mechanisms because they affect their capacity to process a wide range of nonverbal stimuli in the various modalities (tactile, visual, auditory). As the context of social interactions is conveyed primarily through nonverbal means (tone and melody of voice, facial and body gestures, social touch), individuals with AS may miss the value and meaning of the interaction, resorting to the more explicit, and verbal, aspects of the contact. As a consequence, they may hold on to the explicit and literal value of communications, which can only approximate (and may often mislead, e.g., in teasing, humor) the actual valence of the social interchange. Devoid of nonverbal and intuitive social understanding, the emotions, motivations, and intentions of other people may present individuals with AS with an ongoing puzzle, leading them to take charge of the interaction by talking incessantly and one-sidedly about a topic that they know well as a result of their drive to amass factual information. By so doing, they may adjust to the reciprocity demands inherent in social conversation by presenting with a semblance of competent communication. This strategy is only partially successful, as this eccentricity and one-sidedness often alienate others, leading to repeated experiences of social failure and the resultant feelings of despondency and negativism. In other words, the neuropsychological disability prevents them from fulfilling their wish to establish relationships, a wish that is normally not encountered in individuals with autism.

Summary

The ultimate value of a scientific idea is in its generative power in areas other than the ones in which it was first conceived. Mental retardation research has been for years propelled by Ed Zigler's conviction in the need to investigate syndrome specific profiles taking the view of disabled persons beyond their primary disability, and looking at their patterns of adjustment vis-à-vis the social environment. In the field of the pervasive developmental disorders, these lessons have been associated with a new nosology and with a new understanding of profiles of adjustment, thus better preparing us for future etiological research. This model of moving toward increasingly fine-grained distinctions in our study of the behavior and development of persons with organic forms of mental retardation reflects the importance of the syndrome specific approach advocated by Zigler.

The study of the applicability of the developmental model to autism and related conditions has had considerable value in clarifying important aspects of similarity and difference in the development of children with autism. It has also led to an increased appreciation of the role of differing developmental processes in the unfolding of social-communicative competence. The current work on neuropsychological profiles of higher-functioning autism and Asperger's syndrome exemplified this approach. There is little doubt that in terms of their social manifestations HFA and AS are more alike than different. Differences are striking, however, in terms of a number of features such as preservation of certain language skills in AS, better visual spatial abilities in HFA, and so on. These differences are also supported by noteworthy differences in family genetic data and information on course and long-term prognosis. While the distinctiveness of the conditions from each other cannot presently be regarded as absolutely established, available research provides directions for future work, including family genetic and neuroanatomic investigations. Progress in these areas is predicated on an empirical approach with due emphasis on developmental (and longitudinal) courses of adaptation consistent with Zigler's view (1967) of the "whole person" (Zigler and Hodap, 1986).

References

American Psychiatric Association. (1980). *Diagnostic and statistical manual of mental disorders,* 3rd ed. Washington, DC.

American Psychiatric Association. (1987). *Diagnostic and statistical manual of mental disorders,* 3rd ed. rev. Washington, DC.

American Psychiatric Association. (1994). *Diagnostic and statistical manual of mental disorders,* 4th ed. rev. Washington, DC.

Asperger, H. (1944/1991). Autistic psychopathy in childhood (Uta Frith, trans.). In U. Frith (ed.), *Autism and Asperger syndrome.* (pp. 37–92). Cambridge: Cambridge University Press.

Asperger, H. (1979). Problems of infantile autism. *Communication, 13,* 35.

Brothers, L. (1989). A biological perspective on empathy. *American Journal of Psychiatry, 146,* 10–19.

Burack, J. & Volkmar, F. R. (1992). Development of Low- and High-Functioning Autistic Children. *Journal of Child Psychology and Psychiatry, 33,* 607–616.

Cicchetti, D. V., & Cohen, D. J. (Eds.). (1995). *Developmental Psychopathology.* New York: Wiley.

Cicchetti, D. V., & Pogge-Hesse, P. (1982). Possible contributions of the study of organically retarded persons to developmental theory. In E. Zigler & D. Balla (Eds.), *Mental retardation: The developmental-difference controversy.* Hillsdale, NJ: Erlbuam.

Cohen, D. J., Paul, R., & Volkmar, F. R. (1986). Issues in the classification of pervasive developmental disorders: Toward DSM-IV. *Journal of the American Academy of Child and Adolescent Psychiatry, 25,* 213–220.

Cohen, D. J., Volkmar, F. R., Anderson, G., & Klin, A. (1993). Integrating biological and behavioral perspectives in the study and care of autistic individuals: The future ahead. *Israel Journal of Psychiatry, 30* (1), 15–32.

Cohn, J. F., & Tronick, E. Z. (1987). The sequence of dyadic states at 3, 6, and 9 months. *Developmental Psychology, 23,* 68–77.

Corbett, J. (1987). Development, disintegration, and dementia. *Journal Mental Deficiency Research, 31,* 349–356.

DeMyer, M. (1976). Motor, perceptual and intellectual disabilities of autistic children. In L. Wing (ed.), *Early childhood autism.* Oxford: Pergamon.

Dykens, E., Volkmar, F. R., & Glick, M. (1991). Thought disorder in high-functioning autistic adults. *Journal of Autism and Developmental Disorders, 21,* 291–231.

Earl, C. J. C. (1934). The primitive catatonic psychosis of idiocy. *British Journal of Medical Psychology, 14,* 230–253.

Fish, B., Shapiro, T., Halpern, F., & Wile, R. (1965). The prediction of schizophrenia in infancy. *American Journal of Psychiatry, 121,* 768–775.

Ghaziuddin, M., Tsai, L. Y., & Ghaziuddin, N. (1992a). A comparison of the diagnostic criteria for Asperger syndrome. *Journal of Autism and Developmental Disorders, 22,* 643–649.

Ghaziuddin, M., Tsai, L. Y., & Ghaziuddin, N. (1992b). A reappraisal of clumsiness as a diagnostic feature of Asperger syndrome. *Journal of Autism and Developmental Disorders, 22,* 651–656.

Harper, J., & Williams, S. (1975). Age and type of onset as critical variables in early infantile autism. *Journal of Autism and Childhood Schizophrenia, 5,* 25–35.

Heller, T. (1954). About dementia infantilis (translation). *Journal of Nervous and Mental Disease, 119,* 471–477.

Hodapp, R. M., Burack, J. A., & Zigler, E. (Eds.). (1990). *Issues in the developmental approach to mental retardation.* Cambridge: Cambridge University Press.

Hodapp, R. M., & Dykens, E. M. (1991). Toward an etiology-specific strategy of early intervention for handicapped children. In K. Marfo (Ed.), *Early intervention in transition: Current perspectives on programs for handicapped children.* New York: Praeger.

Hodapp, R. M., & Zigler, E. (1995). Past, present, and future issues in the developmental approach to mental retardation and developmental disabilities. In D. Cicchetti & D. Cohen (Eds.), *Handbook of developmental psychopathology* (Vol. 2, 299–331). New York: Wiley.

Hodapp, R. M., & Zigler, E. (in press). Applying the developmental perspective to individuals with Down syndrome. In D. Cicchetti & M. Beeghly (Eds.), *Down syndrome: The developmental perspective.* Cambridge, MA: Harvard University Press.

Hoshino, Y., Kaneko, M., Yashima, Y., Kumashiro, J., Volkmar, F. R., & Cohen, D. J. (1987). Clinical features of autistic children with setback course in their infancy. *Japanese Journal of Psychiatry and Neurology, 41,* 237–26.

Kanner, L. (1943). Autistic disturbances of affective contact. *Nervous Child, 2,* 217.

Klein, M. (1930/1975). The importance of symbol-formation in the development of the ego. In M. Klein, *Love, guilt and reparation and other works, 1921–1941.* London: Hogarth Press.

Klin, A. (1989). Understanding early infantile autism: An application of G. H. Mead's Theory of the Emergence of Mind. *L.S.E. Quarterly, 4* (3), 336–356.

Klin, A. (1991). Young autistic children's listening preferences in regard to speech: A possible characterization of the symptom of social withdrawal. *Journal of Autism and Developmental Disorders, 21* (1), 29–42.

Klin, A. (1994). Asperger syndrome. *Child and Adolescent Psychiatry Clinics of North America, 3*(1), 131–148.

Klin, A., Mayes, L. C., Volkmar, F. R., & Cohen, D. J. (1995). Multiplex developmental disorder. *Journal of Developmental and Behavioral Pediatrics, 16* (3), S7–S11.

Klin, A., Sparrow, S. S., Volkmar, F. R., Cicchetti, D. V., & Rourke, B. P. (1995). Asperger syndrome.

In B. P. Rourke (Ed.), *Syndrome of nonverbal learning disabilities: Manifestations in neurological disease, disorder, and dysfunction* (pp. 93–118). New York: Guilford Press.

Klin, A., & Volkmar, F. R. (1993). The development of individuals with autism: Implications for the Theory of Mind Hypothesis. In S. Baron-Cohen, H. Tager-Flusberg, & D. J. Cohen, (Eds.), *Understanding other minds: Perspectives from autism* (pp. 317–331). Oxford: Oxford University Press.

Klin, A., & Volkmar, F. R. (1997). Autism and the pervasive developmental disorders. In J. D. Noshpitz (Ed.), *Basic handbook of child psychiatry,* 2nd ed. New York: Basic Books.

Klin, A., & Volkmar, F. R. (1995). Autism and the pervasive developmental disorders. *Child and Adolescent Psychiatric Clinics of North America, 4* (3), 617–630.

Klin, A., & Volkmar, F. R. (1996). Asperger syndrome. In D. J. Cohen & F. R. Volkmar (Eds.), *Handbook of autism and pervasive developmental disorders,* 2nd ed. New York: Wiley.

Klin, A., Volkmar, F. R., & Sparrow, S. S. (1992). Autistic social dysfunction: Some limitations of the Theory of Mind hypothesis. *Journal of Child Psychology and Psychiatry, 33,* 861–876.

Klin, A., Volkmar, F. R., Sparrow, S. S., Cicchetti, D. V., & Rourke, B. P. (1995). Validity and neuropsychological characterization of Asperger syndrome. *Journal of Child Psychology and Psychiatry, 36*(7), 1127–1140.

Kolvin, I. (1971). Studies in the childhood psychoses: I. Diagnostic criteria and classification. *British Journal of Psychiatry, 118,* 381–384.

Loveland, K. L., & Kelley, M. L. (1988). Development of adaptible behavior in adolescents and young adults with autism and Down syndrome. *American Journal of Mental Deficiency, 93,* 84–92.

Mahler, M. (1952). On child psychoses and schizophrenia: Autistic and symbiotic infantile psychoses. *Psychoanalytic Study of the Child, 7,* 286–305.

McKenna, K., Gordon, C. T., Lenane, M., & Rappoport, J. (1994). Looking for childhood-onset schizophrenia: The first 71 cases screened. *Journal of the American Academy of Child and Adolescent Psychiatry, 33,* 636–644.

Minshew, N. J. (1992). Neurological localization in autism. In E. Schopler & G. B. Mesibov (Eds.), *High-functioning individuals with autism* (pp. 65–90). New York: Plenum.

Ornitz, E. M., Guthrie, D., and Farley, A. H. (1977). Early development of autistic children. *Journal of Autism and Childhood Schizophrenia, 7,* 207–229.

Ozonoff, S., Rogers, S. J., and Pennington, B. F. (1991). Asperger's syndrome: Evidence of an empirical distinction from high-functioning autism. *Journal of Child Psychology and Psychiatry, 32,* 1107–1122.

Paul, R. (1987). Communication. In D. J. Cohen & A. M. Donnellan (Eds.), *Handbook of autism and pervasive developmental disorders* (pp. 61–84). New York: Wiley.

Prizant, B., and Wetherby, A. (1987). Communicative intent. *Journal of the American Academy of Child and Adolescent Psychiatry, 26,* 472–479.

Rank, B., & MacNaughton, D. (1950). A clinical contribution to early ego development. *Psychoanalytic Study of the Child,* 53–65.

Rett, A. (1966). *Uber ein cerebral-atrophisches Syndrom bei Hyperammonamie.* Vienna: Bruder Hollinek.

Rourke, B. P. (1989). *Nonverbal learning disabilities: The syndrome and the model.* New York: Guilford.

Rutter, M. (1974). The development of infantile autism. *Psychological Medicine, 4,* 147–163.

Rutter, M. (1978). Diagnosis and definition of childhood autism. *Journal of Autism and Childhood Schizophrenia, 8,* 139–161.

Rutter, M. (1985). Infantile autism and pervasive developmental disorder. In M. Rutter & L. Hersov, (Eds.), *Child and adolescent psychiatry: Modern approaches,* 2nd ed. Oxford: Blackwell.

Rutter, M. (1989). Annotation: Child psychiatric disorders in ICD-10. *Journal of Child Psychology and Psychiatry, 30,* 499–513.

Rutter, M., & Schopler, E. (1992). Classification of pervasive developmental disorders: Some concepts and practical considerations. *Journal of Autism and Developmental Disorders, 22,* 459–482.

Scheerer, M., Rothmann, E., & Goldstein, K. (1945). A case of ''idiot savant'': An experimental study of personality organization. *Psychological Monographs, 58* (4).

Snow, M. E., Hertzig, M. E., and Shapiro, T. (1987). Rate of development in young autistic children. *Journal of the American Academy of Child Psychiatry, 26,* 834–835.

Stern, D. (1987). *The interpersonal world of the human infant.* New York: Basic Books.

Szatmari, P., Tuff, L. Finlayson, M. A. J., & Bartolucci, G. (1990). Asperger's syndrome and autism: Neurcognitive aspects. *Journal of the American Academy of Child and Adolescent Psychiatry, 29,* 130–136.

Tantam, D. (1991). Asperger syndrome in adulthood. In U. Frith, (Ed.), *Autism and Asperger syndrome* (pp. 147–183). Cambridge: Cambridge University Press.

Trevathan, E., & Naidu, S. (1988). The clinical recognition and differential diagnosis of Rett syndrome. *Journal of Child Neurology, 3* (suppl.), S6–S16.

Tronick, E. (1980). The primacy of social skills in infancy. In D. B. Sawin, R. C. Hawkins, L. Olzenski Waker, & J. H. Penticuff (Eds.), *Exceptional infant,* Vol. 4: *Psychosocial risks in infant-environment transactions.* New York: Brunner-Mazel.

Tsai, L. Y. (1994). Rett syndrome. *Child and Adolescent Psychiatric Clinics of North America, 3,* 105–118.

Volkmar, F. R. (1987). Social development. In D. J. Cohen & A. Donnellan, (Eds.), *Handbook of autism* (pp. 41–60). New York: Wiley.

Volkmar, F. R. (1994). Childhood disintegrative disorder. *Child and Adolescent Psychiatric Clinics of North America, 3,* 119–130.

Volkmar, F. R., Burack, J. A., & Cohen, D. J. (in Press). Developmental versus difference approaches to autism. In R. M. Hodapp, J. A. Burack, & E. Zigler (Eds.), *Issues in the developmental approach to mental retardation.* Cambridge: Cambridge University Press.

Volkmar, F. R., & Cohen, D. J. (1988). Issues in the diagnosis and classification of infantile autism. In B. Lahey & A. Kazdin, (Eds.), *Advances in clinical child psychology.* New York: Plenum.

Volkmar, F. R., & Cohen, D. J. (1989). Disintegrative disorder or "late onset" autism. *Journal of Child Psychology and Psychiatry, 30,* 717–724.

Volkmar, F. R., & Cohen, D. J. (1991). Nonautistic pervasive developmental disorders. In R. Michels (Ed.), *Psychiatry* (pp. 1–12). Philadelphia: J. B. Lippincott.

Volkmar, F. R., & Cohen, D. J. (1992). Co-morbid association of autism and schizophrenia. *American Journal of Psychiatry, 148,* 1705.

Volkmar, F. R., Cohen, D. J., & Paul, R. (1986). An evaluation of DSM-III criteria for infantile autism. *Journal of the American Academy of Child and Adolescent Psychiatry, 25,* 190–197.

Volkmar, F. R., Cohen, D. J., Bregman, J. D., Hooks, M. Y., & Stevenson, J. M. (1989). An examination of social typologies in autism. *Journal of the American Academy of Child and Adolescent Psychiatry, 28,* 82–86.

Volkmar, F. R., & Klin, A. (1993). Social development in autism: Historical and clinical perspectives. In S. Baron-Cohen, H. Tager-Flusberg, & D. J. Cohen, (Eds.), *Understanding other minds: Perspectives from autism* (pp. 40–55). Oxford: Oxford University Press.

Volkmar, F. R., Klin, A., Schultz, R. B., Bronen, R., Marans, W. D., Sparrow, S. S., & Cohen, D. J. Grand rounds in child psychiatry: Asperger syndrome. *Journal of the American Academy of Child and Adolescent Psychiatry, 35*(1), 118–123.

Volkmar, F. R., Klin, A., Siegel, B., et al. (1994). DSM-IV autism / pervasive developmental disorder field trial. *American Journal of Psychiatry, 151,* 1361–1367.

Volkmar, F. R., Sparrow, S. A., Goudreau, D., Cicchetti D. V., Paul, R., & Cohen, D. J. (1987). Social deficits in autism: An operational approach using the Vineland Adaptive Behavior Scales. *Journal of the American Academy of Child and Adolescent Psychiatry, 26,* 156–161.

Volkmar, F. R., Stier, D., & Cohen, D. J. (1985c). Age of recognition of pervasive developmental disorder. *American Journal of Psychiatry, 142,* 1450–1452.

Weisz, J., & Yeates, J. (1981). Cognitive development in retarded and nonretarded persons: Piagetian tests of the similar structure hypothesis. *Psychological Bulletin, 90,* 153–178.

Weisz, J., & Zigler, E. (1979). Cognitive development in retarded and nonretarded persons: Piagetian tests of the similar-sequence hypothesis. *Psychological Bulletin, 86,* 831–851.

Wing, L. (1981). Asperger's syndrome: A clinical account. *Psychological Medicine, 11,* 115–130.

Wing, L. (1991). The relationship between Asperger's syndrome and Kanner's autism. In U. Frith, (Ed.), *Autism and Asperger syndrome* (pp. 93–121). Cambridge: Cambridge University Press.

Wing, L., & Attwood, A. (1987). Syndromes of autism and atypical development. In D. J. Cohen & A. M. Donnellan (Eds.), *Handbook of autism and pervasive developmental disorders* (pp. 3–19). New York: Wiley.

World Health Organization (1992). *International classification of diseases,* 10th edition, draft version. Geneva.

Zigler, E. (1967). Familiar mental retardation: A continuing dilemma. *Science, 155,* 292–298.

Zigler, E. (1969). Developmental versus difference theories of mental retardation and the problem of motivation. *Americal Journal of Mental Deficiency, 73,* 536–539.

Zigler, E., & Balla D. (Eds.). (1982) *Mental retardation: The development-difference controversy.* Hillsdale, NJ: Erlbaum.

Zigler, E., & Hodapp, R. M. (1986). *Understanding mental retardation.* New York: Cambridge University Press.

11 The developmental approach to adult psychopathology

Marion Glick

This book attests to Edward Zigler's broad application of developmental theory to many areas of psychology. The developmental approach to adult psychopathology represents one of the major lines of theoretical and empirical work that has spanned his career. This work has been intercoordinated with research on self-image disparity and self-image. Moreover, the developmental approach to adult psychopathology recently has been extended to the examination of psychiatric disorders in people with mild mental retardation. This chapter will briefly review these interrelated lines of research emphasizing interconnections among them. Because so many studies have been conducted and because the aim is to underscore the interrelatedness of the work due to common underlying principles, only some studies 'and certain major findings will be considered.

Although influenced by many developmental theorists (e.g., Lewin, 1946; Piaget, 1951; Rapaport, 1951), the developmental approach to adult psychopathology is most strongly rooted in the organismic-developmental formulation of Heinz Werner and Bernard Kaplan (Werner, 1948; Werner & Kaplan, 1963). Among the major developmental theorists, Werner especially was concerned with extending developmental theory beyond child development to domains such as comparative psychology and adult psychopathology. These roots in Werner's broad reaching framework have enabled the developmental approach to psychopathology to encompass many forms of adult disorder and to be integrated with Zigler's developmental research on mental retardation and self-image.

The underlying developmental formulation that has enabled the principles of developmental theory to be broadly applied for understanding psychopathology will be presented first. These underlying developmental principles have allowed the research on psychopathology to be integrated with work in other areas, such as mental retardation and the development of self-image. Next, the research on adult psychopathology will be summarized, emphasizing the extension of developmental principles to many types of disorder and many issues of clinical concern. In the third section, developmental research on self-image will be

This work was supported by a grant from the National Institute of Child Health and Human Development.

presented. Although this work began with research on psychopathology (Achenbach & Zigler, 1963), the formulation has for many years been elaborated through an intercoordinated series of studies that integrates normative research on child development with work on adult psychopathology, on mental retardation, and on emotional disturbance in childhood. In the fourth section, recent research aimed at integrating Zigler's developmental approaches to psychopathology and mental retardation will be discussed. These two developmental approaches derive from the same underlying formulation. Yet until recently, the developmental approach to psychopathology concentrated entirely on psychiatric patients without mental retardation.

Underlying developmental principles

A major premise of the developmental approach to psychopathology is that even adults can be viewed as functioning at different levels along an underlying developmental continuum. A person's underlying developmental level is presumed to broadly influence social and emotional as well as cognitive aspects of functioning. A further premise is that the individual's underlying developmental level continues to influence behavior after the onset of disorder, just as it did prior to the emergence of psychopathology. In becoming symptomatic, a person is not presumed to change characterological modes of responding by regressing to an earlier level. Rather than reverting to earlier and lower developmental levels with the onset of psychopathology, patients are presumed to maintain their premorbid developmental characteristics. Thus manifestations of psychopathology as well as premorbid behavior should reflect the person's same broad underlying developmental level.

Central to the work on psychopathology have been three principles that are fundamental in developmental theory: Development entails (1) greater differentiation and hierarchic integration, (2) increased expression in thought rather than action, and (3) increased internalization of societal demands.

The first principle that development "proceeds from a state of relative globality and lack of differentiation to a state of increasing differentiation, articulation, and hierarchic integration" (Werner, 1957, p. 126) was elaborated most fully by Werner but shared by many other developmental theorists. Of particular relevance to psychopathology are the implications of the orthogenetic principle for understanding the self in relation to external reality and other people, and for coping and adaptation. At early developmental levels, subjective experience and external events tend to be fused, and neither the boundaries nor the point of view of the self can be adequately distinguished from the boundaries or the point of view of the other. With increasing development, not only are the self and the external world differentiated, they are also reintegrated in complex and relatively stable ways. The ability to view subject and object as differentiated entities, each organized in its own right and interrelated with the other, allows for greater planning and active control over both external events and internal need states (Werner & Kaplan, 1963). Gratification can be delayed, goals can be envisioned, and it becomes possible to employ substitutive means and alternative ends in order to achieve these goals. Adaptive capacities and coping, therefore, increase as a function of the structural changes that define development.

The second principle is that developmentally early behavior is marked by immediate, direct, and unmodulated responses to external stimuli and internal need states, whereas developmentally higher functioning is characterized by indirect, ideational, and symbolic or verbal behavior patterns (Piaget, 1951; Werner, 1948). In the developmental approach to adult psychopathology, this principle has been applied most extensively to the analysis of symptoms.

The third principle is that development entails the capacity to incorporate increasingly complex social demands and values. If they are not fulfilled, the greater internalized demands can lead to increased guilt. This developmental principle underlies the research on role orientation in symptomatology and is central also to the work on self-image.

Psychiatric patients who function at higher developmental levels are thus expected to display greater differentiation and hierarchic integration, more frequent expression in thought and verbal behavior rather than in action, and a greater internalization of societal demands and possible guilt than patients whose functioning is developmentally lower. These broad developmental characteristics would be expected to influence many aspects of psychopathology.

Research on adult psychopathology

Research on the developmental approach to adult psychopathology has been ongoing for over 35 years. In this section, a brief summary of the many relationships that have been found between developmental level and major variables in psychopathology will be presented.

Premorbid social competence

The developmental approach to adult psychopathology assumed that the person's underlying developmental level broadly influenced both adaptive and pathological functioning. Developmental level was conceptualized as encompassing cognitive, social, and emotional realms of functioning and presumed to mediate all behavior. An issue was how to measure this broad construct of underlying developmental level in adulthood. Zigler and Phillips (1960) believed that the developmental level construct was too broad and contained too many facets to permit a practical single measure. Given the inherent relationship between developmental level and coping effectiveness, they chose instead to measure the individual's premorbid social competence. Briefly, this measure examines a patient's placement on six variables thought to reflect cognitive, social, and emotional functioning. These variables are age, education, occupation, employment history, marital status, and intelligence. (In most studies, the intelligence variable has been omitted because IQ scores were not available.) Zigler and Phillips (1960) recognized that each of these variables had a considerable margin of error and that none taken in isolation would be a particularly good indicator of developmental level. The hope was that the general pattern of scores, as reflected in an overall score, would provide a broadly derived reliable gauge of an elusive construct: an adult patient's underlying developmental level.

Scoring has been found to be highly reliable (e.g., Glick, Zigler, & Zigler, 1985; Zigler, Glick, & Marsh, 1979; Zigler & Levine, 1981b). The construct validity of the measure is supported by findings that premorbid social competence scores correlate positively with Rorschach developmental level (Lerner, 1968), maturity in moral reasoning (Quinlan, Rogers, & Kegan, 1980), and Loevinger's (Loevinger & Wessler, 1970) measure of level of ego development (Glick, Luthar, Quinlan, & Zigler, 1994). The construct of premorbid adjustment had been applied previously to patients with schizophrenia in order to designate subtypes with better versus poorer prognoses (e.g., L. Phillips, 1953). By contrast, in construing premorbid social competence as a developmental indicator, Zigler and Phillips (1960) assumed that the construct could be applied to patients with many psychiatric diagnoses and would relate to many major variables in psychopathology in addition to outcome. The many relationships discovered between premorbid social competence and other major variables in psychopathology for patients in many diagnostic groups support the developmental interpretation.

Symptomatology

Three modes of categorizing symptoms developmentally have traditionally been employed in research on the developmental approach to adult psychopathology. The first categorization utilizes the three symptom clusters that L. Phillips and Rabinovitch (1958) isolated empirically and conceptualized as reflecting three patterns of role orientation: self-deprivation and turning against the self, self-indulgence and turning against others, and avoidance of others. Inasmuch as turning against the self implies the internalization of societal values and the ability to take the role of internalized others, this role orientation was conceptualized as reflecting developmentally higher functioning than the other two orientations. The developmentally higher status of the role orientation of turning against the self has been supported by many findings that a greater prevalence of symptoms in the turning against the self category, compared with the other two role orientations, correlates with higher premorbid social competence (Glick et al. 1985; Mylet, Styfco, & Zigler, 1979; Zigler & Phillips, 1960, 1962). These results have been obtained for patients in many diagnostic groups (e.g., affective disorder, personality disorder) as well as schizophrenia.

The second mode of symptom classification, along an action–thought continuum, derives from the fundamental assumption described previously that expression in direct action reflects developmentally lower functioning than expression in thought or verbal behavior. Consistent with this assumption, a predominance of symptoms involving thought or verbal expression, compared with action, has been found to be related to higher premorbid social competence in patients with many psychiatric diagnoses (Glick et al., 1985; L. Phillips & Zigler, 1961).

The third ordering, applicable only to psychotic patients, concerns hallucinations and delusions. Conceptual and ideational modes of organization have been presumed to be developmentally higher than perceptual modes (Freud, 1933; Werner, 1948). Based on this developmental principle, Zigler and Levine (1983) advanced the position that hallucinations ("false perceptions") without accompanying delusions ("false beliefs") reflect developmentally lower functioning. Delusions without hallucinations were conceptualized as reflecting developmentally higher functioning, while the presence of both symptoms was presumed to reflect an intermediate developmental position between the two single symptom groups. In samples of patients with schizophrenia and affective psychoses patients who displayed delusions but not hallucinations obtained the highest social competence scores, patients with hallucinations but not delusions obtained the lowest scores, and patients who displayed both symptoms obtained premorbid social competence scores intermediate between those obtained by patients in the two single symptom groups (Glick, Acunzo, & Zigler, 1993; Zigler & Levine, 1983).

Diagnosis

Although the role orientation and thought–action categories have been found to relate to diagnosis, these relationships have been found to be modest (Phillips, Broverman, & Zigler, 1968; Zigler & Phillips, 1961b). Diagnosis and developmental symptom categories thus retain a considerable degree of independence.

Patients with affective disorder diagnoses have consistently been found to evidence developmentally higher functioning as indicated by premorbid social competence and scores on Loevinger's (Loevinger & Wessler, 1970) measure of ego development; in contrast, patients with schizophrenia, antisocial personality disorder, and other diagnoses involving impulsive or aggressive behavior have been found to function at lower developmental levels as indicated by premorbid competence and level of ego development (Glick et al., 1994; Glick et al., 1985; Lewine, Watt, Prentky, & Fryer, 1980; Zigler et al., 1979; Zigler & Phillips, 1961a). In a sample of treatment-seeking cocaine abusers, a similar relationship appeared with respect to comorbid diagnoses. Addicts with comorbid diagnoses of depression had higher premorbid competence scores than addicts with comorbid antisocial personality disorder (Luthar, Glick, Zigler, & Rounsaville, 1993).

Paranoid–nonparanoid status in schizophrenia

Patients with paranoid schizophrenia frequently have been found to obtain higher premorbid social competence scores than patients with nonparanoid schizophrenia (e.g., Goldstein, Held, & Cromwell, 1968; Zigler & Levine, 1973; Zigler, Levine, & Zigler, 1977), although some studies have reported no relationship between premorbid competence and paranoid–nonparanoid status (see Zigler, Levine, & Zigler, 1976, for a review of this research).

Patients with paranoid and nonparanoid schizophrenia have been found to differ on many variables in addition to premorbid social competence. These variables include age at onset of disorder and many aspects of cognitive and perceptual functioning (see Zigler & Glick, 1984). Moreover, research has disclosed many similarities between paranoid schizophrenia and the affective disorders, particularly mania. In reviewing these many findings, Zigler and Glick (1984, 1988) advanced the hypothesis that paranoid schizophrenia or at least some forms of this disorder may, like mania, represent a defense against depression. Consistent with this formulation, Burack and Zigler (1989) found that patients with paranoid schizophrenia were more similar to affective disorder patients than to patients with nonparanoid schizophrenia with respect to both premorbid social competence and age at onset of disorder.

Outcome

As described earlier, the increased differentiation and hierarchical integration that accompany development inherently allow for greater adaptability and coping effectiveness. With greater adaptive resources at their disposal, individuals who function at higher developmental levels should be able to cope more actively and determinedly with the problems related to their disorders, thus displaying better outcomes. Although higher developmental functioning is presumed to be associated with more favorable prognosis, the developmental formulation does not assume that vulnerability to disorder is reducible to developmental level. As described in the preceding section, higher developmental levels of functioning in fact may lead to an increased frequency of certain kinds of problems – those that reflect greater internalization of societal standards with consequently heightened guilt. The relationship between premorbid social competence or premorbid adjustment and outcome has been demonstrated in many studies conducted over many years. Much of this research has focused exclusively on schizophrenia and derives from the view that premorbid adjustment designates subtypes specific to schizophrenic disorder.

In contrast to the view that good and poor premorbid adjustment or competence merely represent subtypes of schizophrenia, the developmental formulation assumes that premorbid competence as an indicator of coping effectiveness reflects the individual's underlying developmental level. As such, the premorbid competence construct should be applicable across a broad spectrum of disorders and thus be related to outcome for patients with many psychiatric diagnoses. This developmental interpretation is supported by findings that premorbid competence and outcome are related not only in schizophrenia but for patients with such other diagnoses as affective, personality, and neurotic disorders (Glick, Mazure, Bowers, & Zigler, 1993; Glick, Zigler, & Edell, 1995; Glick & Zigler, 1986; Prentky, Lewine, Watt, & Fryer, 1980; Zigler et al., 1979; Zigler & Phillips, 1961c). In these studies of patients in various diagnostic groups, those with higher premorbid social competence have been found to have shorter initial hospitalizations, fewer rehospitalizations, shorter rehospitalizations, better early response to neuroleptic treatment, and better social and work functioning after discharge.

A broader view of prognosis

In addition to displaying better outcomes after hospitalization and treatment, the developmental formulation generates the expectation that individuals at higher developmental levels will be less likely to succumb to psychiatric disorders. If they do, such individuals will be older at the time their disorders become manifest than will individuals who function at lower developmental levels (Zigler & Levine, 1981a). In support of these hypotheses, higher social competence has been found to be related to an older age at first hospitalization for patients with schizophrenia (Zigler & Levine, 1981a) and with affective, personality, and neurotic disorders (Glick et al., 1985). Moreover, Zigler and Phillips (1961a) found that, as a group, hospitalized psychiatric patients displayed lower social competence than did the general population.

Personality variables

Despite the many correlates discovered for premorbid competence, little is known about the processes that underlie competent functioning and contribute to the predictive efficacy of premorbid competence measures. A question that has been raised in regard to childhood competence (e.g., Garmezy, Masten, & Tellegen, 1984) as well as premorbid competence in adult psychopathology (Glick & Zigler, 1990; Zigler & Glick, 1986) is what personality variables underlie the attainments that are used as indices of competence. This question has relevance for treatment. If certain personality characteristics are found to be associated with higher competence, intervention and treatment might profitably be directed toward fostering these characteristics.

Greater disparity between the real and ideal self-images, more positive real self-images, less physical anhedonia (a long-term deficit in the ability to experience pleasure), and less external locus of control have been found in high, compared with low, competence psychiatric patients in many diagnostic groups (Achenbach & Zigler, 1963; Garnet, Glick, & Edell, 1993; Glick et al., 1995; Mylet et al., 1979).

Summary

The relationships between developmental level and many major aspects of adult psychopathology revealed by Zigler and his colleagues are summarized in Table 11.1. These relationships to developmental level have appeared for patients in many diagnostic groups. This body of work thus demonstrates that developmental principles can indeed provide a framework that allows a very broad range of phenomena in psychopathology to be conceptually organized and integrated. The many relationships discovered between premorbid social competence and other clinical variables, including most facets of outcome, point to coping effectiveness and developmental level as central variables in psychopathology. A major implication is that prevention and treatment programs should emphasize and foster these positive characteristics that may be equally or more predictive of outcome than a patient's symptoms and disordered functioning.

In the sections that follow, further evidence of the potential of developmental principles to integrate diverse phenomena and domains of research is presented.

A cognitive-developmental interpretation of self-image

Whereas the variables investigated in the work on psychopathology (e.g., symptomatology, outcome) primarily relate to disordered functioning in adulthood, self-image pertains equally to normal and disordered development and to childhood and adult functioning. Consequently, the developmental interpretation of self-image has been advanced through studies of adult psychiatric patients, of normative child development, and of children with mild mental retardation and those with emotional disorders. The research on self-image has also examined experiential variables that may moderate the unfolding of the developmental sequence. Factors related to how others respond to the individual in everyday social interactions appear to be especially influential.

Although the research on self-image includes diverse populations, the underlying developmental issues remain constant. Developmental differences in self-image initially were examined with adult psychiatric inpatients (Achenbach & Zigler, 1963), and the formulation was then extended to normative child development. Experiential, as well as developmental, influences on self-images were first examined in research with children and adolescents having special needs (e.g., Katz, Zigler, & Zalk, 1975; Zigler, Balla, & Watson, 1972), and subsequently used to illuminate

Table 11.1. *Correlates of developmental level in adult psychopathology*

	Developmental level	
Variable	Lower	Higher
Premorbid social		
competence	Lower	Higher
Symptomatology		
Role orientation	Turning against others (e.g., assaultive, threatens assault) Avoidance of others (e.g., hallucinations, withdrawn)	Turning against self (e.g., depressed, suicidal attempt)
Action–thought orientation	Action (e.g., assaultive, suicidal attempt)	Thought (e.g., delusions, threatens assault)
Hallucinations-delusions (for psychotic patients only)	Hallucinations ("false perceptions")	Delusions ("false beliefs")
Diagnosis	Schizophrenia, antisocial personality disorder	Affective disorders, neurosis
Schizophrenia subtype	Nonparanoid	Paranoid
Outcome		
Initial hospitalization	Longer	Shorter
Rehospitalization	Longer and more frequent	Shorter and less frequent
Early neuroleptic response	Poorer	Better
Posthospital social and work functioning	Poorer	Better
Age at first		
hospitalization	Younger	Older
Personality variables		
Self-image disparity	Less	More
Anhedonia	More	Less
External locus of control	More	Less

findings from adult psychiatric patients (Mylet et al., 1979). This research on self-image, therefore, especially exemplifies the integrative potential of developmental psychopathology whereby knowledge about normal development promotes understanding of atypical development and the study of atypical populations enhances knowledge about normal development.

The initial formulation

Achenbach and Zigler (1963) first advanced the cognitive-developmental interpretation of self-image disparity and tested it in research with adult psychiatric and nonpsychiatric inpatients. They posited that increased disparity between the real self-image (the person's current view of self) and the ideal self-image (the ideal person that he or she would like to be) was a natural concomitant of normal growth and development. This formulation was based on two developmental principles. First, the greater cognitive differentiation that characterizes all development (Piaget, 1951; Werner, 1948) should include increased differentiation and thus disparity between the real and ideal self-images as aspects of the self-concept. Second, with development, individuals incorporate increasingly complex social demands and expectations (Zigler & Phillips, 1960). The greater self-demands at higher developmental levels and the guilt that accompanies them should also lead to greater disparity between the real and ideal self-images at higher developmental levels. This hypothesized relationship between self-image disparity and guilt has been supported by findings that guilt is correlated with greater self-image disparity and a higher ideal self-image in both children and young adults (Bybee & Zigler, 1991).

This cognitive-developmental interpretation of self-image disparity stands in marked contrast to the more traditional view, first advanced by Rogers and Dymond (1954) that greater real–ideal self-image disparity indicates a lack of positive self-regard and hence maladjustment. (Following the Rogerian position, real–ideal disparity continues to be used as an indicator of maladjustment [e.g., Higgins, Klein, & Strauman, 1985].)

Consistent with the developmental formulation, patients who scored higher on premorbid social competence within both psychiatric and nonpsychiatric subgroups displayed more real–ideal self-image disparity (and also greater differentiation in other aspects of self-image) than lower-competence patients (Achenbach & Zigler, 1963). Contrary to the Rogerian interpretation, psychiatric and nonpsychiatric patients did not differ in self-image disparity.

Normative development in childhood

Katz and Zigler (1967) continued to elaborate the cognitive-developmental interpretation of self-image in research on normative child development. Consistent with the assumption that greater self-image disparity is a natural concomitant of normal growth and development, they found that older children and children with advanced cognitive development (IQs in the superior range) displayed more self-image disparity than younger children and children of average cognitive ability. Examination of developmental changes in the real and ideal self-images revealed higher (more positive) ideal self-images for older, compared with younger, children and for children of superior, compared with average, cognitive ability. The older children also displayed lower real self-images than the younger children.

In other studies of children and adolescents, greater self-image disparity and more positive ideal self-images have been found to be related to higher developmental functioning as indicated by each of the following variables: chronological age, mental age, the presence of thought rather than action symptoms, and evidence of nonegocentric thought in a role-taking task and greater maturity in moral reasoning (Bybee, 1986; Katz et al., 1975; Leahy, 1981; Leahy, Balla, & Zigler, 1982; Luthar, Zigler, & Goldstein, 1992; D. Phillips & Zigler, 1980; Zigler et al., 1972). A number of these studies also revealed lower real self-images at higher developmental levels (Leahy, 1981; D. Phillips & Zigler, 1980; Zigler et al., 1972). D. Phillips and Zigler (1980) reported complex interactions between developmental level and a number of variables (socioeconomic status [SES], gender, ethnicity) that can give rise to different day-to-day life experiences.

Because the real and ideal self-images frequently have different correlates (Glick & Zigler, 1985), Bybee (1986) examined the relationship of each of the two types of self-image to adjustment. For middle-class children and adolescents, a higher ideal (but not a higher real) self-image related to better adjustment. Recent studies also have considered spontaneous descriptions of the real and ideal self-images as well as responses to self-image questionnaires (Bybee, Glick, & Zigler, 1990).

Children and adolescents with special needs: The interaction of experiential and developmental determinants of self-image

Pervasive experiential factors constitute a second major influence that may moderate the unfolding of the developmental sequence. The combined influences of cognitive-developmental and experiential variables have been examined in various studies of children and adolescents: those living in institutions compared to home settings (Zigler et al., 1972), those with and without mild mental retardation (Leahy et al., 1982; Zigler et al., 1972), and those with internalizing versus externalizing forms of maladjustment compared with those without maladjustment (Katz et al., 1975).

Zigler et al. (1972) studied institutionalized and noninstitutionalized children with mild mental retardation and average intelligence. The influence of cognitive development was reflected in findings that the children of higher mental age (MA) displayed greater real–ideal self-image disparity, higher ideal self-images, and lower real self-images than children of lower MA. Experiential variables associated with both institutionalization and mild mental retardation were also related to the children's self-images. The institutionalized children, regardless of mental age or mental retardation status, had lower real self-image scores and lower ideal self-image scores than noninstitutionalized children. Even though they displayed lower ideal self-images, the institutionalized children showed greater self-image disparity than the noninstitutionalized children because of their very low real self-images. The children living in institutions, thus, appeared both to have very low senses of self-esteem and to set low standards for themselves. Compared with children of the same MA without mental retardation, the children with mild mental retardation had lower ideal self-images and thus displayed less self-image disparity. Leahy et al. (1982) also reported lower ideal self-images in children with mild mental retardation compared with those without mental retardation.

The self-images of children at two age levels (corresponding to the fifth and eighth grades) and classified as maladjusted or nonmaladjusted were examined by Katz et al. (1975). The maladjusted children were in special education classes because of emotional disturbance, and the nonmaladjusted children were in regular classes in the same school system. In addition, styles of symptom expression displayed by the maladjusted children were classified developmentally along an action–thought continuum and related to their self-images. Based on the distinction in the developmental approach to adult psychopathology between symptom expression in thought versus action, internalizing symptoms (see Achenbach, 1966), which involve expression in thought, were conceptualized as reflecting developmentally higher functioning than externalizing symptoms, which involve expression in action. Thus both age and the internalizing–externalizing dimension in symptomatology were conceptualized as developmental variables. In accordance with the cognitive developmental formulation, greater self-image disparity and higher ideal self-images were found for older as compared with younger children and for children with internalizing, as compared with externalizing, symptoms.

The Rogerian formulation was not supported; the maladjusted and nonmaladjusted children did not differ in self-image disparity. However, the children with externalizing symptoms and, to a lesser degree, those with internalizing symptoms had lower real self-images than the nonmaladjusted children. The lower real self-images of the maladjusted children with externalizing symptoms were interpreted as due to experiential variables. Just as the life history experiences associated with being placed in an institution (Zigler et al., 1972) may lead to lower self-regard, the experiences of being labeled maladjusted, excluded from mainstream school activities, and placed in a special education class for emotional disturbance might lead to an attenuated sense of self-worth. The particularly low real self-images of the children with externalizing symptoms is understandable inasmuch as children with acting-out symptoms are least countenanced by peers, family, school personnel, and community members (Katz et al., 1975).

Further research in adult psychopathology

Consistent with the results of Achenbach and Zigler (1963), Mylet et al. (1979) found greater real–ideal self-image disparity and more differentiation in other aspects of self-image for high as compared with low competence psychiatric and nonpsychiatric inpatients. Lower real self-images were found for higher-, compared

Table 11.2 *Developmental differences in self-image*

Developmental variables	Self-image measure	
	Real–ideal disparity	Ideal
Child development		
Older chronological age	Greater	Higher
Older mental age	Greater	Higher
Internalizing rather than externalizing symptoms	Greater	Higher
Nonegocentric reasoning	Greater	Higher
Greater maturity in moral reasoning	Greater	Higher
Adult psychopathology		
Higher premorbid social competence	Greater	—

with lower-, competence patients and for those with psychiatric rather than non-psychiatric disorders. Mylet et al. (1979) interpreted the lower real self-images of the psychiatric patients as due to experiential factors associated with psychiatric hospitalization.

Summary

The major developmental differences found in the self-image research are presented in Table 11.2. Greater real–ideal self-image disparity has consistently been found to characterize developmentally higher functioning for children with both typical development and special needs and in adult psychopathology. For children with both typical development and special needs, higher ideal self-images have also consistently been found at higher developmental levels. With respect to the moderating influences of experiential variables on self-image development, psychiatric patient status, institutionalization, and mild mental retardation consistently have been associated with lower real self-images and sometimes with lower ideal self-images.

Extending the developmental approach to adult psychopathology to psychiatric patients with mental retardation

The developmental approach to psychopathology has recently been applied to the examination of psychiatric disorders in people with mild mental retardation. Zigler's developmental approaches to psychopathology and to mild mental retardation derive from the same underlying formulation. An integration of these two developmental approaches could thus provide a parsimonious common framework for conceptualizing psychiatric disorders in individuals both with and without mental retardation.

In the developmental approach to mental retardation the principles of development that characterize nonretarded individuals are assumed to apply also to persons with nonorganic mental retardation. This group of individuals with mild mental retardation is presumed to differ from the general population only in that development proceeds more slowly and attains a lower upper limit (e.g., Zigler, 1969; Zigler & Balla, 1982; Zigler & Hodapp, 1986). Recent evidence suggests that aspects of the developmental framework can also be applied to people with various organic forms of mental retardation (Cicchetti & Pogge-Hesse, 1982; Hodapp & Zigler, 1995, in press). Principles from the developmental approach to psychopathology should thus be applicable to patients with mild mental retardation (Glick, in press; Zigler & Burack, 1989).

In the effort to integrate the developmental approaches to psychopathology and mental retardation, Glick and Zigler (1995) compared the types of symptoms displayed by psychiatric inpatients with mild mental retardation with those displayed by a matched sample of patients without mental retardation. The developmental position on mental retardation generates the expectation that developmentally lower functioning will characterize psychiatric patients with mild mental retardation compared with ones without mental retardation. As reported earlier in the chapter, patients without mental retardation who function at lower developmental levels display more symptoms indicative of the role orientation of turning against others and fewer symptoms indicative of turning against the self, more symptoms involving expression in action rather than in thought or verbal behavior, and more hallucinations without accompanying delusions than patients at higher developmental levels. Consistent with the developmental formulation, Glick and Zigler (1995) found that the patients with mild mental retardation displayed developmentally lower functioning than patients without mental retardation with respect to each of the three modes of categorizing symptoms. The assumptions underlying the developmental approach to psychopathology thus allowed the diverse symptoms manifested by psychiatric patients with mild mental retardation to be meaningfully organized and understood in relation to knowledge about psychopathology in individuals without mental retardation.

In a second study, Glick and Zigler (1996) used premorbid social competence to further differentiate developmental level within a sample of psychiatric inpatients with mild mental retardation and investigated relationships among premorbid competence, thought–action orientation in symptomatology, and length of current hospitalization as an outcome indicator. The Zigler-Phillips (1960) Social Competence Index was adapted to be appropriate to the competencies and life circumstances of people with mild mental retardation. As has been found for patients without mental retardation, lower premorbid social competence was associated with a predominance of action-oriented, compared with thought-oriented, symptoms. Moreover, premorbid competence and thought-action orientation were each found to make a significant independent contribution to the overall variance in length of current hospitalization. These results indicate that: (1) there is sufficient heterogeneity in the developmental level of patients with mild mental retardation to further differentiate this group, (2) variables from the developmental approach to adult psychopathology can be applied in making this differentiation, and (3) differentiation based on developmental differences in social competence show the same relations to other clinical variables (symptomatology and outcome) as has been found in patients without mental retardation.

The research thus far points to the value of integrating the developmental approaches to psychopathology and mental retardation. This integration provides a theoretical framework within which symptoms and other aspects of psychopathology in people with mild mental retardation can be organized and understood in relation to the broad body of knowledge about psychopathology in people without mental retardation. All hypotheses derived from the developmental approach to adult psychopathology have been confirmed in the research with patients with mild mental retardation. These findings lend important support to a continued effort to apply principles and findings from the developmental approach to psychopathology to the understanding of emotional disturbances in people with mental retardation. Given the relationships discovered among premorbid social competence, symptomatology, and length of hospitalization, for example, future research might examine relations among adaptive behavior, symptomatology, and outcome for patients with mild mental retardation. Other issues for investigation include whether for people with mental retardation: premorbid social competence (or adaptive behavior) and thought–action orientation in symptomatology relate to other outcome variables in addition to length of hospitalization, for example, social functioning, work functioning, neuroleptic response; and whether developmental variables, symptomatology, and outcome would be related for individuals in outpatient as well as inpatient treatment. The applicability of the developmental approach to psychopathology to people in the moderate range of mental retardation also remains to be investigated.

Conclusion

The developmental approach to adult psychopathology and the cognitive-developmental interpretation of self-image are both lines of research that have spanned much of Edward Zigler's career. They illustrate the integrative power of developmental psychopathology. Principles from classical developmental theory have allowed many major variables in adult psychopathology to be elucidated and understood in relation to each other as manifestations of a broad construct, the patient's underlying developmental level. Cognitive developmental principles led Achenbach and Zigler (1963) to an unorthodox interpretation of self-image disparity that was then expanded through research on normative development, children with special needs, and adult psychiatric patients. A common underlying developmental framework has enabled the research on adult psychopathology and on self-image to be extended for understanding people with mild mental retardation.

Just as normative developmental principles have been instrumental for elucidating many facets of psychopathology, findings from the research with disordered adults and with children and adolescents having special needs have enhanced understanding of normative developmental processes. With respect to self-image, the cognitive developmental interpretation discussed in this chapter was first tested with adult patients. Greater real–ideal self-image disparity and higher ideal self-images continue to be interpreted as indicating low self-regard and hence maladjustment (e.g., Higgins et al., 1985). Research on the cognitive developmental interpretation of self-image with psychiatric patients and maladjusted children counters this view. Rather than having a negative impact, the ideal self-image can provide a concrete vision of possibilities and, in so doing, enhance motivation and give direction to development (Glick & Zigler, 1985; Markus & Nurius, 1986). Recognition that self-image disparity and a higher ideal self-image are positive traits contributes in understanding normative development.

This self-image research also has implications for intervention and treatment. Rather than assuming that a major goal of therapy for all clients is to reduce self-image disparity (e.g., Rogers & Dymond, 1954), the developmental research suggests that different goals may be appropriate for clients who function at different developmental levels (Glick & Zigler, 1985). For individuals who function at lower developmental levels (e.g., adults with lower premorbid social competence and children with externalizing forms of maladjustment), a major aim in clinical treatment might be to increase self-image disparity by attempting to raise the person's level of aspirations. In contrast, for individuals who display higher developmental functioning (e.g., adults with higher social competence and symptoms indicative of turning against the self), the aim might be to reintegrate real and ideal self-images, thereby reducing disparity.

The moderating influences of experiential variables on the development of self-image has been elaborated primarily in research on psychopathology and in studies of children and adolescents with special needs. Yet this principle should apply as well in normative development. Psychiatric hospitalization, institutionalization, and being designated emotionally disturbed are dramatic examples of experiential variables that relate to how others respond to a person in everyday social interactions. Such experiential variables as social class or personal achievement might in a similar manner be expected to influence the unfolding of the developmental sequence in forming self-images in children without special needs. Knowledge about how various experiential factors contribute to or deter self-image development can certainly contribute to more effective prevention and treatment efforts for children.

The developmental approach to adult psychopathology stresses the underlying developmental continuity between adaptive and pathological behavior and thus among premorbid, disordered, and postmorbid functioning. The emphasis has been on positive adaptive aspects of patients' functioning – that is, developmental level as reflected in premorbid social competence or coping effectiveness. Striking are the many relationships that have been discovered between premorbid social competence and other variables in psychopathology. The broad predictive power of competence and coping effectiveness has similarly been underscored in research on normative development. In his 35-year prospective study of Harvard sophomores originally selected on the basis of superior adjustment, Vaillant (1974) concluded, it was the "men's successes . . . not their symptoms or their failures [that] predicted subsequent mental health" (p. 20).

Given the central importance of competence and coping effectiveness for understanding psychopathology and normative development, an implication for treatment is that efforts should be directed toward uncovering and building upon these positive attributes and not focus primarily on symptoms and maladaptive functioning. Research on the developmental approach to adult psychopathology is continuing to investigate personality variables associated with premorbid social competence. Interrelationships found in this research between higher premorbid competence, higher ego development, and less externality in locus of control parallel relationships discovered in research on coping and resilience in adolescents (Luthar, 1991). As the research on psychopathology continues to uncover personality variables associated with higher competence, these findings should illuminate processes underlying competent functioning in normal development and enhance prevention and treatment efforts aimed at bolstering competence.

The developmental approach to psychopathology further suggests that the effectiveness of various treatment modalities should be related to differences in developmental level. For individuals at higher developmental levels, who are presumed to be oriented toward expression in thought and to have greater resources for coping, verbal and cognitive forms of therapy would be expected to be most appropriate. By contrast, individuals at lower developmental levels, who are presumed to be more oriented toward expression in direct action and to possess fewer resources for coping, would be expected to derive greater benefit from forms of treatment that emphasize behavior (action) and concrete reinforcement and that provide training and support for coping efforts. For these individuals, behavior modification, social skills training, and residence in halfway houses might thus be particularly beneficial.

While the matching of the patient's developmental level to treatment modality may be needed initially, a longer-term aim of treatment may be to alter the client's typical mode of response. With respect to individuals who function at lower developmental levels, the aim would be to increase maturity through the development of greater competence, greater self-image disparity, and an increased orientation toward developing thought, rather than action, responses to stress. Higher developmental functioning may contribute to favorable outcome but also appears to increase the likelihood of certain disorders, such as depression. As Nolen-

Hoeksema (1987) suggested with respect to gender differences in depression, ruminative or thought-oriented responses may amplify depression whereas action responses may dampen depressed mood. Thus for individuals at higher developmental levels with disorders such as depression, a longer-term aim in treatment might be to encourage the development of action rather than thought-oriented responses.

References

Achenbach, T. (1966). The classification of children's psychiatric symptoms: A factor-analytic study. *Psychological Monographs, 80* (6, whole no. 615).

Achenbach, T., & Zigler, E. (1963). Social competence and self-image disparity in psychiatric and nonpsychiatric patients. *Journal of Abnormal and Social Psychology, 67,* 197–205.

Burack, J. A., & Zigler, E. (1989). Age at first hospitalization and premorbid social competence in schizophrenia and affective disorder. *American Journal of Orthopsychiatry, 59,* 188–196.

Bybee, J. (1986). *The self-image and guilt: Relationships to gender, developmental level, and classroom behavior.* Unpublished doctoral dissertation, Yale University.

Bybee, J., Glick, M., & Zigler, E. (1990). Differences across gender, grade level, and academic track in the content of the ideal self-image. *Sex Roles, 22,* 349–358.

Bybee, J., & Zigler, E. (1991). The self-image and guilt: A further test of the cognitive-developmental formulation. *Journal of Personality, 59,* 733–745.

Cicchetti, D., & Pogge-Hesse, P. (1982). Possible contributions of the study of organically retarded persons to developmental theory. In E. Zigler & D. Balla (Eds.), *Mental retardation: The developmental-difference controversy* (pp. 277–318). Hillsdale, NJ: Erlbaum.

Freud, S. (1933). *The interpretation of dreams* (A. A. Brill, trans.). New York: Macmillan.

Garmezy, N., Masten, A., & Tellegen, A. (1984). The study of stress and competence in children: A building block for developmental psychopathology. *Child Development, 55,* 97–111.

Garnet, K. E., Glick, M., & Edell, W. S. (1993). Anhedonia and premorbid competence in young, nonpsychotic psychiatric inpatients. *Journal of Abnormal Psychology, 102,* 580–583.

Glick, M. (in press). A developmental approach to psychopathology in people with mild mental retardation. In R. M. Hodapp, E. Zigler, & J. Burack (Eds.), *Handbook of mental retardation and development.* New York: Cambridge University Press.

Glick, M., Acunzo, M. A., & Zigler, E. (1993). *Extending the developmental interpretation of delusions and hallucinations to bipolar affective disorder patients.* Unpublished manuscript.

Glick, M., Luthar, S., Quinlan, D., & Zigler, E. (1994). *Level of ego development, premorbid social competence and diagnosis.* Unpublished manuscript.

Glick, M., Mazure, C., Bowers, M., & Zigler, E. (1993). Premorbid social competence and the effectiveness of early neuroleptic treatment. *Comprehensive Psychiatry, 34,* 396–401.

Glick, M., & Zigler, E. (1985). Self-image: A cognitive-developmental approach. In R. Leahy (Ed.), *The development of self* (pp. 1–42). New York: Academic Press.

Glick, M., & Zigler, E. (1986). Premorbid competence and psychiatric outcome in male and female nonschizophrenic patients. *Journal of Consulting and Clinical Psychology, 54,* 402–403.

Glick, M., & Zigler, E. (1990). Premorbid competence and the courses and outcomes of psychiatric disorders. In J. Rolf, A. Masten, D. Cicchetti, K. Nuechterlein, & S. Weintraub (Eds.), *Risk and protective factors in psychopathology,* (pp. 497–513). New York: Cambridge University Press.

Glick, M., & Zigler, E. (1995). Developmental differences in the symptomatology of psychiatric inpatients with and without mild mental retardation. *American Journal on Mental Retardation, 99,* 407–417.

Glick, M., & Zigler, E. (1996). Premorbid competence, thought-action orientation, and outcome in psychiatric patients with mild mental retardation. *Development and Psychopathology, 8,* 585–595.

Glick, M., Zigler, E., & Edell, W. (1995). [Personality correlates of premorbid social competence]. Unpublished raw data.

Glick, M., Zigler, E., & Zigler, B. (1985). Developmental correlates of age on first hospitalization in nonschizophrenic psychiatric patients. *Journal of Nervous and Mental Disease, 173,* 677–684.

Goldstein, M., Held, J., & Cromwell, R. (1968). Premorbid adjustment and paranoid-nonparanoid status in schizophrenia, *Psychological Bulletin, 70,* 382–386.

Higgins, E. T., Klein, R., & Strauman, T. (1985). Self-concept discrepancy theory: A psychological model for distinguishing among different aspects of depression and anxiety. *Social Cognition, 3,* 51–76.

Hodapp, R. M., & Zigler, E. (in press). New issues in the developmental approach to mental retardation. In W. E. MacLean Jr. (Ed.), *Handbook of mental deficiency, psychological theory and research* (3rd ed.). Hillsdale, NJ: Erlbaum.

Hodapp, R. M., & Zigler, E. (1995). Past, present and future issues in the developmental approach to mental retardation. In D. Cicchetti & D. Cohen (Eds.), *Manual of developmental psychopathology* (Vol. 2, pp. 299–331). New York: Wiley.

Katz, P., & Zigler, E. (1967). Self-image disparity: A developmental approach. *Journal of Personality and Social Psychology, 5,* 186–195.

Katz, P., Zigler, E., & Zalk, S. (1975). Children's self-image disparity: The effects of age, maladjustment, and action-thought orientation. *Developmental Psychology, 11,* 546–550.

Leahy, R. L. (1981). Parental practices and the development of moral judgment and self-image disparity during adolescence. *Developmental Psychology, 17,* 580–594.

Leahy, R., Balla, D., & Zigler, E. (1982). Role-taking, self-image, and imitation in retarded and non-retarded individuals. *American Journal of Mental Deficiency, 86,* 372–379.

Lerner, P. M. (1968). Correlation of social competence and level of cognitive perceptual functioning in male schizophrenics. *Journal of Nervous and Mental Disease, 146,* 412–416.

Lewin, K. (1946). Behavior and development as a function of the total situation. In L. Carmichael (Ed.), *Manual of child psychology* (pp. 791–844). New York: Wiley.

Lewine, R. R. J., Watt, N. F., Prentky, R. A., & Fryer, J. H. (1980). Childhood behavior in schizophrenia, personality disorder, depression, and neurosis. *British Journal of Psychiatry, 132,* 347–357.

Loevinger, J., & Wessler, R. (1970). *Measuring ego development* (Vol. 1). San Francisco: Jossey-Bass.

Luthar, S. S. (1991). Vulnerability and resilience: A study of high risk adolescents. *Child Development, 62,* 600–616.

Luthar, S. S., Glick, M., Zigler, E., & Rounsaville, B. (1993). Social competence among cocaine abusers: Moderating effects of comorbid diagnosis and gender. *American Journal of Drug and Alcohol Abuse, 19,* 283–298.

Luthar, S. S., Zigler, E., & Goldstein, D. (1992). Psychosocial adjustment among intellectually gifted adolescents: The role of cognitive-developmental and experiential factors. *Journal of Child Psychology and Psychiatry, 33,* 361–373.

Markus, H., & Nurius, P. (1986). Possible selves. *American Psychologist, 41,* 954–969.

Mylet, M., Styfco, S. J., & Zigler, E. (1979). The interrelationship between self-image disparity and social competence, defensive style, and adjustment status. *Journal of Nervous and Mental Disease, 167,* 553–560.

Nolen-Hoeksema, S. (1987). Sex differences in unipolar depression: Evidence and theory. *Psychological Bulletin, 101,* 259–282.

Phillips, D. A., & Zigler, E. (1980). Children's self-image disparity: Effects of age, socioeconomic status, ethnicity, and gender. *Journal of Personality and Social Psychology, 39,* 689–700.

Phillips, L. (1953). Case history data and prognosis in schizophrenia. *Journal of Nervous and Mental Disease, 117,* 515–525.

Phillips, L., Broverman, I. K., & Zigler, E. (1968). Sphere dominance, role orientation, and diagnosis. *Journal of Abnormal Psychology, 73,* 306–312.

Phillips, L., & Rabinovitch, M. (1958). Social role and patterns of symptomatic behavior. *Journal of Abnormal and Social Psychology, 57,* 181–186.

Phillips, L., & Zigler, E. (1961). Social competence: The action-thought parameter and vicariousness in normal and pathological behavior. *Journal of Abnormal and Social Psychology, 63,* 137–146.

Piaget, J. (1951). Principle factors in determining evolution from childhood to adult life. In D. Rapaport (Ed.), *Organization and pathology of thought* (pp. 154–175). New York: Columbia University Press.

Prentky, R. A., Lewine, R. R. J., Watt, N., & Fryer, J. H. (1980). A longitudinal study of psychiatric outcome: Developmental variables vs. psychiatric symptoms. *Schizophrenia Bulletin, 6,* 139–148.

Quinlan, D. M., Rogers, L. R., & Kegan, R. G. (1980, April). *Developmental dimensions of psychopathology.* Paper presented at the convention of the Eastern Psychological Association, Hartford, CT.

Rapaport, D. (1951). Toward a theory of thinking. In D. Rapaport (Ed.), *Organization and pathology of thought* (pp. 689–730). New York: Columbia University Press.

Rogers, C. R., & Dymond, R. F. (Eds.). (1954). *Psychotherapy and personality change.* Chicago: University of Chicago Press.

Vaillant, G. E. (1974). Natural history of male psychological health. II. Some antecedents of healthy adult adjustment. *Archives of General Psychiatry, 31,* 15–22.

Werner, H. (1948). *Comparative psychology of mental development.* New York: Follett.

Werner, H. (1957). The concept of development from a comparative and organismic point of view. In D. Harris (Ed.), *The concept of development: An issue in the study of human behavior* (pp. 125–148). Minneapolis: University of Minnesota Press.

Werner, H., & Kaplan, B. (1963). *Symbol formation: An organismic-developmental approach to language and the expression of thought.* New York: Wiley.

Zigler, E. (1969). Developmental versus difference theories of mental retardation and the problem of motivation. *American Journal of Mental Deficiency, 73,* 536–556.

Zigler, E., & Balla, D. (Eds.). (1982). *Mental retardation: The developmental-difference controversy.* Hillsdale, NJ: Erlbaum.

Zigler, E., Balla, D., & Watson, N. (1972). Experiential determinants of self-image disparity in institutionalized and noninstitutionalized retarded and normal children. *Journal of Personality and Social Psychology, 23,* 81–87.

Zigler, E., & Burack, J. (1989). Personality development and the dually diagnosed person. *Research in Developmental Disabilities, 10,* 225–240.

Zigler, E., & Glick, M. (1984). Paranoid schizophrenia: An unorthodox view. *American Journal of Orthopsychiatry, 54,* 43–71.

Zigler, E., & Glick, M. (1986). *A developmental approach to adult psychopathology.* New York: Wiley.

Zigler, E., & Glick, M. (1988). Is paranoid schizophrenia really camouflaged depression? *American Psychologist, 43,* 284–290.

Zigler, E., Glick, M., & Marsh, A. (1979). Premorbid social competence and outcome among schizophrenic and nonschizophrenic patients. *Journal of Nervous and Mental Disease, 167,* 478–483.

Zigler, E., & Hodapp, R. (1986). *Understanding mental retardation.* New York: Cambridge University Press.

Zigler, E., & Levine, J. (1973). Premorbid adjustment and paranoid-nonparanoid status in schizophrenia: A further investigation. *Journal of Abnormal Psychology, 82,* 189–199.

Zigler, E., & Levine, J. (1981a). Age of first hospitalization of male and female paranoid and nonparanoid schizophrenics: A developmental approach. *Journal of Abnormal Psychology, 90,* 458–467.

Zigler, E., & Levine, J. (1981b). Premorbid competence in schizophrenia: What is being measured? *Journal of Consulting and Clinical Psychology, 49,* 96–105.

Zigler, E., & Levine, J. (1983). Hallucinations vs. delusions: A developmental approach. *Journal of Nervous and Mental Disease, 171,* 141–146.

Zigler, E., Levine, J., & Zigler, B. (1976). The relation between premorbid competence and paranoid-nonparanoid status in schizophrenia: A methodological and theoretical critique. *Psychological Bulletin, 83,* 303–313.

Zigler, E., Levine, J., & Zigler, B. (1977). Premorbid social competence and paranoid-nonparanoid status in female schizophrenic patients. *Journal of Nervous and Mental Disease, 164,* 333–339.

Zigler, E., & Phillips, L. (1960). Social effectiveness and symptomatic behaviors. *Journal of Abnormal and Social Psychology, 61,* 231–238.

Zigler, E., & Phillips, L. (1961a). Case history data and psychiatric diagnosis. *Journal of Consulting Psychology, 25,* 258.

Zigler, E., & Phillips, L. (1961b). Psychiatric diagnosis and symptomatology. *Journal of Abnormal and Social Psychology, 63,* 69–75.

Zigler, E., & Phillips, L. (1961c). Social competence and outcome in psychiatric disorder. *Journal of Abnormal and Social Psychology, 63,* 264–271.

Zigler, E., & Phillips, L. (1962). Social competence and the process-reactive distinction in psychopathology. *Journal of Abnormal and Social Psychology, 65,* 215–222.

12   Conduct disorder across the life-span

Alan E. Kazdin

Antisocial behaviors in children refer broadly to a variety of acts that reflect social rule violations and/or that are actions against others. Such behaviors as fighting, lying, and stealing are evident in clinically referred children but also are seen in varying degrees in most children over the course of development. For present purposes, the term "conduct disorder" will be used to refer to antisocial behavior that is clinically significant and clearly beyond the realm of "normal" functioning.[1] Whether antisocial behaviors are sufficiently severe to constitute conduct disorder depends on several characteristics of the behaviors including their frequency, intensity, and chronicity and whether they are isolated acts or part of a larger "package" or syndrome with other deviant behaviors. Typically, conduct disorder is reserved for instances in which antisocial behaviors lead to impairment in everyday functioning, as reflected in unmanageability at home and at school or dangerous acts that affect others (peers, siblings).

Conduct disorder is identified in childhood as a pattern of clinical dysfunction, usually during elementary school years. Yet, for many individuals, conduct disorder is a pattern of functioning over the life-span. The present chapter discusses characteristics of conduct disorder, continuities and discontinuities over the course of development, issues and challenges for research, and implications of selected findings for social policy.

Conduct disorder in childhood and adolescence

Diagnosis and prevalence

Extremes of conduct problems are delineated in contemporary diagnosis, as represented by the *Diagnostic and Statistical Manual of Mental Disorders* (DSM-IV; American Psychiatric Association [APA], 1994). Conduct Disorder (CD) is the diagnostic category for coding antisocial behavior among children and adolescents. The essential feature is a pattern of behavior in which the child ignores the rights

Completion of this research was supported by a Research Scientist Award (MH00353) and a grant (MH35408) from the National Institute of Mental Health.

Table 12.1. *Symptoms included in the diagnosis of conduct disorder (DSM-IV)*

Aggression to people and animals
1. Often bullies, threatens, or intimidates others
2. Often initiates physical fights
3. Has used a weapon that can cause serious physical harm to others (e.g., a bat, brick, broken bottle, knife, gun)
4. Has been physically cruel to people
5. Has been physically cruel to animals
6. Has stolen while confronting a victim (e.g., mugging, purse snatching, extortion, armed robbery).
7. Has forced someone into sexual activity

Destruction of property
8. Has deliberately engaged in fire setting with the intention of causing serious damage.
9. Has deliberately destroyed others' property (other than by fire setting)

Deceitfulness or theft
10. Has broken into someone else's house, building, or car
11. Often lies to obtain goods or favors or to avoid obligations (i.e., "cons" others)
12. Has stolen items of nontrivial value without confronting a victim (e.g., shoplifting, but without breaking and entering; forgery)

Serious violations of rules
13. Often stays out at night despite parental prohibitions, beginning before age 13 years
14. Has run away from home overnight at least twice while living in parental or parental surrogate home (or once without returning for a lengthy period)
15. Is often truant from school, beginning before age 13 years

---

Note: The number of symptoms required to meet criteria for the diagnosis of Conduct Disorder is at least 3 symptoms that have occurred within the past 12 months, at least one of which has been in the last 6 months.
Source: The symptom list here is based on the fourth edition of the DSM-IV (APA, 1994). Reprinted with permission from the *Diagnostic and Statistical Manual of Mental Disorders,* Fourth Edition. Copyright 1994 American Psychiatric Association.

of others or violates age-appropriate norms and roles. Table 12.1 lists the characteristics (symptoms) to convey the scope and type of problems such youths exhibit. A diagnosis of CD is provided if the individual shows at least three symptoms of those listed in Table 12.1, the symptoms were evident within the past 12 months, and at least one of the symptoms was evident in the last 6 months.

Using diagnostic criteria such as those in Table 12.1 or prior versions of the DSM, the prevalence of the disorder among community samples of school-age youth is approximately 2–6% (see Zoccolillo, 1993). One of the most frequent findings is that boys show approximately 3–4 times higher rates of CD than girls. The sex differences may be explained by differences in predispositions toward responding in aggressive ways and in socialization through parent–child interactions in relation to aggression, expression of anger, experience of empathy and guilt (see Zahn-Waxler, Cole, & Barrett, 1991). Differential responding on the part of parents may contribute to greater sensitivity of girls to the emotions of others, to their higher levels of empathy, and their reduced outward expression of aggression, compared with boys. Differences in the base rates of boys and girls for a number of behaviors such as engaging in rough-and-tumble play, bullying others, not complying with requests, and fighting have implications for the greater prevalence of conduct disorder (e.g., Achenbach, 1991; Maccoby, 1986). The symptoms that are listed in the diagnostic criteria emphasize confrontive and violent acts that are more likely in boys than girls. Because of low rates of these behaviors in girls, even a few instances, albeit below the threshold of existing diagnostic criteria, may be clinically important. These base-rate differences have raised the possibility of a sex bias in the diagnostic criteria that would also explain, or at least contribute to, the greater prevalence of CD in boys than in girls (Zoccolillo, 1993). In general, research on normative development has revealed qualitative and quantitative differences between boys and girls in behaviors related to aggression and antisocial acts, but the information has not yet influenced diagnostic practices.

Age variations reveal interesting patterns in prevalence rates. Rates of conduct disorder tend to be higher for adolescents (approximately 7% for youths ages 12–16) than for children (approximately 4% for children age 4–11 years) (Offord, Boyle, & Racine, 1991). The increase seems to be due to increases in onset among adolescent girls and among youths who engage in nonaggressive forms of antisocial behavior (e.g., truancy, running away). Sex differences are apparent in the age of onset of dysfunction. For example, in a study of youths referred for antisocial behavior, the median age of onset of dysfunction was in the 8- to 10-year age range (Robins, 1966). Most boys had an onset before age 10 (median = 7 years old). For girls, onset of antisocial behavior was concentrated in the 14- to 16-year age range (median = 13 years old). Characteristic symptom patterns were different as well. Theft and aggression were more likely to serve as a basis of referral among antisocial boys. For girls, antisocial behavior was much more likely to include sexual misbehavior.

Age of onset and subtypes of conduct disorder

Conduct disorder includes a heterogeneous set of problem behaviors. Research has searched for subtypes in an effort to find meaningful ways of grouping various sets of symptoms and to understand processes leading to onset and course of conduct disorder. Many different ways of delineating subtypes and patterns have emerged (see Kazdin, 1995). Recent attention has focused on age of onset as a way of accounting for prevalence differences over the course of development and sex differences in symptom patterns (see Hinshaw, Lahey, & Hart, 1993; Moffitt, 1993; Patterson, DeBaryshe, & Ramsey, 1989).

Child-onset conduct disorder consists of youths whose dysfunction is evident early in childhood, beginning with stubbornness, noncompliance (e.g., oppositional defiant disorder [ODD]) and hyperactivity (e.g., attention-deficit/hyperactivity disorder [ADHD]). The symptoms may progress to those of CD, even though many of the youths retain the symptoms from these other diagnoses. Youths with child-onset CD are more likely than those with adolescent-onset CD to engage in aggressive and criminal behavior and are more likely to continue their dysfunction into adulthood. Thus, child-onset conduct disorder is the more severe form.

Adolescent-onset conduct disorder is more common than child-onset CD. During adolescence, many youths engage in criminal behavior. For many of these youths, the acts are isolated; for others, the pattern meets criteria for CD. Both child-and adolescent-onset conduct disorder youths engage in illegal behavior during adolescence. However, those with child-onset CD are more likely also to engage in aggressive acts and to be represented primarily by boys. Those with adolescent-onset CD are more equally distributed between girls and boys. Peers group influences are considered to play a central role in emergence and onset of adolescent conduct disorder (Moffitt, 1993).

Different lines of evidence converge to suggest the utility of age of onset as a way of subtyping conduct problems. For example, the increased incidence of non-aggressive CD at about the age of 15, with no corresponding increase in aggressive CD, has served as support for the notion that a group can be identified with adolescent onset (R. McGee, Feehan, Williams, & Anderson, 1992; Patterson, 1992). Differences in neuropsychological, sympathetic, and neuroendocrine functions have been proposed to relate to the different subtypes (see Hinshaw et al., 1993; Moffitt, 1993). Child-onset CD has been particularly well studied in relation to parent–child interaction. Evidence suggests that parent child-rearing practices contribute to child-onset CD by inadvertently promoting aversive behavior in the child (Patterson, Reid, & Dishion, 1992). Negative reinforcement of deviant behavior, inattention to positive, prosocial behavior, and coercive interactions between parent and child lead to escalation of aggressive child behavior. This, in turn, leads to stable patterns of child aggression that has other consequences (e.g., poor peer relations, association with deviant peers, school failure) (Patterson, Capaldi, & Bank, 1991).

Child- and adolescent-onset subtypes, at this point in the research, do not yet offer an explanation of the different patterns. Even so, age of onset may be a useful point of departure for connecting subtypes of conduct disorder to specific developmental processes. Perhaps influences studied in developmental research (e.g., regulation and dysregulation of emotions, bonding to parents, peer relations) and transitions over the course of development (e.g., school entry) can be readily integrated with these different patterns. Also, developmental work on understanding peer socialization may provide clues regarding early patterns and how they lead to different trajectories. In this regard, work on child popularity and rejection may be important because peer reactions predict later dysfunction (Asher & Coie, 1990).

Correlates and associated features

Child characteristics. Children who meet diagnostic criteria for CD are likely to show a number of other problem behaviors than those included in the diagnosis. They are likely to argue with adults, lose their temper, actively defy and refuse to comply with requests, deliberately annoy others, and are angry and resentful. These behaviors, as a group, are occasionally referred to as oppositional behavior and comprise their own diagnostic category (oppositional defiant disorder), alluded to previously. Developmentally, oppositional behaviors are precursors to conduct disorder for many youths. Most children who evince conduct disorder probably have this early history of oppositional problems; but most children with oppositional problems are not likely to progress to conduct problems. Longitudinal research is critical in delineating the conditions leading to the continuation and escalation of behavioral problems.

In addition to oppositional behavior, many youths with severe conduct problems are considered by their teachers and parents to be "hyperactive." There is a reasonable basis for this. A large percentage of children (e.g., 40–70%) diagnosed with CD also meet criteria for attention-deficit/hyperactivity disorder (e.g., Fergusson, Horwood, & Lloyd, 1991; Offord et al., 1991). The core symptoms of ADHD include inattention, impulsiveness, and hyperactivity. The general point to underscore here is that children and adolescents with the diagnosis of CD are likely to have many other symptoms.

There are other characteristics that affect diverse facets of functioning as well. Children with conduct disorder are also likely to show academic deficiencies. They are more likely to be left behind in grades, to show lower achievement levels, and to end their schooling sooner than their peers matched in age, socioeconomic status, and other demographic variables (e.g., Bachman, Johnston, & O'Malley, 1978; Glueck & Glueck, 1968). Such children are often seen by their teachers as uninterested in school, unenthusiastic toward academic pursuits, and careless in their work.

Poor interpersonal relations also are associated with conduct disorder. Youths with conduct disorder often are socially ineffective in their interactions with adults (e.g., parents, teachers, community members) and engage in behaviors that promote deleterious interpersonal consequences such as peer rejection (e.g., Behar & Stewart, 1982; Carlson, Lahey, & Neeper, 1984). Related, conduct disorder youths are often deficient in attributional processes and cognitive problem-solving skills that underlie antisocial behavior (e.g., Crick & Dodge, 1994; Shirk, 1988). For example, such youths are more likely than their peers to interpret gestures of others as hostile and are less able to identify solutions to interpersonal problem situations and to take the perspective of others.

Parent and family characteristics. Several characteristics of the parents and families of conduct disorder children are relevant to conceptualization of the dysfunction (see Kazdin, 1993). Among the salient characteristics are parent psychopathology and maladjustment, criminal behavior, and alcoholism. Parent disciplinary practices and attitudes also are associated with conduct disorder. Parents are likely to show especially harsh, lax, erratic, and inconsistent discipline practices. Dysfunctional relations are also evident, as reflected in less acceptance of their children, and in less warmth, affection, emotional support, and attachment, compared with parents of nonreferred youths. At the level of family relations, less supportive and more defensive communications among family members, less participation in activities as a family, and more clear dominance of one family member are also evident. In addition, unhappy marital relations, interpersonal conflict, and aggression characterize the parental relations of antisocial children. These characteristics are correlated with, and often antecedent to, conduct problems, but do not, of course, necessarily cause or inevitably lead to those problems.

Contextual conditions. Conduct disorder youths are likely to live in conditions of overcrowding, poor housing, and high-crime neighborhoods, and to attend schools that are in disadvantaged neighborhoods (see Kazdin, 1995). Many of the untoward conditions in which families live place stress on the parent or diminish the threshold for coping with everyday stressors. The net effect can be evident in adverse parent–child interaction in which parents inadvertently engage in patterns that sustain or accelerate antisocial and aggressive interactions (Patterson et al., 1992). Also, contextual factors (e.g., poor living conditions) are associated with other influences (e.g., deviant and aggressive peer group, poor supervision of the child) that can further affect the child.

Factors that influence onset of conduct disorder

Risk factors. Risk factors refer to characteristics, events, or processes that increase the likelihood (risk) for the onset of a problem or dysfunction (e.g., conduct disorder). Risk factors, as antecedents to the dysfunction, may provide clues as to development and progression of conduct problems, possible mechanisms and processes through which the dysfunction comes about, and periods during development that might be used to identify cases at risk and to intervene (see Rolf, Masten, Cicchetti, Nuechterlein, & Weintraub, 1990). The factors that predispose children and adolescents to conduct disorder have been studied extensively in the context of clinical referrals and adjudicated delinquents (see Henggeler, 1989; Kazdin, 1995; Patterson et al., 1992; Robins & Rutter, 1990). Numerous factors have been implicated. Table 12.2 highlights several risk factors that have been studied along with a general statement of the relation that has been found.

Merely enumerating risk factors is misleading without conveying some of the complexities in how they operate. These complexities have direct implications for interpreting the findings, for understanding the disorder, and for identifying at-risk children for preventive interventions. First, risk factors tend to come in "packages." Thus, at a given point in time several factors may be present such as low income, large family size, overcrowding, poor housing, poor parental supervision, parent criminality, and marital discord, to mention a few (Kazdin, 1995). Second, over time, several risk factors become interrelated, because the presence of one

Table 12.2 *Factors that place youths at risk for the onset of conduct disorder*

Child factors

Child temperament. A more difficult child temperament (on a dimension of "easy-to-difficult"), as characterized by more negative mood, lower levels of approach toward new stimuli, and less adaptability to change

Neuropsychological deficits and difficulties. Deficits in diverse functions related to language (e.g., verbal learning, verbal fluency, verbal IQ), memory, motor coordination, integration of auditory and visual cues, and "executive" functions of the brain (e.g., abstract reasoning, concept formation, planning, control of attention)

Subclinical levels of conduct disorder. Early signs (e.g., elementary school) of mild ("subclinical") levels of unmanageability and aggression, especially with early age of onset, multiple types of antisocial behaviors, and multiple situations in which they are evident (e.g., at home, school, the community)

Academic and intellectual performance. Academic deficiencies and lower levels of intellectual functioning

Parent and family factors

Prenatal and perinatal complications. Pregnancy and birth related complications including maternal infection, prematurity and low birth weight, impaired respiration at birth, and minor birth injury

Psychopathology and criminal behavior in the family. Criminal behavior, antisocial personality disorder, and alcoholism of the parent

Parent–child punishment. Harsh (e.g., severe corporal punishment) and inconsistent punishment increase risk

Monitoring of the child. Poor supervision, lack of monitoring of whereabouts, and few rules about where youth can go and when they can return

Quality of the family relationships. Less parental acceptance of their children, less warmth, affection, and emotional support, and less attachment

Marital discord. Unhappy marital relationships, interpersonal conflict, and aggression of the parents

Family size. Larger family size, that is, more children in the family

Sibling with antisocial behavior. Presence of a sibling, especially an older brother, with antisocial behavior

Socioeconomic disadvantage. Poverty, overcrowding, unemployment, receipt of social assistance ("welfare"), and poor housing

School-related factors

Characteristics of the setting. Attending schools where there is little emphasis on academic work, little teacher time spent on lessons, infrequent teacher use of praise and appreciation for schoolwork, little emphasis on individual responsibility of the students, poor working conditions for pupils (e.g., furniture in poor repair), unavailability of the teacher to deal with children's problems, and low teacher expectancies

Note: The list of risk factors highlights major influences. The number of factors and the relations of specific factors to risk are more complex than the summary statements noted here. For a more detailed discussion, other sources can be consulted (e.g., Kazdin, 1995; Loeber, 1990; Mrazek & Haggerty, 1994; Yoshikawa, 1994).

factor can augment the accumulation of other risk factors. For example, early academic dysfunction can lead to truancy and dropping out of school, which further increase risk for conduct disorder.

Third, risk factors may interact with (i.e., be moderated or influenced by) each other and with other variables (see Boyle & Offord, 1990). As one example, large family size has been repeatedly shown to be a risk factor for conduct disorder. However, the importance of family size as a predictor is moderated by income. If family income and living accommodations are adequate, family size is less likely to be a risk factor (West, 1982). As another example, risk factors often interact with age of the child (e.g., infancy, early or middle childhood). For example, marital discord or separation appears to serve as a risk factor primarily when it occurs early in the child's life (e.g., within the first 4 or 5 years) (Wadsworth, 1979). How risk factors exert impact in childhood and why some periods of development are sensitive to particular influences underscore the importance of understanding "normal" developmental processes.

Protective factors. Research on risk factors leads naturally to the study of positive outcomes. The reason is that even under very adverse conditions with multiple risk factors present, many individuals will adapt and not experience adverse outcomes (e.g., Richters & Martinez, 1993). A conceptually interesting and potentially critical set of influences that may affect onset are referred to as protective factors. These are characteristics, events, or processes that decrease the impact of a risk factor and likelihood of an adverse outcome. Although protective factors have been less well studied than have risk factors, significant progress has been made (see Cicchetti & Garmezy, 1993).

Researchers have identified protective factors by studying individuals known to be at risk (i.e., show several risk factors) and by delineating subgroups of those who do, versus those who do not, later show conduct disorder. For example, in a longitudinal study from birth through young adulthood, youths were identified as at risk for delinquency based on a number of factors (Werner & Smith, 1992). Yet, not all youths at risk became delinquent. Those who did not evince delinquency by adolescence were more likely to be firstborn, to be perceived by their mothers as affectionate, to show higher self-esteem and locus of control, and to have alternative caretakers in the family (than the parents) and a supportive same-sex model who played an important role in their development. Other factors that reduce or attenuate risk include above average intelligence, competence in various skill areas, getting along with peers, and having friends (e.g., Luthar & Zigler, 1991, 1992; Rae Grant, Thomas, Offord, & Boyle, 1989). In many cases, these protective factors seem to be the absence or inverse of a risk factor. For example, easy temperament, academic success, and good relations with parents reduce risk, as does a good relationship with an emotionally responsive, caregiving adult, whether a parent or nonparent figure.

Among the many protective factors, three general categories help to organize current findings (see Garmezy, 1985; Werner & Smith, 1992). The first is *personal attributes of the child*. Beginning in infancy and unfolding throughout development, these include such factors as easy temperament, sociability, competencies at school, and high self-esteem. The second category is *family factors* and includes such characteristics as caretaking style, education of the parents, and parent social competence. The third category consists of *external supports* and includes friendships, peer relations, and support from another significant adult. The categories are useful ways to describe protective factors, but it is important to bear in mind that they tend to be interdependent and reciprocal. For example, child attachment to the parent is important as a protective factor and probably reflects personal attributes of the child in combination with characteristics of the parent. In general, it is useful to conceptualize many of the protective factors as part of transactions between the child and the environment.

General comments. Risk and protective factors refer to variables that influence the probability of onset of an outcome in a population. Although many risk and protective factors have been identified, we do not understand how most of the factors operate. In some cases, there are clues as to the processes and mechanisms that have direct influences on the outcome. For example, harsh punishment practices serve as a risk factor for conduct problems. Punishment is part of a broader set of inept child-rearing practices that have been shown to escalate coercive and aggressive behavior directly (Patterson et al., 1992). How the parent responds (e.g., coercively or passively) in response to the demands of the child has been shown to increase in a systematic way the level of aggressive child behavior. Moreover, intervenng with special training programs that alter how the parents respond to their children decreases child aggression and antisocial behavior (see Kazdin, 1995). Research on parent discipline practices has made significant gains in moving from identification of a descriptor (risk factor) to the process (means of operation). Understanding the processes leading to dysfunction provides an excellent basis for preventive interventions. Also, understanding discipline practices and their relation to conduct problems draws attention to broader developmental issues. For example, inept discipline practices may not lead to behavior problems in many children. Understanding influences that may attenuate the role of these practices in development could be important. Thus, the study of conduct problems draws attention to discipline practices more generally in development, as well as to the search for protective factors among youths who are subjected to those practices that promote antisocial behavior.

Conduct disorder over the course of development

The manifestations of conduct disorder are likely to change over the course of development (Peters, McMahon, & Quinsey, 1992). Even so, there may be a continuity in the inferred trait or characteristic that underlies these manifestations. For example, young children (3–4 years of age) with conduct problems may be mildly stubborn, break other children's toys, and ''borrow'' (take) things that belong to their friends. These behaviors may not predict these same behaviors 10 years later. Yet, these early behaviors may predict other behaviors, such as stealing from stores and confronting strangers with a weapon, that are conceptually related or that belong to the same general class of behaviors. A life-span perspective emphasizes continuities and discontinuities over time and paths and progressions. Behavioral and other manifestations may be discontinuous but still reflect continuity at a broader level of conceptualization. Charting the course over the life-span begins with descriptive characterization of conduct problems at different points in development. The period of school-age years through early adolescence has been especially well studied. The present discussion of conduct disorder focuses on early development and adult outcomes, to fill out the life course of the problems.

Early development: Infancy and preschool years

Risk factor research suggests that a number of signs may be evident in the child, parent, and family context beginning in infancy. Child characteristics (e.g., difficult temperament, neuropsychological deficits, high activity), parent characteristics (e.g., pre- and perinatal birth complications, parental punishment of the child), contextual characteristics (e.g., stress, marital conflict), and other factors, noted earlier, are likely to be present. In addition, diverse psychological processes and experiences (e.g., development of affect, attachment, and cognition) are likely to be implicated. It is likely that a set of general factors may emerge in early development that increase vulnerability to dysfunction and some set of more specific factors that move the child to conduct disorder.

Charting the influence of any single factor is difficult because characteristics of child, parent, and contexts are dynamic rather than static. The dynamic feature emphasizes complex interrelations such as the reciprocal and mutual influence of the child on the parent and the parent on the child (Bell & Harper, 1977; Patterson, 1992). As the child interacts with others (e.g., peers), reciprocal and dynamic influences continue and have their own consequences (e.g., early aggression may lead to peer rejection).

In addition to dynamic influences at a given point, there is a developmental progression over time. The influences can place children on a trajectory or path. The trajectory or path is not a fixed or determined course, but rather the probabilistic sequences and outcomes. Some outcomes become more probable (e.g., being arrested, bonding with delinquent peers), and other outcomes become less probable (e.g., graduating high school, entering a monastery). A variety of influences can converge to alter the probabilities.

The paths and progressions leading to conduct disorder are not well charted. The range of developmental processes within the child, and how these processes interact with parent and contextual factors for normal development and then for specific types of dysfunction (e.g., internalizing and externalizing behaviors) have only begun to be charted. Nevertheless, many efforts have been made to represent some of the influences and progressions. Figure 12.1 is a summary attempt to chart a pathway to conduct disorder, beginning in infancy and continuing through elemen-

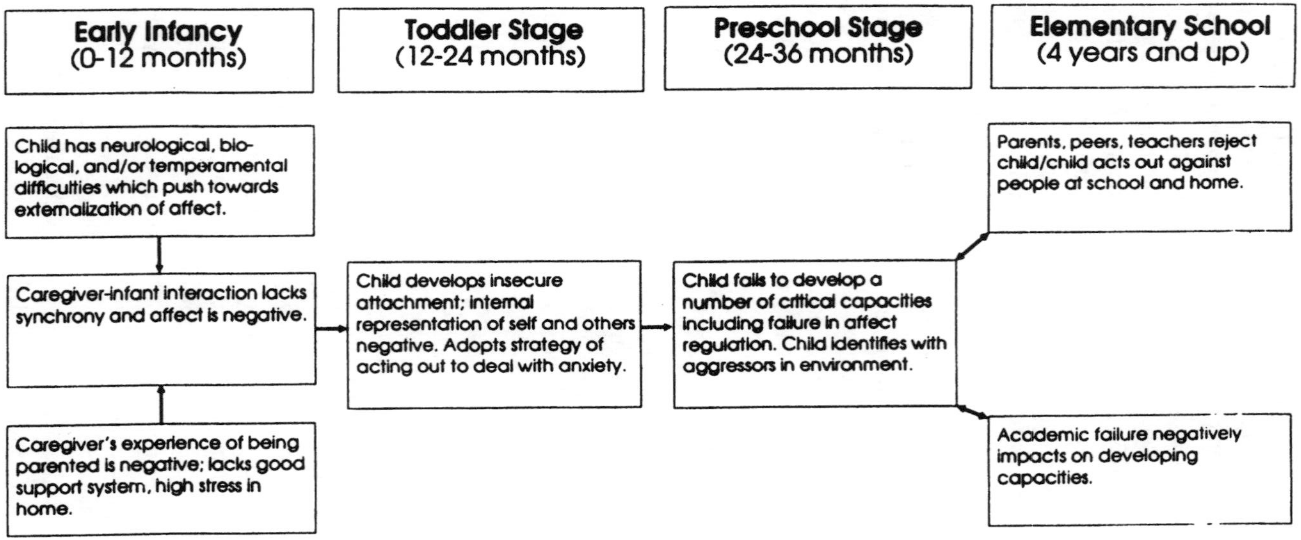

Figure 12.1. Early developmental pathway to conduct problems (Landy & Peters, 1992; reprinted with permission).

tary school (Landy & Peters, 1992). The pathway emphasizes a few of the risk factors, noted previously, and the accretion of dysfunction across such domains as peer relations and academic dysfunction (see Patterson, 1992).

The progression of characteristics in early development toward conduct disorder has been examined in longitudinal studies from birth through adolescence and young adulthood (e.g., Farrington, 1991; Werner & Smith, 1992). In such research, cases are sampled at multiple points (e.g., every few years) and then early predictors of later behavior can be identified. Through longitudinal studies, one can chart the course over short and long periods and identify transitions from one time to another and the relations among proximal and distal manifestations.

Recent research has characterized progressions and different paths and how conduct disorder symptoms and their associated features emerge (Patterson, 1992). Among the salient findings is a progression of severity of conduct problems over time. Trivial antisocial acts precede more severe acts in the child's repertoire. Youths who show the more serious behaviors (e.g., assault, fire setting) are likely to have progressed through the less severe behaviors (e.g., temper tantrums, noncompliance) but, of course, not all youths who engage in less severe antisocial behaviors progress to more severe antisocial behaviors (Lahey, Loeber, Quay, Frick, & Grimm, 1992; Loeber et al., 1993; Patterson, 1982; Patterson & Dawes, 1975).

Adult outcomes

Antisocial personality disorder and psychopathy. Longitudinal studies show that conduct disorder in childhood predicts conduct disorder up to 10, 20, and 30 years later (see Farrington, 1991). Antisocial behavior when continued into adulthood falls into another diagnostic category, namely, antisocial personality disorder (APD). The essential features include a pervasive pattern of disregard of others, violation of the rights of others (APA, 1994). The main symptoms of APD include repeatedly engaging in unlawful behavior, deceitfulness (e.g., repeated lying, conning others), impulsivity, irritability, aggressiveness (repeated fighting), disregard for the safety of others, consistent irresponsibility (e.g., repeated failure to retain a job), and lack of remorse.[2] The presence of CD in one's youth is a prerequisite for the diagnosis of APD. The criteria include many concrete behavioral acts of CD but also encompass more pervasive personality patterns, as reflected in deceit, manipulation, impulsivity, and irresponsibility.

Large-scale epidemiological research has revealed a lifetime prevalence rate of APD of 2.1–3.3% (Robins et al., 1984). Males are approximately 4 to 8 times more likely to be diagnosed with the disorder. The greater prevalence of APD among males compared with females is in keeping with the sex-difference pattern evident in childhood. Follow-up of child conduct disorder has elaborated this sex difference. Boys are much more likely to continue conduct disorder into adulthood and show APD (Quinton, Rutter, & Gulliver, 1990). In contrast, girls are likely to shift into more internalizing types of disorders (e.g., depression, anxiety) in adulthood. This pattern is especially interesting in light of research showing different reactions of boys and girls who are exposed to factors that might increase risk for conduct disorder. For example, exposure to family violence in childhood (ages 6–11) is associated with externalizing and internalizing symptoms in boys but primarily internalizing symptoms among girls (Jaffe, Wolfe, Wilson, & Zak, 1986). The processes leading to symptom pattern differences have yet to be elaborated.

The symptoms required for a diagnosis of APD, noted previously, emphasize overt behavioral signs. Over the history of the study of antisocial behavior in adulthood, emphasis has also been accorded internal experience such as lack of guilt or remorse, lack of empathy, and egocentricity (Cleckley & Thigpen, 1982; W. McCord, 1982). A distinction has been drawn between APD, which emphasizes the behavioral components, and psychopathy which focuses more on the motivational and interpersonal processes (Hare, Hart, & Harpur, 1991; Harpur, Hare, & Hakstian, 1989). APD has as its characteristics adverse family background (e.g., low socioeconomic status) and lower IQ. Psychopathy is correlated negatively with anxiety and positively with narcissism. Interestingly, individuals with both APD and psychopathy are those who exhibit the most severe and enduring patterns of antisocial behavior in adulthood. The distinction in the adult literature between behavioral and motivational/interpersonal components is important from a developmental perspective because it identifies different end points of earlier developmental trajectories. Unfortunately, to date there has been little effort to connect the different outcomes of adulthood with characteristics of early development, with some exceptions (Frick, O'Brien, Wootton, & McBurnett, 1994).

Other outcomes. Robins's classic follow-up study showed that among youths who were severely antisocial during childhood, slightly less than 50% continued their conduct disorder into adulthood. What happens to the remainder of youths? If all diagnoses are considered, rather than continuation of conduct disorder alone, 84% of the full sample received a diagnosis of psychiatric disorder as adults. Moreover, diagnosis of dysfunction does not adequately characterize the scope of adjustment difficulties in adulthood. There are many other outcomes identified by following conduct disorder children (Robins, 1966, 1978). As adults, multiple domains may show continued dysfunction, as reflected in psychiatric symptoms, criminal behavior, physical health, and social maladjustment. The characteristics that conduct disorder youths are likely to show when they become adults are presented in Table 12.3. As the table indicates, individuals with a history of conduct disorder evince a broad range of untoward outcomes.

General comments

From a developmental standpoint, it is important to understand the continuities and discontinuities of conduct disorder over the life-span. Longitudinal studies have

Table 12.3. *Long-term prognosis of youths identified as conduct disorder: Overview of major characteristics likely to be evident in adulthood*

Psychiatric status. Greater psychiatric impairment including antisocial personality, alcohol and drug abuse, and isolated symptoms (e.g., anxiety, somatic complaints); also, greater history of psychiatric hospitalization

Criminal behavior. Higher rates of driving while intoxicated, criminal behavior, arrest records, and conviction, and period of time spent in jail

Occupational adjustment. Less likely to be employed; shorter history of employment, lower status jobs, more frequent change of jobs, lower wages, and dependant more frequently on financial assistance (welfare); served less frequently and performed less well in the armed services

Educational attainment. Higher rates of dropping out of school, lower attainment among those who remain in school

Marital status. Higher rates of divorce, remarriage, and separation

Social participation. Less contact with relatives, friends, and neighbors; little participation in organizations such as church

Physical health. Higher mortality rate; higher rate of hospitalization for physical (as well as psychiatric) problems

Note: These characteristics are based on comparisons of clinically referred children identified for conduct disorder relative to control clinical referrals or normal controls or from comparisons of delinquent and nondelinquent youths (for further discussion see Farrington, 1991; Henggeler, 1989; Patterson et al., 1992).

identified intriguing patterns, yet to be explained. For example, the continuity of conduct disorder among boys (ages 7–12) is influenced by APD of a parent and child intelligence (Lahey et al., 1995). With either an APD parent and lower level of intelligence, boys are likely to continue conduct disorder symptoms. How these characteristics operate and combine and the other variables with which they are associated have yet to be studied.

The continuity of conduct disorder over the life-span warrants mention in another light. The continuity extends beyond the life of the individual, because conduct disorder extends across generations. For example, grandchildren are more likely to show antisocial behaviors if their grandparents have a history of these behaviors (Glueck & Glueck, 1968). Similarly, one of the best predictors of how aggressive a boy will be in childhood is how aggressive his father was when he was about the same age (Huesmann, Eron, Lefkowitz, & Walder, 1984). Thus, the life-span perspective requires consideration of how the dysfunction is extended to one's offspring and whether there are different modes of transmission.

Issues and challenges of developmental perspectives

Continua of dysfunction and risk

Research often focuses on youths who meet diagnostic criteria for CD. In principle, it is quite useful to specify criteria in this fashion so that diagnoses can be made reliably and that research on these samples can be replicated. Yet, the criteria themselves are difficult to defend. Where one draws the cutoff point to decide dysfunction (e.g., 3 symptoms rather than 4 or 8; duration of 12 months rather than 18, 24, or more) is likely to lead to different findings with regard to risk and protective factors, developmental trajectories, responsiveness to treatment, and prognosis.

Clearly, youths who meet the criteria are likely to be significantly impaired. Yet to understand the nature of conduct disorder more generally, it would be important to extend research to the full spectrum of severity of impairment and dysfunction. For example, youths who show symptoms of CD but who are below, at, and above threshold (e.g., ≤ 2 symptoms, 3 symptoms, or ≥ 4 symptoms, respectively, as only one way to operationalize threshold) for meeting the diagnosis would be important to study. This type of analysis would permit evaluation of factors that predict functioning across the spectrum of severity and frequency, as well as those that are only predictive of more severe levels or types of dysfunction. In general, conduct disorder is a "fuzzy" insofar as some individuals are at each extreme (clearly conduct disorder, and clearly not) with many shades in the middle (see Kazdin & Kagan, 1994). Presumably, there are points on the continuum at which there is a particularly poor prognosis, failure to respond to treatment, and so on. The full spectrum warrants much more attention to understand where the points are warranted to be delineated for intervention and for policy decisions as well.

In a similar vein, many of the factors that contribute to conduct disorder can be conceived along continua. In much of the research that focuses on risk factors, groups are selected and compared based on their exposure to and experience of an event. For example, the effects of abusive child-rearing practices on children and adolescents are often studied in this way. Typically in research, one selects abused and nonabused children and then identifies the other characteristics they might show at some later point in time (e.g., symptoms of psychopathology, poor school performance, dysfunctional peer relations). Identification of extreme groups is an excellent point of departure, but we wish to understand the continuum of the risk characteristic. Evaluation of the continua of discipline practices is required to understand the impact of various levels and types of punishment and the point at which these practices become risk factors for various outcomes.

Studying multiple levels of a proposed risk factor is important to reveal the function (or relation) in a more fine-grained fashion than the study of two groups or the presence or absence of a particular characteristic. Many influences are likely to bear curvilinear relations to an outcome of interest, and assessment of different levels of the risk characteristic can reveal this. For example, the degree to which parents try to control their adolescents is related to externalizing symptoms and drug use (Stice, Barrera, & Chassin, 1993). However, the relation between degree of parental control and symptoms is not linear. Extremely high or low parental control, but not intermediate control, is associated with adolescent dysfunction. Similarly, adolescent substance abuse is correlated with current dysfunction and predicts lack of academic pursuits, job instability, and disorganized thought processes years later (Newcomb & Bentler, 1988). Yet, the relation of substance use and untoward consequences is not linear. Heavy alcohol or drug use predicts later problems; no alcohol or drug use or consumption whatsoever is associated with undesirable personal and social characteristics as well. Use of a small amount of alcohol or drugs (primarily marijuana) is associated with several positive outcomes such as decreased loneliness, reduced self-derogation, improved relationships with family, and increased social support (L. McGee & Newcomb, 1992; Shedler & Block, 1990).

The point of these examples is to convey the need to study multiple levels of factors presumed (or indeed known) to increase risk for dysfunction. There may be points at which a given factor has one effect (risk), another at which it has no effect, and another level at which it has an opposite (protective) effect for an outcome of interest. Developmental research examines continuities and disconti-nuities over time for individuals and groups. Research is needed that examines continuities and discontinuities over dimensions of behavior (e.g., conduct disor-der), risk factors (e.g., child-rearing practices), and contextual influences (e.g., so-cioeconomic status). How the dimensions influence development and the points at which risk and impairment are especially likely are not well known.

Packages of influences and outcomes

A significant challenge for research in developmental psychopathology is the find-ing that many influences and outcomes come in "packages." It is difficult to identify simple and singular profiles of risk factors in light of these packages. For example, socioeconomic disadvantage, adverse child-rearing practices, parent ne-glect, and low parental interest in the child's academic accomplishments are inter-related (Rutter & Giller, 1983). The presence of one or two of these risk factors increases the likelihood of a child accumulating more of them. Thus, early child aggression or academic retardation is often associated with peer rejection, associ-ation with deviant peers, and placement in a class designed for socially and emo-tionally disturbed youths. These qualities in turn can lead to a "snowballing" of additional risk factors.

"Packages" are also evident in the outcomes (e.g., problem behaviors, disor-ders). Although we are interested in understanding the development and course of specific emotional and behavioral patterns, many of these are embedded in, or are part of, larger packages. For example, antisocial acts often are part of a larger cluster involving multiple problem behaviors (e.g., substance abuse, early sexual activity, and academic dysfunction) (e.g., Elliott, Huizinga, & Menard, 1988; Jes-sor, Donovan, & Costa, 1991; Newcomb & Bentler, 1988). A challenge is to ex-plain how these behaviors come together developmentally.

Problem behavior theory (Jessor & Jessor, 1977) has been proposed to account for the clustering of problem behaviors in childhood and adolescence. The theory suggests that these behaviors serve similar functions in relation to development.

Autonomy from parents and bonding with peers are two of the functions that may be served by such behaviors. Another theory has proposed that there is a trait or pervasive tendency to engage in deviant, delinquent, and criminal behavior (Gottfredson & Hirschi, 1990). The tendency, referred to as low self-control, refers to a propensity to seek pleasures of the moment and short-term solutions to problems.

What has been well established is that multiple deviant behaviors co-occur. Evidence points to complex interrelations among behaviors and patterns that are idiosyncratic and that vary reliably across individuals, situations, and contexts (see Kazdin, 1982; Mischel & Shoda, 1995). Understanding the organization of affect, cognition, and behavior and how they emerge and evolve developmentally are central to understanding problem behavioral patterns.

No doubt specific factors (e.g., risk and protective) relate to specific outcomes (e.g., conduct disorder), and these are obviously important to identify. Yet from what we know so far, two general conclusions can be reached: (1) multiple paths (e.g., different packages of risk factors) can lead to a specific outcome (e.g., conduct disorder), and (2) a single path (e.g., single or seemingly identical packages of risk factors) can lead to multiple outcomes (e.g., diverse types of dysfunctions or other outcomes). Elaborating specific lines of development and exploring the bases for variation are rich in opportunities for both theory and research.

Moderators of development and dysfunction

Research in development and developmental psychopathology begins with the task of identifying models that explain how affect, cognition, and behavior emerge and the factors that influence them. In this context, models refer to conceptualizations of influences on development, including what the influences are and how they unfold and develop. A challenge for research stems from the prospect that some influences and relations may vary systematically as a function of other variables. For example, the relation between characteristics of early development and outcome in relation to conduct problems varies as a function of child sex. It is not merely the case that boys and girls differ on a particular measure (e.g., degree of aggressiveness), but rather that the relations among other variables differs as a function of sex. We know, for example, that early evidence of aggression in school is a risk factor for conduct disorder, delinquency, and crime in adulthood for boys but not for girls (Quinton et al., 1990; Tremblay et al., 1992). The issue in relation to the present discussion is not merely the fact that there are sex differences, but rather the relation between antecedents and outcomes is moderated (influenced) by sex as a third variable.

Race and ethnicity are also likely to influence relations among factors related to conduct disorder. Differences are known to exist among European American, African American, and Asian American, and Hispanic American children in relation to prevalence, age of onset, and course of dysfunction. For example, among youths with substance abuse, one of many behaviors associated with conduct problems, ethnic variation exists in the specific substances used, degree of family monitoring, and amount of exposure to substance use (Catalano et al., 1993; Maddahian, Newcomb, & Bentler, 1988). In addition, whether a particular influence emerges as a risk factor varies as a function of ethnicity. That is, a relation between a particular antecedent and outcome is moderated by ethnicity.

Sex and ethnic differences are not the only factors that influence the relations among other variables. Yet these two serve as a basis for articulating the challenge for research. Investigators are often interested in developing models or theories of dysfunction with implied widespread generality of explaining conduct disorder. It is likely that key variables such as sex and ethnicity, but no doubt others as well, influence onset, course, and suitability of various interventions. The reason is that many of the psychosocial influences related to development may be moderated by these and other variables. The challenge for research is to identify whether different models of onset and course are needed for youths of different sex, ethnicity, and other groupings. This challenge goes beyond merely noting that research must consider these other variables. In addition, fundamental relations among risk and protective factors may vary.

Social policy and action

Drawing on knowledge for intervention

From a scientific standpoint various fundamental questions remain regarding conduct disorder. What are the best ways of delineating (diagnosing, categorizing) conduct disorder? How do risk and protective factors operate? For whom can the path toward conduct disorder be interrupted or altered completely? Although there are large gaps in the knowledge base, a great deal is known or at least partially known and this can provide a reasonable basis for action that can have social impact. Expert panels have convened to identify what is known and to provide policy recommendations to curb conduct disorder, particularly aggressive and violent behavior. As a recent example, a Commission on Violence and Youth of the American Psychological Association (1993) provided a 2-year study and concluded that, "society can intervene effectively in the lives of children and youth to reduce or prevent their involvement in violence" (p. 5). Several specific suggestions were elaborated to convey how this can be accomplished. Table 12.4 summarizes the categories of actions that can be taken. Each of these was developed in detail to convey their connection to what is known from current research on risk factors, onset of dysfunction, and interventions.

Many prevention programs have been developed to reduce risk factors for conduct disorder, as well as the incidence of aggressive and antisocial behavior (see McCord & Tremblay, 1992; Yoshikawa, 1994; Zigler, Taussig, & Black, 1992). For example, one of the more well-implemented and effective interventions was designed to help children at risk for school failure (Schweinhart & Weikart 1988;

Table 12.4. *Overview of recommendations to curb violence*

Early childhood interventions directed toward parents, child-care providers, and health-care providers to help build the critical foundation of attitudes, knowledge, and behavior related to aggression

School-based interventions to help schools provide a safe environment and effective programs to prevent violence

Heightened awareness of cultural diversity and involvement of members of the community in planning, implementing, and evaluating intervention efforts

Development of the mass media's potential to be part of the solution to violence, not just a contributor to the problem

Limiting access to firearms by children and youth and teaching them how to prevent firearm violence

Reduction of youth involvement with alcohol and other drugs, known to be contributing factors to violence by youth and to family violence directed at youth

Psychological health services for young perpetrators, victims, and witnesses of violence to avert the trajectory toward later involvement in more serious violence

Education programs to reduce prejudice and hostility, which are factors that lead to hate crimes and violence against social groups

Efforts to strengthen the ability of police and community leaders to prevent mob violence by early and appropriate intervention

Efforts by psychologists acting as individuals and through professional organizations to reduce violence among youth

Source: From the executive summary of the report of the American Psychological Association Commission on Violence and Youth (1993). Copyright 1993 by the American Psychological Association. Reprinted with permission.

Weikart & Schweinhart, 1992). Risk of school failure was based on parental lack of education, low income, and living in a stressful environment. The study began with 3- to 4-year-old children who were randomly assigned to intervention or nonintervention groups. The intervention included a classroom program for a 2-year period and weekly teacher home visits. Although the program ended when the children were 5 to 6 years old, follow-up assessments continued for several years. When the youths were 15 and then 19 years of age, those in the preschool intervention group were significantly (statistically) better on several measures than nonintervention group, including the measure "ever arrested" (31% vs. 51%) and the mean number of arrests (1.3 vs. 2.3) (Weikart & Schweinhart, 1992). Although the intervention clearly affected the lives of many individuals, many still engaged in conduct problem behaviors, even if at a lower rate than those in the nonintervention group. In principle as well as practice, there are limits on the impact of prevention or any single type of intervention.

Diverse intervention efforts and a broad portfolio of approaches are central to reduce conduct disorder in childhood and adolescence. As a beginning, large-scale programs for maternal care and child intervention directed to early risk factors for poor adjustment involving maternal nutrition, baby care, child rearing, and early education can have broad effects on mothers and their offspring (Zigler et al., 1992). The pioneering work of Head Start serves as an example of a program designed to address packages of risk factors that are known to have adverse effects (Zigler & Valentine, 1979). Large-scale, universal programs for children and adolescents in the schools are also important to promote positive social competence and resistance to internal and peer pressures that might lead to antisocial behavior. However, universal programs do not necessarily replace more focused or targeted interventions for youths who are at high risk or who show early signs of antisocial behavior. The task is to identify a range of interventions, settings in which they can be deployed, and ages at which they are maximally effective.

There are multiple opportunities to reduce influences that can contribute to conduct problems and aggression more generally. For example, the use of corporal punishment in child rearing and school discipline, violence in the media, especially television and films, and social practices that permit, facilitate, or tacitly condone violence and aggression (e.g., availability of weapons), to mention salient issues, are some of the practices that are relevant to the issue of aggression and antisocial behavior in society. We take as givens a backdrop of factors and practices that contribute in significant ways to aggression and antisocial behavior in society. The factors need to be scrutinized in relation to policy regarding child management and care.

As an illustration, the use of corporal punishment (i.e., physical aggression against children) is already implicated as a contributor to child aggression. The extensive use of corporal punishment is one of the givens in our society – a right that accompanies parenting and often teaching – that might be challenged if there is broad interest in delimiting aggression and antisocial behavior. Corporal punishment in child discipline at home and at school has been banned in a number of countries (e.g., Austria, Denmark, Finland, Norway, and Sweden; Greven, 1992). Large-scale efforts to reduce risk factors in this fashion are critically important in addition to the more common prevention and treatment efforts.

It might be useful to conceptualize the full range of influences in terms of a risk-factor model in which there are multiple influences that contribute to the outcome. Yet, in a risk-factor model, multiple influences add and combine to increase the likelihood of the outcome (e.g., aggression). Small influences can combine (additively and synergistically) and have significant impact, even if their individual contribution would be nugatory. We want to reduce risk factors not because individually they are *the* cause or because they will eliminate the problem, but because they are likely to have a palpable impact.

Limiting violence in the media can be seen as one influence likely to affect the level of violence and aggression in society. Efforts to quell gross displays of violence in the media are countered with arguments noting the benefits of television (e.g., education) and the responsibilities of others (e.g., parents) in policing what children watch. Yet, the significant impact of the media on antisocial and at-risk behaviors already has been well documented (see Strasburger, 1995). Reducing aggression in the media is likely to have an impact, even though media violence is not "the cause" of violence in society.

A commitment at the policy level and at the level that can mobilize social forces that influence, express, or model aggression could have significant impact on the problem. Social influences involving the matrix of societal displays, encouragement, and implicit endorsement of aggression, including the media at all levels, ought to be mobilized more systematically for a broad effort to alleviate aggression and antisocial behavior. Again, this is not the solution nor a reflection on the cause of aggression in society, but rather a way to have impact in one more incremental way.

Final comments

Conduct disorder represents a special challenge given the multiple domains of functioning that are affected. For many individuals, severe antisocial behavior and associated dysfunction in multiple spheres represents a lifelong pattern. Advances have been made in understanding the characteristics and patterns evident in school-age children and adolescents. Much of the work on diagnosis, assessment, and epidemiology has focused on this age group. Yet efforts have been made to chart the life course longitudinally, different paths leading to conduct disorder in childhood and adulthood, and the role that specific influences play (e.g., parent child-rearing practices, peers) at different points in development. Research has identified characteristics of the child, parent, family, and contexts that contribute to the emergence and maintenance of conduct disorder.

The lifelong pattern of conduct disorder and the transmission of the problems within families from one generation to the next underscore the importance of a developmental and life-span perspective. It will be important to identify the course and various paths and to examine developmentally opportune points of intervention. Over the course of development, influences vary in their contribution to conduct disorder. For example, during adolescence, the influence of peers on the appearance of conduct problem behavior is marked. Peer influences have been implicated in the onset, maintenance, and therapeutic change of antisocial behaviors (Elliott, Huizinga, & Ageton, 1985; Feldman, 1992; Newcomb & Bentler, 1988). Identifying how such influences operate and precursors to such influences has obviously important implications for intervening.

Although many fundamental questions remain about conduct disorder over the course of development, sufficient information is available to advance policy recommendations, a few of which were noted previously. A broad range of social interventions are required to have impact on such conduct problems. Specific programs and interventions developed by the mental health professionals play a major role, but it would be unfortunate to consider these as sufficient. Broader social practices warrant scrutiny in ways that balance individual freedoms and responsibilities. Recommendations from research on ways of reducing conduct problems (e.g., American Psychological Association, 1993) require addressing these broader issues.

Notes

1 Two issues related to terminology and meaning warrant comment. First, the term conduct disorder here is used generically to delineate clinically severe levels of dysfunction. The proper noun, Conduct Disorder, will be used to refer specifically to the formal psychiatric diagnosis with its associated criteria. Second, the terms "normal" and "normal development" will be used to refer to youths functioning in the community and who are not referred for mental health services. These terms do not necessarily refer to youths without clinical dysfunction. The reason is that a significant proportion of youths (e.g., 17–22% under age 18) functioning in everyday life and who are not clinically referred show clinical symptoms and impairment (Institute of Medicine, 1989; Zill & Schoernborn, 1990).

2 The symptoms noted here are based on the DSM-IV (APA, 1994), referred to previously. The diagnosis of antisocial personality disorder requires evidence of a pervasive pattern of disregard for and violation of the rights of others occurring since age 15 years, as indicated by 3 or more of the symptoms noted here. In addition, the individual must be at least 18 years of age and with evidence of a history of Conduct Disorder before the age of 15.

References

Achenbach, T. M. (1991). *Manual for the Child Behavior Checklist/4–18 and 1991 Profile.* Burlington: University of Vermont, Department of Psychiatry.

American Psychiatric Association. (1994). *Diagnostic and statistical manual of mental disorders* (4th ed.). Washington, DC.

American Psychological Association, Commission on Violence and Youth. (1993). *Violence and youth: Psychology's response* (Vol. 1). Washington, DC.

Asher, S. R., & Coie, J. D. (Eds.). (1990). *Peer rejection in childhood.* New York: Cambridge University Press.

Bachman, J. G., Johnston, L. D., & O'Malley, P. M. (1978). Delinquent behavior linked to educational attainment and post-high school experiences. In L. Otten (Ed.), *Colloquium on the correlates of crime and the determinants of criminal behavior* (pp. 1–43). Arlington, VA: MITRE Corp.

Behar, D., & Stewart, M. A. (1982). Aggressive conduct disorder of children. *Acta Psychiatrica Scandinavica, 65,* 210–220.

Bell, R. Q., & Harper, L. (1977). *Child effects on adults.* New York: Wiley.

Boyle, M. H., & Offord, D. R. (1990). Primary prevention of conduct disorder: Issues and prospects. *Journal of the American Academy of Child and Adolescent Psychiatry, 29,* 227–233.

Carlson, C. L., Lahey, B. B., & Neeper, R. (1984). Peer assessment of the social behavior of accepted, rejected, and neglected children. *Journal of Abnormal Child Psychology, 12,* 189–198.

Catalano, R. F., Hawkins, J. D., Krenz, C., Gillmore, M., Morrison, D., Wells, E., & Abbott, R. (1993). Using research to guide culturally appropriate drug abuse prevention. *Journal of Consulting and Clinical Psychology, 61,* 804–811.

Cicchetti, D., & Garmezy, N. (Eds.). (1993). Special Issue: Milestones in the development of resilience. *Development and Psychopathology, 5,* 497–783.

Cleckley, H., & Thigpen, C. H. (1982). *The mask of sanity.* St. Louis: C. V. Mosby.

Crick, N. R., & Dodge, K. A. (1994). A review and reformulation of social information processing mechanisms in children's social adjustment. *Psychological Bulletin, 115,* 74–101.

Elliott, D. S., Huizinga, D., & Ageton, S. S. (1985). *Explaining delinquency and drug use.* Beverly Hills, CA: Sage.

Elliott, D. S., Huizinga, D., & Menard, S. (1988). *Multiple problem youth: Delinquency, substance abuse, and mental health problems.* New York: Springer-Verlag.

Farrington, D. P. (1991). Childhood aggression and adult violence: Early precursors and later life outcomes. In D. J. Pepler & K. H. Rubin (Eds.), *The development and treatment of childhood aggression* (pp. 5–29). Hillsdale, NJ: Erlbaum.

Feldman, R. A. (1992). The St. Louis experiment: Effective treatment of antisocial youths in prosocial peer groups. In J. McCord & R. E. Tremblay (Eds.), *Preventing antisocial behavior* (pp. 233–252). New York: Guilford.

Fergusson, D. M., Horwood, L. J., & Lloyd, M. (1991). Confirmatory factor models of attention deficit and conduct disorder. *Journal of Child Psychology and Psychiatry, 32,* 257–274.

Frick, P. J., O'Brien, B. S., Wootton, J. M., & McBurnett, K. (1994). Psychopathy and conduct problems in children. *Journal of Abnormal Psychology, 103,* 700–707.

Garmezy, N. (1985). Stress-resistant children: The search for protective factors. In J. E. Stevenson (Ed.), *Recent research in developmental psychopathology* (pp. 213–233). Oxford: Pergamon.

Glueck, S., & Glueck, E. (1968). *Delinquents and nondelinquents in perspective.* Cambridge, MA: Harvard University Press.

Gottfredson, M., & Hirschi, T. (1990). *A general theory of crime.* Stanford, CA: Stanford University Press.

Greven, P. (1992). Exploring the effects of corporal punishment. *Child, Youth, and Family Services Quarterly, 15* (4), 4–5.

Hare, R. D., Hart, S. D., & Harpur, T. J. (1991). Psychopathy and the DSM-IV criteria for antisocial personality disorder. *Journal of Abnormal Psychology, 100,* 391–398.

Harpur, T. J., Hare, R. D., & Hakstian, A. R. (1989). Two-factor conceptualization of psychopathy: Construct validity and assessment implications. *Journal of Consulting and Clinical Psychology, 1,* 6–17.

Henggeler, S. W. (1989). *Delinquency in adolescence.* Newbury Park, CA: Sage.

Hinshaw, S. P., Lahey, B. B., & Hart, E. L. (1993). Issues of taxonomy and comorbidity in the development of conduct disorder. *Development and Psychopathology, 5,* 31–49.

Huesmann, L. R., Eron, L. D., Lefkowitz, M. M., & Walder, L. O. (1984). Stability of aggression over time and generations. *Developmental Psychology, 20,* 1120–1134.

Institute of Medicine. (1989). *Research on children and adolescents with mental, behavioral, and developmental disorders.* Washington, DC: National Academy Press.

Jaffe, P., Wolfe, D. A., Wilson, S., & Zak, L. (1986). Similarities in behavioral and social maladjustment among child victims and witnesses to family violence. *American Journal of Orthopsychiatry, 56,* 142–146.

Jessor, R., Donovan, J. E., & Costa, F. M. (1991). *Beyond adolescence: Problem behavior and young adult development.* Cambridge: Cambridge University Press.

Jessor, R., & Jessor, S. L. (1977). *Problem behavior and psychological development: A longitudinal study of youth.* New York: Academic Press.

Kazdin, A. E. (1982). Symptom substitution, generalization, and response covariation: Implications for psychotherapy outcome. *Psychological Bulletin, 91,* 349–365.

Kazdin, A. E. (1993). Treatment of conduct disorder: Progress and directions in psychotherapy research. *Development and Psychopathology, 5,* 277–310.

Kazdin, A. E. (1995). *Conduct disorder in childhood and adolescence* (2nd ed.). Thousand Oaks, CA: Sage.

Kazdin, A. E., & Kagan, J. (1994). Models of dysfunction in developmental psychopathology. *Clinical Psychology: Science and Practice, 1,* 35–52.

Lahey, B. B., Loeber, R., Hart, E. L., Frick, P. J., Applegate, B., Zhang, Q., Green, S. M., & Russo, M. F. (1995). Four-year longitudinal study of conduct disorder in boys: Patterns and predictors of persistence. *Journal of Abnormal Psychology, 104,* 83–93.

Lahey, B. B., Loeber, R., Quay, H. C., Frick, P. J., & Grimm, J. (1992). Oppositional defiant and conduct disorders: Issues to be resolved for DSM-IV. *Journal of the American Academy of Child and Adolescent Psychiatry, 31,* 539–546.

Landy S., & Peters, R. D. (1992). Toward an understanding of a developmental paradigm for aggressive conduct problems during the preschool years. In R. Peters, R. J. McMahon, & V. L. Quinsey (Eds.), *Aggression and violence throughout the life span* (pp. 1–30). Newbury Park, CA: Sage.

Loeber, R. (1990). Development and risk factors of juvenile antisocial behavior and delinquency. *Clinical Psychology Review, 10,* 1–41.

Loeber, R., Wung, P., Keenan, K., Giroux, B., Stouthamer-Loeber, M., Van Kammen, W. B., & Maughan, B. (1993). Developmental pathways in disruptive child behavior. *Development and Psychopathology, 5,* 103–133.

Luthar, S. S., & Zigler, E. (1991). Vulnerability and competence: A review of research on resilience in childhood. *American Journal of Orthopsychiatry, 61,* 6–22.

Luthar, S. S., & Zigler, E. (1992). Intelligence and social competence among high-risk adolescents. *Development and Psychopathology, 4,* 287–299.

Maccoby, E. E. (1986). Social groupings in childhood: Their relationship to prosocial and antisocial behavior in boys and girls. In D. Olweus, J. Block, & M. Radke-Yarrow (Eds.), *Development of antisocial and prosocial behavior* (pp. 263–284). Orlando, FL: Academic Press.

Maddahian, E., Newcomb, M. D., & Bentler, P. M. (1988). Risk factors for substance use: Ethnic differences among adolescents. *Journal of Substance Abuse, 1,* 11–23.

McCord, J., & Tremblay, R. E. (Eds.). (1992). *Preventing antisocial behavior.* New York: Guilford.

McCord, W. M. (1982). *The psychopath and milieu therapy.* New York: Academic Press.

McGee, L., & Newcomb, M. D. (1992). General deviance syndrome: Expanded hierarchical evaluations at four ages from early adolescence to adulthood. *Journal of Consulting and Clinical Psychology, 60,* 766–776.

McGee, R., Feehan, M., Williams, S., & Anderson, J. (1992). DSM-III disorders from age 11–15 years. *Journal of the American Academy of Child and Adolescent Psychiatry, 31,* 50–59.

Mischel, W., & Shoda, Y. (1995). A cognitive-affective system theory of personality: Reconceptualizing the invariances in personality and the role of situations. *Psychological Review, 102,* 246–268.

Moffitt, T. E. (1993). Adolescence-limited and life-course persistent antisocial behavior: A developmental taxonomy. *Psychological Review, 100,* 674–701.

Mrazek, P. J., & Haggerty, R. J. (Eds.). (1994). *Reducing risks for mental disorders: Frontiers of preventive intervention research.* Washington, DC: National Academy Press.

Newcomb, M. D., & Bentler, P. M. (1988). *Consequences of adolescent drug use: Impact on the lives of young adults.* Newbury Park, CA: Sage.

Offord, D. R., Boyle, M. H., & Racine, Y. A. (1991). The epidemiology of antisocial behavior. In D. J. Pepler & K. H. Rubin (Eds.), *The development and treatment of childhood aggression* (pp. 31–54). Hillsdale, NJ: Erlbaum.

Patterson, G. R. (1982). *Coercive family process.* Eugene, OR: Castalia.

Patterson, G. R. (1992). Developmental changes in antisocial behavior. In R. D. Peters, R. J. McMahon, & V. L. Quinsey (Eds.), *Aggression and violence throughout the life span* (pp. 52–82). Newbury Park, CA: Sage.

Patterson, G. R., Capaldi, D., & Bank, L. (1991). An early starter model for predicting delinquency. In D. J. Pepler & K. H. Rubin (Eds.), *The development and treatment of childhood aggression* (pp. 139–168). Hillsdale, NJ: Erlbaum.

Patterson, G. R., & Dawes, R. M. (1975). A Guttman scale of children's coercive behaviors. *Journal of Consulting and Clinical Psychology, 43,* 594.

Patterson, G. R., DeBaryshe, B. D., & Ramsey, E. (1989). A developmental perspective on antisocial behavior. *American Psychologist, 44,* 329–335.

Patterson, G. R., Reid, J. B., & Dishion, T. J. (1992). *Antisocial boys.* Eugene, OR: Castalia.

Peters, R. D., McMahon, R. J., & Quinsey, V. L. (Eds.). (1992). *Aggression and violence throughout the life span.* Newbury Park, CA: Sage.

Quinton, D., Rutter, M., & Gulliver, L. (1990). Continuities in psychiatric disorders from childhood to adulthood in the children of psychiatric patients. In L. N. Robins & M. Rutter (Eds.), *Straight and devious pathways from childhood to adulthood* (pp. 259–278). Cambridge: Cambridge University Press.

Rae Grant, N., Thomas, B. H., Offord, D. R., & Boyle, M. H. (1989). Risk, protective factors, and the prevalence of behavioral and emotional disorders in children and adolescents. *Journal of the American Academy of Child and Adolescent Psychiatry, 28,* 262–268.

Richters, J. E., & Martinez, P. E. (1993). Violent communities, family choices, and children's chances: An algorithm for improving the odds. *Development and Psychopathology, 5,* 609–627.

Robins, L. N. (1966). *Deviant children grown up.* Baltimore: Williams & Wilkins.

Robins, L. N. (1978). Sturdy childhood predictors of adult antisocial behavior: Replications from longitudinal studies. *Psychological Medicine, 8,* 611–622.

Robins, L. N., Helzer, J., Weissman, M., Orvaschel, H., Gruenberg, E., Bruche, J., & Regier, D. (1984). Lifetime prevalence of specific psychiatric disorders in three sites. *Archives of General Psychiatry, 41,* 949–958.

Robins, L. N., & Rutter, M. (Eds.). (1990). *Straight and devious pathways from childhood to adulthood.* Cambridge: Cambridge University Press.

Rolf, J., Masten, A. S., Cicchetti, D., Neuchterlein, K. H., & Weintraub, S. (Eds.). (1990). *Risk and protective factors in the development of psychopathology.* Cambridge: Cambridge University Press.

Rutter, M., & Giller, H. (1983). *Juvenile delinquency: Trends and perspectives.* New York: Penguin Books.

Schweinhart, L. J., & Weikart, D. P. (1988). The High/Scope Perry preschool program. In R. H. Price, E. L. Cowen, R. P. Lorion, & J. Ramos-McKay (Eds.), *14 ounces of prevention: A casebook for practitioners* (pp. 53–66). Washington, DC: American Psychological Association.

Shedler, J., & Block, J. (1990). Adolescent drug use and psychological health: A longitudinal inquiry. *American Psychologist, 45,* 612–630.

Shirk, S. R. (Ed.). (1988). *Cognitive development and child psychotherapy.* New York: Plenum.

Stice, E., Barrera Jr., M., & Chassin, L. (1993). Relation of parental support and control to adolescents' externalizing symptomatology and substance use: A longitudinal examination of curvilinear effects. *Journal of Abnormal Child Psychology, 21,* 609–629.

Strasburger, V. C. (1995). *Adolescents and the media: Medical and psychological impact.* Thousand Oaks, CA: Sage.

Tremblay, R. E., Masse, B., Perron, D., Leblanc, M., Schwartzman, E., & Ledingham, J. E. (1992). Early disruptive behavior, poor school achievement, delinquent behavior, and delinquent personality: Longitudinal analyses. *Journal of Consulting and Clinical Psychology, 60,* 64–72.

Wadsworth M. (1979). *Roots of delinquency: Infancy, adolescence and crime.* New York: Barnes & Noble.

Weikart, D., & Schweinhart, L. J. (1992). High/Scope preschool program outcomes. In J. McCord & R. E. Tremblay (Eds.), *Preventing antisocial behavior* (pp. 67–86). New York: Guilford.

Werner, E. E., & Smith, R. S. (1992). *Overcoming the odds: High risk children from birth to adulthood.* Ithaca, NY: Cornell University Press.

West, D. J. (1982). *Delinquency: Its roots, careers and prospects.* Cambridge, MA: Harvard University Press.

Yoshikawa, H. (1994). Prevention as cumulative protection: Effects of early family support and education on chronic delinquency and its risks. *Psychological Bulletin, 115,* 28–54.

Zahn-Waxler, C., Cole, P. M., & Barrett, K. C. (1991). Guilt and empathy: Sex differences and implications for the development of depression. In J. Garber & K. A. Dodge (Eds.), *The development of emotion regulation and dysregulation* (pp. 243–272). New York: Cambridge University Press.

Zigler, E., Taussig, C., & Black, K. (1992). Early childhood intervention: A promising preventative for juvenile delinquency. *American Psychologist, 47,* 997–1006.

Zigler, E., & Valentine, J. (1979). *Project Head Start: A legacy of the war on poverty.* New York: Free Press.

Zill, N., & Schoenborn, C. A. (1990). Developmental, learning, and emotional problems: Health of our nation's children, United States 1988. *Advance Data: National Center for Health Statistics,* No. 190 (November).

Zoccolillo, M. (1993). Gender and the development of conduct disorder. *Development and Psychopathology, 5,* 65–78.

13 Ontogenesis, depressotypic organization, and the depressive spectrum

Dante Cicchetti, Fred A. Rogosch, and Sheree L. Toth

Depression and its effects on the human condition have constituted a prominent area of inquiry since antiquity. Jackson (1986), in chronicling the historical interest in depression, concluded that there has been considerable continuity over the past 2,500 years in the importance of understanding and alleviating this condition, despite evolving conceptualizations and treatments. In this chapter, we examine the emerging insights that a developmental psychopathology perspective provides for understanding the etiology, course, and sequelae of depressive disorders. Additionally, treatment and social policy implications derived from this perspective are discussed. Mood disorders are of particular interest to developmental psychopathologists because of the complex interplay of psychological (e.g., affective, cognitive, interpersonal) and biological (e.g., genetic, neurophysiological, neurobiological) components that are involved. Further, depressive conditions may be conceived of as forming a spectrum of severity from transient dysphoria universally experienced, to elevated levels of depressive symptoms that do not meet the diagnostic criteria for disorder, to long-term periods of dysthymia and episodes of major depressive disorder. Even within more narrowly defined disorders, for example, major depressive disorder, there are likely to be heterogeneous conditions with phenotypic similarity, despite differences in etiology. Although there are diverse pathways leading to depressive disorders, potential risk factors for depression may result in a multitude of outcomes, of which depression may be one. Moreover, depressive phenomena and disorders are present throughout the life-span, from early childhood through senescence. Because of the continuities and divergences from normal functioning manifested in depressive disorders across the life course, the study of depression holds promise for understanding the interface of normal and abnormal adaptation. Not only does knowledge of normative development and functioning assist in characterizing the deviations evident among those with depression, but also understanding the aberrations in functioning among depressed persons elucidates how normal adaptation is achieved.

Although there has been increased attention to conceptualizing psychopathology

We gratefully acknowledge the support of the Prevention Research Branch of the National Institute of Mental Health (MH45027) and the Spunk Fund, Inc.

273

from a developmental perspective in recent years, for decades Edward Zigler has advocated an appreciation of the developmental underpinnings of serious psychopathology. Many current areas of interest in the field have been presaged by Zigler's work. An organizational or organismic orientation to understanding development has been central to Zigler's formulations (Zigler, 1963; Zigler & Glick, 1986), and this developmental view forms the basis for the ontogenetic perspective on depression espoused in this chapter. Zigler's depiction of premorbid social competence (Zigler & Phillips, 1961) as a developmental attainment achieved through success in adaptive tasks and contributing to individual differences among persons with psychopathological conditions (i.e., in terms of course of disorder, recovery, relapse, and treatment effectiveness) is echoed herein in terms of articulating how incompetent resolutions of stage-salient developmental challenges contribute to the developmentally derived depressotypic organizations. Furthermore, Zigler's analysis of symptom presentations in terms of their underlying developmental level (i.e., action-oriented vs. thought-oriented) (Zigler & Glick, 1986) is reflected in this chapter in the need to understand the ontogenetic origins of depressive symptomatology, particularly the thought-dominated negative attributions regarding the self. Finally, the interest of Zigler and his colleagues in resilient functioning in the face of adversity (Luthar, Doernberger, & Zigler 1993; Luthar & Zigler, 1991) is but one example of his striving to understand diversity in developmental pathways and outcomes, a theme reflected in the formulation of depression that will be discussed. Moreover, Luthar et al. (1993) have shown that depressive features may exist among resilient individuals despite their high level of functioning, attesting to the potential for continuity of vulnerability even in the midst of successful adaptation.

Epidemiology of mood disorders

Before examining developmental processes in depressive conditions, knowledge of the prevalence and course of the depressive disorders across the life-span provides important background for understanding how these disorders are represented within broad periods of the life-span.

Childhood

Prior to adolescence, the prevalence of depression in prepubertal children is approximately 2% (Kashani et al., 1983). In a prospective investigation of major depressive disorder in children in a school-age, clinically referred sample, Kovacs and her colleagues examined the duration of the first illness, the course of recovery from the first episode, and the time period before relapse (Kovacs, Feinberg, Crouse-Novak, Paulauskas, & Finkelstein, 1984; Kovacs, Feinberg, Crouse-Novak, Paulauskas, Pollock, & Finkelstein, 1984). Dysthymia, persisting on the average for three years, was found to have an earlier age of onset than major depressive disorder, which averaged 8 months in duration. Of these children, 42% developed a subsequent depression with all of those relapsing doing so within two years. Children with an underlying dysthymic disorder were more likely to experience recurrent and periodic depression. Further, when dysthymic disorder, as compared with major depressive disorder, is the first to emerge in children, Kovacs, Akiskal, Gatsonis, and Parrone (1994) have shown that, in addition to earlier onset, children with dysthymic disorder also are at greater risk for developing subsequent mood disorders, with 76% of these children developing a subsequent major depressive disorder and 69% of the children having combined dysthymia and depression (i.e., "double depression"). Comorbidity with other disorders also was found to be common among children with dysthymic disorder, including 40% experiencing comorbid anxiety disorders and 31% experiencing comorbid conduct disorders. Moreover, 13% of the dysthymic children later were diagnosed with bipolar disorder. Thus, contrary to a Piagetian position positing that difficulties encountered by children will be more transient and dissipate when they occur during the period of preoperational thought when cognition and affects are more situational, the early occurrence of a childhood mood disorder contributes to risk for later, recurrent disturbance.

Adolescence

The prevalence of depression increases during adolescence, with 5% to 10% of teenagers manifesting a major depressive disorder at any point in time (Fleming & Offord, 1990; Lewinsohn, Hops, Roberts, Seeley, & Andrews, 1993; A. Peterson et al., 1993). In a randomly selected community sample of adolescents, Lewinsohn, Clarke, Seeley, and Rohde (1994) found that the average age of onset for first depressive episode was approximately 15 years. These depressive episodes on the average were 26 weeks in duration (median of 8 weeks) with earlier onset and suicidal ideation related to more extended episodes. Following recovery, 5% relapsed within 6 months, 12% relapsed within 1 year, and almost 30% relapsed within 4 years. While anxiety and conduct disorders are common comorbid disorders among children with depressive disorders (Angold & Costello, 1993; Caron & Rutter, 1991), in adolescence, alcohol and substance abuse also increasingly co-occur (Kovacs, 1989). Mania is rare before puberty, although it increases in frequency by midadolescence (Rutter, 1986). When psychotic symptoms accompany a depressive episode among adolescents, the risk for mania increases. Moreover, the rate of subsequent bipolar disorder among psychotically depressed adolescents is higher (28%) (Strober, Lambert, Schmidt, & Morrell, 1993) than the rate of subsequent mania in depressed adults (4–8%) (Dunner, Dwyer, & Fieve, 1976).

Adulthood

Major depressive disorder among adults has been regarded as the most common serious mental health problem (Weissman, Bruce, Leaf, Florio, & Holzer, 1991) with estimates that nearly 20% of the population experiences a serious clinical depression at some point over the life course (Institute of Medicine, 1985; Kessler et al., 1994). In addition, more chronic dysthymic disorders are found in 3% to 6% of individuals sometime in their lives (Kessler et al., 1994; Weissman et al., 1991), and have been associated with poorer outcomes (Wells, Burnam, Rogers, Hays, & Camp, 1992). Adults with unipolar depression on the average experience five or six depressive episodes, with these episodes averaging from 6 to 9 months, although 20% persist for nearly 2 years (Post & Ballenger, 1984). When subsequent episodes occur, recurrence becomes more likely and the severity of episodes often increases (Maj, Veltro, Pirozzi, Lobrace, & Magliano, 1992). Among the elderly, research tends to show that there is no increase in mood disorders with age (Stoudemire & Blazer, 1985). Moreover, recent large-scale epidemiological studies of the elderly have found lower lifetime prevalence rates of depression and dysthymia (Kessler et al., 1994; Weissman, et al., 1991). As in adolescence, alcohol and substance abuse often co-occur with depressive disorders in adulthood, and comorbid anxiety disorders are common (Maser & Cloninger, 1990). Personality disorders also are frequently comorbid, and this comorbidity is related to earlier onset, poorer recovery, more life stress, and greater risk of suicide (Pfol, Stangl, & Zimmerman, 1984).

Sex differences

In adulthood, depression has consistently been found to be more common among women than men, with twice as many women as men developing depressive disorders (Nolen-Hoeksema, 1990). However, this sex difference does not emerge until adolescence. In childhood, some studies have found higher rates of depression in boys than girls (Andreason, Williams, McGee, & Silva, 1987; Kashani et al., 1983). Angold and Rutter (1992) examined a sample of 3,519 8- to 16-year-olds in treatment and found no sex differences prior to age 11 in the rate of depression, defined by various criteria. However, although the rate of depression increased for both sexes during adolescence, by age 16 girls evidenced twice the rate of depression as boys. Moreover, despite the potential for the biological changes associated with puberty to be involved in this sex and age differentiation in depression, Angold and Rutter (1992) found that pubertal status did not predict depression beyond the effect of age. Nolen-Hoeksema and Girgus (1994) suggest that gender differences in personality or behavioral style (e.g., higher rumination among females) that may exist prior to adolescence interact with increased developmental challenges for girls in adolescence resulting in the gender differences in rates of depression.

Children of depressed parents

The offspring of parents with mood disorders are at greater risk for the development of a range of psychopathological outcomes and, in particular, mood disorders (Weissman et al., 1987). In this context, it is noteworthy that persons with mood disorders often select mates who are more likely to have a psychiatric illness or a family history of psychopathology (Merikangas & Spiker, 1982). This assortative mating further contributes to chronic interpersonal difficulties and a high rate of marital discord (Downey & Coyne, 1990), compromising the family functioning experienced by children reared by a mood-disordered parent. Hammen, Burge, Burney, and Adrian (1990) studied school-age children of mothers with unipolar depression, bipolar disorder, a chronic medical condition, or no disorder. Children of mothers with unipolar depression had the highest rates of disorder, including unipolar depression, whereas the children of bipolar and medically ill mothers had rates exceeding that of the children of well mothers. The majority of children with a psychiatric diagnosis had their first episode in preadolescence and continued on an intermittent or chronic course over the 3-year follow-up period. In another 2-year prospective study of 174 children of parents with major depression (Warner, Weissman, Fendrich, Wickramaratne, & Moreau, 1992), the incidence rate of major depression in these offspring was 8.5% with 16.1% of these children experiencing a recurrent episode. On the average, the episodes of these children were 54 weeks in duration, with prepubertal onset and/or the experience of multiple parental episodes contributing to protracted episodes.

Given the prevalence of depressive disorders across large periods of development and the risk for depression exhibited by offspring of mood-disordered parents, it is essential to understand developmental processes that contribute to the emergence of depressive disorders. In order to structure our understanding of depression across the life course, we next examine central developmental principles, important in both normal and abnormal development.

Concepts in a developmental psychopathology approach to depression

Although developmental psychopathology is frequently equated with the study of psychiatric disorders among children and youth, this perspective encompasses a much broader approach to studying development across the life-span (Cicchetti, 1993). In contrast to developmental psychology which seeks to understand central tendencies and uniformities in normative processes of growth and development, developmental psychopathology is concerned with expanding the knowledge base of developmental psychology by focusing on the extremes of adaptation and non-normative processes of development. In so doing, the dialectic between normal and abnormal development is emphasized. By contrasting abnormal development with expected, normative developmental patterns, the aberrations of psychopathology are highlighted. Equally important, however, is the contrast of normal with abnormal for illuminating the understanding of normal developmental processes. The unique deficits, delays, and atypicalities of psychopathological conditions can provide insights into essential aspects of normal development that would not be otherwise apparent (Cicchetti, 1984; Cicchetti & Cohen, 1995).

Developmental psychopathology has been characterized as a macroparadigm

(Achenbach, 1990). As such, developmental psychopathology seeks to unify multiple fields of inquiry (e.g., psychology, biology, the neurosciences, psychiatry, neurology) in order to understand diverse levels of individual adaptation and development, the interrelations and integrations of these varied systems across the life course, the spectrum of potential developmental pathways that evolve, and the causal processes contributing to these varied trajectories (Cicchetti, 1993). Depression constitutes a particularly important area of study because of the diverse systems that are influenced by the disorder. Aberrations in the broad domains of cognition, affect, and interpersonal relations, as well as anomalies in genetic and neurobiological systems are present to varying degrees among individuals with mood disorders (see Figure 13.1). Notably, these varied systems do not exist in isolation. Rather, they are complexly interrelated and mutually interdependent. Thus, understanding the interrelations among these systems is vital for delineating the nature of the disorder, as well as elucidating how these systems also promote adaptive functioning. More important, a developmental analysis strives to move beyond identification of the interrelated components of depressive disorders to articulate how those aberrations in and among multiple systems have evolved over the course of ontogenesis.

This developmental perspective necessitates that knowledge of normal development and its variations be applied to the study of the development of depressive disorders. Given the multiplicity of systems affected by the disorder, the approach also directs attention to an examination of early developmental attainments that may be theoretically related to later appearing patterns of depressive symptomatology. For example, obtaining an understanding of the deviations in affective regulation or the core negative attributions about the self observed in depressed persons may begin by examining the early development of these features, their developmental course, and their interrelations with other psychological and biological systems of the individual.

Organizational approach to development

In this regard, an organizational perspective on development (Werner, 1948; Werner & Kaplan, 1963) has offered developmental psychopathologists a valuable framework for conceptualizing developmental phenomenon as they relate to the evolution of depression and other forms of psychopathology (Cicchetti & Schneider-Rosen, 1986; Cicchetti & Toth, 1995; Sroufe & Rutter, 1984; Zigler, 1963; Zigler & Glick, 1986). The organizational perspective conceptualizes development via Werner's orthogenetic principle as a series of structural reorganizations that occur within and among biological and psychological systems of the individual, achieved through the processes of differentiation and hierarchical integration. Across development, the maturing individual moves from a state of globality and diffusion to progressive states of greater differentiation, articulation, complexity,

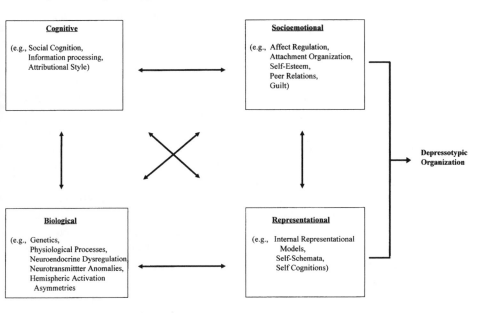

Figure 13.1. Integration of biological and psychological systems in the emergence of depressotypic organization.

and consolidation as various systems and subsystems of the individual are increasingly hierarchically organized and integrated (von Bertalanffy, 1968; Werner, 1948). Thus, depressive presentations of individuals at different developmental stages and periods of the life course must be understood within the context of the patterns of capabilities inherent at a specific developmental level, as well as in terms of individual differences in the developmental course of the person that have occurred up to any specific point in the life-span. Development is viewed in terms of qualitative reorganization rather than accretion of additive components, and similarly symptomatic presentations are examined in terms of qualitative, rather than quantitative, organization.

At each period of reorganization in ontogenesis, the concept of hierarchic motility maintains that prior developmental structures are incorporated into successive structural organizations through the process of hierarchic integration. As such, early experience and consequent strengths or liabilities are not replaced, but rather are integrated into subsequent reorganizations. Although such prior strengths or liabilities may not be prominent at a particular developmental period, they are nevertheless latent and may be activated at later developmental stages depending on experience. As a result, symptomatic presentations of a depressed individual may appear at odds with the current context, but may be consistent when prior developmental vulnerabilities are considered.

At each stage of ontogenesis, the individual is confronted with new developmental challenges (i.e., stage-salient developmental issues) that are posed and to which the individual must adapt. The quality of the resolution of these stage-salient tasks influences how the particular developmental issue is incorporated into psychological and biological systems as reorganization occurs. Positive adaptation to a developmental challenge contributes to competence and better preparedness for resolving subsequent tasks of development adaptively. In contrast, compromised or inadequate resolution of a stage-salient developmental challenge likewise is integrated as reorganization proceeds, resulting in poorer preparedness for adapting to later developmental demands. Thus, although not inevitable, early competence tends probabilistically to promote later competence, and, similarly, early incompetence tends to promote later incompetence, because the quality of resolving developmental demands is maintained systematically through the process of hierarchic integration. As an example, for individuals who later develop a depressive disorder, early difficulties in emotion regulation, perhaps as a consequence of insensitivity in parenting experienced from a depressed caregiver, could subsequently be related to difficulties in forming a secure attachment to the caregiver. These difficulties in affective regulation and insecure attachment pose a greater challenge for the infant in successfully individuating from the caregiver and forming an integrated self-system. Although these developmental liabilities are likely to constrain the ease of adapting to emerging developmental tasks, changes in the caregiving environment could foster the development of adequate relations with peers and a successful adaptation to school. Reworking of earlier developmental liabilities may occur. Nevertheless, vestiges of earlier difficulties, although not currently prominent, may remain latent. These early vulnerabilities could reappear later in development when the individual is confronted with difficult life circumstances. The earlier vulnerabilities in affective regulation, interpersonal relations, and self-system organization may then be accentuated as the individual struggles to cope with current stressors, thereby contributing to a depressive episode.

Transactional understanding of development

Despite the probabilistic tendency for early competence to promote later competence and early incompetence to promote later incompetence, the developmental course is malleable, and a diversity of outcomes is to be expected. Development needs to be conceptualized within a framework that recognizes the transactional nature of influence over time, both within and among internal (e.g., psychological, constitutional, neurobiological, biochemical) and external (e.g., familial, contextual, sociological) systems. Across development, a transactional model posits that the organizational structure of both the individual and the environment are in a state of mutual or bidirectional influence. For example, early temperamental difficultness may meet with responses from a depressed mother that are insensitive or psychologically unavailable. As a result, the infant's developing affect regulatory capacities are less adaptively structured, contributing to more displays of infant distress that are more exasperating for the depressed mother and instill further feelings of helplessness in her, producing still further deficits in her relational responses to her infant. Thus, both the individual and the environment mutually influence each other at specific as well as at subsequent points in time in an unfolding pattern of dynamic interplay. Furthermore, Cicchetti and Tucker (1994) also emphasize the need to examine transactional processes occurring within the individual, between neurobiological and psychological systems of self-organization. For example, the experience of extreme stress or a depressive episode may alter neurotransmitter functioning; subsequently, the neurotransmitter alterations may generate greater susceptibility to stress and a higher likelihood of experiencing a depressive episode.

Consistent with a transactional understanding of development and psychopathology, the study of risk, vulnerability, and protective factors is important for understanding the malleability of the developmental course and the variability in successive developmental outcomes (Rolf, Masten, Cicchetti, Nuechterlein, & Weintraub, 1990). Vulnerability factors typically are regarded as enduring and long-standing conditions or circumstances that commonly promote difficulty in successful adaptation. Vulnerability factors are comprised of both internal (e.g., biological, psychological) and external (e.g., familial, social-environmental) influences. For example, a genetic predisposition to depression, biogenic amine anomalies, temperamental difficultness, and an insecure attachment organization constitute individual vulnerabilities that may compromise successful adaptation on a long-term basis, detracting from the attainment of competence at successive developmental stages. Parental psychopathology, marital conflict, child maltreatment, poverty, inadequate schools, and unsupportive social networks are examples of enduring familial and environmental features that also are likely to detract from the attainment of competence. In addition to long-standing vulnerability factors, individuals also are faced with transient challengers, involving short-term stresses and events that tax adaptive capacities. The transaction of these internal and external vulnerability factors and transient challengers over the course of development may be seen as decreasing the odds that successful adaptation will occur, thereby jeopardizing the quality of the successive hierarchical organization of developmental structures (Cicchetti & Toth, 1995).

In contrast, the polar opposites of many of these enduring vulnerability factors and transient challengers are likely to promote competence and protect the quality of adaptation. Thus, for example, the absence of a genetic predisposition for depression, secure attachment relations, marital harmony, nurturant and supportive parenting, and economic advantage are examples of growth-promoting internal and external resources, constituting enduring protective factors that are likely to enhance the attainment of competence across development. In addition to enduring protective factors, individuals also may experience transient buffers that enhance and support optimal adaptation on a more short-term basis. Moreover, these enduring protective factors and transient buffers also may act in an ameliorative manner, assisting the individual in counteracting the otherwise adverse effects of enduring vulnerability factors.

Thus, in order to understand the course of individual development, a comprehensive delineation of the enduring vulnerability and protective factors involved, as well as of more transient challengers and buffers and their timing in the course of development, needs to be ascertained. Moreover, Rutter (1990) cautions that mere knowledge of the balance of positive and negative influences is not enough. Specifying the processes and mechanisms by which these factors operate to influence adaptation is essential. Further, certain factors may not have intrinsic positive or negative effects, but the valence of their influence will depend on the individual, his or her organization of competencies, and differences in the interpretation of the meaning of events and circumstances. For example, moving to a new neighborhood could create distress for a child who experienced loss of significant friendships, or it could offer opportunities for new relationships and experiences.

Developmental pathways

Clearly, the course of development is marked by considerable variability in successive outcomes, and a diversity of developmental pathways is to be expected (Cicchetti & Rogosch, 1996). Drawing on general systems theory concepts, the principles of multifinality and equifinality are critical. Multifinality specifies that diverse outcomes are likely to result from any one source of influence. For example, although offspring of parents with depressive disorders are considered at risk, including genetic risk, for the development of depression, certainly not all such individuals develop depressive disorders, and a wide spectrum of adaptation is seen. Although children and adolescents with depressive disorder are more likely than comparable psychiatric controls to evidence depressive disorders in adulthood, Harrington and his colleagues (Harrington, Fudge, Rutter, Pickles, & Hill, 1990, 1991) demonstrated that those individuals who also had comorbid conduct disorders tended to be less likely to develop depression in adulthood than those without conduct problems. These findings not only demonstrate a degree of specificity in adult outcomes for depressive disorders, but also illustrate multifinality in developmental pathways through observing alternate patterns of adaptation among children and adolescents who had experienced depressive disorders.

In contrast to multifinality, the principle of equifinality specifies that the same outcome eventuates from diverse routes. Gjerde (1995) provides an illustrative example of equifinality in the development of chronic depressive symptoms by young adulthood as predicted through repeated assessments from the preschool years. Strong predictive patterns were evident for young adult males from the preschool period; undersocialization and antagonistic interpersonal behavior were linked with depression in adulthood, and similar constellations of these personality character-istics in later childhood and adolescence also were related to young-adult chronic depressive symptoms. In contrast, among women this personality organization did not predict adult depressivity. Moreover, early precursors of depressive sympto-matology were not identified for females, and it was not until adolescence that patterns of oversocialization and excessive introspection were found to predict de-pressive symptoms in young women. Thus, very different trajectories to the same depressive outcome in adulthood were identified.

The manner in which continuity in development is conceptualized is crucial for developmental psychopathologists in charting pathways resulting in depression. Homotypic continuity, or the same behavioral manifestation of an underlying pro-cess at different points in development, is likely to be rare (Kagan, 1971). Rather than focusing on continuity of behavior, per se, the meaning and function of be-haviors at different stages of development are important to consider. For example, frequent crying has very different meanings in a toddler as compared with an adolescent. Similarity in behavior may actually represent discontinuity in function and meaning. Sroufe (1979) articulated the concept of coherence in development. Seemingly divergent behavioral presentations may appear to suggest discontinuities in development when isomorphism in behavior is examined. However, when the meaning, function, and organization of behaviors are examined, continuity in terms of underlying process may be discerned, despite seemingly divergent behavioral presentation. Thus, heterotypic continuity, involving a persistence in the underlying organization and meaning of behavior despite changing behavioral manifestation, may frequently be encountered when developmental pathways to depression are investigated. In this regard, it is important to recognize that the same behavior may serve different functions for different individuals or at different points in devel-opment. Similarly, the same function may be served by different behaviors (Werner & Kaplan, 1963).

Blatt (1995) provides an example of what may be considered heterotypic con-tinuity in discussing the suicides of three prominent and highly successful indi-viduals who unpredictably committed suicide. Their high degree of competence and accomplishment would appear to be quite discontinuous with depression se-vere enough to result in suicide. However, Blatt identifies the extreme degree of perfectionism and intense self-criticality that appeared to fuel their striving for inordinately high self-standards. Thus, continuity in underlying process in terms of self-loathing and feelings of inferiority is present, despite the behavioral in-congruity between high competence and suicide. This example of heterotypic continuity illustrates how the same behavior (i.e., great accomplishment) may serve different functions in different individuals, thereby drawing attention to de-lineating diverse meanings and functions of behavior as continuity in develop-ment is examined.

In light of the multiplicity of pathways that are likely to exist in depressive outcomes, developmental psychopathologists are concerned with identifying precursor states or depressotypic developmental organizations that may increase the likelihood that depressive disorders may occur. Examining adaptational failures on stage-salient issues of particular developmental periods is an important strategy for identifying early contributors to depressive trajectories (Cicchetti & Aber, 1986; Noam & Valiant, 1994). Exploration of how early developmental failures are integrated into subsequent developmental structures and how resulting behavioral expression becomes transformed over development is an important goal for developmental psychopathologists. Hammen (1992) has emphasized the need to move beyond the isolated study of cognitive, life stress, and interpersonal features of depression in adulthood to identify the developmental processes and precursors that contribute to those features of depressed individuals. There are likely to be numerous and diverse depressotypic organizations that carry the potential for evolving into depressive conditions given subsequent experiences and the balance of risk and protective factors. Diathesis-stress models are consistent with this approach. The diathesis for depression may evolve in diverse systems within the individual, with depressive outcomes emerging when stressful events or conditions are encountered that overwhelm the individual's capacities to maintain adequate adaptation. Examples of potential prototypical depressotypic organizations include a negative attributional style (Abramson, Seligman, & Teasdale, 1978) and dependent and self-critical personality styles (Blatt, 1995; Blatt, Quinlan, Chevron, McDonald, & Zuroff, 1982). These prototypes are developmentally derived, and although not psychopathological themselves, may eventuate in depressive outcomes when the individual is confronted with experiences that tax his or her capacity to maintain adequate coping.

We next turn to examining early patterns of adaptation to a series of stage-salient developmental tasks. The quality of the resolution of these early tasks may contribute to early aberrations that are hierarchically integrated and portend the development of pathways to depressive disorder via depressotypic organizations of developmental structures.

Illustrative developmental processes in depressotypic organizations

For heuristic purposes, we focus on four early stage-salient developmental issues that bear theoretical relevance for diverse components of evolving depressotypic organizations and depressive disorders. These issues include the development of homeostatic and physiological regulation; affect differentiation and the modulation of attention and arousal; the development of a secure attachment relationship; and the development of the self-system. As development proceeds, each of these areas sequentially reaches ascendancy and becomes a primary arena for which internal resources must be elaborated and extended to hierarchically integrate the imposed developmental challenge in order to further adaptation. Moreover, rather than subsequently declining in importance, each issue remains a lifelong component of adaptation. Evidence for aberrations in these areas will be drawn from research on the offspring of parents with depressive disorders as well as from findings regarding children, adolescents, and adults with mood disorders. While contrasts with nonrisk and nondisordered groups help to specify a progression of potential developmental atypicalities present among individuals with depression and offspring of depressed parents, these contrasts also broaden the understanding of normal developmental processes by illuminating the importance of early developmental attainments in successful adaptation. The influence of these early achievements for normal development becomes more readily apparent when contrasts are made with the significant deviations in expected developmental patterns observed in risk and disordered conditions. These differences illustrate how the study of development of abnormal and risk conditions extends and amplifies the understanding of normal developmental processes.

Homeostatic and physiological regulation

In the early months of life, the infant is challenged to maintain homeostatic equilibrium of internal, physiological states. Homeostatic systems strive to maintain a "set point" of functioning, and departure from this optimal level generates tension with behavioral systems activated to dissipate the tension in order to return to a state of equilibrium. These early fluctuations are related to early infant affect expression, with discomfort and distress as a result of disequilibrium and pleasure related to regaining equilibrium. Early innate motoric reflexes allow the infant some capacity to regain equilibrium. However, the infant requires significant environmental support to regulate physiological states in order to maintain equilibrium. Thus, early physiological regulation is an "open system" requiring support from caregivers. Infants develop capacities to communicate their needs to caregivers through affective responses, and sensitive caregivers must be able to read these signals accurately (Izard & Malatesta, 1987).

As neuroregulatory systems develop, the infant becomes increasingly self-sufficient in modulating arousal generated by physiological tension. This growing capacity corresponds to maturation of forebrain inhibitory tracts and neurotransmitter systems, which allow increasing control of lower hindbrain and midbrain limbic structures. Right brain activation has been associated with distress, whereas left brain activation and inhibition of right brain activity have been linked to positive affect, and the development of interhemispheric connections enhances the infant's ability to self-regulate (Tucker & Williamson, 1984).

The development of these neurological systems is "experience expectant," necessitating external input from caregivers (Greenough, Black, & Wallace, 1987). Moreover, the quality of experiences with caregivers is likely to contribute to variations in neurological growth and development, with long-term effects on the organization and development of the brain. Parents vary in how well they attend to assisting their infants in the maintenance of homeostatic regulation, thereby indirectly influencing the process of brain development. Further, extremely frequent, novel experiences and an unstable environment may more routinely activate the right brain with ensuing negative affect expression. In contrast, stability and consistency in the environment may support dominance of the left brain which may strengthen the inhibitory effects on negative arousal. Thus, parents may influence the development of interhemispheric connections and the quality of emotion regulation that the infant develops.

Early appearing differences in homeostatic regulation have been investigated in the infants of parents with mood disorders. As early as the neonatal period, these infants have been found to have greater difficulty self-quieting, lower activity levels, and more negative affect, suggesting more difficult temperaments (Sameroff, Seifer, & Zax, 1982).

Even simulated depression portrayed by nondepressed mothers has been shown to result in negative infant affectivity and disruption in the infant's effective self-regulation (Cohn & Tronick, 1983). In a sample of depressed mothers and their 2-month-old infants, more negative contingent responsiveness and less positive behavior than among nondepressed mothers and their infants have been observed (Cohn, Campbell, Matias, & Hopkins, 1990). Field and her colleagues (Field, Healy, Goldstein, & Guthertz, 1990; Field, Healy, & LeBlanc, 1989) have studied behavior-state matching and synchrony in depressed and nondepressed mothers and their infants. Negative behavior matching was observed more often among depressed mothers and their babies, with positive behavior matching occurring less often. Additionally, less synchrony between maternal heart rate and infant behavior was found among depressed mothers as compared with nondepressed mothers and their infants, suggesting less physiological attunement between depressed mothers and their offspring. These differences illustrate the early emergence of deviations in regulatory processes occurring among offspring of depressed parents. Moreover, the findings also highlight the importance of synchronous interactive behavior between mother and infant in the development of normative patterns of infant self-regulation.

Beyond infancy, affect regulatory difficulties also have been observed among older offspring of parents with mood disorders. Toddlers of unipolar depressed mothers have been shown to exhibit more dysregulated, out-of-control behavior than toddlers of nondepressed mothers (Zahn-Waxler, Iannotti, Cummings, & Denham, 1990). These differences predicted externalizing behaviors as perceived by mothers at age 5 and as reported by the child at age 6. These differences were found to occur predominantly for children of depressed mothers who were less able to modulate, control, and provide structure and organization to their toddler's play. Youngsters of parents with unipolar or bipolar disorder also have been found to prolong the experience and expression of negative affect (i.e., fear), and in so doing exhibit affects that did not correspond to current situational contexts (Gaensbauer, Harmon, Cytryn, & McKnew, 1984).

These difficulties in regulation of affect may contribute to difficulties in peer relations as these children form relationships with agemates. Zahn-Waxler, Denham, Cummings, and Iannotti (1992) note that preschool-aged children of parents with mood disorder characteristically engage in uncontrolled and poorly regulated social exchanges with peers. Boys of depressed mothers have been found to suggest aggressive strategies in order to solve hypothetical peer conflicts (Hay, Zahn-Waxler, Cummings, & Iannotti, 1992).

Thus, these findings suggest that early-appearing regulatory difficulties in offspring of parents with mood disorders may continue to affect adaptation as new experiences and situations are encountered. These difficulties may portend problems in modulation of affective reactions that may heighten the risk for the development of depressive disorders. These findings also illustrate the importance of parental behavior in scaffolding the development of competent infant regulatory processes.

Affect differentiation and modulation of tension and arousal

With the foundations of internal homeostatic regulation established, the growing infant increasingly becomes more attentive and responsive to the physical environment, and the infant's abilities rapidly develop in diverse areas of functioning. Affective expression becomes a principal means through which the infant interacts and engages in exchanges with the caregiver, and infants begin to regulate and adapt their affective expressions and behaviors to those of their caregivers. Concomitantly, neurological maturation and cognitive growth contribute to this affect differentiation in the infant's internal experience of emotion and its external expression.

Because the infant remains heavily in need of the caregiver for external scaffolding and support, the quality of care and interactions with the caregiver contributes to "experience dependent" individual differences in patterns of affect differentiation, expression, and regulation that emerge (Greenough et al., 1987; Schore, 1996). The history of interactions and exchanges with the caregiver influences the infant's emerging interpretation and reactions to external events (Bowlby, 1973). As previously, caregivers continue to influence the infant's modulation and management of arousal and physiological tension. However, increasingly, the infant now also evaluates the environment based on past experiences, and tension is cognitively generated by those evaluations (e.g., as threatening, too novel, overstimulating) (Sroufe & Waters, 1976). Caregiver sensitivity and affective attunement to the infant's arousal states assist in helping the infant tolerate and cope with increasing amounts of tension and arousal (Sroufe, 1979). Further, caregivers actively socialize affective expression in their infants. This occurs through infant imitation of prevailing caregiver affects, caregiver imitation of infant affect, and selective attention and differential encouragement/discouragement of the expression of different affects by the caregiver (Hesse & Cicchetti, 1982; Malatesta & Izard, 1984).

Given the central role of affective disturbances in individuals with mood disorders, understanding the early origins and ontogeny of aberrations in affect differentiation, expression, and regulation is important (cf. Schore, 1996). The study of mothers with mood disorders and their offspring provides insights into divergences in normative patterns of affect regulation and expression that are relevant for understanding the organization of affect in developmental systems. Field and her colleagues have conducted a number of studies in this regard. Infants of depressed mothers were found to display more frequent expressions of sadness and anger and fewer expressions of interest than were infants of well mothers (Pickens & Field, 1993). The infants of depressed mothers also were shown to be more physiologically stressed when interacting with their mothers as indicated by elevated heart rate and lower vagal tone (Field et al., 1988). Moreover, in face-to-face interaction, depressed mothers and their infants displayed less positive affect. The "depressive" style of the infants also was accompanied by more gaze and head aversion with the mother, suggesting the infants used self-regulatory behaviors to reduce negative affect associated with maternal unresponsiveness. Field and her colleagues (1988) also demonstrated that when the infants of depressed mothers interacted with nondepressed strangers, they tended to elicit depression-like behavior in the strangers. This pattern suggests transactional processes whereby infant and caregiver affective patterns mutually influence each other over time. These findings also highlight the importance of maternal responsiveness and maternal affect expression in terms of greater positivity and less negativity in the emergence of more normative patterns of infant affect expression.

Cicchetti and Toth (1995) report clinical observations of depressed mothers and their toddlers in treatment. Depressed mothers were observed frequently to be affectively asynchronous with their children, exhibiting tendencies to be overly involved with their own concerns and ignoring of their toddlers or overly intrusive and misreading of their toddlers affective signals. The toddlers of these depressed mothers were very attuned to negative affective expression of their mothers. They frequently engaged in efforts to console the mother or distract her, suggesting the toddlers were taking a "caregiving" stance or assuming responsibility for maternal affective states.

These clinical observations are consistent with work by Zahn-Waxler and her colleagues (Zahn-Waxler & Kochanska, 1990; Zahn-Waxler, Kochanska, Krupnick, & McKnew, 1990) in which patterns of guilt in 5- to 9-year-old children of depressed mothers were examined. The younger children were overaroused to hypothetical situations of interpersonal conflict and distress, whereas the older offspring appeared to engage in an internal struggle against experiencing guilt.

Themes of a striking sensitivity to the problems of others and an empathic over-involvement were evident.

Thus, there is evidence of deviations in the development and socialization of affect in offspring of depressed parents from early in the life course. These aberrations are believed to be hierarchically integrated into other developmental systems as these infants and children develop, thereby generating vulnerabilities for later affective disturbance as subsequent developmental challenges are negotiated.

The development of an attachment relationship

The development of an attachment relationship with the primary caregiver during the latter half of the first year is a fundamental achievement that organizes evolving affect, cognition, and behavior in relation to the quality of physical and emotional availability of the caregiver (Sroufe, 1979). Based on evolutionary needs to maintain safety from environmental threats, the caregiver serves as a secure base to which the infant retreats in order to modulate arousal and maintain internal security (Bowlby, 1969/1982). Variation in the quality of caregiving, particularly in terms of sensitivity and responsivity, contributes to individual differences in the manner in which the infant negotiates the attachment relationship with the primary caregiver. Although infants may experience different types of relationships with various caregivers, the attachment relationship with the primary caregiver, typically the mother, assumes hierarchical salience in influencing the way in which affect, cognition, and behavior are organized. Ainsworth, Blehar, Waters, and Wall (1978), utilizing the Strange Situation laboratory procedure involving a sequence of separations and reunions between the infant and the caregiver, identified three major types of attachment organization, differentiating between securely and insecurely attached infants. The traditional classifications include Type B, securely attached, and two types of insecurely attached infants, Type A, insecure avoidant, and Type C, insecure/resistant. Further investigation, particularly involving high-risk samples, led to the discovery of additional atypical insecure attachment patterns, notably a blending of both avoidant and resistant behaviors (Type A/C) (Crittenden, 1988) or a disorganized/disoriented pattern (Type D) (Main & Solomon, 1990), including a variety of undirected behavioral responses and unusual behaviors such as freezing, stilling, hand flapping, and other stereotypies exhibited in the presence of the caregiver. The traditional and atypical attachment classifications represent individual differences in the strategies that infants employ to regulate emotions and behavior and are related to the history of distress remediation and emotional synchrony experienced with the caregiver.

The differences in attachment types are important for understanding early forms of divergent organization of socioemotional, cognitive, representational, and biological systems that may relate to an emerging depressotypic organization. As development proceeds beyond infancy, the experiences of the attachment relationship increasingly become internally represented, and these internal representational models serve to guide subsequent interpersonal relationships, based on expectations of how important others will relate. As such, representational models will serve to channel the manner in which interpersonal relations are perceived and negotiated, as well as the accompanying affects and cognitions that are exhibited. Infants with Type B attachment organizations freely express negative affects directly and expect to be soothed and comforted by caregivers, resulting in less time spent in distress and more time involved in positive interactions, contributing to greater competence in internal emotion regulation. In contrast, Type A infants develop internal models that anticipate rejection. Avoidance of negative affect expression serves a defensive function utilized to maintain proximity to the caregiver while not evoking further caregiver insensitivity and rejection. Freedom to express negative affect is thus curtailed, with concomitant difficulties in emotion regulation. For Type C infants, representational models of caregiver inconsistency derived from experience contribute to infant impulsiveness and demandingness in order to provoke caregiver responsivity. Helplessness and dependency result, and such individuals are easily overwhelmed and preoccupied by negative emotions. In contrast to the organized strategies of Type A, B, and C infants, Type D babies do not appear to have an organized strategy for negotiating the relationship with the caregiver. Type D infants expect to find interactions with caregivers to be incomprehensible and/or frightening (Main & Hesse, 1990). Activation of fear in relationships that should provide protection contributes to strong conflicting emotions and lack of coherence in behavior and emotional communication with the caregiver.

Although children of depressed caregivers are more at risk of experiencing deviations in care as a consequence of their caregivers' struggles with their disorders, these children also may experience a sense of loss, akin to actual loss of a parent (Bowlby, 1980), when caregivers suffer from episodes of major depression. Insecure representational models may place these children in a more tenuous position in terms of coping with the experience of psychological loss of the availability of caregiver, as episodes occur. Prolonged anxiety, sustained grieving, and difficulty in resolving the loss may further contribute to aberrations in the organization of cognitive, affective, representational, and biological systems. Subsequent loss experiences, either real or symbolic, may precipitate depressive episodes (Beck, 1967).

The quality of attachment in infants and children of parents with mood disorders has been examined in a number of studies. In research conducted before the conceptualization of atypical attachment classifications, Gaensbauer et al. (1984) found that 12-month-old offspring of affectively disordered parents did not differ in the proportion of insecurely attached infants. However, by 18 months of age, there was a shift with only 14% of the infants of affectively ill parents evidencing secure attachments as compared with 58% of infants of well parents. Radke-Yarrow, Cummings, Kuczynski, and Chapman (1985) also found high percentages of insecure attachments among offspring of mothers with mood disorders; 47% of children with mothers with major depression and 79% of children of mothers with bipolar disorder were insecure. Subsequently, using a more age-sensitive coding scheme for attachment that also included the Type D classification (Cassidy & Marvin, 1992) for the older children in this sample, DeMulder and Radke-Yarrow (1991) found that 50% of the offspring of the bipolar mothers evidenced the highly insecure disorganized/disoriented attachments. This high rate of Type D attachments is similar to that found in other types of high-risk samples that also involve social disadvantage (Carlson, Cicchetti, Barnett, & Braunwald, 1989; Lyons-Ruth, Repacholi, McLeod, & Silva, 1991).

Lyons-Ruth and her colleagues (Lyons-Ruth, Connell, Grunebaum, & Botein, 1990; Lyons-Ruth, Connell, Zoll, & Stahl, 1987) found that offspring of affectively disordered mothers were more likely to develop insecure attachments when the mothers were not involved in intervention services. Moreover, 54% of these children of untreated depressed mothers were found to have Type D attachments. Subsequently, 80% of the Lyons-Ruth sample was followed up at between 4 and 6 years of age (Lyons-Ruth, Alpern, & Repacholi, 1993). Teachers completed the Preschool Behavior Questionnaire (Behar & Springfield, 1974), which includes anxious, hostile, and hyperactive factors. Among children who exhibited deviant hostile behavior, 71% of them had been classified as Type D at 18 months. This finding supports the view that disorganized attachment may serve as a precursor to later maladaptation before childhood disorders emerge.

At age 7, 62% of the Lyons-Ruth et al. (1993) sample was again assessed (Easterbrooks, Davidson, & Chazan, 1993), using separation–reunion procedures (Main & Cassidy, 1988) to assess current attachment organization and parent and teacher completions of the Child Behavior Checklist (Achenbach & Edelbrock, 1986) to assess behavior problems. Forty-five percent of the sample was found to exhibit insecure attachments (19% A, 12% C, 14% D), and insecure attachments were shown to relate to higher levels of internalizing and externalizing symptomatology. Moreover, in examining whether children were rated in the clinical range of behavior problems by their teachers or their mothers, very high rates of disturbance (83%) were found among the insecurely attached children, with 88% of A's, 60% of C's, and 100% of D's exhibiting clinical levels of symptomatology. These results not only illustrate the influence of insecure attachment organizations on early emerging behavioral disturbance, but they also suggest the importance of secure attachment organizations in contributing to a more competent functioning.

Insecure attachments among children of depressed mothers also contribute to interpersonal difficulties as these offspring negotiate relationships with peers. Rubin, Booth, Zahn-Waxler, Cummings, and Wilkinson (1991) found that insecurely attached offspring of depressed mothers exhibited withdrawal, passivity, and inhibited behavior when observed with a familiar peer in free play at age 5. Rubin (Rubin, LeMare, & Lollis, 1990; Rubin & Mills, 1988) has hypothesized that insecure resistant attachments are associated with later inhibited/withdrawn behavior and insecure avoidant attachments relate to hostile/aggressive later peer behavior. By contrast, this work also implies the importance of early secure attachment organizations in promoting more competent interpersonal functioning as children begin to form relationships with agemates.

During adolescence, clinically depressed teenagers, as compared with normal or nondepressed psychiatric controls, have been found to express less secure attachments to their parents (Armsden, McCauley, Greenberg, Burke, & Mitchell, 1990). Similarly, Kandel and Davies (1986) found that depression in adolescence was related to problems in the emotional relationship with parents, difficulties in forming an opposite-sex intimate relationship, and spousal difficulties in young adulthood. In late adolescence, an insecure attachment organization has been linked to higher levels of depressive symptomatology (Kobak, Sudler, & Gamble, 1991) and to more interpersonal difficulties in transitioning to college (Kobak & Sceery, 1988). Among mildly depressed college women and those recovering from major depression, Carnelley, Pietromonaco, and Jaffe (1994) found insecure relationships with parents were frequent and romantic relationships were often characterized by preoccupation and/or fearful avoidance. The attachment organization of these women more strongly predicted relationship functioning than did their depression status alone.

Attachment organization also has been linked to depression among adults. Among a sample of outpatients in psychotherapy diagnosed with dysthymia, 83% were classified as insecure, utilizing the Adult Attachment Interview (George, Kaplan, & Main, 1984). Half of the dysthymic patients had an insecure dismissing attachment organization (analogous to insecure-avoidant at younger ages), and 33% had an insecure preoccupied-entangled classification (analogous to insecure-resistant). Additionally, 17% also evidenced unresolved/disoriented components in their attachment organization, indicating difficulties in resolving past loss experiences. Although not all individuals who experience early deficits in the parent–child relationship continue to have difficulties in their attachment organization and not all develop depression, the risk for elevated depressive symptomatology remains. Pearson, Cohn, Cowan, and Cowan (1994), in studying an adult population, identified a subgroup of adults who had experienced negative childhood experiences but had apparently been able to resolve those early experiences and were currently secure in their state of mind regarding attachment. This group of parents, labeled "earned secure," did not differ from the continuously secure (autonomous) parents in the quality of their interaction with their children. Nevertheless, the earned secure group of parents still evidenced vulnerability. Similar to the resilient adolescents studied by Luthar et al. (1993), the earned secure parents had heightened depressive symptomatology relative to continuously secure adults, as did adults with insecure adult attachment organizations.

In summary, there is growing evidence of insecure attachment organizations among offspring of parents with mood disorders as well as among youth and adults with depressive disorders. The quality of early attachment relationships contributes to internal representational models of self and other that organize cognition, affect, and behavior, and these models serve to canalize perceptions and experience as development proceeds. In the case of individuals with insecure attachment organizations, their internal representational models are likely to contribute to a depressotypic organization of psychological and biological systems. Affective regulation and expression are less optimal, and significant others are perceived as unavailable or rejecting while the self is regarded as unlovable. These attachment-related aspects of a depressotypic organization may contribute to a proneness to self-processes that have been linked to depression (e.g., low self-esteem, helplessness, hopelessness, negative attributional biases).

The continuities in attachment organization and linkages to interpersonal functioning at different stages of development also illustrate the importance of secure attachment organization for competent adaptation across the life course. The role of early experience and the importance of available and sensitive caregiving in normal development are accentuated by the contrast with conditions in which maternal behavior is compromised (i.e., maternal depression). As a result, normal developmental theory in predicting the links between maternal availability and sensitivity and attachment security is confirmed and expanded by the perspective that examination of attachment organization in abnormal circumstances provides.

The self-system: Self-awareness and self–other differentiation

Building upon the quality of the attachment relationship that has evolved, toddlers begin to develop a sense of themselves as separate and independent entities in the second half of the second year (Cicchetti & Beeghly, 1990; Emde, Gaensbauer, & Harmon, 1976; Lewis & Brooks-Gunn, 1979; Mahler, Pine, & Bergman, 1975). This achievement corresponds with a transition from sensorimotor to representational capacities. Growing capacities for language and play constitute a means through which children symbolically represent the self and relationships, and these abilities continue to be elaborated and differentiated in the second and third years of life. Increasingly, children are able to use symbolic means to communicate needs and feelings and evidence increased abilities to label emotion states, intentions, and cognitions in self and others (Bretherton & Beeghly, 1982; Kagan, 1981). These representational attainments also correspond to increased capacities for self-regulation.

Emotional and cognitive components are increasingly integrated into internal representational models in which the self becomes represented as well as its relation to the attachment figure (Bowlby, 1973; Bretherton, 1987; Sroufe, 1990). Although the growing toddler increasingly acquires capacities for self-regulation, parental involvement remains vital, and parental availability and responsivity influence how the self is represented. Representations of self correspond to the character of the relationship with the attachment figure. Specifically, caregiver accessibility and responsivity correspond to self-representations as acceptable and valued, whereas parental unavailability or rejection relates to self-representations as unlovable and unworthy (Bowlby 1969/1982, 1973; Bretherton, 1990).

Evidence has been obtained that demonstrates difficulties in self-development and corresponding affective functioning in toddlers of mothers with mood disorders. Maternal attribution patterns may affect the types of self-attributions that children make. For example, Radke-Yarrow, Belmont, Nottelmann, and Bottomly (1990) found that mood-disordered mothers conveyed significantly more negative affect in their attributions, particularly in regard to negative attributions about child emotions. Moreover, among the mood disordered mothers and their toddlers, there was a higher correspondence in the affective tone of attributions and statements about the self (e.g., mother says, "I hate myself;" child says, "I'm bad"). This suggests a heightened vulnerability among these children for negative self-attributions, with negative implications for risk for later depressive tendencies. The findings also illustrate how more positive maternal attributions and affect are important in advancing positive self-attributions in children in more normative family circumstances.

Toddlers of mothers with recent unipolar depression have been shown to exhibit more inhibition to the unfamiliar (Kochanska, 1991). Additionally, P. Cole, Barrett, and Zahn-Waxler (1992) found evidence for suppression of typically seen frustration and tension in toddlers of symptomatic mothers in response to mishap situations. Inhibition and lack of expected emotional reactions in frustrating situations may contribute to diminished perceptions of self-efficacy, potentially posing risk for later affective disturbance.

As development proceeds, early representational features of the self are further elaborated, and these aspects of self-representation have relevance for understanding a depressotypic organization (Cicchetti & Schneider-Rosen, 1986). Self-understanding constitutes cognitive representations of the self with roots in the internal representational models of the self derived from the attachment relationships. In contrast, self-esteem represents an affective component of the self that is positively or negatively valenced. Self-cognitions are particular usages of the cognitive structure in reference to the self. They have both content, in terms of what aspects of the self are the focus, and style, involving the manner in which thoughts about the self are derived. Self-cognitions and self-esteem mutually influence each other, and when self-cognitions and associated affects are repeated over time, they contribute to hierarchically organized structuralized representations of the self known as self-schemata that tend to be enduring over time.

Four component domains regarding the self are represented, including material characteristics (e.g., possessions, physical attributes), active characteristics (e.g., skills, activities), social characteristics (e.g., relationships, roles), and psychological characteristics (e.g., thoughts, emotions, personality) (see Damon & Hart, 1988). Developmental complexity increases across these domains from concrete to more abstract. With the cognitive transition that occurs around age 7 to 8 from preoperational to concrete operational thought, children increasingly move from making specific and concrete attributions about the self to generalizing and abstracting features of the self that are considered more stable and enduring over time (cf. Harter, 1983).

These universal attainments have relevance for understanding processes that have been linked to depression. Vulnerable individuals appear to utilize these expanded developmental capacities in ways that perpetuate negative self-schemata, contributing to depressive outcomes. For example, in the reformulated learned helplessness theory of depression (Abramson, Seligman, & Teasdale, 1978), learned helplessness is conceived of as resulting from the perception of noncontingency between one's actions and resulting punishments and outcomes. Noncontingency is attributed to perceptions of failure that result from personal traits. Moreover, failings are attributed to features of the self that are personal, global, and stable, whereas successes are attributed to universal, situation-specific, and transient causes. The cognitive abstractions about the self required for these attributions become available to the individual after the cognitive transition discussed earlier. Similarly, the cognitive requirements needed for the negative cognitive triad in Beck's (1967) theory of depression – that is, negative cognitions about the self, the world, and the future – are available after the cognitive transition allowing for more abstraction and generalization across time and situations.

The cognitive components of depression in adults are not likely to emerge in adulthood in response to stressors alone, but rather are part of a depressotypic organization that has evolved developmentally. Experiences in early life and biologically based constraints on neural functioning and memory contribute to knowledge structures composed of schemata incorporating past experiences, future expectations, and affective vulnerabilities. Dodge (1993) proposes that these knowledge structures organize the way in which subsequent experiences are processed cognitively. Early experiences of interpersonal loss and/or instability or excessive and unrealistic pressure to achieve may foster the development of negative self-schemata and low self-esteem (see also Blatt & Homan, 1992). As subsequent loss, abandonment, and failure are experienced, heightened attention is paid to the negative aspects of these stressors, and attributions of internal, stable, and global features of the self as to the causes are made. Because of these negative schemata and the manner in which they are used to interpret experience, the likelihood of dysthymia and depression is intensified.

Nolen-Hoeksema, Girgus, and Seligman (1992) investigated children's depressed symptoms, negative life events, explanatory style, and helplessness beginning in third grade and followed these children for 5 years. In early childhood, only negative events were related to depressive symptoms. However, later in childhood and notably after the cognitive transition to concrete operations, a pessimistic explanatory style (cf. Peterson & Seligman, 1984) contributed to depressive symptoms, alone or in combination with negative events. In both interpersonal and achievement contexts, the depressed children exhibited helplessness. Moreover, their negative explanatory style worsened during depressive episodes, and their pessimism persisted subsequently. These findings also suggest that how children interpret events and experience is important for maintaining well-being.

Depressed children may maintain excessively high expectations for themselves, contributing to attributions of failure when those expectations are not met. Lauer, Giordani, Boivin, and their colleagues (1994) investigated memory and metamemory abilities among 9- to 12-year-old depressed children. Whereas only severely depressed children exhibited memory *impairments,* all depressed children were found to have performance *difficulties* on metamemory tasks, involving an overestimation of their abilities. Depressed children appeared to be either overcompensating for feelings of inferiority or setting unrealistic standards for themselves, which would tend to confirm their negative self-cognitions and sense of failure.

In general, children have been found to exhibit enhanced recall of adjectives considered personally descriptive. Nondepressed children show differential facilitated memory for positive adjectives, whereas depressed children are more focused on negative adjectives (Hammen, 1992). Children 8 to 16 years old with current or prior histories of depression evidence greater recall of negative self-descriptive adjectives (Zupan, Hammen, & Jaenicke, 1987). Similarly, D. Cole and Jordan (1995) found that depressed children recalled more negative and fewer positive self-referential words, with a notable increase in negative self-referential words occurring by eighth grade. These differences in recall of self-referential words were related to more negative and less positive peer evaluations of the depressed children, and evidence was provided for the recall differences mediating the relation between unfavorable peer evaluations and depression. Moreover, D. Cole, Peeke, and Ingold (1996) have shown that by ninth grade characterological self-blame for academic and social events was significantly related to depression. Thus, depressed children increasingly appear to be primed to focus on negative self-features. These negative self-appraisals are likely to be consistent with negative self-schemata acquired developmentally.

Depressed adult patients also have been shown to attribute more negative features not only to themselves but also to their parents and significant others (Gara, Woolfolk, Cohen, Goldston, Allen, & Novalany, 1993). Alloy and Abramson (1988) have noted that depressed individuals do not engage in tendencies to overestimate their abilities or their capacities to control the environment. This feature of unrealistic self-optimism is observed among nondepressed individuals (Taylor & Brown, 1988). The "depressive realism" of mood-disordered individuals may diminish self-enhancing cognitions that might otherwise protect these persons from depressive symptomatology. Moreover, the positivity biases found among nondepressed individuals and their contribution to maintaining well-being are highlighted by the contrast with depressed persons.

In the study of adults with depressive disorders, there has been considerable interest in differentiating two types of personality organization that underlie depressive outcomes (Beck, 1983; Blatt, 1995; Blatt & Zuroff, 1992). These two personality types include a dependent style, in which issues of loss, abandonment, and interpersonal neediness are prominent, and a self-critical type, in which the self is denigrated for not living up to high internal standards. Although there is controversy regarding how uniquely these two personality types are differentiated (Coyne & Whiffen, 1995), common to both personality organizations are negative self-schemata that contribute to cognitive distortions in how experiences are interpreted, with biases toward negativity regarding the self and associated dysphoric affects. The dependent and self-critical personality types have been related to the higher prevalence of depression among females that emerges during adolescence (Leadbeater, Blatt, & Quinlan, 1995).

These two personality organizations appear to have clear developmental origins. The dependent type likely has roots in insecure attachment relationships, significant losses, and abandonment. The self-critical type may have stronger linkages to early thwarting of autonomy strivings as well as to exceedingly demanding parental expectations for success and achievement (Blatt, 1995). Our developmental analysis suggests such early adverse experiences may constrain the subsequent manner in which experience is perceived and interpreted. In concert with further interpersonal deprivation and perceived failure experiences and an excess of environmental and familial risks and challenges that detract from resolving these early difficulties, various depressotypic organizations are likely to be consolidated, generating the potential for depressive outcomes over the life course.

Developmental biological systems in depression

Although up until this point we have focused on developmental processes in the psychological domain in relation to mood disorders, equally important are developmental biological processes that transact with psychological processes across development and contribute to depressive outcomes. A brief overview of some of these biological components will now be discussed.

Genetic contributions to depressive disorders

There have been consistent observations of a greater prevalence of mood disorders in the relatives of patients with depressive disorders than in the general population (McGuffin & Katz, 1989, 1993), and of a greater probability of disorder among relatives who are more closely related (Faraone, Kremen, & Tsuang, 1990; Tsuang & Faraone, 1990). Methodological differences in various genetic studies (e.g., varying criteria used to define disorder, prior nondifferentiation of unipolar and bipolar disorder) have contributed to some variation in the rates of heritability observed.

Adoption studies have been used in attempts to disaggregate shared genetic and environmental influences, and these studies document increased rates of mood disorder in biological relatives as compared with adoptees (Cadoret, 1978; McGuffin & Katz, 1989; Mendlewicz & Rainer, 1977; Tsuang & Faraone, 1990). Moreover, twin studies indicate greater concordance of disorder among monozygotic than among dizygotic twins (Gershon, Bunny, Leckman, Van Eerdewegh, & DeBauche, 1976; McGuffin, Katz, Watkins, & Rutherford, 1996).

In considering these genetic findings within a developmental context, the mode of genetic transmission must be questioned as well as what it is that is genetically transmitted. Several models of genetic transmission have been posited, including single major locus models, multifactorial polygenic models, and mixed single and multifactorial polygenic models. Faraone et al. (1990) concluded that no single model has found unique support. In part, difficulty in identifying clear genetic models for mood disorders (and psychiatric disorders, more generally) results from substantial heterogeneity in presentation among individuals with mood disorders, etiologic heterogeneity, involving diverse and differing genetic processes contributing to disorder among different individuals, and pleiotropy involving a single genotype having various behavioral presentations across individuals. Further, some individuals develop mood disorders in the absence of genetic influence. These issues emphasize the importance of equifinality and multifinality in pathways leading to depressive disorders. Clearly, mood disorders are multifactorially determined.

Developmental geneticists maintain that genetic contributions to mood disorders must be conceptualized within a dynamic framework that considers the operation of genetic factors in concert with environmental factors across the life course. Genes are unlikely to operate in a static fashion through development. Rather, their influence may vary across the life course. Although some genes' effects may be enduring, others may be transient. At varying developmental periods, genes may be turned on or off, and diverse factors that regulate gene activation/deactivation are likely to vary developmentally (Gottesman & Goldsmith, 1994; Watson, Hopkins, Roberts, Steitz, & Weiner, 1987). Gene action is not a process that occurs only in early stages of development. Although genes may influence the development of early structures (e.g., receptors for neurotransmitters) that influence normal and pathological dispositions, later gene activation/deactivation (as well as experience) also may modify those structures at subsequent periods in ontogenesis (Gottesman & Goldsmith, 1994). Thus, the changing relative influence of genetics and environment at various stages of the life course within varying individuals must be incorporated into developmental models of mood disorders and evolving depressotypic developmental organizations.

Developmental biology of mood disorders

As is the case with genetics, conceptualizing neurobiological, neurochemical, neuropsychological, psychobiological, and psychophysiological processes within a developmental framework greatly enhances the understanding of how those processes contribute to regulation of normal socioemotional processes as well as to how aberrations contribute to depressive disorders.

Researchers have examined anomalies in the structure of sleep and neuroendocrine functioning of children, adolescents, and adults with depressive disorders. Sleep disturbances (e.g., difficulty falling asleep, disrupted sleep, early morning wakening) are frequently seen with depressive disorders (Dahl, 1996). When deviations in sleep features (e.g., latency to fall asleep, rate of rapid eye movement, arousal thresholds) are examined in terms of normal developmental variations in sleep characteristics occurring as a result of the aging process, differences between depressed children, depressed adolescents, depressed adults, and respective nondepressed controls appear to suggest an acceleration among depressed individuals in normative patterns of age changes in these features (e.g., decreases in duration of sleep) and in EEG activity (Knowles & MacLean, 1990). The developmental view thus provides a more appropriate context for understanding the observed sleep differences than would be obtained with findings restricted to one age period in isolation (Puig-Antich, 1986). Further, the detection of an acceleration in normative age patterns of sleep features among depressed individuals, particularly children and adolescents, raises new questions as to how those differences influence the ongoing development and organization of neuroregulatory processes in depressed persons given their respective ages. Similarly, the importance of the changing structure of sleep in normal development also becomes more evident when contrasted with the deviations observed in depressed individuals.

Along with sleep studies, diverse investigations have examined neuroendocrine differences among depressed individuals and controls at different age periods. For example, variation from normal patterns of growth hormone, cortisol, and prolactin secretion have been observed in response to various psychopharmacological challenges among children (Ryan et al., 1992) and adolescents (Dahl et al., 1991; Dahl et al., 1992) with depressive disorders. Similarly, in depressed adults various regulatory difficulties have been observed in hypothalamic-pituitary-adrenal (HPA) axis regulation (Gold, Goodwin, & Chrousos, 1988a, 1988b). In the aggregate these studies suggest a dysregulation of central serotonergic systems (Ryan et al., 1992) and chronic states of arousal (Gold et al., 1988b) among depressed individuals.

Prior hypotheses regarding neurotransmitter irregularities being too high or too low in depressed individuals have increasingly given way to attempts to understand the dynamic characteristics of neurotransmitter systems (Siever & Davis, 1985). Siever and Davis (1985) propose that an enduring vulnerability to highly variable, unstable, or erratic neurotransmitter output in depressed persons may result from a persistent impairment in one or more neurotransmitter regulatory or homeostatic mechanisms. Similarly, Spoont (1992) has proposed that serotonin, which regulates the flow of information through neural systems, acts as a modulator of neurobiological systems, conferring stability on those systems. Deviations in serotonin in depressed individuals contribute to altered neural processing and a destabilization of affect, cognition, and behavior. As a result, alterations in neurotransmitter functioning do not cause pathological conditions, but rather they result in biased processing of information that affects how neural systems respond to novel input, destabilizing the normal relations among serotonin activity, affect, and behavior.

The occurrence of a depressive episode may create additional vulnerabilities in affected persons. Noting the likelihood of depressive episodes recurring, the increased frequency and rapidity of episode recurrence, and the increasing severity of episodes, Post and his colleagues (Post, 1992; Post, Rubinow, & Ballenger, 1986; Post, Weiss, & Leverich, 1994) have posited that among patients with recurrent mood disorders, episodes become triggered by biological mechanisms more readily through processes akin to electrophysiological kindling and behavioral sensitization. In the electrophysiological model, episodes are analogous to amygdala-kindled seizures in which seizures progress from being triggered by intermittent, previously subconvulsant stimulation current to seizures that take place in the absence of exogenous stimulation. Among patients with unipolar disorder, subsequent episodes may be precipitated more readily by the same events to the point where episodes occur autonomously. Similarly, in the behavioral sensitization model, depressive episodes may be triggered in a manner similar to the way in which the use of stimulants or anesthetics produces behavioral changes that contribute to subsequent altered behavioral responses, including more rapid onset of effects, increased magnitude, and longer duration. Analogous sensitization processes may operate in triggering major depressive episodes with negative events and/or the anticipation of negative events acting as conditioned stimuli. Post (1992) suggests that there is both sensitization to stressors and sensitization to episode occurrences contributing to more ready onset of episodes. This conceptualization is important because it emphasizes a developmental progression in the neurobiology of mood disorders with different effects and processes operative at subsequent points in the course of the disorder.

Another area of active inquiry pertaining to biological contributions to mood disorders has been the investigation of individual differences in cerebral lateralization. Normative emotional functioning across the life-span is influenced by the interplay of the left and right hemispheres, and emotional dysfunctions, as in depressive disorders, may involve distortions of normal emotional processing by the brain. Understanding the neuropsychological aberrations in depressed individuals is important for conceptualizing the normal ontogenesis of hemispheric substrates of emotion.

Lateralization of neurotransmitter systems and hemispheric asymmetries may influence arousability to stimulation and individual differences in emotion processing. Through the interaction of noradrenergic and serotonergic systems, the right hemisphere is sensitive to change, alerts the brain to novelty in the environment, and thus is associated with general arousal and brain activation. In contrast, through domination by dopaminergic and cholinergic systems, the left hemisphere is biased toward redundancy, being relatively uninfluenced by novelty in order to maintain behavior in the face of change (Tucker & Williamson, 1984). Although not conclusive, EEG studies suggest that negative emotional states correspond to relatively less left frontal and/or greater right frontal activation, whereas positive emotional states correspond to the opposite pattern of activation.

At birth, hemispheric interconnections are incomplete and continue to develop. Early individual differences among infants in tendencies to approach versus withdraw from novelty and concomitant emotionality may reflect variations in the relative dominance and reactivity of the left and right hemispheres to stimulation (Davidson, 1991; Fox & Davidson, 1984). Furthermore, experience may influence the manner in which the hemispheric connections develop. Infants with greater right hemisphere activation may be prone to overstimulation with greater sensitivity and distraction to environmental change contributing to distress, whereas infants with greater left activation may appear less distressed by environmental change and may have trouble shifting and refocusing attention. Davidson and Fox (1982) demonstrated that relatively greater left-sided activation was observed when babies were shown a happy video, and greater right-sided activation was observed when a sad video segment was presented. Moreover, babies with relatively greater right activation have been found to cry more upon maternal separation than babies with greater left activation (Davidson & Fox, 1989). These findings suggest the involvement of hemispheric asymmetries in the early development of predispositions to positive and negative affective styles, and adult studies have related resting EEG differences among subjects to differences in emotional style.

Davidson and his colleagues have conducted a series of studies on hemispheric asymmetries among college students with subclinical and clinical levels of depression (Davidson, 1991, 1993; Henriques & Davidson, 1991; Tomarken & Davidson, 1994). Depressive symptomatology often relates to decreased left hemisphere activation (Allen, Iacono, Depue, & Arbisi, 1993), and Davidson (1991) has suggested that depression is a disorder of inhibited approach (i.e., lack of interest, anhedonia, withdrawal, motor retardation). Depressed persons were found to display decreased left hemisphere activation and concomitant greater relative right frontal activation (Davidson, 1991). Moreover, decreased activation of the left frontal area also was observed among individuals who were previously depressed, but who had been asymptomatic for a year. Thus, hypoactivation of the left hemisphere may represent a trait marker for depression or, alternatively, may suggest a biological anomaly that is a consequence of a depressive episode (cf., Post, 1992). Additionally, these findings, through the contrast of depressed and nondepressed groups, illuminate how differential hemispheric activation may be involved in the more adaptive functioning of normal individuals.

D. CICCHETTI, F. A. ROGOSCH, S. L. TOTH

Dawson and her colleagues (Dawson, Grofer Klinger, Panagiotides, Hill, & Spieker, 1992; Dawson, Grofer Klinger, Panagiotides, Spieker, & Frey, 1992) examined the electroencephalograms (EEGs) of 14-month-olds of mothers with elevated depressive symptomatology and of nonsymptomatic mothers during various emotion-eliciting situations. Evidence was found that infants of the symptomatic mothers displayed reduced left frontal brain activation during baseline and playful interactions. This finding is reminiscent of the Davidson and Fox (1989) study with depressed adults that demonstrated left frontal activation asymmetries. These infants may similarly be evidencing a tendency toward developing negative emotionality. Moreover, securely attached infants of symptomatic mothers evidenced this left frontal hypoactivation compared with securely attached infants of nonsymptomatic mothers. Further, during distress-eliciting maternal separation, the infants of the symptomatic mothers did not display a greater right frontal activation or the same degree of distress that was seen in the infants of the nonsymptomatic mothers, and these differences were observed regardless of the attachment status of the high-risk infants. Dawson and her colleagues interpret these findings to suggest that both maternal depressive symptoms and attachment security are reflected in infant frontal lobe functioning and emotional behavior. The findings support the view that a genetic diathesis for depression and the quality of caregiving experienced both have an impact on neurobiological development. Convergence between biological and psychological systems is suggested, providing a window on the complexity of developmental organization that may heighten risk for depression. These findings also are important for accentuating the importance of the interrelations among parent behavior, infant behavior, and brain development in normal adaptation. The organization of biological and behavioral domains in normal development and the influence of caregiving are brought into relief by the contrast of the groups of depressed and nondepressed mothers and their infants.

Summary and intervention/policy implications

In this chapter, we have outlined and illustrated a developmental conceptualization of depression. Central to this approach is an emphasis on a broad view of human development that integrates developmental processes at multiple levels of biological and psychological complexity over the life course. Depressive disorders are seen as heterogeneous conditions that are likely to be arrived at developmentally through a variety of developmental pathways. Single risk factors can rarely be conceived of as resulting in depressive outcomes. Rather, the organization of biological and psychological systems, as they have been structured over development, must be fully considered. The concept of a depressotypic developmental organization has much heuristic value in guiding thinking about the diverse processes that underly symptom expression and depressive outcomes. The developmental position challenges us to move beyond identifying isolated aberrations in cognitive, affective, interpersonal, and biological components of depressive presentations, to understand how those components have evolved developmentally and how they are integrated within and across biological and psychological systems. Moreover, in viewing depressive disorders from this organizational-developmental perspective, much is learned, by contrast, regarding the organization of normal developmental processes contributing to successful adaptation.

The developmental psychopathology perspective provides important insights useful for efforts to prevent depressive disorders as well as to intervene once depression has occurred. Consistent with the developmental perspective of Zigler and Glick (1986), understanding the organization of developmental competencies among depressed persons is invaluable for conceptualizing the meaning of symptom expression and the capacities of different depressed persons to benefit from different types of treatment. For example, understanding the attachment organization of adults and the manner in which that attachment organization is involved in symptom expression have important implications for how treatment will succeed and for choosing what types of treatment are likely to be efficacious. Dozier (1990), in studying adults with severe psychopathology, found that patients with affective disorders were more likely to have greater security in their adult attachment organizations than were patients with thought disorders. Greater security was associated with more effective treatment compliance whereas increased rejection of therapists, less self-disclosure, and poorer treatment involvement occurred with patients having avoidant attachment organizations. Additionally, in another study involving dysthymic patients, Patrick, Hobson, Castle, Howard, and Maughan (1994) found that 83% were insecurely attached, with 50% exhibiting dismissing and 33% exhibiting preoccupied adult attachment organizations. These different attachment orientations suggest different approaches may be needed to address how affect, cognition, and interpersonal behaviors are organized within individual patients' depressive presentations. Similarly, the differentiation of dependent and self-critical personality styles among depressed individuals (Blatt, 1995; Blatt & Zuroff, 1992) implies that different domains of developmental deficit are involved for the two types of depressed individuals, and, as a result, alternative foci of treatment are required.

Treatment for depression also may need to vary depending on the history of prior depressive episodes. In studying the developmental progression of episodes among mood-disordered patients, Post (1992) notes that the more automatic triggering of episodes later in the course of these disorders likely requires different treatments. For first episodes of depressive disorder, interpersonal psychotherapies may have greater utility in reorganizing the affective, cognitive, and interpersonal difficulties depressed patients exhibit. However, as later episodes may become increasingly primed biologically, psychopharmacological intervention with more directive cognitive-behavioral techniques is likely to be more essential. Additionally, alternative drug treatments may become necessary, as the progression of episodes and concomitant biological alterations may make previously effective drugs no longer effective. (See also Post et al., 1996.)

For younger depressed patients, interventions must always be mindful of the varying capacities children at different development levels have to make use of various child therapy approaches (Shirk, 1988). Moreover, children continue to develop in an ongoing matrix of risk and protective factors that influences the course of their adaptation. Interventions to alter parental, familial, and social-contextual sources of risk are necessary in order to alleviate ongoing contributors to the difficulty depressed children have in resolving stage-salient issues of development. Because depressed children are likely to have experienced maladaptive resolutions of prior stage-salient issues (e.g., homeostatic and physiological regulation, affect differentiation and regulation, attachment organization, self-system), attention to reorganizing these critical domains through therapeutic interventions is crucial. Moreover, helping children to attain adaptive functioning in current stage-salient domains (e.g., peer relations, school achievement) is likely to be beneficial in beginning to reorganize and rework prior developmental incompetencies.

Given that the roots of depressotypic developmental organizations may extend down to infancy, prevention efforts that focus on early intervention in high-risk conditions are likely to be important for promoting competent early developmental attainments on the sequence of stage-salient developmental issues. Although parental depression as a risk condition has been a focus in this chapter, numerous disadvantageous familial and societal circumstances (e.g, parental psychopathology, parental substance abuse, marital violence, child maltreatment, poverty) constitute situations that may detract from children competently resolving developmental challenges, thereby contributing to risk for depressive outcomes. Broad-based community programs to promote child competence and to support adaptive family relationships are likely to be important for preventing developmental failures associated with depressotypic organizations, thereby reducing the prevalence of depression on a population level. Zigler, in his devotion and diligence to promote early childhood competence, has proposed models for a school of the 21st century (Zigler, 1989; Zigler & Ennis, 1989) in which formal schooling, child care, and family education and support are integrated. We believe such an approach, requiring collaboration of educational, mental health, community, and governmental systems, would be instrumental in reducing long-term risks for depression.

Because of the potential for increased genetic as well as psychological risk with which offspring of depressed parents are faced, preventive interventions for such families may be particularly important. Such prevention strategies, beginning at an early age, should incorporate multiple foci and strategies, including attention to alleviating the parental depression, enhancing parent–child adaptive communication and interaction, and reducing larger family stresses, such as marital discord. In so doing, the likelihood of promoting competence as these children confront the universal challenges of development will be enhanced, and depressive outcomes may be prevented. The need for and provision of preventive services for offspring of depressed parents will likely require changes in social and health care policy. All too often services are designated restrictively for the individual with the "disorder," while the larger needs of family systems, offspring, and the functioning of depressed adults as parents are neglected.

Despite the fact that depression is a treatable illness, considerable social stigma continues to be associated with seeking treatment for depression, and large numbers of individuals who are clinically depressed remain untreated (Institute of Medicine, 1985, 1989). Increased awareness of the availability and utility of treatments for depression, both for children and adults, and reducing the negative public attitudes toward treatment necessitates social and health policies that educate the public regarding depression, its effects, and the importance of intervention, as well as increase the availability and accessibility of treatment. Dedicated efforts to incorporate developmental knowledge into efforts to change and develop social policies to advance the prevention and treatment of depression would do well to follow the lead of Edward Zigler in his tireless efforts to advance social policies to meet the broad-based needs of children and families.

References

Abramson, L., Seligman, M., & Teasdale, J. (1978). Learned helplessness in humans: Critique and reformulation. *Journal of Abnormal Psychology, 87,* 49–74.
Achenbach, T. M. (1990). What is "developmental" about developmental psychopathology? In J. Rolf, A. Masten, D. Cicchetti, K. Nuechterlein, & S. Weintraub (Eds.), *Risk and protective factors in the development of psychopathology* (pp. 29–48). New York: Cambridge University Press.
Achenbach, T. M., & Edelbrock, C. S. (1986). *Child Behavior Checklist and profile for ages 2–3.* Burlington: University of Vermont, Department of Psychiatry.
Ainsworth, M. D. S., Blehar, M. C., Waters, E., & Wall, S. (1978). *Patterns of attachment: A psychological study of the Strange Situation.* Hillsdale, NJ: Erlbaum.
Allen, J., Iacono, W., Depue, R., & Arbisi, X. (1993). Regional EEG asymmetries in bipolar seasonal affective disorder before and after phototherapy. *Biological Psychiatry, 33,* 642–646.
Alloy, L., & Abramson, L. (1988). Depressive realism: Four theoretical perspectives. In L. Alloy (Ed.), *Cognitive processes in depression* (pp. 223–265). New York: Guilford.
Andreason, J. C., Williams, S., McGee, R., & Silva, P. A. (1987). DSM-III disorders in preadolescent children: Prevalence in a large sample from the general population. *Archives of General Psychiatry, 44,* 69–76.
Angold, A., & Costello, E. J. (1993). Depressive comorbidity in children and adolescents: Empirical, theoretical and methodological issues. *American Journal of Psychiatry, 150,* 1779–1791.
Angold, A., & Rutter, M. (1992). Effects of age and pubertal status on depression in a large clinical sample. *Development and Psychopathology, 4,* 5–28.
Armsden, G., McCauley, E., Greenberg, M., Burke, P., & Mitchell, J. (1990). Parent and peer attachment in early adolescent depression. *Journal of Abnormal Child Psychology, 18,* 683–697.
Beck, A. T. (1967). *Depression: Clinical, experimental, and theoretical aspects.* New York: Harper & Row.
Beck, A. T. (1983). Cognitive therapy of depression: New perspectives. In P. J. Clayton & J. E. Barrett (Eds), *Treatment of depression: Old controversies and new approaches* (pp. 265–290). New York: Raven.

Behar, L. B., & Stringfield, S. (1974). A behavior rating scale for the preschool child. *Developmental Psychology, 10,* 601–610.

Blatt, S. J. (1995). The destructiveness of perfectionism: Implications for the treatment of depression. *American Psychologist, 50,* 1003–1020.

Blatt, S. J., & Homann, E. (1992). Parent-child interaction in the etiology of dependent and self-critical depression. *Clinical Psychology Review, 12,* 47–91.

Blatt, S. J., Quinlan, D., Chevron, E., MacDonald, C., & Zuroff, D. (1982). Dependency and self-criticism: Psychological dimensions of depression. *Journal of Consulting and Clinical Psychology, 50,* 113–124.

Blatt, S. J., & Zuroff, D. (1992). Interpersonal relatedness as self-definition: Two prototypes for depression. *Clinical Psychology Review, 12,* 527–562.

Bowlby, J. (1969/1982). *Attachment and loss.* Vol. 1: *Attachment.* New York: Basic Books.

Bowlby, J. (1973). *Attachment and loss.* Vol. 2: *Separation.* New York: Basic Books.

Bowlby, J. (1980). *Attachment and loss.* Vol. 3: *Loss: Sadness and depression.* New York: Basic Books.

Bretherton, I. (1987). New perspectives on attachment relations: Security, communication, and internal working models. In J. Osofsky (Ed.), *Handbook of infant development* (2nd ed., pp. 1061–1100). New York: Wiley.

Bretherton, I. (1990). Open communication and internal working models: Their role in the development of attachment relationships. In R. Thompson (Ed.), *Nebraska symposium on motivation.* Vol. 36: *Socioemotional development* (pp. 57–113). Lincoln: University of Nebraska Press.

Bretherton, I., & Beeghly, M. (1982). Talking about internal states: The acquisition of an explicit theory of mind. *Developmental Psychology, 18,* 906–921.

Cadoret, R. J. (1978). Evidence for genetic inheritance of primary affective disorder in adoptees. *American Journal of Psychiatry, 135,* 463–466.

Carlson, V., Cicchetti, D., Barnett, D., & Braunwald, K. (1989). Disorganized/disoriented attachment relationships in maltreated infants. *Developmental Psychology, 25,* 525–531.

Carnelley, K., Pietromonaco, P., & Jaffe, K. (1994). Depression, working models of others, and relationship functioning. *Journal of Personality and Social Psychology, 66,* 127–140.

Caron, C., & Rutter, M. (1991). Comorbidity in child psychopathology: Concepts, issues, and research strategies. *Journal of Child Psychology and Psychiatry, 32,* 1063–1080.

Cassidy, J., & Marvin, R. (1992). *Attachment organization in preschool children: Procedures and coding manual.* Unpublished manuscript. Pennsylvania State University and University of Virginia.

Cicchetti, D. (1984). The emergence of developmental psychopathology. *Child Development, 55,* 1–7.

Cicchetti, D. (1993). Developmental Psychopathology: Reaction, reflections, projections. *Developmental Review, 13,* 471–502.

Cicchetti, D., & Aber, J. L. (1986). Early precursors to later depression: An organizational perspective. In L. Lipsitt & C. Rovee-Collier (Eds.), *Advances in infancy* (Vol. 4, pp. 87–137). Norwood, NJ: Ablex.

Cicchetti, D., & Beeghly, M. (Eds.) (1990). *The self in transition.* Chicago: University of Chicago Press.

Cicchetti, D., & Cohen, D. J. (1995). Perspectives on developmental psychopathology. In D. Cicchetti & D. J. Cohen (Eds.), *Developmental Psychopathology.* Vol. 1: *Theory and method* (pp. 3–20). New York: Wiley.

Cicchetti, D., & Rogosch, F. A. (Eds.) (1996). Developmental pathways: Diversity in process and outcome. [Special Issue] *Development and Psychopathology, 8* (4).

Cicchetti, D., & Schneider-Rosen, K. (1986). An organizational approach to childhood depression. In M. Rutter, C. Izard, & P. Read (Eds.), *Depression in young people: Clinical and developmental perspectives* (pp. 71–134). New York: Guilford.

Cicchetti, D., & Toth, S. L. (1995). Developmental psychopathology and disorders of affect. In D. Cicchetti & D. J. Cohen (Eds.), *Developmental psychopathology,* Vol. 2: *Risk, disorder, and adaptation* (pp. 369–420). New York: Wiley.

Cicchetti, D., & Tucker, D. (1994). Development and self-regulatory structures of the mind. *Development and Psychopathology, 6,* 533–549.

Cohn, J., Campbell, S., Matias, R., & Hopkins, J. (1990). Face-to-face interactions of postpartum depressed and nondepressed mother-infant pairs. *Developmental Psychology, 26,* 15–23.

Cohn, J., & Tronick, E. (1993). Three-month-old infants' reaction to simulated maternal depression. *Child Development, 54,* 185–193.

Cole, D. A., & Jordan, A. E. (1995). Competence and memory: Integrating psychosocial and cognitive correlates of child depression. *Child Development, 66,* 459–473.

Cole, D. A., Peeke, L. G., & Ingold, C. (1996). Characterological and behavioral self-blame in children: Assessment and developmental considerations. *Development and Psychopathology, 8,* 381–397.

Cole, P., Barrett, K., & Zahn-Waxler, C. (1992). Emotion displays in two-year-olds during mishaps. *Child Development, 63,* 314–324.

Coyne, J. C., & Whiffen, V. E. (1995). Issues in personality as diathesis for depression: The case of sociotropy-dependency and autonomy-self-criticism. *Psychological Bulletin, 118,* 358–378.

Crittenden, P. (1988). Relationships at risk. In J. Belsky & T. Nezworski (Eds.), *Clinical implications of attachment theory* (pp. 136–174). Hillsdale, NJ: Erlbaum.

Dahl, R. (1996). The regulation of sleep and arousal. *Development and Psychopathology, 8,* 3–27.

Dahl, R., Ryan, N., Puig-Antich, J., Nyugen, N., Al-Shabbout, M., Meyer, V., & Perel, J. (1991). 24-hour cortisol measures in adolescents with major depression: A controlled study. *Biological Psychiatry, 30,* 25–36.

Dahl, R., Ryan, N., Williamson, D., Ambrosini, P., Rabinovich, H., Novacenko, H., Nelson, B., & Puig-Antich, J. (1992). Regulation of sleep and growth hormone in adolescent depression. *Journal of the American Academy of Child and Adolescent Psychiatry, 31,* 615–621.

Damon W., & Hart, D. (1988). *Self-understanding in childhood and adolescence.* New York: Cambridge University Press.

Davidson, R. (1991). Cerebral asymmetry and affective disorders: A developmental perspective. In D. Cicchetti & S. L. Toth (Eds.) *Rochester symposium on developmental psychopathology,* Vol. 2: *Internalizing and externalizing expressions of dysfunction* (pp 123–154). Hillsdale, N.J.: Erlbaum.

Davidson, R. (1993). Parsing affective space: Perspectives from neuropsychology and psychophysiology. *Neuropsychology, 7,* 464–475.

Davidson, R., & Fox, N. (1982). Asymmetrical brain activity discriminates between positive versus negative affective stimuli in human infants. *Science, 218,* 1235–1237.

Davidson, R., & Fox, N. (1989). Frontal brain asymmetry predicts infants' response to maternal separation. *Journal of Abnormal Psychology, 98,* 127–131.

Dawson, G., Grofer Klinger, L., Panagiotides, H., Hill, D., & Spieker, S. (1992). Frontal lobe activity and affective behavior of infants of mothers with depressive symptoms. *Child Development, 63,* 725–737.

Dawson, G., Grofer Klinger, L., Panagiotides, H., Spieker, S., & Frey, K. (1992). Infants of mothers with depressive symptoms: Electroencephalographic and behavioral findings related to attachment status. *Development and Psychopathology, 4,* 67–80.

DeMulder, E. & Radke-Yarrow, M. (1991). Attachment with affectively ill and well mothers: Concurrent behavioral correlates. *Development and Psychopathology, 3,* 227–242.

Dodge, K. (1993). Social-cognitive mechanisms in the development of conduct disorder and depression. *Annual Review of Psychology, 44,* 559–584.

Downey, G., & Coyne, J. (1990). Children of depressed parents: An integrative review. *Psychological Bulletin, 106,* 50–76.

Dozier, M. (1990). Attachment organization and treatment use for adults with serious psychopathological disorders. *Development and Psychopathology, 2,* 47–60.

Dunner, D., Dwyer, T., & Fieve, R. (1976). Depressive symptoms in patients with unipolar and bipolar affective disorder. *Comprehensive Psychiatry, 17,* 447–451.

Easterbrooks, M. A., Davidson, C., & Chazan, R. (1993). Psychosocial risk, attachment, and behavior problems among school-aged children. *Development and Psychopathology, 5,* 389–402.

Emde, R. N., Gaensbauer, T., & Harmon, R. (1976). *Emotional expression in infancy: A biobehavioral study.* New York: International Universities Press.

Faraone, S., Kremen, W., & Tsuang, M. (1990). Genetic transmission of major affective disorders: Quantitative models and linkage analyses. *Psychological Bulletin, 108,* 109–127.

Field, T., Healy, B., Goldstein, S., & Guthertz, M. (1990). Behavior-state matching and synchrony in mother-infant interactions of nondepressed versus depressed dyads. *Developmental Psychology, 26,* 7–14.

Field, T., Healy, B., Goldstein, S., Perry, S., Bendell, D., Schanberg, S., Zimmerman, E., & Kuhn, C. (1988). Infants of depressed mothers show "depressed" behavior even with nondepressed adults. *Child Development, 59,* 1569–1579.

Field, T., Healy, B., & LeBlanc, W. (1989). Sharing and synchrony of behavior states and heart rate in nondepressed versus depressed mother-infant interactions. *Infant Behavior and Development, 12,* 357–376.

Fleming, J., & Offord, D. (1990). Epidemiology of childhood depressive disorders: A critical review. *Journal of the American Academy of Child and Adolescent Psychiatry, 29,* 571–580.

Fox, N., & Davidson, R., (1984). Hemispheric substrates of affect. In N. A. Fox & R. J. Davidson (Eds.), *The psychobiology of affective development,* (pp. 353–381). Hillsdale, NJ: Erlbaum.

Gaensbauer, T. J., Harmon, R. J., Cytryn, L., & McKnew, D. H. (1984). Social and affective development in infants with a manic-depressive parent. *American Journal of Psychiatry, 141,* 223–229.

Gara, M., Woolfolk, R., Cohen, B., Goldstron, R., Allen, L., & Novalany, J. (1993). Perception of self and other in major depression. *Journal of Abnormal Psychology, 102,* 93–100.

George, C., Kaplan, N., & Main, M. (1984). *Attachment interview for adults.* Unpublished manuscript. University of California, Berkeley.

Gershon, E., Bunney, W., Leckman, J., Van Eerdewegh, M., & Debauche, B. (1976). The inheritance of affective disorders: A review of data and of hypotheses. *Behavior Genetics, 6,* 227–261.

Gjerde, P. F. (1995). Alternative pathways to chronic depressive symptoms in young adults: Gender differences in developmental trajectories. *Child Development, 66,* 1277–1300.

Gold, P., Goodwin, F., & Chrousos, G. (1988a). Clinical and biochemical manifestations of depression: Relation to the neurobiology of stress (Part I). *New England Journal of Medicine, 319,* 348–353.

Gold, P., Goodwin, F., & Chrousos, G. (1988b). Clinical and biochemical manifestations of depression: Relation to the neurobiology of stress (Part II). *New England Journal of Medicine, 319,* 413–420.

Gottesman, I. I., & Goldsmith, H. (1994). Developmental psychopathology of antisocial behavior: Inserting genes into its genesis and epigenesis. In C. A. Nelson (Ed.), *Minnesota symposia on child psychology,* Vol. 27: *Threats to optimal development: Integrating biological, psychological, and social risk factors* (pp. 69–104). Hillsdale, NJ: Erlbaum.

Greenough, W., Black, J., & Wallace, C. (1987). Experience and brain development. *Child Development, 58,* 539–559.

Hammen, C. (1992). Cognitive, life stress, and interpersonal approaches to a developmental psychopathology model of depression. *Development and Psychopathology, 4,* 189–206.

Hammen, C., Burge, D., Burney, E., & Adrian, C. (1990). Longitudinal study of diagnoses in children of women with unipolar and bipolar affective disorder. *Archives of General Psychiatry, 47,* 1112–1117.

Harrington, R., Fudge, H., Rutter, M., Pickles, A., & Hill, J. (1990). Adult outcomes of childhood and adolescent depression: I. Psychiatric status. *Archives of General Psychiatry, 47,* 465–473.

Harrington, R., Fudge, H., Rutter, M., Pickles, A., & Hill, J. (1991). Adult outcomes of childhood and adolescent depression: II. Risk for antisocial disorders. *Journal of American Academy of Child and Adolescent Psychiatry, 30,* 434–439.

Harter, S. (1983). Developmental perspectives on the self-system. In P. H. Mussen (Ed.), *Handbook of child psychology,* Vol. 4: *Socialization, personality, and social development* (4th ed., pp. 275–385). New York: Wiley.

Hay, D., Zahn-Waxler, C., Cummings, E. M., & Iannotti, R. (1992). Young children's views about conflict with peers: A comparison of the daughters and sons of depressed and well women. *Journal of Child Psychology and Psychiatry, 33,* 669–693.

Henriques, J., & Davidson, R. (1991). Left frontal hypoactivation in depression. *Journal of Abnormal Psychology, 100,* 535–545.

Hesse, P., & Cicchetti, D. (1982). Perspectives on an integrated theory of emotional development. *New Directions for Child Development, 16,* 3–48.

Institute of Medicine. (1985). Research on mental illness and addictive disorders: Progress and prospects. [Supplement to] *American Journal of Psychiatry, 1142,* 1–41.

Institute of Medicine. (1989). *Research in children and adolescents with mental, behavioral, and developmental disorders.* Washington: DC: National Academy Press.

Izard, C., & Malatesta, C. (1987). Perspectives on emotional development. I. Differential emotions theory of early emotional development. In J. Osofsky (Ed.), *Handbook of infant development* (2nd ed., pp. 494–554). New York: Wiley.

Jackson, S. (1986). *Melancholia and depression: From Hippocratic times to modern times.* New Haven: Yale University Press.

Kagan, J. (1971). *Change and continuity in infancy.* New York: Wiley.

Kagan, J. (1981). *The second year: The emergence of self-awareness.* Cambridge, MA: Harvard University Press.

Kandel, D., & Davies, M. (1986). Adult sequelae of adolescent depressive symptoms. *Archives of General Psychiatry, 43,* 255–262.

Kashani, J., McGee, R. O., Clarkson, S. E., Anderson, J. C., Walton, L., Williams, S., Silva, P., Robins, A., Cytryn, L., & McKnew, D. (1983). The nature and prevalence of major and minor depression in a sample of nine-year-old children. *Archives of General Psychiatry, 40,* 1217–1227.

Kessler, R., McGonagle, K., Zhao, S., Nelson, C., Hughes, M., Eshleman, S., Wittchen, H., & Kendler, K. (1994). Lifetime and 12-month prevalence of DSMII-R psychiatric disorders in the United States: Results from the national comorbidity survey. *Archives of General Psychiatry, 51,* 8–19.

Knowles, J., & MacLean, A. (1990). Age-related changes in sleep in depressed and healthy subjects. *Neuropsychopharmacology, 3,* 251–259.

Kobak, R., & Sceery, A. (1988). Attachment in late adolescence: Working models, affect regulation and perceptions of self and others. *Child Development, 59,* 135–146.

Kobak, R., Sudler, N., & Gamble, W. (1991). Attachment and depressive symptoms during adolescence: A developmental pathways analysis. *Development and Psychopathology, 3,* 461–474.

Kochanska, G. (1991). Patterns of inhibition to the unfamiliar in children of normal and affectively ill mothers. *Child Development, 62,* 250–263.

Kovacs, M. (1989). Affective disorders in children and adolescence. *American Psychologist, 44,* 209–215.

Kovacs, M., Akiskal, H., Gatsonis, C., & Parrone, P. (1994). Childhood-onset dysthymic disorder: Clinical features and prospective naturalistic outcome. *Archives of General Psychiatry, 51,* 365–374.

Kovacs, M., Feinberg, T., Crouse-Novak, M., Paulauskas, S., & Finkelstein, R. (1984). Depressive disorders in childhood. I. A longitudinal prospective study of characteristics and recovery. *Archives of General Psychiatry, 41,* 229–237.

Kovacs, M., Feinberg, T., Crouse-Novak, M., Paulauskas, S., Pollock, M., & Finkelstein, R. (1984). Depressive disorders in childhood. II. A longitudinal study of the risk for a subsequent major depression. *Archives of General Psychiatry, 41,* 643–649.

Lauer, R., Giordani, B., Boivin, M., Halle, N., Glasgow, B., Alessi, N., & Berent, S. (1994). Effects of depression on memory performance and metamemory in children. *Journal of the American Academy of Child and Adolescent Psychiatry, 33,* 679–685.

Leadbeater, B., Blatt, S., & Quinlan, D. (1995). Gender-linked vulnerabilities to depressive symptoms, stress, and problem behaviors in adolescence. *Journal of Research on Adolescence, 5,* 1–29.

Lewinsohn, P., Clarke, G., Seeley, J., & Rohde, P. (1994). Major depression in community adolescents: Age at onset, episode duration, and time to recurrence. *Journal of the American Academy of Child and Adolescent Psychiatry, 33,* 809–818.

Lewinsohn, P., Hops, H., Roberts, R., Seeley, J., & Andrews, J. (1993). Adolescent Psychopathology: I. Prevalence and incidence of depression and other DSM-III-R disorders in high school students. *Journal of Abnormal Psychology, 102,* 133–144.

Lewis, M., & Brooks-Gunn, J. (1979). *Social cognition and the acquisition of self.* New York: Plenum Press.

Luthar, S., Doernberger, C., & Zigler, E. (1993). Resilience is not a unidimensional construct: Insights from a prospective study of inner-city adolescents. *Development and Psychopathology, 5,* 703–717.

Luthar, S., & Zigler, E. (1991). Vulnerability and competence: A review of research on resilience in childhood. *American Journal of Orthopsychiatry, 61,* 6–22.

Lyons-Ruth, K., Alpern, L., & Repacholi, B. (1993). Disorganized infant attachment classification and maternal psychosocial problems as predictors of hostile-aggressive behavior in the preschool classroom. *Child Development, 64,* 572–585.

Lyons-Ruth, K., Connell, D., Grunebaum, H., & Botein, S. (1990). Infants at social risk: Maternal depression and family support services as mediators of infant development and security of attachment. *Child Development, 59,* 1569–1579.

Lyons-Ruth, K., Connell, D., Zoll, D., & Stahl, J. (1987). Infants at social risk: Relations among infant maltreatment, maternal behavior, and infant attachment behavior. *Developmental Psychology, 23,* 223–232.

Lyons-Ruth, K., Repacholi, B., McLeod, S., & Silva, E. (1991). Disorganized attachment behavior in infancy: Short-term stability, maternal and infant correlates, and risk-related subtypes. *Development and Psychopathology, 3,* 377–396.

Mahler, M., Pine, F., & Bergman, A. (1975). *The psychological birth of the human infant.* New York: Basic Books.

Main, M., & Cassidy, J. (1988). Categories of response to reunion with a parent at age 6: Predictable from infant attachment classifications and stable over a 1-month period. *Developmental Psychology, 24,* 415–426.

Main, M., & Hesse, E. (1990). Parents' unresolved traumatic experiences are related to infant disorganized attachment status: Is frightened and/or frightening parental behavior the linking mechanism? In M. T. Greenberg, D. Cicchetti, & E. M. Cummings (Eds.), *Attachment in the preschool years* (pp. 161–182). Chicago: University of Chicago Press.

Main, M., & Solomon, J. (1990). Procedures for identifying infants as disorganized/disoriented during the Ainsworth Strange Situation. In M. Greenberg, D. Cicchetti, & E. M. Cummings (Eds.), *Attachment during the preschool years* (pp. 121–160). Chicago: University of Chicago Press.

Maj, M., Veltro, F., Pirozzi, R., Lobrace, S., & Magliano, L. (1992). Pattern of recurrence of illness after recovery from an episode of major depression: A prospective study. *American Journal of Psychiatry, 149,* 795–800.

Malatesta, C. Z., & Izard, C. (1984). The ontogenesis of human social signals: From biological imperatives to symbol utilization. In N. A. Fox & R. J. Davidson (Eds.), *The psychobiology of affective development* (pp. 161–206). Hillsdale, NJ: Erlbaum.

Maser, J., & Cloninger, C. R. (Eds.). (1990). *Comorbidity of mood and anxiety disorders.* Washington, DC: American Psychiatric Press.

McGuffin, P., & Katz, R. (1989). The genetics of depression and manic-depressive illness. *British Journal of Psychiatry, 155,* 294–304.

McGuffin, P., & Katz, R. (1993). Genes, adversity, and depression. In R. Plomin & G. McLearn (Eds.), *Nature, nurture, and psychology* (pp. 217–230). Washington, DC: American Psychological Association.

McGuffin, P., Katz, R., Watkins, S., & Rutherford, J. (1996). A hospital-based twin register of the heritability of DSM-IV unipolar depression. *Archives of General Psychiatry, 53,* 129–136.

Mendlewicz, J., & Rainer, J. (1977). Adoption study supporting genetic transmission in manic-depressive illness. *Nature, 268,* 327–329.

Merikangas, K., & Spiker, D. (1982). Assortative mating among inpatients with primary affective disorder. *Psychological Medicine, 12,* 753–764.

Noam, G., & Valiant, G. (1994). Clinical-developmental psychology in developmental psychopathology: Theory and Research of an emerging perspective. In D. Cicchetti & S. L. Toth (Eds.), *Rochester symposium on developmental psychopathology,* Vol. 5: *Disorders and dysfunctions of the self.* (pp. 299–331). Rochester, NY: University of Rochester Press.

Nolen-Hoeksema, S. (1990). *Sex differences in depression.* Stanford, CA: Stanford University Press.

Nolen-Hoeksema, S., & Girgus, J. (1994). The emergence of gender differences in depression during adolescence. *Psychological Bulletin, 115,* 424–443.

Nolen-Hoeksema, S., Girgus, J., & Seligman, M. (1992). Predictors and consequences of childhood depressive symptoms; A 5-year longitudinal study. *Journal of Abnormal Psychology, 101,* 405–422.

Patrick, M., Hobson, R. P., Castle, D., Howard, R., & Maughan, B. (1994). Personality disorder and the mental representation of early social experience. *Development and Psychopathology, 6,* 375–388.

Pearson, J. L., Cohn, D. A., Cowan, P., & Cowan, C. P. (1994). Earned and continuous-security in adult attachment: Relation to depression and parenting style. *Development and Psychopathology, 6,* 359–373.

Petersen, A., Compas, B., Brooks-Gunn, J., Stemmler, M., Ey, S., & Grant, K. (1993). Depression in adolescence. *American Psychologist, 48,* 155–168.

Peterson, C., & Seligman, M. (1984). Causal explanations as a risk factor for depression: Theory and evidence. *Psychological Review, 91,* 347–374.

Pfol, B., Stangl, D., & Zimmerman, M. (1984). The implications of DSM-III-R personality disorders for patients with major depression. *Journal of Affective Disorders, 7,* 309–318.

Pickens, J., & Field, T. (1993). Facial expressivity in infants of depressed mothers. *Developmental Psychology, 29,* 986–988.

Post, R. (1992). Transduction of psychosocial stress into the neurobiology of recurrent affective disorder. *American Journal of Psychiatry, 149,* 999–1010.

Post, R., & Ballenger, J. (Eds.) (1984). *Neurobiology of mood disorders.* Baltimore: Williams & Wilkins.

Post, R., Rubinow, D., & Ballenger, J. (1986). Conditioning and sensitization in the longitudinal course of affective illness. *British Journal of Psychiatry, 149,* 191–201.

Post, R., Weiss, S., & Leverich, G. (1994). Recurrent affective disorder: Roots in developmental neurobiology and illness progression based on changes in gene expression. *Development and Psychopathology, 6,* 781–813.

Post, R., Weiss, S., Leverich, G., George, M., Frye, M., & Ketter, T. (1996). Developmental psychobiology of cyclic affective illness: Implications for early therapeutic intervention. *Development and Psychopathology, 8,* 273–305.

Puig-Antich, J. (1986). Psychobiological Markers: Effects of Age and Puberty. In M. Rutter, C. C. Izard, & P. B. Read (Eds.), *Depression in young people: Developmental and clinical perspectives.* (pp. 341–381). New York: Guilford.

Radke-Yarrow, M., Belmont, B., Nottelmann, E., & Bottomly, L. (1990). Young children's self-conceptions: Origins in the natural discourse of depressed and normal mothers and their children. In D. Cicchetti & M. Beeghly (Eds.), *The self in transition* (pp. 345–361). Chicago: University of Chicago Press.

Radke-Yarrow, M., Cummings, E. M., Kuczynski, L., & Chapman, M. (1985). Patterns of attachment in two- and three-year-olds in normal families and families with parental depression. *Child Development, 56,* 884–893.

Rolf, J., Masten, A., Cicchetti, D., Nuechterlein, K., & Weintraub, S. (Eds.). (1990). *Risk and protective factors in the development of psychopathology.* New York: Cambridge University Press.

Rubin, K. H., Both, L., Zahn-Waxler, C., Cummings, E. M., & Wilkinson, M. (1991). Dyadic play behaviors of children of well and depressed mothers. *Development and Psychopathology, 3,* 243–251.

Rubin, K. H., LeMare, L., & Lollis, S. (1990). Social withdrawal in childhood: Developmental pathways to peer rejection. In S. Asher & J. Coie (Eds.), *Peer rejection in childhood* (pp. 217–249). New York: Cambridge University Press.

Rubin, K. H., & Mills, R. S. L. (1988). The many faces of social isolation in childhood. *Journal of Consulting and Clinical Psychology, 56,* 916–924.

Rutter, M. (1986). The developmental psychopathology of depression: Issues and perspectives. In M. Rutter, C. Izard, & P. Read (Eds.), *Depression in young people* (pp. 3–30). New York: Guilford.

Rutter, M. (1990). Psychosocial resilience and protective mechanisms. In J. Rolf, A. S. Masten, D.

Cicchetti, K. H. Nuechterlein, & S. Weintraub (Eds.), *Risk and protective factors in the development of psychopathology* (pp. 181–214). New York: Cambridge University Press.

Ryan, N., Birmaher, B., Perel, J., Dahl, R., Meyer, V., Al-Shabbout, M., Iyengar, S., & Puig-Antich, J. (1992). Neuroendocrine response to L-5-Hydroxytryptophan challenge in prepubertal major depression. *Archives of General Psychiatry, 49,* 843–851.

Sameroff, A. J., Seifer, R., & Zax, M. (1982). Early development of children at risk for emotional disorder. *Monographs of the Society for Research in Child Development, 47* (Serial No. 199).

Schore, A. N. (1996). The experience-dependent maturation of a regulatory system in the orbital prefrontal cortex and the origin of developmental psychopathology. *Development and Psychopathology, 8,* 59–87.

Shirk, S. R. (Ed.) (1988). *Cognitive development and child psychotherapy.* New York: Plenum Press.

Siever, L., & Davis, K. (1985). Overview: Toward a dysregulation hypothesis of depression. *American Journal of Psychiatry, 142,* 1017–1031.

Spoont, M. (1992). Modulatory role of serotonin in neural information processing: Implications for human psychopathology. *Psychological Bulletin, 112,* 330–350.

Sroufe, L. A. (1979). The coherence of individual development: Early care attachment, and subsequent developmental issues. *American Psychologist, 34,* 834–841.

Sroufe, L. A. (1990). An organizational perspective on the self. In D. Cicchetti & M. Beeghly (Eds.), *The self in transition* (pp. 13–40). Chicago: University of Chicago Press.

Sroufe, L. A., & Rutter, M. (1984). The domain of developmental psychopathology. *Child Development, 55,* 17–29.

Sroufe, L. A., & Waters, E. (1976). The ontogenesis of smiling and laughter: A perspective on the organization of development in infancy. *Psychological Review, 83,* 173–189.

Stoudemire, A., & Blazer, D. (1985). Depression in the elderly. In E. Beckham & W. Leber (Eds.), *Handbook of depression: Treatment, assessment, and research* (pp. 556–586). Homewood, IL: Dorsey Press.

Strober, M., Lampert, C., Schmidt, S., & Morrell, W. (1993). The course of major depressive disorder in adolescents: I. Recovery and risk of manic switching in a follow-up of psychotic and nonpsychotic subtypes. *Journal of the American Academy of Child and Adolescent Psychiatry, 32,* 34–42.

Taylor, S. E., & Brown, J. D. (1988). Illusion and well-being: A social-psychological perspective on mental health. *Psychological Bulletin, 103,* 193–210.

Tomarken, A., & Davidson, R. (1994). Frontal brain activation in repressors and nonrepressors. *Journal of Abnormal Psychology, 103,* 339–349.

Tsuang, M., & Faraone, S. (1990). *The genetics of mood disorders.* Baltimore: Johns Hopkins University Press.

Tucker, D., & Williamson, P. (1984). Asymmetric neural control systems in human self-regulation. *Psychological Review, 91,* 185–215.

von Bertalanffy, L. (1968). *General system theory.* New York: Braziller.

Warner, V., Weissman, M., Fendrich, M., Wickramaratne, P., & Moreau, D. (1992). The course of major depression in the offspring of depressed parents: Incidence, recurrence, and recovery. *Archives of General Psychiatry, 49,* 795–801.

Watson, J., Hopkins, N., Roberts, J., Steitz, J., & Weiner, A. (1987). *Molecular biology of the gene.* Vol. 1: *General Principles.* Vol. 2: *Specialized Aspects.* Menlo, Park, CA: Benjamin/Cummings Publishing Company.

Weissman, M., Bruce, M., Leaf, P., Florio, L., & Holzer, C. (1991). Affective disorders. In L. Robins & D. Reigier (Eds.), *Psychiatric disorders in America.* (pp. 53–80). New York: Free Press.

Weissman, M., Gammon, G., John, K., Merikangas, K., Warner, V., Prusoof, B., & Sholmskas, D. (1987). Children of depressed parents. *Archives of General Psychiatry, 44,* 847–853.

Wells, K., Burnam, A., Rogers, W., Hays, R., & Camp, P. (1992). The course of depression in adult outpatients: Results from the medical outcomes study. *Archives of General Psychiatry, 49,* 788–794.

Werner, H. (1948). *Comparative psychology of mental development.* New York: International Universities Press.

Werner, H., & Kaplan, B. (1963). *Symbol formation: An organismic-developmental approach to language and the expression of thought.* New York: Wiley.

Zahn-Waxler, C., Denham, S., Cummings, E. M., & Iannotti, R. (1992). Peer relations in children with a depressed caregiver. In R. Parke & G. Ladd (Eds.), *Family-peer relationships: Modes of linkage* (pp. 317–344). Hillsdale, NJ: Erlbaum.

Zahn-Waxler, C., Iannotti, R., Cummings, E. M., & Denham, S. (1990). Antecedents of problem behaviors in children of depressed mothers. *Development and Psychopathology, 2,* 271–291.

Zahn-Waxler, C., & Kochanska, G. (1990). The origins of guilt. In R. Thompson (Ed.), *Nebraska symposium on motivation,* Vol. 36: *Socio-emotional development* (pp. 183–258). Lincoln: University of Nebraska Press.

Zahn-Waxler, C., Kochanska, G., Krupnick, J., & McKnew, D. (1990). Patterns of guilt in children of depressed and well mothers. *Developmental Psychology, 26,* 51–59.

Zigler, E. (1963). Metatheoretical issues in developmental psychology. In M. Marx (Ed.), *Theories in contemporary psychology* (pp. 341–369). New York: Macmillan.

Zigler, E. (1989). Addressing the nation's child care crisis: The school of the twenty-first century. *American Journal of Orthopsychiatry, 59,* 484–491.

Zigler, E., & Ennis, P. (1989). The school of the twenty-first century. *Division of Child, Youth, and Family Services Newsletter, 12,* 1, 12–13.

Zigler, E., & Glick, M. (1986). *A developmental approach to adult psychopathology.* New York: Wiley.

Zigler, E., & Phillips, D. (1961). Social competence and outcome in psychiatric disorder. *Journal of Abnormal and Social Psychology, 61,* 231–238.

Zupan, B. A., Hammen, C., & Jaenicke, C. (1987). The effects of current mood and prior depressive history on self-schematic processing in children. *Journal of Experimental Child Psychology, 43,* 149–158.

Part III

Risks associated with the macrosystem, microsystem, and ontogenic development

14 Transactional ecological systems in developmental psychopathology

Dante Cicchetti and Sheree L. Toth

The study of risk and resilience has an illustrious history in the field of developmental psychopathology. The seminal works in this area include Murphy and Moriarty's (1976) investigation of vulnerability and coping from infancy through adolescence; Rutter's (1966) epidemiological studies on the Isle of Wight; Werner and Smith's (1992) longitudinal examination of the developmental trajectories of a birth cohort of infants born on the Hawaiian island of Kauai and currently followed up into early adulthood; Luthar and Zigler's (Luthar, 1991; Luthar, Doernberger, & Zigler, 1993) studies of disadvantaged inner-city adolescents that illustrate how resilient individuals may be at risk for difficulties in other realms of functioning; Sameroff's discovery in the Rochester Longitudinal Study that cumulative risk factors exert a deleterious impact on developmental outcome (Sameroff, Seifer, Baldwin, & Baldwin, 1993; Sameroff, Seifer, Barocas, Zax, & Greenspan, 1987); and Garmezy and Masten's investigations of the resilient adaptation of high-risk youth in Project Competence (Garmezy, Masten, & Tellegen, 1984; Masten & Coatsworth, 1995). Examinations of risk and resilience across the life course are essential in order to elucidate the role that various biological, psychological, and environmental factors play in fostering or inhibiting positive adaptation, as well as for informing theories of normal development.

In this chapter, we apply a developmental psychopathology perspective to conceptualizing risk and resilience during childhood and adolescence. After describing a developmental psychopathology approach, we discuss the operation of risk and resilience within a transactional model of development. We then present an ecological-transactional framework for understanding the emergence of maladaptation and psychopathology as it relates to broad ecological forces such as divorce, persistent poverty, child maltreatment, parental psychopathology, and substance abuse. Within the context of this framework, we then focus our discussion specifically on the effects of child maltreatment on ontogenic development by reviewing illustrative research from our laboratory. Our goal therein is to examine the effects that proximal ecological factors play in the development of adaptive and maladaptive

We gratefully acknowledge the support of grants from the William T. Grant Foundation, the National Center on Child Abuse and Neglect, the National Institute of Mental Health, and the Spunk Fund, Inc.

ontogenic outcomes in maltreated children. We conclude the chapter by discussing the implications of this work for informing normal developmental theory, as well as for influencing advocacy efforts and social policy formulation and implementation for high-risk and disordered populations (see Cicchetti & Toth, 1993; Gerbner, Ross, & Zigler, 1980; Melton, 1995; Thompson & Wilcox, 1995).

A developmental psychopathology approach

Theory and research emanating from the discipline of developmental psychopathology provide a powerful framework for unifying diverse contributions to the study of high-risk and mentally disordered populations. Developmental psychopathology represents a movement toward understanding the causes, determinants, course, sequelae, prevention, and treatment of mental disorders by integrating knowledge from multiple disciplines within an ontogenetic framework (Cicchetti, 1984, 1993). Utilization of a developmental psychopathology approach requires that those invested in understanding risk and psychopathology move beyond simple cause-and-effect explanations of behavior and grapple with issues such as the mechanisms and processes that eventuate in adaptive versus maladaptive outcome, the reciprocal relations that exist between normality and pathology and how this interface can inform theories of normal development, and the role of individual-versus variable-level analyses in informing theory and approaches to prevention and intervention (Cicchetti, 1984, 1993; Luthar, Chapter 20, this volume; Sroufe & Rutter, 1984).

Attempting to understand the diversity in process and outcome is integral to a developmental psychopathology perspective on risk and disorder. For example, although it cannot be disputed that child maltreatment is a significant risk factor for maladaptation in childhood, as well as throughout the life course, not all maltreated children develop similar, or even any, disorders (Cicchetti, 1989). In this regard, equifinality, which refers to varied pathways eventuating in a similar outcome, and multifinality, which posits that a single component may act differently depending on the organization of the system in which it operates, are relevant (Cicchetti & Rogosch, 1996; von Bertalanffy, 1968). Moreover, some maltreated children appear to escape the potential adverse effects of maltreatment, underscoring the potential diversity in ontogenic outcome, regardless of similarity in risks experienced (Cicchetti, Rogosch, Lynch, & Holt, 1993).

Many of the processes that are implicated in the etiology of mental disorder do not occur in isolation, thereby further complicating efforts to elucidate mediating and moderating influences on development (Garmezy & Masten, 1994; Rutter, 1990; Sameroff et al., 1987). For example, in children with depressed parents, it is extremely difficult to ascertain what factor or factors may be contributing to child maladaptation. Because depressed caregivers reside in environments that typically include marital discord, spousal vulnerability or psychopathology, and genetic loadings for affective disorders, isolating causal influences on child outcome is difficult, if not impossible (Cicchetti, Rogosch, & Toth, Chapter 13, this volume; Downey & Coyne, 1990). Developmental psychopathology strives to recognize multiple influences on ontogenesis and to devise investigations that separate the varied influences of multiple risks.

One strategy that holds potential for disentangling multiple interacting influences on development involves studying the adaptation of individuals who exhibit particular functioning deficits and not others. Multiple processes studied individually in this manner may provide insights into the roles that these single deficits exert on normal adaptation, and on how those influences may change and require reconceptualization within a broader matrix of functioning deficits among children exhibiting a given disorder (Richters & Cicchetti, 1993).

Risk and resilience within a transactional model of development

As we have discussed, a developmental psychopathology approach maintains that reductionistic efforts to delimit unitary, main effects causes of maladaptation or psychopathology are inadequate. Such linear models of causality deny the complexity of development and the mutually influencing nature of constitutional, biological, psychological, environmental, and sociological influences over time (Sameroff & Chandler, 1975). A transactional conceptualization of risk and resilience recognizes the ongoing dynamic interplay that occurs between both distal and proximal factors and strives to investigate risk, disorder, and resilience by developing models that can account for a multiplicity of influences on ontogenesis.

The transactional model maintains that interrelations between the organization of developmental domains, including biological, emotional, cognitive, linguistic, representational, and interpersonal, and environmental influences, including intrafamilial, societal, community, and cultural, are mutually interacting systems. The child is not only influenced by environmental inputs that lead to biological and psychological transformations and reorganizations, but also the environment is affected by and responds to the characteristics of the child. Thus, across the course of development the organizational structure of both the child and the environment are in a state of flux involving bidirectional influences. These transactions generate variations in the quality of the organization of their different biological and behavioral systems. Moreover, variability in the adaptation of the child (i.e., competent vs. incompetent) alters the child's capacity to respond to new experiences, whether they be positive or negative, as well as the pathways toward future adaptation or maladaptation that the child takes.

In accord with a transactional developmental formulation, it is likely that a multitude of general factors across broad domains of development will be related to maladaptive, psychopathological, or resilient outcomes. Therefore, a comprehensive approach to delimiting the processes and mechanisms that have contributed to the course of ontogenesis may be more fruitful than efforts to identify specific predictors of the immediate or proximal onset of maladaptation or resilience. The model proposed by Cicchetti and Rizley (1981) is useful in this regard.

According to Cicchetti and Rizley, vulnerability factors are generally regarded as enduring circumstances or conditions that promote maladaptation and/or psychopathology. Major domains of influence on ontogenic development, including external (intrafamilial, social-environmental) and internal (biological, psychological), may serve as sources of vulnerability because they can detract from the attainment of competence and successful adaptation. For instance, parental psychopathology and substance abuse, child maltreatment, domestic violence, and divorce all may exert detrimental effects on the developing child (see, e.g., Chase-Lansdale, Cherlin, & Kiernan, 1995; Cicchetti, 1989; Cicchetti, Rogosch, & Toth, Chapter 13, this volume; Hetherington, Chapter 15, this volume; Luthar, Cushing, & McMahon, Chapter 19, this volume; Mayes & Bornstein, Chapter 8, this volume; McCloskey, Figueredo, & Koss, 1995; Sternberg, Lamb, & Dawud-Noursi, Chapter 18, this volume). Similarly, stressors such as chronic poverty, unsupportive social networks, community violence, and ethnic and political violence also may detract from competent development (see, e.g., Belsky, 1993; Cairns & Dawes, 1996; Huston, McLoyd, & Garcia Coll, 1994; Macksoud & Aber, 1996; Richters & Martinez, 1993a, 1993b; Zigler, 1976). Over the course of development, vulnerability factors transact with the developing child to compromise positive adaptation and to promote a pathological organization among biological, emotional, cognitive, linguistic, interpersonal, and representational systems (cf. Cicchetti, Rogosch, & Toth, Chapter 13 this volume).

Conversely, enduring protective factors act so as to promote competence in the child. Protective or compensatory factors can best be conceptualized as opposites of the vulnerability factors previously described. For example, examples of protective factors include parental mental health, marital harmony, adequate income levels, and low levels of community violence. All of these factors are likely to enhance the emergence of child competence and adaptation, thereby contributing to the emergence of resilience in children otherwise expected to be at risk for negative developmental outcome (Cicchetti & Garmezy, 1993).

In addition to these enduring vulnerability and protective factors, transient influences also exert a role on the process of development. Although short-term in nature, transient vulnerability (challengers) and protective (buffers) factors also can be instrumental in fostering or hampering positive ontogenesis. Importantly, the extent of the influence exerted by more transient factors is likely to vary as a function of the developmental period during which they occur. Additionally, the same transient vulnerability factor may operate differently depending on the context in which it emerges. For example, sexual abuse perpetrated by a distant relative of a child who resides within a supportive and nurturant family is likely to be less detrimental than a similar event transpiring within the nuclear family. Similarly, the effects of parental job loss are likely to vary depending on the overall economic circumstances of the family. Examples such as these serve to emphasize the importance of considering the effects of vulnerability and protective factors in relation both to the developmental and social environmental context in which they occur. For any child, the influence exerted by specific vulnerability and protective factors will vary. Moreover, outcome will be affected by the dynamic balance that exists between risk and protective factors. Developmental maladaptation is more likely to occur when vulnerability and risk factors outweigh protective and buffering influences (Cicchetti 1989; Cicchetti & Schneider-Rosen, 1984, 1986), whereas adaptation is more likely when the converse is present (Cicchetti & Garmezy, 1993; Cicchetti & Rizley, 1981). Maladaptation and/or disorder are likely to be evidenced in those individuals where a pathological organization has evolved transactionally over the course of development and whose coping capacities and protective resources are unable to counter the influences of enduring vulnerabilities in conjunction with transient stressors (cf. Cicchetti & Rizley, 1981).

In such a conceptualization of risk for maladaptive development and/or psychopathological outcome, it is important to keep in mind that risk and vulnerability factors do not *cause* maladaptation, but rather that they are indicators of a complex matrix of processes and mechanisms that impact on individual development (cf. Rutter, 1990). According to a developmental psychopathology conceptualization, risk and vulnerability factors operate via their influences on competence or incompetence at progressive stages of development. Overall developmental outcome is affected not simply by the presence or absence of risk or vulnerability, but through the interplay that occurs between these factors and prior levels of adaptation (Cicchetti & Tucker, 1994; Sroufe, Egeland, & Kreutzer, 1990; Zigler & Glick, 1986).

An ecological/transactional framework

An ecological/transactional model serves as heuristic for understanding how multiple factors can influence children's development. According to such a perspective, an individual's environment is seen as being comprised of several co-occurring levels (Belsky, 1993; Bronfenbrenner, 1979; Cicchetti & Lynch, 1993). The influence of these levels operates both proximally and distally to the individual and, depending on how immediate the influence is, it may be more or less easily perceived as exerting direct influences on individual development. Specifically, more proximal influences are most readily evaluated as affecting ontogenic development. The two most distal levels of the environment include the *macrosystem,* which contains the beliefs and values of the culture, and the *exosystem,* which involves aspects of the community in which families and children reside. Other levels of the environment that exert more proximal influences on individual development include the *microsystem,* or the immediate setting in which the individual lives, typically the family, and *ontogenic development,* more specifically including factors within the person that contribute to development and adaptation.

Forces from each level of the environment are conceived of as mutually influencing entities that contribute to the outcomes of child development (cf. Sameroff

& Chandler, 1975). Factors present at one level of the ecology influence outcomes in surrounding levels, thereby determining the extent of risk posed to the individual. Interestingly, the ways in which children cope with the challenges presented by different levels of their ecologies are reflected in their own ontogenic development, which, in turn, affects their adaptation or maladaptation.

Researchers and policy advocates who have invested in understanding the effects of trauma and negative life experiences on children have increasingly turned their attention toward the examination of areas such as community and domestic violence, war, child maltreatment, parental divorce, and parental psychopathology and substance abuse (Cicchetti & Toth, 1993; Gerbner et al. 1980; Osofsky, 1995; Thompson & Wilcox, 1995). The application of an ecological/transactional framework is useful in elucidating how experiences such as these can exert a negative impact on children's development. A confluence of influences stemming from culture, community, and family, in conjunction with the prior developmental adaptation attained by the child, interact to influence child developmental outcome. Additionally, potentiating and compensatory factors associated with these life experiences are present at each level of the ecology and also influence the course of development. Occurrences in the various levels of the ecology act to increase or decrease the likelihood of a given event occurring (e.g., substance abuse, maltreatment, divorce), as well as affect occurrences within the microsystem. Although all levels of the ecology exert important influences on development, characteristics associated with the more proximal environment have the most direct effect on children's development. Research conducted within a developmental psychopathology framework can help to explain how aspects of the macro-and exosystem impact upon the more proximal, microsystemic environments that mediate the effects of the more distal ecological systems, thereby exerting a more direct influence on children's ultimate adaptation.

In order to examine the effects of various levels of the ecology on development, we next discuss how factors within the macro-, exo-, and microsystem relate to a variety of high-risk conditions and psychopathological disorders.

The macrosystem

The macrosystem encompasses those aspects of cultural values and beliefs that foster violence within nations, communities, and families. It is in the macrosystem that overarching values about family also are contained. Thus, the effects on children of occurrences such as war, maltreatment, or divorce can be mitigated or exacerbated by the overall societal view of these issues. Additionally, because resources and supports made available to those confronted with such stressors as violence are determined by cultural attitudes, the macrosystem can exert a significant impact on the adaptation of the individual.

The exosystem

The exosystem includes social structures such as the neighborhood, informal and formal support groups, employment opportunities, socioeconomic status, and the availability of services. The *mesosystem,* defined by Bronfenbrenner (1979) as reflecting interconnections among community settings with which the family interfaces, including schools, peer groups, churches, and employment settings, also is contained within the exosystem.

The exosystem is likely to assume a central role in affecting the individual's development when conditions such as community violence, maltreatment, substance abuse, and divorce are present. In examining the area of community violence, Richters and Martinez (1993b) found that a significant number of children who resided in violent neighborhoods had themselves been victims of violence. However, these children were two to four times more likely to have witnessed community violence than to have been victims of violence. Importantly, despite the fact that these children were residing in violent neighborhoods, had been exposed to high levels of community violence, and were experiencing associated symptoms of distress, community violence exposure levels were not predictive of adaptational failure or success. Rather, adaptation was related to characteristics of the children's homes. Specifically, the probability of adaptational failure rose significantly when children resided in unstable and/or unsafe homes. This investigation underscores the importance of caregiver functioning in moderating the effects of adverse life events and suggests that the more proximal microsystem need not be eroded by more distal exosystem influences.

In addition to the role of caregiver functioning, the availability and quality of schools, employment opportunities, and community support systems also are likely to affect the microsystems of children exposed to ecological stress. For example, if a maltreated child can attain support at school, the adverse sequelae of the maltreatment may be reduced (Cicchetti, Toth, & Hennessy, 1993; Lynch & Cicchetti, 1992). Similarly, during times of war, the supports available through the community can significantly buffer the potentially adverse consequences of the war experience (Cicchetti, Toth, & Lynch, 1993; Garbarino, Kostelny, & Dubrow, 1991).

The microsystem

In accord with Bronfenbrenner's conceptualization (1979), the microsystem is not limited to the developmental histories and psychological resources of the family. Rather, it encompasses any environmental setting that contains the developing person, such as the home, school, or work setting. This conceptualization, which extends beyond the immediate family context, allows for a more comprehensive incorporation of events in the community that are proximal to the developing child. For example, children who observe a shooting at their school have experienced an occurrence that is likely to affect their current and future development. Of course, the overall consequences of such an event will be influenced by the way in which the school, as well as the family, deals with the trauma.

The immediate family context plays a central role in determining how a given child will cope with adversity. Whether one is striving to understand the effects of parental psychopathology and substance abuse, divorce, community and intrafamilial violence, or war, if the home environment has not contributed to a positive level of adaptation prior to the inception of the stressor, then the child's ability to function adaptively in the face of the trauma is likely to be compromised. For example, if a child has experienced loving caregiving that has fostered a positive sense of self, the effects of parental divorce may be less traumatic than if the child grew up in a highly conflictual home in which marital discord precluded the provision of positive parenting. Overall, the family can provide a supportive function, or contribute further to the negative consequences associated with a traumatic event. The occurrence of sexual abuse, and issues such as whether or not the child is believed, and the provision of support subsequent to the revelation of the abuse, serve as yet another example of the role that the family can play in influencing child outcome. Similar scenarios occur in instances of parental psychopathology or substance abuse, where it is not the illness per se, but the impact that the illness exerts on parenting and the availability of other supports that will influence the child's ontogenic development in response to stressors.

Of course, the role of the family in affecting children's coping is often intimately related to the traumatic event that is experienced. For example, the probability of a maltreating family providing a support function is highly unlikely, whereas a family may be able to function adaptively during times of war, in instances of occurrences of community violence, or during divorce. To address the influence of the family on children's adaptation more fully, we briefly examine child maltreatment and parental depression as they affect parenting.

In maltreating families, disruptions in all aspects of family relationships are frequently present. Maltreating parents interact with their children less and display more negative affect toward their children than do nonmaltreating parents (Burgess & Conger, 1978). Additionally, anger and conflict are pervasive in maltreating families (Trickett & Susman, 1988). Moreover, husbands and wives in maltreating families are less warm and supportive, less satisfied with their spouses, and more aggressive and violent with their marital partners than are parents in nonabusive families (P. Howes & Cicchetti, 1993; Rosenbaum & O'Leary, 1981; Rosenberg, 1987; Straus, Gelles, & Steinmetz, 1980). Overall, family interactions in maltreating families are unsupportive and the family system is characterized by chaos and instability (Cicchetti & Howes, 1991). Thus, it is not surprising that pervasive family dysfunction compounds the experience of child maltreatment.

Dysfunctional parenting also has been linked to a number of difficulties experienced by children with depressed caregivers. Depressed parents have been described as more inconsistent, lax, and ineffective in their child management and discipline than nondepressed parents (Zahn-Waxler, Iannotti, Cummings, & Denham, 1990). Depressed caregivers also have been alternately described as less engaged and involved with their children (DeMulder, Tarullo, Klimes-Dougan, Free, & Radke-Yarrow, 1995), as well as more forceful in their use of control strategies (Fendrich, Warner, & Weissman, 1990). Overall, depressed caregivers appear to try to avoid conflict with their children by accommodating to child demands. When effects are made to set limits, however, depressed caregivers are less likely to reach a compromise with their children (Kochanska, Kuczynski, Radke-Yarrow, & Welsh, 1987).

Now that aspects of the macro-, exo-, and microsystems that can contribute to child maladaptation or resilience have been explored, we turn our attention specifically to the microsystemic influences of child maltreatment on ontogenic development.

Ontogenic development

It is in children's ontogenic development that the effects of maltreatment, and the environmental failure that maltreatment represents, can be seen. At the level of ontogenic development, the most critical determinant of eventual adaptation or maladaptation is the negotiation of the central tasks of each developmental period (Cicchetti, 1989). Although certain issues may be salient at particular periods in time and subsequently decrease in importance, each issue must be coordinated and integrated with the environment, as well as with subsequently emerging issues across the life-span (Cicchetti, 1993; Sroufe, 1979). As such, each new development builds on and incorporates previous developments. The manner in which these issues are handled plays a pivotal role in determining subsequent adaptation. While the previously described features of the macro-, exo-, and microsystems continue to transact with the individual to influence overall development, poor resolution of these issues ultimately may contribute to the development of psychopathology.

Thus, growing up in a maltreating family, an experience that deviates from the average expectable environment (cf. Scarr, 1992), impacts upon children's individual development. Our review is organized around ascertaining how maltreated children resolve some of the central developmental tasks of infancy and childhood with an emphasis placed on our work. Because each issue is operative throughout the life course, we begin with each task's period of ascendance as a salient issue and track what is known about each issue as it unfolds to become coordinated and integrated with later emerging developmental tasks.

Affect regulation and differentiation

Affect regulation is defined as the intra- and extraorganismic factors by which emotional arousal is redirected, controlled, modulated, and modified so that an individual can function adaptively in emotionally challenging situations (Cicchetti,

Ganiban, & Barnett, 1991; Thompson, 1990). Early parent–child interactions play an important role in the development of this emotional competency (Cicchetti & Schneider-Rosen, 1986; Kalin, Shelten, & Snowdon, 1993).

Unfortunately, maltreated children evidence numerous deficits in their emotional self-regulation. Because serotonin is the neurotransmitter involved in the fine tuning of arousal and aggression (Spoont, 1992), it is conceivable that maltreatment experiences bring about a dysregulation of the neuromodulating serotonergic system. Moreover, maltreated children exhibit distortions in the initial patterns of affect differentiation (Gaensbauer & Hiatt, 1984; Gaensbauer, Mrazek, & Harmon, 1981). Specifically, they display either excessive amounts of negative affect or, in contrast, blunted patterns of affect where they express neither positive nor negative emotions. Maltreated children also exhibit difficulties in the processing of emotional stimuli. Because maltreated children reveal problems in effectively modulating physiological arousal, these youngsters often have significant difficulties coping with emotionally stressful circumstances. Their dysregulated arousal and hypervigilant states seriously hinder their capacity to make rational assessments of stressful or ambiguous situations (Rieder & Cicchetti, 1989).

Other irregularities are observed in maltreated children's affective development. The facial expressions of 3- to 4-month-old physically abused infants reveal the early manifestation of a number of negative affects, including fear (Gaensbauer, 1980; Gaensbauer & Hiatt, 1984). This early emergence of fear in abused infants contrasts with the normal pattern seen in nonabused infants, where fear does not appear until approximately 8 to 9 months of age (Sroufe, 1995). It is possible that early maltreatment experiences accelerate the development of fear in infancy, and that this brings about corresponding neurobiological changes in the negative affect pathways in the brain (cf. Eisenberg, 1995). However, lacking the cognitive capacity at this early age to process fear-inducing stimuli adequately may create problems for infants as they attempt to modulate powerful negative affect. The early emergence of fear, in combination with the existence of distorted patterns of affective communication with their caregivers (Gaensbauer et al., 1981), may result in severe impairments in the regulation and organization of emotions for young maltreated children.

In addition to the affective anomalies found among maltreated infants, physically abused children also demonstrate later affect regulatory problems in the coping that they employ when they are confronted with interadult anger. For example, physically abused boys who observe simulated anger directed at their mothers by an adult female confederate experimenter evidence more aggression (e.g., physical and verbal expressions of anger directed toward the female experimenter), as well as more coping designed to minimize their mother's distress (e.g., helping mother, comforting mother) than do nonabused boys (Cummings, Hennessy, Rabideau, & Cicchetti, 1994). It appears that physically abused boys do not habituate to anger as a result of their history of being exposed to familial hostility, but rather that they are more aroused and angered by it, and more likely to try to stop it. In general, the hypervigilance and arousal in response to hostility seen among abused children might contribute to the development of aggressive behavior in them, especially if conflict in the home is chronic.

In a related line of inquiry, Hennessy, Rabideau, Cicchetti, and Cummings (1994) presented physically abused and nonabused boys with videotaped vignettes of adults in angry and friendly interactions. After viewing the vignettes, abused boys report experiencing more distress than nonabused boys in response to interadult hostility, especially when the hostility involves unresolved anger between adults. Moreover, physically abused boys described more fear in response to different forms of angry adult behavior. These results support a sensitization model in which repeated exposure to anger and familial violence leads to greater, rather than less, emotional reactivity. Similarly, the distress responses to interadult anger that abused children display may provide an early indication of an increased potential for developing internalizing problems among children exposed to high levels of familial violence.

Additional evidence about the affective coping strategies of maltreated children can be seen in studies of cognitive control functioning. Rieder and Cicchetti (1989) have found that maltreated children are more hypervigilant to aggressive stimuli and recall a greater number of distracting aggressive stimuli than do nonmaltreated children. Maltreated children also assimilate aggressive stimuli more readily even though this impairs their efficiency on cognitive control tasks. Hypervigilance and ready assimilation of aggressive stimuli may develop originally as an adaptive coping strategy in the maltreating environment, alerting the child to signs of imminent danger and keeping affects from rising so high that they would incapacitate the child. Although hypervigilance and quick assimilation of aggressive stimuli may emerge as an adaptive coping response in a maltreating environment, this strategy becomes less adaptive when children are faced with nonthreatening situations.

Evidence on affect regulatory abilities in maltreated youngsters also is being obtained in the physiological domain. Physiological and behavioral responses to maltreatment are expected to be interrelated and to lead children to make choices and respond to experiences in ways that foster pathological development (Cicchetti & Tucker, 1994). Even though we possess limited knowledge about the neurobiology of children who have grown up in a maltreating environment, information is accumulating on the functioning of the hypothalamic-pituitary-adrenocortical (HPA) system in maltreated children.

Although interest in the neuroendocrine correlates of maltreatment has increased, there are relatively few studies comparing neuroendocrine activity in maltreated and nonmaltreated children. Many of the studies that do exist have focused primarily on sexually abused girls and have been conducted in a clinical laboratory (see Trickett, Chapter 17, this volume). Several neuroendocrine studies of more heterogeneous groups of maltreated children have been carried out in complex social settings, a context that does not allow the same level of experimental control as that available in a clinical laboratory.

One such study, conducted by Hart, Gunnar, and Cicchetti (1995) examined the salivary cortisol concentrations and social behavior (via observations and teacher reports) of maltreated and nonmaltreated children. The maltreated youngsters were studied while they attended a therapeutic preschool for abused and neglected children, and the nonmaltreated children were studied while they were enrolled in a preschool that served economically disadvantaged families. Each child's cortisol values over a number of days were used to compute measures of basal activity (median cortisol) and reactivity (ratio of quartile ranges). A child with a reactive HPA system would be expected to have a larger positive than negative quartile range.

Hart and colleagues (1995) discovered that median cortisol was not significantly correlated with social behavior measures. Moreover, these investigators found that cortisol reactivity was positively correlated with social competence and negatively correlated with shy/internalizing behavior. Furthermore, maltreated children exhibited less cortisol reactivity than did comparison children. Maltreated children also scored lower in social competence and higher in shy/internalizing and acting out/ externalizing behaviors. In additional analyses, maltreated children failed to show elevations in cortisol on days of high versus low social conflict in the classroom. Social competence also was found to correlate positively with cortisol levels on high conflict days. Taken in tandem, the results suggest a reduction in cortisol reactivity in maltreated children related to the impairment in social competence frequently noted among these children (cf. Kaufman & Cicchetti, 1989; Trickett, Chapter 17, this volume).

Hart, Gunnar, and Cicchetti (1996) also examined the effects of maltreatment on physiological and affective functioning in a large group of school-age maltreated and nonmaltreated children attending a summer day camp setting. These investigators discovered that maltreated children had slightly elevated afternoon cortisol concentrations, whereas their morning concentrations did not differ significantly from those of nonmaltreated children. Neither clinical levels of depression, nor internalizing or externalizing problems were predictive of these elevated afternoon values. Depression among maltreated children was, however, associated with altered activity of the HPA system. Specifically, depressed maltreated children displayed lower morning cortisol concentrations compared with nondepressed maltreated children and were more likely to show a rise rather than the expected decrease in cortisol from morning to afternoon. In addition, there was no evidence that depressed, nonmaltreated children exhibited this change in diurnal cortisol activity.

Formation of attachment relationships

The capacity for preferential attachment originates during early affect regulation experiences and interactions with the caregiver. The preattachment parent–child environment helps to shape children's physiological regulation and biobehavioral patterns of response (Gunnar & Nelson, 1994; Hofer, 1987; Pipp & Harmon, 1987). More overt manifestations of attachment become salient near the end of the first year of life when infants derive feelings of security from their caregivers and use them as a base from which to explore the environment (Sroufe, 1995). Parent–child dyadic interactions, characterized by relatedness and synchrony, and appropriate affective interchange are associated with successful adaptation during this stage of development. The knowledge that a caregiver is reliable and responsive also is critical because the absence of contingent responsiveness on the part of the caregiver can impede infants' ability to develop feelings of security in their primary attachment relationship (Sroufe & Waters, 1977). Ultimately, the task for the child is to be able to enter into a goal-corrected partnership where the caregiver and the child share internal states and goals (Bowlby, 1969/1982; Cicchetti, Cummings, Greenberg, & Marvin, 1990). Based on the relationship history with their primary caregivers, children form representational models of attachment figures, of themselves, and of themselves in relation to others (Bowlby, 1969/1982). Through these mental representational models, children's affects, cognitions, and expectations about future interactions are organized and carried forward into subsequent relationships (Sroufe & Fleeson, 1986, 1988).

A number of studies, using the Strange Situation (Ainsworth & Wittig, 1969), have shown that maltreated children are more likely to form insecure attachments with their caregivers than are nonmaltreated children. Using traditional attachment classification schemes (cf. Ainsworth, Blehar, Waters, & Wall, 1978), approximately two-thirds of maltreated children have insecure attachments to their mothers (either anxious avoidant Type A or anxious resistant Type C), while the remaining one-third of these children have secure attachments (Type B). The reverse pattern is observed in nonmaltreated children (Youngblade & Belsky, 1989). In addition, both cross-sectional and longitudinal studies that employ only the traditional ABC attachment typology reveal that, with increasing age, maltreated infants' attachments are more likely to be classified as insecure-avoidant (see, e.g., Schneider-Rosen, Braunwald, Carlson, & Cicchetti, 1985; Youngblade & Belsky, 1989).

A number of investigators have observed patterns of attachment behavior that do not fit smoothly into the original attachment rating system. For example, unlike infants from nonrisk samples who commonly form one of the three typical patterns of attachment, infants from high-risk and maltreating populations often lack organized strategies for dealing with separations from and reunions with their caregiver. Main and Solomon (1990) describe this pattern of attachment as disorganized/disoriented (Type D). In addition, these infants display other bizarre symptoms in the presence of their caregiver such as interrupted movements and expressions, dazing, freezing and stilling behaviors, and apprehension.

Distortions in affect regulation may play a role in the disorganization found in maltreated children's attachment relationships. The early emergence of fear that is elicited in these children may paralyze or severely impair maltreated children's ability to regulate and organize their affects when their attachment system is activated (Cicchetti & Lynch, 1993). In fact, frightened and frightening behavior associated with the caregiver is believed to be a key factor in the emergence of disorganized attachments (Main & Hesse, 1990). When fear is connected to the caregiver, the child in effect loses the attachment figure as a secure base and a haven of safety, and the result can be a disorganized/disoriented orientation toward the attachment relationship with the caregiver. This type of loss is a devastating psychological insult and may lead to long-term psychobiological impairments, such as those found in posttraumatic stress disorder (PTSD), dissociative disorder, and multiple personality disorder (Cicchetti, 1991; van der Kolk, 1987).

Within a revised attachment classification scheme that includes the atypical Type D pattern, maltreated infants demonstrate a preponderance of disorganized/disoriented attachments. Approximately 80% of maltreated infants exhibit disorganized attachments (Carlson, Cicchetti, Barnett, & Braunwald, 1989; Lyons-Ruth, Repacholi, McLeod, & Silva, 1991). This is in comparison to only 20% of demographically matched nonmaltreated infants having disorganized attachments. Moreover, maltreated children show substantial stability of insecure attachment, whereas, over time, securely attached maltreated children generally develop insecure attachments (Cicchetti & Barnett, 1991; Schneider-Rosen et al., 1985). In contrast, for nonmaltreated children, secure attachments are highly stable, whereas insecure attachments are more likely to change (Lamb, Thompson, Gardner, & Charnov, 1985).

Throughout the preschool years, maltreated children continue to be more likely than nonmaltreated children to be insecurely attached (Crittenden, 1988; Trickett, Chapter 17, this volume). As maltreated children grow older, though, it appears less certain that they will have atypical patterns of attachment. In an investigation of the attachments of preschool-aged maltreated children, Cicchetti and Barnett (1991) discovered that 30-month-old children who had been maltreated were significantly more likely to evidence atypical patterns of attachment than were nonmaltreated children. However, even though approximately one-third of 36-month- and 48-month-old maltreated children manifested these atypical patterns, this was not significantly greater than the proportion of same-aged nonmaltreated children who have such patterns.

In a study of maltreated school-aged children, a preponderance of nonoptimal (i.e., insecure) patterns of relatedness was obtained, indicating continued disturbance in the representations of their relationships (Lynch & Cicchetti, 1991). Lynch and Cicchetti (1991) also found that approximately 30% of maltreated children between the ages of 7 and 13 years report having a "confused" pattern of relatedness to their mothers. This pattern of relatedness is characterized by children reporting that they feel warm and secure with their mothers despite not feeling close to them. The identification of a confused pattern of relatedness may be consistent with our prior discussion that some maltreated children manifest a basic confusion, disorganization, or disorientation in how they mentally represent their relationships with their mothers. The finding of significantly more confused patterns of relatedness among maltreated school-aged children than nonmaltreated agemates suggests that distortions in maltreated children's relationships with, and mental representations of, their caregivers may persist up through the preadolescent years at rates comparable with those during the preschool years, but at lower rates than those observed during infancy.

The development of an autonomous self

The infant's self-concept is believed to emerge from within the context of caregiving relationships (Mahler, Pine, & Bergman, 1975; Ryan, 1991; Sroufe, 1990; Stern, 1989). In fact, attachment security to mother is associated with more complex self-knowledge in children aged 12 to 16 months (Pipp, Easterbrooks, & Harmon, 1992). Even among maltreated children, attachment security is associated with an increased likelihood of an early onset of visual self-recognition (Schneider-Rosen & Cicchetti, 1984), higher linguistic functioning (Gersten, Coster, Schneider-Rosen, Carlson, & Cicchetti, 1986), an absence of internal-state language deficits (Beeghly & Cicchetti, 1994), and higher levels of perceived competence (Toth & Cicchetti, 1996) in comparison with insecurely attached maltreated children.

As development proceeds and the task of self-management begins to move away from the context of the caregiver–infant relationship into the realm of autonomous functioning, the toddler becomes increasingly invested in self-management because of the development of new capabilities, as well as a more developed understanding of self and other. Increasingly during this period, self-regulation and the regulation of affect are transferred from the caregiver–child dyad to the child alone. The caregiver's sensitivity to, and tolerance of, the toddler's strivings for autonomy, in addition to the caregiver's ability to set age-appropriate limits, are necessary for the successful resolution of this issue. Caregivers who feel rejected as a result of their toddler's increasing independence, or who are stressed by their child's new demands, may inhibit the emergence of autonomy in their children (Rogosch, Cicchetti, Shields, & Toth, 1995).

As self-organization is brought forward to the new tasks of development, a number of aspects of maltreated children's self-development are likely to be affected, with possible implications for their subsequent interpersonal relationships. Studies on the self-recognition of maltreated children provide some insight into their emerging self-concept. Whereas there are no deficits in maltreated infants' ability to recognize their rouge-marked selves in a mirror, they are more likely than nonmaltreated infants to display neutral or negative affect upon visual self-recognition (Schneider-Rosen & Cicchetti, 1984, 1991). Other delays in maltreated children's self-systems have been noted as well. For example, maltreated children talk less about themselves and about their internal states than do nonmaltreated children (Beeghly & Cicchetti, 1994). Maltreated children with insecure attachments display the most compromised internal state language (Beeghly & Cicchetti, 1994). The ability to talk about internal states and feelings is a development of late toddlerhood that is believed to reflect toddlers' emergent self–other understanding and to be fundamental to the regulation of social interaction (Beeghly & Cicchetti, 1994). Maltreated children's negative feelings about themselves and their inability to talk about their own activities and states may impede their ability to engage in successful social relationships.

In particular, maltreated children are most reluctant to talk about their negative internal states (Beeghly & Cicchetti, 1994). This finding is corroborated by studies revealing that maltreated children may actually inhibit negative affect, especially in the context of their relationship with their primary caregiver (Crittenden & DiLalla, 1988; Lynch & Cicchetti, 1991). It is possible that some maltreated children adopt a strategy designed to suppress the expression of their own negative feelings in order to avoid eliciting adverse responses from their caregivers (Cicchetti, 1991). Whereas this approach may be adaptive in the context of a maltreating relationship, it can become maladaptive and lead to incompetence in other interpersonal contexts such as the peer and school arenas. Additionally, the inability of maltreated children to identify and discuss their own distress may play a major role in these children's difficulties in displaying empathy toward their peers (Main & George, 1985; Troy & Sroufe, 1987).

In general, school-aged physically abused children show deficits in self-esteem when compared with nonabused children. However, consistent with the work of Katz and Zigler (1967), there appear to be different patterns of findings for children of different ages. Young maltreated children actually express an exaggerated sense of self-competence in comparison to nonmaltreated children (Vondra, Barnett, & Cicchetti, 1989). By the age of 8 to 9 years, maltreated children perceive themselves as being less competent than do nonmaltreated children. Teachers' ratings of these children's competence indicate that the older maltreated children's perceptions are more accurate and in accord with their own ratings. Initially, young maltreated children's inflated sense of self may help them to gain feelings of competence in the midst of family relationships that are chaotic and uncontrollable. As maltreated children mature, enter the school arena, and are forced to make social comparisons between themselves and others, they begin to make more negative (and accurate) self-appraisals. These negative appraisals likely become internalized as part of their self-representations. Feeling less competent in comparison to others may exert a further negative impact on maltreated children's ability to interact with others successfully. Evidence of the presence of exaggerated and overinflated as well as impaired perceptions of competence (Vondra et al., 1989) and denial of authentic needs and feelings has contributed to the belief that maltreated children are prone to develop a "false self." According to this conceptualization, maltreated children often act compulsively compliant with their caregivers and display insincere positive affect (Crittenden & DiLalla, 1988).

In the most extreme cases, maltreatment experiences may lead to basic and severe disturbances in self-definition and self-representation. Utilizing a narrative story stem completion task, Toth, Cicchetti, Macfie, and Emde (1995) investigated the interrelations among preschool-age maltreated youngsters' maternal representations, self-representations, and relationships with an examiner. Maltreated children differed substantially from nonmaltreated children in terms of their maternal and self-representations. Specifically, maltreated preschoolers had more negative representations of maternal figures and of themselves; moreover, as would be expected based on these negative representations, maltreated children also were more controlling and less responsive to the examiner. However, these differences between maltreated and nonmaltreated children obfuscated some of the more complex differences found among subtypes of maltreated children. While the data from physically abused and neglected youngsters generally mirror that obtained for the overall maltreated sample, sexually abused youngsters exhibited a pattern that differed from that of physically abused and neglected children. In particular, sexually abused children revealed a high level of both positive and negative self-representations. The findings that positive maternal and self-representations of the sexually abused children did not co-occur with a positive relationship with the examiner is equally interesting, and further suggest a disorganization of the self-system among these children. The findings with regard to sexually abused children also are consistent with research on split self-representations in sexually abused adolescents.

Calverley, Fischer, and Ayoub (1994) investigated the perceptions and representations that sexually abused adolescents had of themselves and their worlds. Calverley and her colleagues found that the sexually abused adolescents attributed significantly more negative self-perceptions to their core selves, and displayed greater "polarized affective splitting" (e.g., described the self as "happy," "sad," "lonely," and "good" in the absence of any obvious conflict) than did non–sexually abused adolescent females. Despite their differences in self-representation, the sexually abused adolescents revealed no delays in their level of self-development and, in fact, operated on the same level or better than their non–sexually abused counterparts. Consistent with the viewpoint of developmental psychopathologists, the experience of trauma did not necessarily result in developmental delay. Rather, it eventuated in an alternative and unique path of adaptation to the adolescents' extreme experiences and not to a developmental fixation or regression to an earlier developmental level.

The formation of peer relationships

Another important task of ontogenic development is the formation of effective peer relationships. Because of their negative early relationship histories, peer relationships and friendships may provide an important opportunity for promoting positive adaptation in maltreated children.

Unfortunately, maltreated children's relationships with their peers typically mirror the maladaptive representational models that they carry with them into this task of development. In general, maltreated children exhibit more disturbed patterns of interaction with peers than do nonmaltreated children. They interact less with their peers and they display fewer prosocial behaviors than do nonmaltreated children (Mueller & Silverman, 1989). A number of investigations have demonstrated that maltreated children display general maladjustment and incompetence in interactions with their peers (Kaufman & Cicchetti, 1989; Rogosch & Cicchetti, 1994). In addition, physically abused children are less popular with their peers, show less positive reciprocity in their interactions, and have social networks that are more insular and atypical, with higher levels of negativity (Rogosch & Cicchetti, 1994; Salzinger, Feldman, Hammer, & Rosario, 1993). Maltreated children also express greater mistrust of peers (Bernath, Feshbach, & Gralinski, 1993). This lack of trust is related to maltreated youngsters' diminished concern about affect and future interpersonal relationships, somewhat heightened concern about the past (Bernath et al., 1993), and the display of less intimacy in interactions with friends (Parker & Herrera, in press).

Overall, two main themes regarding maltreated children's relationships with their peers emerge from the literature (Mueller & Silverman, 1989). One set of findings indicates that maltreated children, particularly physically abused children, show heightened levels of physical and verbal aggression in their interactions with peers. Another set of results demonstrates that there are high degrees of withdrawal from and avoidance of peer interactions among maltreated children, especially those who have been neglected (Mueller & Silverman, 1989). In many cases, it appears that this social withdrawal is an active strategy of avoidance on the part of maltreated children, and not merely a passive orientation toward peer interaction.

Rogosch and Cicchetti (1994) have identified a subgroup of maltreated and non-maltreated children who are perceived by their peers as demonstrating a combination of aggressive and withdrawn behavior. In particular, maltreated children who are perceived as relatively high on both aggression and withdrawal by their peers evidence substantially lower social effectiveness than is the case for nonmaltreated comparison youngsters. This co-occurrence of aggression and withdrawal may represent the continued operation of disorganized representational models of relationships carried forward from the attachment relationship into new social encounters, resulting in disturbances in social adaptation. The aggressive-withdrawn strategy may be used protectively to diminish the anticipated negative aspects of interpersonal relations; aggression may be employed to terminate perceived interpersonal threats while isolation may be utilized to avoid threats.

Adaptation to school

As children grow older, they increasingly begin to function in contexts that extend beyond the home and family. School is the major extrafamilial environment in which children operate, beginning in early childhood and extending through adolescence. In the school setting, children are exposed to a new community of unfamiliar peers and adults, and they are presented with a new set of context specific challenges. In particular, integration into the peer group, acceptable performance in the classroom, and appropriate motivational orientations for achievement are all part of this stage-salient developmental task.

Once again, however, maltreated children are at risk for an unsuccessful resolution of this central issue of development. For example, Eckenrode and his colleagues have shown that maltreated children, in comparison with nonmaltreated children, perform worse on standardized tests, obtain lower grades, and are more likely to repeat a grade (Eckenrode, Laird, & Doris, 1993). In addition, they receive significantly more discipline referrals and suspensions than nonmaltreated children (Eckenrode et al., 1993). Moreover, Rogosch and Cicchetti (1994) found that teachers consistently perceive maltreated children as evidencing greater maladaptation in social functioning than nonmaltreated children. Specifically, teachers evaluate maltreated children as less socially competent, as less socially accepted by their peers, and as displaying higher levels of behavioral disturbance, particularly externalizing problems. Classroom peers also distinguish maltreated children as more rejected or isolated by peer groups. Physically abused children show the greatest differentiation from their nonmaltreated peers.

An especially important factor in resolving the task of adaptation to school may be "secure readiness to learn." Aber, Allen, Carlson, and Cicchetti (1989) have proposed that effectance motivation, which is the intrinsic desire to deal competently with one's environment (see Lepper, Sethi, Dialdin, & Drake, Chapter 2, this volume; Zigler, Abelson, Trickett, & Seitz, 1982) and successful relations with novel adults (i.e., relations that are characterized by neither dependency nor wariness – cf. Zigler & Balla, 1982) are important factors related to children's being able to adapt to their first major out-of-home environment. "Secure readiness to learn" is characterized by high effectance motivation and low dependency. Maltreated children consistently score lower than comparison children on secure readiness to learn (Aber et al., 1989). Secure readiness to learn appears to represent a dynamic balance between establishing secure relationships with adults and feeling free to explore the environment in ways that will promote cognitive competence. The findings of Aber and his colleagues with school-age children are particularly compelling because the results are congruent with prior research on how maltreatment affects development in infants and toddlers. At both of these developmental periods, maltreatment interferes with the balance between the motivation to establish secure relationships with adults and the motivation to explore the world in competency-promoting ways.

In efforts to examine the links between relationship patterns and school adaptation, Toth and Cicchetti (1996b) studied a sample of maltreated and demographically comparable nonmaltreated children. These investigators found that the security that a child experienced in relation to his or her mother, in interaction with maltreatment status, significantly affected school functioning. Nonmaltreated children who reported secure patterns of relatedness to their mothers exhibited less externalizing symptomatology, more ego resilience, and fewer school record risk factors (e.g., attendance problems, poor achievement test performance, suspensions, failure in 50% of courses, grade retention) than did maltreated children who reported insecure patterns of relatedness. Additionally, nonmaltreated children with secure patterns of relatedness to their mothers exhibited more positive adaptation in school than did nonmaltreated children who reported insecure patterns of relatedness. For maltreated children, the positive effects of secure relatedness on school functioning were evident only in school record data, suggesting that a positive relationship with a maltreating parent may actually exert a negative impact on some aspects of school adaptation.

Maladaptation: The emergence of behavior problems and psychopathology

As opposed to what is expected in response to an average expectable environment, the ecological conditions associated with maltreatment set in motion a probabilistic path of ontogenesis for maltreated children that is characterized by an increased likelihood of failure on many of the stage-salient issues of development. These failures may be isolated to particular domains of functioning, or they may occur in combination with failures in other domains. Specifically, maltreated children are likely to exhibit atypical physiological responsiveness, difficulties in affect differentiation and regulation, dysfunctional attachment relationships, anomalies in self–system processes, problematic peer relationships, and trouble adapting to school. These repeated developmental disruptions create a profile of relatively enduring vulnerability factors that places maltreated children at high risk for future maladaptation. Although not all maltreated children who have trouble successfully resolving stage-salient issues will develop psychopathology, let alone the same form of psychopathology, later disturbances in functioning are likely to occur.

In addition to increased rates of adjustment problems, studies of maltreated children reveal a greater prevalence of psychiatric symptoms and diagnoses than is observed in nonmaltreated children. Maltreated children exhibit a significantly higher incidence of attention deficit hyperactivity disorder, oppositional disorder, and posttraumatic stress disorder (PTSD) than do nonmaltreated children (Famularo, Kischerff, & Fenton, 1992). Child interviews reveal that maltreated children present a significant incidence of psychotic symptomatology, as well as personality and adjustment disorders. Parent interviews assessing child symptomatology also show a greater incidence of conduct and mood disorders among maltreated children (Famularo et al., 1992). In general, maltreatment, especially physical and sexual abuse, is related to a number of psychiatric complaints in childhood and adulthood, including panic disorders, anxiety disorders, depression, eating disorders, somatic complaints, dissociation and hysterical symptoms, sexual dysfunction, and borderline personality disorder (Cicchetti & Olsen, 1990; Kendall-Tackett, Williams, & Finkelhor, 1993; Putnam & Trickett, 1993).

Many studies show evidence of more depressive symptomatology in maltreated children than in nonmaltreated children (Sternberg et al., 1993; Toth, Manly, & Cicchetti, 1992). Moreover, numerous maltreated children meet diagnostic criteria for major depression and/or dysthymia (Kaufman, 1991). Various factors appear to mediate the impact of maltreatment on depression, including the subtype of maltreatment experienced, children's patterns of relatedness to their mother, their social supports and stressful life events, their attributional styles, and their psychophysiological responsivity (Hart et al., 1996; Kaufman, 1991; Toth & Cicchetti, 1996a).

As knowledge on the sequelae of child maltreatment has burgeoned, investigators have become increasingly interested in examining the links between maltreatment and psychopathology. The aforementioned findings of increased depressive symptomatology in maltreated children, taken in conjunction with studies documenting insecure attachment relationships among maltreated children, suggest that insecure attachment relationships and the resulting negative representational models of the self and of the self in relation to others may be a central mechanism contributing to the emergence of disturbances in children who have been maltreated (Toth et al., 1992). In fact, investigators are directing increased attention toward elucidating the effects of various types of maltreatment experiences on the etiology of self-disorders.

Specifically, considerable effort has been directed toward examining the effects of sexual abuse on self-pathology. With respect to long-term consequences of childhood sexual abuse, a number of adult psychiatric outcomes have been identified, including borderline personality disorder, eating disorders, PTSD, dissociative disorder, multiple personality disorder, somatization disorder, and substance abuse (see Putnam, 1995; Putnam & Trickett, 1993). Research is less clear regarding the acute impact of childhood sexual abuse, with as many as half of sexually abused children seeming to be asymptomatic on initial evaluation (Kendall-Tackett et al., 1993). Of those children evidencing problems, common symptoms include sexualized behavior, PTSD, fears, depression, low self-esteem, and behavior problems.

Toth and Cicchetti (1996) applied an attachment theory–based framework to examining the possible mechanisms contributing to increased depressive symptomatology in sexually abused, physically abused, and neglected children. These investigators found that maltreated children with confused patterns of relatedness to mother reported more depressive symptomatology than maltreated children with optimal/adequate (i.e., secure) relatedness to mother. Especially noteworthy was the finding that sexually abused children who had confused patterns of relatedness to their mothers reported extremely elevated levels of depressive symptomatology that were consistent with depression considered to be of clinical significance. These results contrasted markedly with the low level of depressive symptomatology endorsed by sexually abused children who reported optimal/adequate relatedness to mother. Importantly, the results of this investigation are a step toward elucidating the possible mechanisms that may account for the heterogeneity in functioning (i.e., multifinality) among samples of maltreated children. Because developmental psychopathologists must grapple with the heterogeneity of outcome *among* maltreated children, efforts to identify moderating and mediating factors that may be contributing to diverse outcome are critical.

Resilient outcomes

The notion that an average expectable environment is necessary for species-typical development suggests that competent outcomes in maltreated children are highly improbable due to wide-ranging disturbances in the maltreatment ecology (Scarr, 1992). However, whereas there is documented risk for maladaptation associated with maltreatment, the absence of an average expectable environment does not necessarily condemn maltreated children to negative developmental outcomes later in life. Despite the relatively low probability of adaptive outcomes for maltreated children, individuals' inherent self-righting tendencies (Waddington, 1942, 1957), in combination with the presence of any additional intraorganismic as well as environmental protective mechanisms or factors, may result in some maltreated children achieving developmental competence.

In an investigation of resilience in school-aged children, Cicchetti, Rogosch, Lynch, and Holt (1993) discovered that maltreated children as a group show lower overall competence across multiple areas of adaptation than nonmaltreated children. However, whereas more maltreated children than nonmaltreated children exhibited low levels of competence, an equal proportion of maltreated and nonmaltreated children demonstrated moderate to high levels of competence. Ego resiliency, ego control, and self-esteem have been found to predict individual differences in competent functioning in these children. In particular, ego resiliency, ego overcontrol, and positive self-esteem account for significant amounts of variance in the adaptive functioning of maltreated children. In contrast, only ego resiliency and positive self-esteem contribute to adaptation in nonmaltreated children. This finding of a differential contribution of ego control for the two groups in predicting adaptive or resilient functioning suggests that ego overcontrol may serve a protective function for maltreated children. A reserved, controlled approach to the environment may help these children to be more attuned to adapting to the adverse conditions of their home environments, and may protect them from being targets of continued maltreatment (cf. Werner, 1993). Clearly, pulling back from conflict in the family, detaching from high-intensity affect in the family, and being compliant with the wishes of one's caregiver all can help one to escape abuse and/or to attain competent adaptation.

Lessons for normal and abnormal development

Developmental psychopathologists believe that it is possible to learn more about the normal functioning of individuals by studying their pathology and, likewise, more about their pathology by studying their normal condition (Burack, Chapter

7, this volume; Cicchetti, 1984, 1990; Rutter, 1986; Sroufe & Rutter, 1984). To theorize about development without considering the deviations that might be expected from prominent and wide-ranging intra- and extraorganismic disturbances, as well as the transactions that occur among them, would result in incomplete and ambiguous accounts of ontogenesis. The study of child maltreatment provides researchers with an excellent opportunity to examine such developmental deviations and the ecological disturbances that are associated with them (Cicchetti, 1996).

There are numerous lessons about development that can be learned through the study of child maltreatment. For example, adopting an ecological-transactional approach toward understanding normal development may help to organize current thinking about ontogenesis and its multiple influences, as well as to guide future research. As applied to the study of maltreatment, an ecological-transactional model of development points out that factors from many levels of the individual's ecology are operating simultaneously to influence ontogeny and adaptation. It emphasizes the linkages among the various psychological and biological domains of development, and stresses that factors internal and external to the individual continually affect each other and influence the direction of the individual's developmental pathway.

By studying the effects of severe environmental disturbances (such as maltreatment) on individual development, it may be possible to examine processes that normally are so subtle and gradual that they are not observed (Chomsky, 1968; Cicchetti & Sroufe, 1976; Lenneberg, 1967). For example, through investigating the neurobiological development of children who have not received a benign rearing environment, such as youngsters who have been maltreated, the impact that caregiving experiences can exert on brain structure, function, and organization can be elucidated (cf. Cicchetti & Tucker, 1994; Eisenberg, 1995).

Furthermore, the kind of ecological-transactional approach that has been applied to child maltreatment allows researchers to focus on periods of developmental transition, and on how vulnerability and protective processes associated with each of these transitions operate for different children (Masten, 1989). In particular, it is clear from studies of maltreated children that failure on the major tasks of development results in cumulative risk for future maladaptation and psychopathology. Additionally, there is evidence for various critical periods in development associated with different caregiving experiences. This idea is supported by the different experience-dependent effects that emerge when maltreatment occurs at different points in development (Cicchetti & Tucker, 1994). Overall, the study of child maltreatment provides a good initial test of the ecological-transactional model of development. However, additional theory and model testing needs to be carried out on other high-risk and mentally disordered samples.

Research on child maltreatment also has shed light on several putative mechanisms of development. As has been discussed, maltreated children's emerging patterns of physiological responsiveness play a role in their subsequent biobehavioral organization. These early patterns of responsiveness and organization are important factors in shaping the nature of children's interactions with the environment and, as a result, in influencing their developmental trajectories.

Representational models also are believed to be a mechanism in the continuity and coherence of individual development. Research with maltreated children has helped to inform us about the nature and function of these models. For example, there is evidence that people activate both specific and generalized representational models of themselves and others as they deal with their interpersonal environment (Bretherton, 1985, 1987). Maltreated children may be predisposed to employing generalized models that are closed to the processing of new information (Crittenden & DiLalla, 1988; C. Howes & Segal, 1993; Lynch & Cicchetti, 1991). This preconscious cognitive strategy of utilizing generalized or closed representational models may be used as a defense to protect maltreated children from having to deal with the negative and angry affects that are characteristic of their family interactions. Rather than openly evaluating and adjusting their representational models on the basis of new interpersonal information, the models of maltreated children may be more defensive in nature, thus closing these children off to new experiences with caregivers and nonfamily members. However, such a strategy may be maladaptive in other contexts, because it inhibits maltreated children from incorporating alternative information about themselves and others. If this is true, then it would suggest that having representational models that are open to new information, and that being able to appropriately employ both generalized and specific models, might be associated with more competent development in normal children. Children's representational models also influence the manner in which they process social information more generally. Evidence of this can be seen in the hypervigilance maltreated children display in attending to threatening stimuli (Rieder & Cicchetti, 1989) and in their imputing aggressive intent to ambiguous acts (Dodge, Pettit, & Bates, 1994).

Research on child maltreatment also informs, and can be informed by, information regarding the significant functions of normal parenting (Rogosch et al., 1995). The specific acts and omissions that define child maltreatment are salient features of maltreated children's microsystems (Aber & Zigler, 1981; Barnett, Manly, & Cicchetti, 1993). It is in this immediate context of deviant parenting that maltreated children's atypical development takes shape. Closer analysis of the maltreating caregiving environment and its links with poor developmental outcomes can shed light on the protective factors and processes associated with appropriate, normal parenting.

Finally, studies of resilience in maltreated children provide information about the multiple possible pathways of development. To begin, there is evidence for the principles of both equifinality and multifinality (von Bertalanffy, 1968; Cicchetti & Rogosch, 1996) in maltreated children's attempts at adaptation. Despite having different specific experiences, many maltreated children exhibit similar failures in the tasks of development (i.e., equifinality). On the other hand, not all maltreated children are equally affected by their experiences, with some children displaying resilient outcomes and the rest exhibiting developmental incompetence (i.e., multifinality). Examination of maltreated children's development and struggles with adaptation teaches us about the range and variability of individual response to challenge and adversity. Cases of maltreated children who succeed at particular tasks of development (such as forming a secure attachment) or who otherwise achieve competent levels of adaptation teach us about the self-righting properties inherent to development that result in a type of canalization of species-typical outcomes despite poor quality care (Sameroff & Chandler, 1975; Scarr, 1992; Waddington, 1957). Conversely, findings that indicate the extreme rarity with which maltreated children display resilient outcomes point out some of the real constraints on children's self-righting abilities.

Conclusion and social policy implications

In this chapter we have utilized a developmental psychopathology perspective to examine risk and resilience during childhood and adolescence. We first discussed aspects of the social ecology more broadly, including the macro-, exo-, and micro-systems. Examples were provided from a number of high risk conditions, including parental divorce, persistent poverty, domestic violence, child maltreatment, parental psychopathology, and substance abuse. We then focused more specifically on a microsystemic occurrence, child maltreatment, in order to elucidate the effects of aberrant parenting on ontogenesis. Finally, we discussed the importance of work on the consequences of child maltreatment for informing normal developmental theory. We would be remiss, however, not to explore the implications of work on the sequelae of child maltreatment for advocacy efforts and for social policy development and implementation.

The research reported in this chapter clearly elucidates the potentially devastating effects of residing within a maltreating, dysfunctional family. Moreover, the ability of the microsystem to mitigate against the effects of more distal ecologies also was discussed. Thus, the importance of fostering adaptive parenting by supporting vulnerable families cannot be minimized.

Despite the pervasive rhetoric about the importance of "family," current political attitudes and fiscal conservatism threaten to erode many of the gains that have been made in helping families to parent effectively. This troubling state of affairs is illustrated graphically by the fact that the United States was one of the last Western nations to ratify the United Nations "International Bill of Rights for Children," a document endorsed by 159 member states of the United Nations General Assembly in 1989.

While fiscal reforms certainly may be necessary in order to stem overspending, such initiatives must consider the effects of reducing supports available to impoverished, isolated families. So-called entitlements, if eliminated, must be replaced with programs designed to empower and educate parents who have historically been welfare dependent. Moreover, the effects of any social action on the children who reside within such families must be considered carefully.

Decades of research have demonstrated the importance of providing early intervention to preschool children who reside within disadvantaged families (Meisels & Shonkoff, 1990; Zigler & Valentine, 1979; see also Luthar, Chapter 20, this volume). However, despite the preponderance of evidence on the value of early intervention, it is the children most in need who are in the minority with respect to the receipt of such services. For example, in 1986 50% of 3-year-olds and 67% of 4-year-olds residing in families with incomes of $35,000 or more attended preschools. This contrasts dramatically with the 16% of 3-year-olds and 38% of 4-year-olds enrolled in preschools from families with incomes under $10,000 (National Center for Children in Poverty, 1990). Moreover, despite the potential of schools to serve as a resource for children and families that can far exceed the academic arena, partnerships among schools, families, and the mental health community continue to be rare. Zigler's vision of the school of the 21st century (Zigler, 1989; Zigler & Ennis, 1989), where a system to integrate formal schooling, child care, and family education and support was proposed, is far from fruition, though the dawn of the next century is near.

Equally disconcerting has been the reluctance of the United States Congress to support the continuation of the Child Abuse and Treatment Act (CAPTA), initially enacted in 1974. CAPTA was charged with authorizing the provision of financial assistance for identifying, preventing, and treating child abuse and neglect, as well as with supporting the creation of the National Center on Child Abuse and Neglect, an agency developed to provide research, data collection, information dissemination, and coordination activities related to child maltreatment. While other federal institutions may be charged with assuming some of these responsibilities, the possible demise of the first legislative effort designed specifically to protect children from maltreatment should be of considerable concern to all individuals who are committed to fostering positive child development. Although cost-containing acts such as this may provide some immediate financial relief, the long-term consequences are likely to be far more costly in terms of the lost productivity and the extensive needs of the children whom we fail to protect.

We have learned much from research efforts in the areas of risk and resilience, yet unfortunately this knowledge has been too infrequently infused into the policy arena. The work of child advocates and researchers such as Edward Zigler, as well as of those whom he has influenced, has been a bright beacon on an otherwise dim horizon.

References

Aber, J. L., Allen, J. P., Carlson, V., & Cicchetti, D. (1989). The effects of maltreatment on development during early childhood: Recent studies and their theoretical, clinical, and policy implications. In D. Cicchetti & V. Carlson (Eds.), *Child maltreatment: Theory and research on the causes and consequences of child abuse and neglect* (pp. 579–619). New York: Cambridge University Press.

Aber, J. L., & Zigler, E. (1981). Developmental considerations in the definition of child maltreatment. *New Directions for Child Development, 11*, 1–29.

Ainsworth, M. D. S., Blehar, M. C., Waters, E., & Wall, S. (1978). *Patterns of attachment: A psychological study of the Strange Situation.* Hillsdale, NJ: Erlbaum.

Ainsworth, M. D. S., & Wittig, B. A. (1969). Attachment and the exploratory behavior of one-year-olds in a strange situation. In B. M. Foss (Ed.), *Determinants of infant behavior* (Vol. 4, pp. 113–136). London: Methuen.

Barnett, D., Manly, J. T., & Cicchetti, D. (1993). Defining child maltreatment: The interface between policy and research. In D. Cicchetti & S. L. Toth (Eds.), *Child abuse, child development, and social policy* (pp. 7–73). Norwood, NJ: Ablex.

Beeghly, M., & Cicchetti, D. (1994). Child maltreatment, attachment and the self system: Emergence of an internal state lexicon in toddlers at high social risk. *Development and Psychopathology, 6,* 5–30.

Belsky, J. (1993). Etiology of child maltreatment: A developmental-ecological analysis. *Psychological Bulletin, 114,* 413–434.

Bernath, M. S., Feshbach, N. D., & Gralinski, J. H. (1993, March). *Physical maltreatment and trust in peers: Feelings, reasons, and behavioral intentions.* Paper presented at the biennial meeting of the Society for Research in Child Development, New Orleans, LA.

Bowlby, J. (1969/1982). *Attachment and loss* (Vol. 1): *Attachment.* New York: Basic Books.

Bretherton, I. (1985). Attachment theory: Retrospect and prospect. In I. Bretherton & E. Waters (Eds.), *Growing points of attachment theory and research. Monographs of the Society for Research in Child Development, 50,* (Social No. 209), pp. 3–38.

Bretherton, I. (1987). New perspectives on attachment relations: Security, communication, and internal working models. In J. Osofsky (Ed.), *Handbook of infant development* (2 ed., pp. 1061–1100). New York: Wiley.

Bronfenbrenner, U. (1979). *The ecology of human development: Experiments by nature and design.* Cambridge, MA: Harvard University Press.

Burgess, R. L., & Conger, R. D. (1978). Family interaction in abusive, neglectful, and normal families. *Child Development, 49,* 1163–1173.

Cairns, E., & Dawes, A. (1996). Children: Ethnic and political violence – a commentary. *Child Development, 67,* 129–139.

Calverley, R., Fischer, K., & Ayoub, C. (1994). Complex splitting of self-representations in sexually abused adolescent girls. *Development and Psychopathology, 6,* 195–213.

Carlson, V., Cicchetti, D., Barnett, D., & Braunwald, K. (1989). Disorganized/disoriented attachment relationships in maltreated infants. *Developmental Psychology, 25,* 525–531.

Chase-Lansdale, P. L., Cherlin, A., & Kiernan, K. (1995). The long-term effects of parental divorce on the mental health of young adults: A developmental perspective. *Child Development, 66,* 1614–1634.

Chomsky, N. (1968). *Language and mind.* New York: Harcourt Brace Jovanovich.

Cicchetti, D. (1984). The emergence of developmental psychopathology. *Child Development, 55,* 1–7.

Cicchetti, D. (1989). How research on child maltreatment has informed the study of child development: Perspectives from developmental psychopathology. In D. Cicchetti & V. Carlson (Eds.), *Child maltreatment: Theory and research on the causes and consequences of child abuse and neglect* (pp. 377–431). New York: Cambridge University Press.

Cicchetti, D. (1990). A historical perspective on the discipline of developmental psychopathology. In J. Rolf, A. Masten, D. Cicchetti, K. Nuechterlein, & S. Weintraub (Eds.), *Risk and protective factors in the development of psychopathology* (pp. 2–28). New York: Cambridge University Press.

Cicchetti, D. (1991). Fractures in the crystal: Developmental psychopathology and the emergence of the self. *Developmental Review, 11,* 271–287.

Cicchetti, D. (1993). Developmental psychopathology: Reactions, reflections, projections. *Developmental Review, 13,* 471–502.

Cicchetti, D. (1996). Child maltreatment: Implications for developmental theory. *Human Development, 39,* 18–39.

Cicchetti, D., & Barnett, D. (1991). Attachment organization in preschool aged maltreated children. *Development and Psychopathology, 3,* 397–411.

Cicchetti, D., Cummings, M., Greenberg, M., & Marvin, R. (1990). An organizational perspective on attachment beyond infancy: Implications for theory, measurement, and research. In M. Greenberg, D. Cicchetti, & E. M. Cummings (Eds.), *Attachment in the preschool years: Theory, research and intervention* (pp. 3–49). Chicago: University of Chicago Press.

Cicchetti, D., Ganiban, J., & Barnett, D. (1991). Contributions from the study of high risk populations to understanding the development of emotion regulation. In J. Garber & K. Dodge (Eds.), *The development of emotion regulation* (pp. 15–48). New York: Cambridge University Press.

Cicchetti, D., & Garmezy, N. (Eds.). (1993). Milestones in the development of resilience. Special Issue of *Development and Psychopathology, 5* (4), 497–774.

Cicchetti, D., & Howes, P. (1991). Developmental psychopathology in the context of the family: Illustrations from the study of child maltreatment. *Canadian Journal of Behavioural Science, 23,* 257–281.

Cicchetti, D., & Lynch, M. (1993). Toward an ecological/transactional model of community violence and child maltreatment: Consequences for children's development. *Psychiatry, 56,* 96–118.

Cicchetti, D., & Olsen, K. (1990). Borderline disorders in childhood. In M. Lewis & S. Miller (Eds.), *Handbook of developmental psychopathology* (pp. 355–370). New York: Plenum Press.

Cicchetti, D., & Rizley, R. (1981). Developmental perspectives on the etiology, intergenerational transmission, and sequelae of child maltreatment. *New Directions for Child Development, 11,* 31–55.

Cicchetti, D., & Rogosch, F. A. (Eds.). (1996). Developmental pathways. Special Issue of *Development and Psychopathology, 8* (4).

Cicchetti, D., Rogosch, F. A., Lynch, M., & Holt, K. (1993). Resilience in maltreated children: Processes leading to adaptive outcome. *Development and Psychopathology, 5,* 629–647.

Cicchetti, D., & Schneider-Rosen, K. (1984). Toward a developmental model of the depressive disorders. *New Directions for Child Development, 26,* 5–27.

Cicchetti, D., & Schneider-Rosen, K. (1986). An organizational approach to childhood depression. In M. Rutter, C. Izard, & P. Read (Eds.), *Depression in young people, clinical and developmental perspectives* (pp. 71–134). New York: Guilford.

Cicchetti, D., & Sroufe, L. A. (1976). The relationship between affective and cognitive development in Down's syndrome infants. *Child Development, 47,* 920–929.

Cicchetti, D., & Toth, S. L. (Eds.). (1993). *Child abuse, child development, and social policy.* Norwood, NJ: Ablex.

Cicchetti, D., Toth, S. L., & Hennessy, K. (1993). Child maltreatment and school adaptation: Problems and promises. In D. Cicchetti & S. L. Toth (Eds.), *Child abuse, child development, and social policy* (pp. 301–330). Norwood, NJ: Ablex.

Cicchetti, D., Toth, S. L., & Lynch, M. (1993). The developmental sequelae of child maltreatment: Implications for war-related trauma. In L. A. Leavitt & N. A. Fox (Eds.), *Psychological effects of war and violence on children* (pp. 41–71). Hillsdale, NJ: Erlbuam.

Cicchetti, D., & Tucker, D. (1994). Development and self-regulatory structures of the mind. *Development and Psychopathology, 6,* 533–549.

Crittenden, P. M. (1988). Relationships at risk. In J. Belsky & T. Nezworski (Eds.), *Clinical implications of attachment theory* (pp. 136–174). Hillsdale, N.J.: Erlbaum.

Crittenden, P. M., & DiLalla, D. (1988). Compulsive compliance: The development of an inhibitory coping strategy in infancy. *Journal of Abnormal Child Psychology, 16,* 585–599.

Cummings, E. M., Hennessy, K., Rabideau, G., & Cicchetti, D. (1994). Responses of physically abused boys to interadult anger involving their mothers. *Development and Psychopathology, 6,* 31–42.

DeMulder, E., Tarullo, L., Klimes-Dougan, B., Free, K., & Radke-Yarrow, M. (1995). Personality disorders of affectively ill mothers: Links to maternal behavior. *Journal of Personality Disorders, 9,* 199–212.

Dodge, K. A., Pettit, G. S., & Bates, J. E. (1994). Effects of physical maltreatment on the development of peer relations. *Development and Psychopathology, 6,* 43–55.

Downey, G., & Coyne, J. C. (1990). Children of depressed parents: An integrative review. *Psychological Bulletin, 108,* 50–76.

Eckenrode, J., Laird, M., & Doris, J. (1993). School performance and disciplinary problems among abused and neglected children. *Developmental Psychology, 29,* 53–62.

Eisenberg, L. (1995). The social construction of the human brain. *American Journal of Psychiatry, 152,* 1563–1575.

Famularo, R., Kinscherff, R., & Fenton, T. (1992). Psychiatric diagnoses of maltreated children: Preliminary findings. *Journal of the American Academy of Child and Adolescent Psychiatry, 31,* 863–867.

Fendrich, M., Warner, V., & Weissman, M. M. (1990). Family risk factors, parental depression, and psychopathology in offspring. *Developmental Psychology, 26,* 40–50.

Gaensbauer, T. (1980). Anaclitic depression in a three-and-one-half-month-old child. *American Journal of Psychiatry, 137,* 841–842.

Gaensbauer, T., & Hiatt, S. (1984). Facial communication of emotion in early infancy. In N. A. Fox & R. J. Davidson (Eds.), *The psychobiology of affective development* (pp. 207–230). Hillsdale, NJ: Erlbaum.

Gaensbauer, T., Mrazek, D., & Harmon, R. (1981). Emotional expression in abused and/or neglected infants. In N. Frude (Ed.), *Psychological approaches to child abuse* (pp. 120–135). Totowa, NJ: Rowman and Littlefield.

Garbarino, J., Kostelny, K., & Dubrow, N. (1991). *No place to be a child: Growing up in a war zone.* New York: Lexington Books.

Garmezy, N., & Masten, A. S. (1994). Chronic adversities. In M. Rutter, E. Taylor, & L. Hersov (Eds.), *Child and adolescent psychiatry: Modern approaches* (3rd ed., pp. 191–208). London: Blackwell Scientific Publications.

Garmezy, N., Masten, A. S., & Tellegen, A. (1984). The study of stress and competence in children: A building block for developmental psychopathology. *Child Development, 55,* 97–111.

Gerbner, G., Ross, C. J., & Zigler, E. F. (Eds.). (1980). *Child abuse: An agenda for action.* New York: Oxford University Press.

Gersten, M., Coster, W., Schneider-Rosen, K., Carlson, V., & Cicchetti, D. (1986). The socioemotional bases of communicative functioning: Quality of attachment, language development, and early maltreatment. In M. E. Lamb, A. L. Brown, & B. Rogoff (Eds.), *Advances in developmental psychology* (Vol. 4, pp. 105–151). Hillsdale, NJ: Erlbaum.

Gunnar, M., & Nelson, C. A. (1994). Event-related potentials in year-old infants: Relations with emotionality and cortisol. *Child Development, 65,* 80–94.

Hart, J., Gunnar, M., & Cicchetti, D. (1995). Salivary cortisol in maltreated children: Evidence of relations between neuroendocrine activity and social competence. *Development and Psychopathology, 7,* 11–26.

Hart, J., Gunnar, M., & Cicchetti, D. (1996). Altered neuroendocrine activity in maltreated children related to depression. *Development and Psychopathology, 8,* 201–214.

Hennessy, K., Rabideau, G., Cicchetti, D., & Cummings, E. M. (1994). Responses of physically abused children to different forms of interadult anger. *Child Development, 65,* 815–828.

Hofer, M. A. (1987). Early social relationships: A psychobiologist's view. *Child Development, 58,* 633–647.

Howes, C., & Segal, J. (1993). Children's relationships with alternative caregivers: The special case of maltreated children removed from their homes. *Journal of Applied Developmental Psychology, 14,* 71–81.

Howes, P., & Cicchetti, D. (1993). A family/relational perspective on maltreating families: Parallel processes across systems and social policy implications. In D. Cicchetti & S. L. Toth (Eds.), *Child abuse, child development and social policy* (pp. 249–300). Norwood, NJ: Ablex.

Huston, A. C., McLoyd, V., & Garcia-Coll, C. T. (Eds.). (1994). Special issue on child and poverty. *Child Development, 65* (2), 275–718.

Kalin, N. H., Shelton, S. E., & Snowdon, C. T. (1993). Social factors in regulating security and fear in infant rhesus monkeys. *Depression, 1,* 137–142.

Katz, P., & Zigler, E. (1967). Self-image disparity: A developmental approach. *Journal of Personality and Social Psychology, 5,* 186–195.

Kaufman, J. (1991). Depressive disorders in maltreated children. *Journal of the American Academy of Child and Adolescent Psychiatry, 30,* 257–265.

Kaufman, J., & Cicchetti, D. (1989). The effects of maltreatment on school-aged children's socioemotional development: Assessments in a day camp setting. *Developmental Psychology, 25,* 516–524.

Kendall-Tackett, K. A., Williams, L. M., & Finklehor, D. (1993). The impact of sexual abuse on children: A review and synthesis of recent empirical studies. *Psychological Bulletin, 113,* 164–180.

Kochanska, G., Kuczynski, L., Radke-Yarrow, M., & Welsh, J. D. (1987). Resolution of control episodes between well and affectively ill mothers and their young child. *Journal of Abnormal Child Psychology, 15,* 441–456.

Lamb, M., Thompson, R., Gardner, W., & Charnov, E. (1985). *Infant-mother attachment.* Hillsdale, NJ: Erlbaum.

Lenneberg, E. (1967). *Biological foundations of language.* New York: Wiley.

Luthar, S. S. (1991). Vulnerability and resilience: A study of high-risk adolescents. *Child Development, 62,* 600–616.

Luthar, S. S., Doernberger, C. H., & Zigler, E. (1993). Resilience is not a unidimensional construct: Insights from a prospective study on inner-city adolescents. *Development and Psychopathology, 5,* 703–717.

Lynch, M., & Cicchetti, D. (1991). Patterns of relatedness in maltreated and nonmaltreated children: Connections among multiple representational models. *Development and Psychopathology, 3,* 207–226.

Lynch, M., & Cicchetti, D. (1992). Maltreated children's reports of relatedness to their teachers. *New Directions for Child Development, 57,* 81–107.

Lyons-Ruth, K., Repacholi, B., McLeod, S., & Silva, E. (1991). Disorganized attachment behavior in infancy: Short-term stability, maternal and infant correlates, and risk-related subtypes. *Development and Psychopathology, 3,* 377–396.

Macksoud, M., & Aber, J. L. (1996). The war experiences and psychosocial development of children in Lebanon. *Child Development, 67,* 70–88.

Mahler, M., Pine, F., & Bergman, A. (1975). *The psychological birth of the human infant.* New York: Basic Books.

Main, M., & George, C. (1985). Response of abused and disadvantaged toddlers to distress in agemates: A study in the day care setting. *Developmental Psychology, 21,* 407–412.

Main, M., & Hesse, E. (1990). Parents' unresolved traumatic experiences are related to infant disorganized attachment status: Is freighted and/or frightening parent behavior the linking mechanism? In M. Greenberg, D. Cicchetti, & E. M. Cummings (Eds.), *Attachment in the preschool years* (pp. 161–182). Chicago: University of Chicago Press.

Main, M., & Solomon, J. (1990). Procedures for identifying infants as disorganized/disoriented during the Ainsworth Strange Situation. In M. Greenberg, D. Cicchetti, & E. M. Cummings (Eds.), *Attachment during the preschool years* (pp. 121–160). Chicago: University of Chicago Press.

Masten, A. (1989). Resilience in development: Implications of the study of successful adaptation for developmental psychopathology. In D. Cicchetti (Ed.), *Rochester symposium on developmental psychopathology, Vol. 1: The emergence of a discipline* (pp. 261–294). Hillsdale, NJ: Erlbaum.

Masten, A., & Coatsworth, D. J. (1995). Competence, resilience, and psychopathology. In D. Cicchetti & D. Cohen (Eds.), *Developmental psychopathology, Vol. 2: Risk disorder, and adaptation* (pp. 715–752). New York: Wiley.

McCloskey, L., Figueredo, A., & Koss, M. (1995). The effects of systemic family violence on children's mental health. *Child Development, 66,* 1239–1261.

Meisels, S., & Shonkoff, J. (Eds.) (1990). *Handbook of early childhood intervention.* New York: Cambridge University Press.

Melton, G. (1995). Bringing psychology to Capitol Hill: Briefings on child and family policy. *American Psychologist, 50,* 766–770.

Mueller, E., & Silverman, N. (1989). Peer relations in maltreated children. In D. Cicchetti & V. Carlson (Eds.), *Child maltreatment: Theory and research on the causes and consequences of child abuse and neglect* (pp. 529–578). New York: Cambridge University Press.

Murphy, L. B., & Moriarty, A. (1976). *Vulnerability, coping, and growth: From infancy to adolescence.* New Haven, CT: Yale University Press.

National Center for Children in Poverty (1990). *Five million children: A statistical profile of our poorest young citizens.* New York: Columbia University.

Osofsky, J. (1995). The effects of exposure to violence on young children. *American Psychologist, 50,* 782–788.

Parker, J. G., & Herrera, C. (in press). Interpersonal processes in friendship: A comparison of maltreated and nonmaltreated children's experiences. *Developmental Psychology, 32.*

Pipp, S., Easterbrooks, M. A., & Harmon, R. J. (1992). The relation between attachment and knowledge of self and mother in one-to three-year-old infants. *Child Development, 63,* 738–750.

Pipp, S., & Harmon, R. J. (1987). Attachment as regulation: A commentary. *Child Development, 58,* 648–652.

Putnam F. W. (1995). Development of dissociative disorders. In D. Cicchetti & D. Cohen (Eds.), *Developmental psychopathology,* Vol. 2: *Risk, Disorder, and Adaptation* (pp. 581–608). New York: Wiley.

Putnam, F. W., & Trickett, P. (1993). Child sexual abuse: A model of chronic trauma. *Psychiatry, 56,* 82–95.

Richters, J. E., & Cicchetti, D. (1993). Mark Twain meets DSM-III-R: Conduct disorder, development, and the concept of harmful dysfunction. *Development and Psychopathology, 5,* 5–29.

Richters, J. E., & Martinez, P. E. (1993a). The National Institute of Mental Health Community Volence Project: I. Children as victims of and witnesses to violence. Special issue on children and violence. *Psychiatry: Interpersonal and Bilogical Processes, 56,* 7–21.

Richters, J. E., & Martinez, P. E. (1993b). Violent communities, family choices, and children's chances: An algorithm for improving the odds. *Development and Psychopathology, 5,* 609–627.

Rieder, C., & Cicchetti, D. (1989). An organizational perspective on cognitive control functioning and cognitive-affective balance in maltreated children. *Developmental Psychology, 25,* 382–393.

Rogosch, F. A., & Cicchetti, D. (1994). Illustrating the interface of family and peer relations through the study of child maltreatment. *Social Development, 3,* 291–308.

Rogosch, F., Cicchetti, D., Shields, A., & Toth, S. L. (1995). Facets of parenting disturbance in child maltreatment. In M. H. Bornstein (Ed.), *Handbook of parenting* (Vol. 4, pp. 127–159). Hillsdale, NJ: Erlbaum.

Rosenbaum, A., & O'Leary, D. (1981). Marital violence: Characteristics of abusive couples. *Journal of Consulting and Clinical Psychology, 49,* 63–71.

Rosenberg, M. S. (1987). New directions for research on the psychological maltreatment of children. *American Psychologist, 42,* 166–171.

Rutter, M. (1966). *Children of sick parents: An environmental and psychiatric study.* London: Oxford University Press.

Rutter, M. (1986). Child psychiatry: The interface between clinical and developmental research. *Psychological Medicine, 16,* 151–160.

Rutter, M. (1990). Psychosocial resilience and protective mechanisms. In J. Rolf, A. S. Masten, D. Cicchetti, K. H. Nuechterlein, & S. Weintraub (Eds.), *Risk and protective factors in the development of psychopathology* (pp. 181–214). New York: Cambridge University Press.

Ryan, R. (1991). The nature of the self in autonomy and relatedness. In J. Strauss & G. R. Goethals (Eds.), *The Self: Interdisciplinary approaches* (pp. 208–238). New York: Springer-Verlag.

Salzinger, S., Feldman, R. S., Hammer, M., & Rosario, M. (1993). The effects of physical abuse on children's social relationships. *Child Development, 64,* 169–187.

Sameroff, A. J., & Chandler, M. J. (1975). Reproductive risk and the continuum of caretaking casualty. In F. D. Horowitz (Ed.), *Review of child development research* (Vol. 4, pp. 187–244). Chicago: University of Chicago Press.

Sameroff, A. J., Seifer, R., Baldwin, A., & Baldwin, C. (1993). Stability of intelligence from preschool to adolescence: The influence of social and family risk factors. *Child Development, 64,* 80–97.

Sameroff, A. J., Seifer, R., Barocas, R., Zax, M., & Greenspan, S. (1987). Intelligence quotient scores of 4 year children: Social-environmental risk factors. *Pediatrics, 79,* 343–350.

Scarr, S. (1992). Developmental theories for the 1990s: Development and individual differences. *Child Development, 63,* 1–19.

Schneider-Rosen, K., Braunwald, K., Carlson, V., & Cicchetti, D. (1985). Current perspectives in at-
tachment theory: Illustration from the study of maltreated infants. In I. Bretherton & E. Waters
(Eds.), *Growing points in attachment theory and research* (pp. 194–210). *Monographs of the
Society for Research in Child Development, 50* (Serial No. 209).

Schneider-Rosen, K., & Cicchetti, D. (1984). The relationship between affect and cognition in maltreated infants: Quality of attachment and the development of visual self-recognition. *Child Development, 55,* 648–658.

Schneider-Rosen, K., & Cicchetti, D. (1991). Early self-knowledge and emotional development: Visual
self-recognition and affective reactions to mirror self-image in maltreated and nonmaltreated toddlers. *Developmental Psychology, 27,* 481–488.

Spoont, M. (1992). Modulatory role of serotonin in neural information processing: Implications for
human psychopathology. *Psychological Bulletin, 112,* 330–350.

Sroufe, L. A. (1979). The coherence of individual development: Early care, attachment, and subsequent
developmental issues. *American Psychologist, 34,* 834–841.

Sroufe, L. A. (1990). An organizational perspective on the self. In D. Cicchetti & M. Beeghly (Eds.),
The self in transition (pp. 281–307). Chicago: University of Chicago Press.

Sroufe, L. A. (1995). *Emotional development: The organization of emotional life in the early years.*
Cambridge: Cambridge University Press.

Sroufe, L. A., Egeland, B., & Kreutzer, T. (1990). The fate of early experience following developmental
change: Longitudinal approaches to individual adaptation in childhood. *Child Development, 61,*
1363–1373.

Sroufe, L. A., & Fleeson, J. (1986). Attachment and the construction of relationships. In W. Hartup &
Z. Rubin (Eds.), *Relationships and development* (pp. 51–76). Hillsdale, NJ: Erlbaum.

Sroufe, L. A., & Fleeson, J. (1988). The coherence of family relationships. In R. A. Hinde & J.
Stevenson-Hinde (Eds.), *Relationships within families: Mutual influences* (pp. 27–47). Oxford:
Oxford University Press.

Sroufe, L. A., & Rutter, M. (1984). The domain of developmental psychopathology. *Child Development,
55,* 17–29.

Sroufe, L. A., & Waters, E. (1977). Attachment as an organizational construct. *Child Development, 48,*
1184–1199.

Stern, D. (1989). The representation of relational patterns: Developmental considerations. In A. Sameroff & R. Emde (Eds.), *Relationship disturbances in early childhood* (pp. 52–69). New York:
Basic Books.

Sternberg, K., Lamb, M., Greenbaum, C., Cicchetti, D., Dawud, S., Cortes, R., & Krispin, O. (1993).
Effects of domestic violence on children's behavior problems and depression. *Developmental Psychology, 29,* 44–52.

Straus, M. A., Gelles, R. J., & Steinmetz, S. K. (1980). *Behind closed doors: Violence in the American
family.* New York: Anchor Press.

Thompson, R. (1990). Emotions and self-regulation. In R. Thompson (Ed.), *Nebraska Symposium on motivation, Vol. 36: Socioemotional development* (pp. 367–467). Lincoln: University of Nebraska Press.

Thompson, R., & Wilcox, B. (1995). Child maltreatment research: Federal support and policy issues.
American Psychologist, 50, 789–793.

Toth, S. L., & Cicchetti, D., (1996a). Patterns of relatedness, depressive symptomatology, and perceived
competence in maltreated children. *Journal of Consulting and Clinical Psychology, 64,* 32–41.

Toth, S. L., & Cicchetti, D. (1996b). The impact of relatedness with mother on school functioning in
maltreated youngsters. *Journal of School Psychology, 34,* 247–266.

Toth, S. L., Cicchetti, D., Macfie, J., & Emde, R. (1995, March). *Representational development in
maltreated children.* Paper presented at the biennial meeting of the Society for Research in Child
Development, Indianapolis, IN.

Toth, S. L., Manly, J. T., & Cicchetti, D. (1992). Child maltreatment and vulnerability to depression.
Development and Psychopathology, 4, 97–112.

Trickett, P. K., & Susman, E. J. (1988). Parental perceptions of childrearing practices in physically
abusive and nonabusive families. *Developmental Psychology, 24,* 270–276.

Troy, M., & Sroufe, L. A. (1987). Victimization among preschoolers: The role of attachment relationship history. *Journal of the American Academy of Child and Adolescent Psychiatry, 26,* 166–172.

van der Kolk, B. (1987). The compulsion to repeat the trauma: Re-enactment, revictimization, and masochism. *Psychiatric Clinics of North America, 12,* 389–411.

von Bertalanffy, L. (1968). *General system theory.* New York: Braziller.

Vondra, J., Barnett, D., & Cicchetti, D. (1989). Perceived and actual competence among maltreated and comparison school children. *Development and Psychopathology, 1,* 237–255.

Waddington, C. H. (1942). Canalization of development and the inheritance of acquired characters. *Nature, 150,* 563–564.

Waddington, C. H. (1957). *The strategy of genes.* London: Allen and Unwin.

Werner, E. (1993). Risk, resilience, and recovery: Perspectives from the Kauai Longitudinal Study. *Development and Psychopathology, 5,* 503–515.

Werner, E., & Smith, R. (1992). *Overcoming the odds: High-risk children from birth to adulthood.* Ithaca, NY: Cornell University Press.

Youngblade, L. M., & Belsky, J. (1989). Child maltreatment, infant-parent attachment security, and dysfunctional peer relationships in toddlerhood. *Topics in Early Childhood Special Education, 9,* 1–15.

Zahn-Waxler, C., Iannotti, R. J., Cummings, E. M., & Denham, S. (1990). Antecedents of problem behaviors in children of depressed mothers. *Development and Psychopathology, 2,* 271–291.

Zigler, E. (1976). Controlling child abuse in America: An effort doomed to failure? In W. A. Collins (Ed.), *Newsletter of the Division on Developmental Psychology, American Psychological Association* (pp. 17–30). Washington, DC: American Psychological Association.

Zigler, E. (1989). Addressing the nation's child care crisis: The school of the twenty-first century. *American Journal of Orthopsychiatry, 59,* 484–491.

Zigler, E., Abelson, W., Tricket, P., & Seitz, V. (1982). Is an intervention program necessary in order to improve economically disadvantaged children's IQ scores? *Child Development, 53,* 340–348.

Zigler, E., & Balla, D. (1982). Atypical development: Personality determinants in the behavior of the retarded. In E. Zigler, M. Lamb, & I. Child (Eds.), *Socialization and personality development* (pp. 238–245). New York: Oxford University Press.

Zigler, E., & Ennis, P. (1989). The school of the twenty-first century. *Division of Child, Youth, and Family Services Newsletter, 12,* 1, 12–13.

Zigler, E., & Glick, M. (1986). *A developmental approach to adult psychopathology.* New York: Wiley.

Zigler, E., & Valentine, J. (Eds.) (1979). *Project Head Start: A legacy of the War on Poverty.* New York: Free Press.

15   Teenaged childbearing and divorce

E. Mavis Hetherington

This chapter involves an appraisal of issues pertaining to two family constellations that are frequently labeled as nontraditional but which are becoming increasingly common. These are families involving mothers who are single teenagers, and those involving divorced mothers. Impetus for this review derived from five major factors.

First, these two family forms occur often enough to no longer be viewed as atypical and they serve as the setting for the development of an increasing number of children. Over half of the children in the United States will spend some time in a mother-headed family (Cherlin, 1992).

Second, this is an especially auspicious time in which to review these two topics, given the quality and breadth of research data that are now available on each. Both large sample, longitudinal survey data and smaller longitudinal studies involving more intensive study of family process, but usually using samples of convenience, are now available. However, more multimethod, multimeasure studies including observations are available in research on divorce than on teenaged parenting. In addition, most intensive studies of teenaged parents involve blacks and intensive studies of divorce are of whites.

Third, teenaged childbearing and divorce share some similar associated psychosocial risks. Both occur more often in poor and in black families, both are associated with income loss and at least temporary welfare dependency, both result in low contact with or absence of a father and in residence in a single-parent household with or without kin. There are several notable differences we also must keep in mind in discussing these two family changes. Although cohabiting couples account for one-quarter of births to single mothers (Bumpass & Raley, 1993), divorce is more likely to have involved a sustained period in a two-parent household that may have been terminated with considerable acrimony and conflict. Moreover, divorce involves a parent, usually the father, moving out of the home, which may result in disruptions in already formed bonds of attachment. In addition, the child will be more aware of family reorganization, changes in roles and relationships,

Appreciation is extended to Kristen Moore and Child Trends for their information on the teenaged childbearing section of this paper.

350

and separation and loss associated with divorce. Finally, the immediate decline in income for mothers following divorce is greater than that following a birth to a single mother. Note we are talking about decline in income rather than the absolute level of economic resources. Thus, conflict, loss, separation, and change may be more salient factors, at least in the short run, for the adjustment of children in divorced families than for children born to unwed mothers.

Fourth, researchers are moving from a deficit model to risk and resiliency models in studying teenaged childbearing and divorce. Mothers and children in both types of families often experience adverse high levels of multiple life stressors; however, a large proportion do not have problems in adjustment and are resilient in the face of the challenges in their family situation.

Finally, a well-known tenet in the field of developmental psychopathology is that in trying to understand developmental processes within a particular population, it is often useful to look at insights that have been obtained from other, similar populations. The study of atypical children and families has yielded rich infor-mation about developmental processes and family functioning in normative groups of children and families. The converse is also true. Given the many similarities that occur across families headed by a single teenaged mother or a divorced mother, the objective in this review was to identify adaptive processes that might be com-mon, or idiosyncratic, to each. The ultimate aim of this exercise was to further our understanding of risk and protective mechanisms associated with single-parent fam-ily status, an approach that would be useful for both theoretical and practical (in-tervention) purposes.

In discussing these issues, a brief review of changes in dating, mating and pro-creating that have occurred in the past 35 years will be presented, followed by a discussion of risk and protective factors associated with long-term outcomes of teenaged childbearing and divorce for mothers and their children. In the concluding section of this chapter, themes that are common or specific to the two constellations are discussed and interventions and future research directions are presented.

Dating, mating, and procreating

Underlying contemporary shifts in family structure, relationships, and functions are economic, social, cultural, and political changes that have led to alterations in attitudes and laws about intimate relationships, marriage, childbearing, and divorce. In examining the patterns of these family changes, it is obvious that marriage is becoming a more optional, less permanent relationship. Sexuality, cohabitation, marriage, and childbearing are becoming increasingly less closely linked. It has been proposed that for black families, marriage and childbearing should be viewed as separate trajectories (Cherlin, 1992). However, for all groups sexual activity is being initiated at an earlier age, cohabitation, out-of-wedlock births, and divorce are increasingly common, marriage is being delayed, and fertility is declining. Both divorce and out-of-wedlock childbearing are contributing to the high numbers of children living in single-parent households.

The early initiation of sexual activity accompanied by inept contraception and the decline in teenaged marriages are the main contributors to increasing numbers of births to single teenaged mothers. In 1960, 40% of all 19-year-olds had been married compared with less than 10% of current 19-year-olds. Although marriage is being delayed, sexual activity and cohabitation are not. Two out of five males and one out of four females are sexually active by age 15 with blacks initiating sexual activities at an earlier age than whites (Zabin & Hayward, 1993). Furthermore, since young teenagers are less likely to use contraception and since the pressure on pregnant women to marry has declined, an increase in births to single teenaged women has resulted. Marriage in black teenagers is minimal with less than 4% marrying by the age of 19. It is not teenaged parenthood but it is births to single teenagers that has increased notably in the past 20 years. In 1992, 93% of the births to black teenagers and 61% to white teenagers were to unmarried adolescents (National Center for Health Statistics, 1993; Snyder & Fromboluti, 1993). Young teenaged mothers are at greater risk than older mothers for having a second child out of wedlock. Of all teen births in 1992, 25% were not first births (Moore, Snyder, & Glei, 1995).

Although there is a perception that the increase in sexuality and in nonmarital childbearing primarily occurs with black teenagers, nonmarital childbearing has increased in all groups since the mid-1970s and over 70% of the births to single women are to women in their 20s and 30s. Thus, sexual and childbearing patterns of black teenagers in the late 1960s and 1970s were anticipating future shifts across a broader range of the population. Marriage and childbearing are becoming less linked across a wide range of ethnic and age groups (Furstenberg, 1991a, 1991b; Moore et al., 1995; Snyder & Fromboluti, 1993).

In addition to childbearing among single mothers, a second contribution to the increase in single-parent households is high rates of divorce. Although divorce rates have declined over the past decade, it is still estimated that almost half of first marriages will end in separation or divorce (Norton & Miller, 1992). Most children will find themselves in a home with a custodial mother following divorce and will remain in a single-parent household for an average of 5 years (Castro-Martin & Bumpass, 1989). Many of these single-parent households will include kin and co-habiting male partners. Remarriage rates have been dropping since the 1960s and it is now estimated that only two-thirds of separated and divorced women and three-quarters of men will ever remarry (Bumpass, Sweet, & Castro-Martin, 1990; Cherlin & Furstenberg, 1994). Since divorce rates are somewhat higher in remarriages, more adults and children are finding themselves going through multiple marital transitions and family reorganizations with their accompanying life changes, challenges, and stresses.

Births to single mothers, cohabitation, separation, and divorce are higher for blacks than whites. Black couples are less likely to marry, more likely to separate, to remain separated longer before obtaining a divorce or to never legally divorce, and less likely to remarry. Thus, black children are more likely than white children to spend longer periods of time in a household with a single or divorced mother often living with a grandmother or other kin.

Teenaged mothers and their children

We turn now to an examination of the adjustment of children of teenaged mothers and the economic, individual, and family risk and protective factors associated with single adolescent parenthood and the well-being of teenaged parents and their children. A discussion of factors associated with teenaged pregnancy is included since the characteristics and background of the mother will influence the risks, resources, and experiences of children in single-parent families.

The adjustment of children of single teen mothers

Evidence documents that children of single teen mothers do have problems in various areas of functioning. Differences in the children of teenaged and older mothers are more consistently found in cognitive and academic functioning than in psychopathology, and are more often obtained in the offspring of very young teenagers. Even with statistical controls for mother's background, early problems in health and increased premature birth associated with poor prenatal care and nutrition in teen mothers, as well as differences in cognitive functioning, academic performance, and self-regulation are found, especially for boys in the preschool and elementary school years (Zabin & Hayward, 1993). In high school, misbehavior, learning problems, retention in a grade, truancy, school dropout, and idleness are more likely to occur (McLanahan & Sandefur, 1994; Zabin & Hayward, 1993). In addition, running away from home, early sexual activity, and teenaged childbearing are more common in adolescents who had teenaged rather than older mothers (Zabin & Hayward, 1993). Some of the major risk factors contributing to these problems involve attributes of the mother and her life circumstances associated with teenaged childbearing.

Economic and educational risk factors

In examining family transitions, such as teenaged pregnancy, divorce, and remarriage, investigators have become increasingly aware that some or all of what they viewed as consequences of the transition may actually have anteceded and contributed to the transition (Furstenberg, 1991a; McLanahan & Sandefur, 1994; Zabin & Hayward, 1993). Two of the most notable examples of this in teenaged childbearing are poverty and academic problems, such as low academic attainment, truancy, and school dropout, which are present before and increase after the birth of a child. However, even with antecedent conditions controlled, teenaged childbearing is likely to increase economic and academic problems and the length of time on welfare for mothers, which in turn expose their children to economic duress and less cognitively stimulating parenting. It is estimated that more than half of all welfare recipients were teenagers at the time their first child was born (Hardy & Zabin, 1991; Moore, 1994).

The younger the mother, the more disadvantaged her background (Moore, 1994), with differences in social disadvantage between those teenagers who bear children and those who do not being greater for white than black adolescents (Hardy & Zubin, 1991). Furthermore, the effects of early childbearing on later poverty is more sustained for whites than blacks. However, although the early conspicuous disadvantages for teenaged mothers in education and income diminish with age, at least for blacks, their marital histories are highly unstable (Furstenberg, 1991a, 1991b), presenting further risks for their children.

Family factors

Teenaged mothers often have experienced suboptimal family relationships that constrain the quality of parenting they offer to their own children. There is some evidence of intergenerational transmission of out-of-wedlock childbearing. Teenaged mothers are more likely to have a poorly educated, nonreligious, single mother who also bore a child out of wedlock (Moore, Peterson, & Furstenberg, 1984; Newcomber & Udry, 1984; Zabin & Hayward, 1993) and to have had an older sister who was a single parent. In addition to role modeling, parent–child relations and parenting style are related to teenaged childbearing (Furstenberg, Brooks-Gunn, & Chase-Lansdale, 1989; Zabin & Hayward, 1993). Teenagers who are alienated from their families and have little supervision are more likely to engage in early sexual activities and become teenaged mothers. A close relationship with authoritative parents and parental monitoring of adolescent activities are associated with lower rates of adolescent sexual activities. Although a belief that children who are well informed about sexual processes and contraception will inhibit sexual activity underlies most sex education programs, the role of parental communication in protecting against early sexual activities and teenaged pregnancy is more ambiguous than that of maternal warmth and supervision. Evidence that open communication by mothers about sex may deter sexual activity in both boys and girls is inconsistent; however, open communication between fathers and sons may actually lead to earlier sexual activity and procreation, as fathers may condone or even encourage this as a sign of fulfillment of the masculine role. How are these family background factors reflected in the parenting of teenaged parents?

The parenting of teenaged parents

There is evidence that teenaged mothers are less competent caregivers than older mothers. This has been attributed to the fact they exhibit more personal problems and have fewer resources than nonteenaged parents, are less desirable role models, and are coping with the competing demands of adolescence and offtime parenting. Evidence in both survey and observational studies indicates that, in contrast to older mothers, teenaged mothers are less warm, verbally stimulating, contingent, reciprocal, and nurturant in their caretaking with infants (Chase-Lansdale, Brooks-Gunn, & Paikoff, 1991; Hayes, 1987).

As the children grow older, teen mothers continue to be less verbally and cognitively stimulating, reading to their children less, being less involved in school activities, and having lower educational aspirations for their children (McLanahan & Sandefur, 1994). Teen mothers are also less authoritative in child rearing of older children and adolescents, exerting less responsive control and consistent monitoring of children's behavior (McLanahan & Sandefur, 1994).

Although differences between early and later childbearers are found more often in early nurturance and verbal stimulation and in later control and supervision of children's activity than in punitiveness, there are some findings of greater inappropriate aggressive behavior, abuse, and neglect in young mothers (Lamb & Elster, 1986; Luster & Mittelslaedt, 1993).

In summary, there is evidence that adolescent mothers, especially very young teenaged mothers from stressful circumstances, may engage in suboptimal child care that may be associated with later problems found in the cognitive and socioemotional development of their children. Many of the personal and socioeconomic factors that put very young teenagers at risk for childbearing also create stresses that may erode nurturant, responsive, and authoritative child rearing.

Early marriage as a risk factor

In comparison with our knowledge about the backgrounds and parenting of teenaged mothers, little is known about their marriages and their partners. On average, teenaged mothers are younger than their partners and the age discrepancy is greater for whites than for blacks. White fathers average 4 years older than teenaged mothers whereas black fathers are only 2 to 3 years older (Hardy & Zabin, 1991). However, one-quarter of the partners of teenaged mothers are over 20.

Young mothers in comparison with older mothers are less likely to marry the father of their child and less likely to receive child support (Furstenberg & Harris, 1993). In addition, pregnant black teenagers are less likely than white teenagers to marry. When a pregnant teenager marries, she is likely to expose her child not only to the risks associated with single parenthood, but also with divorce. If a pregnant teenager marries she is more likely to divorce not only because young marriages are associated with higher dissolution rates and the early birth of a second child, but also because her spouse is more likely to have fewer resources – to be lacking in educational and vocational training, and to be poor and economically dependent on his family. Furthermore, partners of teenage mothers are more likely to have a history of poor relationships with their own family, school difficulties, and behavior problems (Furstenberg & Harris, 1993; Lamb & Elster, 1986; Parke, 1995). Just as differences between teenaged mothers and nonmothers were greatest for whites, differences between characteristics of teenaged fathers and nonfathers are greater for non-Hispanic whites and Hispanics than for blacks.

Protective factors for teenaged mothers and their children

Births to teenaged mothers occur in settings with many risks and few resources. A teenager's life chances and those of her children are compromised at least temporarily by early childbearing. What are some of the protective factors that might alleviate the effects of the multiple risks confronting single teenaged mothers and their children?

Protective aspects of the mother's life

Longitudinal studies such as the Baltimore Study of Furstenberg and his colleagues (Furstenberg, Brooks-Gunn, & Morgan, 1987) are yielding rich information on how some teenaged mothers and their children exposed to the multiple risks and early adversity associated with teenaged childbearing eventually emerge as competent individuals. Educational attainment, limits on future fertility, and a successful marriage in the long run can equalize the outcomes for early and later childbearers, but it should be noted that this combination of conditions is not frequent for teenaged mothers. Social support and involvement of grandmothers and extended kin in the early years following the birth of a child also can help teenaged mothers, especially very young teenaged mothers, cope with their new life situation, continue their education, become economically self-sufficient, stay off of welfare, and continue relationships with peers. Prolonged coresidence with a grandmother into the time when the grandchild is an adolescent is less common (4%) and may be associated with sustained economic problems and welfare dependency.

White teenagers are less likely than black teenaged mothers to reside with kin and to get help in child care from kin, although they are more likely to receive economic aid (Hayes, 1987). In addition, support from kin declines over time. Moreover, even in black families support from kin is less to older teens than younger teens and to single teenagers having a second rather than a first birth. Furthermore, young grandmothers may be unwilling to assume the responsibility of caring for their grandchild and the task may fall on an already overburdened great-grandmother (Burton, 1995; Burton & Bengston, 1985).

Evidence is stronger in indicating long-term problems in the offspring of teenaged mothers than to the mothers themselves, perhaps because of the adverse economic situation and stressful environment in which they spend their early years, and stresses that negatively impact on the psychological well-being of single teen mothers and their child rearing. Many of the protective factors for children of teenaged mothers are associated with changes in the mother's situation. If the mother moves off welfare and becomes economically independent and increases her education or enters a stable marriage before the child reaches adolescence, her child's adjustment and academic performance are enhanced (Furstenberg, 1991a).

McLanahan and Sandefur (1994) argue that about half of the contribution to adverse outcomes in children of single mothers is due to poverty and the other half to family and community factors. Other investigators (Amato, 1993; Chase-Lansdale, Wakschlag, & Brooks-Gunn, in press; Hetherington, 1989) report that much of the effect of poverty is not direct but is mediated by correlates of poverty such as instability in residence, distress, depression, and psychological problems in the mother, and disruptions in parenting. Whether the effects of poverty are direct or indirect, poverty is associated with a multiplicity of stressors that have adverse effects on the well-being of children.

Protective influences of fathers

Considerable controversy exists over the extent, quality, and effects of the fathers' relationship with children born to teenaged mothers (Furstenberg & Harris, 1993; Lamb & Elster, 1986; Parke, 1995). However, evidence is accruing that fathers can play a protective role in the development of children born to single teenaged mothers.

Contact of fathers of children born to teen mothers with their offspring is higher than was once believed, with non-Hispanic whites (30%) and Hispanic (37%) fathers more likely to have no contact than black fathers (12%). McLanahan and Sandefur (1994) in their analysis of data from the National Survey of Families and Households report considerable variability in the contact never married, divorced, and remarried fathers have with their children. A larger percentage of never married fathers than of divorced fathers shows both no contact with their children and contact at least once a week, and remarriage diminishes contact.

Furstenberg and his colleagues found long-term effects of a positive relationship with the father on the adjustment of late adolescents and young adults born to teenaged parents, especially in the case of offspring living with their fathers. The quality but not the quantity of the relationship with the father was associated with higher educational attainment, less depression, and less likelihood of imprisonment in the children of teenaged parents (Furstenberg & Harris, 1993). In addition, McLanahan and Sandefur (1994) report that having a stepfather in the household increases the likelihood of success among the offspring of black but not white single mothers. Young black men born to single mothers who lived in a stepfamily had high school dropout rates comparable with those in two parent households and the rate of teen pregnancy in daughters of single mothers who later married also was comparable to that in two parent households. They propose that the resources black stepfathers bring to single mothers and their children may have more impact than those of white fathers because they reside in communities with fewer resources and social controls. On the other hand, it may be that black mothers who remarry are already more socially advantaged, which might be related to the greater success of their children.

Protective factors of grandparents

Although early studies (Kellam, Ensminger, & Turner, 1977; Luster & Mittelslaedt, 1993) indicated that coresidence with a grandmother was effective in facilitating her daughter's parenting, in protecting her grandchild against the deleterious effects of an irritable or insensitive mother (Crockenberg, 1981), and in protecting children from some of the adverse circumstances associated with being born to single teen-aged mothers, newer studies are suggesting that these buffering effects may have diminished.

McLanahan and Sandefur (1994) report that the average adolescent raised by a mother and grandmother is doing about as well as the average child raised by a single mother and that both of these are doing less well than children raised in a dual-parent home. The risk of teenaged childbirth for adolescent children of single mothers in coresident households is the same as in single-mother households, and the risk of high school dropout is twice as great in homes with a grandmother present. Direction of effects must be considered in these findings. It is unusual for a single parent to be living with her mother when her child is an adolescent, and only 4% do so. McLanahan and Sandefur speculate that the grandmother may be in coresidence because the mother and child are having problems or because the grandmother is in need of care.

In addition, a few scattered studies are indicating that under some circumstances coresident multigenerational families may have home environments and child-care practices by mother and grandmothers that are no better or even worse than non-coresiders (Chase-Lansdale, Brooks-Gunn, & Zamsky 1994; Speiker, 1991; Wasserman, Brunelli, & Raub, 1990).

Why should there be these differences in the findings of earlier studies which report protective effects of extended families and some later studies that find no such buffering effect for the offspring of single parents? There are many studies indicating that social support is most effective at moderate levels of stress. Under high levels of stress and multiple, massed risk factors, social supports often are found not to be able to protect individuals from adverse outcomes. Many scholars (Hogan, Hao, & Parish, 1990; McLanahan & Sandefur, 1994; McLloyd, 1990; Wilson, 1987) have speculated that due to a decline in economic conditions, to technological changes that make it more difficult for unskilled workers to obtain jobs, and an increasing concentration of urban poverty, unemployment, crime, hom-icides, substance abuse, declining educational standards, and lack of social mobility in the environments in which teenaged mothers and their children live, it has become more difficult for supportive kin to buffer them from the adverse consequences of massed adversity.

Ethnicity

Some of the most intriguing findings on teenaged parents and their children are those that relate to ethnicity. A brief summary of these findings follows. Although black adolescents are more likely to become teenaged mothers, adverse outcomes for them and for their children in comparison with those in two-parent households appears to be somewhat less than for whites. This may be because of ethnic differences in the backgrounds of teen parents and in resources available to teen mothers and their children.

The differences in disadvantaged background between teenaged mothers and older mothers and between single teenagers who do and do not have a child is greater for whites than for blacks. This same pattern of ethnic differences in disadvantaged backgrounds also holds for fathers. Thus, single teen black parents may not be as culturally deviant as single white parents. In addition, single black fathers maintain more contact with their children with the concomitant salutary effects on child development of a positive father–child relationship. Stepfathers also promote positive outcomes for black children but not for white children. Finally, black teen mothers are more likely to live with their extended family and to get assistance in child care.

Summary

Let me briefly summarize the findings on risk and resiliency associated with teenaged childbearing. Teenaged mothers are more likely to come from extremely disadvantaged circumstances, to be poor and black, and have problems in educational attainment. They are at greater risk for poor educational attainment, economic disadvantage, welfare dependency, and marital instability than are older mothers. Black mothers are more likely to recover economically from the adverse effects of single-teen childbearing. Economic and social disadvantages of teenaged childbearing can be overcome if the mother completes high school, has no more children, and forms a stable conjugal relationship. However, adolescents who are in their very early teens when a child was born may have more difficulty in going through these protective processes, and may have greater long-term problems than those who were older.

Long-term adverse consequences are more marked in the children of teen mothers than in the mothers themselves, with these children being at risk for poorer health, reduced cognitive performance and educational attainment, teenaged pregnancy, and other problem behaviors. However, improvement in the mothers' circumstances and a positive relationship with a father are associated with fewer behavior problems and greater academic achievement in children.

Divorced mothers and their children

Let us turn now to a second area of marked change in families, that of the increased rates of divorce that occurred between the early 1960s and late 1970s and the high levels that have been sustained since then. The discussion in this chapter will focus on parents and children in mother custody families, not only because this is the most frequent arrangement following divorce, but also because their situation is more analogous to that found with single teenaged mothers.

Divorce sets in motion a series of changes in residential arrangements, economic circumstances, and family roles and relationships that have major implications for the well-being and adjustment of family members. Although divorce may confront family members with increased risks and diminish the availability of economic, family, and community resources, it also may reduce stress and offer opportunities for personal growth and more fulfilling, harmonious family and personal relationships. The initial response to divorce to a considerable extent may depend on the quality of the family situation that has preceded it and the uncertainty, change, and conflict accompanying the divorce; the longer-term response will depend more on the current experiences of the family.

Most children respond initially with distress, anxiety, behavior problems, and disruptive angry responses to their parents' separation and divorce; however, most children and parents, if their life situation is not made more difficult by continued conflict or new stresses, are able to adapt to their new life in a single-parent household within 2 to 3 years. The problem is that stressful life circumstances that compromise the well-being of parents and children are more common in divorced than nondivorced families.

The adjustment of children in divorced families

There is general agreement among researchers that divorce is associated with a greater risk of problems in adjustment and less well-being both in the children and the adult offspring of divorced parents. Children from divorced families are more likely than those in nondivorced families to have academic problems, drop out of school, exhibit both externalizing, noncompliant, antisocial behavior and internalizing depressed anxious behavior, be less socially responsible, become sexually active earlier, and to bear children out of wedlock (for reviews, see Amato, 1993; Amato & Keith, 1991a; Hetherington & Stanley-Hagan, 1995). In addition, as adults they have lower socioeconomic attainment, more adjustment problems, and less stable marital relationships (Amato & Keith, 1991b). Many of these problems are similar to those of children born to single mothers; however, they cannot be attributed solely to absence of a father. Children whose mothers are widowed show substantially fewer problems than those of divorced or single mothers (McLanahan & Sandefur, 1994).

Although on the average children in divorced families show more behavior problems than those in nondivorced families, there is considerable disagreement about the size of the effect of divorce on childrens' adjustment. Some investigators report that these effects are relatively modest (Amato & Keith, 1991a), others report an average of about a twofold increase associated with divorce in such things as total behavior problems, academic problems, school dropout, employment, teenaged pregnancy, and conduct disorders (Hetherington, 1989, 1991a; Hetherington et al., 1992; Hetherington & Jodl, 1994; McLanahan & Sandefur, 1994; Zill, Morrison, & Corio, 1993). About 10% of children in nondivorced families have such problems in contrast to 20% in divorced and remarried families. McLanahan and San-defur (1994) report that outcomes are fairly similar for children in divorced families and children born to single mothers.

Even if these are worst-case estimates, what is interesting about such findings is that, although they indicate a twofold increase in problems of adjustment in children from divorced families, most children from divorced families and children born to single mothers do not have serious behavior problems, do not drop out of high school, do not become single teenaged parents, and are not unemployed. They are able to adapt to challenges and changes in their family situation. Their long-term adjustment is characterized by resiliency. This does not mean that divorce is not a painful event in the lives of most children. Even as adults, children frequently look back on divorce as the most traumatic experience in their lives; however, in spite of children's unhappiness with divorce the majority are able to cope with this difficult transition without sustained adverse effects.

Let us turn now to some of the factors that may contribute to the children's diverse adjustments in response to divorce and life with a divorced, custodial mother.

Problems in family conditions preceding divorce

Just as was found in teenaged parenting, recent research suggests that many of the family circumstances and children's adjustment problems presumed to be conse-quences of divorce are present before marital dissolution.

Parents who are poor, stressed, alcoholic, physically violent, and antisocial and have severe emotional disorders and poor interpersonal and problem-solving skills are more likely to get divorced (Amato, 1993; Capaldi & Patterson, 1991; Forgatch, Patterson, & Ray, 1995; Gotlib & McCabe, 1990). Conflict, parental anxiety, de-pression, irritability, and disrupted parenting antecede as well as follow divorce.

These factors seem likely to contribute to behavior problems in children both before and after divorce, and studies that permit a prospective analysis of divorce indicate that children whose parents will later divorce have more problems (Block, Block, & Gjerde, 1986; Capaldi & Patterson, 1991; Cherlin et al., 1991) and are exposed to more inept parenting (Block, Block, & Gjerde, 1988) preceding the divorce than those whose parents remain together. Several alternative interpreta-tions of these findings can be made. First, it is likely that family problems leading to divorce have already taken their toll on children's adjustment before the divorce occurred (Block et al., 1988). Second, it is possible that the divorce may in part be an outcome of having to deal with a difficult child. Third, personality problems in the parent that lead to both divorce and inept socialization practices may be genetically linked to behavior problems in children.

Whatever the causes of these findings may be, when antecedent levels of behavior problems are controlled, the differences in problem behaviors between children in divorced and nondivorced families remain but are reduced.

Economic factors

As was true for teenaged mothers, primary factors underlying the difficulties faced by custodial mothers and their children include the poverty, economic duress, and job instability they encounter following divorce (Garfinkel & McLanahan, 1986). This leads to changes in housing often associated with a move to a less desirable more disorganized neighborhood, with poorer schools and fewer resources to support raising competent children. It has been estimated that 1 year after divorce, custodial mothers retain only 67% of their predivorce income while noncustodial fathers retain 90% of their predivorce income (McLanahan & Booth, 1989). Fortunately, most divorced mothers eventually return to their predivorce income level, but it is a slow, painstaking process and is usually because of remarriage rather than any substantial career gains of their own (Duncan & Hoffman, 1985).

The extent of the contribution of economic factors to problem behaviors in children following divorce is controversial. Some investigators such as McLanahan and Sandefur (1994) argue that about half of the adverse effects of divorce and single parenting on children's adjustment are due to economic factors, whereas others find that most of the effects are indirect and are mediated by concomitants of economic decline such as increased negative life events, the well-being or distress of the custodial parent, and the quality of parenting. Most studies show that significant differences attributable to divorce persist even when income is controlled (Amato, 1993). In addition, in spite of the fact that the economic status of father-custody families and stepfather families is similar to nondivorced families, children in these families show about the same level of problem behaviors as those in mother-custody families (Amato, 1993; Maccoby & Mnookin, 1992).

Parent–child relationships

Both mothers and fathers, regardless of custodial arrangement, are at risk for physical and psychological disorders and show marked changes in behavior and in child rearing during the early phase after divorce (Hetherington, 1989, 1991a, 1991b; Hetherington & Stanley-Hagan, 1986; Kiecolt-Glaser et al., 1987). One of the critical results of this is that children are faced with a less physically and emotionally competent parent, who may be more preoccupied with his or her own problems than the child's well-being at a time when children need stability and support the most.

Most children following divorce find themselves in the custody of their mother. Because of multiple role demands and stressors, the ability of many divorced mothers effectively to support, control, monitor, and discipline their children diminishes in the immediate aftermath of divorce (Hetherington, 1993; Hetherington et al., 1992). Children in divorced families are said to grow up faster, being required to function more independently, receiving less supervision, and spending less time in the company of adults.

Although the parenting of divorced mothers recovers notably in the second year following divorce, conflictual, mutually coercive relationships with sons are particularly intense and enduring (Hetherington, 1989, 1991a, 1991b, 1993). Mother–daughter relationships are also conflictual immediately after the divorce, but gradually may become close and supportive (Hetherington, 1989). However, in adolescence renewed conflict between divorced mothers and daughters frequently emerges, often in response to adolescent daughters' precocious sexual or acting-out behavior (Hetherington et al., 1992).

The relationship between children and their noncustodial parents also undergoes transformations during the period following divorce. As we have noted, contact with fathers declines markedly and as was found for fathers of children born to single teen mothers, less contact is maintained by white than by black fathers. It is not just the quantity but the quality of relationships with the noncustodial father that changes. Noncustodial fathers become either more permissive and indulgent or more disengaged from their children. They are more likely to assume a recreational, companionate role than the instrumental role of teacher or disciplinarian (Furstenberg & Cherlin, 1991). However, there is little congruence between the quality of father–child relationships before the divorce and the postdivorce noncustodial father–child relationship. Some previously disengaged fathers become very involved with their children after the breakup whereas some previously involved fathers gradually fade out of their children's lives (Hetherington, 1989). Fathers are more likely to maintain contact with sons than with daughters, but the primary determinants of the noncustodial father's ultimate relationship with his children are geographical proximity, remarriage, the quality of his relationship with the custodial mother (Furstenberg & Cherlin, 1991), and his feeling of having some power over decisions regarding his children (Selzer, 1991).

Conflict between parents

In a substantial group of families, conflict is sustained or accelerates following divorce (Hetherington, Cox, & Cox, 1982; Kline, Johnston, & Tschann, 1991; Maccoby, Depner, & Mnookin, 1990). Parental conflict is associated with inconsistent discipline, provides children with an opportunity to exploit parents and play one off against the other, and, when older, to escape careful monitoring of their activities. In addition, in such conflicted relationships, children may feel caught in the middle as they are sometimes asked to carry messages between parents, to inform each parent of the other's activities, to defend one parent against the other's disparaging remarks, or to justify wanting to spend time with the other parent (Buchanan, Maccoby, & Dornbusch, 1991; Hetherington, 1993). Being "caught in the middle," rather than divorce per se, or loss of contact with a noncustodial parent, has the most adverse effect on children's behavior and psychological well-being. Conflict has pervasive detrimental effects in both nondivorced and divorced families. An escape from conflict may be one of the most salutary effects of divorce for some children. Children in harmonious, divorced, single-parent households with an authoritative custodial parent show fewer problems than children in high-conflict nondivorced families.

Protective factors in coping with divorce

What are some protective factors that might alleviate the effects of these risks? Characteristics of the child, the relationship between the divorced parents, quality of parenting, and supports outside of the household have all been found to moderate the adverse effects of divorce and its concomitant stresses.

Individual characteristics of children

Many investigators have examined individual characteristics such as age at the time of divorce, gender, intelligence, temperament, and personality in attempting to explain diversity in children's response to divorce.

The role of age and gender is still open to question. Studies of age are inconclusive because children's age at divorce, time passed since divorce, and children's current age are confounded. Some studies suggest that children who are preschoolers at the time of divorce are most adversely affected (Zill et al., 1993); however, it seems most accurate to say that children of different ages respond in different ways to divorce, because of their varying developmental competencies and resources and because of the differing developmental tasks confronting them.

The results of gender are similarly inconclusive. Although some earlier studies and studies using preadolescent children reported that boys are more adversely affected by divorce and girls by remarriage, these effects have not been consistently found and they are less likely to be found in newer studies or those using adolescents.

Children's personality and temperamental characteristics are also important determinants of adjustment to disruptions in family life following divorce. Children with adjustment problems prior to the divorce are likely to exhibit increased problems following divorce. Moreover, more intelligent children with an easy temperament, high self-esteem, and an internal locus of control adapt more readily to disruptions in family life (Hetherington, 1989, 1991a, 1991b). Temperamentally difficult boys are more likely to evoke and to be the target of negative behavior from their divorced custodial mothers, especially if the mother is depressed, under high stress, and has little social support (Hetherington, 1989). On the other hand, the experience of divorce may actually strengthen the coping skills of temperamentally easy girls in situations where the divorce is only moderately stressful and support is available to the child (Hetherington, 1989, 1991a, 1991b). This phenomenon has been referred to as a "steeling" or "inoculation" effect, in which children's ability to deal with later stressors is enhanced because of exposure to and successful coping with current stressors (Rutter, 1987). Thus, the psychologically poor get poorer and the psychologically rich may get richer when confronting the changes and challenges of divorce.

Coparenting

The quality of the relationship with the noncustodial father and the existence of a good relationship between the divorced parents promotes positive adjustment in children. The move toward facilitating visitation and joint custody has been based on the premises that continued contact with both parents is desirable and that noncustodial parents with joint custody will be more likely to maintain contact and financial support. The response to the first premise must be that it depends on who is doing the visiting and on the relationship between the parents. As was true with fathers of children born to single teenaged mothers, it is the quality not the quantity of the relationship that is significant. Correlations between frequency of contact of the noncustodial father and child outcome are rarely found to be significant. If the noncustodial parent is reasonably well adjusted, competent in parenting, and has a close relationship with the child and if the child is not exposed to conflict between the two parents, continued contact can have a salutary effect on the child's adjustment. However, it takes an exceptionally close relationship with a noncustodial father to buffer a child from the deleterious effects of a conflictual, nonsupportive relationship with a custodial mother (Hetherington, et al., 1982). If there is high conflict between the parents, joint custody and continued contact can have adverse effects on the child (Maccoby & Mnookin, 1992; Wallerstein & Blakeslee, 1989). Although cooperative, consensual coparenting following divorce is the ideal relationship (Camara & Resnick, 1988), in most cases the best that can be attained is one of parallel parenting – that is, one of independent but noninterfering parental relations.

Authoritative parenting

Authoritative parenting, in contrast to disengaged, authoritarian, or permissive parenting, is associated with higher levels of social and academic competence and lower levels of psychopathology in children from both nondivorced and divorced families (Baumrind, 1989, 1991; Hetherington et al., 1992; Steinberg, Mounts,

Lamborn, & Dornbusch, 1991). The effects on children of a wide range of eco-logical stressors are, to a large extent, moderated or mediated by competent par-enting (Forgatch et al., 1995; Hetherington et al., 1992). Authoritative parenting by the custodial parent is more influential than that of the noncustodial parent, particularly as the salience of the noncustodial parent decreases with time. How-ever, a very close relationship with an authoritative noncustodial parent or, for preadolescent boys, with a stepfather can to some extent protect the child from a rejecting or incompetent custodial mother. With younger children, authoritative parenting by the custodial parent can eventually almost eliminate the effects of divorce. However, adolescents in restabilized divorced families or in stepfamilies with an authoritative custodial mother exhibit more behavior problems than do children in nondivorced families with authoritative parents (Hetherington et al., 1992). This suggests that factors other than parent–child relations, such as rela-tionships with siblings and peers and experiences in extrafamilial settings, play an increasingly salient role as children grow older.

It must be recognized that the parent–child relationship involves bidirectional processes. It is much easier to be an authoritative parent when dealing with a competent, well-adjusted, responsive child. There is considerable evidence that, as children grow older, and are under stressful life conditions or are part of a family in a state of transition or disequilibrium, adolescents become more influential in shaping their parents' behavior (Hetherington, 1993; Hetherington et al., 1992; Hetherington & Jodl, 1994). In contrast to relationships in nondivorced families, in divorced but especially in stepfamilies in the early stage of a remarriage an adolescent's behavior is more influential in shaping subsequent behavior of parents than vice versa (Hetherington et al., 1992; Hetherington & Jodl, 1994).

Support by others: Siblings, grandparents, peers, and schools

As children grow older, relationships in addition to those with the parents become more salient. A supportive relationship with a female sibling for girls, with a sup-portive authoritative stepfather for boys and with other adults such as grandparents and teachers can in some families play a protective role for children coping with their parents' marital transitions and concomitant stresses. However, these effects are not as powerful as those associated with authoritative parenting by the custodial parent (Hetherington, 1989; Hetherington et al., 1992) and are most likely to be-come salient when the custodial parent is nonauthoritative.

There is little evidence that grandparents are influential in the social, emotional, and cognitive development of their grandchildren from divorced families, unless they live in the home (Cherlin & Furstenberg, 1986). In general, the effects of support by grandmothers are largely mediated by changed maternal behavior in response to such support (Hetherington, 1989). However, involved grandfathers and other male relatives may have direct salutary effects on the social behavior and achievement of boys in divorced-mother-custody families (Hetherington, 1989).

As children age, schools and peers play an increasingly significant role in their adjustment. The social and cognitive development of children and adolescents from divorced families is enhanced if they are in schools with explicitly defined schedules, rules, and regulations and with consistent, warm discipline and expectations for mature behavior (Hetherington, 1993). Just as authoritative parents play a protective function for children going through family transitions, authoritative schools play a buffering role for children undergoing stress. Under stress, children gain security in a structured, safe, predictable environment. Authoritative teachers and school environments attenuate adverse outcomes for children in divorced and remarried families and in nondivorced families with high conflict. This protective effect of authoritative schools is most marked for boys, for children with difficult temperaments, for children exposed to multiple stressful life events, and for children with no authoritative parent in the home (Hetherington, 1993).

About one-third of adolescent children in divorced and remarried families become disengaged from the family (Hetherington, 1993). They become involved in school activities and the peer group or, if they are fortunate, they attach themselves to a responsive adult or to the family of a friend. The outcomes of this disengagement depend on the child's family situation and on the particular activities and type of associates with which the child becomes involved. If they are socially constructive activities and the child's associates are well adjusted, this move can be advantageous. Undesirable activities and an antisocial or delinquent peer group, on the other hand, usually have disastrous consequences (Steinberg, 1987). When disengagement from the family occurs, however, contact with an interested, supportive adult plays a critically important role in buffering the child against the development of behavior problems.

Common themes across the two family constellations

In divorced-mother-custody families as in families with children born to a single teenaged mother, the adjustment of children depends to a large extent on the well-being of mothers. However, mothers and children in both types of families encounter common adverse circumstances that may directly or indirectly jeopardize their mental health. Some socioeconomic and personal risk factors may have anteceded, as well as increased as a result of, teenaged childbearing or divorce.

Poverty, social isolation, task overload, and circumstances such as multiple geographic moves and changes in housing, job instability, and residence in disorganized neighborhoods that make raising competent children more difficult are common for both types of families. Single and divorced mothers must juggle multiple roles, balancing child care while pursuing education or employment outside of the home.

There are also some similarities in protective factors for single teenaged mothers and their children, such as support from extended kin and the father. However, in both types of families, contact and support from fathers tend to diminish with time and constructive cooperative coparenting relationships are rare. The most important protective factor in the well-being of children from both types of families is authoritative parenting by the mother, which serves to moderate or mediate the outcomes of the multiple risk factors to which children with a single teen mother or a divorced mother are exposed.

Finally, in spite of the difficult circumstances in their lives, the adjustment in these families is characterized by considerable resiliency. Although, on the average, children born to single teenaged or divorced mothers show more problems than children in two-parent, nondivorced families, most emerge as competent individuals with few psychological, social, academic, or conduct problems.

Implications for future research

Whereas there are clearly many similarities across the research on teenaged mothers and divorced families, there are several differences as well in terms of salient constructs examined, research designs employed, and findings obtained. Given such differences, the cumulative evidence that has been obtained within either one of these research areas has implications for future research directions in the other. For example, most of the research on family process in families with a teenaged mother, especially those involving observations, focus on mothers with infants or younger children. Following the leads obtained from research on divorce, there needs to be more scrutiny of individual difference variables such as age, gender, temperament, intelligence, and personality in the adjustment of children born to a single teenaged mother. In addition, as is beginning to be done in studies of divorce, more attention in studies of families with single teen mothers needs to be paid to the role of fathers, stepparents, peers, and schools as potential risks or protective factors for children.

Finally, more longitudinal studies of both single teen and divorced families need to be carried out. Adaptation in these families is a dynamic process that takes place over time with different challenges, risks, and resources being confronted along the way. The timing and sequence of experiences and events that may influence child and family outcomes vary widely. Cross-sectional studies take a single slice out of adaptive, developmental trajectories, giving a static, often misleading picture of single mothers and their children.

Implications for intervention

Ideally interventions should be aimed at preventing single teenaged parenthood, by delaying sexual activity and improving contraception, supporting marriage, reducing conflict and stress in families, and promoting responsibility in interpersonal relations. Such preventative programs would help to avert the necessity of dealing with problems related to single teenaged parenting and divorce.

The key elements in successful preventative interventions in teenaged childbearing involve initiating the program before high-risk behavior has begun or teenaged conception has occurred and in having an accessible multifaceted program that is designed to build trust among recipients (Zabin & Hayward, 1993). Sex education programs by themselves change levels of sexual knowledge but often have little impact on sexual activity or pregnancy. Explicit counseling about sexuality and contraception in combination with reproductive health care and access to contraception does delay sexual onset, reduces the frequency of intercourse, and enhances contraceptive use.

Encouraging programs that support marriage does not mean forcing couples to remain in persistently dysfunctional marriages. Children adapt better in a harmonious, authoritative single-parent household than in a conflict ridden two-parent household (Hetherington & Stanley-Hagan, 1986). However, most couples at sometime encounter problems in their relationship or temporary periods of stress, associated with such things as birth of their first child (Cowan & Cowan, 1992), the presence of early teenaged children (Hetherington et al., 1992), job loss or economic duress (Elder, 1974; McLanahan & Sandefur, 1994) that may cause them to question the value of the relationship and to consider separation. A wide array of supportive interventions, many focused on conflict resolution and improving family communication, have been found effective in temporarily alleviating family problems and reducing the likelihood of divorce (Gottman, 1994). However, many of the needs of married couples and programs and policies that contribute to their well-being and marital stability are similar to those of single-parent, mother-headed households. Although not available to many families in the United States, economic security, education and job training, adequate and accessible health care and child care, and universal nonstigmatizing income support plans have been found to enhance family functioning and child development in diverse family forms (see Hartman, 1993, and McLanahan & Sandefur, 1994, for a more detailed discussion of family policy).

Some legal innovations such as no-fault divorce, the introduction of presumptive standards with specified amounts of child support, joint custody, and mandatory mediation have been introduced with the goal of reducing litigation, and conflict in divorce (Emery, 1994). Although many have been successful in this goal, some have had unanticipated consequences. For example, although in most families joint custody had led to greater involvement of fathers with their children and greater maintenance of child support payments (Maccoby & Mnookin, 1992; Seltzer, 1991), in couples who have continuing hostile, acrimonious relationships it is associated with increased conflict and problems in the adjustment of children (Maccoby & Mnookin, 1992).

Finally, policies that facilitate or enforce nonresidential fathers' responsibility for support of their children are essential. To improve the economic condition of

single mothers and their children, some of the burden must be taken from the single
mothers and placed on fathers and society (McLanahan & Sandefur, 1994).

References

Achenbach, T. M., & Edelbrock, C. S. (1983). *Manual for the Child Behavior Checklist and Revised Child Behavior Profile*. New York: Queen City Printer.

Amato, P. R. (1993). Children's adjustment to divorce: Theories, hypotheses and empirical support. *Journal of Marriage and the Family, 55,* 23–38.

Amato, P. R., & Keith, B. (1991a). Parental divorce and the well-being of children: A meta-analysis. *Psychological Bulletin, 110,* 26–46.

Amato, P. R., & Keith, B. (1991b). Parental divorce and adult well-being: A meta-analysis. *Journal of Marriage and the Family, 53,* 43–58.

Baumrind, D. (1989, April). *Sex-differentiated socialization effects in childhood and adolescence in divorced and intact families*. Paper presented at the biennial meetings of the Society for Research on Child Development, Kansas City, MO.

Baumrind, D. (1991). Effective parenting during the early adolescent transition. In P. A. Cowan & E. M. Hetherington (Eds.), *Family transitions* (pp. 111–163). Hillsdale, NJ: Erlbaum.

Block, J. H., Block, J., & Gjerde, P. F. (1986). The personality of children prior to divorce: A prospective study. *Child Development, 57,* 827–840.

Block, J. H., Block, J., & Gjerde, P. F. (1988). Parental functioning and the home environment in families of divorce: Prospective and concurrent analyses. *Journal of the American Academy of Child and Adolescent Psychiatry, 27,* 207–213.

Buchanan, C. M., Maccoby, E. E., & Dornbusch, S. M. (1991). Caught between parents: Adolescents' experience in divorced homes. *Child Development, 62,* 1008–1029.

Bumpass, L. L. (1990). What's happening to the family? Interactions between demographic and institutional change. *Demography, 27,* 483–498.

Bumpass, L. L., & Raley, R. K. (1993). Trends in durations of single-parent families. National Survey of Families and Households Working Paper No. 58. Center for Demography, University of Wisconsin, Madison.

Bumpass, L. L., Sweet, J. A., & Castro-Martin, T. (1990). Changing patterns of remarriage. *Journal of Marriage and the Family, 52,* 747–756.

Burton, L. M. (1995). The timing of childbearing, family structure and the role responsibilities of aging black women. In E. M. Hetherington & E. A. Blechman (Eds.), *Stress, coping and resiliency in children and families* (pp. 55–171). Hillsdale, NJ: Erlbaum.

Burton, L. M., & Bengston, V. L. (1985). Black grandmothers: Issues of timing and continuity of roles. In V. L. Bengston & J. Robertson (Eds.), *Grandparent research and policy perspectives* (pp. 61–77). Beverly Hills, CA: Sage.

Camara, K. A., & Resnick, G. (1988). Interparental conflict and cooperation: Factors moderating children's post-divorce adjustment. In E. M. Hetherington & J. Arasteh (Eds.), *Divorced, single-parent, and stepparent families* (pp. 169–195). Englewood Cliffs, NJ: LEA.

Capaldi, D. M., & Patterson, G. R. (1991). Relation of parental transitions to boys' adjustment problems: I. A linear hypothesis. II. Mothers at risk for transitions and unskilled parenting. *Developmental Psychology, 3,* 489–504.

Castro-Martin, T., & Bumpass, L. (1989). Recent trends and differentials in marital disruption. *Demography, 26,* 37–51.

Chase-Lansdale, P. L., Brooks-Gunn, J., & Paikoff, R. L. (1991). Research and programs for adolescent mothers: Missing links and future promises. *Family Relations, 40,* 396–403.

Chase-Lansdale, P. L., Brooks-Gunn, J., & Zamsky, E. S. (1994). Young African-American multigenerational families in poverty: Quality of mothering and grandmothering. *Child Development, 65,* 373–393.

Chase-Lansdale, P. L., Wakschlag, L. S., & Brooks-Gunn, J. (in press). A psychological perspective on the development of caring in children and youth: The role of the family. *Journal of Adolescence.*

Cherlin, A. J. (1992). *Marriage, divorce and remarriage.* Cambridge, MA: Harvard University Press.

Cherlin, A. J., & Furstenberg, F. F., Jr. (1986). *The new American grandparent: A place in the family, a life apart.* New York: Basic Books.

Cherlin, A. J., & Furstenberg, F. F., Jr. (1994). Stepfamilies in the United States: A reconsideration. In J. Blake & J. Hagen (Eds.), *Annual Review of Sociology* (pp. 359–381). Palo Alto, CA: Annual Reviews.

Cherlin, A. J., Furstenberg, F. F., Jr., Chase-Lansdale, P. L., Kiernana, K. E., Robins, P. K., Morrison, D. R., & Teitler, J. O. (1991). Longitudinal studies of effects of divorce on children in Great Britain and the United States. *Science, 252,* 1386–1389.

Cowan, C. P., & Cowan, P. A. (1992). *When partners become parents.* New York: Basic Books.

Crockenberg, S. (1981). Infant irritability, responsiveness and social support influences in the security of infant-mother attachment. *Child Development, 52,* 857–865.

Duncan, G. J., & Hoffman, S. D. (1985). A reconsideration of the economic consequences of marital dissolution. *Demography, 22,* 485–497.

Elder, G. H. (1974). *Children of the Great Depression.* Chicago: University of Chicago Press.

Emery, R. E. (1994). *Renegotiating family relationships.* New York: Guilford.

Forgatch, M. S., Patterson, G. R., & Ray, J. A. (1995). Divorce and boys' adjustment problems: Two paths with a single model. In E. M. Hetherington & E. A. Blechman (Eds.), *Stress, coping and resiliency in children and families* (pp. 67–105). Hillsdale, NJ: Erlbaum.

Furstenberg, F. F., Jr. (1991a). As the pendulum swings: Teenage childbearing and social concern. *Family Relations, 40,* 127–138.

Furstenberg, F. F., Jr. (1991b). Coming of age in a changing family system. In S. S. Feldman & G. R. Elliott (Eds.), *At the threshold: The developing adolescent* (pp. 147–170). Cambridge, MA: Harvard University Press.

Furstenberg, F. F., Jr., Brooks-Gunn, J., & Chase-Lansdale, P. L. (1989). Teenaged pregnancy and childbearing. *American Psychologist, 44* (2), 313–320.

Furstenberg, F. F., Jr., Brooks-Gunn, J., & Morgan, S. P. (1987). *Adolescent mothers in later life.* Cambridge: Cambridge University Press.

Furstenberg, F. F., Jr., & Cherlin, A. (1991). *Divided families: What happens to children when parents part.* Cambridge, MA: Harvard University Press.

Furstenberg, F. F., Jr., & Harris, K. M. (1993). When and why fathers matter: Impacts of father involvement on children of adolescent mothers. In R. I. Herman & T. J. Ooms (Eds.), *Young unwed fathers* (pp. 117–138). Philadelphia: Temple University Press.

Garfinkel, I., & McLanahan, S. (1986). *Single mothers and their children: A new American dilemma.* Washington, DC: Urban Institute Press.

Gotlib, I. H., & McCabe, S. B. (1990). Marriage and psychopathology. In F. Fincham & T. Bradbury (Eds.), *The psychology of marriage* (pp. 226–257). New York: Guilford.

Gottman, J. M. (1994). *What predicts divorce?* Hillsdale, NJ: Erlbaum.

Hardy, J. B., & Zabin, L. S. (1991). *Adolescent pregnancy in an urban environment: Issues, programs and evaluation.* Washington, DC: Urban Institute Press.

Hartman, A. (1993). Challenges for family policy. In F. Walsh (Ed.), *Normal family process* (pp. 474–500). New York: Guilford.

Hayes, C. D. (1987). *Risking the future: Adolescent sexuality, pregnancy and childbearing* (Vol. 1). Washington, DC: National Academy Press.

Hetherington, E. M. (1989). Coping with family transitions: Winners, losers and survivors. *Child Development, 60,* 1–14.

Hetherington, E. M. (1991a). Presidential address: Families, lies, and videotapes. *Journal of Research on Adolescence, 1,* 323–348.

Hetherington, E. M. (1991b). The role of individual differences and family relationships in children's coping with divorce and remarriage. In P. Cowan & E. M. Hetherington (Eds.), *Family transitions* (pp. 165–174). Hillsdale, NJ: Erlbaum.

Hetherington, E. M. (1993). A review of the Virginia Longitudinal Study of Divorce and Remarriage: A focus on early adolescence. *Journal of Family Psychology, 7,* 39–56.

Hetherington, E. M., Clingempeel, W. G., Anderson, E. R., Deal, J. E., Stanley-Hagan, M., Hollier, E. A., & Lindner, M. S. (1992). Coping with marital transitions: A family systems perspective. *Monographs of the Society for Research in Child Development, 57* (Serial No. 227).

Hetherington, E. M., Cox, M., & Cox, R. (1982). Effects of divorce on parents and children. In M. Lamb (Ed.), *Nontraditional families* (pp. 233–288). Hillsdale, NJ: Erlbaum.

Hetherington, E. M., & Jodl, K. M. (1994). Stepfamilies as settings for child development. In A. Booth & J. Dunn (Eds.), *Stepfamilies: Who benefits? Who does not?* (pp. 55–79). Hillsdale, NJ: Erlbaum.

Hetherington, E. M., & Stanley-Hagan, M. S. (1986). Divorced fathers: Stress, coping, and adjustment. In M. E. Lamb (Ed.), *The father's role: Applied perspectives* (pp. 103–134). New York: Wiley.

Hetherington, E. M., & Stanley-Hagan, M. S. (1995). Parenting in divorced and remarried families. In M. Bornstein (Ed.), *Handbook of parenting* (Vol. 3, pp. 233–254). Hillsdale, NJ: Erlbaum.

Hofferth, S. L. (1987). Social and economic consequences of teenage childbearing. In S. L. Hofferth & C. D. Hayes (Eds.), *Risking the future: Adolescent sexuality, pregnancy and childbearing* (Vol. 2, pp. 123–144). Washington, DC: National Academy Press.

Hogan, D. P., Hao, L. X., & Parish, W. L. (1990). Race, kin networks and assistance to mother-headed families. *Social Forces, 68,* 797–812.

Kellam, S. G., Ensminger, M. E., & Turner, R. J. (1977). Family structure and the mental health of children. *Archives of General Psychiatry, 34,* 1012–1022.

Kiecolt-Glaser, J. K., Fisher, L. D., Ogrocki, P., Stout, J. C., Speicher, C. E., & Glaser, R. (1987). Marital quality, marital disruption, and immune function. *Psychosomatic Medicine, 49,* 13–34.

Kline, M., Johnston, J. R., & Tschann, J. M. (1991). The long shadow of marital conflict: A model of children's postdivorce adjustment. *Journal of Marriage and the Family, 53,* 297–309.

Lamb, M. E., & Elster, A. B. (1986). Parental behavior of adolescent mothers and fathers. In A. B. Elster & M. E. Lamb (Eds.), *Adolescent fatherhood.* Hillsdale, NJ: Erlbaum.

Luster, T., & Mittelslaedt, J. (1993). Adolescent mothers. In T. Luster & L. Okagaki (Eds.), *Parenting: An ecological perspective.* Hillsdale, NJ: Erlbaum.

Maccoby, E. E., Depner, C. E., & Mnookin, R. H. (1990). Co-parenting in the second year after divorce. *Journal of Marriage and the Family, 52,* 141–155.

Maccoby, E. E., & Mnookin, R. H. (1992). *Dividing the child.* Cambridge, MA: Harvard University Press.

McLanahan, S., & Booth, K. (1989). Mother-only families: Problems, prospects, and politics. *Journal of Marriage and the Family, 51,* 557–580.

McLanahan, S., & Sandefur, G. (1994). *Growing up with a single parent: What hurts, what helps.* Cambridge, MA: Harvard University Press.

McLoyd, V. C. (1990). The impact of economic hardship on black families and children: Psychological distress, parenting, socioemotional development. *Child Development, 61,* 311–346.

Miller, B. C., & Moore, K. A. (1990). Adolescent sexual behavior, pregnancy and parenting: Research through the 1980s. *Journal of Marriage and the Family, 52,* 1025–1044.

Moore, K. A. (1994). *Facts at a glance.* Washington, DC: Child Trends.

Moore, K. A., Peterson, J. E., & Furstenberg Jr., F. F. (1984). *Starting early: The antecedents of early premarital intercourse.* Paper presented at the annual meeting of the Population Association of America.

Moore, K. A., Snyder, N. O., & Glei, D. (1995). *Facts at a glance.* Washington, DC: Child Trends.

National Center for Health Statistics. (1993, September). *Advance report of final natality statistics, 1991. Monthly Vital Statistics Report, 42(3), Supplement.* Hyattsville, MD: Public Health Service.

Newcomer, S. F., & Udry, J. R. (1984). Mothers' influence on the sexual behavior of their teenage children. *Journal of Marriage and the Family, 43,* 477–485.

Norton, A. J., & Miller, L. F. (1992). Marriage, divorce and remarriage in the 1990's. In *Current Population Reports* (pp. 23–180). Washington, DC: Bureau of the Census.

Parke, R. D. (1995). Fathers and families. In M. Bornstein (Ed.), *Handbook of parenting* (Vol. 3, pp. 27–64). Hillsdale, NJ: Erlbaum.

Rutter, M. (1987). Psychosocial resilience and protective mechanisms. *American Journal of Orthopsychiatry, 57,* 316–331.

Seltzer, J. A. (1991). Relationships between fathers and children who live apart: The father's role after separation. *Journal of Marriage and the Family, 53,* 79–101.

Snyder, T. D., & Fromboluti, C. S. (1993). *Youth Indicators 1993.* Washington, DC: National Center for Education Statistics.

Speiker, S. J. (1991, April). *Mothers in adolescence: Factors related to infant attachment and disorganization.* Paper presented at the biennial meeting of the Society for Research in Child Development, Seattle, WA.

Steinberg, L. (1987). Single parents, stepparents, and the susceptibility of adolescents to antisocial peer pressure. *Child Development, 58,* 269–275.

Steinberg, L., Mounts, N. S., Lamborn, S. D., & Dornbusch, S. M. (1991). Authoritative parenting and adolescent adjustment across varied ecological niches. *Journal of Research on Adolescence, 1,* 19–36.

Udry, J. R., Billy, T. O. G., Morris, N. M., Groffe, T. R., & Raj, M. H. (1985). Serum androgenic hormones motivate sexual behavior in adolescent boys. *Fertility and Sterility, 43,* 90–94.

Udry, J. R., Talbert, R., & Morris, M. N. (1986). Biosocial foundations for adolescent female sexuality. *Demography, 23,* 217–230.

Wallerstein, J. S., & Blakeslee, S. (1989). *Second chances: Men, women, and children a decade after divorce.* New York: Ticknor & Fields.

Wasserman, G., Brunelli, S. A., & Raub, V. A. (1990). Social supports and living arrangements of adolescent and adult mothers. *Journal of Adolescent Research, 5,* 54–66.

Wilson, W. J. (1987). *The truly disadvantaged: The inner city, the underclass and public policy.* Chicago: University of Chicago Press.

Zabin, L. S., & Hayward, S. C. (1993). *Adolescent sexual behavior and childbearing.* New York: Sage.

Zill, N., Morrison, D. R., & Corio, M. J. (1993). Long-term effects of parental divorce on parent-child relationships, adjustment, and achievement in young adulthood. *Journal of Family Psychology, 7,* 91–103.

16 Children of depressed mothers: A developmental and interactional perspective

Marian Radke-Yarrow and Bonnie Klimes-Dougan

Children of depressed parents have come to be viewed as part of a lineage of pathology: from grandparents and relatives to parents to children. Being born to and reared by a depressed parent carries the expectation of problems. From several decades of research on children of affectively ill parents, the findings have quite uniformly confirmed this expectation (see reviews by Beardslee, Bemporad, Keller, & Klerman, 1983; Downey & Coyne, 1990). There are, however, important amendments: Not all offspring develop problems; their problems are not all of the same kind. Few guides have emerged from research studies regarding the mechanisms through which problems are or are not transmitted from parent to offspring. The challenge now is to understand the processes by which some children of depressed parents succumb to psychiatric disorders, especially depression, and/or to painful impairments in social functioning, and some develop adaptively.

In order to achieve this objective, there is a need for the kind of studies that will allow us to see the parent and child and the environment in which they live in the degree of detail that reveals the phenomena. The depressed parent is not simply a diagnosis and the offspring are not simply sets of problems. The behavior of child and parent is embedded in a history of relationships and in multiple contexts that cannot be ignored if we are to understand the intergenerational successions that have been repeatedly documented. Knowing that children of depressed parents are at risk for problems poses the questions, Why and how does this occur?

There have been many studies of offspring of depressed parents, beginning especially in the 1970s. They had as an initial goal to determine the prevalence rates of psychiatric disorders in the offspring. But in researching rates of problems, it soon became evident that although rates are consistently elevated, there is vast diversity in offspring outcomes – in the presence of disorder and in the kind of disorder. The picture of diversity in the depressed parents' impairments, in the offspring characteristics, and in correlates of depression, and particularly in the family contexts, has significantly changed the research focus. The change in focus provides the bases for many hypotheses regarding processes through which children's lives are affected and through which disorders are transmitted across generations.

If children of depressed parents are studied over the course of their development,

374

in reciprocal interaction with parental characteristics and with the distal and proximal factors in their behavioral environments (Magnusson & Bergman, 1988), we can perhaps acquire some understanding of the mechanisms involved. From the evidence now available, one must anticipate diverse mechanisms of transmission.

It is from this perspective that we are reporting data from a longitudinal study of depressed mothers and their children and a comparison group of well parents and their children. We are using three organizing propositions through which to examine the data.

First, the developmental stage of the child is a determining factor in the impact of maternal depression on the child. Developmental capabilities and needs interact with maternal depression and its correlates. We examine child behavior at successive ages to explore the effects of maternal depression in the context of development.

Second, maternal illness characteristics and correlated family conditions and relationships are significant determinants of how the child is involved with the mother's depression. The child is likely to be involved in multiple ways. The mechanisms of influence depend on the nature of these involvements. Moreover, influences on child functioning are likely to depend on how factors exist in combination.

Third, mechanisms of influence on children's functioning, we believe, are not to be found in single, isolated causal links, but in interacting combinations of factors that include the child as an active participant (e.g., Zigler & Glick, 1986). The same outcomes are not necessarily the result of the same processes. The task for research is to identify particularistic mechanisms as well as "main effects" in processes of transmission.

Our propositions are phrased in terms of problems, and specifically problems of children of depressed parents. Processes in adaptive development and in the development of children of well parents pose complementary questions.

Study description

The families on whom we are reporting are participants in a larger longitudinal study (Radke-Yarrow, 1989) of parental psychopathology and child development. The families in the present analysis are 42 mothers with major (unipolar) depression and 30 mothers without past or current psychiatric problems. Parents' diagnoses are based on the Schedule for affective Disorders Schizophrenia – lifetime version SADS-L; (Spitzer & Endicott, 1977) administered at the beginning of the study, and on the interval SADS administered 6 years into the study. The mothers are moderately to severely depressed. In all families, the mother is the primary caregiver. In the families of depressed mothers, the fathers had a diagnosis at intake (limited to depression or anxiety) or were without a diagnosis. In the families of well mothers, both parents were without diagnoses at the beginning of the study. The families are predominantly middle to upper middle class (Hollingshead, 1975).

Of the well families, 87% are Caucasian, 10% are African American, and 3% are Asian American. Of the depressed families, 83% are Caucasian, 14% are African American, and 2% are Hispanic. In approximately 80% of the families, both parents are present throughout this study.

Two children in each family participated in this study. Families were studied intensively at three transitional developmental stages. At the time of the *first assessment* (T_1), the younger sibling (1½ to 3½ years) was leaving toddlerhood and dealing with early developmental demands regarding autonomy, self-control, and socialization. Normative expectations for the older sibling (5 to 7 years) in the early school years included the additional demands and opportunities of school requirements and peer relationships. At the *second assessment* period (T_2) about 3 years later, the younger child was in the early school years (5 to 6 years) and the older sibling (8 to 11 years) was in middle childhood, a period of consolidation of earlier developmental accomplishments with broader and more complex views of the self and others. The *third assessment* (T_3) was taken approximately 3 years later, bringing the younger sibling to middle childhood (8 to 11 years) and the older sibling into adolescence (12 to 15 years), a period of changing parent–child relationships and increased prominence of extrafamilial relationships. The gender in children of depressed mothers was, respectively, 50% and 43% male in the younger and older cohorts and children of the well mothers were, respectively, 53% and 47% males in the younger and older cohorts.

Procedures

In the larger study, the measurement procedures include interviews, standard tests, psychiatric interviews, and extensive behavior observation. Systematic observations provide information on the mothers and children. The families came to a research apartment for many half-day visits over the years. At T_1 and T_2, time in the apartment was planned to mimic aspects of an ordinary day in the lives of mother and young children. Situations were planned to sample critical day-to-day aspects of child rearing, such as usual routines (e.g., preparing lunch, cleaning up), ambiguities of new experiences, burdening multiple demands, separations, frustrations, relaxing, and pleasant activities. Standard paradigms (e.g., the Strange Situation to measure attachment) were also introduced into the sessions. Behavior in the apartment was videotaped.

Psychiatric evaluations of the children were made at each developmental stage (Child Assessment Schedule, [CAS] – Hodges, Kline, Fitch, McKnew, & Cytryn, 1981; Diagnostic Interview for Children and Adolescents [DICA] – Herjanic & Reich, 1982) and reports by mother at each developmental stage (Child Behavior Check List [CBCL] – Achenbach & Edelbrock, 1919; the parent's report on the child [DICA-P] – Herjanic & Reich, 1982). For the youngest children at T_1, a psychiatric play "interview" was used, combined with mother's report. At each age, the child was given a "diagnosis" based on DSM-III-R criteria. At the younger ages, "problem of clinical concern" better represents the meaning of the diagnostic label. (For details of assessment procedures, see Radke-Yarrow, Nottelmann, Martinez, Fox, & Belmont, 1992; Tarullo, Richardson, Radke-Yarrow, & Martinez, 1995).

Children's problems were assessed in psychiatric terms (DSM-III-R) as clusters of symptoms: *disruptive disorders* – conduct disorder, oppositional defiant disorder, and attention deficit hyperactivity disorder; *mood disorders* – major depression, dysthymia, mania, hypomania, suicidal ideation, adjustment disorder with depressive mood; and *anxiety disorders* – separation anxiety, avoidant disorder, overanxious disorder, and obsessive compulsive disorder.

Overall, measures of behavioral control, affect expression and regulation, quality of relationships, cognitive capacity, school functioning, and attitudes regarding self were included in assessments of the children. Thus, the possible effects of maternal depression on children's lives were evaluated across a broad range of psychosocial functioning.

Data on the mother, as on the child, came from observations of behavior in the apartment. These observations furnished information on the individual mother's expression of depression and on her patterns of interacting with her children. Characteristics of the mother's depression in terms of its episodic quality – recurrence of episodes – were determined from the SADS interview. And personality disorders on which mother's depression was superimposed (or of which it was a part) were diagnosed through an interview (Personality Disorder Examination; Loranger, 1988).

Mothers were the informants concerning family conditions and relationships (a modified Brown and Harris interview, 1978). Marital relationships, other family relationships, losses of significant persons, and economic and health factors in the family were covered.

In the present report, we have focused on the psychiatric evaluations of the children in relation to mothers' psychiatric characteristics and family conditions. Success in bringing insights to the three propositions that we have stated depends on the sensitivity of our developmentally repeated measures of mother, family, and child. The intent has been to provide a description as well as conceptualization of the phenomena that are changing as they are being studied.

Maternal depression and children's functioning at successive developmental stages

We are reporting on each sibling cohort, following the younger children from preschool to late childhood (a mean age of approximately 10 years) and the older siblings to early adolescence (a mean age of approximately 13 years). In a truly developmental analysis, we are following the same child from age to age.

To set the stage for examining developmental origins and changes in children's behavior as a function of mothers' depression, we begin with the late childhood

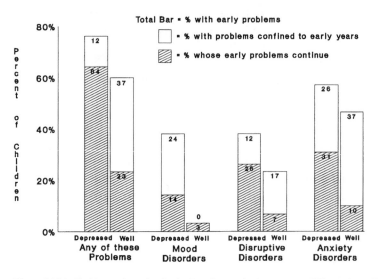

Figure 16.1A. Problems appearing in the first 6 years in the younger sibling cohort: Trajectories up through middle childhood.

and early adolescent status of these children. What kinds of inroads into psychosocial functioning have been made by the end of childhood? Do the children of depressed mothers differ appreciably from the children whose psychiatrically well parents place them at low risk for developmental difficulties?

At 13 years, 69% of the older children of depressed mothers have a diagnosed problem; at 10 years, 62% of the younger siblings have a diagnosed problem of depression, anxiety, or disruptive behavior. These figures are double the corresponding figures (37% and 30%) for children of well parents. At 13 years and 10 years, children (12% and 20%, respectively) are showing clinically severe problems in relationships with peers (the CBCL scale with items such as "doesn't get along with other children," "is teased a lot"). Seventeen percent of the children in each cohort have clinically high CBCL scores on social withdrawal, and equal numbers are not meeting school performance requirements, either academically or in behavior. None of the children of well parents is having serious difficulties in these domains. These outcomes are reasons to turn to earlier periods in the children's lives to look for origins of specific problems and to observe their developmental evolution.

A developmental profile was constructed for each child indicating the problem(s) present at each stage and their fate at subsequent ages. We are reporting first on the younger sibling cohort, summarizing data from 6 years (early childhood; assessment periods T_1 and T_2) and following the developmental course to the 8- to 11-year stage (refer to Figure 16.1A). The profiles make a strong point: At or before 6 years, a majority of children of well (60%) and depressed (76%) mothers alike are manifesting difficulties with important tasks to be accomplished in the early years, namely, socialized control of behavior and affect regulation (any of these problems). There is, however, a notable difference in the fate of these problems. Among the children of well parents, 37% have problems in early childhood that are confined to those years; 23% have early problems that continue into later years. In contrast, among children of depressed mothers, problems in early childhood do not go away (only 12% of the children have problems confined to the first 6 years). In 64% of the children, problems begin in the early years and recur later or simply continue.

Children's vulnerabilities to specific affective and control problems make an early appearance. This is especially true for depressive problems. Only one child of a well mother is so diagnosed. Among children of depressed mothers, mood disturbance appears under the age of 6 in 24% of the children without recurrence in childhood, and in 14% with recurrence in later childhood. For disruptive behavior, the early problems in well families have mainly disappeared by late childhood. In children of depressed mothers, however, 38% are disruptive in the early years, and 26% continue a disruptive developmental path. Early anxiety is high (47% and 57% in well and depressed groups, respectively). It continues to be high (31%) in children of depressed mothers.

What is the message in these childhood profiles? Filtering out problems that can be counted as normative socialization difficulties of the early years, we are left with an extra load of disorders carried by many of the children of depressed mothers more or less throughout their childhood.

Analysis of the age profiles of the older siblings allows us to continue to explore development as a variable in the effects of maternal depression (refer to Figure 16.1B). For these children, we are comparing early childhood (up to about 6 years; T_1 assessment) with middle childhood and adolescence (8 to 15 years; assessments at T_2 and T_3). Only 9% of the children of depressed parents have not presented a problem by early adolescence. The comparable figure for children of well mothers is 40%.

While mood disturbance appears at some time in 20% of the children of well mothers, a high frequency, it appears recurrently in only 3%. Mood disturbances occur in 62% of the children of depressed mothers, recurrently in 36% of the children. Diagnoses of disruptive behavior show a similar course. Disruptive disorders appear in 58% of the children of depressed mothers, recurrently in 29% (in the well group, 10% and 7%, respectively). There is little difference in the patterns of anxiety disorders between children of depressed and well mothers.

The profiles of both sibling groups suggest that high vulnerability in the offspring of depressed mothers is present early and that maternal depression makes a difference in the childhood of many of the offspring. An ''outcome'' diagnosis in the pubertal or adolescent period does not tell the full account of the impact on the child.

These data raise many questions for research. They bring attention to early de-

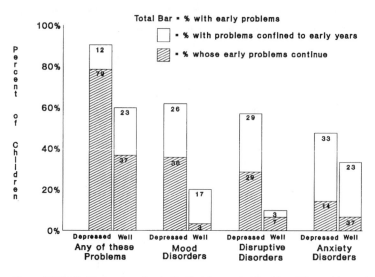

Figure 16.1B. Problems appearing in the first 6 years in the older sibling cohort: trajectories up through middle childhood and adolescence.

velopment, and to differences in timing and course of problems. They raise questions of prediction: What are the high-risk early problems? Is there predictability in the progression of problems? How often do children's problems involve disturbances that do not fit neatly (or fit multiply) into the familiar DSM diagnostic categories of adult origin?

In the literature, externalizing problems or conduct disorders have been shown to exhibit continuity over time. Data from the present study suggest that early depressive problems need a closer look with regard to long-term continuities. For example, nine children in the older sibling cohort – offspring of depressed mothers – were diagnosed with depressive disturbance in an age range of 5 to 7 years. All of these children had recurrent diagnoses of internalizing problems by adolescence. Is it possible that depressive disorders, which are less easily assessed in children, have as much continuity as disruptive problems?

Thus far, we have seen the child only within the abstraction of developmental stage. We turn now to our second proposition, to examine how maternal depression directly and indirectly involves children, and how these varied involvements relate to child functioning.

Effects of maternal illness characteristics on child functioning

Characteristics of the individual mother's illness influence the amount and nature of the child's exposure to her depression (e.g., Keller et al., 1986). We examined two aspects of maternal illness in relation to child functioning; the chronicity of illness (number of episodes) and the presence of comorbid disorders (personality disorders). Major depressive episodes would be expected to expose the child to magnified maternal symptomatic behavior and, quite likely, behavior interfering with supportive mothering. Children's problems were examined in relation to maternal episode characteristics: a single episode in the child's experience (M = 42 weeks) or multiple episodes (M = 146 weeks). Maternal depression, however, is not simply a matter of major episodes. Evidence from studies such as those by Billings and Moos (1985) and Stein et al. (1991) points to "residuals" of chronic depression, linked to maternal behavior independent of episodes. To assess the "chronic" differences in depressed mothers' behavior, mother's personality disorders were examined in relation to children's problems.

The percents of children exhibiting problems in relation to mother's single or multiple depressive episodes are presented in Figure 16.2 (A and B). The effects of recurrent maternal episodes are, at best, modest. Differences are mainly accounted for by contrasts between mothers with multiple depressive episodes and well mothers. Although the overall pattern in child problems is one of progressive increase from well – to one episode – to multiple episode groups, differences between children of mothers with single or multiple episodes do not differ significantly. The relatively weak effect of this variable probably reflects the considerable variance within each category in this dichotomy as well as variance in mothers' interepisodic functioning. The data on the effects of personality disorders in the depressed mothers support this speculation.

Three-quarters of the depressed mothers have personality disorders, which is to say that problematic functioning is ongoing. Of the well mothers, 19% have a personality disorder. Personality disorders (using a dimensional measure based on the Personality Disorders Examination, [PDE]) in depressed mothers are significantly positively correlated with children's total behavior problem scores on the CBCL, ranging from $r = +.38*$ to $r = +.53*$. There are no significant associations in the children of well mothers.

These data allow us to move toward mechanisms by inquiring into the ways in which mothers' personality disorders involve their children by influencing mothers' parenting behavior. Here we are drawing upon findings reported from the larger longitudinal study (DeMulder, Tarullo, Klimes-Dougan, Free, Radke-Yarrow, 1995). Depressed mothers with a personality disorder were more critical, irritable, and psychologically unavailable in interactions with their children than the depressed mothers without a disorder. Especially with the preschool-age child, a subgroup of mothers showed a lack of engagement with the child. This we would interpret as a serious interference with the mother–child relationship at a critical developmental period. This is consistent with the findings of early and persistent problems in children of depressed mothers.

We hypothesize that it is the history and chronicity of maternal dysfunctional behavior more than acute expressions of depression that bring about the greatest damage to children's well-being. It should be noted that these maternal character-

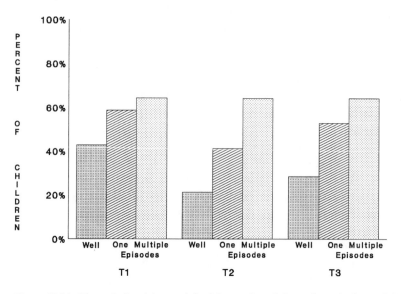

Figure 16.2A. Maternal chronicity, as defined by number of depressive episodes, and the percent of children in the younger cohort with any problems. X^2 analyses yielded significant group differences at the $p < .05$ level for children of mothers with multiple depressive episodes and children of well mothers at T_2 and T_3.

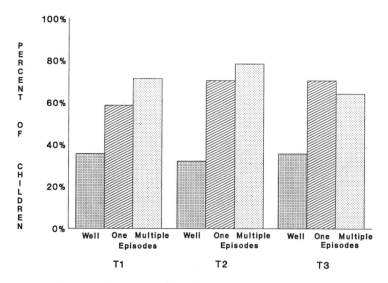

Figure 16.2B. Maternal chronicity, as defined by number of depressive episodes, and the percent of children in the older cohort with any problems. X^2 analyses yielded significant group differences at the $p < .05$ level for children of mothers with multiple depressive episodes and children of well mothers at T_1, T_2, and T_3. Significant group differences were also found between children of mothers with one depressive episode and children of well mothers at T_2 and T_3.

istics do not have a unique child outcome of mood disorders but interfere more generally with adaptive development.

Effects on children of family conditions correlated with maternal depression

Maternal depression and offspring functioning take place in the context of family conditions and relationships. Our first intention was to compare effects of family stress in the well- and depressed-mother groups. However, because our well families were recruited as low-risk families, and they tended to remain so over the years, only 14% have high levels of persistent family stress. In contrast, 77% of the families of depressed mothers have high levels of stress, of many kinds – again, over the years. Much stress is interpersonal, such as marital discord and conflict involving other members of the family. These extreme differences between the well and depressed families pose problems for analyses comparing the effects of family stress on the children of the two groups. The results may just as well be due to the effects of maternal depression. (See Figure 16.3 showing the stress distributions in well- and depressed-mother groups as they relate to child problems.)

Moreover, quantitative ratings of stress do not do justice to the qualitative differences in family environments of the children of well and depressed mothers. In our well families, severe stress is generally severe in ways that are "normal" (e.g., illness, death, loss of job, husband–wife incompatibility). In the depressed families, there is a compounding of stress, not only of the "normal" sort but also of a less normal nature (e.g., husband throws the family out of the house; the depressed mother disappears and neighbors and church members take over the running of the family; the children are abused by a live-in uncle; mother cannot manage the daily routines, so the 8-year-old takes over). In many ways, the stresses are not on the same continua in the well and depressed groups, and identical scores on ratings indicate far from equal experiences for children. Yet it is important to consider the contributions of family stress to children's development and specifically to the etiology of depression, for in theories of depression, stress versus diagnosis or stress as adjunct to diagnosis have occupied much debate.

A concise summary of the findings on family conditions and stress in relation to children's problems is that when children of well mothers and children of depressed mothers are analyzed separately, family stress ratings are not related to measures of children's functioning (CBCL) or very modestly (DICA).

There are reasons to question the validity of the conclusion that stress has little effect on children. A statistical answer fixes the blame on the limited variance within each of our groups. We propose also a psychological answer: Family stresses, as generally reported, do not necessarily reflect the experiences of the individual child. The assessment of stress is focused instead on the family unit. And with this focus, effects of stresses have been measured on single dimensions or in ratings of "total stress." Neither of these approaches gets us closer to the

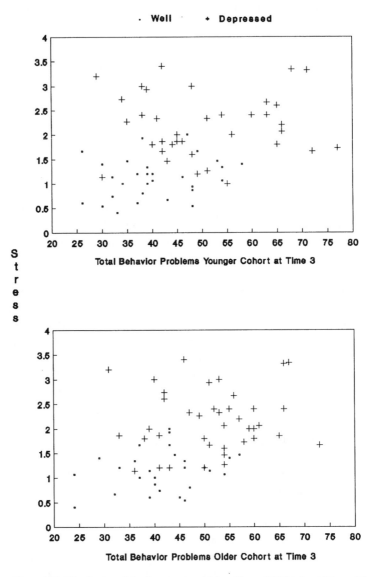

Figure 16.3. Distribution of family stress by child problems (CBCL) for children of depressed and well mothers.

ways in which family contexts, in combination, are encountered by the child. Until the experience of the individual child becomes the focus, we are not likely to learn a great deal about the operation of family variables as mediators of the effects of maternal depression. Reconceptualizations of family influences that take developmental theory into account offer promise. In developmental theory, the child's relationship with the mother has an important bearing on the child's coping. The child's relationship with the depressed mother in the presence of severe family stress, we suggest, needs to be considered in conceptualizing and measuring the influences of family stress. Luthar and Zigler (1991) discuss additional constraints of the literature with regard to assessing the influence of stress on child adaptation.

The effects of marital discord on children's problems provide an example. In the context of this conflict, does the mother become psychologically unavailable to the child? Does the child become the depressed mother's security? Does the mother protect or insulate her relationship with her child from the turmoil in the marital relationship? Our data furnish only a descriptive example, which suggests promise in this direction of inquiry. Families with high ongoing marital discord were identified along with the depressed mother's observed behavior with each child. The mother's behavior was coded on negativity toward the child and supportive and positive engagement with the child. Mothers with low negativity and high engagement and with high negativity and low engagement were classified as good and poor, respectively, in their relationship with each child separately. Thirteen families could be classified in extreme groups at the T_3 assessment. For the younger sibling cohort, 37.5% of the children with a good relationship with the depressed mother (N = 8) presented a diagnosis; 80% of the children with a poor relationship with the depressed mother (N = 5) presented a diagnosis. For the older siblings in the same families, 80% of the children with a good relationship (N = 10) had a diagnosis; 100% with a poor relationship (N = 3) had a diagnosis. These are only descriptive findings, but they suggest something of the intricacies of relationships that have effects on children.

The methodological conclusion that we draw is that if family stresses are to be understood as mechanisms that affect children's psychosocial state, information on family environment will need to be obtained with the individual child in mind.

Multiple interacting influences, multiple developmental paths, multiple outcomes

Combinations of factors have consequences that are not discovered by considering variables one at a time. The meaning or the effect of a given variable is often dependent on the coexistence of another variable. It is not so much the relative weights of influence from different variables but the psychological transformation of the variable defined within a configuration.

From this perspective, it is important to give serious research attention to a search for diverse mechanisms (as opposed to main effects) through which pathology passes from parents to children. A number of changes follow from this shift in approach. Broadly defined variables (e.g., number of episodes of depression; "good" vs. "poor" mother–child relationship) will need to be replaced by variables that have finer theoretical tuning. Inevitably this approach brings in the neglected contributions of the child to his or her own developmental path.

One example of child contributions is individual differences in coping. The detailed lifetime information on the children of this study emphasizes the marked individual differences in their active coping with mother's depression: At the end of childhood, the children were asked about their ways of dealing with their parents' illness and problems. About half the children described actions and impulses of denial, avoidance, and withdrawal (e.g., "I stay out of it"; "I go to the neighbors"; "I just think – be patient, it will work out"). Others referred to their own feelings (e.g., "I keep my feelings in 'til I explode"; "My stomach gets tight"; "I felt I could kill"). Their immediate escapes are interesting in their specificity (e.g., reading, turning on the television, walking in the woods, walking with the dog, going out of the house "where I can't hear the yelling," getting into a vigorous sports activity, praying). A few children partly blame themselves, others take care of their parents, others get help (e.g., "I feel the load has been lifted from me" [as a result of understanding he has achieved through therapy]; "I talked to my class about my parents' problems"). These immediate coping actions also become long-term patterns: Avoidance takes the form of moving out of the house. Escapes become enduring dedications, such as "working like a lion" in school, excelling in sports, becoming "spiritual," idealizing the parent who has died, and aiming for college. What influences have their diverse coping strategies had on their development? When and how did their strategies develop?

Discussion

The longitudinal study from which the data in this paper are drawn grew out of a close collaboration between numerous investigators from developmental psychology, clinical psychology, and child psychiatry. Looking back, it seems incomprehensible for the study to have been conceived and carried out otherwise. The disciplines brought very different perspectives to the formulation of the central questions of the study, which translated into differences in every aspect of the research: What are the important child variables to be considered? How important is development as a variable? How shall children be assessed – in procedures and concepts? Psychiatric interviews and observed behavior do not always tell the same story. Which is correct? How much can we rely on retrospective reports? How necessary are environmental measures? By building on the differing views, concepts, and methods of the disciplines, a rich body of data on both normal and psychopathological development has resulted. Neither discipline alone could produce such a level of integration.

Despite the differences just noted, important issues and orientations in the fields are shared: No field is poised to investigate a grand theory of development. Investigators in the various fields are oriented similarly with respect to accepting the multidetermined nature of behavior and development.

What has this multidisciplinary study taught us about normal and abnormal development? How have theories and concepts and methods of normal development influenced our study of high-risk children? Having focused on pathology in a high-risk population, what messages do we carry to studies of low-risk populations and normal development?

Research on normal development brings to the study of child psychopathology a special sensitivity to development by having identified the specific capacities of and "tasks" imposed on children at given developmental stages. This sensitivity has a bearing on the diagnostic concepts of child psychiatry and on the investigation of the developmental course of child pathological behavior. When is "disturbed" behavior quite "normal"? Is anxiety at 6 years the same underlying problem as anxiety at 16 years? Adult-derived conceptual systems of psychopathology have, we believe, applicability to children if interpreted in a developmental context.

In the joint study of normal development and developmental psychopathology, there is a natural eagerness to apply to one domain the concepts that have proved useful in the other. Beyond the obvious advantages, there are hazards, some of which have become evident in the present study. Our data on family stress highlight a hazard in the use of this concept with low-risk and high-risk populations. The same concept of family stress was imposed on phenomena that are qualitatively very different in the well and depressed families. Therefore, comparisons across groups of the influences of family stress are open to serious question. A closer look at the stress concept in normal and psychopathological development also draws attention to the contrasting contexts of family relationships and family resources in which any particular stressful event or condition is embedded and the importance of the contexts in determining the impact of the stress.

In the joint study of normal and pathological development, this lesson of noncomparability of concepts applies also to conceptualizations of the parent and the child. Maternal personality disorders, we found, were influential in increasing problems in children of depressed mothers but not children of well mothers. But can we come to this conclusion? Personality disorders, at least in the present sample, are of different quality in normal and depressed mothers. Dependent, obsessive-compulsive, and histrionic disorders appear as single problems in a few of the well mothers, whereas borderline, avoidant, dependent, and paranoid disorders often appear in multiples in the depressed mothers (see DeMulder et al., 1995). Again, joint study of the normal and pathological processes increases sensitivity to the need for careful description of the concepts by which we classify individuals.

Furthermore, the problem of noncomparability from normal to pathological conditions exists with respect to assessments of children. If our data are generalizable, a sizable proportion of high-risk children have multiple problems (Radke-Yarrow et al., 1992). This is not the case for children of well parents. Therefore, children from high- and low-risk backgrounds, though given the same diagnosis, may be quite different with respect to the presence of other problems. These differences may mark differences in etiologies and prognoses.

Bringing research on normal and risk groups into the same study can make one very aware of how differently children are being viewed and dealt with in research in the two domains. Diagnoses are severe or extreme cut points that designate children when pathology is the focus. In studies of normal development, extreme children tend to be regarded as measurement error and they are "brought in" the distribution of scores. Both approaches distort our lenses for viewing children. The child characteristics or variables that are studied in normal and abnormal development overlap only partly. Morality, capacities for good interpersonal relationships, masteries, and achievements may be "comorbid" with some diagnoses, but we seldom bring these qualities together. Bringing normal and abnormal development face to face in research may result in a changed view of children.

Although our longitudinal study was not designed with a prevention objective, there are implications for prevention and intervention in the data we have presented. First, the high rate of problems in children of depressed mothers suggests that as a group these children are appropriate targets for prevention. Second, the early childhood histories of mood and disruptive problems – prior to the usual prepubertal and pubertal clinical identification of problems – single out a vulnerable group of children for whom intervention may be especially important. These are the children who show recurrent problems, often at subclinical levels, of depressed affect and/or disruptive-oppositional disturbances. Their exposure to depressed mothers who are chronically emotionally unavailable or are negatively imposing on their children may set up high-risk combinations. For them early intervention might interrupt the continuity or acceleration of their disorders.

References

Achenbach, T. M., & Edelbrock, C. S. (1979). The child behavior profile: II. Boys aged 12–16 and girls aged 6–11 and 12–16. *Journal of Consulting and Clinical Psychology, 47,* 223–233.

Beardslee, W., Bemporad, J., Keller, M. B., & Klerman, G. L. (1983). Children of parents with a major affective disorder: A review. *American Journal of Psychiatry, 140,* 825–832.

Billings, A., & Moos, R. (1985). Children of parents with unipolar depression: A controlled 1-year follow-up. *Journal of Abnormal Child Psychology, 14,* 149–166.

Brown, G. W., & Harris, T. (1978). *Social origins of depression.* New York: Free Press.

DeMulder, E., Tarullo, L., Klimes-Dougan, B., Free, K., & Radke-Yarrow, M. (1995). Personality disorders of affectively ill mothers: Links to maternal behavior. *Journal of Personality Disorders, 9,* 199–212.

Diagnostic and Statistical Manual of Mental Disorders. DSM-III-R. (1987). Washington, DC: American Psychiatric Association.

Downey, G., & Coyne, J. C. (1990). Children of depressed parents: An integrative review. *Psychological Bulletin, 108,* 50–76.

Herjanic, B., & Reich, W. (1982). Development of a structured psychiatric interview for children: Agreement between child and parent on individual symptoms. *Journal of Abnormal Child Psychology, 10,* 307–324.

Hodges, K., Kline, J., Fitch, P., McKnew, D., & Cytryn, L, (1981). The child assessment schedule: A diagnostic interview for research and clinical use. *Catalog of Selected Documents in Psychology, 11,* 56.

Hollingshead, A. (1975). *Four-Factor Index of Social Status.* New Haven, CT: Yale University, Sociology Department.

Keller, M., Beardslee, W., Dorer, D., Lavori, P., Samuelson, H., & Klerman, G. (1986). Impact of severity and chronicity of parental affective illness on adaptive functioning and psychopathology in children. *Archives of General Psychiatry, 43,* 930–937.

Loranger, A. (1988). *Personality Disorder Examination (PDE) Manual.* Yonkers, NY: DV Communications.

Luthar, S. S., & Zigler, E. (1991). Vulnerability and competence: A review of the research on resilience in childhood. *American Journal of Orthopsychiatry, 61,* 6–22.

Magnusson, D., & Bergman, L. (1988). Individual and variable-based approaches to longitudinal research on early risk factors. In M. Rutter (Ed.), *Studies of psychosocial risk: The power of longitudinal data* (pp. 45–61). Cambridge: Cambridge University Press.

Radke-Yarrow, M. (1989). Family environments of depressed and well parents and their children: Issues of research methods. In G. R. Patterson (Ed.), *Aggression and depression in family interactions* (pp. 48–67). Hillsdale, NJ: Erlbaum.

Radke-Yarrow, M., Nottelmann, E., Martinez, P., Fox, M. B., & Belmont, B. (1992). Young children of affectively ill parents: A longitudinal study of psychosocial development. *Journal of American Academy of Child and Adolescent Psychiatry, 31,* 68–77.

Spitzer, R. L., & Endicott, J. (1977). *The schedule for affective disorders and schizophrenia: Lifetime version.* New York: New York State Psychiatric Institute, Biometrics Research.

Stein, A., Gath, D. H., Bucher, T., Bora, K. A., Day, A., & Cooper, P. J. (1991). The relationship between prenatal depression and mother-child interaction. *British Journal of Psychiatry, 150,* 46–52.

Tarullo, L. B., Richardson, D. T., Radke-Yarrow, M., & Martinez, P. (1995). Multiple sources in child diagnosis: Parent-child concordance in affectively ill and well families. *Journal of Clinical Child Psychology, 24,* 173–183.

Zigler, E., & Glick, M. (1986). *A developmental approach to adult psychopathology.* New York: Wiley Interscience.

17   Sexual and physical abuse and the development of social competence

Penelope K. Trickett

In the past several decades, much research has been conducted on the impact on children's development of sexual and physical abuse (see, e.g., Ammerman, Cassis, Hersen, & Van Hasselt, 1986; Beitchman, Zucker, Hood, daCosta, & Akman, 1991; Beitchman et al. 1992; Kendall-Tackett, Williams, & Finkelhor, 1993; Trickett & McBride-Chang, 1995; Widom, 1989, for recent reviews of this literature). Much of this research has focused on the development of psychopathology, psychiatric symptomatology, or behavior problems in victims of these forms of maltreatment. This chapter will take a different slant and focus on the impact of sexual and physical abuse on the development of social competence. This is important to do for several reasons. One is that to understand the impact of child maltreatment on a developing child, one must consider its impact on the normative development of competencies during childhood and adolescence. Simply put, a child is more than the sum of his or her psychopathologies or problem behaviors and to understand the full impact of child maltreatment one must consider its impact on the "whole child" (Zigler, 1970). Also, one frequent finding in research on sexual and physical abuse is that there is considerable variability in impact: Some children exhibit many more problems or psychiatric symptoms than others. It seems that some abused children may exhibit more *resilience* than others (Garmezy, 1985). As is true in other areas of research on resilience in children at risk for psychopathology, understanding children's competencies and the possible mediating role of these competencies may be one of the keys to understanding this variability in response to abuse.

The focus of the chapter is on the development of social competence in sexually and physically abused children. The goal is to understand how these forms of child maltreatment may interfere with the development of social competence at the time the maltreatment is experienced and how it may continue to affect the individual as he or she goes through adolescence and then adulthood. Thus the interest is in both the short-term and long-term impact of these forms of child maltreatment with a focus on impact that interferes with the normal development of social competence during childhood and adolescence. A second goal is to integrate knowledge about the impact of these different forms of abuse, that is, to try to determine and dis-

390

tinguish the common effects on social competence of any type of maltreatment and the specific effects of sexual versus physical abuse.

Defining social competence

In the late 1970s, Zigler and Trickett (1978, 1979) defined the construct of social competence in children as it pertained to evaluating the impact of early childhood interventions for poor children. This concept had its roots in the work of R. White (1959) and others (e.g., Baumrind & Black, 1967; Garmezy, 1974) and in earlier work by Zigler on "premorbid" social competence of adult schizophrenics (e.g., Zigler, Levine, & Zigler, 1976; Zigler & Phillips, 1961) and on social competence as a factor in adaptive behavior in mentally retarded adults (Zigler, 1967).

In these writings, Zigler and Trickett (1978, 1979) defined social competence by stating that measures of this construct should meet two criteria: "The first is that social competence must reflect the success of the human being in meeting societal expectancies. Second, these measures of social competence should reflect something about the self-actualization or personal development of the human being" (1978, p. 795).

This notion of social competence is quite consistent with that of R. White (1959, 1979) who, for example, has stated that "we are curious, probing, learning, coping, adapting creatures who build up competence through action on our surroundings. ... Being effective, being able to have effects, seem[s] to be the heart of the matter" (1979, p. 8). This notion of competence has been reiterated recently by Masten and others (Masten, Morison, Pelligrini, & Tellegen, 1990), who defined competence "in terms of effective functioning in important environments." These authors also point out the importance of a developmental perspective when considering what "effective functioning is" and, for that matter, what "important environments" are. For children and adolescents, school environments and peer settings, as well as family contexts, are especially developmentally salient.

If anything distinguishes the Zigler and Trickett definition from other early conceptualizations (e.g., R. White, 1959), it is suggested by the use of the term "social competence" rather than just "competence." As the first definitional criterion stated by Zigler and Trickett should make clear, the authors emphasized the importance of "societal expectancies" and thus viewed the "social" in social competence more in its "societal" rather than its "interpersonal" meaning, although the latter is one important component of social competence.

In these same articles, Zigler and Trickett (1978, 1979) also detailed what an index of social competence should include. First, there should be measures of physical health and capabilities. While not a sine qua non, this is viewed as a major determinant of social competence. Children develop their physical capabilities to a great extent during the school years. These capabilities and skills contribute to and are integrated into their perception of themselves as competent (Harter, 1982; Trickett, 1993). Second, there should be measures of cognitive ability and school performance or achievement. As noted already, schools are "important environments" for children and functioning effectively in these environments is a critical part of social competence. Third, Zigler and Trickett suggested that a social competence index should include measures of a number of social, emotional, and motivational variables. These should include indices of effectance motivation (e.g., curiosity, variation seeking, learned helplessness, locus of control); aspects of self-image and self-esteem (and what we now call "perceived competence"; Harter, 1982); indices of interpersonal skills with both peers and adults (e.g., sociometric ratings of peer rejection or popularity, overresponsiveness or wariness of adults); and indices of achievement motivation, expectancy of success, optimism, attitudes toward school, and the like.

Zigler and Trickett (1978, 1979) noted that measures of these components might well take the form of both standardized tests and other psychometric techniques and more "molar" measures, for example, incidence of delinquency, teenage pregnancy, dropping out of school or being retained in grade.

Social competence in sexually and physically abused children

As noted earlier, research on the impact of child sexual and physical abuse has proliferated in recent years. Although the focus of this research has been on psychopathology and behavior problems, numerous studies have considered aspects of children's development that are components of social competence, as just described. These studies will be reviewed here. But, first, a few caveats are in order. With a very few notable exceptions the research on the impact of sexual and physical abuse has consisted of two basic designs, each of which has some inherent limitations. First, short-term or acute impact of abuse has been assessed using cross-sectional designs in samples of children and adolescents after maltreatment has been officially identified or disclosed. Long-term impact, on the other hand, has been assessed using retrospective designs in samples of adults who report themselves to have been abused as children. There are almost no longitudinal studies and, with rare exceptions (e.g., Egeland, Sroufe, & Erickson, 1983), none that have followed maltreated children more than 1 or 2 years. While cross-sectional designs can provide knowledge on developmental processes and change if carefully designed, most of the cross-sectional studies concerning child abuse have not been so designed. In fact, many do not consider age or developmental stage as a variable even when samples include subjects who range widely in age (e.g., from 6 to 17 years of age).

There are particular difficulties with cross-sectional designs in the area of child maltreatment since aspects of the maltreatment can easily be confounded with the age or developmental stage of the research subjects. For example, the type of maltreatment, its frequency or duration, or many other characteristics are likely to differ depending on whether the child is 3 or 8 or 12, and a cross-sectional design often does not allow one to disentangle these factors.

Retrospective designs also have some inherent limitations. The most serious problem concerns the distortions of memory that can occur with the passage of time and with experience (see Brewin, Andrews, & Gotlib, 1993, for a recent review of the limits of retrospective reports). In the area of child maltreatment this is particularly problematic for two reasons. First, maltreatment has been shown to affect memory under certain circumstances as yet not fully understood. In some cases maltreatment has been shown to be associated with amnesias and other types of forgetting (see, e.g., Feldman-Summers & Pope, 1994; Putnam & Carlson, 1993; Williams, 1994). There is also the concern, currently, that "false" memories of maltreatment can be induced under certain circumstances (see, e.g., Loftus, 1994). A second problem with the use of retrospective designs in studies of the impact of child maltreatment on adults is that the information used to classify a research subject as maltreated has been based entirely on that person's memory and perceptions, which is quite different from the way this classification takes place in the studies involving children. In these latter studies, samples almost always come from an agency (such as a county child protective services agency) that determines the presence of maltreatment based on a number of sources of evidence, including but not limited to self-report.

Although these characteristics of the adult studies can be viewed as problematic, it is important to review this research since it is so far the only existing evidence on the long-term effects of child abuse. And these studies have strengths as well. They are quite varied when it comes to sampling strategy – there are large and not so large community samples (e.g., Stein, Golding, Siegel, Burnam, & Sorenson, 1988), university samples (e.g., Sedney & Brooks, 1984), samples coming from professional organizations, such as those for nurses (Greenwald, Leitenberg, Cado, & Tarran, 1990). Also, in general, the samples are larger than the child studies with sample sizes most often in the hundreds, so they do not share the power problems that some of the smaller child studies have.

Besides the limitations coming from the research designs employed, the extant research on child sexual and physical abuse has other shortcomings. Detailing many of these is beyond the scope of this chapter (see the reviews previously cited or National Research Council, 1993). A few need to be described, because they affected how the review was conducted and how the conclusions can be interpreted. First, many studies on abuse, especially early ones, did not include an appropriate control or comparison group. This is a basic flaw, given the clear research evidence that many of the outcome measures of interest in maltreatment research are adversely influenced by poverty or low social class status and thus, without an appropriate comparison group, one cannot distinguish between abuse effects and poverty effects (see Trickett, Aber, Carlson, & Cicchetti, 1991). For the present review, only studies with an appropriate comparison group have been considered – that is, studies with no comparison group are not reviewed nor are those which compare maltreatment groups to test norms or those which have a clinical comparison group only (e.g., studies that compare abused psychiatric patients with nonabused psychiatric patients only). A further requirement for inclusion is that evidence was provided that the groups are comparable on relevant demographic characteristics, especially socioeconomic status, or statistical methods were used to control for differences.

Another problem with the extant research is that the definition of the different forms of maltreatment has been inconsistent and, in some cases, too sketchy to allow the reader to understand what it is, exactly, that the child experienced. In a number of studies, samples were selected that purposely and explicitly included children with a variety of maltreatment histories – some of the children in the sample were physically abused, some neglected, and some both abused and neglected. The rationale for this is that children often experience more than one type of maltreatment – that this is the reality of the situation. In other studies, this may have been the case without the reader being aware of it. That is, groups defined as "sexually abused" may have experienced varying amounts of physical abuse or neglect, but this was not measured nor reported. The difficulty here is that where groups consist of several forms of maltreatment whether by design or not, sorting out specific effects of different forms of maltreatment is especially difficult if not impossible.

The present review covers three types of abuse, as identified by the researchers: sexual abuse, physical abuse, and what is usually termed, by researchers, "maltreatment" but, in this chapter, is called "mixed maltreatment." Although the definitions of the different forms of maltreatment used by the researchers vary somewhat, and as noted already are not always clear, for the most part one can consider the definitions to be as follows. Physical abuse is defined as a physical injury perpetrated by a parent or other caretaker. Sexual abuse is defined as sexual activity with a minor child perpetrated by a person (not necessarily a parent or other relative) significantly older than the child. (See National Research Council, 1993, for a discussion of definitional issues.) Mixed maltreatment studies have samples that consist of individuals who have experienced more than one form of maltreatment and/or individuals who have experienced different forms of maltreatment. Usually these samples consist of a varying proportion of children who have experienced physical abuse or are considered "at risk" of physical abuse and/or neglect with occasionally a few sexual abuse victims as well. It is probably accurate to say that the maltreatment experiences of the children in the "mixed maltreatment" studies are more like those of the children in the physical abuse studies than the sexual abuse studies. It should also be pointed out that sexual abuse differs from the other forms of maltreatment in that it varies more in terms of whether parents (or parent figures) or persons other than a parent are the perpetrators. In some cases samples were limited to intrafamilial abuse (which includes perpetrators who are parents as well as other relatives such as uncles or siblings). In other cases, extrafamilial cases are also included. At times it is unclear what types of sexual abuse are included.

A third limitation of extant research is that, despite what is known about the different forms of behavior problems that predominate in boys and girls (Zahn-Waxler, 1993), little attention has been paid to potential sex differences in the impact of maltreatment. Adding to this problem is the fact that the proportion of males and females in studies varied considerably, which may well influence the results. In the sexual abuse studies with samples of children or adolescents reviewed here, 70% of the samples were all female. All the remaining have more females than males in the sample and only one of these examined gender differences. For the physical abuse studies with samples of children and adolescents, all samples had both males and females and about two-thirds had more males than females. Most (89%) examined gender differences. All of the studies that investigated mixed maltreatment also include both males and females. Here the gender breakdown is more complicated: In almost a third of these it is not clear what the gender breakdown is in the different groups. In the remainder about half had equal numbers of males and females and most of the rest had more males than females. Of these studies, 62% did not examine gender differences. Almost 80% of the studies with adult samples have samples of one gender only – all female (68%) or all male (11%). In Table 17.1, gender is indicated if gender differences were examined and established.

The results of this review of research are summarized in Table 17.1, organized by age or development stage. First listed are studies with samples of subjects in infancy and early childhood (roughly birth to age 6), then those with samples in middle childhood (the elementary school years, roughly 6 to 11 or 12), then adolescence (the secondary school years), and finally adulthood. It is important to note that not infrequently samples overlap the age grouping listed here, for example, ages 4 to 11 or 6 to 17. If, in these cases, a significant group effect is found for the sample as a whole, it is entered in both the appropriate categories. (About half of all the studies reviewed analyzed or controlled for age differences. Only two that did not had samples spanning more than one age grouping.)

Table 17.1 is organized in columns according to type of abuse experienced. The rows of the table organize the findings into the three general domains of social competence defined earlier in this chapter: (1) physical health and capability, which include motor development, chronic physical effects of the maltreatment (e.g., scarring), physiological or other biological effects, and somatic complaints (such as headaches or stomachaches), but excludes immediate acute injuries associated with the maltreatment (e.g., bruises, broken bones, anal tears, etc.); (2) cognitive and academic development; and (3) social, emotional, and motivational development, which includes findings concerned with self-esteem, effectance motivation, interpersonal relationships, and the like, as well as certain behavior problems, psychopathology, and social deviancy. The latter have been included because, as they

Table 17.1. *Summary of research findings on the impact of sexual and physical abuse*

	Sexual abuse	Physical abuse	Mixed maltreatment
Infancy and early childhood			
Physical/ motor	Enuresis (esp. girls); somatic complaints (esp. boys)[1]	No difference in gross or fine motor coordination;[2] not elevated somatic complaints[3]	Delayed motor development (infants);[4] disregulated cortisol;[68] lower physical competence (mother & teacher ratings)[5]
Cognitive/ academic	Developmental delay (girls)[1]	Low cognitive maturity[2,3]	Low Bayley scores;[4] low readiness to learn (low cognitive maturity, ability to follow directions, greater dependency, less novelty seeking);[6] Lower IQ[5]
Social/ emotional	Internalizing problems – anxiety, social withdrawal;[1,7] inappropriate sexual behavior[1,7]	Insecure attachment;[8,9] Aggressive, noncompliant, demanding (esp. boys), withdrawn and wary (esp. girls), poor social problem solving, less prosocial with peers[2,9,10,11]	Insecure attachment, esp. disorganized/disoriented;[4,12] Disturbed peer relationships, including heightened verbal and physical aggression, inappropriate anger and hostility, less prosocial behavior, avoidance of interaction, poor social problem solving;[5,13,14,15,16,17] no difference in ability to discriminate emotions if IQ controlled[18]

Middle childhood			
Physical/motor	Genital abnormalities;[19] enuresis;[3] not greater somatic complaints;[7] disregulated cortisol[21,22]	Scars, soft neurological signs;[19] no difference in gross and fine motor coordination;[2] no difference in motor development;[23] no difference in height & weight;[25] decreased heart rate (indicating hypervigilence) in boys only[24]	More school problems, rated as less hardworking (boys), retained in grade;[29] impaired cognitive controls;[30] ADHD[31]
Cognitive/academic	Not lower grades but lower overall academic performance and more learning problems (teacher & mother ratings);[26] low overall academic performance;[27] not lower grades and test scores (school records);[28] ADHD[3]	Low cognitive maturity and school competence;[23] low school grades and test scores, more likely to repeat a grade;[23,28] ADHD & developmental disabilities;[19] low IQ & reading scores[25]	
Social/emotional	Internalizing (esp. depression) and externalizing (esp. aggression, conduct disorder) problems;[20,7,35] dissociation;[36] anxiety higher nitially but not at follow up;[37] anxiety and PTSD not higher;[20] inappropriate sexual activity;[19,32,33,34] small and unsatisfactory peer networks[38]	Internalizing & externalizing problems, including aggression, conduct disorders, noncompliant demanding (esp. boys), withdrawn and wary (esp. girls), pessimism;[2,19,23,24,39,40,41] atypical stimulant drug use;[19] low peer status and peer ratings, low empathy[25,40,41,42]	Low perceived competence, esp. older schoolaged;[29] low self-esteem, low prosocial behavior, withdrawn and anxious, rated by peers as more disruptive and starting fights, maladaptive response to peer provocation;[43,44,45] PTSD and oppositional disorder[31]

Table 17.1 (*cont.*)

	Sexual abuse	Physical abuse	Mixed maltreatment
Adolescence			
Physical/ motor	Disregulated cortisol[21,22]	No difference in somatic complaints;[46] no difference in motor development[23]	
Cognitive/ academic	Not lower grades but lower overall academic performance and learning problems;[26] not lower grades and test scores (school records);[28] lower IQ & school achievement;[33] lower overall academic performance[27]	Lower overall school performance, more grade repeats[23,28]	
Social/ emotional	Internalizing and externalizing problems;[20,33,35] suicidal or self-injurious behavior;[47] classroom behavior problems;[26] more male peers in social network;[38] earlier sexual activity, including coitus and more sex partners;[48] illegal acts, running away[47]	Internalizing and externalizing problems (parent rating);[46,23,49] externalizing problems – girls only (teacher ratings);[23] lower self-esteem, social competence, poorer school, peer, and self-adjustment[23,46]	Delinquency, running away[50]
Adulthood			
Physical/ motor	Somatic complaints[51]		Smaller hippocampal volume[69]
Cognitive/ academic			Poor short-term memory[70]

emotional

women);[52,53] DSM-III diagnoses of
antisocial personality (men &
women) affective disorders and
anxiety disorders (women);[53]
depression;[54,55] anxiety;[51,55,56] high
Global Severity Index and
symptomatology of depression,
anxiety, and psychoticism;[51] same
for males in one sample, but not
another sample (both all men);[58]
poor social adjustment and more
social isolation;[59] more marriage
disruption and dissatisfaction with
sex (men & women);[60]
maladaptive sexual adjustment
relative to physical abuse victims
(women);[61] little difference in
sexual adjustment (men);[58]
revictimization (e.g., rape,
battering);[56,62] child rearing
problems[63,64]

violent offenses (men);[
aggressive and angry relative to
sexual abuse victims (women);[61]
symptomatology including
anxiety, depression,
obsessiveness, dissociation
(women);[66] antisocial behavior
(men)[67]

Notes: [1]White, Halpin, Strom, & Santilli, 1988; [2]Trickett, 1993; [3]Trickett, Aber, Carlson, & Cicchetti, 1991; [4]Lyons-Ruth, Connell, & Zoll, 1989; [5]Vondra, Barnett, & Cicchetti, 1990; [6]Aber & Allen, 1987; [7]Friedrich, Beilke, & Urquiza, 1987; [8]Crittenden, 1981; [9]Erickson & Egeland, 1987; [10]Dodge, Bates, & Pettit, 1990; [11]Hoffman-Plotkin & Twentemann, 1984; [12]Carlson, Cicchetti, Barnett, & Braunwald, 1989; [13]Mueller & Silverman, 1989; [14]Cicchetti, Lynch, Shonk, & Manly, 1992; [15]George & Main, 1979; [16]Howes & Eldredge, 1985; [17]Herrenkohl & Herrenkohl, 1981; [18]Frodi & Smetana, 1984; [19]Kolko, Moser, & Weldy, 1990; [20]Trickett & Putnam, 1991; [21]DeBellis et al., 1993; [22]Putnam & Trickett, 1991; [23]Wodarski, Kurtz, Gaudin, & Howing, 1990; [24]Hill, Bleichfeld, Brunstetter, Hebert, & Stecklere, 1989; [25]Oates, Peacock, & Forrest, 1984; [26]Trickett, McBride-Chang, & Putnam, 1994; [27]Tong, Oates, & McDowell, 1987; [28]Vondra, Barnett, & Cicchetti, 1989; [29]Rieder & Cicchetti, 1989; [30]Rieder & Cicchetti, 1989; [31]Famularo, Kinscherff, & Fenton, 1992; [32]Deblinger, McLeer, Atkins, Ralphe, & Foa, 1989; [33]Einbender & Friedrich, 1989; [34]Goldston, Turnquist, & Knuston, 1989; [35]McBride-Chang, Trickett, Horn, & Putnam, 1992; [36]Putnam, Helmers, & Trickett, 1993; [37]Mannarino, Cohen, Smith, & Moore-Motily, 1991; [38]Helmers, Everett, & Trickett, 1991; [39]Burgess & Conger, 1978; [40]Barahal, Waterman, & Martin, 1981; [41]Salzinger et al., 1989; [42]Dodge, Pettit, & Bates, 1994; [43]Cicchetti et al., in press; [44]Kaufman & Cicchetti, 1989; [45]Downey & Walker, 1989; [46]Wolfe & Mosk, 1983; [47]Kendall-Tackett, Williams, & Finkelhor, 1993; [48]Wyatt, 1988; [49]Garbarino, Sebes, & Schellenbach, 1984; [50]Widom, 1989; [51]Greenwald, Leitenberg, Cado, & Tarran, 1990; [52]Peters, 1988; [53]Stein, Golding, Siegel, Burnam, & Sorenson, 1988; [54]Mullen, Romans-Clarkson, Walton, & Herbison, 1988; [55]Sedney & Brooks, 1984; [56]Fromuth, 1986; [57]Murphy et al., 1988; [58]Fromuth & Burkhart, 1989; [59]Harter, Alexander, & Neimeyer, 1988; [60]Finkelhor, Hotaling, Lewis, & Smith, 1989; [61]Briere & Runtz, 1990; [62]Russell, 1986; [63]Cole, Woolger, Power, & Smith, 1992; [64]Burkett, 1991; [65]Rivera & Widom, 1990; [66]Briere & Runtz, 1988; [67]Pollack et al., 1990; [68]Hart, Gunnar, & Cicchetti, 1995; [69]Bremner et al., 1995b; [70]Bremner et al., 1995a.

have been measured, they tend to be inextricably tied to aspects of social competence, for example, "withdrawn," "socially isolated," "aggressive with peers."

Entries in the table indicate that significant group differences have been found between the maltreated group and the comparison group (e.g., at the top of Table 17.1, the entry, "enuresis," in column 1 means that sexually abused children were found to have a significantly higher frequency of this problem than were children in a nonmaltreated comparison group). What follows is a summary of the findings from the reviewed research studies.

Infancy and early childhood

Physical and motor development

There is scattered evidence about the physical and motor development of sexually and physically abused infants and young children, but it is neither systematic nor conclusive. One study with mixed maltreated infants (neglected and/or physically abused) found developmental delays (Lyons-Ruth, Connell, & Zoll, 1989). There is some evidence of somatic complaints among sexually abused preschoolers (S. White, Halpin, Strom, & Santalli, 1988). There is no evidence of somatic complaints or of motor delays among young physically abused children. But the evidence is scant. One study with mixed maltreated preschoolers found evidence of disregulated cortisol to be associated with maltreatment and further that such disregulation predicted low social competence in the classroom (Hart, Gunnar, & Cicchetti, 1995).

Cognitive and academic development

The evidence is consistent that physically abused and "mixed" groups of infants and young children show cognitive developmental delays and poor early academic progress (Aber & Allen, 1987; Lyons-Ruth et al., 1989; Trickett, 1993; Vondra, Barnett, & Cicchetti, 1990). The evidence concerning sexually abused children is scant. It consists of one study with small numbers that found the sexually abused girls but not the boys to be developmentally delayed (S. White et al., 1988).

Social and emotional development

Numerous studies have examined attachment to parental and other caregivers in infants and toddlers (especially physically abused and mixed). Considerable consistency in these findings (Carlson, Cicchetti, Barnett, & Braunwald, 1989; Crittenden, 1981; Erickson & Egeland, 1987; Lyons-Ruth et al., 1989) suggest disturbed attachment, especially of the newly identified "disorganized/disoriented" type (Main & Solomon, 1990). As is predicted by attachment theory, disturbed peer relationships have also been found in these and slightly older children. These peer problems take the form of heightened aggression, inappropriate anger, and low prosocial behavior (e.g., Dodge, Bates, & Pettit, 1990; George & Main, 1979; Hoffman-Plotkin & Twenteyman, 1984; Howes & Eldredge, 1985; Trickett, 1993). Attachment has not been examined in sexually abused infants and toddlers.

At this young age there is an apparent relation between sexual abuse and internalizing problems, especially anxiety, but not externalizing problems (Friedrich, Beilke, & Urquiza, 1987; S. White et al., 1988). Physically abused and mixed maltreatment groups, on the other hand, show both internalizing and externalizing problems, especially noncompliance and aggression (e.g., Dodge et al., 1990; Hoffman-Plotkin & Twenteyman, 1984; Trickett, 1993). Although the evidence is scant, a possible sex difference exists here with physically abused boys showing more externalizing behavior and girls more internalizing behavior (Dodge et al., 1990; Trickett, 1993). A consistent finding is that sexually abused young children exhibit inappropriate sexual behavior (Friedrich et al., 1987; S. White et al., 1988).

Middle childhood

Physical and motor development

As was true for the younger children, the research on the physical and motor development of abused children is sketchy and nonsystematic. One consistency is in the lack of findings of problems in motor development of physically abused children. There is a scattering of evidence of some chronic problems that could have broader psychological consequences associated with the abusive incidents in both sexually and physically abused children (e.g., scars, genital abnormalities) (Kolko, Moser, & Weldy, 1990). And, as was found in the Hart et al. (1995) study with preschoolers, there is some evidence of psychobiological effects in middle childhood similar to those that have been found to be associated with high levels of stress (e.g., disregulated cortisol, decreased heart rate) in both sexually and physically abused children (DeBellis et al., 1993; Hill, Bleichfeld, Brunstetter, Hebert, & Steckler, 1989; Putnam & Trickett, 1991).

Cognitive and academic development

For physically abused and "mixed maltreated" children, school problems, including maladaptive behavior in the classroom, low grades, poor standardized test scores, and frequent grade retention, are consistently found (Eckenrode, Laird, & Doris, 1993; Oates, Peacock, & Forrest, 1984; Vondra, Barnett, & Cicchetti, 1989; Wodarski, Kurtz, Gaudin, & Howing, 1990). For sexually abused children, the findings are not as consistent: Some studies have found school problems (Tong, Oates, & McDowell, 1987; Trickett, McBride-Chang, & Putnam, 1994), others have not (Eckenrode et al., 1993). For the most part it seems that studies which use grades as the index of school performance have not found deficits in sexually abused children, but those that have used teacher or parent ratings or individualized testing have. Most studies that have measured IQ have found deficits in sexually abused and physically abused children (Oates et al., 1984; Trickett, 1993; Trickett et al., 1991; Wodarski et al., 1990). One intriguing finding in this domain is that different studies have shown high levels of attention deficit hyperactivity disorder among sexually abused, physically abused, and "mixed" groups of children (Famularo, Kinscherff, & Fenton, 1992; Kolko et al., 1990; Trickett & Putnam, 1991).

Social and emotional development

There is a relationship between all types of maltreatment and disturbed peer relationships in middle childhood. For physically abused and "mixed" children, these peer problems include disruptiveness and aggression often associated with peer rejection (e.g., Dodge et al., 1990; Kaufman & Cicchetti, 1989; Salzinger et al., 1989). For sexually abused children, the evidence is less extensive, but the problems seem to have more to do with withdrawn, isolated behavior (Helmers, Everett, & Trickett, 1991). In contrast to younger children, in middle childhood both sexually abused and physically abused (and "mixed") groups of children exhibit *both* internalizing and externalizing behavior problems (Burgess & Conger, 1978; Friedrich et al., 1987; McBride-Chang, Trickett, Horn, & Putnam, 1992; Trickett, 1993; Wodarski et al., 1990). As was true for the younger children, sexual abuse is associated with inappropriate sexual behavior and even the onset of sexual activity in middle childhood (Deblinger, McLeer, Atkins, Ralphe, & Foa, 1989; Einbender & Friedrich, 1989; Goldston, Turnquist, & Knuston, 1989; Kolko et al., 1990). Sexually abused children have also been shown to exhibit high levels of dissociation (a psychophysiological process that produces a disturbance or alteration in the normally integrative functions of memory and identity (Putnam & Carlson, 1993). Also, a positive correlation has been found between high levels of dissociation and presence of inappropriate sexual behaviors (Putnam, Helmers, & Trickett, 1993). Findings are inconsistent concerning the elevation of anxiety disorders including posttraumatic stress disorder (PTSD) among different types of maltreated children (Mannarino, Cohen, Smith, & Moore-Motily, 1991; Trickett & Putnam, 1991).

Adolescence

Physical and motor development

There is less research evidence in general concerning adolescence and this is especially true for physical and motor development. What evidence there is is similar to that for middle childhood. That is, no differences or problems in motor development have been established for physically abused adolescents and there is some evidence of psychobiological effects associated with stress (disregulated cortisol) in sexually abused girls (DeBellis et al., 1993; Putnam & Trickett, 1991). This has apparently not been investigated in adolescents for other types of maltreatment.

Cognitive and academic development

Again the patterns are similar to those found during middle childhood. School performance of physically abused adolescents is poor (Eckenrode et al., 1993; Wodarski et al., 1990). As was true for the younger children, the evidence for sexually abused adolescents is not so consistent (Eckenrode et al., 1993; Tong et al., 1987; Trickett et al., 1994). One additional complicating factor here is that an unknown number of abused adolescents may drop out of school so that assessment of only those who remain in school may underestimate the school performance problems that do exist.

Social and emotional development

As was true for younger children, both sexually abused and physically abused adolescents exhibit both internalizing and externalizing problems (Garbarino, Sebes, & Schellenbach, 1984; McBride-Chang et al., 1992; Wodarski et al., 1990; Wolfe & Mosk, 1983). Poor peer relationships may still be a problem in adolescence especially among the physically abused adolescents, but there is not much research on this and what there is is inconsistent (Wodarski et al., 1990; Wolfe & Mosk, 1983). New problems have been identified in adolescence. Delinquency, of a number of forms, has been shown to be higher in mixed maltreated and sexually abused adolescents (Kendall-Tackett et al., 1989). Also, for sexually abused adolescents, earlier onset of sexual activity, including coitus, and suicidal or self-injurious behavior have been found (Kendall-Tackett et al., 1993; Trickett & Putnam, 1991; Wyatt, 1988).

Adulthood

As the large number of empty cells in this part of the table attest, almost all of the research on adults has been concerned with the social and emotional domain and most of that has focused on psychopathology. There are two findings concerning physical or motor development in adults: (1) sexually abused women have greater somatic complaints (Greenwald et al., 1990) and (2) sexually and/or physically abused adults have smaller hippocampal volume (Bremner et al., 1995b) than controls. Only one study concerning academic or cognitive development or occupational attainment, satisfaction, or success in adults maltreated as children has been conducted: Physically and/or sexually abused adults have been found to have poor short-term memory as compared with controls (Bremner et al., 1995a).

Social and emotional development

Adults who report being sexually abused or physically abused as children demonstrate both externalizing and internalizing problems such as antisocial and aggressive behavior (men and women) and depression and anxiety (especially women) (e.g., Greenwald et al., 1990; Mullen, Romans-Clarkson, Walton, & Herbison, 1988; Stein et al., 1988). Physical abuse has been linked to violent criminal acts in adulthood (Rivera & Widom, 1990). Drug abuse and alcohol abuse have been found to be associated with a sexual abuse history (Peters, 1988; Stein et al., 1988). Child-rearing problems have been found in women who were sexually abused (Burkett, 1991; Cole, Wooleger, Power, & Smith, 1992). There is considerable inconsistency in the findings concerning sexual maladjustment and/or intimate relationships among adults with a history of sexual abuse. By and large, the studies that find no differences in marital and sexual adjustment are those with university samples (e.g., Fromuth & Burkhart, 1989), which may well consist of individuals who experienced less severe abuse and/or less severe consequences of abuse than wider community samples. Sexual and marital adjustment have apparently not been investigated for adults who were physically abused as children.

Moderators of the deleterious impact of sexual and physical abuse

The findings summarized in Table 17.1 are essentially "main effects." Prior to summarizing these main effects and to seeing what can be concluded about how maltreatment affects the development of social competence, it is important to consider possible moderators or mediators of maltreatment impact. This is so for two reasons. First, it can aid in understanding the processes underlying impact and, second, it can aid in understanding why impact tends to be so variable. What is not clear from Table 17.1, but is when one reads the individual research studies and the recent reviews, is the degree of variability of impact. This variability manifests itself in a number of ways – especially the percentage of different samples who manifest a problem and the heterogeneity of severity of a problem within a sample. For example, Putnam, Helmers, and Trickett (1993) found significantly greater scatter (variance) in the dissociation scores of a group of sexually abused girls as compared with nonabused girls. Kendall-Tackett et al. (1993) and Conte and Schuerman (1987) have noted the variability from study to study in the percentage of a sample that manifests a particular problem. It has also been suggested that much of this variability may be due to important moderators of the impact of abuse, moderators that have frequently been overlooked.

Potential moderators that have been considered in a few studies include age or developmental stage, gender, other characteristics of the abused individual, various abuse characteristics, family context, and demographic characteristics such as socioeconomic status and race. Many of these, and especially the studies on abuse characteristics as moderators of impact, are beyond the scope of this chapter (see

Beitchman et al., 1992; Kendall-Tackett et al., 1993; and Trickett & McBride-Chang, 1994, for reviews). What follows is a selective look at research on some possible moderators of impact that are especially relevant for the understanding of how social competence may be affected by abuse or how social competence, in turn, may affect the development of problems in abused children.

A few of the child studies examined age differences in impact of maltreatment and the results of these analyses suggest the promise of this approach. For example, Vondra and her colleagues (Vondra et al., 1990) found that younger elementary mixed maltreated children had especially positive perceptions of their social and academic competence as compared with their nonmaltreated peers. Older elementary-age children, on the other hand, perceived their social and academic competence to be lower than their nonmaltreated peers, which was in accord with their teacher's perceptions (and thus judged realistic). Trickett (1993) found a negative relationship between age and IQ in physically abused school-aged children, but not in comparison children. In combination, these studies suggest that maltreatment may have a cumulatively negative impact on competence and that, with age, children become more aware of their deficiencies.

As has been mentioned repeatedly, few studies have examined sex differences. Those that did include the following: Carlson et al. (1989), with a mixed maltreatment sample, found young lower-social-class boys, regardless of maltreatment status, to exhibit more disorganized attachment patterns to caregivers than girls. Boys seemed especially vulnerable to other adverse aspects of the family environment as well as maltreatment. White and her colleagues (S. White et al., 1988) found young sexually abused boys to exhibit more internalizing problems than girls, but girls to exhibit greater developmental delays. Dodge et al. (1990) found that physically abused boys and girls show similar levels of externalizing problems (as rated by teachers and observers in kindergarten), but girls show more internalizing problems. Trickett (1993) found that parents report both physically abused, school-aged boys and girls to be elevated in internalizing and externalizing problems. Observers and testers, on the other hand, rated abused boys as negativistic and demanding, but abused girls as withdrawn and wary. In adult studies, antisocial behavior problems and substance abuse have been found in both men and women sexually abused as children, but problems with depression and anxiety are significantly elevated in women only (Stein et al., 1988). Finkelhor, Hotaling, Lewis, and Smith, (1989) found that sexually abused women and men were equally likely to report marital and sexual dissatisfaction. In sum, the available evidence does not conclusively indicate that abused males are at an absolute disadvantage relative to abused females, or the converse. Whereas some studies have shown gender differences in specific domains of adjustment, there is little consistency in the patterns documented across studies.

Other attributes within the individual that have been considered as moderators of the impact of abuse include cognitive ability, which Frodi and Smetana (1984) found to mediate social-cognitive deficits in young maltreated children, and self-esteem and internal locus of control, which Moran and Eckenrode (1992) found to mediate depression in mixed maltreated adolescents. Peddell (1991) also found that locus of control mediated the level of teacher-rated behavior problems in sexually abused girls. In women who were sexually abused as children, Wyatt and Newcomb (1990) found that attributions of self-blame for the abuse were related to the severity of negative outcomes. Taken together, these studies suggest the promise of examining components of social competence as *moderators* of adverse outcomes for sexually and physically abused individuals.

Child abuse occurs within the family, and other aspects of the family context, besides the specific acts of abuse, need to be considered as potentially affecting the child and the development of social competence. Among physically abusive parents, considerable evidence has now accrued to show that the child rearing of these parents, as a group, differs in a number of important ways from the child rearing of nonabusive parents. Abusive parents are not only more punitive in their disciplinary style, they are less likely to use reasoning and other educative types of discipline; they are less flexible and adaptive in their use of discipline; they are less open to new experiences and less encouraging of the development of autonomy and independence in their children; they report more anger and conflict in the family and in their reaction to the abused child; they express more dissatisfaction with their child and with the parenting role; they report smaller social networks, especially networks that characteristically provide support for child rearing; and they report greater isolation from the wider community (see Trickett & McBride-Chang, 1994, for more details on these research studies). The child-rearing environment of sexually abusive homes has not been examined as extensively. Mothers in sexually abusive families have not been shown to hold beliefs in harsh punishment or authoritarian control similar to physically abusive parents, but they are similar to physically abusive parents in their greater dissatisfaction with their children and in their social isolation as compared with nonmaltreating parents (Helmers et al., 1991; Trickett, Everett, & Putnam, 1995).

Although these widespread and important differences in the child-rearing environment of abusive homes are well established and we know a great deal about how differences in child rearing affect normal development (see, e.g, Maccoby & Martin, 1983), little research has considered how these child-rearing styles may mediate the impact of abuse on children. Trickett (1993) has shown that several of these dimensions of child rearing (especially amount of parental anger and conflict and expressed enjoyment of the child) predict the development of school-aged, physically abused and nonabused children in cognitive and academic development and in level of behavior problems, and that, after these dimensions are controlled for, abuse status, per se, does not significantly add to the prediction. On the other hand, in this same study, in the area of interpersonal competence, child-rearing measures do not predict development, but, after controlling for these, abuse status does. (See, also, Rogosch and Cicchetti, 1994, for a similar finding.) Egeland and his co-workers (e.g., Egeland et al., 1983) have also shown the deleterious effects of verbal abuse and psychological unavailability, whether or not accompanied by physical abuse, on young children's development.

In sexual abuse research, one other family variable that has been considered as a possible moderator is parental or maternal support. This has sometimes been examined in terms of the nature of the overall relationship between parent and child, and sometimes more narrowly in terms of the mother believing the child's reports of sexual abuse and supporting her disclosure. Several researchers have demonstrated a relationship between amount of support and less severe long-term impact of sexual abuse (Conte & Schuerman, 1987; Wyatt & Mickey, 1987). Friedrich et al. (1987) found a relationship between measures of family conflict and family cohesion and sexually abused children's internalizing and externalizing behavior problems. This area is ripe for further research.

General conclusions

What general conclusions can be derived from this review about the impact of sexual and physical abuse on the development of social competence? Findings will be discussed in terms of the three domains of social competence described at the outset of this chapter.

Physical health and capability

The research findings concerning the physical health and development of maltreated individuals of any type or any age are scant and how this evidence affects social competence directly or indirectly is at best suggestive rather than conclusive. What they do suggest is that, first, there may be some lasting physical problems, such as scarring, from the trauma itself in some victims of sexual or physical abuse. This could well lead to body image problems and, concomitantly, low self-esteem or perceived competence. The presence of enuresis could have the same effect. Second there is some evidence of problems with motor development among maltreated infants. Gara, Rosenberg, and Herzog (1995) describe a similar finding, and suggested that this may result from the disturbed attachment relations in maltreating families, which lead, literally, to less exploration of the physical environment and thus delayed motor development. This same result, as measured by fine and gross motor skills, is not found in older children and adolescents. However, older physically abused children are rated as less physically competent on measures that include a social component, such as participating in team sports. This may result from another maltreating family characteristic – social isolation. This characteristic has not been examined in sexual abuse.

Although not entirely consistent, there is evidence of somatic complaints, including headaches, stomachaches, and abdominal pain, in sexual abuse victims from early in childhood to adulthood. What little evidence there is suggests that this is not the case for physical abuse victims. Why this is so is unclear and more research is sorely needed.

There is beginning to accrue evidence that there may be psychobiological consequences of physical or sexual abuse. Some of this, at least, looks like stress reactions. Recent research has linked physiological indicators of stress with a number of behavior and psychiatric problems, many of which are similar to the behavioral and psychiatric problems exhibited by abuse victims. (For a review, see Susman, Nottelmann, Dorn, Inoff-Germaine & Chrousos, 1989.) The hippocampal damage reported by Bremner et al. (1995b) is also posited to result from stress and concomitant changes in cortisol and other hormones. If this finding holds up under replication, it has very important ramifications for understanding many deficiencies and maladaptations including cognitive and memory problems and different forms of psychopathology. That is, more research in this area could elucidate the mechanistic relationships between specific psychological and biological developmental processes impacted by child abuse and some of the adult outcomes of the abuse.

Cognitive ability and school performance or achievement

The research results seem clearest in the cognitive/academic domain. Consistently, from the earliest ages, physically abused children show poorer cognitive development and poorer school performance than comparison group children. This is so even when socioeconomic status is carefully controlled. For sexual abuse the findings are mixed, although how school performance is measured seems to be important: Those studies that use teacher or parent ratings or individual testing of children are more likely to find deficits in school performance than those studies which rely on grades or other school records. Why this is so is not clear, but it could relate to the fact that many schools, especially but not only secondary schools, may have a number of sections of a certain class that vary in difficulty (e.g., honors vs. standard) and that students are graded relative to other students in their class rather than to all students, thus masking achievement differences. This does not explain why this effect should be seen only in sexual abuse samples and not other maltreatment samples. Another factor in the inconsistency of the sexual abuse studies may be differences in the characteristics of the sexual abuse experienced by the samples in different studies. That is, greater overlap with physical abuse (or neglect that has found to be related to severe academic problems) could be present in the samples that find cognitive and academic problems. Another finding with important implications for classroom behavior and performance is the prevalence of attentional problems in both sexually and physically abused children. The few maltreatment studies that have considered cognitive competence as a possible mediator of risk for psychopathology have shown the same promising findings as the studies previously conducted in the area of childhood risk (e.g., Rolf, Masten, Cicchetti, Neuchterlein, & Weintraub, 1990).

It is striking that, with one exception, no studies with adults have included outcome variables in the cognitive/achievement domain. One could expect, given the consistency of findings in childhood and adolescence, that a major long-term impact of physical abuse and sexual abuse would be lower educational attainment and, as a result, lower occupational attainment. This is important to determine since occupational setting is clearly an ''important environment'' (Masten et al., 1990) for effective functioning for adults and work satisfaction is an important component of overall well-being in adulthood. These findings also have implications for the selection of adult samples. A university sample is clearly problematic to study the long-term effects of physical abuse and sexual abuse, because of the likely overselection of adults with less severe impact of child abuse. Also, these findings should be taken into account in adult research when matching abuse and comparison groups on socioeconomic status since one may be matching on one of the outcomes of the maltreatment.

Social, emotional, and motivational development

In the social, emotional, and motivational domain, the following conclusions seem justified. First, there can no longer be any doubt that maltreatment – whether it be sexual abuse, physical abuse, or some mixture – has significant adverse effects on the development of this domain of social competence in children, adolescents, and adults. Second, the largest and most consistent body of evidence concerns interpersonal skills, including problems with relationships with adults and peers. Sexually and physically abused children show problems with aggression and undercontrol and problems with social withdrawal and isolation. Sexually abused children, especially when young, are most likely to show problems of social withdrawal and isolation. Physically abused children also show these problems as well as problems with aggressive, disruptive interpersonal behavior leading sometimes to peer rejection. The social networks of both physically and sexually abused children tend to be small and the support derived from these networks deemed to be unsatisfactory. One consistent finding, with important ramifications for interpersonal competence, is that sexually abused children from early ages exhibit unusual and inappropriate sexual behavior. Sexual activity seems to start at an early age and may include promiscuity. Although there are no longitudinal studies with evidence in this regard, there is more and more evidence from studies of teen pregnancy of a link between sexual abuse in childhood and pregnancy during adolescence. This is one of the few instances in which, for the present at least, an outcome (sexual maladaptation) is associated unequivocally with only one type of maltreatment (sexual abuse). Third, in adolescence and adulthood evidence of another aspect of poor social competence in this domain emerges – social deviancy, as indexed by delinquency and criminality, drug and alcohol abuse, and other antisocial behaviors.

Much less is known about other components of social competence in the social, emotional, and motivational domain such as self-image, self-esteem, and effectance motivation. Most of the evidence that exists is from studies of mixed maltreated children. Low secure readiness to learn, a concept that includes elements of effectance motivation, has been found among preschool-aged maltreated children. Low self-esteem and low perceived competence have been found among elementary school children.

Except for sexual maladaptation as noted earlier, it is not clear at present how these various social competence problems may differ depending on the type of maltreatment. This confusion is most obvious for studies involving children and is due, at least in part, to the way samples have been developed and defined. Except for the youngest sexually abused children (who have not been found to exhibit externalizing problems), both sexually abused and physically abused children, adolescents, and adults show *both* internalizing and externalizing problems. It *may* be, but the evidence is not completely consistent, that physically abused children, adolescents, and adults show more externalizing problems, including physical aggression, substance abuse, and delinquency, relative to sexually abused individuals who show more internalizing problems, especially depression, low self-esteem, and social withdrawal. What is confounding here, though, is that females predominate in the samples of sexual abuse studies, which is not true in studies of physical abuse or mixed maltreatment. To what degree this apparent type-of-abuse finding reflects instead the tendency for females to develop internalizing problems relative to males is not clear (Zahn-Waxler, 1993).

In sum, the research reviewed here makes clear that both sexual and physical abuse interfere with the normal development of social competence in childhood and adolescence. This seems particularly clear in the areas of interpersonal competence, behavioral and emotional regulation, and cognitive competence. There are hints also that physical competence may be compromised as well, particularly in those areas where there is a social component, for example, athletic achievement. Also there is beginning to accrue evidence that physiological regulatory systems may be adversely affected by abuse with potentially important ramifications for development and adaptation across the life-span.

Thinking of the impact of child abuse in terms of social competence forces one to consider the whole developing child rather than focusing more narrowly on the presence or absence of symptoms or problems. While in one sense this approach results in a realization of more pervasive effects of abuse on development, it also suggests more avenues for intervention. That is, the more traditional "psychopathology" orientation to the impact of child abuse has resulted in an emphasis on individual psychotherapy (Becker et al., 1995), which has often been too expensive and/or a scarce resource unavailable to many. A "social competence" approach on the other hand suggests different types of intervention. For example, group interventions would be appropriate for intervening in the problems with interpersonal competence. And knowledge about the adverse effects of abuse on both interpersonal and cognitive competence suggests a greater emphasis on school-based interventions since school is such a developmentally salient environment (for both cognitive and social development) for children and adolescents. While this has been done to some extent, especially with preschool-aged children (see Becker et al., 1995, for a review), it is an approach that could be expanded with good effect. Secondary prevention programs in the schools are another promising approach. Wolfe and his colleagues (Wolfe, Wekerle, Reitzel-Jaffee, & Gough, 1995) have developed one such program for high school students.

Similarly, a social competence orientation reminds us that adults who have been abused as children may well have problems in social and cognitive domains that are reflected in problems in a number of areas, including marital relationships and occupational attainment and satisfaction. Designing interventions that attend to these domains could result in greater well-being across the life-span for victims of child abuse.

References

Aber, J. L., & Allen, J. P. (1987). The effects of maltreatment on young children's socioemotional development: An attachment theory perspective. *Developmental Psychology, 23,* 406–414.

Ammerman, R. T., Cassis, J. E., Hersen, M., Van Hasselt, V. B. (1986). Consequences of physical abuse and neglect in children. *Clinical Psychology Review, 6,* 291–310.

Barahal, R. M., Waterman, J., & Martin, H. P. (1981). The social cognitive development of abused children. *Journal of Consulting and Clinical Psychology, 49,* 508–516.

Baumrind, D., & Black, A. E. (1967). Socialization practices associated with dimensions of competence in preschool boys and girls. *Child Development, 38,* 291–327.

Becker, J. V., Alper, J. L., BigFoot, D. S., Bonner, B. L., Geddie, L. F., Henggeler, S. W., Kaufman, K. L., & Walker, C. E. (1995). Empirical research on child abuse treatment: Report by the Child Abuse and Neglect Treatment Working Group, American Psychological Association. *Journal of Clinical Child Psychology, 24,* 23–46.

Beitchman, J. H., Zucker, K. J., Hood, J. E., daCosta, G. A., & Akman, D. (1991). A review of the short-term effects of child sexual abuse. *Child Abuse and Neglect, 15,* 537–556.

Beitchman, J. H., Zucker, K. J., Hood, J. E., daCosta, G. A., Akman, D., & Cassavia, E. (1992). A review of the long-term effects of child sexual abuse. *Child Abuse and Neglect, 16,* 101–118.

Bremner, J. D., Randall, P., Scott, S., Capelli, S., Delaney, R., McCarthy, G., & Charney, D. S. (1995a). Deficits in short-term memory in adult survivors of childhood abuse. Unpublished manuscript. Yale University.

Bremner, J. D., Randall, P., Vermetten, E., Staib, L., Bronen, R. A., Capelli, S., McCarthy, G., Innis, R. B., & Charney, D. S. (1995b). *MRI-based measurement of hippocampal volume in posttraumatic stress disorder related to childhood physical and sexual abuse.* Paper presented at the annual meetings of the American Psychiatric Association.

Brewin, C. R., Andrews, B., & Gotlib, L. H. (1993). Psychopathology and early experience: A reappraisal of retrospective reports. *Psychological Bulletin, 113,* 82–98.

Briere, J., & Runtz, M. (1988). Multivariate correlates of childhood psychological and physical maltreatment among university women. *Child Abuse and Neglect, 12,* 331–341.

Briere, J., & Runtz, M. (1990). Differential adult symptomatology associated with three types of child abuse histories. *Child Abuse and Neglect, 14,* 357–364.

Burgess, R. L., & Conger, R. D. (1978). Family interaction in abusive, neglectful, and normal families. *Child Development, 49,* 1163–1173.

Burkett, L. P. (1991). Parenting behaviors of women who were sexually abused as children in their families of origin. *Family Processes, 30,* 421–434.

Carlson, V., Cicchetti, D., Barnett, D., & Braunwald, K. (1989). Disorganized/disoriented attachment relationships in maltreated infants. *Development Psychology, 25,* 525–531.

Cicchetti, D., Lynch, M., Shonk, S., & Manly, J. T. (1992). An organizational perspective on peer relations in maltreated children. In R. D. Parke & G. W. Ladd (Eds.), *Family-Peer Relationships: Modes of Linkage* (pp. 345–383). Hillsdale, NJ: Erlbaum.

Cole, P. M., Woolger, C., Power, T. G., & Smith, K. D. (1992). Parenting difficulties among adult survivors of father-daughter incest. *Child Abuse and Neglect, 16,* 239–249.

Conte, J. R., & Schuerman, J. R. (1987). Factors associated with an increased impact of child sexual abuse. *Child Abuse and Neglect, 11,* 201–211.

Crittenden, P. M. (1981). Abusing, neglecting, problematic, and adequate dyads: Differentiating by patterns of interaction. *Merrill-Palmer Quarterly, 27,* 201–208.

DeBellis, M. D., Chrousos, G. P., Dorn, L. D., Burke, L., Helmers, K., Kling, M. A., Trickett, P. K., & Putnam, F. W. (1993). Hypothalamic-pituitary-adrenal axis dysregulation in sexually abused girls. *Journal of Clinical Endocrinology and Metabolism, 78,* 249–255.

Deblinger, E., McLeer, S. V., Atkins, M. S., Ralphe, D., & Foa, E. (1989). Post-traumatic stress in sexually abused, physically abused, and nonabused children. *Child Abuse and Neglect, 13,* 403–408.

Dodge, K. A., Bates, J. E., Pettit, G. S. (1990). Mechanisms in the cycle of violence. *Science, 250,* 1678–1683.

Dodge, K. A., Pettit, G. S., & Bates, J. E. (1994). Effects of physical maltreatment on the development of peer relations. *Development of Psychopathology, 6,* 43–55.

Downey, G., & Walker, E. (1989). Social cognition and adjustment in children at risk for psychopathology. *Developmental Psychology, 25,* 835–845.

Eckenrode, J., Laird, M., & Doris, J. (1993). School performance and disciplinary problems among abused and neglected children. *Developmental Psychology, 29,* 53–62.

Egeland, B., Sroufe, L. A., & Erickson, M. (1983). The developmental consequence of different patterns of maltreatment. *Child Abuse and Neglect, 7,* 459–469.

Einbender, A. J., & Friedrich, W. N. (1989). Psychological functioning and behavior of sexually abused girls. *Journal of Consulting and Clinical Psychology, 57,* 155–157.

Erickson, M. F., & Egeland, B. (1987). A developmental view of the psychological consequences of maltreatment. *School Psychology Review, 16,* 156–168.

Famularo, R., Kinscherff, R., & Fenton, T. (1992). Psychiatric diagnoses of maltreated children: Preliminary findings. *Journal of the American Academy of Child and Adolescent Psychiatry, 31,* 863–867.

Feldman-Summers, S., & Pope, K. S. (1994). The experience of "forgetting" childhood abuse: A national survey of psychologists. *Journal of Consulting and Clinical Psychology, 62,* 636–639.

Finkelhor, D., Hotaling, G. T., Lewis, I. A., & Smith, C. (1989). Sexual abuse and its relationship to later sexual satisfaction, marital status, religion, and attitudes. *Journal of Interpersonal Violence, 4,* 379–399.

Friedrich, W. N., Beilke, R. L., & Urquiza, A. J. (1987). Children from sexually abusive families: A behavioral comparison. *Journal of Interpersonal Violence, 2,* 391–402.

Frodi, A., & Smetana, J. (1984). Abused, neglected and nonmaltreated preschoolers' ability to discriminate emotions in others: The effects of IQ. *Child Abuse and Neglect, 8,* 459–465.

Fromuth, M. E. (1986). The relationship of childhood sexual abuse with later psychological and sexual adjustment in a sample of college women. *Child Abuse and Neglect, 10,* 5–15.

Fromuth, M. E., & Burkhart, B. R. (1989). Long-term psychological correlates of childhood sexual abuse in two samples of college men. *Child Abuse and Neglect, 13,* 533–542.

Gara, M. A., Rosenberg, S., & Herzog, E. P. (1995). The abused child as parent. Unpublished manuscript.

Garbarino, J., Sebes, J., & Schellenbach, C. (1984). Families at risk for destructive parent-child relations in adolescence. *Child Development, 55,* 174–183.

Garmezy, N. (1974). The study of competence in children at risk for severe psychopathology. In E. Anthony & C. Koupernick (Eds.), *The child in his family,* Vol. 3: *Children at psychiatric risk* (pp. 77–78). New York: Wiley.

Garmezy, N. (1985). Stress-resistant children: The search for protective factors. In J. E. Stevensen (Ed.), *Recent research in developmental psychopathology* (pp. 213–33). *Journal of Child Psychiatry and Psychology* (Book Supplement 4). Oxford: Pergamon Press.

George, C., & Main, M. (1979). Social interactions of young abused children: Approach, avoidance, and aggression. *Child Development, 50,* 306–318.

Goldston, D., Turnquist, D. C., & Knutson, J. F. (1989). Presenting problems of sexually abused girls receiving psychiatric services. *Journal of Abnormal Psychology, 98,* 314–317.

Greenwald, E., Leitenberg, H., Cado, S., & Tarran, M. J. (1990). Childhood sexual abuse: Long-term effects on psychological and sexual functioning in a nonclinical and nonstudent sample of adult women. *Child Abuse and Neglect, 14,* 503–513.

Hart, J., Gunnar, M., & Cicchetti, D. (1995). Salivary cortisol in maltreated children: Evidence of relations between neuroendocrine activity and social competence. *Development and Psychopathology, 7,* 11–26.

Harter, S. (1982). The perceived competence scale for children. *Child Development, 53,* 87–97.

Harter, S., Alexander, P. C., & Neimeyer, R. A. (1988). Long-term effects of incestuous child abuse in college women: Social adjustment, social cognition, and family characteristics. *Journal of Consulting and Clinical Psychology, 56,* 5–8.

Helmers, K., Everett, B. A., & Trickett, P. K. (1991). *Social support of sexually abused girls and their mothers.* Paper presented at the biennial meetings of the Society for Research in Child Development, Seattle, WA.

Herrenkohl, R. C., & Herrenkohl, E. C. (1981). Some antecedents and developmental consequences of child maltreatment. In R. Rizley & D. Cicchetti (Eds.), *Developmental perspectives on child maltreatment* (pp. 57–76). San Francisco: Jossey-Bass.

Hill, S. D., Bleichfeld, B., Brunstetter, R. D., Hebert, J. E., Steckler, S. (1989). Cognitive and physiological responsiveness of abused children. *Journal of the American Academy of Child and Adolescent Psychiatry, 28,* 219–224.

Hoffman-Plotkin, D., & Twentyman, C. T. (1984). A multimodel assessment of behavioral and cognitive deficits in abused and neglected preschoolers. *Child Development, 55,* 794–802.

Howes, C., & Eldredge, R. (1985). Responses of abused, neglected, and non-maltreated children to the behaviors of their peers. *Journal of Applied Developmental Psychology, 6,* 261–270.

Kaufman, J., & Cicchetti, D., (1989). Effects of maltreatment on school-age children's socioemotional development: Assessment in a day-camp setting. *Developmental Psychology, 25,* 516–524.

Kendall-Tackett, K. A., Williams, L. M., & Finkelhor, D., (1993). Impact of sexual abuse on children: A review and synthesis of recent empirical studies. *Psychological Bulletin, 113,* 164–180.

Kolko, D. J., Moser, J. T., & Weldy, S. R. (1990). Medical/health histories and physical evaluation of physically and sexually abused child psychiatric patients: A controlled study. *Journal of Family Violence, 5,* 249–267.

Loftus, E. (1994). Memories of child sexual abuse, *Psychology of Women Quarterly, 18,* 67–84.

Lyons-Ruth, K., Connell, D. B., & Zoll, D. (1989). Patterns of maternal behavior among infants at risk for abuse: Relations with infant attachment behavior and infant development at 12 months of age. In D. Cicchetti & V. Carlson (Eds.), *Child maltreatment: Theory and research on the causes and consequences of child abuse and neglect* (pp. 464–493). New York: Cambridge University Press.

Maccoby, E. E., & Martin, J. A. (1983). Socialization in the context of the family: Parent-child interaction. In P. H. Mussen (Series Ed.) and E. M. Hetherington (Vol. Ed.), *Handbook of child psychology,* Vol 4: *Socialization, personality, and social development.* New York: Wiley.

Main, M., & Solomon, J. (1990). Procedures for identifying infants as disorganized/disorientated during the Ainsworth Strange Situation. In M. Greenberg, D. Cicchetti, & E. M. Cummings (Eds.), *Attachment during the preschool years: Theory, research, & intervention,* (pp. 121–168). Chicago: University of Chicago Press.

Mannarino, A. P., Cohen, J. A., Smith, J. A., & Moore-Motily, S. (1991). Six- and twelve-month follow-up of sexually abused girls. *Journal of Interpersonal Violence, 6,* 494–511.

Masten, A. S., Morison, P., Pellegrini, D., & Tellegen, A. (1990). Competence under stress: Risk and protective factors. In J. Rolf, A. S. Masten, K. H. Cicchetti, K. H. Neuchterlein, S. Weintraub

(Eds.), *Risk and protective factors in the development of psychopathology* (pp. 236–256). New York: Cambridge University Press.

McBride-Chang, C., Trickett, P. K., Horn, J. L., & Putnam, F. W. (1992). *The CBCL and behavior problems in sexually abused girls.* Paper presented at the annual meetings of the American Psychological Association, Washington, DC.

Moran, P. B., & Eckenrode, J. (1992). Protective personality characteristics among adolescent victims of maltreatment. *Child Abuse and Neglect, 16,* 743–754.

Mueller, E., & Silverman, N. (1989). Peer relations in maltreated children. In D. Cicchetti & V. Carlson (Eds.), *Child maltreatment: Theory and research on the causes and consequences of child abuse and neglect,* (pp. 529–578). New York: Cambridge University Press.

Mullen, P. E., Romans-Clarkson, S. E., Walton, V. A., & Herbison, G. P. (1988). Impact of sexual and physical abuse on women's mental health, *Lancet, 1,* 841–845.

Murphy, S. M., Kilpatrick, D. G., Amick-McMullen, A., Veronen, L. J., Paduhovich, J., Best, C. L., Villeponteaux, L. A., & Saunders, B. E. (1988). Current psychological functioning of child sexual abuse survivors. *Journal of Interpersonal Violence, 3,* 55–79.

National Research Council. (1993). *Understanding child abuse and neglect.* Washington, DC: National Academy Press.

Oates, R. K., Peacock, A., & Forrest, D. (1984). The development of abused children. *Developmental Medicine and Child Neurology, 26,* 649–656.

Peddell, H. M. (1991). Locus of control and problem behaviors in young female incest victims. Unpublished doctoral dissertation, George Washington University, Washington, DC.

Peters, S. D. (1988). Child sexual abuse and later psychological problems. In G. E. Wyatt & G. J. Powell (Eds.), *Lasting effects of child sexual abuse.* Newbury Park, CA: Sage.

Pollack, V. E., Briere, J., Schneider, L., Knop, J., Mednick, S. A., & Goodwin, D. W. (1990). Childhood antecedents of antisocial behavior: Parental alcoholism and physical abusiveness. *American Journal of Psychiatry, 147,* 1290–1293.

Putnam, F. W., & Carlson, E. B. (1993). Hypnosis, dissociation and trauma: Myths, metaphors and mechanisms. Unpublished manuscript.

Putnam, F. W., Helmers, K., & Trickett, P. K. (1993). Development, reliability, and validation of a child dissociation scale. *Child Abuse and Neglect, 17,* 731–740.

Putnam, F. W., & Trickett, P. K. (1991). *Cortisol abnormalities in sexually abused girls.* Paper presented at the annual meetings of the American Psychological Society, Washington, DC.

Rieder, C., & Cicchetti, D., (1989). Organizational perspective on cognitive control functioning and cognitive-affective balance in maltreated children. *Developmental Psychology, 25,* 382–393.

Rivera, B., & Widom, C. S. (1990). Childhood victimization and violent offending. *Violence and Victims, 5,* 19–35.

Rogosch, F. A., & Cicchetti, D. (1994). Illustrating the interface of family and peer relations through the study of child maltreatment. *Social Development, 3,* 291–308.

Rolf J., Masten, A. S., Cicchetti, D., Neuchterlein, K. H., Weintraub, S. (Eds.). (1990). *Risk and protective factors in the development of psychopathology.* New York: Cambridge University Press.

Russell, D. E. H. (1986). *The secret trauma: Incest in the lives of girls and women.* New York: Basic Books.

Salzinger, S., Rosario, M., Feldman, R. S., Hammer, M., Alvarado, L., Carabello. L., & Ortega, A. (1989). *Social relationships of physically abused preadolescent urban school children.* Paper presented at the biennial meeting of the Society for Research in Child Development in Kansas City, MO.

Sedney, M. A., & Brooks, B. (1984). Factors associated with a history of childhood sexual experience in a nonclinical female population. *Journal of the American Academy of Child Psychiatry, 23,* 215–218.

Stein, J. A., Golding, J. M., Siegel, J. M., Burnam, M. A., & Sorenson, S. B. (1988). Long-term psychological sequelae of child sexual abuse: The Los Angeles Epidemiologic Catchment Area Study. In G. E. Wyatt & G. J. Powell (Eds.), *Lasting effects of child sexual abuse.* Newbury Park, CA: Sage.

Susman, E. J., Nottelmann, E. D., Dorn, L. D., Inoff-Germaine, G. E., & Chrousos, G. P. (1989). Physiological and behavioral reactivity to stress in adolescents. In G. P. Chrousos, D. L. Louraiux, & P. W. Gold (Eds.), *Mechanisms of physical and emotional stress* (pp. 341–352). New York: Plenum Press.

Tong, L., Oates, K., & McDowell, M. (1987). Personality development following sexual abuse. *Child Abuse and Neglect, 11,* 371–383.

Trickett, P. K. (1993). Maladaptive development of school-aged, physically abused children: Relations with the child rearing context. *Journal of Family Psychology, 7,* 134–147.

Trickett, P. K., Aber, J. L., Carlson, V., & Cicchetti, D. (1991). Relationship of socioeconomic status to the etiology and developmental sequelae of physical child abuse. *Developmental Psychology, 27,* 148–158.

Trickett, P. K., Everett, B. A., & Putnam, F. W. (1995). Child rearing practices of mothers of sexually abused girls and female adolescents. Paper presented at the meeting of the Society for Research on Childhood Development, Indianapolis, Indiana.

Trickett, P. K., & McBride-Chang, C. (1994). The developmental impact of different types of child abuse and neglect. *Developmental Review.*

Trickett, P. K., McBride-Chang, C., & Putnam, F. W. (1994). The classroom performance and behavior of sexually abused females. *Development and Psychopathology, 6,* 183–194.

Trickett, P. K., & Putnam, F. W. (1991). *Patterns of symptoms in prepubertal and pubertal sexually abused girls.* Paper presented at the annual meeting of the American Psychological Association, San Francisco, CA.

Vondra, J. I., Barnett, D., & Cicchetti, D. (1989). Perceived and actual competence among maltreated and comparison school children. *Development and Psychopathology, 1,* 237–255.

Vondra, J. I., Barnett, D., & Cicchetti, D. (1990). Self-concept, motivation, and competence among preschoolers from maltreating and comparison families. *Child Abuse and Neglect, 14,* 525–540.

White, R. W. (1959). Motivation reconsidered: The concept of competence. *Psychological Review, 66,* 297–333.

White, R. W. (1979). Competence as an aspect of personal growth. In M. W. Kent & J. Rolf (Eds.), *Primary prevention of psychopathology* (Vol. 3, pp. 5–22). Hanover, NH: University Press of New England.

White, S., Halpin, B. M., Strom, G. A., & Santilli, G. (1988). Behavioral comparisons of young sexually abused, neglected, and nonreferred children. *Journal of Clinical Child Psychology, 17,* 53–61.

Widom, C. S. (1989). The cycle of violence. *Science, 244,* 160–166.

Williams, L. M. (1994). Recall of childhood trauma: A prospective study of women's memories of child sexual abuse. *Journal of Consulting and Clinical Psychology, 62,* 1167–1176.

Wodarski, J. S., Kurtz, P. D., Gaudin, J. M., & Howing, P. T. (1990). Maltreatment and the school-age child: Major academic, socioemotional, and adaptive outcomes. *Social Work, 35,* 506–513.

Wolfe, D. A., & Mosk, M. D. (1983). Behavioral comparisons of children from abusive and distressed families. *Journal of Consulting and Clinical Psychology, 51,* 702–708.

Wolfe, D. A., Wekerle, C., Reitzel-Jaffe, D., & Gough, R. (1995). Strategies to prevent violence in the lives of high-risk youth. In E. Peled, P. G. Jaffe, & J. L. Edleson (Eds.), *Ending the cycle of violence: Community responses to children of battered women* (pp. 255–274). Thousand Oaks, CA: Sage.

Wyatt, G. E. (1988). The relationship between child sexual abuse and adolescent sexual functioning in Afro-American and white American women. *Annals of the New York Academy of Sciences, 528,* 111–122.

Wyatt, G. E., & Mickey, M. R. (1987). Ameliorating the effects of child sexual abuse: An exploratory study of support by parents and others. *Journal of Interpersonal Violence, 2,* 403–414.

Wyatt, G. E., & Newcomb, M. (1990). Internal and external mediators of women's sexual abuse in childhood. *Journal of Clinical and Counseling Psychology, 60,* 167–173.

Zahn-Waxler, C. (1993). Warriors and worriers: Gender and psychopathology. *Development and Psychopathology, 5,* 79–90.

Zigler, E. (1967). Mental retardation. *Science, 157,* 578–579.

Zigler, E. (1970). The environmental mystique: Training the intellect versus development of child. *Childhood Education, 46*, 402–412.

Zigler, E., Levine, J., & Zigler, B. (1976). The relation between premorbid competence and paranoid-nonparanoid status in schizophrenia: A methodological and theoretical critique. *Psychological Bulletin, 83*, 303–313.

Zigler, E., & Phillips, L. (1961). Social competence and outcome in psychiatric disorder. *Journal of Abnormal and Social Psychology, 63*, 264–271.

Zigler, E., & Trickett, P. K. (1978). I.Q., social competence, and the evaluation of early childhood intervention programs. *American Psychologist, 33*, 789–798.

Zigler, E., & Trickett, P. K. (1979). The concept of competence and national social policy in the child and family life area. In N. W. Kent & J. E. Rolf (Eds.), *Primary prevention of psychopathology*, Vol. 3: *Social competence of children*. (pp. 280–296). Hanover, NH: University Press of New England.

18 Using multiple informants and cross-cultural research to study the effects of domestic violence on developmental psychopathology: Illustrations from research in Israel

Kathleen J. Sternberg, Michael E. Lamb, and Samia Dawud-Noursi

It is widely assumed that child abuse has profound effects on child development. Most researchers correspondingly believe that children who are victims or witnesses of domestic violence have more social and emotional problems than nonabused counterparts, but there is considerable inconsistency across studies. For example, some researchers have found that physically abused children have more behavior problems than children in comparison groups (Aber, Allen, Carlson, & Cicchetti, 1989) whereas others report no such differences (Kravic, 1987; Wolfe & Mosk, 1983). Similarly, some researchers have reported that witnesses of domestic violence have more behavior problems than children in comparison groups (Jaffe, Wolfe, Wilson, & Zak, 1986) but other studies have found no such differences (Wolfe, Zak, Wilson, & Jaffe, 1986).

What might account for these inconsistencies across studies? Differences in research design are surely relevant for, as Zigler and Finn-Stevenson (1992) observed, research on applied topics is difficult to conduct and generalization from the results is often complicated and compromised by awkward research designs. For example, few researchers have carefully distinguished among types of domestic violence or taken into account differences among their informants' perspectives and few have attempted to distinguish the effects of domestic violence from the effects of the many traumatic or pathogenic experiences that abused children may also suffer. The goal of the program of research discussed here was to consider these issues in an effort to achieve clearer answers to questions about the effects of domestic violence. In this chapter, we hope to illustrate the value of cross-cultural research, the importance of clear sample selection criteria, and the value of multiple informants in research on developmental psychopathology.

In previous attempts to explain inconsistencies in the research literature, reviewers such as Aber and Cicchetti (1984) and Lamphear (1985) have raised concerns about the appropriateness of control groups employed, the adequacy of the samples recruited, and the degree to which the severity, frequency, and type of abuse have been specified. In addition, because most of the research on domestic violence has been conducted in the United States, our understanding of the prevalence, etiology, and effects of domestic violence are limited by the characteristics of the U.S. population in general and the welfare population in particular.

In North America, the occurrence of child maltreatment is associated with a variety of social and demographic characteristics (Gerbner, Ross, & Zigler, 1980). Domestic violence is likely to be higher in areas characterized by high crime rates and tolerance for ownership of weapons (Garbarino, Kostelny, & Dubrow, 1991). High rates of single parenthood, divorce, poverty, substance abuse, shelter residence, and institutionalization typically characterize the samples studied, and all have been identified as conditions that increase children's vulnerability to negative developmental outcomes. Some scholars have questioned whether domestic violence per se, rather than factors associated with it, is responsible for the negative "outcomes" that have been empirically linked to abuse (Elmer, 1977; Emery, 1989), however. Similar concerns have been raised by other researchers about the co-occurrence of child maltreatment and other harmful factors like single parenting, substance abuse, and step-parenting (Gelles, 1989; Malkin & Lamb, 1994); these problems also pertain to research on children who experience psychological maltreatment and witness spousal violence (Hart & Brassard, 1987; Jaffe, Wolfe, & Wilson, 1990). Studies examining the effects of witnessing violence on children have almost exclusively involved mothers and children in battered women's shelters (Jaffe et al., 1990). Although the results of these studies suggest that children who witness violence may be at risk for a variety of developmental problems, the conclusiveness of the research is limited by the fact that these children have experienced other stressful life events, like separation from their fathers and familiar neighborhoods, as well as transitions to the often chaotic life-style of the shelters. Furthermore, researchers often fail to document exposure to multiple forms of domestic violence, although both witnessing and being victimized by violence appear to have harmful consequences. Such failures may also explain the inconsistent research findings.

Societies with cultural, economic, and demographic circumstances different from those in North America may provide natural laboratories for studying and understanding the etiology and effects of child maltreatment. The structure of Israeli society in general, and that of the social welfare system in particular, provided us with an opportunity to explore the effects of domestic violence independent of the other potentially pathogenic circumstances with which it is often confounded when comparable research is conducted in the United States. Our goals in this chapter are to discuss the theoretical approaches that guided the design of our research and to show how this unique sociocultural venue made it possible to explore family violence and its impact on children. In addition, we hope to illustrate Zigler and Finn-Stevenson's (1992) dictum that applied research must be rigorous if it is to inform public policy usefully.

Understanding domestic violence and its effects: Conceptual underpinnings

Because no comprehensive theory of family violence exists, this study drew liberally and eclectically on the conceptions of vulnerability, risk and resilience (Cicchetti & Rizley, 1981; Luthar & Zigler 1991; Rutter, 1983; Werner, 1989), social learning theory (Bandura, 1977, 1982), ecological approaches to the study of human development (Belsky, 1980; Bronfenbrenner, 1979), and attachment theory (Crittenden & Ainsworth, 1989) in attempting to understand the impact of domestic violence on children's development.

Vulnerability and resilience

The notions of vulnerability, resilience, and risk are based on a model of human development emphasizing the interactions between individual capabilities and the circumstances in which individuals live. Solnit (1984) suggested that "vulnerability refers particularly to the weaknesses, deficits, or defects of the child whereas risks refer to the interaction of the environment and the child" (p. 135). This approach implies that each individual has a unique constellation of resources and weaknesses that interact in an idiosyncratic style with environmental challenges. Consideration of vulnerabilities and resilience enhances our understanding of the relation between family violence and human development by encouraging us to examine closely: (1) whether the type and severity of maltreatment affect different developmental systems differently depending on the age and gender of the child; (2) which factors place children "at risk" or protect children from the effects of negative experiences; and (3) which conditions might lead to a mismatch between parents and children and thus result in abuse.

Recent research suggests that various types of maltreatment may affect children differently depending on their age or developmental status (Aber et al., 1989; Crittenden, 1985; Egeland & Sroufe, 1981; Schneider-Rosen, Braunwald, Carlson, & Cicchetti, 1985) and that children of different ages may be more likely to experience different types of maltreatment (Crittenden, Clausen, & Sugarman, 1994). According to Schneider-Rosen et al. (1985, p. 198), "The recent evidence that various types of maltreatment may have different impacts on the child's development requires a consideration of the potential interaction between the form of maltreatment and the developmental subsystem most at risk at a given stage of life."

In order to better understand the relationship between domestic violence and developmental outcomes, therefore, studies must be designed to assess developmental differences in exposure to different types of maltreatment in order to explore how various types of maltreatment affect children at different developmental stages. Most studies of domestic violence have not been sufficiently precise to permit such attempts to determine when particular developmental systems are more or less vulnerable to specific types of maltreatment. Because our research studies are longitudinal in nature, we are able to compare the coping styles of children in middle childhood and in adolescence. And because we carefully identified the perpetrators of child and spousal violence, we are able to examine whether children's relationships with perpetrating and nonperpetrating parents are similarly or differentially affected by different types of violence, as well as whether observing spouse abuse and being a victim of child abuse have comparable and cumulative effects on children's perceptions of their parents.

Why is it that some children who experience adverse life experiences cope better than others? To date, researchers have tended to study the vulnerabilities and risks that exacerbate the effects of maltreatment more than the protective factors that limit the adverse effects of domestic violence. Additional research is necessary to understand the individual coping skills as well as the kinds of personal and environmental circumstances that serve to protect children. Others claim that it is important to examine more thoroughly the environmental circumstances, which can either increase or decrease the impact of aversive experiences on developing children (Cicchetti & Rizley, 1981; Cicchetti & Toth, 1987; Martin & Beezley, 1974). Positive social relationships as well as stressful circumstances like poverty and divorce interact with various negative life experiences in shaping children's development (Kaufman & Cicchetti, 1989; Rutter, 1983; Zigler, 1980). In the Kauai longitudinal study, for example, Werner (1989) found three types of protective factors that appeared to discriminate between successful and less successful children who faced equivalently risky circumstances. Resilient children were more likely to have affectionate ties with family members, external support systems, and such dispositional attributes as high activity levels, average intelligence, and competency in communication. Furthermore, the relationship between the risk and protective factors varied over the life-span depending on the developmental stage and gender of the individuals. Factors such as positive relationships with teachers or relatives may modulate the impact of abusive parent–child relationships.

The longitudinal nature of our research permits us to examine how protective factors (including aspects of relationships with peers and family members) and negative life events (like continued abuse or the death or separation from a parent) together influence children's adaptation. In this regard, the availability of information from multiple sources on multiple occasions (schoolteachers, truancy officers, probation officers, peers, family members, and the target children themselves) is of great value. Our assessments of the children's adjustment and psychopathology include data obtained from psychological assessments (e.g., clinical interviews, behavior problem inventories) as well as information concerning performance on standardized tests, truancy, school dropout, delinquency, and acceptance to mandatory military service, in order to achieve a comprehensive evaluation of the children's functioning.

As noted earlier, some scholars question whether domestic violence per se, rather than factors associated with it, affects children's development. As Emery (1989) warned, ''The experience of being a victim of violence may not be the principal factor responsible for many of the psychological disturbances that have been found among abused children'' (p. 11). Such claims are often supported by reference to Elmer's longitudinal study of children who had been abused. Elmer concluded that child maltreatment per se had little effect on children's development; negative life circumstances and the ecology of poverty were much more influential, she opined, and although her study had some important methodological limitations (Aber & Cicchetti, 1984), it was very influential in drawing attention to the fact that abuse is often confounded with other negative life events, making it difficult to assess the independent contribution of abuse (Toro, 1982). Starr (1979) partially replicated Elmer's results, failing to find differences between abused and nonabused children on a large number of measures when the effects of other negative life events were controlled. By contrast, several researchers have reported that abused and non-abused children from families with low socioeconomic status do differ on various dimensions (Egeland & Sroufe, 1981; Egeland, Sroufe, & Erickson, 1984; Kaufman & Cicchetti, 1989; Trickett, Aber, Carlson, & Cicchetti, 1991), suggesting that maltreatment may indeed have adverse effects on children's development. Interestingly, however, no researchers have examined the independent effects of socioeconomic status and maltreatment on older children and adolescents (Crittenden et al. 1994).

Although the participants in our research program were drawn from relatively impoverished neighborhoods, the degree of poverty was less severe than in comparable studies conducted in the United States. In addition, we selected our sample in a way that excluded multiproblem families in the most extreme circumstances. By including only children who lived at home with both biological parents, and excluding families with a history of neglect, psychiatric disorder, and drug and alcohol abuse, we were able to examine the effects of maltreatment independent of these confounding circumstances.

Bandura's social learning theory

Albert Bandura's (1977, 1982) social learning theory also had a major influence on the conceptualization of this study. Social learning theory differs from traditional learning theories in three ways. First, it emphasizes that new behaviors can be learned without direct reinforcement. Bandura claims that vicarious reinforcement – observing how others behave and are treated – is a sufficient condition for learning to take place. Second, this approach emphasizes the relationship between what children think and do and how the responses of others affect their thoughts and actions. The individual is viewed as an active force in his or her own development rather than as a ''tabula rasa'' upon which actions are performed. Finally, social learning theorists emphasize that mental representations of actions can be developed upon observation, encoded, and then be performed later.

By emphasizing how models play a crucial role in the acquisition of behavior, social learning theory advances our understanding of domestic violence in two important ways. First, the emphasis on models as sources of influence suggests that both victims and observers can be affected by experiencing family violence. It implies that exposure to multiple models of violence may affect development more than exposure to one model. Using social learning theory, furthermore, it is possible to predict that the more one's environment is permeated by violent acts, the greater the chances of acquiring aggressive modes of behavior.

In addition to explaining how children might be influenced by exposure to "violent models," some of Bandura's later work helps explain how children exposed to such negative models might nevertheless develop effective coping skills. Bandura emphasizes that cognitive processes play important mediating roles, with "self-percepts" functioning as cognitive mediators of action such that high levels of perceived self-efficacy are associated with high levels of performance. Bandura believes that the individual's subjective evaluations may actually be better predictors of success than objective measures of competence. These subjective evaluations are especially influenced by interactions with family members and significant others and play a particularly important role when fear has been aroused, as it is when individuals think about aversive events. "From the social learning perspective it is mainly perceived inefficacy in coping with potentially aversive events that makes them fearsome" (Bandura, 1982, p. 136). By contrast, self-percepts can reduce fear prior to, during, or after aversive events.

In sum, social learning theory suggests that the effects of exposure to violent experiences can be modulated by feelings of self-efficacy and by cognitive processing and interpretation. In our research, we have been able to examine the differential and combined effects of victimization by child abuse and observation of spousal violence as a means of comparing the impact of direct and vicarious experiences. Furthermore, by examining the children's perspectives and coping strategies, we hope to explore how children's "self-percepts" concerning their ability to cope with violence as victims and/or witnesses affects the impact of family violence on their development.

Bronfenbrenner's ecological approach

Bronfenbrenner's (1979) ecological approach emphasizes that development is influenced by a variety of factors in the individual's immediate and more distal environment and that it is important to examine the interrelations among these factors instead of attempting to identify individual factors or causes. This multivariate-interactional approach represents the true nature of human behavior more accurately than more simplistic theories, Bronfenbrenner argues, thus offering more explanatory power and providing a more useful heuristic device for describing and predicting human development than does the traditional univariate-linear approach.

Bronfenbrenner (1979) lists three defining characteristics of ecological studies. First, the individual must be viewed as an active growing organism who "moves into and restructures the milieu in which it resides" (p. 21). Second, researchers must recognize that environments constantly act upon and adjust themselves to each other. Finally, researchers must study the individual's behavior in a variety of settings, paying attention to the interconnections among factors and considering the impact on development of more remote conditions and events.

This study was designed with these "defining characteristics" in mind. First of all, the study was focused on children who were themselves the victims of abuse. Not only was it assumed that the subjects were "active organisms," but the study was also designed so as to "discover empirically how situations are perceived by the people who participate in them" (Bronfenbrenner, 1979, p. 24). Instead of limiting the investigation to preconceived notions of what it is like to experience abuse (emic measures), those focusing attention on the subjects' construction of reality (etic measures) were also included.

Second, the contrasting and complementary perceptions of the children and of their significant others were explored. Neither the views of the children nor the views of the important people in their environments were believed to represent "the truth." Instead, we focused on the processes by which these perceptions, and the realities to which they pertain, affect children's development.

As recommended by Bronfenbrenner, we attempted to sample across contexts and ecological levels by examining three physical contexts and at least four interpersonal contexts. The children were asked to describe their experiences within their homes, neighborhoods, and schools, as well as their relationships with their mothers, fathers, teachers, friends, and significant others.

Attachment theory

Finally, the contributions of attachment theory must be mentioned. Attachment theorists believe that children's expectations of their parents (their "working models") are revised and adjusted on the basis of children's continuing interactions with them (Bowlby, 1982; Bretherton & Waters, 1990; Crittenden, 1990; Lamb, 1981; Lamb, Thompson, Gardner, & Charnov, 1985). According to attachment theory (Crittenden & Ainsworth, 1989), repeated experiences with abusive parents should make abused children mistrustful and predispose victims to form insecure attachment relationships. Researchers have indeed reported that abusive mothers are more hostile and intrusive than nonabusive mothers from similar socioeconomic backgrounds (Crittenden, 1981; Lyons-Ruth, Connell, & Zoll, 1989) and that abused infants are often insecurely attached to their abusive parents (Carlson, Cicchetti, Barnett, & Braunwald, 1989; Crittenden, 1988; Lamb, Gaensbauer, Malkin, & Schultz, 1985). According to Cassidy and Kobak (1988), however, abused children may protect themselves from the effects of inconsistent parenting by processing information about intimate relationships in ways that minimize their feelings of rejection, and this may result in the formation of somewhat inaccurate representations of their parents. Such defensive processes may help children cope in the short term, but they may foster distorted interpersonal relationships. Researchers have thus found that children who have insecure attachment relationships as infants and toddlers have more trouble developing healthy peer relationships (Sroufe, 1983). Although researchers have generalized from these populations to abusive samples, few researchers have followed children longitudinally in a way that makes it possible to explore maturing relationship patterns (Lynch & Cicchetti, 1991). We thus plan to follow these children's relationships with their parents from middle childhood through adolescence and into young adulthood as they form intimate adult relationships.

Researchers have also questioned the extent to which children generalize the internal representations of their primary attachment relationships to relationships with other attachment figures (Lamb, Gaensbauer, et al., 1985). Many clinicians believe that physically abused children hold their nonperpetrating parents partially responsible for the behavior of abusive parents and generalize negative perceptions of abusive parents to nonabusive parents. Although abused children were often insecurely attached to abusive parents, Lamb, Gaensbauer, et al. (1985) reported that they commonly established secure attachments to nonabusive care providers. Similarly, Lynch and Cicchetti (1991) reported that abused children developed representational models of relationships with specific social partners. Because we specifically identified the perpetrators of abuse in the families we studied, we were able to explore children's ability to discriminate between abusive and nonabusive parents.

Finally, both ecological and attachment theories underscored the importance of studying the children's relationships with both of their parents. There is ample evidence that most children establish formatively important relationships with both mothers and fathers (Lamb, 1997a, 1997b), although researchers – particularly those concerned with family violence (Sternberg, 1997) – consistently ignore the formative importance of father–child relationships. A review of the literature on children's victimization and observation of violence in the family reveals a conspicuous lack of information from and about fathers in abusive families (Sternberg, 1997). Although fathers are frequently portrayed as the perpetrators of family violence, little is actually known about the roles they play in their children's lives.

In sum, our research program was informed by a variety of theoretical perspectives as we sought to undertake research that was both theoretically and methodologically sound and likely to inform social policy. In the next section, we briefly describe central aspects of the research program, before articulating some of the implications for clinicians and social service agencies in the final section.

Research on domestic violence in Israel

In our research, Israeli mothers, fathers, teachers, peers, children, and official records provided information about the behavior of children who were either victims of physical child abuse, witnesses of spouse abuse, both victims and witnesses, or neither victims nor witnesses. As indicated earlier, the research was undertaken in Israel because we were able to recruit a relatively large sample while avoiding some of the methodological problems that often plague research on domestic violence in the United States. Most researchers have studied abused children from single-parent families and/or children living with their mothers in battered women's shelters. In such contexts, it is difficult, if not impossible, to distinguish the effects of domestic violence from the effects of such potentially traumatic events as parental separation/divorce, relocation, or poverty. In addition, most children have both experienced and witnessed domestic violence, with few researchers making efforts to distinguish the effects of these quite distinct experiences.

In the present study, by contrast, all children were drawn from the case files of social welfare agencies, the families were matched with respect to size, ethnicity, religious fervor, and socioeconomic status; all children were still living with both of their biological parents during the first wave of data collection and had never been placed outside the home or lived in a shelter. Exhaustive efforts, using data from all family members and official records, were also made to recruit groups of children whose exposure to different forms of domestic violence was known so that comparisons could be made among the groups identified.

The longitudinal study was designed to explore the effects of child and spouse abuse on a wide range of developmental outcomes, including children's behavior problems, depression, relationships with family members, children's attributions about peers and parents, children's self-concepts, children's perceptions of their social networks, the relationships with their peers, and their academic performance (Sternberg et al., 1993; Sternberg et al., 1994; Sternberg & Dawud-Noursi, in press). Instead of attempting a review of our findings to date, our goal here is simply to illustrate some important issues, particularly the importance of obtaining information from multiple informants when evaluating children for clinical and empirical purposes.

The longitudinal study involved 110 children (61 boys, 49 girls) and their parents who were recruited with the assistance of child protection workers from the Department of Family Services in Jerusalem and Tel Aviv, Israel, when the children were 8 to 12 years old (M = 10 years and 7 months). Instead of relying on case records, we asked the child protection workers who had intensive contact with the families to complete detailed questionnaires about family violence. The initial measure we developed for classifying families involved a specific 50-item inventory of specific acts of abuse, which was based on the questionnaire developed by Giovannoni and Becerra (1979). The social workers were asked to indicate whether either parent directed such acts toward the other or toward the target child. To our surprise, the social workers were unable to answer many of these specific questions in spite of their close contact with the families and we thus revised our instrument. The caseworkers were instead asked to provide detailed descriptions of at least one incident of domestic violence in the past 6 months. If the child was identified by records as an abused witness, the social workers were asked to describe one incident of physical abuse by a parent as well as one incident of spousal violence. The social workers were also asked questions about the severity and history of violence as well as about any developmental problems the children were having, and then all families that met our selection criteria were invited to participate in the study. In order to obtain a homogeneous sample, the sample was limited to lower-class, two-parent families of Jewish origin. Mentally retarded children and children who were victims of sexual abuse were excluded from the study. Likewise, children whose parents were mentally retarded or had diagnosed psychiatric disorders and children who were only victims of psychological maltreatment or neglect were not included in this study.

The families included in this study were representative of the Jewish social welfare population with respect to ethnic origin (75% had parents born in Middle Eastern or North African countries) and background characteristics. On average, mothers and fathers in this study had completed 9.4 years of formal education. All children lived with their biological parents; they had an average of three siblings. There were no differences among the four study groups with respect to background characteristics sometimes related to abuse and its effects – including socioeconomic status, apartment size, unemployment, stressful life events, birth order, birth complications, and chronic or serious health problems.

The sample was divided into four groups. Three groups of children who had experienced some form of chronic domestic violence (with at least one incident in the previous 6 months) were compared with each other and with children in a matched comparison group. Group I – *child abuse* ($N = 33$: 18 boys, 15 girls) – included children who had experienced physical abuse by one or both parents. Group II – *spouse abuse* ($N = 16$: 8 boys, 8 girls) – included children who had witnessed physical violence between their parents, but were not themselves abused. Group III – *abused witnesses* ($N = 30$: 21 boys, 9 girls) – included children who had both witnessed and been physically abused by one or both parents. Group IV – *comparison* ($N = 31$: 14 boys, 17 girls) – comprised a group of children who had neither observed nor been victims of physical violence, but were matched with the other groups on a variety of demographic variables.

Multiple perspectives on developmental psychopathology

Like us, many clinicians and researchers have raised concerns about the tendency to rely on one source of information when assessing children's adjustment. Although mothers or teachers have traditionally been the sole informants about children's behavior and adjustment (Fantuzzo & Lindquist, 1989), recent studies suggesting that these informants may have unique and differing perspectives have fostered discussion about the importance of obtaining information about children's behavior and adjustment from multiple informants.

Over the past decade, there has been a growing interest in the differences between the types of information about children's social and emotional development obtained from different informants (Achenbach, McConaughy, & Howell, 1987). Some of these disagreements have been attributed to differences in informants' perspectives, whereas others have been attributed to differences in the children's behavior across contexts and relationships (Richters, 1992; Tein, Roosa, & Michaels, 1994). Initially, agreements and disagreements among mothers, fathers, teachers, and mental health professionals with respect to children's behavior problems were treated like traditional inter-observer reliability assessments with discrepancies among informants believed to reflect inaccuracy, error, or bias on the part of one or more of the informants. Many researchers considered ways to identify the "optimal informant" and the various deficiencies of each information source were pointed out (Achenbach et al., 1987; Loeber, Green, Lahey, & Stouthamer-Loeber, 1989; Reid, Kavanagh, & Baldwin, 1987). These issues have recently been reframed, however, with reviewers suggesting that the discrepancies among informants may have a variety of origins, which do not necessarily reflect inaccuracy or "inter-rater unreliability" (Achenbach et al., 1987; Reid et al., 1987). Unlike objective observers who are trained to code children's behavior in specific contexts, mothers, fathers, teachers, and mental health workers observe and interact with children in different contexts, and thus should not be expected to report the same behaviors and behavior problems. Unlike objective observers, furthermore, parents, teachers, mental health workers, and peers have investments of different sorts in these children, which by definition prevent them from being objective.

Disagreements among informants are of particular concern when examining the effects of domestic violence on children's adjustment. When mothers are variously the victims of spouse abuse, the perpetrators of physical abuse, or the partners of child abusers, their perceptions of their children's behavior problems may vary too (Wolfe et al., 1986; Wolfe, Jaffe, Wilson, & Zak, 1985). For example, mothers may project their own frustrations or guilty feelings onto their children, and distressed mothers are known to evaluate their children's behavior more harshly than objective observers do (Brody & Forehand, 1986; Hughes, 1988; Hughes & Barad, 1983; Kazdin, Moser, Colbus, & Bell, 1985). Abusive parents also appear more likely than other parents to attribute negative motives to their children's behavior (Bauer & Twentyman, 1985) and more likely than independent observers to view their children's behavior as problematic (Reid et al., 1987).

For purposes of the present discussion, we focus on evaluations of the children's behavior using the Child Behavior Checklist and the corresponding teacher- and self-report forms of that instrument (Achenbach & Edelbrock, 1981, 1983, 1986, 1987). As reported elsewhere (Sternberg et al., 1993, 1994; Sternberg, Lamb, & Dawud-Noursi, in press), our results highlight the importance of obtaining information from multiple informants when evaluating the effects of domestic violence on child development. They also raise many interesting questions about ways in which different types of information can be integrated to yield meaningful representations of children's adjustment.

In Phase I, children's reports of their behavior problems suggested that victims and abused witnesses were more likely than children in the comparison group to report internalizing and externalizing behavior problems. These children acknowledged that they behaved in ways likely to get them in trouble with significant others (i.e., parents and teachers) and reported that they felt sad, unwanted, and less healthy than their peers. In fact, children from the child abuse and abused witness groups were significantly more likely to obtain scores in the intervention range on the internalizing scale of the Youth Self-Report (YSR) than were the children in the comparison group.

Mothers painted very different pictures of the children in the various groups. On the Child Behavior Checklist, mothers who were abused by their husbands (spouse abuse and abused witness groups) reported more externalizing behavior problems than did mothers of children in the comparison group and a similar trend on the internalizing dimension approached significance. Thus mothers reported effects of domestic violence on their children only when they were the victims of spousal violence. When their children alone were victimized, mothers did not report more behavior problems than mothers of children in the comparison groups.

Discrepancies in the patterns of group differences reported by the mothers and children raise many interesting questions about how one should interpret information provided by different informants. Inspired by social learning theory, we had originally predicted that the children in the abused witness group would have the most problems and that they would be followed by children in the child abuse, spouse abuse, and comparison groups, respectively. We did not expect to find that group differences varied systematically depending on the informants' identity, or that mothers of physically abused children and mothers of children in the comparison group would report similar levels of problematic behavior. It may be that the mothers of abused children in this sample were less sensitive to the behavior problems displayed by their children or that they preferred not to recognize signs of the damage wrought by abusive parental behavior. It was also surprising that the two groups of mothers who reported the highest levels of behavior problems were those who were themselves abused. Perhaps these mothers were so taxed by their own distress that ''negative filters'' compromised their ability to provide accurate information about their children's behavior.

Of course, one must consider the type of biases that might cloud children's reports of their own behavior problems as well. Loeber and his colleagues (1989) have suggested that children tend to be underreporters, acknowledging fewer symptoms than other informants. Although this pattern was replicated in this study – mothers, fathers, and teachers all reported higher rates of behavior problems than the children did – it is important to underscore the unique information provided by the children. Children were the only informants to identify group differences on the internalizing dimension, with approximately one-quarter of the child abuse victims assigning themselves internalizing scores high enough to suggest the need for intervention. Other researchers have also found that children are more likely than their parents to report internalizing problems (Kazdin et al., 1985; Earls, Smith, Reich, & Jung, 1988; Reich & Earls, 1987).

Contrary to our expectations, fathers of children who were victims and/or witnesses of physical abuse were no more likely to report problem behaviors than fathers of children in the comparison group. There are several possible explanations. Because fewer fathers than mothers and children responded to the behavior problem questionnaire, there may not have been sufficient statistical power to detect group differences in their reports. It is also possible that the fathers were not sufficiently familiar with their children's problems, were unused to describing their children's development and functioning, or had difficulty completing standardized measures, or that the children exposed to domestic violence did not in fact display more behavior problems than their counterparts in the comparison group. Researchers and mental health professionals often forfeit potentially valuable information from fathers because they are less accessible than mothers, as they were in the present study. Instead of continuing to ignore fathers in the future, we believe that it is important to develop and explore alternative methods for interviewing fathers (Lamb, in press b). Fathers' perspectives are especially important when, as in this study, fathers are the primary perpetrators of abuse. In Phase II of our study, we used open-ended interviews to encourage fathers to describe their relationships with their children in their own words. In the next section of this chapter, we describe how the problems we encountered and the results we obtained in Phase I guided later phases of the research project.

Profiting from experience: Follow-up

When the target children averaged 12 years of age, we began obtaining further information from social workers, teachers, guidance counselors, and probation and truancy officers about their academic and psychosocial status. We began reinterviewing the adolescents (and their parents) when they averaged 14 years of age, including assessments of the same constructs we had assessed in Phase I although the specific measures sometimes differed to accommodate the developmental level of the adolescents. Psychological adjustment was evaluated using standardized measures such as the Child Depression Index (CDI: Kovacs, 1981), the Child Assessment Schedule (CAS: Hodges, 1991), and the Child Behavior Checklist (Achenbach & Edelbrock, 1983). Children's relationships with their parents, peers, and best friends were evaluated using the Inventory for Peer and Parent Attachment (IPPA; Armsden & Greenberg, 1987) and subscales of the Neighborhood Walk (Bryant, 1985). Children's perceptions of conflict and violence in the family were assessed using the Family Interaction Questionnaire (Salzinger, Feldman, Hammer, & Rosario, 1993), Children's Perceptions of Interparental Conflict (CPIC: Grych & Fincham, 1993), and the Issues Checklist (Robin & Foster, 1989). As in Phase I, we again collected information from multiple informants.

Preliminary analyses suggested that earlier exposure to child and spouse abuse had little impact on the adolescents' later relationships with their parents, their behavior problems, or their psychological status, although we await the completion of data collection to begin examining the complex array of buffers and negative life events that may moderate and modulate the effects of violence on adolescent adjustment. The rich array of constructs we assessed in this project will allow us to examine differences between the resilient and less resilient children in detail. These findings will inform not only the area of child and adolescent maltreatment but have broader implications for the understanding of developmental psychopathology.

Because 4 years had passed since we conducted our first interviews, it was necessary to collect information about current patterns of child and spouse abuse in these families as well as about other important life events that had occurred since the first interviews. Interviews with the social workers revealed that they were less familiar with the target adolescents and their families than they had been when we began the study in 1988. In fact, only half of the social workers were able to provide us with detailed information about the target families, underscoring the importance of obtaining information from multiple informants about the extent and severity of family violence (e.g., Kaufman, Jones, Stieglitz, Vitulano, & Mannarino, 1994), particularly when studying adolescents, who may be less likely than younger children to share their concerns and problems with social welfare agencies (Crittenden et al., 1994; Finkelhor & Dziuba-Leatherman, 1994; McGee, Wolfe, Yuen, Wilson, & Carnochan, 1995). Preliminary analyses suggest that information provided by the adolescents and their fathers about family violence enriched the pictures painted by mothers and social workers. In fact, fathers agreed with their children more often than mothers did, not only in cases where abuse was reportedly absent.

Because we had tried so hard to locate and interview the fathers, we were disappointed with the initial data that cast some doubts on the meaning of the fathers' responses. Instead of abandoning our efforts to incorporate fathers' perspectives, however, we decided to expand our interviews with fathers, relying more heavily on qualitative interview strategies. A preliminary review of the data suggests that fathers are willing to discuss both violent and nonviolent aspects of their relationships with their children and to share their perspective and beliefs. These data may promote a better understanding of the father's role in violent families and suggest new directions for future research (Sternberg, 1997).

Implications for research, intervention, and policy

The results summarized here have several important implications for the design of research on domestic violence, as well as for the design of clinical interventions and public policies. When conducting research on the effects of domestic violence, first of all, extensive efforts must be made to obtain detailed descriptive information about the severity and nature of domestic violence in order to accurately document the scope of maltreatment to which children have been exposed. We learned that in order to obtain a comprehensive account of children's maltreatment experiences, it is not sufficient to review case records, as is often the practice in research on maltreatment. We found it was extremely valuable to interview the social workers, parents, and target children about violent events that had occurred. Each of these informants provided us with unique information. The information collected from different informants would undoubtedly assist caseworkers in making decisions about children who live in violent families.

Although the children who experienced violence as both victims and witnesses did not appear to have more behavior problems than children who were either victims or witnesses, other researchers have suggested that they often do and the literature on the vulnerability to stress suggests that cumulative effects are likely to occur (Luthar & Zigler, 1991). Researchers thus need to determine exactly which types of violence their subjects have experienced if they are to avoid misattributions about the effects of various types of maltreatment. Furthermore, because the dynamics of sexual and physical abuse appear quite different, it would be wise to refrain from including children who have experienced sexual abuse in samples of children who have experienced domestic violence, or to document the histories of sexual abuse carefully.

The results summarized in this chapter also underscore the importance of obtaining reports from multiple informants concerning children's adjustment. Although many researchers have noted that maternal reports may be biased in systematic ways, most have relied primarily on information provided by mothers to assess children's functioning. This was the first study focusing on child abuse and witnessing spousal violence in which four different informants – mothers, fathers, teachers, and children – reported on the incidence of the same set of behavior problems using the same measure. Like their teachers, the fathers of children in the different groups saw no differences in their children's behavior; mothers reported elevated levels of behavior problems associated with domestic violence, but only when they themselves were also abused; and children who were abused reported clear behavior problems. This suggests that mothers tend to report behavior problems with their children as a function of their own victimization rather than as a function of their children's victimization. The discrepancies between maternal and child reports suggest that the exclusive reliance on information provided by mothers is undesirable because it may bias practitioners' diagnoses and evaluations of children in violent families. More generally, the discrepancies among informants illustrate the danger of relying on only one informant, even though each may provide a valuable perspective on children's functioning. Had reliance been placed on any one of these sources of information, the results and conclusions would have been very different. On the other hand, it is particularly important to pay attention to what children have to say about their own adjustment. In order to assess children's perspectives, researchers need to develop valid and reliable measures with which to evaluate young children's perceptions of their own feelings and behaviors in research and clinical settings.

It may also be necessary to develop and explore alternative methods for assessing fathers' perspectives. Fathers' perspectives are especially important when, as in this study, fathers are the perpetrators of abuse or are married to women who are violent. Perhaps their abusive behavior would be reduced or controlled if they were more sensitive to the impact of their actions. Although it was three to four times more difficult and costly to interview fathers than to interview either mothers or children, we continue to believe that their perspectives should not be ignored in future research. The lessons we have learned about how to obtain information from fathers are certainly relevant to social welfare and clinical settings in which contacts with mothers have traditionally been emphasized (Jaffe, 1983; Sternberg, 1997; Wolins, 1983).

References

Aber, J. L., Allen, J. P., Carlson, V., & Cicchetti, D. (1989). The effects of maltreatment on development during early childhood: Recent studies and their theoretical, clinical, and policy implications. In D. Cicchetti & V. Carlson (Eds.), *Child maltreatment: Theory and research on the causes and consequences of child abuse and neglect* (pp. 579–619). Cambridge: Cambridge University Press.

Aber, J. L., & Cicchetti, D. (1984). The socio-emotional development of maltreated children: An empirical and theoretical analysis. In H. Fitzgerald, B. Lester, & M. Yogman (Eds.), *Theory and research in behavioral pediatrics* (Vol. 2, pp. 147–199). New York: Plenum.

Achenbach, T. M., & Edelbrock, C. S. (1981). Behavioral problems and competencies reported by parents of normal and disturbed children aged four through sixteen. *Monographs of the Society for Research in Child Development, 46* (Serial No. 188).

Achenbach, T. M., & Edelbrock, C. S. (1983). *Manual for the Child Behavior Checklist and Revised Child Behavior Profile.* Burlington: University of Vermont.

Achenbach, T. M., & Edelbrock, C. S. (1986). *Manual for the teacher's report form and teacher's version of the Child Behavior Profile.* Burlington: University of Vermont, Department of Psychiatry.

Achenbach, T. M., & Edelbrock, C. S. (1987). *Manual for the Youth Self-report and Profile.* Burlington: University of Vermont.

Achenbach, T. M., McConaughy, S., & Howell, C. T. (1987). Child/adolescent behavioral and emotional problems: Implications of cross-informant correlations for situational specificity. *Psychological Bulletin, 87,* 213–232.

Armsden, G. C., & Greenberg, M. T. (1987). The Inventory of Parent and Peer Attachment: Relationships to well-being in adolescence. *Journal of Youth and Adolescence, 16* (5), 427–454.

Bandura, A. (1977). *Social learning theory.* Englewood Cliffs, NJ: Prentice-Hall.

Bandura, A. (1982). Self-efficacy mechanism in human agency. *American Psychologist, 37,* 122–147.

Bauer, W. D., & Twentyman, C. T. (1985). Abusing, neglectful, and comparison of mothers' responses to child-related and non-child-related stressors. *Journal of Consulting and Clinical Psychology, 53,* 335–343.

Belsky, J. (1980). Child maltreatment: An ecological integration. *American Psychologist, 35,* 320–335.

Bowlby, J. (1982). Violence in the family as a disorder of the attachment and caregiving systems. *American Journal of Psychoanalysis, 44,* 9–27, 29–31.

Bretherton, I., & Waters, E. (1990). Attachment theory: Retrospect and prospect. Growing points of attachment theory and research. *Monographs of the Society for Research in Child Development, 50* (Serial No. 20a).

Brody, G. H., & Forehand, R. (1986). Maternal perceptions of child maladjustment as a function of the combined influence of child behavior and maternal depression. *Journal of Consulting and Clinical Psychology, 54,* 237–240.

Bronfenbrenner, U. (1979). *The ecology of human development.* Cambridge, MA: Harvard University Press.

Bryant, B. K. (1985). The neighborhood walk: Sources of support in middle childhood. *Monographs of the Society for Research in Child Development, 50* (3) (Serial No. 210).

Carlson, V., Cicchetti, D., Barnett, D., & Braunwald, K. G. (1989). Finding order in disorganization: Lessons from research on maltreated infants' attachments to their caregivers. In D. Cicchetti & V. Carlson (Eds.), *Child maltreatment* (pp. 494–528). Cambridge: Cambridge University Press.

Cassidy, J., & Kobak, R. R. (1988). Avoidance and its relationship to other defensive processes. In J. Belsky & T. Nezworski (Eds.), *Clinical implications of attachment* (pp. 300–323). Hillsdale, NJ: Erlbaum.

Cicchetti, D., & Rizley, R. (1981). Developmental perspectives on the etiology, intergenerational transmission, and sequelae of child maltreatment. *New Directions in Child Development, 11,* 31–55.

Cicchetti, D., & Toth, S. (1987). The application of a transactional risk model to intervention with multi-risk, maltreating families. *Zero to Three, 7,* 1–8.

Crittenden, P. M. (1981). Abusing, neglecting, problematic and adequate dyads: Differentiating by patterns of interaction. *Merrill Palmer Quarterly, 27,* 1–18.

Crittenden, P. M. (1985). Social networks, quality of child-rearing and child development. *Child Development, 56,* 1299–1313.

Crittenden, P. M. (1988). Relationships at risk. In J. Belsky & T. Nezworski (Eds.), *Clinical implications of attachment* (pp. 136–174). Hillsdale, NJ: Erlbaum.

Crittenden, P. M. (1990). Internal representational models of attachment relationships. *Infant Mental Health Journal, 11,* 259–277.

Crittenden, P. M., & Ainsworth, M. D. S. (1989). Child maltreatment and attachment theory. In D. Cicchetti & V. Carlson (Eds.), *Child maltreatment* (pp. 432–463). Cambridge: Cambridge University Press.

Crittenden, P. M., Claussen, A. H., & Sugarman, D. B. (1994). Physical and psychological maltreatment in middle childhood and adolescence. *Development and Psychopathology, 6,* 145–165.

Earls, F., Smith, E., Reich, W., & Jung, K. (1988). Psychopathological consequences of a disorder in children: Findings from a pilot study incorporating a structured diagnostic interview. *Journal of the American Academy of Child and Adolescent Psychiatry, 27,* 90–95.

Egeland, B., & Sroufe, L. A. (1981). Developmental sequaelae of maltreatment in infancy. In R. Rizley & D. Cicchetti (Eds.), *Developmental perspectives in child maltreatment* (pp. 77–92). San Francisco: Jossey-Bass.

Egeland, B., Sroufe, L. A., & Erickson, M. (1984). The developmental consequence of different patterns of maltreatment. *Journal of Child Abuse and Neglect, 7,* 459–469.

Elmer, E. (1977). A follow-up study of traumatized children. *Pediatrics, 59,* 273–279.

Emery, R. E. (1982). Interparental conflict and the children of discord and divorce. *Psychological Bulletin, 92,* 310–330.

Emery, R. E. (1989). Family violence. *American Psychologist, 44,* 321–328.

Fantuzzo, J. W., & Lindquist, C. U. (1989). The effects of observing conjugal violence on children: A review of research methodology. *Journal of Family Violence, 4,* 77–94.

Finkelhor, D., & Dziuba-Leatherman, J. (1994). Children as victims of violence: A national survey. *Pediatrics, 94* (4), 413–420.

Garbarino, J., Kostelny, K., & Dubrow, N. (1991). *No place to be a child: Growing up in a war zone.* Lexington, MA: Lexington Books.

Gelles, R. J. (1989). Child abuse and violence in the single parent families: Parent-absence and economic deprivation. *American Journal of Orthopsychiatry, 59,* 492–501.

Gerbner, G., Ross, C. J., & Zigler, E. F. (Eds.). (1980). *Child abuse: An agenda for action.* New York: Oxford University Press.

Giovannoni, J. M., & Becerra, R. M. (1979). *Defining child abuse.* New York: Free Press.

Grych, H. J., & Fincham, F. D. (1993). Children's appraisals of marital conflict: Initial investigations of the cognitive-contextual framework. *Child Development, 64,* 215–230.

Hart, S. N., & Brassard, M. R. (1987). A major threat to children's mental health: Psychological maltreatment. *American Psychologist, 42,* 160–165.

Hodges, K. (1991). Guidelines to aid in establishing interrater reliability for the Child Assessment Schedule (CHS).

Hughes, H. (1988). Psychological and behavioral correlates of family violence in child witnesses and victims. *American Journal of Orthopsychiatry, 58,* 77–90.

Hughes, H., & Barad, S. (1983). Psychological functioning of children in a battered women's shelter: A preliminary investigation. *American Journal of Orthopsychiatry, 53,* 525–531.

Jaffe, E. D. (1983). Fathers and child welfare services: The forgotten clients. In M. E. Lamb & A. Sagi (Eds.), *Fatherhood and family policy* (pp. 129–137). Hillsdale, NJ: Erlbaum.

Jaffe, P., Wolfe, D., & Wilson, S. K. (1990). *Children of battered women.* Newbury Park, CA: Sage.

Jaffe, P., Wolfe, D. A., Wilson, S. K., & Zak, L. (1986). Family violence and child adjustment: A comparative analyses of girls' and boys' behavioral symptoms. *American Journal of Psychiatry, 143,* 74–77.

Kaufman, J., & Cicchetti, D. (1989). Effects of maltreatment on children's socioemotional development: Assessments in a day-camp setting. *Developmental Psychology, 25,* 516–524.

Kaufman, J., Jones, B., Stieglitz, E., Vitulano, L., & Mannarino, A. P. (1994). The use of multiple informants to assess children's maltreatment experiences. *Journal of Family Violence, 9,* 227–248.

Kazdin, A. E., Moser, J., Colbus, D., & Bell, R. (1985). Depressive symptoms among physically abused and psychiatrically disturbed children. *Journal of Abnormal Psychology, 94,* 298–307.

Kovacs, M. (1981). Rating scales to assess depression in school-age children. *Acta Paedopsychiatry, 46,* 305–315.

Kravic, J. N. (1987). Behavior problems and social competence of clinic-referred abused children. *Journal of Family Violence, 2,* 111–120.

Lamb, M. E. (1981). The development of social expectations in the first year of life. In M. E. Lamb & L. Sherrod (Eds.), *Infant social cognition* (pp. 155–175). Hillsdale, NJ: Erlbaum.

Lamb, M. E. (1997a). The development of father-infant relationships. In M. E. Lamb (Ed.), *The role of the father in child development* (3rd ed.). New York: Wiley.

Lamb, M. E. (1997b). The role of the father: An introductory overview and guide. In M. E. Lamb (Ed.), *The role of the father in child development* (3rd ed.). New York: Wiley.

Lamb, M. E., Gaensbauer, T. S., Malkin, C. M., & Schultz, L. A. (1985). The effects of abuse and neglect on security of infant-adult attachment. *Infant Behavior and Development, 8,* 35–45.

Lamb, M. E., Teti, D. M., Sternberg K. J., & Malkin, C. M. (1991). Child maltreatment and the child welfare system. In F. Kessel, M. H. Bornstein, & A. J. Sameroff (Eds.), *Contemporary constructions of the child: Essays in honor of William Kessen* (pp. 195–208). Hillsdale, NJ: Erlbaum.

Lamb, M. E., Thompson, R. A., Gardner, W., & Charnov, E. L. (1985). *Infant-mother attachment: The origins and developmental significance of individual differences in Strange Situation behavior.* Hillsdale, NJ: Erlbaum.

Lamphear, V. S. (1985). The impact of maltreatment on children's psychosocial adjustment: A review of the research. *Child Abuse and Neglect, 9,* 251–263.

Loeber, R. M., Green, S. M., Lahey, B. B., & Stouthammer-Loeber, M. (1989). Optimal informants on childhood disruptive behaviors. *Development and Psychopathology, 1,* 317–337.

Luthar, S. S., & Zigler, E. (1991). Vulnerability and competence: A review of research on resilience in childhood. *American Journal of Orthopsychiatry, 61,* 6–22.

Lynch, M. & Cicchetti, D. (1991). Patterns of relatedness in maltreated and nonmaltreated children: Connections among multiple representational models. *Development and Psychopathology, 3,* 207–226.

Lyons-Ruth, K., Connell, D. B., & Zoll, D. (1989). Patterns of maternal behavior among infants at risk for abuse: Relations with infant attachment behavior and infant development at 12 months of age. In D. Cicchetti & V. Carlson (Eds.), *Child maltreatment* (pp. 464–493). Cambridge: Cambridge University Press.

Malkin, C. M., & Lamb, M. E. (1994). Child Maltreatment: A test of sociobiological theory. *Journal of Comparative Family Studies, 25*(1), 121–133.

Martin H. P., & Beezley, P. (1974). Prevention and consequences of child abuse. *Journal of Operational Psychology, 6,* 68–74.

McGee, R. A., Wolfe, D. A., Yuen, S. A., Wilson, S. K., & Carnochan, J. (1995). The measurement of maltreatment: A comparison of approaches. *Child Abuse and Neglect, 19*(2), 233–249.

Reich, W., & Earls, F. (1987). Rules for making psychiatric diagnoses in children on the basis of multiple sources of information: Preliminary strategies. *Journal of Abnormal Child Psychology, 15,* 601–616.

Reid, J. B., Kavanagh, K., & Baldwin, D. V. (1987). Abusive parents' perceptions of child problem behaviors: An example of parental bias. *Journal of Abnormal Child Psychology, 15,* 457–466.

Richters, J. E. (1992). Depressed mothers as informants about their children: A critical review for the evidence for distortion. *Psychological Bulletin, 112,* 485–499.

Robin, A. L., & Foster, S. L. (1989). Issues Checklist. In A. L. Robin & S. L. Foster (Eds.), *Negotiating parent-adolescent conflict: A behavioral-family systems approach* (pp. 296–299). New York: Guilford.

Rutter, M. (1983). Stress, coping, and development: Some issues and some questions. In N. Garmezy & M. Rutter (Eds.), *Stress, coping, and development in children.* New York: McGraw Hill.

Salzinger, S., Feldman, R. S., Hammer, M., & Rosario, M. (1993). The effects of physical abuse on children's social relationships. *Child Development, 64,* 169–187.

Schneider-Rosen, K., Braunwald, K. G., Carlson, V., & Cicchetti, D. (1985). Illustrations from the study of maltreated infants. In I. Bretherton & E. Waters (Eds.), *Growing points in attachment theory and research* (pp. 194–210). *Monographs of the Society for Research on Child Development, 72* (Serial No. 209).

Solnit, A. J. (1984). Keynote address: Theoretical and practical aspects of risks and vulnerability in infancy. *Child Abuse and Neglect, 8,* 133–144.

Sroufe, L. A. (1983). Individual patterns of adaptation from infancy to preschool. In M. Perlmutter (Ed.), *Development and policy concerning children with special needs: Minnesota symposium on child psychology.* Hillsdale, NJ: Erlbaum.

Starr, R. H., Jr. (1978). The controlled study of the ecology of child abuse and drug abuse. *Child Abuse and Neglect, 2,* 19–28.

Starr, R. H., Jr. (1979). Child abuse. *American Psychologist, 34,* 872–878.

Sternberg, K. J. (1997). Fathers: The missing parents in research on family violence. In M. E. Lamb, (Ed.), *The role of the father in child develpment* (3rd ed., pp. 284–308, 292–297). New York: Wiley.

Sternberg, K. J., & Dawud-Noursi, S. D. (in press). Effects of domestic violence on children's behavior problems: Multiple perspectives. In R. Tessier & G. M. Tarabulsy (Eds.), *Enfance et famille: Contextes de developpements* [Child and family: Contexts for development]. Quebec, Canada: Les Presses de l'Université Laval.

Sternberg, K. J., Lamb, M. E., & Dawud-Noursi, S. (In press). Understanding domestic violence and its effects: Making sense of divergent reports and perspectives. In G. W. Holden, R. Geffner, & E. W. Jouriles (Eds.), *Children exposed to family violence.* Washington, DC.: American Psychological Association.

Sternberg, K. J., Lamb, M. E., Greenbaum, C., Cicchetti, D., Dawud, S., Cortes, R. M., Krispin, O., & Lorey, F. (1993). Effects of domestic violence on children's behavior problems and depression. *Developmental Psychology, 29,* 44–52.

Sternberg, K. J., Lamb, M. E., Greenbaum, C., Dawud, S., Cortes, R. M., & Lorey, F. (1994). The effects of domestic violence on children's perceptions of their perpetrating and nonperpetrating parents. *International Journal of Behavioral Development, 17,* 779–795.

Tein, J., Roosa, M. W., & Michaels, M. (1994). Agreement between parent and child reports on parental behaviors. *Journal of Marriage and the Family, 56,* 341–355.

Toro, P. A. (1982). Developmental effects of child abuse: A review. *Child Abuse and Neglect, 6,* 423–431.

Trickett, P. K., Aber, J. L., Carlson, V., & Cicchetti, D. (1991). Relationship of socioeconomic status to the etiology and developmental sequelae of physical child abuse. *Developmental Psychology, 27,* 148–158.

Werner, E. E. (1989). High-risk children in young adulthood: A longitudinal study from birth to 32 years. *American Journal of Orthopsychiatry, 59,* 72–81.

Wolfe, D. A., Jaffe, P., Wilson, S. K., & Zak, L. (1985). Children of battered women: The relations of child behavior to family violence and maternal stress. *Journal of Consulting and Clinical Psychology, 5,* 657–665.

Wolfe, D. A., & Mosk, M. (1983). Behavioral comparisons of children from abusive and distressed families. *Journal of Consulting and Clinical Psychology, 51,* 702–708.

Wolfe, D. A., Zak, L., Wilson, S. K., & Jaffe, P. (1986). Child witnesses to violence between parents: Critical issues in behavioral and social adjustment. *Journal of Abnormal Child Psychology, 14,* 95–104.

Wolins, M. (1983). The gender dilemma in social welfare: Who cares for children. In M. E. Lamb & A. Sagi (Eds.), *Fatherhood and family policy* (pp. 113–128). Hillsdale, NJ: Erlbaum.

Zigler, E. (1980). Controlling child abuse: Do we have the knowledge and/or the will? In G. Gerbner, C. J. Ross, & E. Zigler (Eds.), *Child abuse: An agenda for action* (pp. 3–32). New York: Oxford University Press.

Zigler, E. F., & Finn-Stevenson, M. (1992). Applied developmental psychology. In M. H. Bornstein & M. E. Lamb (Eds.), *Developmental psychology: An advanced textbook* (3rd ed.). Hillsdale, NJ: Erlbaum.

19 Interdisciplinary interface: Developmental principles brought to substance abuse research

Suniya S. Luthar, Gretta Cushing, and Thomas J. McMahon

Substance abusers are a group at high risk for a range of negative mental and physical health outcomes. Individuals addicted to cocaine and opioids frequently have serious comorbid psychiatric disorders such as depression and antisocial personality disorder, as well as physical health problems, such as neurological, cardiovascular, and obstetrical complications, and high vulnerability to HIV infections.

In terms of risk factors linked with addiction, among the most potent – and still inadequately understood – are those related to family functioning. Research has established that diagnoses of drug abuse and associated psychopathology in a given individual connote high levels of vulnerability for his or her family members as well. While this global risk index has been identified, little is currently understood about the etiological pathways that might underlie the emergence of psychiatric dysfunction among affected families. Working within the framework of developmental psychopathology, this chapter describes research-based explorations of familial factors associated with drug abuse, with a special focus on different pathways to disorder.

The goal underlying this chapter is to foster more cross-disciplinary research in the arena of substance abuse. More specifically, we seek to highlight the value of applying insights from developmental psychology to paradigms that have traditionally encompassed work on familial factors in drug abuse, that is, psychiatry and family-genetic research. We pursue our underlying objectives, first, by illustrating some of the scientific gains of such cross-disciplinary empirical efforts and, second, by exploring potential impediments to, and directions for, future work of this integrative nature.

In the first section of the chapter, we present background information regarding the design and central findings of the existing psychiatric-epidemiology studies that set the stage for the interdisciplinary efforts discussed here. In describing the in-

This research was supported by funding to the first author by Research Scientist Development Award K21-DA00202 and P50-DA09241. We thank Jacob Burack for his suggestions on organization and presentation of ideas within this paper. Also gratefully acknowledged are comments from Dante Cicchetti and John Weisz, from Linda Mayes, M.D., and from the Child and Family Research Group members at the Yale Substance Abuse Center.

437

terdisciplinary efforts themselves, our attempt is to specify areas of interface between developmental psychology and other social science disciplines. Their interdisciplinary nature is highlighted in various aspects of the efforts described: in the formulation of research questions, in the identification of areas requiring further empirical or clinical attention, as well as in the implications of the results obtained. The final section of the chapter presents a commentary on future directions for research with drug abusers and their families that is in the tradition of developmental psychopathology.

Background research: Paradigm and methodology

During the past decade, researchers have conducted a series of studies on familial vulnerability to psychiatric disorders among cocaine and opioid addicts and their relatives (see Ripple & Luthar, 1996, for a review). Designed within the paradigm of family-genetic studies in psychiatric epidemiology (Weissman et al., 1986), much of this research has been aimed at examining patterns of transmission of serious psychopathology among drug abusers and their first-degree relatives, that is, their biological parents and siblings.

The broad aim of family-genetic studies is to examine the role of the family in transmitting particular disorders. This research paradigm involves, at the outset, the ascertainment of a group of "probands," or individuals with the disorder of interest – say depression – and a comparable group of individuals who are unaffected by that disorder. The first-degree relatives of both groups are then assessed for the presence or absence of major psychiatric disorders. Familial transmission of depression might be suggested if, for instance, a higher rate of depression were found among a depressed proband's relatives (parents, siblings, or offspring), as compared with relatives of individuals unaffected by depression (see Weissman et al., 1986).

A limitation of the family-genetic research paradigm is that it precludes the disentangling of genetic versus environmental influences linked with the recurrence of particular disorders among related individuals. This limitation notwithstanding, family-genetic studies are often a critical first step in guiding the conduct of studies that more conclusively indicate genetic linkages – but that are far more difficult to implement – such as twin studies or cross-fostering studies (Rounsaville, Kosten, et al., 1991; Weissman et al, 1986).

Two family-genetic studies of substance abusers and their relatives lie at the core of discussions in this section. The first (Rounsaville, Kosten, et al., 1991) included 201 opioid addicts and 877 of their first degree relatives (400 parents and 476 siblings), and the second (Rounsaville, Anton, et al., 1991) involved 298 cocaine abusers and 1,165 relatives (492 parents and 673 siblings). The participating families were generally of lower socioeconomic status, with approximately 75% of the proband addicts belonging to Hollingshead (Hollingshead & Redlich, 1958) Classes IV or V. The opioid sample included only Caucasian families, whereas the sample of cocaine abusers included both Caucasians and African Americans.

Using methods and analyses deriving from psychiatric epidemiology, this research has involved in-depth assessments of the psychiatric status of addicted probands and their relatives. Psychiatric diagnoses were made based on structured interviews utilizing the Schedule for Affective Disorders and Schizophrenia, Lifetime Version (SADS-L, Endicott & Spitzer, 1978), Research Diagnostic Criteria (RDC; Spitzer, Endicott, & Robins, 1978), family history from multiple informants, and available medical records.

Major findings have indicated vulnerability to substance abuse, as well as to other psychiatric disorders, among addicts' first-degree relatives. Substantially higher rates of alcoholism and drug abuse were found among families of addicts as compared with those of a control group (Rounsaville, Kosten, et al., 1991), indicating the aggregation of substance use problems within families. In addition, like substance abusers themselves, relatives of drug abusers also showed elevations in several other psychiatric disorders such as depression and antisocial personality disorder (Rounsaville, Kosten, et al., 1991; see also Mirin, Weiss, Griffin, & Michael, 1991).

Familial factors and substance abuse: Developmentally informed research

While the previously cited studies collectively establish high risk linked with a family history of substance abuse, they do not address questions about factors that might influence the transmission of disorders among related individuals. As Rende and Plomin (1993) indicate, once family studies document aggregation, the next step is to identify etiological factors contributing to the aggregation of pathology within families. Given that all family members are not affected in the same manner, the critical question from a research perspective is, Who gets affected, how, and why, in families at risk for psychopathology? Or to rephrase the query from the perspective of resilience research, Within these at-risk families, who does *not* get affected and why?

Previous family-study research findings therefore served as the backdrop for three developmentally informed inquiries, each focused on factors that might affect outcomes among individuals at risk for drug abuse and associated pathology. The first study examined differences in patterns of familial transmission depending on whether the affected parent in a particular family was the mother or the father. The second and third inquiries examined different dimensions of vulnerability to psychopathology among adult siblings of drug abusers.

Gender of affected parent

A question of interest – hitherto neglected in the family-genetic literature on substance abuse – was whether patterns of familially transmitted disorders might differ according to the gender of the affected parent. In contrast to the abundant epidemiological evidence regarding gender differences in the *incidence* of major forms of psychopathology, there have been few family-genetic studies on potential *ramifications* for children, of the presence of particular disorders among fathers versus mothers.

Rates of disorders among addicts' siblings were therefore examined separately as a function of psychopathology among their mothers versus their fathers (Luthar, Merikangas, & Rounsaville, 1993). Offspring disorders were examined in terms of four major categories: drug abuse, alcoholism, depressive/anxiety disorders, and antisocial personality disorder (ASPD). These disorders were each examined in relation to two categories of parent disorders, that is, alcoholism and depression/anxiety. Analyses of these associations involved the previously described sample of opioid abusers' families (Rounsaville, Kosten, et al., 1991), as well as those of cocaine addicts (Rounsaville, Anton, et al., 1991). The availability of both African American and Caucasian families in the latter case enabled scrutiny of variations in the transmission of disorders by ethnicity.

The findings indicated varying trends in the familial aggregation of disorders depending on the gender of affected parent as well as on the disorder in question. Across both sets of addicts' families, maternal depression, but not alcoholism, showed significant associations with almost all categories of offspring psychopathology. By contrast, among fathers, depression was unrelated to offspring psychopathology. The only paternal associations found were between paternal alcoholism and offspring substance use, and further analyses within the cocaine sample indicated that these effects were restricted to the African American families.

Results deriving from this research can be interpreted based on previous evidence in the fields of developmental psychology, psychiatry, and epidemiology. In the context of developmental psychology, for example, the strong links between various types of offspring psychopathology and maternal – but not paternal – depression may at least partly reflect the role of socializing influences. Depressed fathers may, in fact, show behaviors such as those documented among depressed mothers in interactions with their children (e.g., high child-directed negativity and constriction of affective/behavioral expression; see Cicchetti and Toth, 1995). However, the effects of maternal depression may be more insidious since mothers, being primary caregivers, often have greater exposure than fathers to their children. Differences in this context may be particularly pronounced among substance abusers' families: Many of these are single-parent families where the children are often raised without fathers (Hawley & Disney, 1992; Levy & Rutter, 1992).

Drawing on psychiatric and epidemiological research, the weak links involving maternal *alcoholism* – that contrasted with the apparently far-reaching effects of maternal depression – possibly reflect lower severity of this disorder as compared with depression among mothers in this study. In analyses involving the cocaine sample, for example, the single association found between maternal alcoholism and child pathology involved African American mothers; there is evidence that alcoholism is generally a more severe problem among African American women as compared with others (e.g., Corrigan & Anderson, 1982; Dawkins & Harper, 1983). Explanations involving severity of disorders might, similarly, be advanced for findings of links between paternal alcoholism and offspring substance abuse only among the African American families of cocaine addicts. Compared with men in other ethnic groups, African American alcoholics are more likely to be older, unemployed or laborers, and divorced; they also tend to have more years of heavy drinking and higher daily consumption of alcohol (Babor & Mendelson, 1983; National Institute on Alcohol Abuse and Alcoholism, 1981).

As the research questions and interpretation of findings within this effort drew on insights from different disciplines, so did the findings carry implications relevant to different fields. Most important, perhaps, are the implications for psychiatric epidemiology research: The results indicate the value of examining gender of the affected parent in studying patterns of familial aggregation of psychiatric disorders. As noted previously, the underlying aim of most family studies is to ascertain whether there might be a genetic component in the transmission of particular disorders (Weissman et al., 1986). If analyses suggest gender-linked components in the aggregation of particular disorders (as they did here), this evidence might guide the further study of potential environmental influences, and/or genetic pathways, with other more complicated and difficult designs and methodology.[1]

For developmental psychology, the results are perhaps most relevant to the understanding of the role of fathers in children's psychosocial adjustment. As Phares (1992; Phares & Compas, 1992) indicates, fathers have been dramatically underrepresented as compared with mothers in previous research on parental factors in child psychopathology. Noting that while the extant research indicates that paternal psychopathology is a sufficient but not necessary condition for child maladjustment, Phares stresses the need for further research that will allow for more specific prediction of the *circumstances* under which fathers are involved in child pathology. The present findings on the specificity of paternal effects to alcoholism among African American but not Caucasian families suggest that ethnicity may be an important construct to consider in this growing body of work.

Addicts' siblings: Vulnerability to substance abuse and psychopathology

In studying aggregation of disorders among first-degree relatives, another potentially useful distinction proposed (Luthar, Anton, Merikangas, & Rounsaville, 1992b) was that involving affected individuals' siblings as opposed to their parents. It was argued that particularly when the research focus is on issues related to substance use, analyses of familial transmission might be best limited to persons within the same age cohort, for whom one can assume similarity in exposure to particular substances (e.g., in terms of availability of severely addictive drugs) (see also Plomin, Rende, & Rutter, 1991).

Patterns of psychopathology were therefore scrutinized among siblings of drug abusers, using the previously mentioned sample of families of opioid addicts (Rounsaville, Kosten, et al., 1991). This inquiry (Luthar et al., 1992b) involved ascertainment of rates of major psychiatric disorders among addicts' siblings vis-à-vis rates in community cohorts of comparable age, using reports from the Epidemiological Catchment Area (ECA) study (Robins & Regier, 1991); rates among their parents; and major comorbid disorders in the addict proband (depression, antisocial personality disorder, or neither of these).

Findings indicated that in comparison with rates in the community, addicts' siblings had elevated rates of all major psychiatric disorders. Almost *two-thirds* of the addicts' siblings themselves had psychiatric diagnoses of drug abuse, with relative risk (RR) rates[2] in comparison to the community sample of 10 for males and 14 for females. In other words, as compared with individuals in the community, drug abusers' siblings showed a 10- to 14-fold increase in the risk of serious substance abuse problems. Heightened vulnerability was also found for other disorders. In comparison with community adults, relative risk rates for male and female addicts' siblings respectively were 4 and 12 for alcoholism, 15 and 5 for major depression, and 7 and 12 for antisocial personality disorder.

Rates of drug abuse were also substantially higher among addicts' siblings as compared with their parents, with incidence rates of 70% and 6% respectively among brothers versus fathers, and 59% and 3% respectively among sisters versus mothers. This pattern of greater vulnerability among siblings was echoed in trends with other psychiatric disorders. Incidence of ASPD was 40% versus 6% (males), and 16% versus 0 (females); furthermore, twice as many siblings as compared with parents had developed major depression (among males) and alcoholism (among female relatives).

When sibling disorders were viewed in terms of comorbid psychopathology among addicted probands, results indicated a general conveyance of risk rather than specificity of aggregation of disorders within families. Brothers and sisters typically displayed vulnerability to several psychiatric disorders and not just the specific diagnosis evidenced by their substance abusing relative. For example, the prevalence of ASPD among siblings was about the same whether or not the addict proband had a comorbid diagnosis of ASPD.

Among the various results of this study, particularly intriguing were findings of substantial differences in psychopathology reported by siblings as opposed to their parents. What might these intergenerational differences reflect? One of the most obvious explanations rests on cohort effects in psychiatric disorders (e.g., Klerman et al., 1985). In the case of substance abuse, higher rates over time may be directly linked to the increased availability of drugs such as heroin and cocaine since the 1960s.

The marked differences in rates of antisocial personality among parents and siblings may also be associated with cohort effects, and possibly with reporting biases. There is evidence that in providing retrospective self-report data, people tend to forget rather quickly even important personal events such as surgery and hospitalization (Cannell, 1977). Furthermore, since antisocial behaviors are typically manifested during the early adulthood years, older respondents may have been less likely to report lifetime symptoms of ASPD than were those closer to that period in their lives.

Biases such as these must be weighed against another equally plausible factor that could have loaded the findings in the *opposite* direction; that is, that parents, having lived longer, had a greater chance than siblings of developing lifetime disorders. Even considering diagnoses such as depression and alcoholism, rates that parents reported were considerably lower than those among siblings. In short, wherever substantial differences in incidence of disorders were found, siblings were inevitably worse off than their parents.[3]

The considerably elevated rates of disorders among siblings may, at least in part, reflect high levels of environmental vulnerability among these individuals, particularly with regard to drug use and related problems. Developmental research has shown, for example, that older siblings may serve as persistent role models for drug abuse for their adolescent brothers and sisters, and may also serve as sources for illicit substances (Brook, Whiteman, Gordon, & Brook, 1990). Studies have also established that older siblings can play an important role in younger siblings' drug use, often more so than parents (Brook et al., 1990; Needle, McCubbin, Wilson, Reineck, & Lazar, 1986).

The high rates of disorders among siblings might also be explained by developmental evidence on shared versus nonshared family environments. Hetherington, Reiss, and Plomin (1994) have noted that in general, concordance rates for psychopathology among siblings are less than 10%. Contrast this with rates of 66% for drug abuse among siblings of addicts, and lower, though still high, concordance rates of about 30% for both depression and ASPD. In instances such as these – where concordance for psychopathology among siblings far exceeds expected levels – researchers have suggested that shared environmental influences that derive from salient extreme environmental conditions are likely to be operating (see Bouchard, Lykken, McGue, Segal, & Tellegen, 1990; Rutter, 1994). For example, Bouchard et al. (1990) argued that shared effects can be particularly high in homes where children are grossly deprived or mistreated.

Also relevant to the present findings is evidence that shared environmental influences among siblings can be particularly important among individuals with extreme forms of psychopathology, particularly for disorders such as delinquency and substance use (e.g., Cloninger & Gottesman, 1987; McGue, Pickens, & Svikis, 1992; Rende, Plomin, Reiss, & Hetherington, 1993). Opiate addiction typically occurs in individuals with multiple dysfunctional attributes, including personality disturbances and psychiatric difficulties, medical complications, disturbed family relations, and frequent negative life events (Mirin et al., 1991; Rounsaville et al., 1982). It is therefore entirely plausible that their siblings would show a variety of forms of serious psychopathology, and not just the particular comorbid psychiatric disorder manifested by the addicted proband.

Risk/protective factors for drug abuse among addicts' siblings

In a third study (Luthar, Anton, Merikangas, & Rounsaville, 1992a), the focus was on risk or protective factors linked with the most frequently noted disorder among addicts' siblings, that is, problems of substance abuse. As noted previously, almost two-thirds of the addicts' siblings interviewed themselves had problems of drug addiction.

In exploring potential vulnerability and protective processes, guided by developmental research on resilience, the approach in this study was multifaceted. Investigators have argued for the inclusion of variables at different levels of individual, family, or societal organization as potential etiological factors, given strong evidence that multiple risk/protective constructs can each contribute significant independent variance to psychosocial outcomes among children (see Garmezy, 1985; Luthar & Zigler, 1991; Seifer & Sameroff, 1987).

Based on such recommendations and existing evidence in the substance use literature (discussed in the ensuing paragraphs), the variables examined in this study were as follows. At the level of the individual, two constructs were included: experimentation with drugs as a teenager and levels of sensation seeking. Examination of early experimentation with drugs was based on clinical observations that among such high-risk populations, having ever *tried* a substance seemed linked with elevated risk for eventually developing serious problems of drug abuse and dependence. Sensation seeking and impulsive expression have repeatedly been documented as among the most important personality characteristics associated with the use of drugs (Andrucci, Archer, Pancoast, & Gordon, 1987; Jaffe & Archer, 1987).

At the level of the family, birth order relative to the addicted proband was examined, given evidence that older siblings can play a vital role in younger siblings' drug use (Brook et al., 1990; Needle et al., 1986). Finally, given the importance of the peer group in the initiation and maintenance of adolescent drug use (Brook, Whiteman, & Gordon, 1983; Huba, Wingard, & Bentler, 1979), two types of peer influences during the respondents' adolescent years were examined: drug use among peers and whether peers offered drugs to the individual.

Analyses involved the sample of siblings of opioid addicts described earlier (Rounsaville, Kosten, et al., 1991). Associations between the various risk factors and drug abuse among siblings were examined via logistic regressions. Results showed that with the six risk variables and two demographic factors (age and gender) predicting sibling drug abuse, a single significant effect emerged, that is, the variable "Ever Tried Drugs."[4] The odds ratio for this variable was 4.7 (95% confidence interval of 1.6–14.2), indicating that individuals who had ever tried drugs were almost *five times as likely* to be substance abusers during adulthood as compared with those who never experimented with drugs. Descriptive data showed that of all the siblings who had ever experimented with drugs, 77% went on eventually to develop psychiatric diagnoses of drug abuse.

To follow up on these analyses, two additional regression analyses were performed to ascertain which constructs other than early experimentation with drugs might be related to adult diagnoses of substance abuse. In these analyses, "Ever Tried Drugs" was (a) excluded from the list of predictor variables in the equation, and (b) was treated as the criterion variable with all other variables as predictors. In both analyses, results indicated significant effects of sensation seeking, and of peers' use of drugs. Thus, although clearly secondary to early experimentation with drugs, the trait of sensation seeking and peers' drug use appeared to be of some importance in terms of links with the siblings' eventual drug abuse.

The results of this study suggest various causal associations among risk factors for substance abuse, which might be usefully explored in future prospective research. Based on the present results, for example, one might speculate that sensation seeking and peer use each influence early experimentation with drugs, which, in turn, affects eventual drug abuse. Alternatively, it is possible that drug use tends to alter personality traits such as sensation seeking (instead of the converse), or that drug-using adolescents would be more likely to seek out drug-using peers. In the future, longitudinal developmental research could help to clarify such causal associations among groups at risk for substance abuse, such as younger siblings of adult drug abusers and addicts' offspring.

Results of this study differ dramatically from previous developmental findings on experimentation with drugs among more mainstream teens. In an innovative investigation of this issue, Shedler and Block (1990) demonstrated that in their sociodemographically heterogeneous sample, adolescents who had engaged in some drug experimentation (chiefly with marijuana) showed more positive adjustment patterns than either those who used drugs frequently or those who abstained completely. The findings were interpreted in terms of stage-salient developmental issues: Given the apparent acceptability of marijuana in the contemporary teen culture, as well as the developmental appropriateness of limit testing during adolescence, it was not surprising that the more psychologically healthy, sociable individuals had at least tried marijuana by the age of 18 years.

Shedler & Block's (1990) findings with a relatively low-risk group are in stark contrast to the previously described results based on addicts' siblings, among whom teenage experimentation with drugs was linked with a fivefold increase in serious drug abuse problems in adulthood. Viewed together, the findings underscore cautions noted in the developmental and resilience literature (Baldwin, Baldwin, & Cole, 1990; Luthar, 1995) that links between risk/protective factors and outcomes can differ substantially with variations in contextual, ecocultural factors.

The trends identified on early drug experimentation are also important in that they indicate intervention directions that are both specific and delimited. Frequently, variables that are identified as being high risk are difficult to modify through intervention efforts (e.g., personality traits, characteristics of the neighborhood, or use of drugs by significant others). Although often refractory to change itself, experimentation with drugs by addicts' teenage siblings or offspring is a risk dimension that is comparatively more delimited and may be more easily targeted for preventive interventions. Adoption of intervention strategies based on research findings such as these could, therefore, yield high gains in terms of reducing the incidence of drug addiction among highly vulnerable groups.

Summary

Research described in the preceding section involves the application of various principles of developmental psychology to research conducted in the paradigm of psychiatric epidemiology, and the findings, in turn, have implications for different social science domains. In the first study, developmental principles led to the scrutiny of familial aggregation of psychiatric disorders separately according to gender of the affected parent. Results corroborated the value of such gender-based differentiation. The findings showed, for example, that whereas maternal depression had strong links with offspring psychopathology, paternal depression did not; further, associations involving paternal alcoholism appeared to vary by ethnicity. In terms of implications for future research within the family-genetic paradigm, these data underscore the importance of considering gender of the affected parent when examining aggregation of psychiatric disorders within families. The results also have relevance to efforts in developmental psychology aimed at identifying the circumstances under which fathers' influences on their children may be particularly pronounced.

In a second inquiry departing from the tradition of examining familial transmission among relatives as a single group, patterns of psychopathology were contrasted among addicts' siblings versus their parents. Results showed that drug abusers' siblings had higher rates of substance abuse as well as other psychiatric disorders. The magnitude of intergenerational differences found, and their consistency across different diagnostic categories, suggest that these variations are unlikely to be purely artifactual (e.g., reflecting cohort effects). Instead, resonating as they do with developmental research indicating high concordance of serious forms of psychopathology among sibling pairs, the data raise important concerns about shared environmental adversities to which siblings in drug abusers' families might be exposed.

Given that almost two-thirds of addicts' siblings had diagnoses of drug abuse, a third inquiry was focused on exploring risk and protective factors associated with this disorder among siblings. Guided by the literature on child resilience, constructs examined included those at the level of the individual, the family, and the wider social group. Results indicated that a single construct shared by far the most variance with the outcome, that is, experimentation with any illegal substance as a teenager. Of all the drug abusers' siblings who had ever tried drugs, more than three-quarters eventually developed serious problems of substance abuse. Contrasting sharply with findings with more mainstream groups (which suggest that moderate experimentation with drugs might be adaptive during adolescence), these data emphasize the importance of considering contextual factors in the study of links between risk/protective processes and psychosocial outcomes. The results also have implications for interventions, indicating that in terms of pathways to eventual drug abuse among addicts' siblings, early experimentation with drugs – a fairly delimited construct and one that could be a relatively "modifiable modifier" – appears to be of particular salience.

Future directions

Dovetailing with foregoing illustrations of insights gleaned by applying developmental principles to psychiatric research on substance abuse, the section that follows presents specific directions for future research of this interdisciplinary nature. In turn, the ensuing discussions focus on the relative paucity of studies of addicts and their families within the developmental psychology literature, followed by a delineation of salient issues in the context of research, intervention, and social policy, that might benefit from the contributions of child development experts.

Developmental research on substance abusers

Addicted individuals have traditionally been studied by psychiatrists, from a medical or pharmacological perspective. There are comparatively few methodologically sound studies on psychosocial aspects of addiction that are based in developmental theory. The bulk of the extant developmental research in the area has been focused on *use* of substances such as alcohol and marijuana among children and adolescents; there has been relatively little empirical attention to abuse of or dependence on substances such as heroin or cocaine.[5]

The dearth of developmentally oriented research on drug abusers is particularly striking given the high relevance of many aspects of addicts' lives to areas of expertise of developmentalists. To illustrate, the childhood histories of substance-abusing women typically reflect poor attachments with primary caregivers and exposure to inconsistent patterns of parenting, physical and/or sexual abuse, and parental separations or divorce (Davis, 1990; Dembo et al., 1988; Hawley & Disney, 1992; Rohsenow, Corbett, & Devine, 1988). Each of these aspects of child rearing, considered individually, has received abundant attention in the developmental research literature. Why, then, have substance abusers, who experience a combination of them, been neglected?

The relative neglect of addiction in the child development literature may partly reflect an uneasiness within the professional community that mirrors, to some extent, the discomfort among society in general toward groups that are seriously disenfranchised. As McLoyd & Wilson (1991) and others (Belle, 1984) have asserted, mental health professionals often have an attitude of contempt toward women living in poverty. Sentiments of this kind are likely to be exacerbated when the poor people concerned are also those with serious psychopathology and histories of addiction, and probably still further heightened when these addicts are parents of young children (Chang, Carroll, Behr, & Kosten, 1992; Eliason & Skinstad, 1995; Mackie-Ramos & Rice, 1988).

Second, stereotypes about addiction may lead to views that drug abusers are characterologically antisocial individuals with problems that are largely immutable to change (Imhof, 1991); thus, they are less worthy of research resources than are other disadvantaged or disenfranchised groups. The evidence in support of such stereotypes, however, is not commanding. Admittedly, antisocial personality disorder is among those most refractory to psychotherapeutic intervention. However, this disorder has been found in less than half of all addicts in studies (at least those in treatment), and in only 5% to 20% of female addicts (Rounsaville et al., 1982; Rounsaville, Anton, et al., 1991). Furthermore, clinical trials have shown the efficacy of thoughtful treatments that are geared to addicts' specific areas of comorbid psychopathology, *including* those for substance abusers with comorbid antisocial personality disorder (see Carroll & Rounsaville, 1995; Gerstley et al., 1989; Woody et al., 1985).

Third, more so than other psychiatrically disordered groups, addicts may often be seen as responsible for creating and perpetuating many of the problems in their lives (see Beck, Steer, & Shaw, 1984; Kandall & Gaines, 1991; Mayes & Bornstein, 1995; Murphy & Irwin, 1992). A schizophrenic mother living in poverty, for example, is likely to receive far less societal censure than a heroin-abusing mother in similar circumstances, chiefly because the former is seen as a victim whereas the other is seen as responsible not only for destroying her own life but also the lives of her children (Eliason & Skinstad, 1995; Mackie-Ramos & Rice, 1988). Stereotypes such as these can strongly affect scientists' and service providers' efforts with the populations they serve (Imhof, 1991; Imhof, Hirsch, & Terenzi, 1983); yet, in the context of substance abusers, they have little basis in empirical data (Mayes & Bornstein, 1995). This leads back, once again, to the need for more developmental research with this population. The success of future interventions that might *help* addicts assume control of their lives necessitates a sound research-based understanding of the multiple pathways that lead to addiction and associated psychopathology (Brady, Grice, Dustan, & Randall, 1993; Ripple & Luthar, 1996).

Directions for developmentally informed research

If, in the future, developmentally trained psychologists were to lend their expertise in working with addicts and their families, especially useful would be studies of risk and protective factors associated with the onset, maintenance, and cessation of drug abuse. As suggested earlier in this chapter, there is a need for such research on the children of addicts and/or their younger siblings. Whereas these youngsters are faced with multiple and serious risks, it is clear that not all succumb to serious psychopathology; some, in fact, function remarkably well (Luthar, Cushing, Merikangas, & Rounsaville, 1995). Using existing models and research trends in the field of childhood resilience, developmentalists could provide vital information about what distinguishes these relatively well adjusted children from those that succumb to the adversities associated with familial drug abuse (Glantz, 1992).

In examining risk and protective processes among addicts' children, studies of school-age and adolescent offspring are particularly needed. Most of the existing methodologically rigorous, developmentally oriented research in the area (see note 5) has focused on in-utero drug exposure, or on infant and preschool children of drug addicts. The evidence regarding these young children is mixed, with some studies indicating specific areas of deficit in comparison with socioeconomically matched controls, and others reporting few such differences (see Hawley & Disney, 1992; Mayes & Bornstein, Chapter 8, this volume). By contrast, the little evidence that currently exists on school-age and adolescent offspring is less equivocal regarding the presence of psychopathology (Goldstein et al., 1995; Wilens, Biederman, Kiely, Bredin, & Spencer, 1995). For example, in our own research with school-age and teen offspring living with addicted mothers (Luthar, Cushing, Merikangas, & Rounsaville, in press), we have found high rates of psychiatric disorders. In our sample of 119 children, 61% were found to have at least one lifetime DSM-III-R psychiatric disorder, with 30% manifesting one or more disruptive childhood disorders, and 40% showing at least one anxiety or affective disorder. Data such as these underscore the need for developmentally informed inquiry into factors that might exacerbate or ameliorate the cumulative adversities of living with an addicted mother through the preteen and adolescent years.

Intervention research

Another critical direction for developmental efforts is intervention research, particularly that focused on improving the parenting behaviors of drug-abusing mothers. This suggestion stems from four converging threads of evidence in the literature. First, epidemiological data have shown substantial increases in the incidence of cocaine and opioid abuse among women in the past three decades (Levy & Rutter, 1992). Second, most women in treatment for drug abuse are single parents of children less than 18 years of age (Colten, 1980; Deren, 1986; Levy & Rutter, 1992). Third, addicted mothers show several deficits in their parenting behaviors (for reviews, see Hawley & Disney, 1992; Mayes & Bornstein, Chapter 8, this volume). They tend, for example, to be relatively disengaged and uncommunicative with their infants and, with their older children, often use threatening and authoritarian disciplinary approaches. Child abuse and neglect are also problems encountered frequently among addicted mothers.

Fourth, despite their several deficits in parenting, concern for the well-being of their children is frequently identified as a primary source of motivation for addicted women to seek treatment (Colten, 1980). Contrary to the rampant biases that convey a severely negative judgment toward these individuals, studies have found that opiate-addicted women are concerned about the welfare of their children (Levy &

Rutter, 1992; Tunving & Nilsson, 1985). Clinical and empirical evidence also indicate that addicted mothers experience a range of negative feelings in relation to their role as parents, including feelings of guilt, confusion regarding appropriate child-rearing strategies, inadequacy in the parenting role, and fear about child outcomes (Colten, 1982; Grossman & Schottenfeld, 1992; Levy & Rutter, 1992). Each of these "problem areas" falls squarely within the purview of developmental psychologists' expertise.

While considering parenting interventions from a developmental perspective, it is also important to acknowledge the role of fathers in addicts' families. In the substance abuse literature, children are discussed almost exclusively in terms of women's (their mothers') issues. Understanding of parenting issues among drug-dependent fathers remains very limited despite evidence that drug-dependent men also demonstrate deficits in their capacity to function effectively as parents – often by simply being absent from the lives of their children (Luthar, Cushing, Merikangas, & Rounsaville, 1996). Although clinicians and researchers may be influenced by value systems that accept paternal abandonment of children to the care of their mothers, there are important questions about the ways in which fathers' drug dependence might affect child outcomes. Even when estranged from families of procreation, addicted fathers may have concerns about their role as parents, and might still have significant influences on the well-being of their children (see, e.g., Zimmerman, Salem, & Maton, 1995). By allowing children to remain largely a women's issue, researchers, clinicians, and policy makers may be contributing to the perpetuation of stereotypes regarding addicted fathers, and may be tacitly condoning these men's continued revocation of important responsibilities at tremendous cost to their children, families, and society.

For maximal efficacy, future developmentally informed parenting interventions with substance abusers must be designed within the context of rigorous evaluative research (see Zigler, 1980; Zigler & Trickett, 1978). Recognizing the many areas of adversity faced by addicted parents and their children, there have been several efforts to develop multifaceted treatment packages in recent years (e.g., Catalano, Hagerty, & Gainey, in press; Finnegan, Hagan, & Kaltenbach, 1991; Grossman & Schottenfeld, 1992; Hawley & Disney, 1992; Levy & Rutter, 1992; Scherling, 1994). Unfortunately, few programs, so far, have provided detailed manualization of therapeutic procedures used or have been subjected to empirical evaluation of their therapeutic efficacy and cost effectiveness as compared to other treatments. Gaps such as these limit the extent to which existing therapies might be extended to treatment facilities other than those they originated in (Hawley & Disney, 1992; Luthar & Walsh, 1995).

Aside from contributing in the design of clinical interventions, developmental research could also yield vital information for social policy concerns. Too frequently, health and legal policies concerning addicts and their families are not based on research data; they have tended to be punitive toward substance-abusing parents and are not always in the best interest of the child (Garrity-Rokous, 1994). As Mayes and Bornstein (1995) note, for example, policies regarding mandatory reporting to child protective agencies of positive urine screens among pregnant women is based on the presumption that these women will be unfit parents to their newborn offspring. While these policies may seem resonant with extant evidence of vulnerability among addicts' offspring, not all children living with drug-dependent parents are abused or neglected. Further, mandates such as these often dissuade drug-abusing women from seeking prenatal or perinatal medical attention due to fears of losing child custody. Reviewing several such concerns, Mayes and Bornstein conclude that future policies regarding the care of these multiply disadvantaged women and their children must be based on research data on their developmental and health care needs, such as the specific parenting capacities and deficits of addicted mothers, and the neurodevelopmental status of drug-exposed infants and children.

Summary and conclusions

There is a pressing need for more research on developmental issues in drug addiction. The problems experienced by substance abusers are certainly the domain of medicine, psychiatry, and psychopharmacology. There is no question, however, that individuals trained in psychosocial aspects of child development could make valuable contributions in attempts to understand the issues confronting this population and efforts to intervene with them. Further research is necessary to understand the developmental pathways to addiction and positive versus negative mental health outcomes among substance abusers and their family members. Additionally, given the recent increases in numbers of drug-abusing women who have minor children in their custody, there is a need for the design of developmentally based interventions targeting these women's parenting skills, and for the evaluation of such interventions via rigorous empirical research. The role of substance-abusing fathers in the adjustment of their children and partners is yet another area that requires the empirical scrutiny of interdisciplinary teams.

In conclusion, child development experts could make substantial contributions in the future to the research-based understanding of psychopathology and competence among substance abusers and their family members. Over the past three decades, pioneering developmental psychopathologist Edward Zigler has forcefully argued that the empirical study of pathways to adjustment is essential to develop, ultimately, effective interventions for at-risk children and their families (Zigler, 1980; Zigler & Berman, 1983; Zigler, Taussig, & Black, 1992; Zigler & Trickett, 1978). Perhaps more so than any subgroup of disenfranchised individuals in contemporary society, substance abusers and their families urgently require the attention of scholars with expertise in psychosocial issues and child development.

Notes

1 For illustrations of approaches to investigating genetic versus environmental influences in disorders showing gender effects in familial transmission, see Gatz, Pederson, Plomin, Nesselroade, & McClearn, 1992.
2 All rates presented in this chapter have been rounded in the interest of brevity.
3 The ECA study indicated that in the general community as well, rates of major psychiatric disorders were higher among adults younger than 45 years of age as compared with those between 45 and 65 years of age, possibly because psychiatric disorder accounts for premature deaths, leaving psychiatrically healthy older survivors (Robins & Regier, 1991). In general, however, the disparity between incidence rates across these two adult ECA cohorts was narrower than that found across siblings versus parents in the study under discussion.
4 This construct included a range of substances, including those more commonly experimented with by teenagers, such as marijuana and solvents, as well as the more "end stage" drugs such as cocaine and opiates.
5 For some illustrations of exemplary developmentally based research on children of addicts, see Alessandri, Sullivan, Imaizumi, & Lewis, 1993; Brinker, Baxter, & Butler, 1994; de Cubas & Field, 1993; Mayes, 1994; and Rodning, Beckwith, & Howard, 1991.

References

Alessandri, S. M., Sullivan, M. W., Imaizumi, S., & Lewis, M. (1993). Learning and emotional responsivity in cocaine-exposed infants. *Developmental Psychology, 29,* 989–997.

Andrucci, G. L., Archer, R. P., Pancoast, D. L., & Gordon, R. A. (1987). The relationship of MMPI and sensation seeking scales to adolescent drug use. *Journal of Personality Assessment, 53,* 253–266.

Babor, T. F., & Mendelson, J. H. (1983, May). *Ethnic-religious differences in the manifestation and treatment of alcoholism.* Paper presented at the Conference on Alcohol and Culture: Comparative Perspectives from Europe and America. Farmington, CT.

Baldwin, A. L., Baldwin, C., & Cole, R. E. (1990). Stress-resistant families and stress-resistant children. In J. Rolf, A. S. Masten, D. Cicchetti, K. H. Nuechterlein, & S. Weintraub (Eds.), *Risk and protective factors in the development of psychopathology* (pp. 257–280). New York: Cambridge University Press.

Beck, A. T., Steer, R. A., & Shaw, B. F. (1984). Hopelessness in alcohol-and heroin-dependent women. *Journal of Clinical Psychology, 40,* 602–606.

Belle, D. (1984). Inequality and mental health: Low income and minority women. In L. Walker (Ed.), *Women and mental health policy* (pp. 135–150). Beverly Hills, CA: Sage.

Bouchard, T. J., Lykken, D. T., McGue, M., Segal, N. L., & Tellegen, A. (1990). Sources of human psychological differences: The Minnesota study of twins reared apart. *Science, 250,* 223–228.

Brady, K. T., Grice, D. E., Dustan, L., & Randall, C. (1993). Gender differences in substance use disorders. *American Journal of Psychiatry, 150,* 1701–1711.

Brinker, R. P., Baxter, A., & Butler, L. S. (1994). An ordinal pattern analysis of four hypotheses describing the interactions between drug-addicted, chronically disadvantaged, and middle-class mother-infant dyads. *Child Development, 65,* 361–372.

Brook, J. S., Whiteman, M., & Gordon, S. (1983). Stages of drug abuse in adolescence: Personality, peer, and family correlates. *Developmental Psychology, 19,* 269–277.

Brook, J. S., Whiteman, M., Gordon, S., & Brook, D. W. (1990). The role of older brothers in younger brothers' drug use viewed in the context of parent and peer influences. *Journal of Genetic Psychology, 151,* 59–75.

Cannell, C. F. (1977). *A summary of studies of interviewing methodology.* (Pub. No. [HRA] 77–1343.) Washington, DC: Department of Health, Education, and Welfare.

Carroll, K. M., & Rounsaville, B. J. (1995). Psychosocial treatments for substance dependence. In J. M. Oldham & M. B. Riba (Eds.), *American Psychiatric Press Review of Psychiatry* (Vol. 14, pp. 127–149). Washington, DC: American Psychiatric Press.

Catalano, R. F., Haggerty, K. P., & Gainey, R. R. (in press). Prevention approaches in methadone treatment settings: Children of drug abuse treatment clients. In W. J. Bukoski & Z. Amsel (Eds.), *Drug abuse prevention: Sourcebook on strategies and research.*

Chang, G., Carroll, K. M., Behr, H. M., & Kosten, T. R. (1992). Improving treatment outcome in pregnant opiate-dependent women. *Journal of Substance Abuse Treatment, 9,* 327–330.

Cicchetti, D., & Toth, S. L. (1995). Developmental psychopathology and disorders of affect. In D. Cicchetti & D. J. Cohen (Eds.), *Developmental psychopathology: Risk, disorder, and adaptation* (Vol. 2, pp. 369–420). New York: Wiley.

Cloninger, C. R., & Gottesman, I. I. (1987). Genetic and environmental factors in antisocial behavior disorders. In S. Mednick, T. Moffitt, & S. Stack (Eds.), *The causes of crime* (pp. 92–109). New York: Cambridge.

Colten, M. E. (1980). A comparison of heroin-addicted and non-addicted mothers: Their attitudes, beliefs and parenting experiences. In *Heroin-addicted parents and their children: Two reports* (pp. 1–18). Rockville, MD: National Institute on Drug Abuse.

Colten, M. E. (1982). Attitudes, experiences, and self-perceptions of heroin-addicted mothers. *Journal of Social Issues, 38,* 77–92.

Corrigan, E. M., & Anderson, S. C. (1982). Black alcoholic women in treatment. *Journal of Addictions and Health, 3,* 49–58.

Davis, S. K. (1990). Chemical dependency in women: A description of its effects and outcome on adequate parenting. *Journal of Substance Abuse Treatment, 7,* 225–232.

Dawkins, M. P., & Harper, F. D. (1983). Alcoholism among women: A comparison of Black and White problem drinkers. *International Journal of the Addictions, 18,* 333–349.

de Cubas, M. M., & Field, T. (1993). Children of methadone-dependent women: Developmental outcomes. *American Journal of Orthopsychiatry, 63,* 266–276.

Dembo, R., Williams, L., Wish, E. D., Dertke M., Berry, E., Getreu, A., Washburn, M., Schmeidler, J. (1988). The relationship between physical and sexual abuse and illicit drug use: A replication among a new sample of youths entering a juvenile detention center. *International Journal of Addictions, 23,* 1101–1123.

Deren, S. (1986). Children of substance abusers: A review of the literature. *Journal of Substance Abuse Treatment, 3,* 77–94.

Eliason, M. J., & Skinstad, A. H. (1995). Drug/alcohol addictions and mothering. *Alcohol Treatment Quarterly, 12,* 83–96.

Endicott, J., & Spitzer, R. L. (1978). A diagnostic interview: The Schedule for Affective Disorders and Schizophrenia. *Archives of General Psychiatry, 37,* 837–844.

Finnegan, L., Hagan, T., & Kaltenbach, K. (1991). Scientific foundation of clinical practice: Opiate use in pregnant women. *Bulletin of the New York Academy of Medicine, 67,* 223–239.

Garmezy, N. (1985). Stress-resistant children: The search for protective factors. Recent research in developmental psychopathology (pp. 213–233). *Journal of Child Psychology and Psychiatry* (Book supplement no. 4). Oxford: Pergamon Press.

Garrity-Rokous, F. E. (1994). Punitive legal approaches to the problem of prenatal drug exposure. *Infant Mental Health Journal, 15,* 218–237.

Gatz, M., Pederson, N. L., Plomin, R., Nesselroade, N. R., & McClearn, G. E. (1992). Importance of shared genes and shared environments for symptoms of depression in older adults. *Journal of Abnormal Psychology, 101,* 701–708.

Gerstley, L., McLellan, A. T., Alterman, A. I., et al. (1989). Ability to form an alliance with the therapist: A possible marker of prognosis for patients with antisocial personality disorder. *American Journal of Psychiatry, 146,* 508–512.

Glantz, M. D. (1992). A developmental psychopathology model of drug abuse vulnerability. In M. D. Glantz & R. W. Pickens (Eds.), *Vulnerability to drug abuse* (pp. 389–418). Washington, DC: American Psychological Association.

Goldstein, R. B., Weissman, M. M., Sobin, C. A., Nunes, E. V., Adams, P. B., & Yu, Q. (1995, May 20–25). *Comorbidity in parents and disorders in children.* Paper presented at the annual meeting of the American Psychiatric Association, Miami.

Grossman, J., & Schottenfeld, R. (1992). Pregnancy and women's issues. In T. Kosten & H. Kleber (Eds.), *Clinician's guide to cocaine addiction* (pp. 374–388). New York: Guilford.

Hawley, T. L., & Disney, E. R. (1992). Crack's children: The consequences of maternal cocaine abuse. *Society for Research in Child Development Social Policy Report, 6,* (Winter 1992).

Hetherington, E. M., Reiss, D., & Plomin, R. (1994). *Separate social worlds of siblings: The impact of nonshared environment on development.* Hillsdale, NJ: Erlbaum.

Hollingshead, A. B., & Redlich, F. C. (1958). *Social class and mental illness.* New York: Wiley.

Huba, G. J., Wingard, J. A., & Bentler, P. M. (1979). Beginning adolescent drug use and peer and adult interaction patterns. *Journal of Consulting and Clinical Psychology, 47,* 265–276.

Imhof, J. E. (1991). Countertransference issues in alcoholism and drug addiction. *Psychiatric Annals, 21,* 292–306.

Imhof, J. E., Hirsch, R., & Terenzi, R. E. (1983). Countertransferential and attitudinal considerations in the treatment of drug abuse and addiction. *International Journal of the Addictions, 18,* 491–510.

Jaffe, L. T., & Archer, R. P. (1987). The prediction of drug use among college students from MMPI, MCMI, and sensation seeking scales. *Journal of Personality Assessment, 51,* 243–253.

Kandall, S. R., & Gaines, J. (1991). Maternal substance use and subsequent sudden infant death syndrome (SIDS) in offspring. *Neurotoxicology and Teratology, 13,* 235–240.

Klerman G. L., Lavori P. W., Rice J., et al. (1985). Birth-cohort trends in rates of major depressive disorder among relatives of patients with affective disorder. *Archives of General Psychiatry, 42,* 689–693.

Levy, S. J., & Rutter, E. (1992). *Children of drug abusers.* New York: Lexington Books.

Luthar, S. S. (1995). Social competence in the school setting: Prospective cross-domain associations among inner-city teens. *Child Development, 66,* 416–429.

Luthar, S. S., Anton, S. F., Merikangas, K. R., & Rounsaville, B. J. (1992a). Vulnerability to drug abuse among opioid addicts' siblings: Individual, familial, and peer influences. *Comprehensive Psychiatry, 33,* 190–196.

Luthar, S. S., Anton, S. F., Merikangas, K. R., & Rounsaville, B. J. (1992b). Vulnerability to substance abuse and psychopathology among siblings of opioid abusers. *Journal of Nervous & Mental Disease, 180,* 153–161.

Luthar, S. S., Cushing, G., Merikangas, K. R., Rounsaville, B. J. (1995). May 20–25. *Psychiatric disorders and resilience among drug abusers' offspring.* Paper presented at the annual meeting of the American Psychiatric Association, Miami.

Luthar, S. S., Cushing, G., Merikangas, K. R., Rounsaville, B. J. (in press). Multiple jeopardy: Risk/ protective processes among addicted mothers' offspring. *Development and Psychopathology.*

Luthar, S. S., Merikangas, K. R., & Rounsaville, B. J. (1993). Parental psychopathology and disorders in offspring: A study of relatives of drug abusers. *Journal of Nervous and Mental Disease, 181,* 351–357.

Luthar, S. S., & Walsh, K. (1995). Treatment needs of drug-addicted mothers: Integrated parenting psychotherapy interventions. *Journal of Substance Abuse Treatment, 12* 341–348.

Luthar, S. S., & Zigler, E. (1991). Vulnerability and competence: A review of research on resilience in childhood. *American Journal of Orthopsychiatry, 61,* 6–22.

McGue, M., Pickens, R., & Svikis, D. S. (1992). Sex and age effects on the inheritance of alcohol problems: A twin study. *Journal of Abnormal Psychology, 101,* 3–17.

Mackie-Ramos, R., & Rice, J. (1988). Group psychotherapy with methadone maintained pregnant women. *Journal of Substance Abuse Treatment, 5,* 151–161.

McLoyd, V. C., & Wilson, L. (1991). The strain of living poor: Parenting, social support, and child mental health. In A. C. Huston (Ed.), *Children in poverty.* (pp. 105–135). New York: Cambridge University Press.

Mayes, L. C. (1994). Neurobiology of prenatal cocaine exposure effect on developing monoamine systems. *Infant Mental Health Journal, 15,* 121–133.

Mayes, L. C., & Bornstein, M. (1995). The context of development for young children from cocaine-abusing families. In P. Kato & T. Mann (Eds.), *Health psychology of special populations.* New York: Plenum.

Mirin, S. M., Weiss, R. D., Griffin, M. L., & Michael, J. L. (1991). Psychopathology in drug abusers and their families. *Comprehensive Psychiatry, 32,* 36–51.

Murphy, S. & Irwin, J. (1992). "Living with the dirty secret": Problems of disclosure for methadone maintenance clients. *Journal of Psychoactive Drugs, 24,* 257–264.

National Institute on Alcohol Abuse and Alcoholism. (1981). *Black clients treated in NIAAA-funded programs: Calendar year 1979.* Rockville, MD.

Needle, R., McCubbin, H., Wilson, M., Reineck, R., & Lazar, A. (1986). Interpersonal influence in adolescent drug use: The role of older siblings, parents, and peers. *International Journal of the Addictions, 31,* 739–766.

Phares, V. (1992). Where's Poppa? The relative lack of attention to the role of fathers in child and adolescent psychopathology. *American Psychologist, 47,* 656–664.

Phares, V., & Compas, B. E. (1992). The role of fathers in child and adolescent psychopathology: Make room for daddy. *Psychological Bulletin, 111,* 387–412.

Plomin, R., Rende, R., & Rutter, M. (1991). Quantitative genetics and developmental psychopathology. In D. Cicchetti & S. L. Toth (Eds.), *Internalizing and externalizing expressions of dysfunction: Rochester symposium on developmental psychopathology* (Vol. 2, pp. 155–202). Hillsdale, NJ: Erlbaum.

Rende, R., & Plomin, R. (1993). Families at risk for psychopathology: Who becomes affected and why? *Development and Psychopathology, 5,* 529–540.

Rende, R. D., Plomin, R., Reiss, D., & Hetherington, E. M. (1993). Genetic and environmental influences on depressive symptomatology in adolescence: Individual differences and extreme scores. *Journal of Child Psychology and Psychiatry, 34,* 1387–1398.

Ripple, C. H., & Luthar, S. S. (1996). Familial factors in illicit drug abuse: An interdisciplinary perspective. *American Journal of Drug and Alcohol Abuse, 22,* 147–172.

Robins, L., & Regier, D. (Ed.). (1991). *Psychiatric disorders in America: The Epidemiologic Catchment Area Study.* New York: Free Press.

Rodning, C., Beckwith, L., & Howard, J. (1991). Quality of attachment organization and play organization in prenatally drug-exposed toddlers. *Development and Psychopathology, 3,* 351–366.

Rohsenow, D. J., Corbett, R., & Devine, D. (1988). Molested as children: A hidden contribution to substance abuse? *Journal of Substance Abuse Treatment, 5,* 13–18.

Rounsaville, B. J., Anton, S. F., Carroll, K., Budde, D., Prusoff, B. A., & Gawin, F. (1991). Psychiatric diagnoses of treatment-seeking cocaine abusers. *Archives of General Psychiatry, 48,* 43–51.

Rounsaville, B. J., Kosten, T. R., Weissman, M. M., Prusoff, B., Pauls, D., Foley, S., & Merikangas, K. (1991). Psychiatric disorders in the relatives of probands with opiate addiction. *Archives of General Psychiatry, 48,* 33–42.

Rounsaville, B. J., Weissman, M. M., Wilber, C. H., et al. (1982). Pathways of opiate addiction: An evaluation of differing antecedents. *British Journal of Psychiatry, 141,* 437–466.

Rutter, M. (1994). Stress research: Accomplishments and tasks ahead. In R. J. Haggerty, L. R. Sherrod, N. Garmezy, & M. Rutter (Eds.). *Stress, risk, and resilience in children and adolescents* (pp. 354–385). New York: Cambridge University Press.

Scherling, D. (1994). Prenatal cocaine exposure and childhood psychopathology: A developmental analysis. *American Journal of Orthopsychiatry, 64,* 9–19.

Seifer, R., & Sameroff, A. J. (1987). Multiple determinants of risk and invulnerability. In E. J. Anthony & B. J. Cohler (Eds.), *The invulnerable child* (pp. 51–59). New York: Guilford.

Shedler, J., & Block, J. (1990). Adolescent drug use and psychological health: A longitudinal inquiry. *American Psychologist, 45,* 612–630.

Spitzer, R. L., Endicott, J., & Robins E. (1978). Research diagnostic criteria: Rationale and reliability. *Archives of General Psychiatry, 36,* 733–782.

Tunving, K., & Nilsson, K. (1985). Young female drug addicts in treatment: A 12 year perspective. *Journal of Drug Issues, 15,* 367–382.

Weissman, M. M., Merikangas, K. R., John, K., Wickramaratne, P., Prusoff, B. A., & Kidd, K. K. (1986). Family-genetic studies of psychiatric disorders. *Archives of General Psychiatry, 43,* 1104–1116.

Wilens, T. E., Biederman, J., Kiely, K., Bredin, E., & Spencer, T. J. (1995). Pilot study of behavioral and emotional disturbances in the high-risk children of parents with opioid dependence. *Journal of the American Academy of Child and Adolescent Psychiatry, 34,* 779–785.

Woody, G. E., McLellan, A. T., Luborsky, L., et al. (1985). Sociopathy and psychotherapy outcome. *Archives of General Psychiatry, 42,* 1081–1086.

Zigler, E. (1980). Welcoming a new journal. *Journal of Applied Developmental Psychology, 1,* 1–6.

Zigler, E., & Berman, W. (1983). Discerning the future of early childhood intervention. *American Psychologist, 38,* 894–906.

Zigler, E., Taussig, C., & Black, K. (1992). Early childhood intervention: A promising preventative for juvenile delinquency. *American Psychologist, 47,* 997–1006.

Zigler, E., & Trickett, P. K. (1978). IQ, social competence, and evaluation of early childhood intervention programs. *American Psychologist, 33,* 789–798.

Zimmerman, M. A., Salem, D. A., & Maton, K. I. (1995). Family structure and psychosocial correlates among urban African-American adolescent males. *Child Development, 66,* 1598–1613.

Part IV

Exosystemic risks: Sociodemographic disadvantages

20 Sociodemographic disadvantage and psychosocial adjustment: Perspectives from developmental psychopathology

Suniya S. Luthar

In discussing developmental psychopathology perspectives on adjustment in the context of disadvantage, this chapter focuses on two distinct sets of issues. The first half of the chapter describes empirical research involving inner-city adolescents by our research group. The effort here is twofold: to elucidate ways in which this program of research reflects principles of developmental psychopathology, and to examine the broad canvas of findings obtained across different studies in order to identify themes that emerge consistently.

Moving beyond research by our own group, the second half of this chapter focuses more broadly on contemporary issues involved in studying adjustment in the context of disadvantage. Rather than discussing empirical findings, the focus here is on theoretical issues in the field, with particular emphasis on directions for future theoretical efforts that fall within the tradition of developmental psychopathology. The task of theory building in the future is approached from various positions, that is, by (1) identifying specific domains in which theoretical models are particularly lacking, (2) specifying aspects of theories that make them exemplary in terms of guiding future developmental psychopathology research, (3) illustrating processes by which accumulating empirical evidence might be integrated with extant theoretical perspectives, and (4) addressing precautions or caveats to be considered in undertaking such theoretical ventures.

Empirical research involving inner-city adolescents

Over the past decade, we have conducted a series of investigations on psychosocial adjustment among inner-city teens. These studies have involved four central principles of developmental psychopathology (Cicchetti, 1993; Sroufe & Rutter, 1984): They focus on departures from normative developmental trajectories, they are based in developmental theory, they involve an integration of principles and evidence

This work was supported by P50-DA09241 and Research Scientist Development Award K21-DA00202. I am grateful for suggestions offered by my coeditors, Jake Burack, Dante Cicchetti, and John Weisz, and from Gretta Cushing and other members of the Child and Family Research Group at the Yale Substance Abuse Center.

459

from diverse social science disciplines, and they have implications for intervention efforts.

Rather than targeting atypical outcomes in the context of maladjustment, the focus in this body of research has generally been on the opposite end of the curve, that is, on aspects of positive adjustment. Resonant with the "wellness" perspective (Cowen, 1994) – a close bedfellow of developmental psychopathology (see Cicchetti & Garmezy, 1993; Cowen, Work, & Wyman, Chapter 23, this volume) – our studies on disadvantaged teens have involved three facets of "atypically positive" adjustment: resilience, or the maintenance of high competence despite adversities; high cognitive abilities; and popularity within the peer group.

In discussing these three domains of adolescent adjustment within this chapter, a description of the research design that encompassed all the studies presented is outlined at the outset. Subsequently and for each area, aspects of interface between this research and tenets of developmental psychology are elucidated.

Design overview

Our research with disadvantaged teens has been school-based, and has involved two cohorts of ninth-grade students – of approximately 150 teenagers each – in an inner-city public school in Connecticut. The first cohort (Luthar, 1991) participated in a cross-sectional study during the 1987–1988 academic year, and the second cohort, assessed during 1990–1991, was part of a 6-month longitudinal study designed to build upon initial findings (Luthar, 1995; Luthar, Doernberger, & Zigler, 1993).

As the two cohorts were recruited from the same school, they had similar sociodemographic characteristics. On average, parents' socioeconomic status fell in the second lowest of the five categories on the Hollingshead-Redlich (1958) scale, and most of the children were from minority group families (74% in the first study, and 84% in the second cohort).

Interest in the construct of psychosocial adaptation among disadvantaged teens was piqued by epidemiological data showing that inner-city teenagers are highly vulnerable to a range of behavior problems, such as delinquency, substance use, and teenage pregnancy (e.g., Farrington, 1987; Snyder & Patterson, 1987). Given these trends, and the then rapidly burgeoning literature on childhood resilience (Garmezy, Masten, & Tellegen, 1984; Werner & Smith, 1982), the pivotal question that propelled this body of research was, what might enable some inner-city youth to remain relatively competent in spite of the many adversities they face?

Operationalization of competence in everyday life, the central construct in this research, was guided by developmental theory. In assessing individuals' levels of overall adjustment, social competence has often been viewed as the measure of choice (Garmezy et al., 1984; Masterpasqua, 1989; Zigler & Trickett, 1978). This construct reflects behavioral manifestations of success at meeting societal expectations that are associated with a particular developmental stage (Zigler & Trickett, 1978).

Given the school-based nature of the research, and applying Havighurst's (1972) schema of stage specific "developmental tasks," social competence in this adolescent population was defined in terms of three aspects of behavioral competence: doing well academically, getting along well with peers, and maintaining positive behaviors in the classroom. These indices were assessed using a multimethod, multiagent approach, based on school records of academic grades as well as ratings by both teachers and peers. Data reduction of peer and teacher ratings led to the derivation of three composite competence indices, two of which essentially involved peer ratings. The first of the peer-rated dimensions represented conformity of behaviors (prosocial leadership versus aggressive, disruptive behaviors), and the second encompassed global ratings of acceptance within the peer group (popularity and sociability versus isolation by peers). The teacher rating composite reflected assertive, responsible behaviors in the classroom (Luthar, 1991; Luthar et al., 1993).

Discussions that follow present findings around three major constructs examined within this research program, that is, resilience, high intelligence, and peer popularity. In each case, the presentation is organized around elucidating the interface with the following tenets of developmental psychopathology: the application of developmental principles in designing research on atypical adjustment patterns; implications of findings, within such research, for theory on "normal" developmental processes; links with social science disciplines other than developmental psychology; and ramifications of results for intervention planning with underprivileged teens.

Domain specificity of resilience

One of the first issues to be scrutinized in this research concerned the degree to which resilient functioning might extend across different domains of adjustment. The operational definition of the construct of resilience rested on two criteria, namely, the manifestation of high behavioral competence in any one of the school-based domains assessed (as rated by peers or by teachers, or based on school grades) and, concurrently, the presence of high levels of negative life events in the preceding months. The question at issue was whether apparently resilient children – those who excelled in at least one domain despite high life stress – might experience significant difficulties in *other* areas of adjustment.

This question was first examined in the context of covert, emotional difficulties that might coexist with overt indices of successful coping among at-risk youth (Luthar, 1991). Interest in this issue was sparked by two threads of evidence in the literature. First, as Zigler and his colleagues have established, individuals at relatively high developmental levels are more likely to show their distress in the form of internalizing, thought-oriented symptoms, rather than disruptive, externalizing ones (Glick, Zigler, & Zigler, 1986; Phillips & Zigler, 1961; Zigler & Glick, 1986;

Zigler & Phillips, 1962). Second, children identified as resilient are typically at relatively high developmental levels, as indicated, for example, by their greater intellectual maturity (Masten, Morison, Pellegrini, & Tellegen, 1990). Given these considerations, then, it seemed plausible that manifestly resilient children might have elevated levels of symptoms such as depression and anxiety, in spite of their profiles of superior competence on behavioral indices.

Results of the investigation did in fact indicate that apparently resilient teens – those who showed high social competence despite stressful life circumstances – showed elevations in self-reported depressive symptoms. In point of fact, these manifestly sturdy youngsters reported symptom levels that were statistically comparable with those of high-stress youngsters who had the lowest levels of behavioral competence in the sample (Luthar, 1991).

These preliminary findings were further explored with the second cohort of adolescents using a 6-month prospective design (Luthar et al., 1993). In this inquiry, attempts were made to address three limitations of the previous study, each of which may have compromised the interpretability of findings on manifest resilience and distress. These included the cross-sectional design of the initial study, the use of a relatively small number of children in the (individual-based) analyses, and the potential for confounds in the measurement of negative life events, given the inclusion of "controllable" events such as failing a grade, as well as "uncontrollable" ones (e.g., death of a parent). Accordingly, with the second cohort of children, analyses were prospective in nature, continuous data analyses were used to allow for the inclusion of the entire sample in the analyses, and life stress was measured based on only uncontrollable events.

Results of this inquiry supported earlier suggestions. High-stress children who showed impressive behavioral competence initially were found to display vulnerability to emotional distress over time. Rather than manifesting stress resistance on emotional indices, high-stress children who had high social competence at Time 1 reported substantially more distress at Time 2, than did their high-competence peers who had low levels of life stress.

Variations in adjustment across different domains were then further examined from a third perspective; the focus here was on differences *among* spheres of behavioral competence at school (Luthar et al., 1993). The question addressed was as follows: Of a group of high-stress children who excel in one domain of school-based competence, what proportion might show significant difficulties in other areas of behavioral competence?

Findings of this study provided still more evidence for the relative domain specificity of resilience. A subset of 25 apparently resilient children was identified: These youngsters each reported frequent uncontrollable negative life events and also excelled on any one of four indices of school-based behavioral competence. Of these teens, 60% (N = 15) were found to have significant *difficulties* in a competence domain other than the one(s) on which they were initially identified as resilient. With additional "exclusionary criteria" applied, for example, relatively high levels of self-reported symptoms, this proportion went up to 84%. Put differently, of the children who seemed resilient based on excellence in one domain of functioning, only 16% had managed to evade significant adjustment difficulties in other areas of behavioral competence/symptomatology, over the course of a 6-month period.

Trends among the resilient children were mirrored by those among others in the sample. In other words, the data indicated that resilient children did not necessarily differ from relatively "unexceptional" children in terms of the stability of functioning maintained across different domains. For children with moderate levels of life stress, as well as those who had experienced unusually few negative life events, over 70% of youngsters who excelled in one domain showed significant problems in another sphere of behavioral functioning at school.

The findings described here carry implications for theoretical views of resilience, for perspectives on normal developmental processes, as well as for intervention planning. With respect to the first of these, the present results warn against conceptualizing the construct of resilience in overly broad, global terms. Early works in the resilience literature carried cautions against the use of terms such as "invulnerable," noting that stress resistance is not necessarily continuous over time but that it can be interspersed with periodic setbacks (Anthony, 1987; Felsman & Vaillant, 1987; Murphy & Moriarty, 1976). Going a step further, the question raised by our research was whether even phases of apparently successful coping are in fact as trouble-free as they might seem. Over the years, empirical findings reported by various investigative groups (e.g., Radke-Yarrow & Sherman, 1990; Werner & Smith, 1982, 1992) have established that resilience is not a unidimensional construct: At-risk individuals can excel in one domain yet concurrently experience significant difficulties in other areas. In theoretical accounts, then, as well as in research efforts deriving from these, it is critical that the notion of domain specificity of resilience be clearly articulated. Such qualifications are imperative, if social scientists are to avoid conveying to the lay public and policy makers that some children are somehow inherently able to emerge completely unscathed from traumatic life situations.

In the context of insights concerning normal developmental processes, the data presented here suggest that among inner-city teens in general, and not just the apparently resilient subgroup, successful functioning in one sphere of adjustment may often coexist with significant problems in other areas. Issues pertaining to inconsistencies across different school-based competence domains are discussed at some length later in this chapter, in the section on positive peer reputation among inner-city teens.

The trends found regarding emotional difficulties among manifestly resilient children are arresting in terms of implications for future interventions. Typically, the most likely recipients of child mental health services are youngsters who present management problems for authority figures. Among the many disadvantaged children who experience significant and serious adversities in their lives, the select few whose behaviors reflect *positive* adaptation in everyday life are in fact those least likely to be recruited for professional services. The message regarding these children is clear. As teachers, clinicians, and educators, even as we extol the fortitude of these manifestly stress-resistant children, we must remain attentive to the considerable difficulties they might experience across some areas of their lives.

Intelligence and adaptation

In a second set of investigations, the focus was on intelligence and psychosocial adaptation. This line of inquiry began with a scrutiny of intelligence as a potential protective factor against stress: the question was, Are bright children better able than others to cope with adversity? Interest in this question was kindled by prior developmental research. In their seminal study of resilience among school-age children, Garmezy et al. (1984) found that unlike their less intelligent peers, bright children seemed to do well at school regardless of whether life stress was high or low.

Cross-sectional findings obtained with the first cohort of inner-city teens (Luthar, 1991) were contrary to those presented by Garmezy et al. (1984): It was the *brighter* adolescents, rather than the less intelligent ones, who showed lower levels of school-based competence when life stress was high rather than low. The data indicated that intelligent inner-city teens displayed more variability than others in their performance at school, depending on whether their life circumstances were stressful or benign (Luthar, 1991).

In interpreting these trends, two arguments were raised with interrelated yet somewhat different foci. Drawing on developmental and ecocultural considerations, it was argued that bright inner-city teenagers may be drawn to using their talents in areas other than academics, unless they are "protected" by positive or ameliorative forces (in this case, low negative life events). Second, based on evidence in the giftedness literature, it was asserted that bright inner-city adolescents – like other groups of intelligent youngsters (Zigler & Farber, 1985) – may have been more sensitive than others to *negative* forces in their lives.

To pursue the first of these interpretations further, we examined interactions between intelligence and two other constructs, internal locus of control and high levels of ego development (Luthar & Zigler, 1992). The argument extended was that these personal attributes, like low levels of life stress, are also psychosocial constructs typically conducive to overall adjustment. Thus, the apparently ameliorative effects linked with infrequent life stressors should presumably replicate with these constructs as well. Results supported this reasoning. Again, as compared with their less intelligent peers, bright disadvantaged teens showed greater deficits at low as compared with high levels of both internal locus of control and ego development.

The second interpretation mentioned earlier, that is, that bright children may be more sensitive than others to vicissitudes of their lives, was explored in prospective analyses with the second cohort. Rather than examining environmental stressors, however, the focus here was on interactions between intelligence and negative intrapsychic experiences (Luthar & Ripple, 1994). The expectation was that more so than others, bright youth would show high sensitivity to subjective emotional distress associated with feelings of depression and anxiety. Results were consistent with expectations. Bright youngsters who reported high levels of depression and anxiety symptoms at baseline showed decreases in school-based functioning across a period of 6 months, whereas those low on initial distress showed improvements in social competence levels over time. Such associations between initial distress and subsequent social competence were not found among the less intelligent children.

The trends involving intelligence and emotional distress are consonant with both developmental theory and clinical research evidence. The findings obtained suggested that (a) bright youngsters may have been more keenly attuned than others to their emotional distress, and (b) this, in turn, may have adversely affected their adjustment over time. Several developmental theorists have asserted that cognitive maturity is, in fact, associated with heightened consciousness of inner experience (e.g., Loevinger & Wessler, 1983; Zigler & Glick, 1986). Similarly, there is support in the clinical literature for the premise that keen consciousness of one's inner distress can be detrimental to adjustment (or, conversely, that *not* dwelling on distress can be beneficial) (see Nolen-Hoeksema, Parker, & Larson, 1994; Pyszczynski, Holt, & Greenberg, 1987; Schwartz, 1990; Taylor & Brown, 1988).

These empirical trends on intelligence carry implications, again, for theory as well as intervention efforts. From a theoretical perspective, the data belie the tacit view among developmentalists that intelligence inevitably leads to, or is associated with, positive social-emotional outcomes among children. Whereas links between intelligence and psychosocial adaptation have typically been discussed in terms of main effect models (White, Moffitt, & Silva, 1989), the data described here indicate that cognitive sophistication is not necessarily an unmitigated blessing. Bright inner-city teens appeared to do very well in the presence of positive psychosocial forces. However, in the presence of negative forces, they seemed to be hurt more than did their less intelligent peers.[1]

From an intervention perspective, the importance of these findings is underscored by the fact that intelligent inner-city teens – who could potentially be a valuable resource for society – are often among the most vulnerable to negative influences in their lives. As the anthropologist John Ogbu and others have noted, youngsters in the urban underclass do not necessarily believe that traversing the "straight and narrow" path leads to success in later life. Rather than striving for excellence in school, many bright youth in these circumstances tend to turn their talents instead to illegal activities (Ogbu, 1978, 1982; Myers, 1990). Recognizing, then, the high potential of intelligent inner-city teens, and the risk for their diversion to (and likely success at) nonacademic, possibly antisocial pursuits, there is clearly a need for preventive interventions that are targeted specifically at this group of youngsters.

Acceptance by peers: Cross-domain associations

Among the results obtained early in our research, particularly intriguing were findings that levels of peer group acceptance were essentially unrelated to other facets
of adaptive functioning at school. Contrary to an abundance of studies showing
that popular children generally have good grades and positive teacher ratings (see
Wentzel, 1991, for a review), among the first cohort of inner-city teenagers, no
such links were found involving the composite construct of peer acceptance (high
popularity and low isolation). The absence of associations in this context was further accentuated given findings with the second of the two composite peer-rated
indices in this research: A peer reputation of prosocial versus aggressive orientation
was positively associated with both grades and teacher ratings (Luthar, 1991).

Interest in further exploring cross-domain links involving peer acceptance was
whetted when considering suggestions by Cauce, Felner, and Primavera (1982) that
popularity may sometimes run *counter* to academic performance among inner-city
teens. These investigators demonstrated that among disadvantaged males, high levels of informal support were negatively associated with academic achievement. In
view of these trends, prospective analyses were conducted with the second cohort
of teens (Luthar, 1995), examining ways in which peer acceptance might relate to
other aspects of school functioning both as an antecedent and as a consequent
variable.

These analyses showed that teenagers' globally rated peer acceptance was, in
fact, negatively related to academic competence over time. Adolescents who were
initially rated as being relatively friendly and easy to get along with were those
who showed the greatest declines in academic functioning over the course of the
school year (Luthar, 1995). The findings were interpreted in the context of antipathy
toward academics within the inner-city peer group. In general, inner-city students
often have little interest in doing well at school (e.g., Fordham & Ogbu, 1986;
Luthar & Blatt, 1995; Ogbu, 1978). It is possible, then, that more so than others,
popular youngsters might be particularly susceptible to peer pressure against scholastic achievement, resulting in their deteriorating grades over time (Luthar, 1995).

The disconcerting implications of these findings led, finally, to a more fine-
grained scrutiny of the correlates of disadvantaged teens' peer reputation. In this
inquiry (Luthar & McMahon, in press), the four dimensions of peer reputation
which had hitherto been examined only as two composite constructs, were each
examined individually. Apart from carefully examining the reliability of our measurement of the four peer reputation dimensions, variable-based and individual-
based analyses (see Cicchetti, 1993; Magnusson & Berman, 1988) were both used
to examine the associations *between* each peer reputation dimension and other
adjustment indices, as well as links *among* the four aspects of peer reputation
themselves. To maximize robustness of the analyses, these questions were addressed within a relatively large sample involving both of the independently ascertained cohorts of inner-city teenagers.

Results extended previous findings suggesting that among disadvantaged teens, peer acceptance and academic success may run counter to each other. This investigation showed, for example, that adolescents who were socially isolated by their peers were among those with the best academic performance, and also those with the most positive teacher ratings on task orientation and frustration tolerance in the classroom.

Another startling and quite unexpected finding concerned associations involving peer reputations of aggression: This construct showed *positive* links with popularity among peers. More specifically, the data suggested that there were two diametrically opposed routes to popularity among inner-city teens: the "conventional" route, involving prosocial, altruistic behaviors and good grades, and a more atypical one that was associated with disruptive, aggressive behaviors and poor academic performance. Simple correlations involving peer ratings on popularity, and peer ratings on both prosocial leadership and aggressiveness, were virtually identical (.36 versus .30). Cluster analyses, similarly, revealed two distinct clusters of popular children, those who were popular and prosocial, and those who were popular and highly disruptive and aggressive (Luthar & McMahon, in press).

Resonating with these trends involving aggressive behaviors and peer acceptance were findings involving aggression and rejection by peers. Again, variable- and individual-based data analyses converged in indicating no associations between aggressive-disruptive reputations and rejection, or even isolation, within the disadvantaged teen peer group. These findings are in sharp contrast to those of a host of studies involving other child populations, in which robust links between aggressive behaviors and rejection by peers have been demonstrated (see Newcomb, Bukowski, & Pattee, 1993).

The apparent endorsement of aggression by the inner-city peer group was interpreted, again, in the light of sociocultural factors (Luthar & McMahon, in press). In disenfranchised, impoverished communities besieged by crime and violence, aggressive behaviors among youth may be not only normative but also, in some situations, possibly adaptive. Within such communities, behaviors considered deviant by mainstream society may sometimes be viewed as effective ways to achieve personal goals, and may be associated with relatively high prestige and status within the immediate subcultural group (e.g., Coie & Jacobs, 1993; Richters & Cicchetti, 1993; Simmons 1987).[2]

The patterns of findings on peer reputation have implications for contemporary theories of psychosocial development. Evidence that among inner-city teenagers, successful negotiation of one developmental task (e.g., peer acceptance) might be a proxy for *failure* on another stage-specific task (academic success), implies the need for modifications or extensions of mainstream developmental theories when considering adolescents facing multiple aspects of socioeconomic deprivation. Such theoretical issues are addressed in some detail in the second section of this chapter.

In terms of implications for interventions, findings on peer reputation suggest the value of interventions that target adolescents with antiestablishment behavior patterns. Several theorists, including Coie and Jacobs (1993), Caspi (1993), and Moffitt (1993), have argued for the application of theories of resocialization of social identity, wherein deviant peer leaders, helped to access socially conventional bases for authority and prestige, may in turn help shift the tenor of values in the wider peer system. Another body of work that resonates with recommendations offered here is studies on the effectiveness of interventions with at-risk youth (for reviews, see Takanishi, 1993; Weisz, Weiss, Alicke, & Klotz, 1987; Weisz, Weiss, Han, Granger, & Morton, 1995). Research has shown that peers can be highly influential in socializing teens away from maladaptive behavior patterns and, in addition, that adolescents' participation in activities that contribute to the welfare of others can be highly rewarding in terms of self-esteem and feelings that they can indeed "make a difference" (see Price, Gioci, Penner, & Trautlein, 1993).

Summary

The previously described body of research with inner-city adolescents involved the application of various principles from child development theory. At the very outset, developmental theory was used in defining the pivotal construct of interest, that is, positive adaptation in everyday life. Applying paradigms regarding stage-salient tasks and social competence, adolescents were seen as showing positive adjustment if they performed well academically, got along with peers, and/or were viewed positively by authority figures (in this case, teachers).

Developmental perspectives were also applied in articulating the central research hypotheses. The first of these – that emotional distress would often underlie manifest resilience – was based on prior evidence that children at high developmental levels typically express their distress in the form of internalizing symptoms rather than externalizing ones. Results were consistent with predictions. Additionally, further inquiry showed variations not only across overt (behavioral) versus covert (emotional) indices, but among overt aspects of adjustment in the school setting.

Indicating as they do that resilience is not a unidimensional construct, trends documented have implications for burgeoning theories about resilience in the face of adversity. The findings also have implications for interventions: They point to the need for educators, clinicians, and parents to be attentive to the fact that while at-risk youth might be overtly resilient – excelling in some areas – they may, at the same time, experience considerable difficulties in other domains.

The second set of questions discussed concerned intelligence. This line of research was spurred by findings from other studies showing that among younger children, the brighter ones seemed relatively unperturbed by high levels of life stress. Among inner-city teenagers, however, a series of investigations converged in indicating that the more intelligent children showed more variations in adjustment than others, depending on the level of positive or negative psychosocial forces – intrapsychic and environmental – in their lives. This evidence underscores the need to incorporate, in contemporary developmental theories, not just main effect models regarding intelligence, but also those which address the complexity of interactive phenomena involving intelligence and adjustment. The findings also suggest the value of interventions targeted at intelligent inner-city teens, who, while a potentially valuable resource for society, may be among the most susceptible to negative influences in their lives.

Peer acceptance was at the core of the third set of questions addressed here. As noted previously, theories about developmental tasks formed the very basis for the inclusion of peer reputation as a central index of social competence. In turn, the pattern of findings obtained over time has yielded implications for prevailing theories on "normal" adolescent development. Among disadvantaged teens, success at one major developmental task (peer acceptance) may often mitigate success in other areas of social competence (academic performance and the maintenance of socially conforming behavior). Data such as these underscore the need to extend classic theories of psychosocial development to incorporate ecological considerations and suggest, as well, the potential value of interventions targeting "deviant" peer leaders in the adolescent peer group.

Theories of psychosocial development: Applications among disadvantaged groups

Moving beyond research by our own group, discussions in the rest of this chapter involve issues that apply to the field as a whole, with attention, specifically, to directions for future efforts in studying adjustment in the context of disadvantage. In contemplating future directions, the focus in this chapter is specifically on the refinement of theoretical models on psychosocial adjustment among disadvantaged children and their families.

Why this focus on theory development, rather than just empirical research? Exhortations for theory-building efforts derive from five underlying factors. First (and most obviously), the ultimate aim of any science is theory. Theories offer explanations of interrelations among sets of phenomena, and provide directions for subsequent scientific research by guiding the selection of variables, research design, and analytic approach (Kerlinger, 1986; Pedhazur & Schmelkin, 1991).

Second, the articulation of theories pertaining to disadvantage has been a relatively neglected enterprise within the developmental psychology literature. Whereas there have been several calls for more studies involving nonmainstream children (e.g., Compas, Hinden, & Gerhardt, 1995; Graham, 1992; MacPhee, Kreutzer, & Fritz, 1994; Zaslow & Takanishi, 1993), less noted is the need for attention to theoretical paradigms that assimilate and subsequently guide these research efforts. Resonant with these thoughts, Spencer (1988) has asserted that since the 1970s, there have in fact been many innovative and sophisticated studies on development among nonmainstream youth. Yet, insights from these efforts have rarely been integrated into the academic literature on child development: "textbooks continued

to be written during this period as though new research findings did not exist''
(Spencer, 1988, pp. 66).

Third, there is a rapidly increasing segment of the population to whom such
theories would apply: The number of disadvantaged children in contemporary society has grown rapidly in recent years. Considering just the United States, for
example, statistics have shown that by the year 1992, 26% of this nation's children
between the ages of 0 and 6 were growing up in poverty (Knitzer & Aber, 1995).
Similarly, citing projections that by the year 2030 most children in the United States
will be from minority group families, Spencer (1988) has drawn attention to the
incompleteness of existing theoretical models of human development as they apply
to nonmainstream groups.[3]

Aside from their relevance to increasing numbers of children, the value of theoretical models on disadvantage is evident in the substantial real-life ramifications
of this life circumstance. Perhaps as much as any aspect of the contextual environment, exposure to chronic poverty can have insidious and far-reaching implications for various aspects of children's and their families' development (Huston,
1994; Huston, McLoyd, & Garcia Coll, 1994).

Finally, considering the extant psychologically based models on development
and disadvantage, it is clear that some themes or phenomena are more explored
than others. A review of the existing literature indicates that, paralleling the state
of empirical research (see MacPhee et al., 1994), conceptual models on disadvantaged groups more often pertain to negative outcomes among children and their
parents, with less attention to positive adaption, and still less work with normal
developmental trajectories in the context of disadvantage.

The following section presents a review of some contemporary theoretical models in the field that are developmentally based. This exercise is undertaken not to
provide a comprehensive review of the literature but rather to compile a ''representative sample'' of existing models, with a view toward identifying themes that
have received relatively widespread attention as opposed to those that clearly require further thought.

Current theoretical models: Themes well represented in the literature

The developmental psychology literature encompasses several carefully stated and
empirically verified theoretical models that pertain to negative outcomes among
disadvantaged children. Among the most widely cited and tested of these is the
model proposed by McLoyd and colleagues (McLoyd, 1989; 1990; McLoyd &
Wilson, 1991). Building upon Elder's pioneering studies of families of the Great
Depression (Elder, 1979; Elder, Liker, & Cross, 1984; Elder, Nguyen, & Caspi,
1985), McLoyd postulates that scant economic resources affect child maladjustment
indirectly, through the quality of parenting (McLoyd, 1989; 1990; McLoyd & Wilson, 1991). This conceptual model has held up to empirical scrutiny in several

studies employing various subject populations and diverse approaches to defining and measuring the central constructs encompassed (e.g., Brody et al., 1994; Conger et al., 1992; Conger, Ge, Elder, Lorenz, & Simons, 1994; Dodge, Pettit, & Bates, 1994; Harnish, Dodge, & Valente, 1995; Leadbeater & Bishop, 1994; McLoyd, Jayaratne, Ceballo, & Borquez, 1994; Sampson & Laub, 1994).

Another widely cited model on environmental stressors and psychosocial outcomes is that posited by Rutter (1979) and Sameroff and colleagues (Sameroff, Seifer, Zax, & Barocas, 1987), which holds that, more than any one aspect of sociodemographic disadvantage, it is the total number of risk factors experienced that is predictive of negative child outcomes. Considering multiple risk factors that are typically associated with poverty – such as single parenthood, large family size, minority group status, and low parental occupation and education – several studies have supported the notion that such indices have a synergistic effect, where the effects of coexisting stressors far exceed the effects of any one considered individually (Allen, Moore, & Kuperminc, Chapter 24, this volume; Egeland, Carlson, & Sroufe, 1993; Richters & Martinez, 1993; Rutter, 1979; Sameroff et al., 1987; Sameroff, Seifer, & Bartko, Chapter 22, this volume; Williams, Anderson, McGee, & Silva, 1990).

There are comparatively fewer models in the literature that pertain to positive adaptation in the context of disadvantage, and much of the work that exists is couched within the conceptual framework of child resilience (Garmezy et al., 1984; Rutter, 1987; Werner & Smith, 1992), aimed at identifying risk and protective factors in adjustment (e.g., Baldwin et al., 1993; Chase-Lansdale, Brooks-Gunn, & Zamsky, 1994; Connell, Spencer, & Aber, 1994; Dubois, Felner, Meares, & Krier, 1994; Spencer, Cole, DuPree, Glymph, & Pierre, 1993; Richters & Martinez, 1993; Werner & Smith, 1992). These efforts have often yielded interesting insights regarding vulnerability and protective processes that may be relatively unique to the risk condition of sociodemographic disadvantage. Salient in this context, for example, are works by Baldwin and colleagues (Baldwin, Baldwin, & Cole, 1990; Baldwin, Baldwin, Sameroff, & Seifer, 1989), which indicate that the child-rearing strategies that work well among impoverished families can differ substantially from those that are effective among more affluent families. Whereas authoritative, democratic styles are typically viewed as beneficial for child outcomes, in dangerous, lower-socioeconomic-status neighborhoods, the most optimal parenting styles were autocratic ones, involving frequent monitoring of children in order to shield them from environmental risks (Baldwin et al., 1990).

Also noteworthy among developmentally based conceptualizations involving positive adjustment are models that distinguish between distal and proximal influences, that is, where associations between child outcomes and disadvantage are explained in terms of intervening proximal processes that directly affect the child. Baldwin's model is a case in point, in which parenting styles constitute the critical construct that mediates the effects of distal environmental adversities. Similarly,

Richters and Martinez (1993) present – and validate – a model where the adaptation of children living in violent communities is related to the stability and safety of their own homes.

Theoretical perspectives on normative development

One set of conceptual issues remains noticeably underexplored in the literature (and these, paradoxically, involve assumptions that *any* model of negative or positive adaptation must necessarily rest upon): These issues concern what exactly constitutes "normal development" in the context of disadvantage. The pressing need for thought in this regard is underscored by accumulating evidence that what mainstream developmental psychologists typically view as normal may differ from what is normative or adaptive within the immediate subculture of poverty and violence.

Before delving any further into these issues, a point of clarification is in order. Discussions in this section do not, in any way, derive from assumptions that existing mainstream theories are entirely inapplicable to, or inappropriate for, disadvantaged youth. The suggestion is merely that in some instances, it may be useful to extend or elaborate upon current theories, so that they incorporate themes that are prominent, ubiquitous – and unique – in the lives of underprivileged children and families (see Katz & Kofkin, Chapter 3, this volume; Zimmerman, Salem, & Maton, 1995).

The need for further attention to conceptualizations of "normative development" in the context of disadvantage has been eloquently argued by Richters and Cicchetti (1993), in an article questioning the view that conduct disturbances inevitably indicate underlying psychiatric dysfunction. These authors distinguish between two broad pathways to conduct disturbances: dysfunctional pathways – associated, for example, with neuropsychological or social cognition deficits – and normal pathways, where conduct problems are essentially the outcome of extrinsic, environmental factors rather than internal dysfunctions. In reference to the latter, Richters and Cicchetti provide vignettes from the life histories of adults with criminal records, drawing attention to the insistent, seductive allure of antisocial activities in their childhood environments. Underscoring the critical distinction between the moral implications of individuals' behaviors versus the concept of underlying psychopathology, the authors conclude that antisocial behaviors may often occur among essentially *normally functioning* individuals, reflecting their adaptation to the prevailing mores and norms of a counterculture subculture.

These arguments are resonant with the tenor of empirical findings described in the first half of this chapter. To recapitulate, across two independent cohorts of inner-city adolescents, the evidence indicated that acceptance within the peer group ran counter to academic success, and to socially conventional patterns of behavior at school. These broad empirically derived findings by our own group are supported by trends reported by several other researchers as well (e.g., Coie & Jacobs, 1993; Ogbu, 1991a; Seidman, Allen, Aber, Mitchell, & Feinman, 1994; Spencer et al.,

1993). Collectively, the data emphasize that conceptions of "normal" developmental trajectories can vary substantially among children and families living in poverty as opposed to those who live in more affluent, ecoculturally mainstream families.

Integrating empirical findings with developmental theory. As Kerlinger (1986) has indicated, science has a cyclical aspect; whereas theory must guide research, accumulating empirical data must guide the revision and refinement of theory. The available evidence on developmental processes among disadvantaged youth points to several possibilities in terms of integration with current theoretical perspectives. Illustrations are provided here in the context of two major theories of psychosocial development: Eriksonian theory, and organizational-developmental perspectives advanced by Sroufe and Rutter (1984) and Cicchetti and Schneider-Rosen (1986).

Given the conflicting value systems they constantly encounter, the Eriksonian psychosocial stage of "identity formation versus identity diffusion" presents a unique set of challenges for inner-city teenagers. Adolescents' emerging sense of identity involves integration of issues relating to career choices, to specific subgroups to which allegiance is avowed, and to ideologies regarding what succeeds in the adult world (Erikson, 1963). Across these various fronts, the messages that disadvantaged teens receive are contradictory. On the one hand, they are faced with the emphasis in society on effort at conventional activities (schoolwork) as being critical for success in adult life. On the other hand, the value system of the immediate subculture reinforces antiestablishment behavior due, for example, to ongoing experiences involving racism and marginalization, high aggression and violence in the neighborhood, and perceptions of "job ceilings" that deny disadvantaged youth access to jobs with high prestige and power (Arroyo & Zigler, 1995; Coie & Jacobs, 1993; Ogbu, 1991b; Richters & Cicchetti, 1993; Spencer et al., 1993).

Choosing from among these contradictory sets of messages must inevitably pose a risk for what Diana Baumrind has called "alienation" among these teenagers. This construct encompasses several component attitudes, namely the belief that socially disapproved behaviors are required to achieve one's goals, the conviction that one's personal goals are not rewarded by society, and the withdrawal of value attribution from one's acts (Baumrind, 1987). Thus defined, the construct of alienation encapsulates much of what disadvantaged teens must inevitably struggle with in the development of a sense of identity. For youngsters facing chronic sociocultural disadvantage, then, rather than "identity formation versus diffusion," the constructs "identity *coherence* versus *alienation*" – which subsume but go beyond the constructs in the Eriksonian scheme – may more completely capture the dilemmas associated with this stage-specific adolescent task, specifically within the inner-city setting.

To summarize, in future theoretical conceptualizations of psychosocial development among inner-city teens, it may be useful to acknowledge at the outset not only those developmental tasks that confront all adolescents (related to identity formation in general), but also those that are unique, significant, and inevitable, in the lives of most disadvantaged teenagers. These include substantial challenges in developing a sense of coherence as opposed to alienation, given the ongoing tussle between values endorsed by mainstream society on the one hand, and those held personally and by those in the immediate subculture, on the other.

We turn, then, to a second prominent psychosocial theory, that is, the structural-organizational perspective (Cicchetti & Schneider-Rosen, 1986; Sroufe & Rutter, 1984; Waters & Sroufe, 1983). Within this perspective, competence is viewed as a molar construct reflecting the integration of behavioral, cognitive, and affective responses in producing positive developmental outcomes. Mirroring the Eriksonian principle of epigenesis, a central belief is that although manifestations of competence vary across the developmental span – depending on the relevant stage-salient tasks, for example – coherence is typically maintained in an individual's competence patterns ontogenetically.

Elaborating on this perspective in the context of development of disadvantaged youth, it might be argued (a) that rather than a single trajectory, there coexist two – often opposed – trajectories of "competent" behaviors, and (b) that coherence of competence is maintained ontogenetically *within,* but necessarily across, each of these. As noted previously, broad, behavior-based designations of an inner-city teen as "doing well in life" can differ depending on the value system applied in making such labels – that espoused by authority figures in mainstream society or that of peers in the immediate subculture (see also Richters & Cicchetti, 1993; Weisz et al., 1995; Weisz, McCarty, Eastman, Chaiyasit, & Suwanlert, Chapter 25, this volume). Disadvantaged youth whose early behaviors reflect conformity to mainstream society's beliefs (e.g., high motivation for academic success or to gain teachers' approval) may, more likely than not, continue along this path later in life. By contrast, those highly invested in maintaining a sense of connection and solidarity with their immediate subcultural group (which strongly repudiates academic achievement and associated conforming behaviors) may continue on this general trajectory later in life as well. In short, considering any one of the broad value systems that confront disadvantaged teens, coherence in the unfolding of competence may well, as predicted by the structural-organizational perspective, be displayed over time.

For future research on inner-city youth, what are the implications of these theoretical contentions regarding alternative pathways of competence? Assuming that there do in fact exist at least two often mutually opposed sets of criteria for labeling adolescent competence, researchers must consider each of these in defining the construct. For adolescents in general, academic success and acceptance by peers both constitute major developmental tasks; one could not convincingly argue that there is any absolute difference in competence between a high-achieving youngster – who is marginalized by peers and who struggles with feelings of "racelessness" in his emerging sense of identity (see Arroyo & Zigler, 1995) – and a high school dropout who is respected and liked by peers, and who feels a strong sense of connection with his immediate subcultural group. In sum, then, in future research on behavioral competence among disadvantaged youth, it is critical that both sets of value systems are considered in theoretically defining the construct.

Parameters for the development of theoretical models

Concluding this discussion on theoretical issues, this final section of the chapter presents some broad guidelines for the articulation of theoretical models on adaptation and disadvantage that are in the tradition of developmental psychopathology. General attributes of promising theoretical models are first briefly reviewed, followed by an elucidation of some dilemmas that are specifically relevant to the theoretician concerned with disadvantage.

What makes for useful theoretical models on development and disadvantage? Like any good scientific theory, such models must involve specific, clear predictions that lend themselves to empirical verification, and explanations of phenomena that are couched in terms of general constructs, rather than in relation to highly specific events or phenomena (Kerlinger, 1986; Pedhazur & Schmelkin, 1991).

From a developmental psychopathology perspective, there are three additional criteria to be considered in developing theoretical paradigms in this domain (see Cicchetti, 1990, 1993). First, these models must involve an integration of insights from a range of social science disciplines. As Sameroff and colleagues (Chapter 22, this volume) have indicated, the analysis of social-ecological environments has typically fallen in the domain of sociologists. For the developmental theorist concerned with disadvantage, there is much to be gained by drawing upon the expertise of those for whom ecological issues have, historically, constituted the focal area of scholarly effort.

Second, it is important that these models carry specific implications for interventions and social policy. In an early and seminal paper, Zigler (1963) noted that much of the value of a promising developmental theory lies in its ability to guide human action: With validation of central principles, a good theory directs us toward appropriate courses of action for intervention. In the context of existing theories on disadvantage, exemplary in this regard is the model put forth by McLoyd and colleagues, which, to recapitulate, holds that parental behavior mediates the effect of economic hardship on children. McLoyd has delineated specific implications stemming from the empirical validation of her model. At the level of the individual, for example, she calls for treatment focusing on intrapsychic processes and parent education; at the community level, she underscores the need for advocacy activities concerning housing, employment, and child care, and at a macrolevel, she reviews social policy issues related to welfare recipients (McLoyd & Wilson, 1991).

From the perspective of developmental psychopathology, a third important objective to be considered in developing theories on disadvantage is the incorporation of insights derived from individual-based analyses, as well as those from variable-based research. Examination of individual profiles can often provide invaluable supplements to variable-based analyses of entire groups, particularly when the objective is to understand complex psychological phenomena such as psychopathology (Chess & Thomas, 1990; Cicchetti, 1990, 1993; Magnusson & Berman, 1988). The potential contributions of individualized approaches are effectively illustrated in several recent studies on adaptation of disadvantaged children (see Apfel & Seitz, Chapter 21, this volume; Brinker, Baxter, & Butler, 1994).

In closing this section, three considerations are appraised which each relate to a bugaboo that plagues any theorist – that is, the tussle between comprehensiveness versus specificity of models presented. A major concern in this context pertains to the many demographic parameters that might be subsumed within the broad construct of poverty. Consider, for example, the issue of ethnicity. Noting that, in general, there is a disproportionate representation of minority individuals among the lower socioeconomic strata of contemporary American society, several leading researchers (McLoyd, 1990; Ogbu, 1988) discuss disadvantage in the context of the dual criteria of non-Caucasian ethnicity and economic insubordination. Precautions in adopting this strategy, however, have been raised by some. MacPhee and colleagues (1994), for example, caution against the perpetuation of racist stereotypes if poverty and ethnicity are treated by scholars as synonymous: The authors strongly argue for the examination of developmental processes that might be unique to particular ethnic groups.

Aside from variations across ethnic groups, connotations and implications of the term disadvantage can vary substantially depending on the specific demographic indices on which it is based, such as parents' income, occupation, education, or social class, income-to-need ratios in particular families, or neighborhood of residence (see Brooks-Gunn, Duncan, Klebanov, & Sealand, 1993; Duncan, Brooks-Gunn, & Klebanov, 1994; Garrett, Ng'andu, & Ferron, 1994; Entwisle & Astone, 1994; Hauser, 1994). Still other important parameters have been noted that might interact with socioeconomic status in influencing psychosocial processes and outcomes, including culture and language (Garcia Coll, 1990; Laosa, 1980; McLoyd, 1990), and the nature of poverty experiences in terms of being chronic versus acute (Huston et al., 1994).

Glancing through this list of myriad approaches to operationalizing "disadvantage," the task of developing theoretical models on this construct may seem impossibly broad. While disheartening at first blush, the task presented is by no means insurmountable. What is necessary is a clear specification of what Lakatos (cited in Pedhazur & Schmelkin, 1991) has called the "hard core" of the theory – the central principles that should apply across samples and with various ways of operationalizing central constructs – as opposed to the "protective belt" surrounding it (which may or may not generalize across different samples or settings). As an analogy, consider the Piagetian theory of cognitive development. Central principles within the Piagetian scheme, such as that of assimilation, accommodation, and equilibration, are likely to be substantiated across settings and studies, whereas other aspects of the model, such as those pertaining to the specific ages of onset of discrete stages – may vary across cultures and with methodologies employed (Flavell, 1985; Gelman & Baillargeon, 1983).

A second difficult issue to be grappled with stems from the sheer complexity of constructs subsumed within the overall association between disadvantage and child adaptation. There are myriad links in this chain that one might choose to focus on – that is, any of sundry proximal processes intervening between poverty and variously operationalized adjustment outcomes, links among different groups of child outcomes, and protective or vulnerability processes that might modify the effects of overall disadvantage, or of individual proximal influences.

Because we lack the capacity to approach or even understand this complex set of interrelated influences, we are compelled, as scientists, to reach into the matrix and scrutinize only a subset of constructs at a time (Burack, Chapter 7, this volume; Richters & Martinez, 1993). This, in turn, should by no means be cause for consternation. As Pedhazur and Schmelkin (1991) have asserted, conceptions of theory in the social sciences run a wide gamut. On one extreme are those calling for tests of single hypotheses (not necessarily within any theoretical framework), and on the other are those who maintain that what is really needed are grand theories. In the sociobehavioral sciences, neither of these extreme approaches is likely to be as useful or productive as the more moderate and realistic strategy, that is, attempts to work with what Merton (1968) has dubbed "minitheories" or theories of middle range.

The third issue to be negotiated is somewhat of an offshoot of the second and involves the question of whether, for developmental psychopathologists, there are any "preferred" points of focus in this overall chain of associations between disadvantage and outcomes. This question is germane to oft-heard concerns regarding the study of disadvantage by leading developmentalists. As Zigler and colleagues (Zigler, Lamb, & Child, 1982) and Bronfenbrenner (1986) have noted, for psychologists, it is important to understand in *psychological* terms the ways in which the molar sociological construct of poverty might affect child outcomes. Studies of sociodemographic disadvantage as a "social address" (Bronfenbrenner, 1986) – defined simply in terms of low status on indices such as education and occupation – convey little about the processes that underlie associations between socioeconomic status and outcomes. Consonant with these views (as indicated earlier in the chapter), efforts of several researchers have been focused on the in-depth study of proximal processes that might mediate the effects of the global risk index of life in challenging environments (e.g., Baldwin et al., 1993; Richters & Martinez, 1993; Spencer et al., 1993).

The preceding statements should not, however, be construed as necessarily negating the value of research that *does* treat disadvantage as a distal construct. Notwithstanding psychologists' typically greater comfort with constructs of a psychological nature, Zigler and Child (1969) noted that there is no single "correct" level of analysis of behavior; depending on the objectives of the researcher, psychogenic and sociogenic approaches each can be valuable in trying to explain variations in outcomes. Second, concerns about imprecision of measurement of the social address construct must be weighed against its parsimony. As Cohler, Stott, and Musick (1995) point out, social address is a shorthand reference to a host of environmental characteristics that affect psychosocial development (e.g., poor nutrition, substandard housing, exposure to violence), as well as to a world of meanings regarding the self, others, and the course of life. Third, there are invaluable lessons to be learned from developmental efforts that, rather than exploring *how* exactly poverty affects children, are focused instead on understanding protective processes that *modify* its effects, such as the processes associated with high-quality day care, interventions with parents, social support for the family, or attributes of the children themselves (e.g., Caughy, DiPietro, & Strobino, 1994; Chase-Lansdale et al., 1994; Connell et al., 1994; Hashima & Amato, 1994; Posner & Vandell, 1994; Ramey, Byant, & Suarez, 1985; Seitz & Apfel, 1994; Vandell & Ramanan, 1991).

In the arena of developmental psychopathology, there clearly is a place for sociodemographic status in its many incarnations, ranging from the more psychological and molecular to those primarily sociogenic and molar. In seeking to understand better the nature and determinants of outcomes among disadvantaged individuals, there is much to be learned by exploring specific proximal processes that might mediate the effects of poverty. Equally valuable, however, are studies focused on the web of protective processes that alter the effects of distal risks. As indicated in the resilience literature (Luthar & Cushing, in press; Masten, Best, & Garmezy, 1990; Rutter, 1990), unquestionably there are times when it is profitable to examine "who beats the odds" even if the "odds" themselves – global, sociogenic risks – remain incompletely understood in terms of the precise mechanisms via which adversity is conferred.

Summary

In considering future directions for developmental psychopathology, there is a need to refine theoretical models on development in the context of disadvantage. Whereas historically, disadvantaged children were neglected in the empirical literature, recent years have seen a range of sophisticated studies in the area. As these empirical efforts continue, it is critical that theoretical efforts stay abreast. There must be ongoing attempts to integrate, in conceptual models, threads of evidence accumulated across studies, in order to guide more effectively subsequent research in the area.

In terms of existing theoretical models, a review of the current developmental literature indicates that some aspects of life in disadvantaged settings have been considered more often than others. There are several carefully conceptualized, empirically substantiated models on maladjustment among impoverished youth; these models have directed research toward identifying important processes in the links between poverty and negative psychosocial outcomes. Additionally, the broad theoretical framework of childhood resilience has been used increasingly in studying positive adaptation among disadvantaged groups. Studies conducted within this paradigm have identified various vulnerability and protective processes, some of which may be relatively unique to the ecological risk condition of poverty.

In particular, there is a need for greater attention to theoretical conceptualizations regarding "normative development" in the context of poverty. The core principles of classic developmental theories are likely to hold across diverse populations. In some instances, however, it could be helpful to elaborate on existing models, so that they specifically incorporate issues that are invariably prominent in, and often unique to, the lives of children and families in the underclass.

Finally, in articulating future models on adaptation in the context of disadvantage, it would be useful for developmental psychopathologists to draw on insights from different social science disciplines (particularly sociology and anthropology), to incorporate data from individual- as well as variable-based analyses, and to attend to the implications for interventions associated with empirical verification of their models. Recognizing the many and complex associations involved in links between disadvantage and child outcomes, the theoretician must perforce focus on a subset of links in the overall chain. In so doing, however, it would be useful to specify the "core" of the model presented – principles likely to hold across diverse settings, and with different methodological approaches – as opposed to the "protective belt" around it, facets that may vary somewhat with changes in specific parameters.

In conclusion, developmental psychopathology provides a framework that is especially well suited to studies of psychosocial adjustment in the context of disadvantage. Research conducted from this perspective has begun to yield a set of important insights; sustained attention to theoretical efforts – that integrate accumulated empirical findings – is vital in order to steer future research in meaningful directions. The continuing interface between theory and research is a prerequisite for the ultimate design of effective interventions targeting the needs of children and families exposed to the insidious life circumstance of ongoing socioeconomic deprivation.

Notes

1 In considering these statements, a point of clarification is in order. The contention is not that being bright is generally associated with more negative psychosocial outcomes; to the contrary, our own research corroborates other evidence in indicating that the performance of bright inner-city youth was typically superior to that of others. The assertion here is simply that bright youth may be particularly reactive to both internal and external forces, tending to lose somewhat of their advantage over others in the presence of negative forces in their lives.

2 In considering such interpretations, there is an important caveat, that is, trends found here may not be unique to inner-city teens but may apply, to some extent, to their more privileged counterparts as well. Moffitt (1993), for example, has argued that during the developmental moratorium of adolescence in contemporary Western society, antisocial

behaviors can take on a positive value because they symbolize maturity, independence, and the attendant prestige and power. Similarly, Steinberg (1987) has noted that American teens in general, regardless of their sociocultural status, do not particularly admire hard work at school.

3 The issue of distinctions versus overlaps across poverty, minority group status, and other demographic indices is discussed at some length later in this chapter, in the section on "Parameters for the development of theoretical models."

References

Anthony, E. J. (1987). Risk, vulnerability, and resilience: An overview. In E. J. Anthony & B. J. Cohler (Eds.), *The invulnerable child* (pp. 3–48). New York: Guilford.

Arroyo, C. G., & Zigler, E. (1995). Racial identity, academic achievement, and the psychological well-being of disadvantaged adolescents. *Journal of Personality and Social Psychology, 69,* 903–914.

Baldwin, A. L., Baldwin, C., & Cole, R. E. (1990). Stress-resistant families and stress-resistant children. In J. Rolf, A. S. Masten, D. Cicchetti, K. H. Nuechterlein, & S. Weintraub (Eds.), *Risk and protective factors in the development of psychopathology* (pp. 257–280). New York: Cambridge University Press.

Baldwin, A. L., Baldwin, C. P., Kasser, T., Zax, M., Sameroff, A., & Seifer, R. (1993). Contextual risk and resiliency during late adolescence. *Development and Psychopathology, 5,* 741–761.

Baldwin, A. L., Baldwin, C., Sameroff, A. J., & Seifer, R. (1989). *Protective factors in adolescent development.* Paper presented at the biennial meeting of the Society for Research in Child Development, Kansas City, MO.

Baumrind, D. (1987). A developmental perspective on adolescent risk taking in contemporary America. In C. E. Irwin (Ed.), *New directions for child development,* Vol. 37: *Adolescent social behavior and health* (pp. 93–125). San Francisco: Jossey-Bass.

Brinker, R. P., Baxter, R. P., & Butler, L. S. (1994). An ordinal pattern analysis of four hypotheses describing the interactions between drug-addicted, chronically disadvantaged, and middle-class mother-infant dyads. *Child Development, 65,* 361–372.

Brody, G. H., Stoneman, Z., Flor, D., McCrary, C., Hastings, L., & Conyers, O. (1994). Financial resources, parent psychological functioning, parent co-caregiving, and early adolescent competence in rural two-parent African-American families. *Child Development, 65,* 590–605.

Bronfenbrenner, U. (1986). Ecology of the family as a context for human development: Research perspectives. *Developmental Psychology, 22,* 723–742.

Brooks-Gunn, J., Duncan, G., Klebanov, P. K., & Sealand, N. (1993). Do neighborhoods influence child and adolescent development? *American Journal of Sociology, 99,* 353–395.

Caspi, A. (1993). Why maladaptive behaviors persist: Sources of continuity and change across the life course. In D. C. Funder, R. D. Parke, C. Tomlinson-Keasey, & K. Widman (Eds.), *Studying lives through time.* (pp. 343–376). Washington, DC: American Psychological Association.

Cauce, A. M., Felner, R. D., & Primavera, J. (1982). Social support in high-risk adolescents: Structural components and adaptive impact. *American Journal of Community Psychology, 10,* 417–428.

Caughy, M. O., DiPietro, J. A., & Strobino, D. M. (1994). Day-care participation as a protective factor in the cognitive development of low-income children. *Child Development, 65,* 457–471.

Chase-Lansdale, P. L., Brooks-Gunn, J., & Zamsky, E. S. (1994). Young African-American multigenerational families in poverty: Quality of mothering and grandmothering. *Child Development, 65,* 373–393.

Chess, S., & Thomas, A. (1990). Continuities and discontinuities in temperament. In L. Robins & M. Rutter (Eds.), *Straight and devious pathways from childhood to adulthood* (pp. 205–220). Melbourne, Australia: Cambridge University Press.

Cicchetti, D. (1990). An historical perspective on the discipline of developmental psychopathology. In J. Rolf, A. S. Masten, D. Cicchetti, K. H. Nuechterlein, & S. Weintraub (Eds.), *Risk and protective factors in the development of psychopathology* (pp. 2–28). New York: Cambridge University Press.

Cicchetti, D. (1993). Developmental psychopathology: Reactions, reflections, projections. *Developmental Review, 13,* 471–502.

Cicchetti, D., & Garmezy, N. (1993). Prospects and promises in the study of resilience. *Development and Psychopathology, 5,* 497–502.

Cicchetti, D., & Schneider-Rosen, K. (1986). An organizational approach to childhood depression. In M. Rutter, C. E. Izard, & P. B. Read (Eds.), *Depression in young people: Developmental and clinical perspectives* (pp. 71–134). New York: Guilford.

Cohler, B. J., Stott, F. M., & Musick, J. S. (1995). Adversity, vulnerability, and resilience: Cultural and developmental perspectives. In D. Cicchetti & D. J. Cohen (Eds.), *Developmental psychopathology,* Vol. 2: *Risk, disorder, and adaptation* (pp. 753–800). New York: Wiley.

Coie, J. D., & Jacobs, M. R. (1993). The role of social context in the prevention of conduct disorder. *Development and Psychopathology, 5,* 263–275.

Compas, B. E., Hinden, B. R., & Gerhardt, C. A. (1995). Adolescent development: Pathways and processes of risk and resilience. *Annual Review of Psychology, 46,* 265–293.

Conger, R. D., Conger, K. J., Elder, G. H., Lorenz, F. O., Simons, R. L., & Whitbeck, L. B. (1992). A family process model of economic hardship and adjustment of early adolescent boys. *Child Development, 63,* 526–541.

Conger, R. D., Ge, X., Elder, G. H., Lorenz, F. O., & Simons, R. L. (1994). Economic stress, coercive family process, and developmental problems of adolescents. *Child Development, 65,* 541–561.

Connell, J. P., Spencer, M. B., & Aber, J. L. (1994). Educational risk and resilience in African-American youth: Context, self, action, and outcomes in school. *Child Development, 65,* 493–506.

Cowen, E. L. (1994). The enhancement of psychological wellness: Challenges and opportunities. *American Journal of Community Psychology, 22,* 149–179.

Dodge, K. A., Pettit, G. S., & Bates, J. E. (1994). Socialization mediators of the relation between socioeconomic status and child conduct problems. *Child Development, 65,* 649–665.

Dubois, D. L., Felner, R. D., Meares, H., & Krier, M. (1994). Prospective investigation of the effects of socioeconomic disadvantage, life stress, and social support on early adolescent adjustment. *Journal of Abnormal Psychology, 103,* 511–522.

Duncan, G. J., Brooks-Gunn, J., & Klebanov, P. K. (1994). Economic deprivation and early childhood development. *Child Development, 65,* 296–318.

Egeland, B., Carlson, E., & Sroufe, L. A. (1993). Resilience as process. *Development and Psychopathology, 5,* 517–528.

Elder, G. (1979). Historical change in life patterns and personality. In P. Baltes & O. Brim (Eds.), *Life span development and behavior* (Vol. 2, pp. 117–159). New York: Academic Press.

Elder, G., Liker, J., & Cross, C. (1984). Parent-child behavior in the Great Depression: Life course and intergenerational influences. In P. Baltes & O. Brim (Eds.), *Life span development and behavior* (Vol. 6, pp. 109–158). New York: Academic Press.

Elder, G., Nguyen, T., & Caspi, A. (1985). Linking family hardship to children's lives. *Child Development, 56,* 361–375.

Entwisle, D. R., & Astone, N. M. (1994). Some practical guidelines for measuring youth's race/ethnicity and socioeconomic status. *Child Development, 65,* 1521–1540.

Erikson, E. H. (1963). *Childhood and society.* New York: Norton.

Farrington, D. P. (1987). Epidemiology. In H. C. Quay (Ed.), *Handbook of juvenile delinquency* (pp. 33–61). New York: Wiley.

Felsman, J. K., & Vaillant, G. E. (1987). Resilient children as adults: A 40-year study. In E. J. Anthony & B. J. Cohler (Eds.), *The invulnerable child* (pp. 289–314). New York: Guilford.

Flavell, J. H. (1985). *Cognitive development* (2nd ed.). Englewood Cliffs, NJ: Prentice-Hall.

Fordham, S., & Ogbu, J. U. (1986). Black students' school success: "Coping with the burden of 'acting white.' " *Urban Review, 18,* 176–206.

Garcia Coll, C. T. (1990). Developmental outcome of minority infants: A process-oriented look into our beginnings. *Child Development, 61,* 270–289.

Garmezy, N., Masten, A. S., & Tellegen, A. (1984). The study of stress and competence in children: A building block for developmental psychopathology. *Child Development, 55,* 97–111.

Garrett, P., Ng'andu, N., & Ferron, J. (1994). Poverty experiences of young children and the quality of their home environments. *Child Development, 65,* 331–345.

Gelman, R., & Baillargeon, R. (1983). A review of some Piagetian concepts. In P. H. Mussen (Ed.), *Handbook of child psychology.* New York: Wiley.

Glick, M., Zigler, E., & Zigler, B. (1986). Developmental correlates of age on first hospitalization in nonschizophrenic psychiatric patients. *Journal of Nervous and Mental Disease, 183,* 677–684.

Graham, S. (1992). "Most of the subjects were white and middle class." *American Psychologist, 47,* 629–639.

Harnish, J. D., Dodge, K. A., & Valente, E. (1995). Mother-child interaction quality as a partial mediator of the roles of maternal depressive symptomatology and socioeconomic status in the development of child behavior problems. *Child Development, 66,* 739–753.

Hashima, P. Y., & Amato, P. R. (1994). Poverty, social support, and parental behavior. *Child Development, 65,* 394–403.

Hauser, R. M. (1994). Measuring socio-economic status in studies of child development. *Child Development, 65,* 1541–1545.

Havighurst, R. J. (1972). *Developmental tasks and education* (3rd ed.). New York: David McKay.

Hollingshead, A. B., & Redlich, F. C. (1958). *Social class and mental illness.* New York: Wiley.

Huston, A. C. (1994). *Children in poverty.* New York: Cambridge University Press.

Huston, A. C., McLoyd, V. C., & Garcia Coll, C. (1994). Children and poverty: Issues in contemporary research. *Child Development, 65,* 275–282.

Kerlinger, F. N. (1986). *Foundations of behavioral research* (3rd edition). New York: Harcourt Brace Jovanovich.

Knitzer, J., & Aber, J. L. (1995). Young children in poverty: Facing the facts. *American Journal of Orthopsychiatry, 65,* 174–176.

Laosa, L. M. (1980). Maternal teaching strategies in Chicano and Anglo-American families: The influence of culture and education on maternal behavior. *Child Development, 51,* 759–765.

Leadbeater, B. J., & Bishop, S. J. (1994). Predictors of behavior problems in preschool children of inner-city Afro-American and Puerto Rican adolescent mothers. *Child Development, 65,* 638–648.

Loevinger, J., & Wessler, R. (1983). *Measuring ego development.* San Francisco: Jossey-Bass.

Luthar, S. S. (1991). Vulnerability and resilience: A study of high-risk adolescents. *Child Development, 62,* 600–616.

Luthar, S. S. (1995). Social competence in the school setting: Prospective cross-domain associations among inner-city teens. *Child Development, 66,* 416–429.

Luthar, S. S., & Blatt, S. J. (1995). Differential vulnerability of dependency and self-criticism among disadvantaged teenagers. *Journal of Research on Adolescence, 5,* 431–449.

Luthar, S. S., & Cushing, G. (in press). Measurement issues in the empirical study of resilience: An overview. In M. Glantz, Z. Sloboda, & L. C. Huffman (Eds.), *Resiliency and development: Positive life adaptations.* New York: Plenum.

Luthar, S. S., Doernberger, C. H., & Zigler, E. (1993). Resilience is not a unidimensional construct: Insights from a prospective study on inner-city adolescents. *Development and Psychopathology, 5,* 703–717.

Luthar, S. S., & McMahon, T. (in press). Peer reputation among adolescents: Use of the Revised Class Play with inner-city teens. *Journal of Research on Adolescence.*

Luthar, S. S., & Ripple, C. H. (1994). Sensitivity to emotional distress among intelligent adolescents: A short-term prospective study. *Development and Psychopathology, 6,* 343–357.

Luthar, S. S., & Zigler, E. (1992). Intelligence and social competence among high-risk adolescents. *Development and Psychopathology, 4,* 287–299.

McLoyd, V. C. (1989). Socialization and development in a changing economy. *American Psychologist, 44,* 293–302.

McLoyd, V. C. (1990). The impact of economic hardship on black families and children: Psychological distress, parenting, and socioemotional development. *Child Development, 61,* 311–346.

McLoyd, V. C., Jayaratne, T. E., Ceballo, R., & Borquez, J. (1994). Unemployment and work interruption among African-American single mothers: Effects on parenting and adolescent socioemotional functioning. *Child Development, 65,* 562–589.

McLoyd, V. C., & Wilson, L. (1991). The strain of living poor: Parenting, social support, and child mental health. In A. C. Huston (Ed.), *Children in poverty* (pp. 105–135). New York: Cambridge University Press.

MacPhee, D., Kreutzer, J. C., & Fritz, J. J. (1994). Infusing a diversity perspective into human development courses. *Child Development, 65,* 699–715.

Magnusson, D., & Bergman, L. (1988). Individual and variable-based approaches to longitudinal research on early risk factors. In M. Rutter (Ed.), *Studies of psychosocial risk* (pp. 45–61). Cambridge: Cambridge University Press.

Masten, A. S., Best, K. M., Garmezy, N. (1990). Resilience and development: contributions from the study of children who overcome adversity. *Development and Psychopathology, 2,* 425–444.

Masten, A. S., Morison, P., Pellegrini, D., & Tellegen, A. (1990). Competence under stress: Risk and protective factors. In J. Rolf, A. S. Masten, D. Cicchetti, K. H. Nuechterlein, & S. Weintraub (Eds.), *Risk and protective factors in the development of psychopathology* (pp. 236–256). New York: Cambridge University Press.

Masterpasqua, F. (1989). A competence paradigm for psychological practice. *American Psychologist, 44,* 1366–1371.

Merton, R. K. (1968). *Social theory and social structure* (enlarged ed.). New York: Free Press.

Moffitt, T. E. (1993). Adolescence-limited and life-course-persistent antisocial behavior: A developmental taxonomy. *Psychological Review, 100,* 674–701.

Murphy, L. B., & Moriarty, A. E. (1976). *Vulnerability, coping and growth.* New Haven: Yale University Press.

Myers, L. M., Jr. (1990, June 29–July 3). *Crime, entrepreneurship, and labor force withdrawal.* Paper presented at the 65th annual Western Economic Association Conference, San Diego.

Newcomb, A. F., Bukowski, W. M., & Pattee, L. (1993). Children's peer relations: A meta-analytic review of popular, rejected, neglected, controversial, and average sociometric status. *Psychological Bulletin, 113,* 99–128.

Nolen-Hoeksema, S., Parker, L. E., & Larson, J. (1994). Ruminative coping with depressed mood following loss. *Journal of Personality and Social Psychology, 67,* 92–104.

Ogbu, J. U. (1978). *Minority education and caste: The American system in cross-cultural perspective.* New York: Academic Press.

Ogbu, J. U. (1982). Cultural discontinuities and schooling. *Anthropology and Education Quarterly, 13,* 290–307.

Ogbu, J. U. (1988). Cultural diversity and human development. In D. Slaughter (Ed.), *New directions for child development,* Vol. 42: *Black children and poverty: A developmental perspective* (pp. 11–28). San Francisco: Jossey-Bass.

Ogbu, J. U. (1991a). Low school performance as an adaptation: The case of blacks in Stockton, California. In M. A. Gibson & J. U. Ogbu (Eds.), *Minority status and schooling: A comparative study of immigrant and involuntary minorities* (pp. 249–285). New York: Garland.

Ogbu, J. U. (1991b). Minority coping responses and school experience. *Journal of Psychohistory, 18,* 433–456.

Pedhazur, E. J., & Schmelkin, L. P. (1991). *Measurement, design and analysis: An integrated approach.* Hillsdale, NJ: Erlbaum.

Phillips, L., & Zigler, E. (1961). Social competence: The action-thought parameter and vicariousness in normal and pathological behavior. *Journal of Abnormal and Social Psychology, 63,* 137–146.

Posner, J. K., & Vandell, D. L. (1994). Low-income children's after-school care: Are there beneficial effects of after-school programs? *Child Development, 65,* 440–456.

Price, R. H., Gioci, M., Penner, W., Trautlein, B. (1993). Webs of influence: School and community programs that enhance adolescent health and education. In R. Takanishi (Ed.), *Adolescence in the 1990's: Risk and opportunity* (pp. 29–63). New York: Teachers College Press.

Pyszczynski, T., Holt, K., & Greenberg, J. (1987). Depression, self-focused attention, and expectancies for positive and negative future life events for self and others. *Journal of Personality and Social Psychology, 52,* 994–1110.

Radke-Yarrow, M., & Sherman, T. (1990). Hard growing: Children who survive. In J. Rolf, A. S. Masten, D. Cicchetti, K. H. Nuechterlein, & S. Weintraub (Eds.), *Risk and protective factors in the development of psychopathology* (pp. 97–119). New York: Cambridge University Press.

Ramey, C. T., Bryant, D. M., & Suarez, T. (1985). Preschool compensatory education and the modifiability of intelligence: A critical review. In D. K. Detterman (Ed.), *Current topics in human intelligence.* Norwood, NJ: Ablex.

Richters, J. E., & Cicchetti, D. (1993). Mark Twain meets DSM-III-R: Conduct disorders, development, and the concept of harmful dysfunction. *Development and Psychopathology, 5,* 5–29.

Richters, J. E., & Martinez, P. E. (1993). Violent communities, family choices, and children's chances: An algorithm for improving the odds. *Development and Psychopathology, 5,* 609–627.

Rutter, M. (1979). Protective factors in children's responses to stress and disadvantage. In M. W. Kent & J. E. Rolf (Eds.), *Primary prevention in psychopathology* (pp. 49–74). Hanover, NH: University Press of New England.

Rutter, M. (1987). Psychosocial resilience and protective mechanisms. *American Journal of Orthopsychiatry, 57,* 316–331.

Rutter, M. (1990). Psychosocial resilience and protective mechanisms. In J. Rolf, A. S. Masten, D. Cicchetti, K. H. Nuechterlein, & S. Weintraub (Eds.), *Risk and protective factors in the development of psychopathology* (pp. 181–214). New York: Cambridge University Press.

Sameroff, A. J., Seifer, R., Zax, M., & Barocas, R. (1987). Early indicators of developmental risk: The Rochester Longitudinal Study. *Schizophrenia Bulletin, 13,* 383–393.

Sampson, R. J., & Laub, J. H. (1994). Urban poverty and the family context of delinquency: A new look at structure and process in a classic study. *Child Development, 65,* 523–540.

Schwartz, G. E. (1990). Psychobiology of repression and health: A systems approach. In J. L. Singer (Ed.), *Repression and dissociation* (pp. 405–434). Chicago: University of Chicago Press.

Seidman, E., Allen, L., Aber, J. L., Mitchell, C., & Feinman, J. (1994). The impact of school transitions in early adolescence on the self-system and perceived social context of poor urban youth. *Child Development, 65,* 507–522.

Seitz, V., & Apfel, N. H. (1994). Effects of a school for pregnant students on the incidence of low-birthweight deliveries. *Child Development, 65,* 666–676.

Simmons, R. G. (1987). Social transition and adolescent development. In C. E. Irwin (Ed.), *New directions for child development,* Vol. 37: *Adolescent social behavior and health* (pp. 33–61). San Francisco: Jossey-Bass.

Snyder, J., & Patterson, G. (1987). Family interaction and delinquent behavior. In H. C. Quay (Ed.), *Handbook of juvenile delinquency* (pp. 216–243). New York: Wiley.

Spencer, M. B. (1988). Self-concept development. In D. Slaughter (Ed.), *New directions for child development,* Vol. 42: *Black children and poverty: A developmental perspective* (pp. 59–72). San Francisco: Jossey-Bass.

Spencer, M. B., Cole, S. P., DuPree, D., Glymph, A., & Pierre, P. (1993). Self-efficacy among urban African American early adolescents: Exploring issues of risk, vulnerability, and resilience. *Development and Psychopathology, 5,* 719–739.

Steinberg, L. (1987, April 25). Why Japan's students outdo ours. *New York Times,* p. 15.

Sroufe, L. A., & Rutter, M. (1984). The domain of developmental psychopathology. *Child Development, 55,* 17–29.

Takanishi, R. (1993). *Adolescence in the 1990's: Risk and opportunity.* New York: Teachers College Press.

Taylor, S. E., & Brown, J. D. (1988). Illusion and well-being: A social psychological perspective on mental health. *Psychological Bulletin, 103,* 193–210.

Vandell, D. L., & Ramanan, J. (1991). Children of the National Longitudinal Survey of Youth: Choices in after school care and child development. *Developmental Psychology, 27,* 637–643.

Waters, E., & Sroufe, L. A. (1983). Social competence as a developmental construct. *Developmental Review, 3,* 79–97.

Weisz, J. R., Weiss, B., Alicke, M. D., & Klotz, M. L. (1987). Effectiveness of psychotherapy with children and adolescents: A meta-analysis for clinicians. *Journal of Consulting and Clinical Psychology, 55,* 542–549.

Weisz, J. R., Weiss, B., Han, S. S., Granger, D. A., & Morton, T. (1995). Effects of psychotherapy with children and adolescents revisited: A meta-analysis of treatment outcome studies. *Psychological Bulletin, 117,* 450–468.

Wentzel, K. R. (1991). Relations between social competence and academic achievement in early adolescence. *Child Development, 62,* 1066–1078.

Werner, E. E., & Smith, R. S. (1982). *Vulnerable but invincible: A study of resilient children.* New York: McGraw-Hill.

Werner, E. E., & Smith, R. S. (1992). *Overcoming the odds: High risk children from birth to adulthood.* Ithaca, NY: Cornell University Press.

White, J. L., Moffitt T. E., & Silva, P. A. (1989). A prospective replication of the protective effects of IQ in subjects at high risk for juvenile delinquency. *Journal of Consulting and Clinical Psychology, 57,* 719–724.

Williams, S., Anderson, J., McGee, R., & Silva, P. A. (1990). Risk factors for behavioral and emotional disorder in preadolescent children. *Journal of the American Academy of Child and Adolescent Psychiatry, 29,* 413–419.

Zaslow, M. J., & Takanishi, R. (1993). Priorities for research in adolescent development. *American Psychologist, 48,* 185–192.

Zigler, E. (1963). Metatheoretical issues in developmental psychology. In M. Marx (Ed.), *Theories in contemporary psychology* (pp. 341–369). New York: Macmillan.

Zigler, E., & Child, I. L. (1969). Socialization. In G. Lindzey & E. Aronson (Eds.), *Handbook of social psychology* (2nd ed., pp. 450–589). Reading, MA: Addison-Wesley.

Zigler, E., & Farber, E. A. (1985). Commonalities between the intellectual extremes: Giftedness and mental retardation. In F. Horowitz & M. O'Brien (Eds.), *The gifted and talented: Developmental perspectives* (pp. 387–408). Washington, DC: American Psychological Association.

Zigler, E., & Glick, M. (1986). *A developmental approach to adult psychopathology.* New York: Wiley.

Zigler, E., Lamb, M. E., & Child, I. L. (1982). *Socialization and personality development* (pp. 97–119). New York: Oxford University Press.

Zigler, E., & Phillips, L. (1962). Social competence and the process-reactive distinction in psychopathology. *Journal of Abnormal and Social Psychology, 63,* 69–75.

Zigler, E., & Trickett, P. K. (1978). IQ, social competence, and evaluation of early childhood intervention programs. *American Psychologist, 33,* 789–798.

Zimmerman, M. A., Salem, D. A., & Maton, K. I. (1995). Family structure and psychosocial correlates among urban African-American adolescent males. *Child Development, 66,* 1598–1613.

21 The firstborn sons of African American teenage mothers: Perspectives on risk and resilience

Nancy Apfel and Victoria Seitz

For the past decade and a half we have been studying a population of New Haven school-aged mothers and their firstborn children, who were born in the late 1970s. Earlier long-term studies of adolescent mothers whose children were born in the 1960s have documented the serious repercussions of teenage motherhood in an era even before AIDS and the influx of cocaine had an impact (Brooks-Gunn & Furstenberg, 1986; Furstenberg, Brooks-Gunn, & Morgan, 1987; Horwitz, Klerman, Kuo, & Jekel, 1991a, 1991b). In our study of a more current population of teen mothers and offspring, we have seen that the risks have multiplied for them. Within this population is an especially vulnerable group – the African American male child. Evidence is building that young African American males are truly endangered. They are less likely than African American females, and white males and females, to enter mainstream society through education and employment, to avoid criminality, and even to survive (Gibbs, 1988a, 1988b; Hare & Castenell, 1985; Taylor, 1991).

Resiliency and vulnerability: The children of adolescent mothers

Our research on the development of children born to African American adolescent mothers illustrates many of the issues addressed by the relatively new field of developmental psychopathology. Using both quantitative and qualitative data, we will explore some of these issues. The resiliency and vulnerability literature provides a framework for investigating why some of these children appear to do well, while others do not.

Almost all of the children in our population were born into urban poverty with

This research was funded by grants from the W. T. Grant Foundation, the Smith Richardson Foundation, and the National Institute of Child Health and Human Development. We wish to thank the families who have participated in our study, generously giving of their time and sharing their life events over the years with us. We also thank the New Haven Public Schools and, in particular, the staff of the Polly T. McCabe Center, whose help has been invaluable to us. To our dedicated research staff, without whom we could not have carried out such an endeavor, we express our gratitude: Laurel Bidwell, Jean Davis, Reissa Michaels, Laurie Rosenbaum, Lynn Ugolik, Moira Whitley, and Kathryn Young. We also thank Suniya Luthar, one of the most helpful editors with whom we have ever worked, and our colleague Robert Hodapp for valuable editorial suggestions.

its associated social problems and lack of resources. As Ronald Taylor eloquently describes, "the increasing social and spatial concentration of poverty in the inner-cities of this country, and the growing predominance of social ills long associated with such poverty – family disruption, school failure, drugs, violent crime, housing deterioration, etc. – have quantitatively and qualitatively altered the psychosocial as well as the material foundations of life for most of the inhabitants, intensifying the conditions of economic marginality and social isolation" (Taylor, 1991, p. 140). In addition, most of the children are offspring of young single mothers, whose lack of financial and emotional resources are even more striking than those of other mothers living in poverty.

Many of the children in our study also have experienced other risks associated with being born to an adolescent. One risk is that of being a premature, low-birthweight baby (Institute of Medicine, 1985; Strobino, 1987). In our population, 12% of the children were low birthweight at delivery. Low-birthweight children are more likely than normal-birthweight children to experience school, health, and emotional problems (Brooks-Gunn et al., 1994; Escalona, 1982; Scott, 1987).

Low parental school and cognitive performance is another risk factor for off-spring. About 20% of the teen mothers in our population were categorized as educable mentally retarded (EMR) or placed in special education classes, and another 16% were earning nothing higher than Ds in their academic courses. On the revised Peabody Picture Vocabulary Test (PPVT-R) their average standard score was 68.5 (100 is the average standard score for the PPVT-R). Children of parents with this level of cognitive function often have similar school and cognitive problems.

The risks to an urban adolescent mother's children are multiple and readily apparent. Yet not all such children succumb to the fate of low achievement and social maladjustment. Children who have multiple risk factors, yet who appear to adapt successfully, have been described by some theorists as being "resilient." Researchers have attempted to identify protective factors that help buffer the stressors for such children, and this has been one aim of our study of the children of teen mothers. As we will show later, we have found a number of factors that reduce the probability of negative outcomes in this population. Some of these protective factors are at the institutional level. Services provided to pregnant and parenting adolescents can substantially improve health, social, and educational outcomes for them. Other factors are at the family level, including help from the teenager's parents and extended family and the teenage mother's ability to delay her subsequent childbearing.

Our research also confirms a finding that has been highlighted by developmental psychopathologists, that resilient children may have to pay for their apparent success with other problems, such as high levels of anxiety and depression. Luthar and Zigler (1991), for example, have demonstrated that resilience is not necessarily found in all domains of development and that children who appear resilient may carry vulnerabilities that could jeopardize their future development. As Zigler

(1971) has cautioned throughout his study of the development of typical and atypical children, and as our findings will also show, we must not lose sight of the whole child when we focus on one area of his or her success.

Purposes and history of our longitudinal study

Our continuing longitudinal study has had two main purposes. The first purpose is to describe health, educational, and social outcomes for an unbiased population of inner-city teenage mothers and their children and to determine what factors predict better versus poorer outcomes for them. The second purpose is to determine the effects of early community intervention on the later life outcomes of adolescent mothers and their firstborn children. The community intervention we have been evaluating is the Polly T. McCabe Center, in New Haven, Connecticut, which was established in the late 1960s as a school-based program for pregnant students. The program was begun to prevent school dropout among this population, and also to provide supportive health and social services.

Through hospital and school record review we identified a study sample of 164 young mothers with 166 children, including two sets of twins. This sample represents two partially overlapping populations of New Haven residents who delivered a firstborn child from March 1, 1979, through February 29, 1980: (1) all school-aged mothers, regardless of ethnicity, who were still in school when they conceived (N = 154) and (2) all African American mothers in the city who were younger than 18 years old at delivery (N = 115). We have followed the development of these mothers and children from pregnancy to 12 years postpartum. Attrition in the study has been low: at 12 years, we interviewed 90% of living mothers and 93% of the children's primary caregivers, and we tested 88% of the children. In the present chapter, we will focus on the second population – the young, African American mothers and their children.

Breadth of measures over the 12 years of follow-up

Consonant with the philosophy of developmental psychopathology, we have selected a wide breadth of measures and interdisciplinary approaches to study the adolescents and their firstborns over the years. We felt that we needed to observe growth and development in a variety of domains – social, cognitive, and health – and from multiple points of view, including those of the teen mother and her child, the child's grandmother, and the child's teachers. We gave an extensive interview to the teen mother and her mother at 18 months postpartum, and to the teen mother at 6 and 12 years postpartum. At each time, we also interviewed the child's primary caregiver, if this person was not the teen mother. We interviewed the child at age 12 and the child's teachers when the child was 6 and 12 years old. At the 6-year visit we administered the Peabody Picture Vocabulary Test – Revised to the teen mothers (Dunn & Dunn, 1981). With their permission, we collected information from the mother's and their firstborn's medical records from the pregnancy of the index child to 12 years postpartum, and from the mother's and child's school records.

The maternal interviews covered a wide range of topics including the mother's educational, work, and childbearing history, her residential moves, child-rearing beliefs and practices, family support over time, and the mother's and child's school and community activities. The children were administered the Bayley Scales of Infant Development (Bayley, 1969) at 18 months, the Stanford-Binet Intelligence Test (Thorndike, Hagen, & Sattler, 1986) at 6 years of age, and the Woodcock-Johnson Tests of Achievement (Woodcock & Johnson, 1989, 1990) at 12 years postpartum. To look at the children's social adaptation, we used the Vineland Adaptive Behavior Scales (Sparrow, Balla, & Cicchetti, 1985) administered to the child's main caregiver at 6 and at 12 years of age. For school adaptation, we obtained teacher ratings of the child's personality and classroom behavior attributes, information about the child's receipt of special school services, and the child's school attendance and grades at 6 and 12 years of age.

A brief overview of findings

Reduction of the incidence of low-birthweight babies

To evaluate health consequences of intervention, we used the entire population of all first births to school-aged mothers in the city over 1 full year. We divided this population into the group who were still enrolled in public school at the time they became pregnant (and who therefore should have been referred to the McCabe program) and into the group who were not enrolled in public school at the time they conceived. (Most of this group were known to be prepregnancy school dropouts; some may have been attending parochial schools.)

For the group who were still in public school, we reasoned that their ability to receive the intervention should be affected by its discontinuation during the summer months. Using this rationale, we found strong intervention effects on the incidence of low birthweight (Seitz & Apfel, 1994). Nearly three-quarters of all school-aged primiparas who were enrolled in the city's public schools at conception attended the McCabe Center. Because of summer vacation, however, students who conceived in January through April began attending later in pregnancy than did those who conceived in May through December. The students who were able to attend the McCabe program earlier and longer, due to the timing of their pregnancy relative to the school year, showed startlingly positive effects on the health of their babies at birth. Nearly 12% of the teens who could not attend the program early in their pregnancy because of summer vacation delivered a preterm, low-birthweight baby, whereas fewer than 1% of the ones who could attend early in pregnancy delivered preterm low-birthweight babies ($p < .006$, by Fisher's Exact

Test; Seitz & Apfel, 1994). No seasonal effects were found for other teenagers in the city who were not enrolled in public school at conception.

We considered the role of a number of constructs that might have been confounded with timing of conception, including total number of prenatal visits, consumption of cigarettes, alcohol, or other drugs during pregnancy, and adequacy of the mother's prenatal diet; none of these showed significant differences across the two groups. Thus, the evidence strongly indicates that infant health can be improved if support, supervision, and education are made available to pregnant teens, starting early in their pregnancies.

Prevention of rapid subsequent childbearing

We also found that this intervention had noteworthy effects on the incidence of repeated childbearing among these teen mothers. Elsewhere we have reported findings on the prevention of repeated childbearing for the first 2 years postpartum (Seitz, Apfel, & Rosenbaum, 1991). Performing a median split on duration of postnatal intervention, we found that when students received more than 7 weeks of postnatal McCabe time, they were significantly less likely to have a second baby within the next 2 years than if they received seven weeks or less (12% versus 32% respectively, $p < .01$). In a later follow-up, we found that postnatal intervention at McCabe predicted subsequent childbearing as long as 5 years later (Seitz & Apfel, 1993).

To rule out the possibility that there were preexisting differences between the groups formed by the median split, we examined a variety of other factors. We found that the teenagers in both groups were comparable in age, grade level, academic grades, attendance, prior pregnancy history, family size, and amount of child-care help from family. The only apparent difference we could find between the groups was the amount of time they were allowed to remain at McCabe postnatally, a factor that was controlled by the academic calendar and not by the girls' choice. We felt that the mechanism that led to McCabe's effectiveness in helping teen mothers to limit subsequent childbearing was the availability of advice and support from trusted persons at a critical time, about the time they received their postpartum medical exam. This appears to be a time when a teen is particularly receptive to information on sexuality and fertility. Most of the teenagers in this study received a postpartum check-up, whether they were receiving postnatal intervention or not, and almost three-quarters of them were given an effective form of contraception. However, it appears that the McCabe staff influenced the students' compliance with the medical advice they received in their check-ups (Seitz & Apfel, 1993).

Outcomes for the children

We turn now to the firstborn children and how they were doing as preteens. Although we have detailed assessments of the children when they were younger, the focus of this chapter is on child outcomes at age 12. At this age, the average performance of the children on the Woodcock-Johnson Achievement Tests was 94.1 (34th percentile) on reading, and 90.0 (27th percentile) on mathematics. As these scores indicate, the children's academic performance was relatively low. However, there was a considerable range in performance in children of both sexes, from the 1st percentile to the 99th.

Of particular interest to us was the subgroup of children who showed average or better levels of academic performance. Considering the entire African American sample of children, 42% of the girls and 33% of the boys scored at or above national norms for 12-year-olds on reading, mathematics, or both. The achievement levels of these children were particularly noteworthy to us in view of the substantial risks they faced. The children of young mothers living in conditions of extreme poverty are at high risk for failing and dropping out of school (Furstenberg et al., 1987; Horwitz et al., 1991a, 1991b). The question we addressed and the one on which we focus in this chapter was, What might have contributed to the relative academic success of some of the 12-year-olds in our study?

Having examined a number of possible explanatory factors, quantitative analyses indicated that one of the most important predictive factors was the speed with which the children's mothers had a second child. For firstborn boys, if their mothers had waited at least 5 years before delivering a second child, the benefits were dramatic. Boys who remained only children throughout their preschool years not only had higher school performance at age 12 than did boys who had younger siblings while they were preschoolers, but also their performance was close to national norms for children of their age. Similar findings were obtained for girls, although there was a shorter span of time – 2 years – across which a single-child status was necessary for positive effects to be evident. We discuss the girls' development in greater detail elsewhere (Apfel & Seitz, 1996).

Thus, these children of teen mothers have benefited from their mothers' decisions to limit their early childbearing. This maternal behavior often appears to have resulted from having spent at least 7 weeks in the McCabe school program after they delivered their firstborns. These findings demonstrate how services offered during and after a teenager's pregnancy can lower risk in this population.

It is generally agreed that clinical insight can inform and expand the more traditional developmental study of children. Therefore, to supplement the quantitative outcomes just presented, we now explore some of our findings qualitatively. In the present chapter we focus on the group whose good academic performance as 12-year-olds most surprised us and seemed in need of explanation: the sons of mothers whose own academic achievement and measured cognitive ability were low and whose life outcomes were unusually poor. From among the group of our best-performing boys, we selected two boys whose mothers were among the weakest in our sample in cognitive performance and academic achievement.

We now turn to these case studies to explore in greater depth the question of how very high-risk sons of inner-city African American teenage mothers can nevertheless show good academic achievement as they near adolescence. The question that we ask is, How could these adolescent mothers with their own history of school adjustment problems, extreme youth, and poverty, manage to raise sons who have such academic promise? All names and some details have been changed to protect confidentiality.

Rita and Charles

Sixteen-year-old Rita faded in and out of high school in two ways. The first was her pattern of high absenteeism. In her first attempt to pass 10th grade, she missed about a quarter of the school year. Her second style of school fade-out was her inconsistent achievement; sometimes she would receive Bs and Cs, but at other times, Ds and Fs in the same courses. On the PPVT-R, she scored in the 1st percentile, earning a score of 66.

After missing many days of school at her regular high school program, Rita registered at the McCabe Center in early February 1979, in the first trimester of her pregnancy. Her grades at McCabe improved again for a quarter, but plummeted in the final quarter of that school year as she neared the time of her baby's delivery. Nevertheless, Rita said that McCabe "taught me everything I needed to know about the baby and pregnancy. I ate more [during pregnancy] and I ate broccoli, spinach, and squash for the first time. I took vitamins and iron and didn't drink any alcohol."

In mid-August of 1979, Rita delivered a healthy full-term baby boy weighing 7 pounds 2 ounces, whom she named Charles. This summer delivery meant that Rita received no postnatal intervention at McCabe.

Rita and her baby lived in a large multifamily house with Rita's grandmother, Regina, and grandfather, George, who had raised her. Her mother, Tina, had moved away years earlier, leaving Rita and her sister in the care of their grandparents. When Rita was 12 years old, her mother returned to the household with her three other children to live on the top floor, although Rita and her sister continued to live downstairs with their grandparents.

When Charles was 18 months old, Tina and Rita both reported that they had little to do with each other. Regina, on the other hand, said that she played with Charles, her great-grandson, who made her "happy all the time" and that she loved him. This great-grandmother firmly stated, however, that Rita was primarily responsible for taking care of Charles, and that Regina would only do occasional baby care when Rita was there and babysitting when Rita needed to be out. Regina avoided involvement in Charles's daily routines. "I've raised eleven children," Regina said, implying that she did not intend to end up as Charles's primary caregiver.

Regina expressed her anger and disappointment in Rita's decision not to return to school: "She is very lazy; I felt terrible at the beginning [when Rita dropped out of school in the fall after Charles's birth], but it doesn't bother me now [nearly two years later]." Rita lost the babysitting services of her aunt and then had to drop out of school. Her motivation to replace her sitter may have been low because she commented, "I couldn't get into the schoolwork very much. I felt like I didn't fit in."

In her mothering, Rita showed more enthusiasm. She told us how she taught Charles the names of things, starting with "making sounds back and forth with him." She would read and show him pictures in books and play with blocks and toys with him as a toddler, spending most of her time with her little son. Charles was a well-developing 18-month-old when we administered the Bayley examination, earning a score of 98 on the mental development index.

Charles's father was uninvolved in Rita's and his son's lives. Nevertheless, the paternal grandmother recognized Charles as one of her grandchildren and she was a steady resource for Rita. "Whenever I need anything, I can go to Sophie," Rita said.

Six years postpartum

Rita had a second child, a daughter, in 1982, giving Charles 3 years of being an only child. Because Rita's family was unsupportive of this second pregnancy, Rita established her own independent household. At 6 years postpartum she was working at a factory more than 30 hours a week assembling purses, earning too little to be independent of welfare. Rita had studied for the high school equivalency certificate but had not yet taken the test.

By the time of our 6-year-postpartum follow-up, Rita spoke warmly of her relationship with her grandparents, apparently putting behind her her past feelings that family support was low during her second pregnancy. However, she was still estranged from her biological mother. Rita said of her grandmother, "I followed in her footsteps. She raised me from when I was a baby. Everything I know I got from her. Any problem, I call her." Charles was close to his mother, his paternal grandmother and his maternal great-grandmother, receiving mothering from all three women.

Charles was described as a "cheerful and friendly child who put forth a reasonable effort on the harder problems" by our Stanford-Binet tester. On this measure he received a score of 87, which was neither a particularly strong nor weak score. Charles's teacher described him as one of the most enjoyable students in her class and ascribed to him such characteristics as being reliable and helpful. He was very rarely absent and was rated as an above-average student who needed no remedial school services to do well. Charles was reported by his mother to love school. Rita was a regular visitor, going once a month to his school to see how he was doing. She said of his teachers, "They work with him at school like I do at home."

Twelve years postpartum

In our 12-year interview, Rita told of the difficult times she and her children had been through. By this time she had had four children, ages 12, 9, 2 years old, and 9 months old. Rita had become involved with her thirdborn's father, Sam, 3 years earlier. She had moved from the apartment where she and her two children had lived for many years to live with Sam. Sam and Rita had a healthy, full-term baby girl in the spring of 1989, when Charles was 9 years old. Rita and Sam were happy and excited about the birth of their daughter. However, Sam became addicted to cocaine and led Rita and her children to a life-style of multiple moves, emergency housing, and eventually drug addiction for Rita also. Sam also became physically abusive to Rita. She knew that she and her children were in serious jeopardy so she "kicked Sam out" and asked Regina for help. Regina helped her go through drug withdrawal and to pull her life back together.

Rita formed another relationship with a man who had a stable well-paying job in maintenance at the local community college. This partner proved to be as unreliable as the other men in her life, because he also turned to drugs, leaving his mainstream work for the monetary rewards of selling drugs. Throughout this troubled time, Rita showed remarkable determination to provide educational stability for her children. She managed to keep her children in the same school that they loved, even when they lived in emergency housing across town. While pregnant with her fourth child she walked her two school-aged children long distances in the winter to and from school each day because school bus transportation to that school was unavailable from where they lived.

In the fall of 1991, Rita was taking adult education courses and had nearly completed the credits she needed for her high school diploma. Her plans were to continue in a business school program in January that would take a year to finish.

Rita and Charles independently told us that they felt very close to each other. In a photograph that Rita had brought to show us, Charles looked more like a 16-year-old, than the 12-year-old that he was. Rita was proud of Charles's school accomplishments. "He always gets on the honor roll. Since kindergarten all the teachers love him. He's only missed one day of school in [the last] three years!" When report cards came out Rita would talk to each of Charles's teachers about his progress. She proudly stated that Charles never had any discipline problems at school, "He loves school. All of it." His performance on the Woodcock-Johnson showed him to be at the 50th percentile on the reading tests and the 65th percentile on the mathematics tests. This level of achievement is exceptional among inner-city African American boys (Humphries, 1988; Irvine, 1990).

Charles had an active extracurricular calendar, participating in Boy Scouts, football, and a local university's youth program in which he had been active for the past 3 years. Charles and Rita were also regular church attenders.

On the face of things, Charles seemed to have made good adjustments at home and in school and community life. There were some incidents, however, that revealed undercurrents of anger and hostility in Charles. During his interview, his stance toward our interviewer was, in her words, "indifferent and as if he wanted to be somewhere else." He became agitated and guarded when asked about his father, whom he said he "hated." Charles commented that his father lived with a girlfriend and gave things to her children, but never gave anything to Charles, "not even a pair of pants." Charles also told of times that his father was belligerent to Rita when she asked for financial help for Charles's support: "He kept phoning her and calling her names and stuff." A more generic hostility surfaced during the interview when a telephone that was ringing in a nearby office caused Charles to lose his temper and utter a threat at the phone. Rita also spoke of Charles's occasional temper tantrums, but she did not seem concerned about them.

Rita had firm rules that Charles usually obeyed, limiting how much he could be away from home, and with whom he could socialize. A turning point in Rita and Charles's relationship occurred in the summer of his 12th year. Rita told how Charles became rebellious about her rules and threatened to run away from home because of them. In Rita's words: "One day he said he was going to leave. I can't even remember what it started over, some rule or other. The next thing I knew, he was putting things in a bag to leave me." Rita became emotional as she expressed her fears that her son would fall into the same criminal life-style that his father and father's father lived. They both sold drugs in the neighborhood in which she and Charles lived. She felt that she was going to lose him to the streets unless she could turn the situation around. "I said I'd put him in a military school. He realized he couldn't go nowhere. I let him know his father sells drugs and is in and out of jail. I said, 'I want to send you to college.' " Rita told us that by the end of this highly charged encounter with Charles, he finally said, "I *want* to go [to college]," and began to unpack his bag. Rita explained her style of rearing Charles by saying, "I was young too. We been learning together, more like brother and sister."

Rita and Charles still received strong support from Rita's grandmother and grandfather and her maternal aunt. She spoke of her own mother negatively, "My mother is bad news and out of control. My values are like my grandmother's."

Case analysis

This young mother, who was one of our lowest scorers on the PPVT-R and who had a history of high absenteeism from school, reared a 12-year-old son who scored impressively on the academic achievement test. Rita's comments about how she changed her diet and avoided alcohol after her lessons at McCabe in prenatal nutrition echoed those of many of her classmates. Rita delivered Charles full term, giving him the advantage of a healthy start. She never received postpartum education at McCabe because of her summer delivery. Nevertheless, she did not have a second baby until her firstborn was 3 years old, giving him slightly more than 3 years as her only child. Most students in this population needed the postpartum time at McCabe to delay their childbearing.

In her attempts to find a loving and supportive mate, Rita was unsuccessful. Even when the man appeared to have a stable job, he succumbed to the attraction of the high profits of drug dealing. Rita's story personalizes the bleak statistics on the likelihood of African American young men falling out of the mainstream. However, Rita had extraordinary family support in her grandparents, particularly her grandmother. Charles not only had three mothering figures, but also his maternal great-grandfather whom he named as the person most like a father to him.

A consistent theme in Rita's interviews was her belief in the value of education for her children. Her own academic performance previous to her pregnancy was not indicative of how she came to value education for her children. Rita's story had difficult times of drug addiction, spousal abuse, and homelessness. Out of such unpromising circumstances, she managed to rear a 12-year-old child who loved school and achieved academic success and whose aspirations included a college education.

This was no easy task as Rita's story of tumultuous episodes told. When Charles threatened to run away, it was an urban mother's worst fear – that the seductive influence of a violent drug-infested neighborhood would steal her son from her. Such a child is likely to have an older peer group on his block waiting and watching for someone just like him to run drugs for them. Rita won Charles back that time, but there will be other times when he resists her rules, and the anger that he carries spills over. He has the added vulnerability of an urban male child who looks much older than he is, raising expectations in others of a maturity that he does not yet have. His family's belief in him and his own academic ability are strengths that hopefully will sustain him and keep him from slipping off track.

Bertille and Cassius

Bertille was classified as an educable mentally retarded (EMR) student by the New Haven public schools. When we tested her, her score on the PPVT-R was 73. Her school attendance from her elementary school days through middle school was abysmal. Her ninth grade year was an academic disaster: She failed all her courses in the first half of the year, prompting the school to place her in a modified program, but this too was unsuccessful, and she continued to fail. By January of 1979, when she was beginning the last trimester of her pregnancy she entered the McCabe program. In this smaller, more personalized, environment she did well academically, earning a B average in academic courses. At the end of March, just before Bertille's 16th birthday, Cassius was born, full term and weighing a healthy 7 pounds 3 ounces. The transition to motherhood dampened her school performance and she began failing her academic courses again, earning her only passing grade in the postnatal health course. Bertille attended the McCabe Center for almost 3 months postpartum, but she did not return to school after leaving McCabe in June 1979.

When we interviewed Bertille and her mother, Gertrude, at 18 months postpartum, Gertrude explained, ''Bertille wanted to be home with Cassius the first year, so I let her. She wants to become a beautician and go to Wilfred Beauty Academy, but I can't afford it.''

Bertille and her baby lived with her mother, her 14-year-old sister, and her 13-year-old brother. Bertille's mother and sister helped in caring for Cassius, but

Bertille was his primary caregiver. She described him as a very active infant who did not like to slow down to be cuddled, but who liked to have her read to him every day. In interactions with our Bayley examiner, he enjoyed the tasks, was quick to respond, and performed at his appropriate age level in the mental scale and above age level in the motor scale.

Cassius's father was in prison, and his family was unhelpful and uninvolved with Bertille and Cassius at this time.

Six years postpartum

Cassius was Bertille's only child for his first 6 years; however, before his seventh birthday, she had another child. The medical records showed that soon afterward she was again pregnant. Bertille, Cassius, and his sibling lived with Bertille's mother and sister and her sister's two preschool children. They had been through many moves as they sought suitable housing for their large group. In one of their apartments, which was insect-and rodent-infested, the landlord was not providing heat and hot water. Cassius's home life was described in his medical records as unstable and chaotic, partly due to the frequent changes of address. At about the time when his mother delivered her third child, Cassius began to have abdominal pains and unexplained vomiting; the medical staff wondered if his home situation was taking a toll on his health. He also had a history of asthmatic wheezing episodes and chronic nighttime enuresis that had started when he was 3 years old. Bertille and her family had come to the attention of social services for these issues and for the irregularity of school attendance and medical care Cassius was receiving. They arranged for her to receive the help of a parent aide who would do home visiting and help them find housing.

Cassius's school records indicated that, when he was in kindergarten and first grade, he was not attending school regularly. He missed 45 days in his first-grade year. Despite these difficulties, Cassius's teacher rated him as an outgoing, above-average student who could do his work with little supervision. Even with his absenteeism, he kept up with the schoolwork without extra services or tutoring. On the Stanford-Binet he also did well, earning a score of 102. Our examiner reported that he was enthusiastic, but that he was distractable and needed help with focusing. Cassius had become involved in a few fights at school with peers, but seemed to be doing well overall. On the Vineland Scales he showed below average socialization skills and daily living skills (e.g., taking care of his clothing, using the telephone, and preparing simple food for himself).

Bertille was proud of Cassius's school performance and rewarded his good report card with shopping trips. The early reading that Bertille had done with Cassius was imitated by him, as he read books every day to his baby sister. Bertille told us she felt Cassius found school easy because "I had worked with him with preschool books."

Bertille had firm rules for Cassius's behavior. She described her interactions with

Cassius when he had upset her by going into an unsafe neighborhood without her permission, and she had "grounded" him for 2 weeks by withholding television and outside play after school. However, Bertille spent much less time with school-aged Cassius than she had with preschool-aged Cassius; she said, "There isn't much we do together." This is not surprising considering that she had had two additional children in rapid succession after a 6-year hiatus in which Cassius was the only child for whom she was responsible.

Every day Cassius saw his maternal grandmother and aunt, who had both lived with and helped care for him since his birth. Cassius was also receiving attention from his father's sister, who would visit with him three or four times a week. Cassius's father remained in prison.

Bertille had obtained a student grant to become a beautician, and had successfully become licensed in this. She had also taken some high school equivalency certificate courses, but not the test, at a local community college. Her child-care responsibilities prevented her from seeking a job at a beauty parlor, leaving her dependent on welfare and food stamps.

Twelve years postpartum

By 12 years postpartum Bertille had five children ages 12, 5, 4, 3, and 2 years old. For the past 3 years, she and her children had been living apart from her mother and sister.

Bertille was enthusiastic as she described the academic prowess of Cassius. "He is a whiz at reading and math!" On the Woodcock-Johnson test, Cassius performed extremely well, scoring at the 87th percentile on the reading and the 65th percentile on the mathematics subtests. Bertille was rightly proud of what her firstborn son had achieved academically. In school his grades were solid; he was earning a B-average, which was not as high as one would expect from his achievement test results. This discrepancy between test results and school performance was probably related to the number of school days he missed; he missed 32 days in his seventh-grade year. This was actually an improvement from his absences in fourth and fifth grade when he missed 56 and 61 days, respectively. Given his high absenteeism over the years, his test results were astonishing. When we interviewed him about his schoolwork and aspirations, he said that his mother helped him with his homework most of the time, and that he had high educational goals, "I'll finish college." Bertille spoke in more detail about Cassius's goals, "He's going to be a cop. He thinks he can go to college and be a part-time cop at the same time." The teacher's interview about Cassius was informative for its mixed ratings. Cassius was not rated as one of the teacher's most enjoyable students, but he was categorized as a very good student. He was described as energetic, independent, liked by peers, and not disobedient. Yet he was given ratings that indicated he was sometimes demanding and not always reliable. Our Woodcock-Johnson examiner commented in her notes about Cassius's reaction to her, "He was very personable and charming. He shook hands at the end of the session."

Cassius's main extracurricular activity in school was track; he spent as much as 19 hours a week on his running. His favorite activity was reading. He attended church with his mother and siblings every Sunday for 2 hours. He had a big brother relationship with a man at church who arranged special activities for Cassius, such as a week in a summer church camp. Bertille and Cassius spoke of his involvement in a program run by the local police department that sponsored activities for urban youth. Bertille remarked, "Cassius has a friendship with a policeman in the neighborhood who he follows around and asks questions about police work."

These activities and accomplishments were all positive; however, Cassius's school record and our interviews revealed a darker side. Bertille reported that he had had an altercation with his third-grade teacher in which he had hit her. In seventh grade, he threw a shoe at his teacher, whom he reportedly liked, according to Bertille, but "she got on his nerves." He was also suspended numerous times and expelled once that year. He told us that these disciplinary actions were for bringing weapons to school: he had brought a BB gun one time and a switchblade another time. When another boy had words with him, Cassius took the blade out and threatened the boy. This was seen by school authorities who expelled him. In answer to our questions about whether he had ever hurt anyone badly enough for them to need bandages or a doctor's attention, Cassius told of numerous violent altercations. "A kid tried to steal my new bike that my great-grandmother gave me before she died and I smashed his head into a car door." "A kid slammed his bike on my little brother and I cut him with my switchblade." "A kid called my Mom a name and I beat him up with a baseball bat." Bertille commented that 12-year-old Cassius was a loner: "He stays to himself."

Family history provides some of the explanation for the contrasts that Cassius displayed. When Cassius was 9 years old, his mother entered the local hospital emergency room for a cocaine overdose. She was pregnant at the time with her fifth child. She had sought no prenatal care for this pregnancy, her second one within 12 months. This infant was born at 38 weeks gestation, weighting 6 pounds 13 ounces, and was in the Newborn Special Care Unit for "jitters." The hospital notes say that Bertille showed no interest in her newborn. After this birth, Bertille chose to have a bilateral tubal ligation to prevent any future pregnancies. In the spring and summer of 1990, 1 year later, Bertille was in the hospital for two suicide attempts. She was cocaine dependent, depressed, and overwhelmed with caring for her five children. Her mother, Gertrude, had refused to allow Bertille and her five children to live with her. Gertrude was angry and frustrated with her daughter's drug problem. During this time Bertille was in serious trouble, struggling with addiction and depression. Cassius's home environment was clearly a risky one. He was a fifth grader at that time and, in that year, he missed over 60 days of school.

Cassius never criticized his mother in his interview, and, in fact, he spoke poignantly of times when his mother made him happy, "They are so many; it's not one thing.'' He spoke of how she had grounded him for misbehavior in the recent past, implying that she was trying to maintain rules for him. However, he also knew of a time when his mother had gone to court and had become involved in a fight there and was consequently put into jail. Bertille was not a model of nonviolent behavior.

Family support to Bertille from Cassius's 6th through 12th years had obviously changed dramatically. Bertille's mother had become distant as she rejected Bertille's behavior. Bertille's father, whom she had mentioned as someone she could depend on if she needed help, had died in 1989 of complications of alcoholism. Bertille's younger sister, who had helped to rear Cassius, had succumbed to drug use also and was in a drug rehabilitation program the year we conducted our interviews. Cassius's father, while still in prison, was telephoning and writing Cassius frequently. Cassius reported that nothing his father did made him happy; he rated his relationship with his father as ''not close,'' in spite of the father's efforts. Cassius saw his paternal aunt several times a month and considered her ''like a mother,'' as well as his own mother. Bertille also received support that she felt was helpful from her second child's paternal grandmother. Family support from Bertille's own family had withered away, but she was able to gather help from other female relatives of her children.

Case analysis

Bertille had many children, was a school dropout, welfare dependent, and had a period of drug addiction and suicide attempts. How could such a mother raise a son who excelled in academic achievement? With the help of certain institutional and familial supports, she did a few things right for Cassius. She delivered him healthy and full term; she delayed having subsequent children until Cassius was almost 7 years old; she read to him and helped him with homework, and took pride in his schoolwork. Bertille took her family to church where he found a male role model who gave him opportunities to participate in other programs. Cassius repeated this pattern and sought out another male mentor, a policeman whom he admired.

Cassius's tendency to resort to violence to solve problems is a danger sign, as is his high absenteeism. Cassius has experienced multiple hazards that may have left him with vulnerabilities. He also has strengths that could counter the risks he carries. Perhaps his dream of higher education and a career as a policeman will help channel his considerable energy in positive directions.

Discussion: The interplay of findings from typical and atypical populations

Findings from our study of adolescent mothers and their children demonstrate how understandings gleaned from this high-risk group of children can enrich developmental theory by their similarities to, and differences from, results from more typical populations of parents and children. The studies of how family support can affect a new mother illustrate this point.

Studies of two-parent, middle-class families suggest that support given to a new parent by a spouse or parent is important in a new mother's adjustment, even when she is an adult (Belsky, 1984; Pederson, 1982; Tinsley & Parke, 1984). We and other researchers similarly find that family support is important in an adolescent's adjustment to parenthood (Apfel & Seitz, 1991, 1996; Colletta, 1981; Crockenberg, 1981; Furstenberg & Crawford, 1978; Kellam, Ensminger, & Turner, 1977; Leadbeater & Bishop, 1994).

The sources of family support for teenage mothers, however, may be broader than those in more typical populations. Our findings also agree with those of Kellam and his colleagues (1977) in showing that different family constellations can be just as effective as the traditional two-parent household in rearing impoverished children who adapt well to school. This earlier sociological approach to the study of children has brought valuable insights to developmental psychology from a nonmainstream population. In the Kellam et al. study, inner-city children from grandmother-mother headed households were equivalent to those from mother-father households in their early school adjustment. In our case studies as well, considerable family support was available to bolster the mothers' child rearing. During their preschool years, these boys had at least two, and sometimes more, parental figures who were biologically related to them. Significant support could come from a child's paternal female relatives even when the father himself was uninvolved. The cases also show how support patterns can shift over time. When a source of support is lost from a teen's own family, as in Bertille's case, a young mother can seek help elsewhere, and find it in her firstborn's paternal aunt and her second born's paternal grandmother.

We can draw the conclusion that inner-city teenage mothers and middle-class mature mothers have a common need for family support in order to function at their best as parents. Yet, there is also an apparent difference in the characteristics of the support system from which each group draws its strength. Family constellations providing support to an at-risk population such as ours appear to be more varied and extended than those of traditional two-parent households.

We now turn to another factor to explore the relationship between findings from typical and atypical populations – the spacing of sibling births. One of our key findings – that the preteen firstborn children of teen mothers have higher levels of academic achievement if they are given sufficient time as their mothers' only children – relates to the findings of researchers who have studied the academic achievement of high school students using large, nationally representative samples. Close spacing of sibling births was found to increase the likelihood that high school students would have poor test performance and low grade point averages, and that they would fail to continue their education beyond secondary school (Powell & Steelman, 1990, 1993). Research with sixth-grade-age children has also shown that larger family size and shorter age spacing was associated with lower intelligence test scores, with this effect most pronounced among families of lower socioeconomic status (Lancer & Rim, 1984).

Powell and Steelman (1990, 1993), who found sibship density to be more significant than sibship size, have considered several possible explanations for how close birth spacing affects child outcomes. They suggested that a "resource dilution" hypothesis best explained their findings. That is, when siblings' births are closely spaced, parental attention and economic resources are spread more thinly, and this leads to poorer academic performance in offspring. Whether this dilution of family resources has its strongest impact early, later, or throughout child rearing is still unclear. Nevertheless, it would appear that birth spacing may be an extremely important variable in the lives of impoverished families, and particularly so in the families created by teen mothers.

Bertille's case is striking because, although she delayed repeated childbearing for more than 6 years, she then had four children in rapid succession. In our study, almost all mothers who delayed repeated childbearing also had limited their family size to, at most, three children by the 12-year follow-up (92% had done so), and they were likely to be high school graduates; many were mostly or entirely self-supporting. Such improvements in maternal education and socioeconomic status might themselves provide adequate explanation for why their children were performing well academically. Rita's and Bertille's cases are remarkable because they had larger families, did not complete high school, and were still welfare dependent 12 years after the birth of their first child. Their cases suggest the possibility that, for children of teenagers, the experience of being an only child during the preschool years is so powerful a protective factor that, to some extent, it can override very negative events later in the child's life.

In addition to family support and spacing of sibling births, we found other factors that help to explain the children's success. The case studies suggest that one such factor was the mother's strong belief in the value of education. This belief has been identified by other researchers as an important protective factor (Luthar & Zigler, 1991), but we had not anticipated finding it in the cases we selected, because the mothers were chosen for their extremely poor academic histories.

It was startling to discover that these mothers, whose school records were filled with failure, not only felt that their children's good school performance was important, but also believed they could help their sons achieve academic success through their child-rearing practices. This value was often reflected as early as the child's toddlerhood when these teen mothers tended to read to and otherwise cognitively stimulate their children; and once their children started school, Bertille and Rita helped their sons with their homework, visited their classrooms, and showed deep pride in their sons' academic accomplishments.

The unlinking of maternal academic achievement from children's academic outcomes distinguishes our findings from those of more typical groups. The discovery that mothers who have shown little academic aptitude can nevertheless rear children who are academically successful gives reason for hope. Apparently a pattern of educational failure does not have to be handed down inevitably to the next generation.

Another child-rearing practice that seemed to affect the development of the boys was parental discipline. Both Rita and Bertille spoke of the rules they had for their sons – about where they could go, when they should return home, and requiring the boys to keep them informed of their whereabouts. Research with more typical populations has shown that parental expectations for such behavior in their children lead to higher school achievement (Lamborn, Mounts, Steinberg, & Dornbusch, 1991). Other research with inner-city families has also shown the value of strict parental monitoring of adolescents (Baldwin, Baldwin, & Cole, 1990; Loeber & Stouthamer-Loeber, 1986). We saw much variation in our population on this dimension of parenting; some parents reported that they could not control their 12-year-olds and had apparently given up in the attempt, and others, like our case mothers, were trying to maintain rules for their children. Our work suggests that urban teen parents who have firm guidelines for their sons have sons with higher levels of academic performance.

A final factor that was identified in our study was the availability of community supports that the families utilized. Both teen mothers in our case studies had participated in the McCabe program. The utilization of programs such as Head Start or extended day programs that provide activities after school were also mentioned in both cases. Bertille received family support services in the form of home visits from a parent aide when she and her children were extremely vulnerable. Regular church participation of children and adults was another community involvement often mentioned by the families in our study. Baldwin and his colleagues (1990) also noticed that African American families who raised academically successful children in high-risk environments often reported that church was important in their lives. These researchers speculate that having a social support group that backs up parental disciplinary efforts and that provides peers who are more likely to share the same value system as the parents, could have a positive impact on the children's cognitive outcomes. The case studies and our formal evaluations of the McCabe program strongly suggest that these and other community supports can promote better life outcomes for highly disadvantaged mothers and children.

This interplay of findings from more normative samples of children and the more at-risk groups enriches our understanding of how family life affects the growth and development of children. In this study of a complete, unbiased population of a very high-risk group of children born to young African American mothers, a third of the boys showed average or better-than-average academic achievement in reading, mathematics, or both. The case studies just presented provide some insights as to how some children managed to overcome stressors such as poverty, absent fathers, and multiple moves, and even mothers who were substance abusers.

Resilience researchers have identified three broad categories of protective forces in the lives of at-risk children (Garmezy, 1985; Luthar & Zigler, 1991; Werner & Smith, 1982). In the case of the children of teen mothers, our own analyses point to the salience of several factors within each of these categories. At the level of the community and extended family, the availability of prenatal and postnatal intervention and of support from extended kin is critical. At the level of the immediate family, important factors seem to include maternal spacing of subsequent children, the mother's belief in the value of education for her child, and her attempt to maintain firm rules. Finally, at the level of the individual child, cognitive ability, high educational goals, and interpersonal charm appear to be somewhat protective. Questions that remain to be addressed concern the relative importance of these different factors. Some of these ameliorative forces, such as sibship density and family support, may be more indispensable than are others.

As the case studies show, even with high academic achievement, the successful later life adjustment of these boys is not assured. These 12-year-old boys who have done so well have vulnerabilities that could sabotage their development. As Luthar and her colleagues (Luthar, 1993; Luthar, Doernberger, & Zigler, 1993; Luthar & Zigler, 1992) have reported, resilience is not a unitary concept, and children who appear to be academically resilient may have emotional or other vulnerabilities. The trouble signs in the two boys whom we have described include an underlying hostility and anger, a tendency to resort to fighting and aggressive behavior to solve problems, and the failure to attend school regularly. The influences of their urban environment and future family disruptions could undermine their promise.

There is now considerable evidence that disadvantaged children's IQ scores and/ or school adjustment can be improved through preschool programs that provide cognitive stimulation (Campbell & Ramey, 1994; Garber, 1988; Lazar, Darlington, Murray, Royce, & Snipper, 1982). Our findings suggest that the academic achievement of very high-risk children can also be enhanced by helping their mothers avoid rapid subsequent childbearing. However, as Zigler (1971) noted in his work with children with mental retardation, children are much more than their scores on a test of cognitive competence. The better socialization of children is at least as important a goal as raising their IQs and academic achievement. The present case studies lend force to this concern.

References

Apfel, N. H., & Seitz, V. (1991). Four models of adolescent mother-grandmother relationships in black inner-city families. *Family Relations, 40,* 421–429.

Apfel, N. H., & Seitz, V. (1996). African American adolescent mothers, their mothers, and their daughters: A longitudinal perspective over twelve years. In B. J. R. Leadbeater & N. Way (Eds.), *Urban adolescent girls: Resisting stereotypes, creating identities* (pp. 149–170). New York: New York University Press.

Baldwin, A. L., Baldwin, C., & Cole, R. E. (1990). Stress-resistant families and stress-resistant children. In J. Rolf, A. S. Masten, D. Cicchetti, K. H. Nuechterlein, & S. Weintraub (Eds.), *Risk and protective factors in the development of psychopathology* (pp. 257–280). New York: Cambridge University Press.

Bayley, N. (1969). *Bayley Scales of Infant Development, manual.* New York: Psychological Corporation.

Belsky, J. (1984). The determinants of parenting: A process model. *Child Development, 55,* 83–96.

Brooks-Gunn, J., & Furstenberg, F. F., Jr. (1986). The children of adolescent mothers: Physical, academic, and psychological outcomes. *Developmental Review, 6,* 224–251.

Brooks-Gunn, J., McCarton, C. M., Casey, P. H., McCormick, M. C., Bauer, C. R., Bernbaum, J. C., Tyson, J., Swanson, M., Bennett, F. C., Scott, D. T., Tonascia, J., & Meinert, C. L. (1994). Early intervention in low-birth-weight premature infants: Results through age 5 years from the Infant Health and Development Program. *Journal of the American Medical Association, 272,* 1257–1262.

Campbell, F. A., & Ramey, C. T. (1994). Effects of early intervention on intellectual and academic achievement: A follow-up study of children from low-income families. *Child Development, 65,* 684–698.

Colletta, N. D. (1981). Support and the risk of maternal rejection by adolescent mothers. *Journal of Psychology, 109,* 191–197.

Crockenberg, S. B. (1981). Infant irritability, mother responsiveness, and social support influences on the security of infant-mother attachment. *Child Development, 52,* 857–865.

Dunn, L. M., & Dunn, L. M. (1981). *Manual forms L and M, Peabody Picture Vocabulary Test – revised.* Circle Pines, MN: American Guidance Service.

Escalona, S. K. (1982). Babies at double hazard: Early development of infants at biologic and social risk. *Pediatrics, 70,* 670–676.

Furstenberg, F. F., Jr., Brooks-Gunn, J., & Morgan, S. P. (1987). *Adolescent mothers in later life.* New York: Cambridge University Press.

Furstenberg, F. F., Jr., & Crawford, A. G. (1978). Family support: Helping teenage mothers to cope. *Family Planning Perspectives, 10,* 322–333.

Garber, H. L. (1988). *The Milwaukee Project: Prevention of mental retardation in children at risk.* Washington, DC: American Association on Mental Retardation.

Garmezy, N. (1985). Stress-resistant children: The search for protective factors. In J. E. Stevenson (Ed.), *Recent research in developmental psychopathology* (pp. 213–233). Oxford: Pergamon Press.

Gibbs, J. T. (1988a). Young black males in America: Endangered, embittered, and embattled. In J. T. Gibbs (Ed.), *Young, black, and male in America* (pp. 1–36). Dover, MA: Auburn.

Gibbs, J. T. (1988b). The new morbidity: Homicide, suicide, accidents, and life-threatening behaviors. In J. T. Gibbs (Ed.), *Young, black, and male in America* (pp. 258–293). Dover, MA: Auburn.

Hare, B. R., & Castenell, L. A. (1985). No place to run, no place to hide: Comparative status and future prospects of black boys. In M. B. Spencer, G. K. Bookins, & W. R. Allen (Eds.), *Beginnings: The social and affective development of black children* (pp. 201–214). Hillsdale, NJ: Erlbaum.

Horwitz, S. M., Klerman, L. V., Kuo, H. S., & Jekel, J. F. (1991a). School-age mothers: Predictors of long-term educational and economic outcomes. *Pediatrics, 87,* 862–868.

Horwitz, S. M., Klerman, L. V., Kuo, H. S., & Jekel, J. F. (1991b). Intergenerational transmission of school-age parenthood. *Family Planning Perspectives, 23,* 168–172, 177.

Humphries, L. G. (1988). Trends in levels of academic achievement of blacks and other minorities. *Intelligence, 12,* 231–260.

Institute of Medicine, Committee to Study the Prevention of Low Birthweight. (1985). *Preventing low birthweight.* Washington, DC: National Academy Press.

Irvine, J. J. (1990). *Black students and school failure: Policies, practices, and prescriptions.* New York: Greenwood Press.

Kellam, S. G., Ensminger, M. E., & Turner, R. J. (1977). Family structure and the mental health of children. *Archives of General Psychiatry, 34,* 1012–1022.

Lamborn, S. D., Mounts, N. S., Steinberg, L., & Dornbusch, S. M. (1991). Patterns of competence and adjustment among adolescents from authoritative, authoritarian, indulgent, and neglectful families. *Child Development, 62,* 1049–1065.

Lancer, I., & Rim, Y. (1984). Intelligence, family size and sibling age spacing. *Personality and Individual Differences, 5,* 151–157.

Lazar, I., Darlington, R., Murray, H., Royce, J., & Snipper, A. (1982). Lasting effects of early education: A report from the Consortium for Longitudinal Studies. *Monographs of the Society for Research in Child Development, 47* (2–3, Serial No. 195).

Leadbeater, B. J., & Bishop, S. J. (1994). Predictors of behavior problems in preschool children of inner-city Afro-American and Puerto Rican adolescent mothers. *Child Development, 65,* 638–648.

Loeber, R., & Stouthamer-Loeber, M. (1986). Family factors as correlates and predictors of juvenile conduct problems and delinquency. In M. Tonry & N. Morris (Eds.), *Crime and justice: An annual review of research* (Vol. 7, pp. 129–150). Chicago: University of Chicago Press.

Luthar, S. S. (1993). Annotation: Methodological and conceptual issues in research on childhood resilience. *Journal of Child Psychology and Psychiatry, 34,* 441–453.

Luthar, S. S., Doernberger, C. H., & Zigler, E. (1993). Resilience is not a unidimensional construct: Insights from a prospective study of inner-city adolescents. *Development and Psychopathology, 5,* 703–717.

Luthar, S. S., & Zigler, E. (1991). Vulnerability and competence: A review of research on resilience in childhood. *American Journal of Orthopsychiatry, 61,* 6–22.

Luthar, S. S., & Zigler, E. (1992). Intelligence and social competence among high-risk adolescents. *Development and Psychopathology, 4,* 287–299.

Pedersen, F. (1982). Mother, father, and infant as an interactive system. In J. Belsky (Ed.), *In the beginning: Readings on infancy* (pp. 216–226). New York: Columbia University Press.

Powell, B., & Steelman, L. C. (1990). Beyond sibship size: Sibling density, sex composition, and educational outcomes. *Social Forces, 69,* 181–206.

Powell, B., & Steelman, L. C. (1993). The educational benefits of being spaced out: Sibship density and educational progress. *American Sociological Review, 58,* 367–381.

Scott, D. T. (1987). Premature infants in later childhood: Some recent follow-up results. *Seminars in Perinatology, 11,* 191–199.

Seitz, V., & Apfel, N. H. (1993). Adolescent mothers and repeated childbearing: Effects of a school-based intervention program. *American Journal of Orthopsychiatry, 63,* 572–581.

Seitz, V., & Apfel, N. H. (1994). Effects of a school for pregnant students on the incidence of low-birthweight deliveries. *Child Development, 65,* 666–676.

Seitz, V., Apfel, N. H., & Rosenbaum, L. K. (1991). Effects of an intervention program for pregnant adolescents: Educational outcomes at two years postpartum. *American Journal of Community Psychology, 6,* 911–930.

Sparrow, S. S., Balla, D. A., & Cicchetti, D. V. (1985). *Vineland Adaptive Behavior Scales.* Circle Pines, MN: American Guidance Service.

Strobino, D. M. (1987). The health and medical consequences of adolescent sexuality and pregnancy: A review of the literature. In S. L. Hofferth & C. D. Hayes (Eds.), *Risking the future: Adolescent sexuality, pregnancy, and childbearing* (Vol. 2, pp. 93–122). Washington, DC: National Academy Press.

Taylor, R. L. (1991). Poverty and adolescent black males: The subculture of disengagement. In P. B. Edelman & J. Ladner (Eds.), *Adolescence and poverty: Challenge for the 1990's* (pp. 139–162). Washington, DC: Center for National Policy Press.

Thorndike, R. L., Hagen, E. P., & Sattler, J. M. (1986). *Stanford-Binet Intelligence Scale* (4th ed.). Cambridge, MA: Riverside Publishing.

Tinsley, B. R., & Parke, R. D. (1984). Grandparents as support and socialization agents. In M. Lewis (Ed.), *Beyond the dyad* (pp. 161–194). New York: Plenum Press.

Werner, E. E., & Smith, R. S. (1982). *Vulnerable but invincible: A study of resilient children.* New York: McGraw-Hill.

Woodcock, R. W., & Johnson, M. B. (1989, 1990). *Woodcock-Johnson Psycho-Educational Battery – revised.* Allen, TX: DLM Teaching Resources.

Zigler, E. (1971). The retarded child as a whole person. In H. E. Adams & W. K. Boardman III (Eds.), *Advances in experimental clinical psychology* (Vol. 1, pp. 47–121). New York: Pergamon Press.

22   Environmental perspectives on adaptation during childhood and adolescence

Arnold J. Sameroff, Ronald Seifer, and W. Todd Bartko

The pursuit of happiness is a fundamental right in our society, yet the goal of achieving a sense of satisfaction with one's abilities and achievements is becoming increasingly elusive for large segments of the population. For example, over half of today's 10- to 17-year olds engage in two or more risk behaviors including unsafe sex, teenage pregnancy, drug or alcohol abuse, school failure, delinquency and crime and 10% of these youth engage in all of these risks (Dryfoos, 1991). The roots of these failures are frequently attributed to environmental factors that undermine achievement and mental health, yet efforts to alter these influences have not been generally successful for school-age children. Many have speculated that the long history of adversity that characterizes the lives of many of these children may have solidified problem behavior such that altering their fates is no longer easily accomplished (Zigler, Taussig, & Black, 1992). Zigler (1990) has long maintained that early intervention in the lives of children is the most effective solution for preventing later problem behavior. However, frequent demonstrations of fade-out effects of these programs (Zigler & Berman, 1983) have emphasized that it is not only the contemporary experiences of the child that have to be changed but the child's continuing experiences if a positive long-term outcome is expected. Therefore, attention must be paid to the multiple contexts that support development in the family, the school, and the community from infancy through adolescence.

Few studies have directly tested the premise that it is continuing environmental adversity that undermines development. Many studies have examined the stability of child characteristics over time but few have examined continuities of contextual risk. In a recent study Brooks-Gunn, Duncan, Klebanov, and Sealand, (1993), found the best predictor of competence during early childhood was not the current economic circumstance of the family but the number of previous years that the family had spent in poverty. We, too, have found long-term continuities in the effects of social risk on children which should serve to inform our understanding of what

Research reported here was supported by grants from the National Institute of Mental Health, the W. T. Grant Foundation, and the MacArthur Foundation Research Network on Successful Adolescent Development.

507

can and cannot be expected from environmental interventions during early child-hood.

Assessing environments

Despite the nominal interest of developmentalists in the effects of the environment, the analysis and assessment of context has fallen more in the domain of sociology than of developmental psychology (Clausen, 1968; Elder, 1984; Kohn & Schooler, 1983; Mayer & Jencks, 1989). The magnitude of a social ecological analysis involving multiple settings and multiple systems (Bronfenbrenner, 1979) has daunted researchers primarily trained to focus on individual behavioral processes. A further daunting factor has been the increasing necessity to use multicausal models to explain developmental phenomena (Sameroff, 1983).

To examine the effects of the environment on later mental health we began an investigation of the development of a group of children from the prenatal period through adolescence living in a socially heterogeneous set of family circumstances – the Rochester Longitudinal Study (RLS). The study was focused on the idea that having a parent with a psychiatric diagnosis of schizophrenia was a major risk factor for child development. As the study progressed, we had to modify this belief.

During the early childhood phase of the RLS (Sameroff, Seifer, & Zax, 1982), we assessed children and their families at birth, and then at 4, 12, 30, and 48 months of age both in the home and in the laboratory. At each age we evaluated two major indicators of developmental status, the child's cognitive and social-emotional competence. In our search for family risk factors that would adversely affect the children's growth we considered three major hypotheses: (1) that problem behavior would be related to a specific parental psychiatric diagnosis, for example, schizophrenia; (2) that problem behavior would be attributable to variables associated with parental mental illness in general, especially severity and chronicity of disorder, but no diagnosis in particular; and (3) that problem behavior in the children would be associated with other aspects of the family's condition, especially socioeconomic status (SES). Because many of the families had single parents we focused our assessments of characteristics of the mother. This approach was taken not because we believed that fathers were unimportant, but because there were too few available for participation in our study.

When we examined our data we found little support for the first hypothesis. There was no effect of the parents' specific psychiatric diagnosis on the behavior of their offspring during early childhood. The second hypothesis, that mental illness in general would produce substantial effects, was supported more strongly. General effects of the severity and chronicity of parental psychopathology were ubiquitous throughout the study. Our third hypothesis that differences in family socioeconomic circumstance would produce differences in child behavior was also strongly supported. The social status effects were apparent throughout the first 4 years of life. Children from the poorest families in our sample exhibited the poorest development. They had poorer obstetrical status, more difficult temperaments, and lower developmental test scores at 4 months, less responsivity during the home and laboratory observations at 12 months, and less adaptive behavior in the home and laboratory at 30 and 48 months of age. When the number of differences in child behavior was compared for the diagnostic, mental illness, and social status comparisons, family SES and parental factors of severity and chronicity of mental disturbance were more powerful risks than the specific psychiatric diagnoses we examined. Social status differences were the most frequent (Sameroff & Seifer, 1983).

At that point in our study we had discovered, on the one hand, if the only developmental risk for a child was a mother with schizophrenia, that child was doing fine. On the other hand, if the child had a mother who was schizophrenic, who was also poor, uneducated, without social supports, and with many stressful life events, that child was doing poorly. But, we also found that children whose mothers were poor, uneducated, without social supports, and with many stressful life events had bad outcomes, even if the mother did not have a psychiatric diagnosis. In the RLS social circumstance was a more powerful risk factor than any of the parental mental illness measures. What we learned was the overriding importance of attending to the context of the children in the study in order to understand their development. To better understand the role of SES, more differentiated views of environmental influences needed to be taken. We needed to analyze socioeconomic factors into variables that would have a more direct influence on the child. We had to discover what was different about the experience of children raised in different socioeconomic environments.

Environmental conditions as developmental risks

Although SES is the best single variable for predicting children's cognitive competence, and an important, if less powerful predictor of social-emotional functioning, we decided to add more psychological content to this sociological variable. SES operates at many levels of the ecology of children. It impacts on parenting, parental attitudes and beliefs, their family interactions, and many institutions in the surrounding community. From the data available in the RLS we searched for a set of variables that were related to economic circumstance but not the same as SES. The factors we chose homed in from distal variables such as the financial resources of the family, to intermediate variables like the mother's mental health, to proximal variables like the mother's here-and-now behavioral interaction with the child.

From the 4-year assessment of the children in the RLS, we chose a set of 10 environmental variables that were correlates of SES but not equivalents (Sameroff, Seifer, Barocas, Zax, & Greenspan, 1987). We then tested whether poor cognitive and social-emotional development in our preschool children was a function of the compounding of environmental risk factors found in low-SES groups. The definitions of the 10 environmental risk variables can be seen in Table 22.1: (1) a history

Table 22.1. *Summary of risk variables*

Risk variables	Low risk	High risk
Mental illness	0–1 psychiatric contact	More than 1 contact
Anxiety	75% least	25% most
Parental perspectives	75% highest	25% lowest
Spontaneous interaction	75% most	25% least
Education	High school	No high school
Occupation	Skilled	Semi- or unskilled
Minority status	No	Yes
Family support	Father present	Father absent
Stressful life events	75% fewest	25% most
Family size	1–3 children	4 or more children

Source: Sameroff, Seifer, Barocas, Zax, & Greenspan, 1987.

of maternal mental illness, (2) high maternal anxiety, (3) parental perspectives that reflected rigidity in the attitudes, beliefs, and values that mothers had in regard to their child's development, (4) few positive maternal interactions with the child observed during infancy, (5) minimal maternal education, (6) head of household in unskilled occupations, (7) disadvantaged minority status, (8) single parenthood, (9) stressful life events, and (10) large family size.

We found, indeed, that each of these variables was a risk factor. We compared the high-risk and low-risk group for each variable separately. For both the cognitive and mental health outcomes the low-risk group had higher scores than the high-risk group. Most of the differences were about one-half to two-thirds of a standard deviation, enough to demonstrate the effects for group comparisons but certainly not enough to detect which specific individuals with the risk factor would have an adverse outcome.

Although statistically significant differences in outcome are associated with single environmental risk factors, these differences rarely explain large proportions of outcome variance. In a much cited study, Rutter (1979) argued that it was not any particular risk factor but the number of risk factors in a child's background that led to psychiatric disorder. Psychiatric risk for a sample of 10-year-olds he studied rose from 2% in families with zero or one risk factors to 20% in families with four or more. The six risk factors considered included severe marital distress, low SES, large family size or overcrowding, paternal criminality, maternal psychiatric disorder, and admission of the child to foster care. In another study Williams, Anderson, McGee, & Silva (1990) related behavioral disorders in 11-year-olds to a cumulative disadvantage score based on number of residence and school changes, single parenthood, low SES, marital separation, young motherhood, low maternal cognitive ability, poor family relations, search for marriage guidance, and maternal mental health symptoms. The sample was divided into five groups with increasing

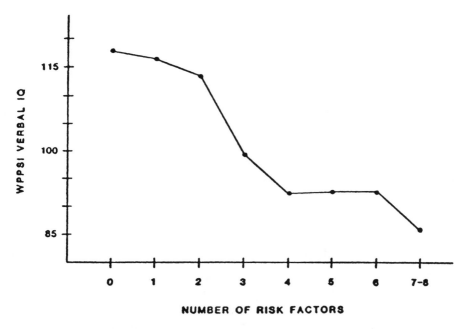

Figure 22.1. Effects of multiple risk scores on 4-year verbal IQ in Rochester Longitudinal Study (Sameroff, Seifer, Barocas, Zax, & Greenspan, 1987).

levels of risk and again a strong relation was found between disadvantage and child behavior score. For the children with less than two disadvantages only 7% had behavior problems, whereas for the children with eight or more disadvantages the rate was 40%.

Accumulating risk factors

In the RLS there were significant effects for the single risk factors, but it was clear that most children with only a single risk factor would not end up with a major developmental problem. But what would be the result if a comparison was made between children growing in environments with many risk factors compared to children with very few. We created a multiple risk score that was the total number of risks for each individual family. In the RLS the range was well distributed between scores of 0 and 8, with one family having as many as 9 risks. When these risk factors were related to the child's intelligence and mental health, major differences were found between those children with few risks and those with many. On an intelligence test children with no environmental risks scored more than 30 points higher than children with 8 or 9 risk factors as can be seen in Figure 22.1. On average, each risk factor reduced the child's IQ score by 4 points.

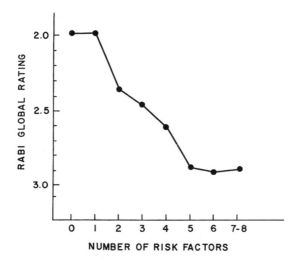

Figure 22.2. Effects of multiple risk scores on 4-year social-emotional competence in Rochester Longitudinal Study (Sameroff, Seifer, Zax, & Barocas, 1987).

The relation between the multiple risk scores and the social-emotional outcome can be seen in Figure 22.2. It is clear that the effect of combining the 10 risk variables was to accentuate strongly the differences noted for the individual scores described previously. As the number of risk factors increased, performance decreased for children at 4 years of age. For the social-emotional scores, the difference between the lowest and highest groups was about two standard deviations. Thus the combination of risk factors resulted in a nearly threefold increase in the magnitude of differences found among groups of children relative to the effect of single variables (Sameroff, Seifer, Zax, & Barocas, 1987).

These analyses of the RLS data were attempts to elaborate environmental risk factors by reducing global measures such as SES to component social and behavioral variables. We were able to identify a set of risk factors that were predominantly found in lower SES groups, but affected child outcomes in all social classes. Moreover, no single variable was determinant of outcome. Only in families with multiple risk factors was the child's competence placed in jeopardy.

We found that the multiple pressures of environmental context in terms of amount of stress from the environment, the family's resources for coping with that stress, the number of children who must share those resources, and the parents' flexibility in understanding and dealing with their children all play a role in the contemporary development of child intelligence test performance and mental health. However, the RLS sample was biased toward families where a parent had a psychiatric diagnosis. Would we find the same effects of multiple risks in a sample more representative of the general community?

The Philadelphia study

The opportunity to examine the effects of multiple environmental risks on child development was provided by data emerging from a study of adolescents in a large sample of Philadelphia families we have been studying under the auspices of the MacArthur Foundation (Furstenberg, Eccles, Elder, Cook, & Sameroff, in preparation). We interviewed mothers, fathers, and children in close to 500 families where there was a youth between the ages of 11 and 14. The sample varied widely in SES and the racial composition was about two-thirds African American and one-third white with a small percentage of Puerto Rican families.

Previous studies of multiple risk factors were important in demonstrating the power of such analyses but did not use an ecological model to identify domains of risk. Typically, there was a selection process in which the risks were chosen from the available measures already in the data set of the study. In the Philadelphia project we took a more conceptual approach in designing the project so that we had environmental measures at a series of ecological levels.

For our analyses of environmental risk we examined variables within systems that affected the adolescent, from those microsystems (Bronfenbrenner, 1979) in which the child was an active participant to those systems more distal to the child where any effect had to be mediated by more proximal variables. We made a distinction between the characteristics of systems that were theoretically independent of the child and those in which the child was an active participant. For example, the family system was subdivided into management processes, where it is difficult to determine if the behavior is influenced more by the parent or the child (e.g., discipline effectiveness), and structural variables like marital status and household density, which were relatively independent of the child.

The risk factors were divided into six groupings reflecting different ecological relationships to the adolescent (see Table 22.2). We selected 20 variables to serve as risk factors, twice as many as in the Rochester study. Our intention was to be able to have multiple factors in each of our six ecological levels. Family process was the first grouping and included variables in the family microsystem that were directly experienced by the child. These included support for autonomy, discipline effectiveness, parental involvement, and family climate. The second grouping was parent characteristics which included the mother's mental health, sense of efficacy, resourcefulness, and level of education. This group included variables that influenced the child but, generally speaking, were less influenced by the child. The third grouping was family structure that included the parents' marital status, and socioeconomic indicators of household crowding and receipt of welfare payments. The fourth grouping, family management of the community, comprised variables that characterized the family's management of its relation to the larger community as reflected in variables of institutional involvement, informal networks, social resources, and adjustments to economic pressure. The fifth grouping, peers, included indicators of another microsystem of the child, the extent to which the youth was

Table 22.2. *Significance tests of risk factors*

Domain	Psychological adjustment	Self-competence	Problem behavior	Activity involvement	Academic performance
Family process					
Support for autonomy	***	***	***	†	***
Discipline effectiveness	***	***	***		***
Parental investment	**		†	***	***
Family climate	***	**	*	***	**
Mothers' education/mental health					
Education				***	***
Efficacy	***	**	***		***
Resourcefulness	***				†
Mental health	***	*	†		**
Family structure/economy					
Marital status			***		***
Household crowding		*	***	†	***
Welfare receipt	**	***			***
Management of community					
Institutional involvement	***		***	***	***
Informal networks				**	***
Social resources	***			***	**
Economic adjustment			**		*
Peers					
Prosocial	*	**	*	***	***
Antisocial	**	***	***		***
Community					
Neighborhood SES				***	**
Neighborhood problems	***		**	*	**
School climate	***		***	*	***

*** $p < .001$.   ** $p < .01$.   * $p < .05$.   † $p < .10$.

associated with prosocial and antisocial peers. Community was the sixth grouping representing the ecological level most distal to the youth and the family. It included a census tract variable reflecting the average income and educational level of the neighborhood the family lived in, a parental report of the number of problems in the neighborhood, and the climate of the adolescent's school.

Adolescent competence

In the Philadelphia study we had a wider array of assessments available for interpreting developmental competence. The five outcomes were psychological adjustment of the adolescent as reported by the parent, self-competence and problem behavior as reported by the youth, activity involvement as reported by the parent and adolescent, and academic performance as reflected in grade reports reported by the parent and the adolescent.

Identifying risks

As in the RLS, once we had determined a representative list of potential risk factors at different levels of the child's ecology, we had to assess whether each of these variables was indeed a risk factor. We used two criteria for identifying each risk factor. The first was that the raw variable was correlated with one of our five outcome variables and the second was that adolescents in families that had the risk factor did significantly worse on at least one of the outcomes than adolescents in families without that environmental risk. For those variables that met the correlational criteria, we chose a cutoff score to optimize the difference between the outcomes for adolescents with the risk factor and those without. In general, the cutoff separated about 25% of the sample as a high-risk group from the remaining 75% defined as low risk. We then compared the groups using *t*-tests and the results of those comparisons are shown in Table 22.2.

The first important conclusion was that, indeed, we were successful in identifying risk factors. The results indicated that there were risks at every ecological level associated with child outcomes. It is not only the parent or the family that has an influence on child competence but the peer group, neighborhood, and community together with their interactions with the family that have an impact. Some of the variables were risks for each of our five outcomes. These included lack of support for autonomy, a negative family climate, and few prosocial peers. At the other extreme were variables that affected only a few outcomes such as having parents who lacked education and resourcefulness, single marital status and much economic adjustment, a lack of informal networks, and low census tract SES.

Many risk factors have been identified in previous research that used only a single adolescent outcome such as delinquency (Stouthamer-Loeber et al., 1993). To examine the generality of risk factors requires that there be multiple outcomes in the study. In the Philadelphia study we found that the pattern of relations between

Table 22.3. *Distribution of multiple-risk scores in Philadelphia study*

Number of risks	Frequency	Percent	Cumulative percent
0	1	0.2	0.2
1	24	4.9	5.1
2	47	9.6	14.7
3	67	13.7	28.4
4	68	13.9	42.3
5	78	16.0	58.3
6	51	10.4	68.7
7	47	9.6	78.3
8	41	8.4	86.7
9	18	3.7	90.4
10	14	2.9	93.3
11	21	4.3	97.5
12	9	1.8	99.4
13	3	0.6	100.0

ecological variables chosen as our risk factors and adolescent behavior was different for each outcome. On the one hand, academic performance, psychological adjustment, and problem behavior were related to risks at every ecological level. On the other hand, the correlates of self-competence and activity involvement presented two more limited and contrasting pictures. Activity involvement was strongly related to family management of the community and community characteristics, whereas self-competence was unrelated to either. In contrast, family structure played a significant role in adolescent self-competence but not in adolescent activity involvement.

As in the Rochester study, when the differences between high- and low-risk groups were examined for each individual risk factor, the effect sizes were small or moderate, rarely exceeding two-thirds of a standard deviation. But as in Rochester we could ask the question of what would be the consequence on adolescent competence if the youth experienced a number of these risk factors? Moreover, what would be the increase in predictive efficiency if we used a cumulative risk score as our predictor for adolescent success?

Multiple-risk scores

Multiple-environmental-risk scores were calculated for each adolescent. The resulting range was from a minimum of 0 to a maximum of 13 out of a possible 20 risk factors. Only one family had no risk factors. The distribution of risk factors can be seen in Table 22.3. The mode in our sample was 5 risk factors with 42% of families with fewer and 42% of families having more. For the multiple-risk analysis we wanted to have adequate sample size in each group so we combined

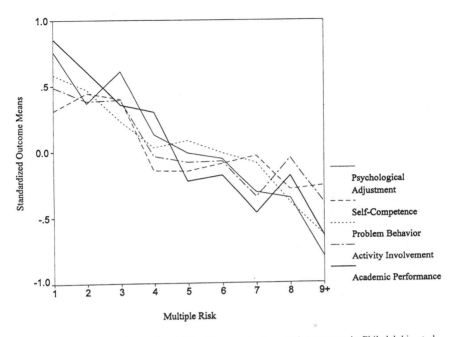

Figure 22.3. Relation of multiple risk score to five youth outcomes in Philadelphia study (Sameroff, Bartko, & Eccles, in preparation).

the single family with no risk factors with the 1-risk factor group and at the other extreme the 65 families with 9 or more risk factors into a single group. When the five normalized adolescent outcome scores were plotted against the number of risk factors, a very large decline in outcome was found with increasing risk.

As can be seen in Figure 22.3 the maximum effect of cumulative risk was on psychological adjustment and academic performance, with a difference of more than one and a half standard deviations between adolescents with only 1 risk factor compared to those with 9 or more. The smallest effects were for the youth's report of self-competence and activity involvement, where the difference was less than a standard deviation.

Protective factors

The concern with preventing developmental failures has often clouded the fact that the majority of children in every social class and ethnic group are not failures. They get jobs, have successful social relationships, and raise a new generation of children. The concern with the source of such success has fostered an increasing concern with the development of competence and the identification of protective factors (Garmezy, Masten, & Tellegen, 1984). However, the differentiation between risk and protective factors is far from clear (Seifer & Sameroff, 1987) and there continue to be many theoretical and methodological limitations in their identification (Luthar & Zigler, 1991).

Although some have argued that protective factors can only have meaning in the face of adversity (Rutter, 1987), in most cases protective factors appear to be simply the positive pole of risk factors (Stouthamer-Loeber et al., 1993). To test this simplification we created a set of protective factors by cutting each of our risk dimensions at the top quartile (Sameroff, Bartko, & Eccles, 1996). So, for example, where a negative family climate had been a risk factor, a positive family climate now became a protective factor, or where a parent's poor mental health was a risk factor, her good mental health became protective. We then summed these protective factors and examined their relation to our five outcomes. The results mirrored our analysis of the effects of multiple risks. There was a similar range of protective factors, from families with none to families with 15 out of a possible 20 and a similar relation to outcomes, families with many protective factors doing substantially better than from contexts with few protective factors. We went further and examined the combination of risk and protective factors and its effect on adolescent behavior. The question here is whether risk or protective factors are more predictive of child competence. For the youth in the Philadelphia sample there does not seem to be much difference. The more risk factors the worse the outcomes, the more protective factors the better the outcomes. In short, when taken as part of a constellation of environmental influences on child development, most contextual variables in the parents, the family, the neighborhood, and the culture at large seem to be dimensional, aiding in general child development at one end and inhibiting it at the other.

Odds ratio analysis

Whether our cumulative risk score meaningfully increases our predictive efficiency can be demonstrated by an odds ratio analyses. We could compare the odds of having a bad outcome in a high-risk versus a low-risk environment. For the typical analysis of relative and attributable risk, the outcome variable is usually discrete, succumbing to a disease or disorder. For our sample of early adolescents, there were few discrete negative outcomes. They were generally too young to have many pregnancies or arrests and the rate of academic failure was not particularly high. We had to create artificially bad outcomes by making cut scores in our outcome measures. We dichotomized each of the five outcomes by making a cut at the 25th percentile for worse performance. These were the 25% of adolescents who were doing the most poorly in terms of mental health, self-competence, problem behavior, activity involvement, or academic performance. To simplify the report we examined the relation between these bad outcomes and adolescent environmental risk scores subdivided into four multiple-risk groups: a low-risk group defined as 3 or less, two moderate-risk groups of 4–5 and 6–7 risks, and a high-risk group with 8 or more (see Figure 22.4).

The relative risk in the high-risk group for each of the bad outcomes was sub-

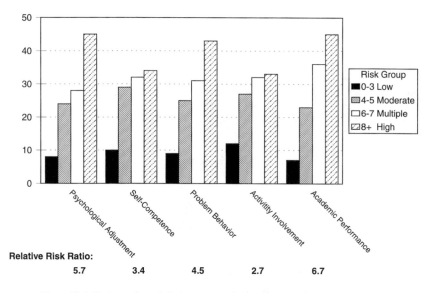

Figure 22.4. Percent of youth in lowest quartile for five youth outcomes in the Philadelphia study separated into four multiple risk groups. Odds are calculated as the ratio between percent of youth in the lowest quartile in the high-risk and low-risk groups (Sameroff, Bartko, & Eccles, in preparation).

stantially higher than in the low-risk group. The strongest effects were for academic performance, where the relative risk for a bad outcome increased from 7% in the low-risk group to 45% in the high-risk group, an odds ration of 6.7 to 1. The weakest effect was for activity involvement, where the relative risk only increased from 12% to 33%, an odds ratio of 2.7 to 1. In some sense this is not unexpected because where everyone would agree that academic failure and poor mental health are bad outcomes, there might be some dispute whether an adolescent's desire not to participate in the scouts, religious activities, or sports reflects a lack of competence. In any case, for the important cognitive and social-emotional outcomes of youth there seem to be powerful negative effects of the accumulation of environmental risk factors.

Group comparisons

A major concern of our study is to seek out interactions where different relations between variables would be found in different contexts. In terms of the effects of multiple-risk scores we examined whether the relation between environmental risks and adolescent outcomes were different for boys and girls, blacks and whites, or youth living in lower-income (< $20,000) versus higher-income (> $20,000) families. The effect of multiple-risk scores on adolescent behavior was robust across all of these comparisons. There were no interactions. The same correlations be-

Table 22.4. *Correlations between multiple-risk scores and outcomes in subgroups of adolescents*

Outcome	Girls	Boys	White	Black	Low income	High income
Psychological adjustment	.49	.40	.52	.39	.40	.47
Self-competence	.24	.19	.24	.22	.17	.22
Problem behavior	.30	.41	.38	.31	.32	.35
Activity involvement	.21	.26	.31	.22	.24	.21
Academic performance	.41	.45	.38	.43	.37	.40

tween risk scores and outcomes were found for boys and girls, blacks and whites, and adolescents living in lower-income and in higher-income families (Table 22.4). What this analysis tells us is that gender, race or ethnicity, and income level taken alone may have statistically significant effects on adolescent behavior, but that these differences pale in comparison with the accumulation of multiple negative influences that characterize our high-risk groups. The overlap in outcomes for boys versus girls, blacks versus whites, and low-income versus high-income families is substantial for any and all psychological outcomes, but the overlap is greatly reduced between groups of children reared in conditions of high versus low multiple risk, where gender, race, and income are only single factors. The important implication is that a focus on individual characteristics of individuals of families, such as whether their skin color is different, can never explain more than a tiny proportion of variance in behavioral development. To appreciate truly the determinants of competency requires attention being paid to a broad constellation of ecological factors in which these individuals and families are embedded.

Continuity of environmental risk

Studies like the RLS that have explored the effects of environmental risk factors on early development have shown major consequences for children living in multiproblem families. What are the long-term consequences of these early adverse circumstances? Will later conditions alter the course for such children or will early experiences lock children into pathways of deviance? To answer this question we must return to a consideration of data from the adolescent phase of the Rochester Longitudinal Study.

Within the RLS our attention has been devoted to the source of continuities and discontinuities in child performance. We completed a new assessment of the sample when the children were 13 and 18 years of age (Sameroff, Seifer, Baldwin, & Baldwin, 1993; Baldwin et al., 1993). Because of the potent effects of our multiple-risk index at 4 years, we calculated new multiple-environmental-risk scores for each family based on their situation 9 and 14 years later. To our surprise there were very few families that showed major shifts in the number of risk factors across the 9-year intervening period. Between 4 and 13 years the factor that showed the most improvement was maternal education where the number of mothers without a high school diploma or equivalent decreased from 33% to 22% of the sample. The risk factor that increased the most was single parenthood with the number of children being raised by their mothers alone increasing from 24% to 41%. In the main, however, there was little change in the environments of the children in our sample.

The typical statistic reported in longitudinal research is the correlation between early and later performance of the children. We too found such correlations. Intelligence at 4 years correlated .72 with intelligence at 13 years. The usual interpretation of such a number is that there is a continuity of competence or incompetence in the child. Such a conclusion cannot be challenged if the only assessments in the study are of the children. In the RLS we examined and were able to correlate environmental characteristics across time as well as child ones. We found a high correlation of .77 between environmental risk scores at the two ages that was as great or greater than any continuity within the child. Whatever the child's ability for achieving higher levels of competence, it was severely undermined by the continuing paucity of environmental support in high-risk contexts and fostered in low-risk contexts. Whatever the capabilities provided to the child by individual factors, the environment acted to limit or expand further opportunities for development.

Because of the very high stability in the number of risks experienced by these families it was impossible to determine if the effects of early adversity or contemporary risk were having the greater effect on the later behavior of the children. Those children who had been living in high risk environments at 4 years of age were still living in them at 13 years of age. Moreover, these contemporary high-risk contexts were producing the same negative effects on behavior as the earlier ones had done. In Figure 22.5 one can see the relation between the IQ outcome and low-, medium-, and high-risk scores at the three assessment ages. The curves overlap substantially with similar ranges of outcomes at each age. We found the same relationship between the number of risk factors and the child's intellectual competence; those children from families with no risk factors scored more than 30 points higher on intelligence tests than those with the most risk factors and had significantly better mental health.

Secular trends

The thrust of a contextual analysis of developmental regulation is not that individual factors in the child are nonexistent or irrelevant but that they must be studied in a context larger than the single child. The risk analyses discussed so far have implicated parent characteristics and the immediate social conditions of family support and life event stress as important moderators of healthy psychological growth in the child. To this list of risks must be added changes in the historical supports

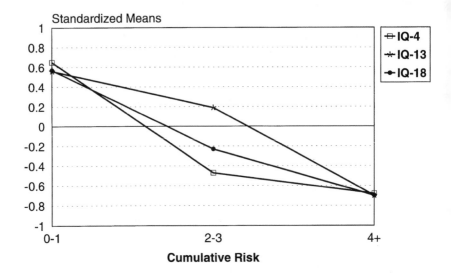

Figure 22.5. Relation of contemporary multiple-risk scores to child IQ at 4, 13, and 18 years of age.

for families in a given society. The importance of this added level of complexity was emphasized when we examined secular trends in the economic well-being of families in the United States.

At 4 years we had divided the sample into high-, medium-, and low-risk groups based on the number of cumulative risks: 0 or 1 in the low-risk group, 2 or 3 in the medium-risk group, and 4 or more in the high-risk group. We found that 22% of the high-risk group had IQs below 85 whereas none of the low-risk sample did. Conversely, 59% of the low-risk group had IQs above 115 but only 4% of the high-risk sample did.

After the 13-year assessment we made the same breakdown into high-, medium-, and low-risk groups and examined the distribution of IQs within risk groups. Again we found a preponderance of low IQ scores in the high-risk group and a preponderance of high IQ scores in the low-risk group indicating the continuing negative effects of an unfavorable environment. But, strikingly, the number of children in the high-risk group with IQs below 85 had increased from 22% to 46%, more than doubling. If our analysis was restricted to the level of the child and family, we would hypothesize that high-risk environments operate synergistically to worsen further the intellectual standing of these children during the period from preschool to adolescence, placing them in a downward spiral of increasing incompetence.

An alternative hypothesis was that society was changing during the 9 years between the RLS assessments. In a study completed by the House of Representatives Ways and Means Committee (Passel, 1989), it was found that between the years 1973 to 1987, during which time we were doing this study, the average household income of the poorest fifth of Americans fell 12% while the income of the richest fifth increased 24%. Elder (1974) has made a strong case for attending to major changes in society as determinants of the life course for growing children. His work centered on the great depression of the 1930s. Similar effects seem to be apparent in our own times.

Protective factors and the search for resiliency

When studies are successful in identifying protective factors, the issue is raised of identification on an individual basis of resilient (or protected) individuals. Ideally, one would like to identify a substantial subset of children who by any measure of competence were doing better than average, despite the adversity they faced in daily life. We selected a high-risk subsample of children who had four or more environmental risks to determine the characteristics of those who were doing better than expected. Only 3 of the 50 high-risk children were above the total sample mean on our 13-year child outcome measures; but all three had also improved in their risk status. They had been in the highest risk category at 4 years of age, but by 13 years were doing better. Thus, it is unclear whether the more favorable outcomes in these children were due to protective factors or to a lessening of risk.

When we examined the whole RLS sample to see what the consequences of moving from high (4 or more) to low (0 or 1) environmental risk or from low to high risk was for children in the study, we found striking effects. The group that changed from high risk at 4 years to low risk at 13 years improved in IQ by 13 points. In contrast the group that changed from low risk at 4 years to high risk at 13 years dropped in IQ by 15 points. These findings make a strong case for the powerful effects of environmental risks on the children. Unfortunately, such changes in number of risk factors are not common. We discussed the stability of risk factors from early childhood to adolescence. Only one child was in the group that went from high to low risk and there was only one child in the group that went from low to high risk. Stability rather than change appeared to be the rule.

Social and political agendas

What we have described here are the results of an academic agenda for understanding the effects of poverty on children. There are many who argue that children do poorly in conditions of poverty because they don't have individual characteristics that would promote resilience, overcome challenge, and eventuate in productive work and family life. By identifying characteristics of children who achieve despite adverse circumstances, some hope that we could instill those characteristics in other children to help them overcome environmental adversity. In contrast is the position that environmental risks are so pervasive that opportunities do not exist for positive development even if the child does have excellent coping skills.

In discussions about the consequences of environmental risk and methods for amelioration, a focus on resiliency can take the form of blaming the victims. If children show poor outcomes, it is because they weren't resilient. Clearly, if one believes it is the resiliency of the individual child that is the determining factor in their outcomes, then the intervention agenda will be different than if one believes it is social and familial risk factors that are more important.

The Holocaust was a major environmental event from which there were few survivors. If one were a scientist seeking methods to survive the Holocaust, a resilience strategy would be to determine the characteristics of those who survived and then instill those characteristics in the rest of the affected population. The stories of how these survivors overcame adversity usually is remarkable. If they weren't remarkable, there would not have been survival. One example is of someone who was in the last row of a group being shot and survived because the rest of the bodies fell on top of him. Other examples of survivors are individuals who worked for the Nazis to administer the rest of the concentration camp inmates. Do such survival stories provide lessons that could have been used to save a larger proportion of the victims of the Holocaust? A more fruitful strategy would have been to change the risk factors, to have prevented or eliminated the Holocaust.

Reducing risk

We have indicated that there are many environmental risk factors associated with poor developmental outcomes. These risk factors can be found in all socioeconomic strata but are most concentrated in areas of poverty. There may be social consequences of this research if changes can be made in the number of risk factors experienced by families. In the natural course of time in the sample we studied, there were few such changes. High-risk families remained high risk and low-risk families remained low risk.

These analyses of the effects of environmental risk on adolescent development have focused on the negative side of each variable. This was intentional in that we were trying to find a way to identify those youth who are likely to be the most troubled and truly in need of intervention services. However, just because we have identified a subset of troubled youth does not mean that we can successfully change their fates. As Zigler (1990) has noted, the fact that in these cases we can identify risk factors at multiple ecological levels may mean that interventions must be addressed to those multiple levels – changing family management strategies, improving maternal education and mental health, increasing family economic resources, enlarging family social support systems, insulating the youth from antisocial peers, and even improving the climate of the school, neighborhood, and community. Clearly this is an enormous enterprise requiring massive infusions of personnel and economic resources. A number of intervention programs have demonstrated some capacity for making changes in children's lives (Ramey & Ramey, 1992). The social and political agendas of our society will determine if the positive results of our research agenda will be extended to making differences in the lives of children living in conditions of risk.

References

Baldwin, A. L., Baldwin, C. P., Kasser, T., Zax, M., Sameroff, A., & Seifer, R. (1993). Contextual risk and resiliency during late adolescence. *Development and Psychopathology, 5,* 741–761.

Bronfenbrenner, U. (1979). *The ecology of human development.* Cambridge, MA: Harvard University Press.

Brooks-Gunn, J., Duncan, G. J., Klebanov, P. K., & Sealand, N., (1993). Do neighborhoods influence child and adolescent development? *American Journal of Sociology, 99,* 353–395.

Clausen, J. A. (1968). *Socialization and society.* Boston: Little, Brown.

Dryfoos, J. G. (1991). Adolescents at risk: A summation of work in the field: Programs and policies. *Journal of Adolescent Health, 12,* 630–637.

Elder, G. H., Jr. (1974). *Children of the Great Depression.* Chicago: University of Chicago Press.

Elder, G. H., Jr. (1984). Families, kin and the life course: A sociological perspective. In R. D. Parke (Ed.), *Review of child development research: The family* (Vol. 7). Chicago: University of Chicago Press.

Furstenberg, F. F., Jr., Eccles, J., Elder, G. H., Cook, T., & Sameroff, A. J. (in preparation). *Urban families and adolescent success.*

Garmezy, N. (1985). Stress-resistant children: The search for protective factors. In J. E. Stevenson (Ed.), *Recent research in developmental psychopathology* (pp. 213–233). Oxford: Pergamon Press.

Garmezy, N., Masten, A. S., & Tellegan, A. (1984). The study of stress and competence in children: A building block of developmental psychopathology. *Child Development, 55,* 97–111.

Kohn, M., & Schooler, C. (1983). *Work and personality: An inquiry into the impact of social stratification.* Norwood, NJ: Ablex.

Luthar, S. S., & Zigler, E. (1991). Vulnerability and competence: A review of research on resilience in childhood. *American Journal of Orthopsychiatry, 61,* 6–22.

Mayer, S. E., & Jencks, C. (1989). Growing up in poor neighborhoods: How much does it matter? *Science, 243,* 1441–1445.

Passell, P. (1989, July 16). Forces in society and Reaganism, helped by deep hole for poor. *New York Times,* pp. 1, 20.

Ramey, C. T., & Ramey, S. L. (1992). Effective early intervention. *Mental Retardation, 30,* 1–9.

Rutter, M. (1979). Protective factors in children's responses to stress and disadvantage. In M. W. Kent & J. E. Rolf (Eds.), *Primary prevention of psychopathology,* Vol. 3: *Social competence in children* (pp. 49–74). Hanover, NH: University Press of New England.

Rutter, M. (1987). Psychosocial resilience and protective mechanisms. *American Journal of Orthopsychiatry, 57:*316–331.

Rutter, M. (1991). Protective factors: Independent or interactive? (Letter to the editor). *Journal of the American Academy of Child and Adolescent Psychiatry, 30,* 151–152.

Sameroff, A. J. (1983). Developmental systems: Contexts and evolution. In W. Kessen (Ed.), *History, theories, and methods.* Volume 1 of P.H. Mussen (Ed.), *Handbook of child psychology* (pp. 237–294). New York: Wiley.

Sameroff, A. J., Bartko, W. T., & Eccles, J. (in preparation). Additive effects of ecological risk factors on adolescent competence.

Sameroff, A. J., & Chandler, M. J. (1975). Reproductive risk and the continuum of caretaking casualty. In F. D. Horowitz, M. Hetherington, S. Scarr-Salapatek, & G. Siegel (Eds.), *Review of child development research* (Vol. 4, pp. 187–244). Chicago: University of Chicago.

Sameroff, A. J., & Seifer, R. (1983). *Sources of continuity in parent-child relationships.* Paper presented at the meeting of the Society for Research in Child Development, Detroit.

Sameroff, A. J., Seifer, R., Baldwin, A., & Baldwin, C. (1993). Stability of intelligence from preschool to adolescence: The influence of social and family risk factors. *Child Development, 64,* 80–97.

Sameroff, A. J., Seifer, R., Barocas, R., Zax, M., & Greenspan, S. (1987). Intelligence quotient scores of 4-year-old children: Social environmental risk factors. *Pediatrics,* 79:343–350.

Sameroff, A. J., Seifer, R., & Zax, M. (1982). Early development of children at risk for emotional disorder. *Monographs of the Society for Research in Child Development,* 47 (Serial No. 199).

Sameroff, A. J., Seifer, R., Zax, M., & Barocas, R. (1987). Early indicators of developmental risk: The Rochester Longitudinal Study. *Schizophrenia Bulletin,* 13:383–393.

Seifer, R., & Sameroff, A. J. (1987). Multiple determinants of risk and vulnerability. In E. J. Anthony & B. J. Cohler (Eds.), *The invulnerable child* (pp. 51–69). New York: Guilford Press.

Seifer, R., Sameroff, A. J., Baldwin, C. P., & Baldwin, A. (1992). Child and family factors that ameliorate risk between 4 and 13 years of age. *Journal of the American Academy of Child Psychiatry, 31,* 893–903.

Stouthamer-Loeber, M., Loeber, R., Farrington, D. P., Zhang, Q., van Kammen, W., & Maguin, E. (1993). The double edge of protective and risk factors for delinquency: Interrelations and developmental patterns. *Development and Psychopathology, 5,* 683–701.

Williams, S., Anderson, J., McGee, R., & Silva, P. A. (1990). Risk factors for behavioral and emotional disorder in preadolescent children. *Journal of the American Academy of Child and Adolescent Psychiatry, 29,* 413–419.

Zigler, E. (1990). Preface. In S. J. Meisels & J. P. Shonkoff (Eds.), *Handbook of early childhood intervention* (pp. ix–xiv). New York: Cambridge University Press.

Zigler, E., & Berman, W. (1983). Discerning the future of early childhood intervention. *American Psychologist, 38,* 894–906.

Zigler, E., Taussig, C., & Black, K. (1992). Early childhood intervention: A promising preventative of juvenile delinquency. *American Psychologist, 47,* 997–1006.

23   The Rochester Child Resilience Project (RCRP): Facts found, lessons learned, future directions divined

Emory L. Cowen, William C. Work, and Peter A. Wyman

When, happily, we were invited to contribute to this volume we were asked to focus on the Rochester Child Resilience Project (RCRP) – a decade-long series of studies of young, highly stressed, urban inner-city children with stress-resilient (SR) and stress-affected (SA) outcomes. That suggestion made eminently good sense on several counts. First, this is an area in which Ed Zigler has long been involved and to which he has made major contributions (e.g., Luthar, Doernberger, & Zigler, 1993; Luthar & Zigler, 1991). Second, we too have been immersed in the area and expect that focus to continue prominently in our future research. And finally, resilience is a very important topic of inquiry in its own right – one that fits naturally into a developmental psychopathology (DP) framework. Indeed, the "hand-in-glove" nature of that fit is well illustrated in a recent, highly contributory special issue of *Development and Psychopathology* entitled: "Milestones in the Development of Resilience" (Cicchetti & Garmezy, 1993a).

Revisiting several definitional anchor points for the field of DP helps to clarify why the topic of resilience fits so well within its framework (Cicchetti & Garmezy, 1993b). At its core, DP applies developmental principles to the study of deviant and at-risk groups in seeking to illuminate developmental trajectories and outcomes (Cicchetti, 1989b). This approach assumes that knowledge of normal development can inform the study of deviant outcomes and conversely, that knowledge of deviant populations can enhance understanding of normal development (Cicchetti, 1984, 1989a). Moreover, given DP's interest in both expected and unexpected aspects of development, the phenomenon of child resilience, vivified by outcomes that run counter to base-rate expectancies, falls neatly within its purview.

To acknowledge, as we do, that DP offers one highly fruitful framework within which to study childhood resilience, however, falls short of saying that it is the only framework within which that topic can be gainfully examined. Thus, Masten (1989) noted that information about the wellsprings of outstanding coping among high-risk children was the stuff from which effective prevention steps could be

Our sincere gratitude to the W. T. Grant Foundation for its support of the research on which this chapter is based.

527

fashioned: "To understand and prevent maladaptation, we will do well to understand resilience in development; they are different parts of the same story" (1989, p. 290). Cowen, Wyman, Work, and Parker (1990) carried this point a step further by suggesting that the study of the nature of, and pathways to, child resilience was a potentially important aspect of developing a needed psychology of wellness. A wellness framework, though not at all inconsistent with DP's, has several different points of emphasis including a more central focus on adaptive outcomes; being more population, and before-the-fact-oriented; and being less driven by the concept of risk.

Thus, importantly in our view, the study of childhood resilience redirects attention from the focus on pathology that has long, and frustratingly, dominated the mental health fields, toward a prime focus on wellness (Cowen, 1994). Antonovsky (1979) coined the term "salutogenesis" to describe processes that subserve wellness outcomes. He proposed this term as an antonym to the older, more widely traveled concept of pathogenesis. His intent was to highlight processes that undergird healthy development rather than pathology.

Hence, even though it might make for more short-term solidarity were all contributions in this volume cast within an exclusive DP matrix, there may be heuristic value in calling attention to other (e.g., wellness-oriented) frameworks within which to consider the intriguing phenomenon of childhood resilience (Staudinger, Marsiske, & Baltes, 1993). Doing so is consistent with the axiom that genetic variation increases the likelihood of evolutionary success. In any case, because the RCRP was, in fact, cast and conducted in a prevention-wellness framework, signposts of that framework are evident in this chapter. This viewing lens, as noted, differs modestly in its core emphasis (i.e., a prime focus on wellness outcomes) from DP's.

Before getting to the nitty-gritty of the RCRP, however, a few words of history and a brief description of the soil in which our interest in resilience sprouted can help to clarify both our "angle of approach" to this topic and the specifics of the work we have done. In actual fact, our interest in resilience has deep roots. Since 1957, we have been actively involved in the development, evaluation, and dissemination of a program in early detection and prevention of school adjustment problems (Cowen et al., 1975). This program, known as the Primary Mental Health Project (PMHP), continues to grow and flourish (Cowen et al., 1996); it is now located in several thousand schools in 700+ school districts across the United States and in foreign countries.

Early in PMHP's unfolding it became clear, both from direct experience with the program and research findings, that school maladaptation was widespread, affecting roughly one of every three primary grade children (Cowen, Zax, Izzo, & Trost, 1966); and the presence of significant early school adjustment problems increased the likelihood of later adaptive problems, including school failure (Cowen, Pederson, Babigian, Izzo, & Trost, 1973). Later reports from task forces of two major presidential commissions on mental health confirmed those findings

(Glidewell & Swallow, 1969; Task Panel Report: Learning Failure and Unused Learning Potential, 1978).

One reason for concern about those stark findings was that virtually all of society's finite mental health resources were being concentrated on efforts to contain, or repair, things that had already gone seriously awry (Albee, 1959). That orientation still exists today. Given the vexing social and human problems that were fallout from that strategy (Zax & Cowen, 1972), we made a calculated decision to redirect our personal efforts toward developing what seemed to be a much needed, socially utilitarian, *do*-able approach, that is ontogenetically early secondary prevention. That way of thinking was PMHP's midwife; it reflects the core of what PMHP has been about over the years.

Although we saw this strategy as a constructive, pragmatic step forward, we realized early on that it was only "second best" conceptually (Cowen et al., 1975). Hence we remained continually attuned to the potential of more primary preventive ways, including efforts to build health, competence, and psychological wellness from the start. In that context, we were intrigued by early formulation of the concept of "invulnerability" and the case made for its place in a prevention framework (Garmezy, 1971; Garmezy & Nuechterlein, 1972).

The concept of invulnerability (a direct ancestor of the current term resilience), in spotlighting the fact that some children exposed to profound stress adjusted outstandingly well, offered one useful beacon to guide turnabout from mental health's classic mode of struggling to repair dysfunction, toward building for wellness. Such a shift in portfolio seemed, in the abstract, to be sensible, pragmatic, egalitarian, cost effective, and much needed.

The preceding way of thinking fueled the start of the RCRP. Two major resilience projects of the time were especially influential in shaping RCRP objectives and methods: Project Competence (Garmezy, Masten, & Tellegen, 1984; Garmezy & Tellegen, 1984) and the Kauai Longitudinal Study (Werner & Smith, 1982). Both these longitudinal projects remain active and productive today (Gest, Neeman, Hubbard, Masten, & Tellegen, 1993; Masten, 1989; Werner, 1993; Werner & Smith, 1992).

RCRP foci

The RCRP has been a slow, pebble-piling effort with both proximal and distal goals. Although we can report extensive findings bearing on the former, for the latter we can offer only a peculiar mix of early exploratory probes and ample fantasy. Within that framework, we first describe RCRP steps thus far taken and summarize some findings from that work.

The RCRP is a decade-old research project built around the concept of childhood resilience. As noted earlier, this concept has typically been defined by good adjustment in the face of exposure to major life stress (which, on base rate, increases risk for diverse maladaptive outcomes). Although that definition of resilience works well as an abstraction, there have been some differences in how the adjustment aspect of the definition has been construed. Whereas some have defined good adjustment as the *absence* of major psychological disorders (as, e.g., those described in DSM-IV), we have defined it more stringently to require *especially good* adaptation – not just the absence of evident maladaptation. That usage is consistent both with Werner and Smith's (1982) depiction of resilient children as those who "worked well, played well, loved well, and expected well" notwithstanding major life adversity, and our own prime focus on wellness outcomes.

Because growing up under conditions of major life stress increases the likelihood of maladaptation, the RCRP has focused on poor, young inner-city children, among whom base rates for such exposure are high. The project has studied two separate cohorts of inner-city children, each over several years – a sample of fourth-, fifth-, and sixth-graders and one of second- and third-graders.

Although some details of methodology and instrumentation differed in these two studies (e.g., test content and formats had to be fine-tuned to the developmental realities of younger children), their central research foci and the procedures used to identify target children were much the same. Both, for example, were organized around two key questions: What are the child test, and parent and child interview – correlates of resilient adaptations under major life stress? Which aspects of the child's developmental history, the parent–child relationship, and the family milieu in which the child grew up antecede SR and SA outcomes?

Concretely, the two studies used the same multistep selection procedure to identify children who comprised their main, contrasting target groups. To qualify for either group the child and his or her family had to have experienced four or more major stressful life events and circumstances (SLE-Cs) as reported by the parent at the time consent for participation was given. Most of these SLE-Cs reflected chronically stressful processes (e.g., child being involved in serious family arguments; sometimes having little food to eat; family known to Protective Services) rather than discrete events. The two study samples (SR and SA) had had roughly comparable histories of exposure to such stressors.

RCRP samples over the years have, on average, experienced eight to nine SLE-Cs. Beyond this stringent stress-exposure criterion, to qualify as SR a child had to have been judged to be in the top one-third or better on at least two of the three brief screening measures completed independently by the child's parent, current teacher, and prior year's teacher, and no worse than the middle one-third on the other. Conversely, to classify as SA the child had to score in the bottom one-third on the same screens, or at least on two of the three, and no better than the middle one-third on the other. Thus, although all selected SR and SA children shared the common risk factor of exposure to chronic and severe early life stress, the two groups were differentially characterized as well or poorly adjusted, based on the agreement of pertinent observers.

These preliminary judgments were confirmed by current teachers' in-depth adjustment ratings showing that SRs, as a group, were at least one-half SD above, and SAs one-half SD below, age and gender-appropriate norms for urban children on all problem behavior and competence subscales and sum scores, on the measure used (Hightower et al., 1986). Further testimony to the outstanding adjustment of SRs comes from the fact that they also significantly exceeded a demographically matched nonstressed (i.e., zero or one stressor) group on this same adjustment measure (Work, Cowen, Parker, & Wyman, 1990).

Two aspects of this subject selection procedure bear underscoring. First, SRs were not just children in whom no significant problems had been identified; rather, at the time of selection, they were adjusting much better than age and sociode-mographic peers according to the independent judgments of parents, and former and current teachers. Second, because *all* selected children had experienced major life stress, and the two criterion groups clearly represented different adjustment outcomes, the essential preconditions for studying correlates and antecedents of resilient outcomes appeared to have been met.

Although the two main RCRP studies shared the preceding common foci and procedures, they differed in several respects beyond developmentally necessary changes in test and interview formats. For one thing, there was a modest amount of Darwinian evolution, over time, in the procedures and instrumentation used. Thus, when battle-line experience identified measures or interview items that were inappropriate, or insensitive to group differences (i.e., nondiscriminating), they were dropped. Conversely, new materials were added in promising areas addressed only superficially on early rounds. Although this modification process somewhat reduced uniformity and comparability across studies, it added new dimensions and important shades of meaning to our inquiry in domains we had overlooked in the project's early stages.

Two other changes in the downward-extension study with second and third graders were more basic. First, in addition to the SR and SA groups, we included a high-stressed intermediate (HSI) adjustment group in the study design, hopefully to provide a more continuous adjustment distribution at Time 1 (T_1). We hoped that step would facilitate later study of stability and change in children's adjustment over time, and the mediating protective factors (i.e., initial status variables, intervening life events) that related to later ($T_2 \ldots T_n$) adjustment status. Second, whereas the initial RCRP study was done cross-sectionally (even though we were able to follow up some of these youngsters later), the new research was set up as a longitudinal study with a first reassessment scheduled 1½ to 2 years after the initial contact. That first follow-up step has been completed; some of its findings are reported later in the chapter.

The rest of the chapter describes how the two RCRP projects proceeded, their main findings, convergences and differences in these findings, and some speculation about future research directions to which these findings point. Given that most findings from the initial sample have already been published, that work is summarized only briefly here. The chapter's main focus is on the second study, and common threads that cut through both sets of findings.

The initial RCRP: Fourth-, fifth-, and sixth-graders

The format of the initial RCRP study was guided both by the then existing knowledge base about child resilience (Garmezy et al., 1984; Garmezy & Tellegen, 1984; Werner & Smith, 1982) and a miniconceptual model that we ourselves developed (Cowen & Work, 1988). These two input strands shaped the selection of an 11-measure child test battery that seemed, on conceptual and empirical grounds, to have potential for differentiating SRs and SAs. In that sense, the battery was intended to sharpen the nomological definitional net for the construct of child resilience, that is, to identify more specifically key correlates of what, to that point, had been called good adjustment globally.

The battery included measures of child self-rated adjustment, self-esteem, perceived competence, empathy, locus of control, realistic control attributions, coping styles, social problem-solving skills, anxiety, depression, and perceived social support. It was given in two 45-minute group sessions, separated by 3–6 weeks. Parker, Cowen, Work, and Wyman (1990) described these measures and provided a rationale for their selection. The battery was supplemented by a 1-hour individual child interview that included 28 open-ended and 144 objective questions. This interview, designed to explore domains in which test measures did not exist, was administered to 136 of the 147 tested SR and SA children in their home schools (Wyman et al., 1992).

In-depth interviews were also conducted with parents of 131 of these children (Wyman, Cowen, Work, & Parker, 1991). The parent interview included 35 open-ended and 244 objective items designed to probe child development and family milieu variables that might shed light on the antecedents of, and pathways to, child resilience under conditions of major life stress. The interview had eight main areas: demographic and family background information, achievement of early developmental milestones, the infancy period (ages 0–2), the preschool period (ages 2–5), the school-age period (ages 6–current), discipline practices, parent psychosocial resources, and parent views of the child's future. At the end, interviewers blind to the subject's group status provided ratings of the parent–child relationship, the parent as a person, and support available to the family, and judged whether the interviewee was the parent of an SR or SA child. The interview's nearly 300 scoreable responses were condensed into 25 "supercategories" that preserved distinctions across the interview's eight main content areas.

On child test measures (Cowen et al., 1992), SRs rated themselves as significantly better adjusted than SAs overall, and on specific factors such as school interest, social skills, and rule conformity. They scored higher on perceived scholastic and social competence, behavioral conduct, self-esteem, and global self-worth. They were less depressed, more empathic, and had both a more internal locus of control and more realistic control attributions. They also reported using more adaptive problem-solving strategies and coping skills, and said they had more support from mothers and friends. A discriminant function analysis (DFA) identified a set of five predictor variables that most sensitively differentiated the groups: global self-worth, empathy, realistic control attributions, social problem-solving skills, and self-esteem. Knowledge of children's status on these five variables correctly classified 84% of the group as SR or SA (Parker et al., 1990).

The preceding findings helped to establish a nomological net of defining variables that concretized the global notion of good adjustment used to select SR children in the study. Although that expanded definitional base is useful in several respects (e.g., identifying potential target domains for preventive interventions with young, highly stressed children), there is a parallel need to identify mechanisms and processes that operate to shape these protective qualities (Masten, 1989; Rutter, 1987) and the developmental pathways, including family milieu and interaction processes, that help them to flower. The parent interviews provided a starting point for exploring these significant issues. Salient findings from that aspect of the initial RCRP are summarized next.

Infancy period variables that predicted later SR outcomes included an easy temperament, early achievement of developmental milestones, the absence of prolonged separation of the infant and primary caregiver, and the availability of child-care support for the mother, both generally and specifically from a father figure. Sensitive preschool-age predictors of later SR outcomes again included easy temperament and, importantly, a sound parent–child relationship. In the school-age period, both the parent–child relationship and the caregiver's sense of parenting efficacy predicted SR status. Other variables that related to SR outcomes included authoritative, age-appropriate, and consistent parent discipline practices, optimistic parent views of the child's future, and parent "resources" – an amalgam of positive self-views, having support available, and overall life satisfaction (Wyman et al., 1991).

A related study analyzing the parent–child relationship at a more "micro" level (Gribble et al., 1993) underscored the central role of a sound parent–child relationship (i.e., warm caring interactions, involvement in common activities, and the use of sound discipline practices) as reported independently by parents and children, in the unfolding of SR outcomes among highly stressed children. Also, SR, compared with SA, parent–child dyads had more congruent perceptions of the parent–child relationship, and were more similar to each other in personal styles and expressive-motor behaviors (Cowen, Work, & Wyman, 1993).

A DFA based on the parent interview findings identified a set of seven variables that discriminated the two groups with maximal sensitivity and correctly classified 86% of the children as SR or SA: positive parent expectations for the child's future, fewer separations of child and primary caregiver in infancy, an easy child temperament, parent's use of age-appropriate, reasoned discipline, the involvement of a father figure in caretaking in infancy, overall child-care help in infancy, and consistent parental discipline. Findings from the parent interview thus underscored the crucial protective role that a parent–child relationship characterized by continuity, nurturance, and positive discipline played in favoring SR outcomes under stressful life conditions. Those findings spotlight the fact that the roots of child resilience in the face of ongoing stress go deep, and thus suggest that effective interventions designed to enhance resilience may need to start early and be family-based, as opposed to later, circumscribed one-shot interventions directed only (primarily) to the child.

This initial set of RCRP findings stimulated several other areas of inquiry. Although none of the latter strands is yet well developed, each bears brief mention. One exploratory study (Fagen, Cowen, Work, & Wyman, 1996) showed a modest relationship between parent–child relational variables, particularly parental warmth, and several child test indicators (e.g., self-rated adjustment, perceived competencies, locus of control). Documenting that type of relationship is a first step toward identifying pathways to resilient outcomes.

Second, although the initial RCRP was a cross-sectional study, we were able to follow up some subjects 2–3 years later. Wyman, Work, Kerley, et al. (1996) probed the extent to which six initial test measures predicted risk for drug and alcohol abuse, assessed when the children were sixth- through ninth-graders. High initial global self-worth and reading achievement predicted low risk for later substance abuse, and exposure to recent life stress predicted greater risk for alcohol and drug use. Another study (Wyman, Cowen, Work, & Kerley, 1993) found that positive expectations for the future, assessed in grades four through six, predicted enhanced socioemotional adjustment in school and a more internal locus of control 2–3 years later, and served as a protective factor in reducing the negative effects of high stress on self-rated competence. Although these two sets of follow-up findings do not reflect the full richness that a longitudinal framework can offer, they at least suggest that the adaptive status (SR vs. SA) of highly stressed urban children at ages 10–12 provides a meaningful baseline for predicting some important aspects of adolescent well-being at ages 13–15.

Another interest strand growing out of original RCRP involves exploratory steps taken to apply its findings in framing a pilot preventive intervention. A first tentative probe in this direction was built on prior identification of attributes that significantly differentiated SRs and SAs (Cowen et al., 1992). We realized that because those attributes form slowly over long time periods, a brief "child-alone" preventive intervention designed to promote them was not likely to produce enduring change at ages 10–11. Even so, we thought it pertinent to explore the utility of such an intervention both as an initial probe toward helping the many children who face serious adaptive problems because of exposure to major life stress, and to clarify how much gain might accrue from this type of time- and scope-limited intervention.

With those objectives in mind, we developed, conducted, and evaluated a pilot (12-session) school-based intervention designed to enhance resilience among highly stressed urban children in fourth and fifth grades (Cowen, Wyman, Work, & Iker, 1994). The curriculum was designed to strengthen the resources of at-risk children in several areas previously shown to be important in differentiating SRs from SAs, for example, understanding feelings in self and others, perspective taking, social problem solving, dealing with solvable and nonsolvable problems, and building self-esteem and a sense of efficacy. This time and goal-limited intervention did, in fact, yield minor, short-term improvements on teacher-rated measures of children's learning problems and task-orientation, as well as child self-ratings of perceived efficacy, anxiety, and realistic control attributions.

Those modestly encouraging findings were hardly definitive, because of the program's limited scope, and major shortcomings in the program evaluation study (e.g., small *n*, lack of a comparison group, no follow-up). Although there was nothing discouraging about the findings per se, both common sense and empirical data suggest that resilience-enhancing qualities in young children can best be promoted through wellness-oriented programs that start at an early age, when such qualities are significantly shaped; include a main focus on, and the active involvements of, primary caregivers; are continuous over time; introduce pertinent new elements as children mature; and provide opportunities to solidify competencies established earlier (Tolan & Guerra, 1994; Yoshikawa, 1994; Zigler, Taussig, & Black, 1992).

Resilience among second–third graders: Early findings from a longitudinal study

The second RCRP study downwardly extended the research to 7–8-year-olds within a longitudinal framework. Although important analyses from this second study remain to be done, and none of its findings have yet appeared in journal outlets, we have enough information to be able to preview those findings.

As noted earlier, this second study both added a highly stressed intermediate (HSI) adjustment group to the well-adjusted (SR) and poorly adjusted (SA) groups used in the prior study; and was set up longitudinally from the start, with a first follow-up 1½–2 years after the initial assessment. These two design modifications were intended to facilitate the study of changes in young, highly stressed children's adjustment over time and factors (e.g., intervening life events) that related to such change.

Several preparatory steps were taken before the study started. First, because it was to involve second- and third-graders, who are less evolved cognitively than fourth-, fifth-, and sixth-graders, test development work was done to determine which prior test measures could, or could not, be used and, among those that seemed usable, what modifications were needed to adapt them to 7–8-year-olds.

Based on developmental considerations, findings from the initial RCRP, and pilot testing, the initial 11-variable test battery reduced to eight measures. One of those (IQ) was new to this study. The other seven assessed self-rated adjustment, anxiety, empathy, social problem solving, realistic control attributions, self-efficacy, and perceived competence. The first two of those measures had had extensive prior use with 7–8-year-olds; the remaining five had to be modified. In making such changes we sought to preserve each measure's intended focus and meaning insofar as possible. Many of the changes were mechanical – for example, converting items to language and response formats that took into account a 7-year-old's cognitive realities. Thus, measures were shortened by eliminating complex and redundant items and by simplifying item wordings, test instructions, and response metrics.

The revised measures were piloted several times to increase the likelihood that they would be clear to 7–8-year-olds, yield acceptable distributions of scores, and be reasonably sound psychometrically. Even so, we recognized that the measures would be less than ideal and that the test responses of 7–8-year-olds would be less reliable or valid than those of 10–12-year-olds, due to item comprehension difficulties, briefer attention spans, and the cognitive limitations of young children in providing sensitive self-appraisals.

The parent interview, as noted, was changed by dropping prior insensitive items and adding questions in seemingly promising areas probed only superficially in the prior study (e.g., seeking more information about *parents*). The full parent interview took about 2¼ hours to administer. It was conducted face-to-face with parents of SR and SA children either at their homes or project headquarters, as the parent preferred. When appropriate, interviews were done in Spanish. HSI parents had an abbreviated (45-minute) phone interview, with about 40% of the questions from the full interview.

Subjects and procedures

Subjects were solicited in all second- and third-grade classes in 11 inner-city schools – 5 in Year 1 and 6 in Year 2. Overall, 2,043 parents were contacted to request permission for their child to participate in the study; 758 consented. This response rate (37.1%) was 5% higher than for the fourth through sixth grades. There were roughly equal numbers of boys and girls as well as second- and third-graders in a predominantly poor, inner-city sample, made up of 55% black, 27% white, 16% Hispanic, and 2% other (Asian American, Native American) children. Fewer than 30% of the children lived with both natural parents.

A group classification procedure similar to the one used in the original RCRP study identified target groups of 74 SAs, 85 SRs, and 115 HSIs, a total of 274 potential children in the combined Year 1 and 2 samples. These three groups did not differ significantly in terms of S-LECs experienced (M = 8.75), nor were they disproportional by gender, grade level, or ethnicity.

A verification analysis based on in-depth teacher ratings of children's current adjustment confirmed that SRs significantly exceeded HSIs and SAs, and HSIs, in turn, significantly exceeded SAs on all seven subscales and the two summary scales (i.e., problem total and competence total) of the Teacher–Child Rating Scale (T-CRS), a measure of young children's school adjustment (Hightower et al., 1986). Moreover, SRs averaged at least one-half SD above relevant age and gender norms for urban children, and SAs at least one-half SD below such norms, on all T-CRS subscale and total scale scores. These data simply confirmed that study children had experienced major life stress and that the intended adjustment differences among groups were present. Thus, the subject-defining conditions that were pre-requisite to comparing target groups on child test and parent interview variables had indeed been met in this new sample, as they had been in the prior RCRP study.

Criterion test measures

Testing was done in two 45-minute sessions. All children with parent permission completed Session 1, administered by project staff and trained assistants to small groups of 4–8 children in their home schools in fall and early winter each year. This session included five measures: child self-rated adjustment (CRS) (Hightower et al., 1987), perceived self-efficacy (Cowen et al., 1991), realistic control attributions (Wannon, 1990), the State-Trait Anxiety Scale for Children (STAIC; Spielberger, 1973), and an empathy scale (Bryant, 1982). Session 2, 3–8 weeks later, included three individually administered tests: social problem solving (Work, 1986), perceived competence (Harter, 1982), and WISC III Vocabulary and Block Design subtests (Wechsler, 1991), given in that order only to the selected SR, SA, and HSI subgroups and several alternates.

Test findings (Hoyt-Meyers et al., 1995) were similar in substance to those from the earlier study, though less robust, very likely because 7–8-year-olds are less reliable test takers and less self-aware (i.e., cognitively evolved) than 10–12-year-olds. Dilution notwithstanding, SRs still significantly exceeded SAs on self-rated adjustment (i.e., CRS total and its anxiety, follows rules, and social skills subscales, and perceived competencies in behavioral conduct, global self-worth, and physical appearance). SRs also exceeded SAs on empathy, social problem-solving skills, realistic control attributions, and IQ. A DFA identified a set of four variables that differentiated the two groups with maximal sensitivity and correctly classified 80% as SR or SA. The two strongest predictors were child self-rated rule compliance and IQ; the behavioral conduct and physical appearance scales of the perceived competence measure added sensitivity to the prediction. These data accord with Radke-Yarrow and Brown's (1993) findings that resilient children exceeded troubled peers on measures of IQ and school achievement, self-perceptions, and peer relationships.

Parent interview findings

The new parent interview had 10 sections, with a total of 261 objective and 18 open-ended items. The first 6 sections, (i.e., demographic and family background information, achievement of developmental milestones, overviews of the infancy, preschool- and school-age periods, and family discipline practices) were similar in format and content to the first 6 segments of the initial RCRP interview (Wyman et al., 1991). Section 7, called parent views, modified a similar section of the prior interview. It included nine objective items reflecting parent views of the child and expectations about his or her future, and a four-part open-ended item: "What do you think (your child's) life will be like ten years from now?" with specific domain probes about anticipated school and work careers, and interpersonal relationships.

The last several sections included new material. The first, based on Bavolek's (1984) child-rearing attitude scale, assessed three types of negative parenting attitudes (i.e., inappropriate expectancies, role reversal, and lack of empathy) and their sum. A second explored the caregiver's early history, including several open-ended questions about her childhood and its influence on her own child-rearing practices, plus 18 objective items assessing three dimensions of her environment when she was a child (i.e., neglect/indifference; aggression/hostility, and warmth/affection) and their sum (Rohner, Saavedra, & Granum, 1983). A third new area called "parent resources" included five sets of information. The first two were part of the initial parent interview. One, "life satisfaction," had 7 objective items describing specific facets of the parent's life (e.g., health, mood, efficacy as a parent). A second 7-item objective scale inquired about the parent's felt support from several sources (e.g., family, friends, community). The third was Rosenberg's (1965) 10-item self esteem scale, and the fourth a 5-item measure adapted from Berwick et al. (1991), assessing the parent's view of key facets of her own mental health status (e.g., happy, nervous, down in the dumps) during the past year. The last measure in the cluster was a set of self-descriptive semantic-differential ratings (Osgood, Suci, & Tannenbaum, 1957) based on 16 scales, each anchored by polar-opposite adjectival descriptors (e.g., strong–weak, happy–sad, tense–relaxed). This measure had also been used in the earlier RCRP study (Wyman et al., 1991). A sum score was derived for these five resource categories.

The interview's several hundred scoreable raw responses were reduced to 10 main clusters – the 9 described plus interviewer (blind) ratings of parents (Wyman, Cowen, et al., 1996). The SR and SA parent groups were first compared on the 10 overall clusters and, when appropriate, on their component variables. Significant differences favoring SRs were found on 8 of the 10 clusters. Thus, SR parents reported that their children achieved basic developmental milestones (motor and language) sooner than SA children. SRs were described as having had easier temperaments than SAs in the infancy and preschool periods. More positive parent–child relationships were reported for SRs in both the preschool- and school-age periods. SR parents tended to use sounder discipline approaches than SA parents in three concrete discipline situations and their discipline was more consistent. They significantly exceeded SA parents on both components of the parent-views cluster, that is, objective items reflecting the parent's perceptions of the child and his or her future, and the four-part open-ended item assessing the parent's future expectations for the child.

SR parents also exceeded SAs in three specific resource areas (i.e., global mental health in the past year, perceived support, and semantic differential self-ratings) and in overall resources. They had significantly less negative child-rearing attitudes on the parenting attitude scales of inappropriate expectations, lack of empathy, and role reversal, and their sum. Only one subscale of the caregiver developmental history cluster (influence of one's own childhood on caregiving practices) significantly favored SR over SA parents. Postinterview ratings favored SR over SA parents both on the judged quality of the parent–child relationship and positiveness of the interviewer's ratings of the parent. Interviewers correctly classified 80% of the sample as SR or SA.

A DFA based on sensitive univariate differentiators identified a set of seven parent interview variables that correctly classified 75.2% of the children as SR or SA: parent views of the child, the open-ended estimate of the child's future, sum of the caregiver's negative attitudes, own childhood influences on caregiving practices, parent discipline style, parent–child relationship (preschool period), and child temperament (infancy). The first three of those variables were stronger contributors to the overall DFA than the last four.

These interview data thus showed clear, consistent differences between SR and SA parents, highlighting the importance of the parent–child relationship, child-rearing attitudes and practices, discipline strategies, and the parent's own competencies and resources as factors that favor SR outcomes among children who grow up under major life stress. This cluster overlaps with the construct of "emotionally responsive parenting" that Egeland, Carlin, and Sroufe (1993) found to facilitate resilient adaptations among profoundly stressed children.

Beyond the preceding "bread-and-butter" analyses, several other analyses of clinical or theoretical interest were done. Hierarchical regression analyses using four key aspects of the child's caregiving environment – the primary caregiver's attachment history, personal resources (e.g., education, mental health), relationship with the child (e.g., discipline, involvement), and parenting attitudes (e.g., inappropriate expectations, lack of empathy) – were used to test a theoretical model predicting that the effects of caregiver attachment history and resources on children's school adjustment and IQ are mediated by parenting attitudes and the parent–child relationship (Wyman, Work, Cowen, & Kim 1996). Findings from these analyses lend support to a mediational model and highlight the importance of proximal parent variables, such as attitudes, in predicting children's development. Specifically, positive parent attitudes accounted for 32% of the variance in children's IQ, and 11% to 14% in teacher-rated classroom adjustment. The study findings also underscored the complexity of the relationship between the parent's own childhood experiences and her child's development. Indeed, many parents with histories of harsh abusive parenting had children who were developing very well.

We have also conducted several exploratory analyses comparing demographically matched, highly stressed, black and white inner-city children on numbers and type of life stressors experienced; frequency of classification as SRs and SAs; "within-race" comparisons of test variables that differentiate SRs and SAs; and interview responses that differentiate their parents. Ultimately we hope to examine relationships between parent interview and child test and adjustment variables within groups, and to compare these relationships across groups in seeking to identify pathways to resilient outcomes under stress that are similar or different for different racial groups. Also planned are studies to identify antecedents and precursors of longer-term (e.g., in adolescence) maladaptive outcomes such as aggression and violence, delinquency and criminal behavior, substance abuse, and teenage pregnancy.

The informative RCRP findings thus far reported point to several structural conclusions not yet highlighted. One, quite obvious in our view, is that childhood resilience is a fertile, socially utilitarian study area that can contribute richly to the vistas and future directions of both a psychology of wellness and developmental psychopathology. Our experience also suggests that the more one learns about the intriguing and challenging phenomenon of childhood resilience, the clearer do needed next steps and challenges become. In this vein, Masten, Best, & Garmezy (1990) recently made a strong case for shifting the focus of resilience research from "what" (descriptive) questions to "how" questions, designed to identify key underlying mechanisms and processes.

Initial longitudinal assessment

As noted already, the RCRP study of second- and third-graders was set in a longitudinal framework with a first reassessment (T_2) scheduled after 1½–2 years. The goals of the T_2 reassessment were to explore stability and change over time in child adjustment and test performance, and parent interview responses; to assess intervening (T_1–T_2) child and family stressors, as well as positive changes in the family situation; and to use combinations of initial child and parent variables, plus intervening life-change indicators, to test the relative sensitivity of several theoretical models in explaining adjustment change among highly stressed urban children over a 2-year period. Although a number of analyses bearing on these issues remain to be done, we can report several findings that have emerged from the initial longitudinal assessment.

The maximal potential n for the initial follow-up was 199 families – all those with complete T_1 child testing and parent interview data. Because these families were highly mobile, it took considerable effort to locate many of them at follow-up. One index of this mobility is the fact that study children, who had initially come from 11 inner-city schools had, within 1½–2 years, scattered to 35 local area schools as well as several distant places (e.g., Michigan, Long Island). After an extensive and persistent search, 183 families consented to participate in the follow-up. Most of the 16 nonconsenting families were "nonlocatables"; only three families in that group declined to participate. Of the pool of 183 consenting families, we were able to interview 181 parents – 65 SRs, 44 SAs, 72 HSIs, based on the T_1 classification – and test 179 children.

Child test data

Five tests given at T_1 were readministered at T_2: self-rated adjustment (CRS); empathy, realistic control attributions, perceived competence, and social problem solving. At T_2, parents and teachers provided ratings of children's current school adjustment on the same measures used at T_1. On most of these measures, SRs continued to exceed SAs 2 years later; indeed the group differentiators were generally sharper at T_2 than they had been at T_1. Specifically, on test measures, SRs exceeded SAs in overall adjustment and competence, as well as on specific CRS subscales assessing ability to follow rules and peer social skills, and perceived competence subscales assessing behavioral conduct and global self-worth. Similar group differences favoring SRs were found on the empathy, social problem solving, and realistic control measures.

Uniformly on the P-CRS total and all its subscales, SR parents rated their children as significantly better adjusted than SA parents at T_2. The same was true for teacher ratings on all seven T-CRS problem and competence subscales and its two summary scores, problem total and competence total. The importance of this latter finding lies in the fact that teacher-raters at T_2 were simply rating children in general, that is, they had no knowledge of children's initial group assignment status, or even that such a thing existed. Also noteworthy is the fact that the intermediate adjustment position of HSI children (i.e., between SRs and SAs) was even more clearly crystallized at T_2 than it had been at T_1.

A DFA based on the five child test measures used both at T_1 and T_2 identified a set of four predictor variables that most sensitively discriminated SRs and SAs at T_2. These four variables – CRS rule conformity, perceived self-worth, fewer poor SPS solutions, and the controllable scale of the realistic control measure – correctly classified 75% of the children as SR or SA. When parent and teacher ratings of child adjustment were added to the DFA, classification accuracy increased to 88.5%.

Relevant to the study questions posed here, the findings cited relate most closely to the issue of the stability of the (SR vs. SA) classification system. This issue was also probed by correlating T_1 and T_2 scores on all 19 child test measures (i.e., subscale scores) and the 16 parent and teacher ratings of child adjustment that were used in the same format for both evaluation points. The median T_1–T_2 correlation for the child measures, constrained by several weak alphas at T_1, was .35; the comparable figure for the adult ratings of child adjustment was .46 notwithstanding the fact that there was *no* overlap in teacher raters from T_1 to T_2. Thus, child test scores and adult ratings of children's adjustment showed modest stability over the 2-year interval between T_1 and T_2.

Follow-up parent interviews

The T_2 parent interview included many questions from the T_1 interview; it also added questions that were not part of that interview. Questions about the child's early development (e.g., developmental milestones, infancy period, preschool period) explored at T_1 were not repeated at T_2. Repeated interview segments included items assessing sense of efficacy as a parent, sources of support available, activities with the child, parent discipline practices, and a parent resources section that assessed life-satisfaction, felt support, self-concept, and global mental health status, all now focused on the T_1–T_2 time interval. Parents also provided a current set of child adjustment ratings, and interviewers did the same postinterview ratings that were used at T_1.

New T_2 interview segments included: (a) 8 objective items reflecting behaviors thought to predict later delinquency (e.g., fighting, theft, lying, truancy), which the parent answered yes or no and, for yes responses, estimated frequency of occurrence; (b) 13 objective items and one global estimate, reflecting changes in the family's situation (family relationships, financial status, living conditions, neighborhood violence) during the T_1–T_2 interval; (c) a 10-item, objective measure of positive and negative parent coping styles derived from Moos (1992); and (d) an expanded 9-item objective measure of the parent's expectations for key aspects of the child's future (e.g., having friends who care about him or her, staying out of trouble, finishing school).

The following main findings have so far emerged from the T_2 interviews. SR parents exceeded SAs on the parent–child relational cluster, including caregiver's self-rated efficacy and judgments of the quality of the parent–child relationship. They also exceeded SAs on caregiver resources and its component scales assessing support received, self-esteem, and global mental health, and interviewer rating clusters assessing the positiveness of the parent–child and parent–interviewer relationships.

On the new T_2 interview items, although the two groups did not differ on the 13-item intervening life-change measure, SR parents tended ($p < .06$) to judge their lives during this period more positively than SAs. They also reported significantly fewer predelinquent behaviors in their children, used more adaptive coping strategies, and had more positive expectations for their children's future.

A DFA identified four predictors that sensitively differentiated the two parent groups: positive expectations for the child's future; absence of predelinquency indicators; parent use of effective coping strategies; and parent's global mental health for the past year. Collectively, these four variables correctly identified 78% of the children as having been SRs or SAs 2 years earlier. Also, for 17 variables in common to two interviews, the median T_1–T_2 correlation was .53. These *r*s which ranged up to .7, suggested that parent responses across this 2-year time interval were reasonably stable.

Summary and implications

The following main conclusions have so far emerged from the second RCRP study exploring correlates and antecedents of resilient outcomes among highly stressed, inner-city children in the second and third grades:

1. Child test correlates of SR and SA outcomes in this study were similar to those found earlier to differentiate SRs and SAs in the fourth, fifth, and sixth grades (Cowen et al., 1992). The new findings, however, were less robust than the prior ones, probably because younger children are less clearly crystallized developmentally, and their test responses are less sensitive and reliable.

2. Parent interviews also identified variables similar to those found to discriminate SRs from SAs in the prior study (Wyman et al., 1991), for example, a sound parent–child relationship, sense of efficacy as a parent, positive expectations about the child's future, and the parent's own sense of well-being.

3. Follow-up, 1½ to 2 years later, showed the T_1 findings to be moderately stable. Thus, children classified as SR and SA at T_1 showed much the same pattern of differences at T_2 on test measures and parent and teacher ratings of child adjustment. Also, the configuration of interview differentiators that had favored SR over SA parents at T_1 remained reasonably constant at T_2.

4. However, several new parent interview indicators that surfaced at T_2 contributed importantly to group discrimination at that time. The combination of variables at T_2 that most sensitively discriminated children classified as SR or SA at T_1 included positive future expectations for the child, absence of reported predelinquent behaviors in the child, positive caregiver's mental health during the T_1–T_2 interval, and caregiver's use of adaptive coping strategies.

In final overview, RCRP findings highlight child test and parent interview indicators that differentiate young urban children who evidence effective versus ineffective adaptation under stressful life conditions. These findings are important in their own right, for their stimulus value in framing preventive interventions for highly stressed children, and for the contribution they can make to the development of a richer psychology of wellness. They also point toward logical next research steps. Based on clearer understandings established of the correlates and antecedents of resilient outcomes among highly stressed urban children, a next challenge is to identify pathways that operate to form the protective qualities that help some children to cope and adjust well in the face of chronic and dire life stress, while other comparably exposed youngsters falter and fall (Masten et al., 1990; Rutter, 1987). Knowledge of such pathways can provide further building blocks for informed preventive intervention designed to strengthen the adaptive potential of many highly stressed children in modern society, otherwise likely to experience major adaptive problems.

RCRP findings to date also suggest that the most effective resilience enhancing (i.e., preventive) interventions will be those that are launched early; are directed to family units, including particularly primary caregivers whose own effectiveness operates compellingly to shape the adaptation of young children; and include continuing inputs and "booster shots" as children's later development and maturity permit. With respect to the first two of those proposed emphases, recent evidence points strongly to the preventive advantages that effective early comprehensive programs can offer (Tolan & Guerra, 1994; Yoshikawa, 1994; Zigler, Taussig, & Black, 1992).

The study of childhood resilience is of central importance both to developmental psychopathology and emergent thrusts in prevention and wellness enhancement (Cowen, 1994). Indeed, one is hard-pressed to think of domains that hold as much potential as resilience for fusing significant basic research with practical applications that can bring major benefits to children and, ultimately, to society at large.

References

Albee, G. W. (1959). *Mental health manpower trends.* New York: Basic Books.

Antonovsky, A. (1979). *Health, stress and coping.* San Francisco: Jossey-Bass.

Bavolek, S. J. (1984). *Handbook for the Adult-Adolescent Parenting Inventory.* Eau Claire, WI: Family Development Resources.

Berwick, D. M., Murphy, J. M., Goldman, P. A., Ware, J. E., Barsky, A. J., & Weinstein, M. C. (1991). Performance of a five-item mental health screening test. *Medical Care, 29,* 169–176.

Bryant, B. K. (1982). An index of empathy for children and adolescents. *Child Development, 53,* 413–426.

Cicchetti, D. (1984). The emergence of developmental psychopathology. *Child Development, 55,* 1–7.

Cicchetti, D. (1989a). Developmental psychopathology: Past, present, and future. In D. Cicchetti (Ed.), *Rochester symposium on developmental psychopathology* (Vol. 1, pp. 1–12). Hillsdale, NJ: Erlbaum.

Cicchetti, D. (1989b). Developmental psychopathology: Some thoughts on its evolution. *Development and Psychopathology, 1,* 1–4.

Cicchetti, D., & Garmezy, N. (Eds.). (1993a). Milestones in the development of resilience. *Development and Psychopathology, 5,* 497–783.

Cicchetti, D., & Garmezy, N. (1993b). Prospects and promises in the study of resilience. *Development and Psychopathology, 5,* 497–502.

Cowen, E. L. (1994). The enhancement of psychological wellness: Challenges and opportunities. *American Journal of Community Psychology, 22,* 149–179.

Cowen, E. L., Hightower, A. D., Pedro-Carroll, J. L., Work, W. C., Wyman, P. A., & Haffey, W. G. (1996). *School-based prevention for children at risk: The Primary Natal Health Project.* Washington, DC: American Psychological Association.

Cowen, E. L., Pedersen, A., Babigian, H., Izzo, L. D., & Trost, M. A. (1973). Long-term follow-up of early detected vulnerable children. *Journal of Consulting and Clinical Psychology, 2,* 438–446.

Cowen, E. L., Trost, M. A., Lorion, R. P., Dorr, D., Izzo, L. D., & Isaacson, R. V. (1975). *New ways in school mental health: Early detection and prevention of school maladapation.* New York: Human Sciences Press.

Cowen, E. L., & Work, W. C. (1988). Resilient children, psychological wellness and primary prevention. *American Journal of Community Psychology, 16,* 591–607.

Cowen, E. L., Work, W. C., Hightower, A. D., Wyman, P. A., Parker, G. R., & Lotyczewski, B. S. (1991). Toward the development of a measure of perceived self-efficacy in children. *Journal of Clinical Child Psychology, 20,* 169–178.

Cowen, E. L., Work, W. C., & Wyman, P. A. (1993). Similarity of parent and child self-views in stress affected and stress resilient urban families. *Acta Paedopsychiatrica, 55,* 193–197.

Cowen, E. L., Work, W. C., Wyman, P. A., Parker, G. R., Wannon, M., & Gribble, P. A. (1992). Test comparisons among stress-affected, stress resilient and non-classified 4th–6th grade urban children. *Journal of Community Psychology, 20,* 200–214.

Cowen, E. L., Wyman, P. A., Work, W. C., & Iker, M. R. (1994). A preventive intervention for enhancing resilience among young highly stressed urban children. *Journal of Primary Prevention, 15,* 247–260.

Cowen, E. L., Wyman, P. A., Work, W. C., & Parker, G. R. (1990). The Rochester Child Resilience Project (RCRP): Overview and summary of first year findings. *Development and Psychopathology, 2,* 193–212.

Cowen, E. L., Zax, M., Izzo, L. D., & Trost, M. A. (1966). Prevention of emotional disorders in the school setting: A further investigation. *Journal of Consulting Psychology, 30,* 381–387.

Egeland, B., Carlson, E., & Sroufe, L. A. (1993). Resilience as process. *Development and Psychopathology, 5,* 517–528.

Fagen, D. B., Cowen, E. L., Wyman, P. A., & Work, W. C. (1996). Relationships between parent-child relational variables and child test variables in highly stressed urban children. *Child Study Journal, 2,* 87–108.

Garmezy, N. (1971). Vulnerability research and the issue of primary prevention. *American Journal of Orthopsychiatry, 41,* 101–116.

Garmezy, N. (1983). Stressors of childhood. In N. Garmezy & M. Rutter (Eds.), *Stress, coping and development in children* (pp. 43–84). New York: McGraw-Hill.

Garmezy, N., Masten, A. S., & Tellegen, A. (1984). Studies of stress-resistant children: A building block for developmental psychopathology. *Child Development, 55,* 97–111.

Garmezy, N., & Nuechterlein, H. (1972). Invulnerable children: The fact and fiction of competence and disadvantage. *American Journal of Orthopsychiatry, 42,* 328–329.

Garmezy, N., & Tellegen, A. (1984). Studies of stress-resistant children: Methods, variables and preliminary findings. In F. Morrison, C. Ford, & D. Keating (Eds.), *Advances in applied developmental psychology* (Vol. 1, pp. 1–52). New York: Academic.

Gest, S. D., Neeman, J., Hubbard, J. J., Masten, A. S., & Tellegen, A (1993). Parenting quality, adversity and conduct problems in adolescence: Testing process oriented models of resilience. *Development and Psychopathology, 5,* 663–682.

Glidewell, J. C., & Swallow, C. S. (1969). *The prevalence of maladjustment in elementary schools: Report prepared for the Joint Commission on the Mental Health of Children.* Chicago: University of Chicago Press.

Gribble, P. A., Cowen, E. L., Wyman, P. A., Work, W. C., Wannon, M., & Raoof, A. (1993). Parent and child views of the parent-child relationship and resilient outcomes among urban children. *Journal of Child Psychology and Psychiatry, 34,* 507–519.

Harter, S. (1982). The Perceived Competence Scale for Children. *Child Development, 53,* 87–97.

Hightower, A. D., Cowen, E. L., Spinell A. P., Lotyczewski, B. S., Guare, J. C., Rohrbeck, C. A., & Brown, L. P. (1987). The Child Rating Scale: The development and psychometric refinement of a socioemotional self-rating scale for young school children. *School Psychology Review, 16,* 239–255.

Hightower, A. D., Work, W. C., Cowen, E. L., Lotyczewski, B. S., Spinell, A. P., Guare, J. C., & Rohrbeck, C. A. (1986). The Teacher-Child Rating Scale: A brief objective measure of elementary children's school problem behaviors and competencies. *School Psychology Review, 15,* 393–409.

Hoyt-Meyers, L. A., Cowen, E. L., Work, W. C., Wyman, P. A., Magnus, K., Fagen, D. B., & Lotyczewski, B. S. (1995). Test correlates of resilient outcomes among highly stressed 2nd–3rd grade urban children. *Journal of Community Psychology, 23,* 326–338.

Luthar, S. S., Doernberger, C. H., & Zigler, E. (1993). Resilience is not a unidimensional construct: Insights from a prospective study of inner-city adolescents. *Development and Psychopathology, 5,* 703–718.

Luthar, S. S., & Zigler, E. (1991). Vulnerability and competence: A review of research on resilience in childhood. *American Journal of Orthopsychiatry, 61,* 6–22.

Masten, A. S. (1989). Resilience in development: Implications of the study of successful adaptation for developmental psychopathology. In D. Cicchetti (Ed.), *Rochester symposium on developmental psychopathology* (Vol. 1, pp. 261–294). Hillsdale, NJ: Erlbaum.

Masten, A. S., Best, K. M., & Garmezy, N. (1990). Resilience development: Contributions from the study of children who overcame adversity. *Development and Psychopathology, 2*, 425–444.

Moos, R. H. (1992). *Coping Responses Inventory: Adult form manual.* Palo Alto, CA: Center for Health Care Evaluation, Stanford University and Department of Veterans Affairs Medical Centers.

Osgood, C. E., Suci, G. J., & Tannenbaum, P. H. (1957). *The measurement of meaning.* Urbana: University of Illinois Press.

Parker, G. R., Cowen, E. L., Work, W. C., & Wyman, P. A. (1990). Test correlates of stress affected and stress resilient outcomes among urban children. *Journal of Primary Prevention, 11,* 19–35.

Radke-Yarrow, M., & Brown, G. (1993). Resilience and vulnerability in children of multiple-risk families. *Development and Psychopathology, 5,* 581–592.

Rohner, R. J., Saavedra, J. M., & Granum, E. O. (1983). *Parental Acceptance-Rejection Questionnaire: Test manual.* Washington, DC: American Psychological Association, Journal Supplement Abstract Service.

Rosenberg, M. (1965). *Society and adolescent self-image.* Princeton, NJ: Princeton University Press.

Rutter, M. (1987). Psychosocial resilience and protective mechanisms. *American Journal of Orthopsychiatry, 57,* 316–331.

Spielberger, C. D. (1973). *State-Trait Anxiety Scale for Children: Preliminary manual.* Palo Alto, CA: Consulting Psychologists Press.

Staudinger, U. M., Marsiske, M., & Baltes, P. B. (1993). Resilience and levels of reserve capacity in later adulthood: Perspectives from life-span theory. *Development and Psychopathology, 5,* 541–566.

Task Panel Report. (1978). Leaning failure and unused learning potential. *Task panel reports submitted to the President's Commission on Mental Health* (Vol. 3) (Stock No. 040-000-00392-4). Washington, DC: U.S. Government Printing Office.

Tolan, P. H., & Guerra, N. G. (1994). Prevention of delinquency: Current status and issues. *Applied and Preventive Psychology, 3,* 251–273.

Wannon, M. (1990). *Children's control beliefs about controllable and uncontrollable events: Their relationship to stress resilience and psychosocial adjustment.* Unpublished doctoral dissertation, University of Rochester, Rochester, NY.

Wechsler, D. (1991). *Manual for the Wechsler Intelligence Scale for Children – revised.* New York: Psychological Corporation.

Werner, E. E. (1993). Risk, resilience and recovery: Perspectives from the Kauai Longitudinal Study. *Development and Psychopathology, 5,* 503–515.

Werner, E. E., & Smith, R. S. (1982). *Vulnerable but invincible: A study of resilient children.* New York: McGraw-Hill.

Werner, E. E., & Smith, R. S. (1992). *Overcoming the odds: High risk children from birth to adulthood.* Ithaca, NY: Cornell University Press.

Work, W. C. (1986). *The social problem solving cognitive measure.* Unpublished manuscript. University of Rochester.

Work, W. C., Cowen, E. L., Parker, G. W., & Wyman, P. A. (1990). Stress resilient children in an urban setting. *Journal of Primary Prevention, 11,* 3–17.

Wyman, P. A., Cowen, E. L., Work, W. C., Hoyt, L., Magnus, K., & Fagen, D. (1996). Developmental and caregiving factors differentiating parents of young stress affected and stress resilient urban children: A replication and extension. Manuscript submitted for publication.

Wyman, P. A., Cowen, E. L., Work, W. C., & Kerley, J. H. (1993). The role of children's future expectations in self-system functioning and adjustment to life-stress. A prospective study of urban at risk children. *Development and Psychopathology, 5,* 649–661.

Wyman, P. A., Cowen, E. L., Work, W. C., & Parker, G. R. (1991). Developmental and family milieu interview correlates of resilience in urban children who have experienced major life-stress. *American Journal of Community Psychology, 19,* 405–426.

Wyman, P. A., Cowen, E. L., Work, W. C., Raoof, A., Gribble, P. A., Parker, G. R., & Wannon, M.

(1992). Interviews with children who experienced major life stress: Family and child attributes that predict resilient outcomes. *Journal of the American Academy of Child and Adolescent Psychiatry, 31,* 904–910.

Wyman, P. A., Work, W. C., Cowen, E. L., & Kim, J. (1996). Testing an attachment-theory based model: Cross-sectional and longitudinal prediction of urban children's adjustment and IQ. Manuscript submitted for publication.

Wyman, P. A., Work, W. C., Kerley, J., Hightower, A. D., Cowen, E. L., & Lotyczewski, B. S. (1996). Predicting substance abuse risk behaviors among inner-city adolescents from childhood competencies and family life-stress: A longitudinal study. Manuscript submitted for publication.

Yoshikawa, H. (1994). Prevention as cumulative protection: Effects of early family support and education on chronic delinquency and its risks. *Psychological Bulletin, 115,* 28–54.

Zax, M., & Cowen, E. L. (1972). *Abnormal psychology: Changing conceptions.* New York: Holt, Rinehart & Winston.

Zigler, E., Taussig, C., & Black, K. (1992). A promising preventative for juvenile delinquency. *American Psychologist, 47,* 997–1006.

24 Developmental approaches to understanding adolescent deviance

Joseph P. Allen, Cynthia M. Moore, and Gabriel P. Kuperminc

The importance of understanding serious externalizing problem behaviors in adolescence – such as delinquency, substance abuse, and school dropout – can be readily grasped by even a brief consideration of their costs, such as the $2.8 billion per year for facilities to detain apprehended juveniles, or the $260 billion in lost lifetime earnings for each year's class of school dropouts (Catterall, 1987; U. S. Bureau of the Census, 1993). These staggering costs may themselves be only pale reflections of the larger cumulative costs of these problems to individual adolescents, many of whom are also enduring lingering effects of growing up in impoverished conditions. Researchers and theoreticians have sought to explain these problems with sociological, psychological, biological, and genetic theories (Becker, 1973; DiLalla & Gottesman, 1989; Gottesman & Goldsmith, in press; Gottfredson & Hirschi, 1990; Patterson, DeBaryshe, & Ramsey, 1989). Yet, for all we have learned about juvenile deviance, our knowledge has yielded only moderate guidance to efforts to prevent or reduce the incidence of such deviance (Kazdin, 1993; Tate, Reppucci, & Mulvey, 1995).

Given the long and extensive history of research and theorizing in this area, what can the relatively new discipline of developmental psychopathology contribute? Perhaps a great deal. A unique facet of developmental psychopathology is that it focuses not on static correlates of deviance, but on developmental precursors and sequelae of deviance (Cicchetti, 1984, 1990). Psychopathology is also not seen as existing in a vacuum, but within a broader social context in which individual development and larger social, economic, and cultural forces interact over time (Richters & Cicchetti, 1993; Zigler & Glick, 1986). This approach is thus intrinsically well suited to inform real-world efforts to modify or produce such change and development.

This chapter was completed with the assistance of grants from the Spencer Foundation and National Academy of Education, the National Institute of Mental Health, and the W. T. Grant Foundation to the first author.

548

Questions raised by a developmental perspective

With its focus upon change and both normative and nonnormative aspects of development, the perspective of developmental psychopathology suggests a need to look afresh at three of the more well established findings about juvenile deviance. These three findings have each been consistently replicated and are strikingly well accepted across numerous disciplines:

1. Problem behavior rates shoot up dramatically at the onset of adolescence.
2. They decline almost as precipitously by the end of adolescence.
3. Delinquency rates are highest among adolescents with troubled family backgrounds.

The increase in problem behavior rates is stark and dramatic at the onset of adolescence with rates of serious criminal behavior increasing more than 10-fold from ages 12 to 17 (Blumstein, Cohen, & Farrington, 1988). The decreases at the end of adolescence are less clear-cut, although by the age of 30, serious criminal behaviors decline to less than one-fourth of their adolescent peak (Blumstein et al., 1988). Finally, a long line of research on families of delinquent adolescents has consistently revealed strong links between deviance and parental histories of delinquency in adolescence, poor parenting practices (particularly disciplinary practices), use of harsh disciplinary strategies, and poor monitoring of teens' behaviors (Cloward & Ohlin, 1960; Dumas, Gibson, & Albin, 1989; Hirschi, 1969; Hirschi & Gottfredson, 1980; Loeber & Dishion, 1983; Patterson & Stouthamer-Loeber, 1984; West, 1982). Taken together, these parenting practices can account for 30% to 40% of the variance in key behaviors such as delinquency or school difficulties (Patterson et al., 1989).

These three recurring findings about adolescent deviance are now accepted as "given" or as background in much research on juvenile delinquency. Yet, if we simply take these three findings for granted and move on to other issues, we miss an immense opportunity to understand the development of adolescent deviance. Specifically, these findings give rise to three parallel questions, that cut to the heart of how and why developmental psychopathology can and must inform our thinking about adolescent problem behaviors:

1. *Why* does the incidence of problematic behavior increase so dramatically in adolescence?
2. Why does it decline following adolescence?
3. How and why do negative family interaction patterns *develop and get maintained* in families with deviant teens?

The first two questions suggest that as we look for the causes of deviance *within* samples of adolescents, we risk overlooking factors that may help us understand why adolescence as an era of development is associated with dramatically increased rates of deviance. Ironically, we spend large sums of money on interventions (particularly punitive and incarceration-based interventions) and action research with frequently disappointing results in the quest to find ways of reducing problem behaviors (Tate et al., 1995; U.S. Bureau of the Census, 1993). Yet, as our field struggles with the apparent intractability of juvenile deviance, millions of teens are literally growing out of problematic patterns of behavior each year, as a result of naturally occurring social, psychological, biological, and interpersonal changes (Moffitt, 1993). These developmental changes occur regularly and predictably with little or no professional intervention, across both normal and at-risk populations. Understanding these developmental processes may be one of our best means for identifying ways of intervening to alter them in a more favorable direction. For example, even slight accelerations in developmental processes that occur naturally at the end of adolescence could lead to sizable reductions in the incidence of problem behavior within our society. Although prior research has identified high degrees of stability of problem behaviors *within* cohorts, these findings should not lead us to ignore the fact that actual levels of deviance for an entire cohort typically change quite substantially over time (Loeber, Stouthamer-Loeber, Van Kammen, & Farrington, 1991). Before we conclude that "nothing works," we may want to examine the normative developmental processes that already routinely have the effects we desire to bring about with intervention efforts.

Deviance and adolescent social development

In the remainder of this chapter we will consider the ways in which problematic patterns of behavior develop and change in adolescence by focusing on their links to adolescents' progress in addressing the major social developmental tasks of this period. These tasks include revising relationships with parents, forming peer relationships that are deep and lasting enough to serve eventually as attachment relationships, and learning a multitude of microskills necessary to cope emotionally, socially, financially, and even physically as an independent adult (Allen & Pfeiffer, 1991; Hauser & Bowlds, 1990). We need to begin to consider, What happens *normally* during the adolescent phase of development to lead to such a dramatic increase followed by a dramatic decline in levels of problem behavior?

We will consider two important aspects of social development in adolescence: increasing autonomy strivings and the changing nature of the attachment relationship as they relate to adolescent deviance. We begin with a consideration of adolescent autonomy strivings, first examining these strivings as a universal developmental challenge for adolescents, and then going on to consider what we are learning about different developmental pathways for handling these strivings, and, in particular, how these different pathways might influence the likelihood of deviant behavior. Next, we consider the growing body of knowledge about the ways in which attachment relationships are maintained and internalized into and beyond adolescence. Here we also begin to suggest some of the more complex interactions that might be expected between different attachment organizations and different paths toward handling autonomy strivings. Because it is impossible to consider social development absent a social context to serve as a backdrop for this development, we conclude this chapter by considering how the individual and familial level developmental processes we describe might interact with major sociodemographic influences that have been linked to deviant behavior.

Autonomy strivings

Normative development

One of the most important tasks for adolescent social development is the gradual attainment of both emotional and behavioral autonomy in relation to parents (Collins, 1990; Grotevant & Cooper, 1985; Hill & Holmbeck, 1986; Moore, 1987; Steinberg, 1990). Without attaining such autonomy in adolescence, meaningful practice in developing judgment about complex life decisions becomes virtually impossible. Yet, while greater autonomy opens up new areas in which teens can explore and gain competence, increased autonomy strivings also bring about the potential for problems. As adolescence begins, teens begin to feel that their parents' judgment should be superseded by their own or by peers' judgment (Berndt, 1979; Smetana, 1988). Serious difficulties may arise as adolescents "try out" ways of behaving other than those prescribed by their parents. In addition, in their strivings for both autonomy and maturity, Moffitt (1993) has argued persuasively that teens may be increasingly likely to mimic deviant peers who appear to have access to markers of maturity – from alcohol to forbidden activities. Thus, deviance may increase normatively both as a result of increased freedom from parental norms and, at least in some cases, as a means of obtaining the appearance of maturity and autonomy when it cannot be otherwise obtained.

One of the most significant gains in research on adolescent autonomy in the past 15 years has been the recognition that such autonomy optimally is developed not at the expense of relationships, but rather *in the context of close, supportive relationships with parents* (Allen, Hauser, Bell, & O'Connor, 1994; Collins, 1990). Although increased autonomy may bring with it increased opportunity for problem behaviors and deviance, a strong relationship with parents may serve as a check on deviant behavior (Hirschi, 1969). Such a relationship does not eliminate teens' ability to explore problem behaviors, but it does increase motivation to conform behavior to limits acceptable within adult society. If we consider autonomy and relatedness with parents as independent dimensions (i.e., adolescents may possess one, the other, both, or neither), we immediately begin raising questions about the different paths adolescents may take toward establishing autonomy within different types of relationships with parents. Based on existing research and theory, we will outline several potential pathways along with their implications for deviant behavior in adolescence.

Autonomy with relatedness

As suggested, establishing autonomy in the context of a positive relationship with parents is one adaptive pathway through which relationships with parents may be redefined during adolescence. Clearly, establishing high levels of both autonomy and relatedness in a single relationship is a complex task, and, until relatively recently, autonomy and relatedness were seen as lying at opposite ends of a continuum (Newman & Newman, 1975). Understanding how adolescents and their parents negotiate this task requires considering both the domains in which autonomy is established and the specific strategies used by both parents and adolescents.

Smetana (1988, 1989) has shown that parent–teen conflicts can be meaningfully distinguished in terms of whether they simply reflect issues of personal style and choice, or larger social conventions and moral issues. When adolescent autonomy is established around issues of personal choice (such as style, taste, and personal preferences), autonomy strivings need not threaten parental authority nor the adolescent's relationship with parents (Smetana, 1988). Questions such as hair length and style might even briefly become "life and death" issues to teens without necessarily threatening their relationship with parents, precisely because these are not "life and death" issues for parents. At the same time, these issues do not necessarily interfere with teen functioning. Quite the opposite, establishing some independence from adult norms – at least in noncritical areas of functioning – appears linked to better overall functioning with peers (Allen, Weissberg, & Hawkins, 1989). Thus, autonomy can be established in some areas, reflecting personal style, while parental authority may be maintained in other areas that are more central to adaptive functioning, such as maintaining adequate academic performance and avoiding serious illegal behavior.

Autonomy strivings that focus primarily around personal choice issues are typically met as the adolescent matures, and is granted increased responsibility and freedom by parents (Smetana, 1988). These strivings may also drive some deviant behavior; however, we would expect that the likelihood of their leading to highly deviant behaviors would decrease to the extent that the strivings were met in adaptive ways (Allen, Aber, & Leadbeater, 1990). From this perspective, the natural rise and fall of autonomy strivings may account for part of the rise and fall of more serious deviant behavior before, during, and after adolescence. Understanding teen autonomy strivings may thus tell us something about why deviance increases as adolescence begins and then decreases as it ends.

A second key quality of the process by which teens establish their autonomy in relation to parents is *how* it is established, whether via negotiation and cooperation or hostility and withdrawal (Allen, Kuperminc, Philliber, & Herre, 1994). Teens need not declare war with their parents to establish their autonomy. They may, however, need to engage in protracted and tense "peace talks" in which they both directly question their parents' authority while also responding to thoughtful responses their parents make in return. In our research, we have examined the extent to which parents and teens handle disagreements by focusing on the reasoning underlying each of their positions. When individuals focus on why they hold their positions, they can consider the merits of their own and others' reasoning as a basis for addressing the disagreement, rather than trying to decide who should give in and to what extent (Allen et al., 1994). Positions may change *not* because of pressure from another person (i.e., via relinquishment of autonomy), but through careful consideration of another person's reasoning about that issue.

In practical terms, an adolescent who becomes convinced of the dangers of drug use may adopt this as his or her own value, rather than seeing it as a compromise with parents. Drug use, then, would no longer be a focus (or a result) of autonomy struggles with parents. Ironically, a successfully negotiated solution can leave both sides feeling autonomous and in control of the outcome, whereas impulsive and unilateral adolescent assertions of autonomy followed by equally unilateral and harsh parental reactions can leave both sides feeling *less* autonomous and in control. Successful negotiating patterns may help teens establish autonomy without forgoing a positive relationship with parents, whereas unsuccessful handling of autonomy strivings may cause teens to feel both less autonomous and more in need of ways to establish their autonomy.

Of course, even a successful negotiation of autonomy issues that maintains the parental relationship may not eliminate deviant behavior. Rather, it may simply provide avenues by which autonomy can be obtained while also allowing the parental relationship to play its normal function of limiting the extent and seriousness of deviant behavior. Although the developmental function of autonomy strivings may help explain overall patterns of change in deviance across adolescence, particular difficulties in handling these strivings may help explain why particular adolescents display high levels of deviant behavior relative to their peers. Some of these difficulties are considered here.

Difficulties in establishing autonomy

Because establishing autonomy is such a critical task for adolescents, teens who are not able to establish autonomy while maintaining positive relationships with parents are likely to be at high risk for a number of disturbances in functioning. For example, in our observations of teens and parents discussing previously identified areas of disagreement about hypothetical moral dilemmas (an area suggested by Smetana [1989] as likely to be in teens' growing province of issues about which they expect to have some control), some families actively undermine one another's emotional and cognitive autonomy. They may do this by overpersonalizing discussions, turning them into battles between persons rather than discussions of ideas, or by placing undue pressure on the other person, rather than by offering reasoned arguments ("You just won't ever understand what I'm saying, you're just too young (or old)," or, "Will you just give up and stop arguing?") Autonomy-undermining behavior in discussions at age 14 has been found to predict *increases* in levels of hostility demonstrated toward parents from age 14 to age 16 (Allen, Hauser, O'Connor, Bell, & Eickholt, 1996). The clearest predictions come not from parents' behaviors undermining autonomy in the discussion, but from teens' own autonomy-undermining behaviors. A likely explanation is that teens who are having difficulty achieving autonomy within relationships with parents may eventually seek to undermine those relationships with hostile behavior – either out of frustration or in a less-than-optimal attempt to gain autonomy through angry confrontations with parents.

In addition, families in which parents undermine teens' autonomy at age 16 have teens who are later viewed as unusually hostile in interactions with peers at age 25 (Allen & Hauser, in press). These correlations are strong ($r = .50$), robust (occurring in both normal and previously psychiatrically hospitalized groups of adolescents), and suggest long-term sequelae of difficulties with this critical developmental task. One possible explanation is that teens who have had their autonomy undermined in interactions with parents carry forward expectations of close relationships in which their basic social and emotional needs are unlikely to be met. They then approach new relationships with a defensive, hostile stance. Such teens may have also developed patterns of seeking autonomy at the expense of relationships, based initially on interactions with parents, but eventually generalizing to interactions with peers.

These findings suggest that the feelings of anger and hostility that are associated with adolescent deviant behavior may be partly understandable as a reaction to failure at a critical developmental task (establishing autonomy vis-à-vis parents) at a critical juncture in development (Allen, et al., 1990). This may not be the only source of such anger and hostility, but it does suggest an explanation of why adolescence may be a time of particularly hostile interactions for some families. Even in families where autonomy-granting takes place *relatively* smoothly, transient difficulties in this process may also lead to hostility or to teens' efforts to establish autonomy by violating parents' behavioral norms. Most important, this perspective suggests that development may well open up different avenues for intervention at different points in the life-span. Whereas behavior management training and mastery-based and skills-training interventions may be most effective with young children (McMahon & Wells, 1990), interventions that offer nondeviant paths toward autonomy – for example, by offering ways of being better accepted in the larger social world beyond the family – may carry the most salience in adolescence (Allen et al., 1994).

Further questions about adolescent pathways to autonomy

There are many other paths besides the two outlined for handling issues of teen autonomy, and many variations off of these paths. For example, teens may simply withdraw from the task and from parents – a behavior pattern that we have observed to be relatively stable over time, and to predict depression more than hostility

(Allen et al., 1994). In addition, this discussion raises other important questions such as, What are the *precursors* at earlier stages of development of teen–parent difficulties handling autonomy strivings? How do strivings to gain cognitive and emotional autonomy, as described earlier, interact with strivings to gain direct control over one's behavior and to escape parental monitoring and control? and, Are there teens for whom increased autonomy from troubled relationships with parents may lead to *decreased* deviance, or ways in which completion of the task of establishing autonomy leads to decreased deviance for most teens?

Even this brief list of questions should make clear that the preceding discussion illustrates only one way in which understanding different pathways for handling teen autonomy strivings may help us understand adolescent deviance. Other pathways clearly exist and warrant equal attention (e.g., see Moffitt, 1993). We now turn to consider one perspective on the history of the parent–adolescent relationship – offered by attachment theory – as an example of ways in which patterns established at prior periods in development might interact with current developmental challenges to influence current levels of problem behaviors.

Adolescent attachment and deviance

Attachment theory and accompanying research have revolutionized the study of infant development in the past 20 years (Ainsworth, Blehar, Waters, & Wall, 1978; Ainsworth, 1989; Bretherton, 1985; van Ijzendoorn, in press). More recently, the development of interview techniques that assess adults' internal representations of attachment experiences and that have strong theoretical and empirical links to attachment as measured in infancy and childhood have brought the promise of understanding a universal human process with substantial implications for behavior across the life-span (Main, Kaplan, & Cassidy, 1985). Strong continuities observed in attachment organization across the life-span and across generations (Benoit & Parker, 1994; Waters, Merrick, Albersheim, & Treboux, 1995) suggest that attachment theory may offer both a mechanism by which disturbed family interactions may be internalized and carried forward into future relationships, *and* a potential way to understand the genesis of patterns of disturbed interactions in families with adolescents.

The consistently observed continuities in attachment patterns across the life-span and across generations suggest the likelihood of substantial continuities in attachment organization between parents and adolescents. This in turn suggests that it may make some sense to speak of the attachment organization of family relationships, rather than just of individuals, in adolescence. Adolescence has long been identified as an era in which models of attachment relationships can be reconsidered and reorganized, and in which the relationships on which those models are based can rapidly change (Main et al., 1985; Ricks, 1985; Sroufe & Fleeson, 1986). In particular, the highly charged stress of impending separation and growing autonomy may well rekindle issues and patterns of interaction from far earlier in the attachment relationship.

As will be outlined, available data suggest relations of attachment insecurity to problem behaviors and deviance more generally. Several possible lines of relation among attachment and deviance in adolescence are presented and ways in which attachment organization would be likely to interact with other aspects of development to lead toward or away from problematic behavior are then considered.

Secure attachment organizations

Security in attachment organization, represented in the infant's secure categorization or in the adolescent's or adult's categorization as "autonomous yet valuing of attachment," is identified as the optimal outcome of attachment processes (Ainsworth et al., 1978; Bowlby, 1980; Main et al., 1985). This organization in infant–caregiver dyads is accompanied by flexibility in attending to new stimuli, and by exploratory behaviors that are sustained and supported by the expectation that the caregiver will be available to provide a secure base that can be returned to in the event of need. In adolescence and adulthood, this security is internalized, and characterized by the ability to think and speak coherently about attachment relationships, describing them in logical, internally consistent, and balanced ways (Main & Goldwyn, in press).

As children with secure attachment relationships to parents enter adolescence, autonomy issues can still be expected to arise and lead to predictable family conflicts. However, in secure dyads one might expect these relationships to be characterized by strong efforts by all parties to maintain strong connections between parent and teen. Kobak has referred to the importance in adolescence of the "goal-corrected partnership" in which both parents and adolescents adjust their behaviors in line with the other's communicated needs and desires as both seek a common goal of fostering adaptive adolescent development (Kobak, Cole, Ferenz-Gillies, & Fleming, 1993). Our own studies have found far better communication patterns in families of secure adolescents, with parents knowing more about what their adolescent thinks, being trusted and confided in more, and having lower levels of conflict and conflict characterized by multilateral (vs. unilateral) decision making (Allen & Bell, 1995). Both parents' and teens' attachment systems may become taxed repeatedly as the adolescent explores values, behaviors, and ultimately residences that are not shared with parents. Such exploration may bring threats, both to adolescents and parents who are resetting life goals and tasks (Hill & Holmbeck, 1986). Yet, these tasks are unlikely to be overly threatening, and such threats are likely to be lessened by the secure expectation that the relationship will remain fundamentally intact and the other person will remain psychologically available. Thus, in secure dyads, teen autonomy strivings are relatively unlikely to undermine the fundamental role of the parental relationship in limiting the most serious forms of deviant behavior.

Various studies in childhood have linked attachment security to fewer problems in compliance and to fewer childhood autonomy struggles with parents (Ainsworth et al., 1978; Alexander, Waldron, Barton, & Mas, 1989; Lay, Waters, & Park, 1989; Russo, Cataldo, & Cushing, 1981; Sroufe et al., 1984; Waters, Wippman, & Sroufe, 1979). In adolescence, research is just beginning to identify ways in which secure parent–teen dyads avoid struggles over autonomy and control issues that their insecure counterparts do not (Allen & Hauser, in press, Kobak et al., 1993). In adolescence and adulthood, secure states of mind regarding attachment have been related to better social functioning with peers and to lower levels of psychological symptomatology in both normal and patient samples (Kobak & Sceery, 1988; Dozier, Stevenson, Lee, & Velligan, 1991). Our own research to date suggests that secure teens have somewhat lower likelihoods of engaging in problem behaviors (Allen & Kuperminc, 1995). However, this research also confirms a recurring finding from childhood – that the attachment system is not isomorphic with other important systems operating in families, such as parents' behavioral control systems.

Clearly, in secure dyads, all behavior will not necessarily be in accord with parents' desires. As already discussed, exploration and autonomy strivings in adolescence mean exploring values and behaviors that are different from those of parents, including deviant behaviors. Experimentation with such behaviors is not necessarily destructive (Shedler & Block, 1990); yet a secure relationship with parents is likely to keep this exploration from going too far and into overly dangerous territory. At the same time, adolescents' interests in exploring autonomy from parents, combined with security in the availability of the relationship with parents, could actually allow the adolescent *heightened* opportunities to explore deviant behavior. This would arise because teens may have the confidence to behave autonomously, with little fear of losing the parental relationship as a result of their behavior, even if it contradicts parental norms. The key term here is "exploration." Secure teens might explore deviant behaviors, but would probably be less likely to engage in serious and destructive *patterns* of behavior of which their parents disapprove.

Insecure attachment organizations

Insecure attachment organizations have been categorized into three basic patterns described slightly differently in infancy and adulthood: dismissing/avoidant (in adulthood/infancy); preoccupied/ambivalent; and unresolved with respect to past loss or trauma/disorganized (Ainsworth et al., 1978; Main & Solomon, 1986; Main & Goldwyn, in press). Each is expected to hold in common past experience with a caregiver who was at some point not adequately sensitive and/or available to meet the attachment needs of the child/adolescent (Bowlby, 1980; Main & Solomon, 1986). In addition, as assessed in adolescence and adulthood, each of these insecure attachment organizations reflects at least some degree of functional deficit or incoherence in thinking about, discussing, and evaluating attachment experiences (Main & Goldwyn, in press). Beyond that, specific manifestations of different types of insecure attachment organizations, particularly as they relate to deviant behavior, can be expected to differ somewhat across classifications.

Individuals with dismissing/avoidant attachment organizations adopt strategies that deemphasize the salience and importance of attachment experiences, in part as a response to consistent experiences of rejection of attachment needs by caregivers (Ainsworth et al., 1978; Belsky & Cassidy, in press; Bretherton, 1985; Sroufe & Fleeson, 1986). Families characterized by this attachment organization are likely to find the impending separations and autonomy struggles of adolescence quite threatening to a relationship that may already appear fragile in terms of its capacity to meet the teen's needs. Parents with dismissing attachment organizations are likely to react to separations by emotionally withdrawing and minimizing the importance of the attachment relationship. This in turn may further threaten the adolescent and may lead to similar behavior or to an angry response (Kobak et al., 1993).

One possible outcome is that adolescent and parent may mutually distance themselves from one another. This dramatically lessens parental influence over adolescent behavior. Such lessened control increases the likelihood of the occurrence of teen problem behaviors, although only when other exacerbating factors are also present. For example, problematic behavior could tend to force avoidant/dismissing teens and parents back into closer (and uncomfortable) contact to address the difficulties, and such behavior would thus be avoided by these teens. Also, firm and strict parental control over behavior may limit problem behaviors even when other qualities of the parent–teen relationship do not. Yet, in families where such controls are lacking, and where parents, for whatever reasons, are not engaged by teens' problematic behavior, there may be little to prevent high levels of deviant behavior (Allen et al., 1990). In our study of a sample of moderately at-risk teens, we have found that such an *interaction* of insecure/dismissing teen attachment strategies with loose parental control strategies was predictive of high levels of violent and aggressive behavior (Allen & Kuperminc, 1995). This dynamic linking of avoidant/ dismissing attachment organization, interacting with parental control strategies, in predicting antisocial behavior need not be limited to adolescence, and would be consistent with observed connections of infant avoidant attachments to later antisocial behavior in childhood (LaFreniere & Sroufe, 1985; Sroufe, 1983).

Individuals with preoccupied/ambivalent attachment organizations typically are hyperattuned to attachment experiences. This is believed in part to be a response to experiences of intermittent and inconsistent parental availability to meet attachment needs (Cassidy & Berlin, 1994). Families with this attachment organization might also be expected to find adolescent autonomy strivings particularly threatening because they also challenge a potentially fragile attachment system. However, drawing analogies from infant and adult attachment research, we might expect the reaction to this challenge to be greatly heightened attachment behavior, potentially with accompanying angry behavior as well (Ainsworth et al., 1978; Cassidy & Berlin, 1994). The rate of deviant behavior in these families depends largely upon how such behavior changes the family interaction pattern in a given family. In families where deviance heightens and intensifies interactions among family members (i.e., leads to long, intense discussions), high levels of deviance might well be expected because deviance may come to function as an overused attachment behavior, just as angry protest does in infancy. The adolescent analogue to insecure-resistant/ambivalent infant behavior in strange situations may well be protracted, angry conflict between parents and teens.

Alternatively, in some preoccupied families, adolescent problem behaviors may produce too great a threat to family relationships, and thus be avoided. In this respect, deviance would function more like exploratory behavior in infancy. The perceived fragility and ongoing hyperactivation of the attachment system precludes opportunity for the adolescent to explore behavior proscribed by the parent. Some researchers have even argued, with some empirical support, that low levels of deviance in adolescence may actually reflect a slightly higher level of competence than the complete absence of deviant behaviors (Shedler & Block, 1990).

The unresolved/disorganized attachment organization constitutes the newest, least studied, and most controversial of attachment organizations that are widely used in research (Main & Hesse, 1990, 1992; Main & Solomon, 1986). This classification typically applies when an attachment figure dies, or behaves in frightening or abusive ways, and the individual is not subsequently able to reorganize attachment thought and behavior to take these factors into account. This status has been linked to aggressive and hostile child behavior and to serious adolescent psychopathology (Allen, Hauser, & Borman-Spurrell, 1996, Lyons-Ruth, Alpern, & Repacholi, 1993), but more specific behavior patterns associated with it have not yet been clearly identified. In addition, one pathway toward this status, a history of abuse at the hands of attachment figures, probably bears particular consideration, as it suggests a further means of understanding the observed relation between violent and abusive parenting and child/adolescent delinquency and violence (Dodge, Bates, & Pettit, 1990; Main & Goldwyn, 1984). One possibility is that disorganized attachments can account for highly disturbed (and often aggressive) patterns of behavior both within and beyond the family. Again, this pattern would not necessarily be expected to be limited to adolescence, although increased family conflict around other issues during adolescence could well intensify disturbances associated with this attachment organization.

Individual development and sociodemographic disadvantage

As mentioned earlier, the developmental processes and attachment relationships that influence the development of deviance in adolescence do not occur in a social and cultural vacuum. Although a detailed consideration of the influences of factors such as poverty, unemployment, racism, and crime within a community upon teen deviance is beyond the goals and scope of this chapter, even a brief consideration of how such factors might interact with the developmental processes just described can fulfill several important functions: It can help place the theoretical speculations presented within a larger context; it can suggest how understanding development can shed light on the specific mechanisms by which sociodemographic risk factors influence deviant behavior; and, ultimately, considering both individual development and larger social contexts together may help to generate a body of theory and research that is useful in developing interventions to aid those most at risk. What follows is a brief revisiting of the developmental processes already described, considered in terms of how they might play out for youths with the greatest exposure to sociodemographic risks such as poverty and neighborhood deterioration.

Adolescent autonomy strivings clearly take on a different cast when placed in the context of high levels of neighborhood poverty, crime, and unemployment. The single most important question in this regard is, What is the ultimate goal of autonomy for an adolescent whose adult role models may well lack stable employment, adequate living circumstances, or much hope for upward mobility? Clearly, autonomy may have unique meanings for youths living in such circumstances. For example, as described earlier, teens may use their peer group as a means of making the transition from dependence upon their parents to eventual autonomy (Berndt, 1979). Yet, when a neighborhood peer group, including older teens, is characterized by unusually high levels of criminal and deviant behavior, then the same autonomy strivings that might lead to small acts of vandalism in one neighborhood may well lead to muggings and acts of larceny in another.

Faced with these prospects, parents may be understandably reluctant to permit their teen the autonomy the teen seeks. Adolescent independence that may be growth promoting in a safe environment may be too threatening for impoverished urban environments where homicide is a leading cause of death among adolescents and young adults. Such factors may also underly observed differences in child-rearing styles among different groups in different social classes. For example, African American parents have been identified as relatively more authoritarian and less authoritative than European American parents with their children (Steinberg, Dornbusch, & Brown, 1992). In essence, they leave less room for discussion and place a higher value upon unquestioning obedience with their children. Such a style certainly has the potential to heighten stress around adolescent autonomy strivings. Yet, for many families living under economic strain, the alternatives – parents' spending time they do not have in extended discussions with their teens, versus allowing their teens too much freedom in a dangerous environment – indicate the Scylla and Charybdis nature of the situation these parents must face daily (Baldwin, Baldwin, & Cole, 1990).

In addition to influences upon teens' autonomy strivings, economic deprivation appears equally or more likely to alter the adolescents' attachment relationships with their parents. Repeatedly and consistently, researchers have found that one of the primary ways in which the effects of economic hardship are transmitted to children and adolescents is via the changes they bring about in their parents' behavior toward them. For example, maternal unemployment has been found to lead to a chain of maternal depression, increased levels of punishment of the adolescent, and adolescents' perceptions of a less functional relationship with their mothers, all of which lead to lower levels of teen socioemotional functioning (McLoyd, Jayaratne, Ceballa, & Borquez, 1994). Similarly, poverty appears to limit the ability of parents' to use their relationship with their teen to set limits on deviant behavior (Sampson & Laub, 1994). When parents are increasingly irritable or hostile, or have increased levels of conflict with their teen, this impairment in the relationship appears likely to lead to higher levels of externalizing behavior on the part of the child or adolescent (Conger, Ge, Elder, Lorenz, & Simons, 1994).

Finally, the effects of sociodemographic stressors are not necessarily additive (Rutter, 1979; Sameroff, Seifer, Barocas, Zax, & Greenspan, 1987). Rather, in the case of deviance, a "multiple gates" model may be most appropriate. Factors such as parental limits on behavior, neighborhood and peer social pressures, the quality of relationship with parents, expectations of positive future societal roles, and basic empathy skills developed in close relationships with caregivers over time may each serve individually as gates to help prevent the most serious deviant behavior. Each of these gates, even functioning in isolation, may be sufficient to rein in the most serious and disturbed deviant behavior even in the face of variations in teens' autonomy strivings and changing attachment relationships with parents. And even completely removing one or two of these gates may lead to only modest increases in deviance. Yet, in situations when *all* or virtually all of these gates are absent – when extreme impoverishment and economic despair combine with family lives in which parents' have been chronically too overtaxed to handle adequately teens' needs for either autonomy or attachment, all in the context of a dangerous neighborhood – there may be little left to limit adolescent deviance. Such a model, and such circumstances may help to account for the development of the violent, extremely high rate offenders who create such tremendous societal problems.

This perspective is clearly sobering in suggesting the limits of purely psychological approaches to teen deviance. Yet, this perspective also suggests that the most serious deviant behavior may in some ways be quite amenable to preventive interventions designed to maintain the presence of at least one of the gates described here. Indeed, intensive psychological interventions are demonstrating success in reducing deviance even among the most violent juveniles (Henggeler, Melton, & Smith, 1992). Similarly, multifaceted interventions aimed at alleviating the effects of poverty and social deprivation across childhood and adolescence continue to be developed and enhanced (Campbell & Ramey, 1994; Zigler, Styfco, & Gilman, 1993), offering the promise of using our knowledge ultimately to prevent serious adolescent problem behaviors.

Conclusions

In this chapter we have sought to illustrate the ways in which an understanding of developmental processes in childhood and adolescence can enhance our understanding of deviant adolescent behavior. We have considered ways in which different paths toward handling one key developmental challenge – adolescents' need to establish autonomy while maintaining relationships with their parents – may interact with other factors, such as an existing insecure attachment relationship, to influence teen problem behaviors. Several conclusions emerge from such an analysis.

First, understanding normative developmental processes in adolescence is critical to understanding the normative, yet costly, increases in deviant behaviors that begin in early adolescence. Although this chapter considered only one example of such normative changes – in levels of autonomy strivings – other kinds of developmental change, ranging from changes in hormone levels, to changes in physical skill and cognitive abilities, also appear likely to be useful in understanding the rise and fall of rates of deviance from preadolescence through adolescence and into adulthood (Moffitt, 1993).

Second, understanding normative developmental changes that are potentially linked to problem behaviors for an entire cohort of teens may also help in understanding individual differences in developmental pathways that may lead to particularly high levels of problem behavior for individual teens. This chapter considered how several different developmental paths in adapting to increased autonomy strivings might lead to different levels of deviance. One point that emerges repeatedly is that not all negative facets of development or of family interactions will necessarily point the teen toward externalizing problem behaviors. Some forms of pathology, such as high anxiety or major depression, may emerge from problems in development such as those discussed here, but may actually paralyze the teen sufficiently so as to *preclude* the possibility of delinquency and related behaviors. To understand the emergence of problem behaviors requires understanding not just the emergence of pathology generally, but the determinants of specific developmental paths that lead to particular forms of pathology.

Third, an implication of the overall perspective taken in this chapter is that a continued search for stable, personality- or family-oriented ''main effect'' explanations of deviant behavior, which act in isolation from other developmental processes, may have little further to add to our understanding of *change and development* in teen deviance. For example, parental monitoring and control behaviors have been highly related to teen deviance (Patterson et al., 1989), yet even if they explained all of the variance in teen deviance, they would not necessarily help in predicting when and how some teens decrease their deviant behavior *after* they leave their families and enter adulthood. Finally, monitoring and control behaviors clearly interact with developmental processes: At the simplest level, these behaviors are linked to high levels of criminal behavior at some but not all stages of development. More complex interactions are also quite likely to exist and warrant exploration, however.

These issues are important to research on adolescent problem behaviors, but are absolutely critical to efforts to intervene to prevent or reduce levels of serious teen problem behavior, in which issues of change and development are focal. Not surprisingly, some of the most successful and well-evaluated interventions, addressing problems from school dropout to teen violence to teen pregnancy, share a recognition of the need to address problematic characteristics of teens and/or their families *in the context of* specific developmental needs (Allen et al., 1994; Henggeler et al., 1992). It is now clearly time for our research efforts to catch up to the level of sophistication implicit in some of our best intervention efforts to date; both research and intervention can only benefit from such progress.

References

Ainsworth, M. D. S. (1989). Attachments beyond infancy. *American Psychologist, 44,* 709–716.

Ainsworth, M. D. S., Blehar, M. C., Waters, E., & Wall, S. (1978). *Patterns of attachment: A psychological study of the strange situation.* Hillsdale, NJ: Erlbaum.

Alexander, J. F., Waldron, H. B., Barton, C., & Mas, C. H. (1989). The minimizing of blaming attributions and behaviors in delinquent families. *Journal of Consulting and Clinical Psychology, 57,* 19–24.

Allen, J. P. (1992, October). *Family interactions and adolescent psychopathology.* National Institute of Mental Health Personality and Social Processes Research Branch, Personality and Emotion Program, Conference on "Affective Processes in Adolescence," Bethesda, MD.

Allen, J. P., Aber, J. L., & Leadbeater, B. J. (1990). Adolescent problem behaviors: The influence of attachment and autonomy. *Psychiatric Clinics of North America, 13,* 455–467.

Allen, J. P., & Bell, K. L. (1995, March). *Attachment and communication with parents and peers in adolescence.* Paper presented at the biennial meetings of the Society for Research in Child Development, Indianapolis, IN.

Allen, J. P., & Hauser, S. T. (in press). Autonomy and relatedness in adolescent-family interactions as predictors of young adults' states of mind regarding attachment. *Development and Psychopathology.*

Allen, J. P., Hauser, S. T., Bell, K. L., & O'Connor, T. G., (1994). Longitudinal assessment of autonomy and relatedness in adolescent-family interactions as predictors of adolescent ego development and self-esteem. *Child Development, 65,* 179–194.

Allen, J. P., Hauser, S. T., & Borman-Spurrell, E. (1996). Attachment insecurity and related sequelae of severe adolescent psychopathology: An eleven-year follow-up study. *Journal of Consulting and Clinical Psychology, 64,* 254–263.

Allen, J. P., Hauser, S. T., O'Connor, T. G., Bell, K. L., & Eickholt, C. (1996). The connection of observed hostile family conflict to adolescents' developing autonomy and relatedness with parents. *Development and Psychopathology, 8,* 425–442.

Allen, J. P., & Kuperminc, G. P. (1995, March). *Adolescent attachment, social competence, and problematic behavior.* Paper presented at the biennial meetings of the Society for Research in Child Development, Indianapolis, IN.

Allen, J. P., Kuperminc, G., Philliber, S., & Herre, K. (1994). Programmatic prevention of adolescent problem behaviors: The role of autonomy, relatedness, and volunteer service in the Teen Outreach Program. *American Journal of Community Psychology, 22,* 617–638.

Allen, J. P., & Pfeiffer, S. I. (1991). Residential psychiatric treatment of adolescents who do not return to their families. *Comprehensive Mental Health Care, 1,* 209–222.

Allen, J. P., Weissberg, R. P., & Hawkins, J. (1989). The relation between values and social competence in early adolescence. *Developmental Psychology, 25,* 458–464.

Baldwin, A. L., Baldwin, C., & Cole, R. E. (1990). Stress-resistant families and stress-resistant children. In J. Rolf, A. S. Masten, D. Cicchetti, K. H. Nuechterlein, & S. Weintraub (Eds.), *Risk and protective factors in the development of psychopathology* (pp. 257–280). Cambridge: Cambridge University Press.

564   J. P. ALLEN, C. M. MOORE, G. P. KUPERMINC

Becker, H. S. (1973). Labeling theory reconsidered. In P. Rock & M. McIntosh (Eds.), *Deviance and social control*. New York: Columbia University Press.

Belsky, J., & Cassidy, J. (in press). Attachment: Theory and evidence. In M. Rutter, D. F. Hay, (Eds.), *Development through life: A handbook for clinicians* (pp. 373–402). Oxford: Blackwell.

Benoit, D., & Parker, K. C. H. (1994). Stability and transmission of attachment across three generations. *Child Development, 65,* 1444–1456.

Berndt, T. J. (1979). Developmental changes in conformity to peers and parents. *Developmental Psychology, 15,* 608–616.

Blumstein, A., Cohen, J., & Farrington, D. P. (1988). Criminal career research: Its value for criminology: *Criminology, 26,* 1–35.

Bowlby, J. (1980). *Attachment and loss.* Vol. 3: *Loss, sadness and depression.* New York: Basic Books.

Bretherton. I. (1985). Attachment theory: Retrospect and prospect. In I. Bretherton & E. Waters (Eds.), *Growing points in attachment theory and research* (pp. 3–35). *Monographs of the Society for Research in Child Development, 50,* (Serial No. 209).

Campbell, F. A., & Ramey, C. T. (1994). Effects of early intervention on intellectual and academic achievement: A follow-up study of children from low-income families. Special issue on children and poverty. *Child Development, 65,* 684–698.

Cassidy, J., & Berlin, L. J. (1994). The insecure/ambivalent pattern of attachment: Theory and research. *Child Development, 65,* 971–991.

Catterall, J. S. (1987). On the social costs of dropping out of school. *High School Journal, 71,* 19–30.

Cicchetti, D. (1984). The emergence of developmental psychopathology. *Child Development, 55,* 1–7.

Cicchetti, D. (1990). An historical perspective on the discipline of developmental psychopathology. In J. Rolf, A. S. Masten, D. Cicchetti, K. H. Nuechterlein, & S. Weintraub (Ed.), *Risk and protective factors in the development of psychopathology* (pp. 2–28). Cambridge: Cambridge University Press.

Cloward, R. A., & Ohlin, L. E. (1960). *Delinquency and opportunity: A theory of delinquent gangs.* New York: Free Press.

Collins, W. A. (1990). Parent-child relationships in the transition to adolescence: Continuity and change in interaction, affect, and cognition (pp. 85–106). In R. Montemayor, G. R. Adams, & T. P. Gullotta (Eds.), *From childhood to adolescence: A transitional period? Advances in Adolescent Development* (Vol. 2). Newbury Park, CA: Sage.

Conger, R. D., Ge, X., Elder, G. H., Lorenz, F. O., & Simons, R. L. (1994). Economic stress, coercive family process, and developmental problems of adolescents. Special issue on children and poverty. *Child Development, 65,* 541–561.

DiLalla, L. F., & Gottesman, I. I. (1989). Heterogeneity of causes for delinquency and criminality: Lifespan perspectives. *Development and Psychopathology, 1,* 339–349.

Dodge, K. A., Bates, J. E., & Pettit, G. S. (1990). Mechanisms in the cycle of violence. *Science, 250,* 1678–1683.

Dozier, M., Stevenson, A. L., Lee, S. W., & Velligan, D. I. (1991). Attachment organization and familial overinvolvement for adults with serious psychopathological disorders. *Development and Psychopathology, 3,* 475–489.

Dumas, J. E., Gibson, J. A., & Albin, J. B. (1989). Behavioral correlates of maternal depressive symptomatology in conduct-disorder children. *Journal of Consulting and Clinical Psychology, 57,* 516–521.

Egeland, B., & Sroufe, L. A. (1981). Attachment and early maltreatment. *Child Development, 52,* 42–52.

Gottesman, I. I., & Goldsmith, H. H. (in press). Developmental psychopathology of antisocial behavior: Inserting genes into its ontogenesis and epigenesis. In C. A. Nelson (Ed.), *Threats to optimal development: Integrating biological, psychological, and social risk factors.* Hillsdale, NJ: Erlbaum.

Gottfredson, D. C. (1985). Youth employment, crime, and schooling: A longitudinal study of a national sample. *Developmental Psychology, 21,* 419–432.

Gottfredson, M., & Hirschi, T. (1990). *A general theory of crime.* Stanford, CA: Stanford University Press.

Grotevant, H. D., & Cooper, C. R. (1985). Patterns of interaction in family relationships and the development of identity exploration in adolescence. *Child Development, 56,* 415–428.

Hauser, S. T., & Bowlds, M. K. (1990). Stress, coping, and adaptation. In S. S. Feldman & G. R. Elliott

(Eds.) *At the threshold: The developing adolescent* (pp. 388–413). Cambridge, MA: Harvard University Press.

Henggeler, S. W., Melton, G. B., & Smith, L. A. (1992). Family preservation using multisystemic therapy: An effective alternative to incarcerating serious juvenile offenders. *Journal of Consulting and Clinical Psychology, 60,* 953–961.

Hill, J. P., & Holmbeck, G. N. (1986). Attachment and autonomy during adolescence. *Annals of Child Development, 3,* 145–189.

Hirschi, T. (1969). *Causes of Delinquency.* Berkeley: University of California Press.

Hirschi, T., & Gottfredson, M. (Eds.). (1980). *Understanding crime: Current theory and research.* Beverly Hills, CA: Sage.

Kazdin, A. E. (1993). Adolescent mental health: Prevention and treatment programs. *American Psychologist, 48,* 127–141.

Kobak, R. R., Cole, H. E., Ferenz-Gillies, R., Fleming, W. S. (1993). Attachment and emotion regulation during mother-teen problem solving: A control theory analysis. *Child Development, 64,* 231–245.

Kobak, R. R., & Sceery, A. (1988). Attachment in late adolescence: Working models, affect regulation and representations of self and others. *Child Development, 59,* 135–146.

LaFreniere, P., & Sroufe, L. A. (1985). Profiles of peer competence in the preschool: Interrelations between measures, influence of social ecology, and relation to attachment history. *Developmental Psychology, 21,* 56–68.

Laub, J. H., & Sampson, R. J. (1993). Turning points in the life course: Why change matters to the study of crime. *Criminology, 31,* 301–325.

Lay, K. L., Waters, E., & Park, K. A. (1989). Maternal responsiveness and child compliance: The role of mood as mediator. *Child Development, 60,* 1405–1411.

Loeber, R., & Dishion, T. (1983). Early predictors of male delinquency: A review. *Psychological Bulletin, 94,* 68–99.

Loeber, R., Stouthamer-Loeber, M., Van Kammen, W. B., & Farrington, D. P. (1991). Initiation, escalation and desistance in juvenile offending and their correlates. *Journal of Criminal Law and Criminology, 82,* 36–82.

Lyons-Ruth, K., Alpern, L., & Repacholi, B. (1993). Disorganized infant attachment classification and maternal psychosocial problems as predictors of hostile-aggressive behavior in the preschool classroom. *Child Development, 64,* 572–585.

Main, M., & Goldwyn, R. (1984). Predicting rejection of her infant from mother's representation of her own experiences: Implications for the abused-abusing intergenerational cycle. *Monograph of the International Journal of Child Abuse and Neglect, 8,* 203–217.

Main, M., & Goldwyn, R. (in press). Adult attachment rating and classification systems. In M. Main (Ed.), *A typology of human attachment organization assessed in discourse, drawings and interviews.* New York: Cambridge University Press.

Main, M., & Hesse, E. (1990). Parents' unresolved traumatic experiences are related to infant disorganized attachment status: Is frightened and/or frightening parental behavior the linking mechanism? In M. T. Greenberg, D. Cicchetti, & E. M. Cummings (Eds.), *Attachment in the preschool years* (pp. 161–184). Chicago: University of Chicago Press.

Main, M., & Hesse, E. (1992). Disorganized/disoriented infant behavior in the Strange Situation, lapses in the monitoring of reasoning and discourse during the parent's Adult Attachment Interview, and dissociative states. In M. Ammaniti & D. Stern (Eds.), *Attachment and psychoanalysis.* Rome: Gius, Laterza, and Figli.

Main, M., Kaplan, N., & Cassidy, J. (1985). Security in infancy, childhood, and adulthood: A move to the level of representation. In I. Bretherton & E. Waters (Eds.), *Growing points in attachment theory and research* (pp. 66–104). *Monographs of the Society for Research in Child Development, 50,* (Serial No. 209).

Main, M., & Solomon, J. (1986). Discovery of a new, insecure-disorganized/disoriented attachment pattern. In T. B. Brazelton & M. Yogman (Eds.), *Affective development in infancy* (pp. 95–124). Norwood, NJ: Ablex.

McLoyd, V. C., Jayaratne, T. E., Ceballo, R., & Borquez, J. (1994). Unemployment and work interruption among African American single mothers: Effects on parenting and adolescent socioemotional functioning. Special issue on children and poverty. *Child Development, 65,* 562–589.

McMahon, R. J., & Wells, K. C. (1989). Conduct disorders. In E. J. Mash & R. A. Barkley (Eds.), *Treatment of childhood disorders* (pp. 73–131). New York: Guilford Press.

Moffitt, T. E. (1993). Adolescence-limited and life-course-persistent antisocial behavior: A developmental taxonomy. *Psychological Review, 100,* 674–701.

Moore, D. (1987). Parent-adolescent separation: The construction of adulthood by late adolescents. *Developmental Psychology, 23,* 298–307.

Newman, B. M., & Newman, P. R. (1975). *Development through life: A psychosocial approach.* Homewood, IL: Dorsey Press.

Patterson, G. R., DeBaryshe, B. D., & Ramsey, E. (1989). A developmental perspective on antisocial behavior. *American Psychologist, 44,* 329–335.

Patterson, G. R., & Stouthamer-Loeber, M. (1984). The correlation of family management practices and delinquency. *Child Development, 55,* 1299–1307.

Richters, J. E., & Cicchetti, D. (1993). Mark Twain meets DSM-III-R: Conduct disorder, development, and the concept of harmful dysfunction. Special Issue: Toward a developmental perspective on conduct disorder. *Development and Psychopathology, 5,* 5–29.

Ricks, M. H. (1985). Social transmission of parental behavior: Attachment across generations. In I. Bretherton & E. Waters (Eds.), *Growing points of attachment theory and research* (pp. 211–227). *Monographs of the Society for Research in Child Development, 50* 1–2, (Serial No. 209).

Russo, D. C., Cataldo, M. F., & Cushing, P. J. (1981). Compliance training and behavioral covariation in the treatment of multiple behavior problems. *Journal of Applied Behavior Analysis, 14,* 209–222.

Rutter, M. (1979). Protective factors in children's responses to stress and disadvantage. In M. W. Kent & J. E. Rolf (Ed.), *Primary prevention in psychopathology* (pp. 49–74). Hanover, NH: University Press of New England.

Sameroff, A. J., Seifer, R., Barocas, R., Zax, M., & Greenspan, S. (1987). Intelligence Quotient scores of 4-year-old children: Social-environmental risk factors. *Pediatrics, 79,* 343–350.

Sampson, R. J., & Laub, J. H. (1994). Urban poverty and the family context of delinquency: A new look at structure and process in a classic study. Special Issue: Children and poverty. *Child Development, 65,* 523–540.

Shedler, J., & Block J. (1990). Adolescent drug use and psychological health. *American Psychologist, 45,* 612–630.

Smetana, J. G. (1988). Adolescents' and parents' conceptions of parental authority. *Child Development, 59,* 321–335.

Smetana, J. G. (1989). Adolescents' and parents' reasoning about actual family conflict. *Child Development, 60,* 1052–1067.

Sroufe, L. A. (1983). Infant-caregiver attachment and patterns of adaptation in the preschool: The roots of maladaptation and competence. *Minnesota symposium in child psychology* (Vol. 16, pp. 41–83).

Sroufe, L. A., & Fleeson, J. (1986). Attachment and the construction of relationships. In W. W. Hartup & Z. Rubin (Eds.), *Relationships and development* (pp. 51–71). Hillsdale, NJ: Erlbaum.

Sroufe, L. A., Schork, E., Motti, E., Lawroski, N., & LaFreniere, P. (1984). The role of affect in emerging social competence. In C. Izard, J. Kagan, & R. Zajonc (Eds.), *Emotion, cognition and behavior* (pp. 289–319). New York: Cambridge University Press.

Steinberg, L. (1990). Interdependency in the family: Autonomy, conflict, and harmony in the parent-adolescent relationship. In S. Feldman & G. Elliott (Eds.), *At the threshold: The developing adolescent* (pp. 255–276). Cambridge, MA: Harvard University Press.

Steinberg, L., Dornbusch, S. M., & Brown, B. B. (1992). Ethnic differences in adolescent achievement: An ecological perspective. *American Psychologist, 47,* 723–729.

Tate, D. C., Reppucci, N. D., & Mulvey, E. P. (1995). Violent juvenile delinquents: Treatment effectiveness and implications for future action. *American Psychologist, 50,* 777–781.

U. S. Bureau of the Census (1993). *Statistical abstract of the United States: 1993.* Washington, DC: U.S. Government Printing Office.

van Ijzendoorn, M. H. (in press). Associations between adult attachment representations and parent-child attachment, parental responsiveness, and clinical status: A Metaanalysis on the predictive validity of the Adult Attachment Interview. *Psychological Bulletin.*

Waters, E., Merrick, S. K., Albersheim, L. J., & Treboux, D. (1995, March). Attachment security from infancy to early adulthood: A 20-year longitudinal study. Paper presented at the Biennial Conference of the Society for Research in Child Development, New Orleans.

Waters, E., Wippman, J., & Sroufe, L. A. (1979). Attachment, positive affect, and competence in the peer group: Two studies in construct validation. *Child Development, 50,* 821–829.

West, D. J. (1982). *Delinquency: Its roots, careers and prospects.* Cambridge, MA: Harvard University Press.

Zigler, E., & Glick, M. (1986). *A developmental approach to adult psychopathology.* New York: Wiley.

Zigler, E., Styfco, S. J., & Gilman, E. (1993). The national Head Start program for disadvantaged preschoolers. In E. Zigler & S. J. Styfco (Eds.), *Head Start and beyond: A national plan for extended childhood intervention* (pp. 1–41). New Haven, CT: Yale University Press.

25   Developmental psychopathology and culture: Ten lessons from Thailand

John R. Weisz, Carolyn A. McCarty, Karen L. Eastman,
Wanchai Chaiyasit, and Somsong Suwanlert

Most of what we know about developmental psychopathology comes from research in Western cultures. Such research is valuable, but the findings from children and adolescents in North America and western Europe may not tell us all we need to know about the diverse paths development may follow, the diverse factors that may contribute to dysfunction, or the diverse definitions of abnormality or ''deviance'' that may be derived from different cultural perspectives on child behavior. In addition, deriving our understanding of developmental psychopathology from a largely Western data base may lead us to blur the distinction – so crucial to our understanding of mental health problems – between phenomena that are culture-specific and those that are culture-general (see Draguns, 1982). It seems particularly important to study cultural variations in psychopathology during childhood and adolescence, when the impact of societal variations on development may be most pronounced. The data and ideas that we present here constitute one attempt to explore that impact, and in the process to help broaden our base of information about child behavior, dysfunction, and psychopathology beyond its Western foundations. We will also suggest that cross-national research can connect importantly to research on subcultural differences within our own society.

This chapter emphasizes the connection between research on culture and child psychopathology, on the one hand, and the perspective that has come to be known as ''developmental psychopathology,'' on the other. Several of the themes addressed here were previewed years ago in the early work of Vygotsky on societal influence (summarized in Vygotsky, 1978), and later in the writings of Edward Zigler and his colleagues on socialization and personality development (see Zigler

The research program described in this chapter was supported through research grants from the National Institute of Mental Health (each numbered R01 MH38240), and John Weisz was supported through a Research Scientist Award from NIMH (K05 MH01161). We are grateful for the support of the Child Mental Health Center in Bangkok, Thailand, and we thank the many colleagues who have participated in the studies described herein, particularly Bahr Weiss for his skilled and insightful contributions. We also thank Kita Curry for her wordsmithery, and the many clinic administrators, clinical practitioners, teachers, parents, and children, who contributed their time, energy, and good ideas to this work.

& Child, 1969; Zigler, Lamb, & Child, 1982). In harmony with some of the ideas of these developmentalists, we will try to illustrate how an understanding of socialization as it relates to developmental psychopathology may be enriched by considering culture.

Theoretical models of cultural influence

Before embarking on cross-national research, it is useful to construct heuristic models describing ways that culture might have an impact. Such models can serve to guide research, to suggest interpretations, and to stimulate theory development. The models may, in turn, be modified or replaced as the data warrant. Our research has been guided by two nascent models of cultural influence – both growing out of an important fact about research on child psychopathology.

That fact is this: The study of child psychopathology is inevitably the study of two phenomena: the behavior of children, and the lens through which adults view child behavior – that is, the attitudes and beliefs that lead adults to regard some forms of child behavior as disturbed or "pathological." The adult lens is particularly important because it is adults, not children, who make the all-important decisions about child classification, referral, and treatment. If adults are not concerned about a child's behavior or psychological state, that child is not likely to receive clinical attention, no matter how concerned the child may be. It follows, then, that to understand the origins of "psychopathology" in childhood, we need to understand the forces that shape both child behavior and adult attitudes toward that behavior. One force that appears to shape both is culture.

This reasoning has led us to two general models of cultural influence, one focused on child behavior, the other on adult attitudes. A focus on child behavior suggests what we have called a "problem suppression-facilitation model" (see Weisz, 1989): Cultural forces may directly influence the likelihood of certain child problems, suppressing (e.g., via punishment or social pressure) the development of behavior that is disapproved, and facilitating (e.g., via teaching, modeling, or reward) the development of behavior that is considered acceptable in the child's society. A focus on the lens through which child behavior is viewed suggests what we have called an "adult distress threshold model" (see Weisz, 1989): Culture may influence adults' attitudes toward child behavior, helping to determine how distressing child problems will be to adults, and what actions adults will take in response to the problems (e.g., whether they will seek professional help for the children involved). Using these models as a starting point, we have sought, in our research program, to determine whether there are types of problems that may show relative suppression or facilitation in one culture relative to another, and to identify similarities and differences between adult thresholds for distress over child problems in different countries.

Selecting a problem focus, comparison countries, and target issues

To maximize the conceptual and empirical yield of research on culture and psychopathology, it is important to select cultures for study that differ in ways that are theoretically interesting and important, and to identify problem patterns or syndromes that theory suggests may be related to those cultural differences.

Problem focus: Over- and undercontrolled syndromes

The syndromes we selected for emphasis are the two most frequently identified in factor analytic research with children: overcontrolled or "internalizing" problems (e.g., shyness, somaticizing, depression) and undercontrolled or "externalizing" problems (e.g., disobedience, fighting, impulsivity). Syndromes in these general forms have been found in more than 20 factor analytic and principal components analytic studies in diverse cultures (many of the studies reviewed by Achenbach and Edelbrock, 1978), including Thailand (Weisz, Suwanlert, Chaiyasit, Weiss, Achenbach, & Eastman, 1993). (To provide a common basis for comparison, in the analyses reported here, overcontrolled and undercontrolled problems are defined as those loading on the internalizing and externalizing factors derived from American data by Achenbach & Edelbrock [1991a].)

Although the two broad syndromes are frequently studied, there is little consensus on what forces may lead to their development – that is, on why some youngsters may develop overcontrolled problems whereas others develop undercontrolled problems (or, for that matter, why some youngsters develop high levels of both). Biological factors related to behavioral inhibition may well play a role (see, e.g., Gray, 1982; Kagan, 1989; Kagan, Reznick, & Snidman, 1987). In addition, some evidence (Achenbach & Edelbrock, 1978; Hetherington & Martin, 1986) and theory (Weisz, 1989) focus on child-rearing and socialization factors. Overcontrolled problems are linked by some models to strict or critical parenting, parental modeling, and socialization that encourages high levels of self-control and emotional restraint (see reviews by Bernstein & Borchardt, 1991; Gotlib & Hammen, 1992); undercontrolled problems are linked in some models to permissive or inconsistent parenting, poor child monitoring, and tolerance of aggression (see review by Kazdin, Chapter 12, this volume). One of our aims has been to contribute to the search for possible causes by studying the prevalence of over- and undercontrolled problems in cultures whose child-rearing and socialization practices differ in ways that seem particularly relevant to the causal debate.

Selecting target cultures: Why Thailand?

To identify some of the relevant differences, let us briefly characterize the literature on child rearing in Thailand. Thai adults, 95% of whom are Buddhist, are said to be unusually intolerant of aggression, disobedience, and disrespectful acts in children (Gardiner & Suttipan, 1977; Moore, 1974; Suvannathat, 1979). Ethnographic reports indicate that children are taught to be peaceful, polite, and deferent – to strive for *krengchai,* an attitude of self-effacement and humility that aims to avoid disturbing others (Phillips, 1965; Suvannathat, 1979). Thai youngsters are also reportedly taught to inhibit outward expression of anger and other strong emotions (Gardiner, 1968; National Identity Office, 1984; Suwanlert, 1974) in ways that seem to foster overcontrolled behavior. One Thai student noted, "parents train their children not to contest the point that they think is right. So, when I am angry with my parents or any elder brother or sister about their regulation or advice, I must be quiet" (Gardiner, 1968, p. 225). Another student commented, "the elders teach their grandchildren to collect their feelings and not show the anger" (p. 225). Some researchers (e.g., Boesch, 1977; Sangsingkeo, 1969; Suwanlert, 1974) have suggested that such Thai customs may foster not only politeness and nonaggression but inhibition and anxiety as well.

Child-rearing patterns and syndrome prevalence

Such literature suggests the possibility that Thai children might differ from their American age-mates in the prevalence of certain problems. Through the kind of suppression-facilitation process described here (and see Weisz, 1989; cf. Draguns, 1973), Thai socialization may produce a somewhat elevated prevalence of overcontrolled or internalizing problems in Thai youngsters, relative to American youngsters. It is also possible that Thai cultural pressures against aggression and disobedience might inhibit the development of undercontrolled problems in Thai youth, but that prediction seems less well supported in the literature and in our findings, as will be seen.

Cultural factors and adult distress thresholds

In addition, several reported differences between Thai and American societies suggest the possibility of cross-national differences in adult attitudes, or "distress thresholds" with respect to child problems. For example, Suvannathat's (1979) analysis of Thai parenting styles indicates that Thais are unusually tolerant of a broad range of child behavior. Moreover, the Buddhist belief in the transience of all human conditions may mitigate concern over child problem behavior at any particular point in time (see Weisz et al., 1988b). Finally, Thai adults certainly have less exposure to child psychology through the media, academic courses, and the like than do American adults; this differential exposure may mean that Thais have not been so primed to think of child adjustment problems as sinister signs, or nascent pathology, that may grow worse without professional intervention. This reasoning suggests that thresholds for adult concern over child problems may be set at a higher level for Thais than for Americans.

Cultural practices and gender differences in problem prevalence

Cross-national research may also contribute to our knowledge about gender as it relates to psychopathology. In the United States, boys are more likely than girls to develop undercontrolled problems (Achenbach & Edelbrock, 1981; Rutter & Garmezy, 1983). Some have suggested that sex typing and parental behavior may foster this pattern (see Maccoby & Jacklin, 1974). In Thailand, socialization of boys and girls seems different in some respects from that in the United States; for example, boys receive rigorous training in Buddhist ideals, including pacifism and respect for all living things, and all boys (but not girls) are expected to reside in the temple for a period of priesthood before marriage, typically during adolescence. (Note, though, that some priesthood terms are too brief for much detailed learning about Buddhism to take place.) Are these patterns of socialization associated with a moderating, or reversal, of sex differences found in the United States? Data from our research can help address this question.

Multiple methodologies used in the research

Given the complexity of any culture, and of the phenomena under study here, we have assumed from the outset that the research will require the use of diverse methods and multiple sources of information about the children under study. Different questions require different approaches, of course, but we also want to be able to test the degree to which compatible findings emerge from different methods. We have used the following approaches thus far.

Surveys of referral problems that prompted child clinic intake

We have surveyed client intake records in Thai and American child mental health clinics, computing frequencies of the referral problems noted by the adults who brought the children for treatment. These data served two purposes. They helped us identify possible cross-national differences in the reasons for which adults seek child treatment (Weisz, Suwanlert, Chaiyasit, & Walter, 1987 – cited as Weisz et al., 1987a). And they provided raw material for the development of our Thai problem-report instrument, described in the next section.

General population prevalence surveys using problem checklists

We have surveyed the prevalence of various behavioral and emotional problems among randomly selected general population samples of youth in the two countries, as reported by parents (Weisz et al., 1987b; Weisz et al., 1993) and teachers (Weisz et. al., 1988a). For the Thai component of these surveys, we constructed the Thai Youth Checklist (TYC), parent and teacher forms. To facilitate comparison with U.S. data from the widely used Child Behavior Checklist (CBCL; Achenbach,

1991a) and Teacher's Report Form (TRF; Achenbach, 1991b), we made the initial items on the two TYC forms the same as the CBCL and TRF, respectively (for translation procedures, see Weisz et al., 1987b, 1988a, 1993). Subsequent TYC items were added based on our survey, just noted, of the most common reasons for child clinic referral in Thailand, and recommendations from Thai child clinicians.

Analyses of the referability of child problems

We have developed a method for assessing *problem referability* – that is, the power of various child problems to stimulate a clinic referral. The referability of a given problem, indexed by a new statistic that we call the *referability index,* reflects the frequency with which that problem stimulates clinic referral (based on our referral surveys), adjusted for its prevalence in the general population (based on our prevalence surveys).

Studies of Thai and American adult attitudes toward child problems

We have used vignettes describing different patterns of child clinical problems (overcontrolled, undercontrolled) to assess attitudes of adults (parents, teachers, and clinical psychologists) in Thailand and the United States (Weisz et al., 1988b; Weisz, Suwanlert, Chaiyasit, Weiss, & Jackson, 1991). We asked the adults to read a vignette, and then answer a series of questions about the child. Some of the questions involved ratings on seven-point Likert scales (e.g., "How serious is this child's problem?"), some were open-ended (e.g., "What do you think is the major cause of this child's behavior problems?").

Direct observations of child behavior problems in both countries

We have also used trained observers to record problem behaviors (and off-task behavior) displayed by Thai and American elementary school children in classroom settings. Certainly, no amount of observational training and reliability assessment can completely eliminate the influence of the observer's personal perspective. But we believe that Thai–American comparisons based on this observational approach can be a useful complement to data based on parent- and teacher-report checklists.

Some lessons learned to date

In the course of the various studies, using this five-method array, we have learned a number of lessons, some of which may generalize beyond the confines of our two target cultures. Here we describe ten of the most important lessons learned.

1. *Cultures that differ markedly in beliefs and child-rearing practices may nonetheless be very similar in the prevalence of various child problems.*

Despite marked cultural differences between Thailand and the United States, Thai and American parent reports in our epidemiologic studies have shown striking similarity in the population prevalence of child problems. In our study of parent reports for children aged 6–11 (Weisz et al., 1987b), for example, Thai and American means for total problems differed by only 3.4 points on a 240-point scale. Of 118 specific problems, 64 showed no significant cross-cultural difference despite the powerful statistical tests afforded by our sample of 960 children. Of the 54 problems on which Thai and American children did differ significantly, only six showed cross-cultural effects accounting for as much as 6% of the variance; thus, only 6 of 118 specific problems could be considered "medium" or "large" in magnitude by Cohen's (1988) standards. Thai and American mean scores were even more similar in our recent parallel study of adolescent problem prevalence (Weisz et al., 1993). In summary, the findings suggest that problem prevalence, as perceived by parents, is generally quite similar among Thai and American children.

This finding is echoed in a recent review of 13 cross-national studies using child problem checklists in 10 different countries (Weisz & Eastman, 1995); surveying the small number (and magnitude) of cross-national differences in individual problem rates left the reviewers "more impressed by the cross-national similarities they reveal than by the differences" (p. 46). The overall similarities found for so many different problems across most cultures studied thus far certainly raise an important developmental possibility: Much of what we see in the way of child problems in various parts of the world may be so strongly influenced by developmental forces that even wide variations in culture may not alter the picture dramatically.

2. *Despite cross-national similarities in the general population prevalence of many problems, certain theoretically meaningful clusters of child problem behavior may still differ in prevalence across cultures.*

The numerous similarities we have identified between American and Thai patterns of child psychopathology have not meant that the differences we found are uninteresting or unimportant. On the contrary, we found that overcontrolled or "internalizing" problems (e.g., fears, refusal to talk, shyness/timidity, constipation) were noted significantly more often for Thai than for American youngsters in our TYC general population prevalence studies using both parent reports (Weisz et al., 1987b, 1993) and teacher reports (Weisz et al., 1993). This difference is consistent with our theoretical interpretation of the literature on Thai culture and its emphasis on inhibition and self-control.

3. *Cultures may differ markedly in the specific problems for which children are referred to mental health specialists.*

We found marked cross-national differences in the problems for which youngsters in clinics had been referred for treatment (see Weisz et al., 1987a). Undercontrolled problems were much more often the cause of clinic referal in the United States than in Thailand, and the reverse was true of overcontrolled problems. Table 25.1 lists the 12 most common problems leading to clinic intake in the two countries. Note that all of the top 12 problems in the U.S. sample were undercontrolled;

Table 25.1. *Twelve most common referral problems in Thailand and the United States*

Problem	Type[a]	U.S. (%)	Thai (%)	x^2	p
United States					
1. Poor school work	U	33.9	35.9	0.4	ns
2. Disobedient at home	U	19.3	6.1	29.5	<.001
3. Temper tantrums, hot temper	U	15.4	11.7	2.2	ns
4. Gets into fights	U	14.3	.8	49.3	<.001
5. Disobedient at school	U	14.1	2.9	30.3	<.001
6. Physically attacks people	U	12.5	7.4	5.4	<.05
7. Lying or cheating	U	11.5	3.5	17.5	<.001
8. Steals outside the home	U	10.4	4.5	9.5	<.005
9. Can't concentrate, pay attention	U	10.2	6.4	3.6	<.10
10. Argues a lot	U	9.9	3.2	13.8	<.001
11. Demands attention	U	8.9	1.1	24.3	<.001
12. Can't sit still, hyperactive	U	8.6	5.6	2.6	ns
Thailand					
1. Poor school work	U	33.9	35.9	0.4	ns
2. Somatic problems (especially headaches) with no known physical cause	O	6.3	29.3	69.3	<.001
3. Absentminded, forgets easily	N	2.6	17.0	44.4	<.001
4. Fearful or anxious	O	3.4	12.8	22.6	<.001
5. Lacks motivation to study or learn	N	4.7	12.0	13.2	<.001
6. Sleep problems	O	1.0	11.7	36.5	<.001
7. Underactive, lacks energy	O	.5	11.7	41.6	<.001
8. Temper tantrums, hot temper	U	15.4	11.7	2.2	ns
9. Stubborn, sullen, irritable	M	4.7	9.8	7.5	<.01
10. Nervous movements, twitching	O	2.1	9.0	17.6	<.001
11. Strange behavior[b]	O	1.0	9.0	25.6	<.001
12. Worrying	O	2.6	7.4	9.4	<.005

[a] Type of problem, as determined by factor analyses of the Child Behavior Checklist (CBCL). U = loads exclusively or predominantly on the undercontrolled syndrome; O = loads exclusively or predominantly on the overcontrolled syndrome; M = loads on both syndromes with about equal frequency across various age X sex groups; N = not included in factor analysis, because it is not listed on CBCL.
[b] This category included behavior that seemed odd to parents but did not fall into any other category. Most was of a type often associated with thought disorder. For example, one child spoke words and sentences that made no sense and another had a habit of laughing out loud for no apparent reason.
Source: Weisz, J. R., Suwanlert, S., Chaiyasit, W. & Walter, B. (1987). Over- and undercontrolled referral problems among children and adolescents from Thailand and the United States: The *Wat* and *Wai* of cultural differences. *Journal of Consulting and Clinical Psychology, 55,* 719–726. Copyright 1987 by the American Psychological Association. Reprinted by permission.

by contrast, more than half the top 12 problems in the Thai sample were overcontrolled, and only two were undercontrolled. Such striking differences suggest a substantial difference between the two countries in the kinds of problems that are receiving clinical attention.

4. *Some problems may have more power to evoke clinic referral in one culture than in another; and the relation between referability and other factors (e.g., gender, problem type) may differ across cultures.*
The fact that a particular problem, or cluster of problems (e.g., overcontrolled) is more often seen in the clinics of Thailand than those of the United States may mean at least two things: the problem has particular power to stimulate a referral – for example, perhaps it is seen as especially serious – when it occurs in Thai children; or the problem is simply more prevalent in the general population of Thailand than of the United States, and thus the problem is more likely, for purely statistical reasons, to show up in Thai clinics. In other words, high prevalence in a clinic sample is hard to interpret unambiguously. This being the case, if we want to examine the first phenomenon – that is, the power of particular problems to evoke referral when they occur within a particular culture – we cannot do so by simply counting rates of problem referral in clinics; instead, we must adjust each problem's clinic referral rate according to its prevalence rate in the general population of that culture.

We have pursued this issue in our research program, developing methods, and a companion statistic, for studying the *referability* of problems in different cultures (Weisz & Weiss, 1991). The statistic, which we call the *referability index* (RI), permits us to assess the referability of various problems in Thailand and the United States – that is, the power of each problem to stimulate referral to a specialist. We compute the RI for each individual problem, within a culture, by applying logit analysis to data on the clinic-referral rate of the problem, adjusting for that problem's general population prevalence within the culture (general population prevalence is assessed in our epidemiologic studies using the TYC – see Lessons 1 and 2).

Using this method, we have found some intriguing cross-national differences. For example, as Figure 25.1 shows, we have found problems in general to be more referable for girls than boys in the United States, but not in Thailand. Our data suggest that this is partly due to the strong tendency of Americans to refer girls more than boys for sex-related problems (e.g., "thinks about sex too much"). As Figure 25.2 shows, we have found undercontrolled problems to be much more referable than overcontrolled problems in the United States, but not in Thailand. The fact that undercontrolled problems are not more referable in Thailand may seem surprising, given the clear risks posed by many kinds of undercontrolled behavior. Our Thai collaborators have suggested that the relatively low level of referability for undercontrolled problems in their country may reflect the fact that such problems are *so* unacceptable in Thai culture; Thai parents may be embarrassed to "go public" with such problems, admitting via clinic referral that they have been unable to prevent such problems within their home.

It is certainly no surprise that gender and problem type are significantly related to the power of child problems to generate referral. What our findings suggest,

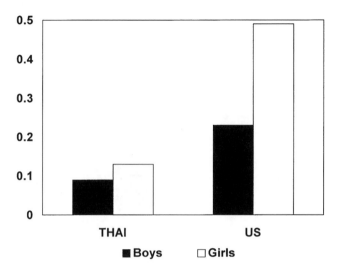

Figure 25.1. Gender x Culture interaction: referability of problems for boys and girls in Thailand and the United States (vertical axis shows mean referability index). *Source:* Weisz, J. R. & Weiss, B. (1991). Studying the referability of child clinical problems. *Journal of Consulting and Clinical Psychology, 59,* 266–273. Copyright 1991 by the American Psychological Association. Reprinted by permission.

however, is that the precise nature of that relationship may be quite different from one culture to the next.

5. *As the referability findings suggest, cultural differences may be linked to sharply contrasting adult attitudes toward the same child problems.*

Our vignette research (Weisz et al., 1988b, 1991) suggested significant cross-national differences in adults' attitudes and beliefs about child problems. After Thai and American parents, teachers, and clinical psychologists read through vignettes depicting children with overcontrolled and undercontrolled problems, they rated (on a seven-point scale) how worried they would be as the child's parent and as the child's teacher, how likely the child would be to improve if no intervention occurred, how serious the child's problems were, and how unusual the child was. Main effects of problem type indicated that undercontrolled problems were viewed as more serious and worrisome, and as less likely to improve, than overcontrolled problems. However, strong main effects of culture (not mitigated by any interaction with problem type) indicated that, averaging across both types of problems, American adults rated children's problems as more serious, more worrisome, more unusual, and less likely to improve, than did Thai adults. This pattern, shown in Figure 25.3, suggests that very different thresholds may exist in the two countries for concern over both undercontrolled and overcontrolled child problems. As suggested earlier, reasons for such threshold differences may include Buddhist versus Western

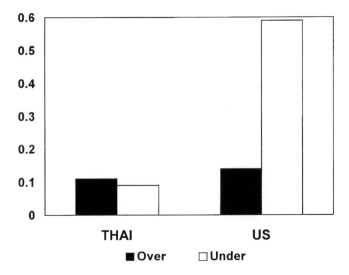

Figure 25.2. Culture x Problem Type interaction: referability of overcontrolled and under-controlled problems in Thailand and the United States (vertical axis shows mean referability index). *Source:* Weisz, J. R. & Weiss, B. (1991). Studying the referrability of child clinical problems. *Journal of Consulting and Clinical Psychology, 59,* 266–273. Copyright 1991 by the American Psychological Association. Reprinted by permission.

philosophical views on the transience versus the tenacity of personality and problems, and even Thai versus American differences in exposure to media on child psychology.

6. *Cultural differences may be associated not only with different adult attitudes toward child problems, but also with different adult beliefs regarding etiology and appropriate remediation.*

To sharpen our picture of cross-national differences in adult constructions of developmental psychopathology, it is useful to understand differences in prevailing beliefs about etiology and treatment. In our vignette research (Weisz et al., 1988b), when we asked Thai and American adults to identify "the major cause" of the vignette child's problem, we found that Thais were particularly likely to attribute the problems to faulty child rearing, socialization, or teaching; more than half made such a causal attribution for both over- and undercontrolled problems. Americans, by contrast, preferred child personality trait and psychodynamic attributions (e.g., the child has internal conflicts); they were much less likely than Thai adults to attribute responsibility to parents or other socializing agents. The findings are shown in Figure 25.4.

We found equally striking cross-national differences in the remediation proposals adults advanced for the children. Responding to our question, "What methods could be used at home to assist this child?" Thai adults favored verbal interventions (e.g., "talk to the child," "reassure him") for both over- and undercontrolled chil-

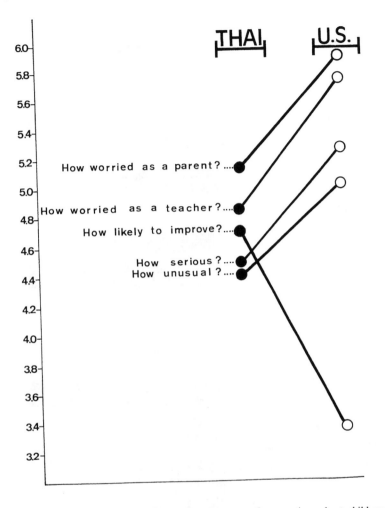

Figure 25.3. Thai and American adults' answers to five questions about child problems (problem types combined). The numbers reflect mean ratings on Likert scales ranging from 1 to 7. *Source:* Weisz, J. R., Suwanlert, S., Chaiyasit, W., Weiss, B., Walter, B., & Anderson, W. (1988). Thai and American perspectives on over- and undercontrolled child behavior problems: Exploring the threshold model among parents, teachers, and psychologists. *Journal of Consulting and Clinical Psychology, 56,* 601–609. Copyright 1988 by the American Psychological Association. Reprinted by permission.

dren, whereas Americans favored more behavioral approaches involving reward and punishment contingencies. Viewed broadly, this collection of findings suggests that a child who shows disturbed behavior may well meet with very different adult interpretations and very different intervention preferences depending on the cultural context within which that child shows the behavior.

7. *Cross-cultural differences may be found not only across nations but across*

OVERCONTROLLED CHILD

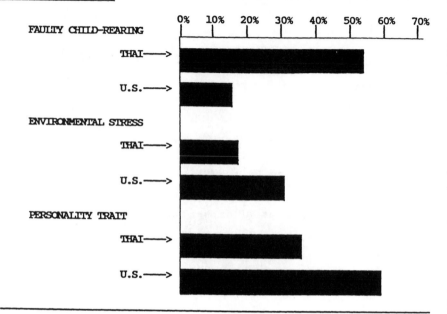

UNDERCONTROLLED CHILD

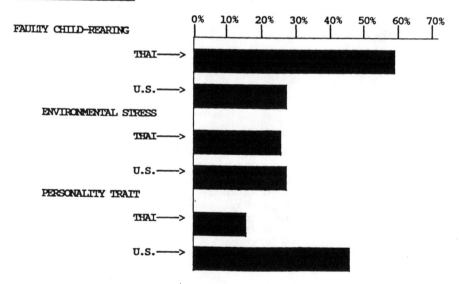

Figure 25.4. Percentage of Thai and American adults identifying various factors as the primary cause of overcontrolled and undercontrolled child problems. *Source:* Weisz, J. R., Suwanlert, S., Chaiyasit, W., Weiss, B., Walter, B., & Anderson, W. (1988). Thai and American perspectives on over- and undercontrolled child behavior problems: Exploring the threshold model among parents, teachers, and psychologists. *Journal of Consulting and Clinical Psychology, 56,* 601–609. Copyright 1988 by the American Psychological Association. Reprinted by permission.

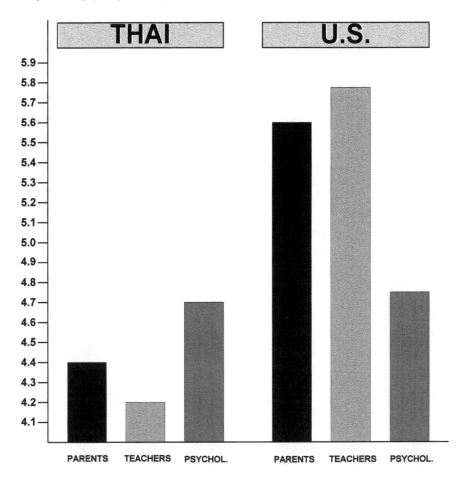

Figure 25.5. Mean responses to the question, "How serious is this child's problem?" Ratings ranged from 1 (*not serious at all*) to 7 (*very serious*). Psychol. = psychologists. *Source:* Weisz, J. R., Suwanlert, S., Chaiyasit, W., Weiss, B., Walter, B., & Anderson, W. (1988). Thai and American perspectives on over- and undercontrolled child behavior problems: Exploring the threshold model among parents, teachers, and psychologists. *Journal of Consulting and Clinical Psychology, 56,* 601–609. Copyright 1988 by the American Psychological Association. Reprinted by permission.

different professional groups; for example, psychologists may form a kind of "professional culture," via a socialization process analogous to socialization within a national culture.

One other finding of our vignette research (Weisz et al., 1988b) bears attention here. Adult ratings of the "seriousness" of the child problem behavior in the vignettes showed marked cross-national differences among parents and teachers, but notable similarity among psychologists from the two countries. As shown in Figure 25.5, this marked cross-national similarity among psychologists actually meant that Thai psychologists "overpathologized" relative to Thai parents and teachers, whereas American psychologists "underpathologized" relative to American parents and teachers. In interpreting this finding, it is useful to note that most Thai psychologists receive instruction via Western textbooks and articles, and from teachers and supervisors who attended Western universities. Indeed, most child clinical training around the world has its origins in the West. Such training is, of course, a kind of professional socialization analogous in some respects to the process of growing up within a national culture. Psychologists – and other professionals, as well – in various parts of the world may thus partake of a "professional culture" so potent as to mitigate some of the effects of their own national culture.

8. *Evidence continues to accumulate that boys show a number of undercontrolled problems more often than do girls, across cultures, even in Thailand, where boys are taught otherwise.*

In our parent-report epidemiologic studies, boys showed significantly higher rates of several undercontrolled problems (e.g., bragging, disobeying, fire setting) than did girls. Boys also showed significantly higher scores than girls on total undercontrolled (externalizing) problems among 6–11-year-olds (Weisz et al., 1987b), but not among adolescents (Weisz et al., 1993). Importantly, there was no significant culture–gender interaction for total undercontrolled problems among either the 6–11-year-olds or the adolescents; this suggests that cultural practices of Thailand were not associated with a significantly different pattern of gender differences than that found in the United States, for either age group. And at the level of individual problems, there were very few gender x culture interactions indicating different gender effects in Thailand than in the United States. By contrast, numerous gender differences seen particularly frequently in other countries (see following paragraph) were replicated as gender main effects cutting across the Thai and U.S. samples. In both the child and adolescent samples (Weisz et al., 1987b, 1993), the majority of problems showing higher prevalence for boys than girls were undercontrolled problems.

As Table 25.2 (adapted from Achenbach, Hensley, Phares, & Grayson, 1990) shows, the gender differences seen in Thailand and the United States are rather consistent with gender differences in problem prevalence reported for other countries (see also Verhulst & Achenbach, 1995; Weisz & Eastman, 1995). However, the Thai findings are of special interest because they arose in a culture where boys receive special training in the tenets of Therevada Buddhism, including nonaggression, politeness, and humility. Indeed, it could be argued that Thailand is one of the few places in the world where cultural traditions might be expected to moderate the traditional sex differences in undercontrolled behavior. Yet the traditional sex differences emerged in Thailand, as in the United States and other countries where similar problem checklist methods have been used. The robustness of these sex differences across such different cultures offers some support for the notion that they reflect relatively culture-transcendent developmental forces that are not easily countered by prosocial, pacific socialization of boys.

Table 25.2. *Problems showing gender differences across multiple national samples*

	Chile	Holland	Ontario	Puerto Rico	Sydney	Thailand	U.S.
Boys > girls							
Bragging	−	+	+	−	+	+	+
Can't concentrate	+	+	+	+	+	−	+
Can't sit still	+	+	+	+	+	+	+
Destroys own things	+	+	+	+	+	+	+
Disobedient at school	+	+	+	+	+	−	+
Impulsive	+	+	+	−	−	+	+
Sets fires	+	+	+	+	+	(+)	+
Showing off	+	+	+	−	+	+	+
Speech problem	−	+	+	(+)	+	+	+
Swearing	+	+	+	(+)	+	−	+
Teases a lot	+	+	+	(+)	+	+	+
Girls > boys							
Fears	+	+	+	+	+	−	+

Note. + indicates gender difference significant at $p < 0.01$; (+) indicates gender differences significant at $p < 0.05$; − indicates nonsignificant gender differences. Data from Chile and Thailand are for ages 6–11 only. This table is constructed from data presented in Achenbach, Hensley, Phares, and Grayson (1990).

9. Cross-cultural research on developmental psychopathology poses methodological challenges; consider the problem of parent reports, and consider the inherent complexity of culture.

Cross-cultural research on child psychological problems poses special methodological problems. Methods that are currently available do not permit us to control, or even gauge, the full impact of diverse cultural influences that may help to shape our findings.

Consider, for example, our use of parent reports to assess the prevalence of child problems. Such parent reports may certainly reflect the actual occurrence and intensity of those problems. However, parent reports may also be influenced by cultural context – in at least three ways. First, the cultural milieu may color adults' judgments about what is *appropriate* for children at a given age; such judgments could help determine whether parents report, for example, that their child "talks too much" (item No. 93 on the TYC and CBCL). An amount of talking considered *appropriate* by American parents might well be considered *too much* by parents in a culture where children are expected to be quiet. Second, cultural context may color adults' judgments about what is *usual* for children at a given age; such judgments could influence the likelihood that parents would report, for example, that their child is "unusually loud" (item No. 104). Third, parent reports may be influenced by culture-bound definitions of concepts embedded in the problem items. For example, the Thai definition of "swearing" (item No. 90) includes language that would be considered merely impolite in the United States; swearing, in Thailand, includes calling a peer a lizard, or insulting a peer's parent. Thus, the fact that Thai parents in our study reported twice as much swearing among their 6–11-year-old children as did American parents may reflect, in part, cross-cultural differences in the breadth of the definition.

Concerns such as these need to be raised for two reasons. First, it is important to recognize the limitations of our methods lest we overinterpret findings. Second, raising such concerns can help point the way to more refined methods, or at least a richer methodological diversity. In the case of child psychopathology, for example, we think it is worthwhile to supplement parent (and other) reports with direct observations of child behavior.

Finally, to make a broader point: Cultures are complex, and this makes clear interpretation of findings an elusive goal at best. In Lesson 8, we noted the persistence of gender differences in undercontrolled behavior despite the messages of nonaggression and prosocial behavior that are emphasized in the socialization of Thai boys. Although this does appear to be generally true in Thailand, it would be an oversimplification to argue that the socialization of Thai boys is devoid of any proaggression messages. Indeed, Thais take great pride in the fierce reputation of their all-male military force. And Thai males across the age spectrum show considerable interest in Thai boxing, which adds to American boxing such features as kicking and kneeing one's opponent. Moreover, in the age of satellite dishes and videocassetes, many of the same displays of undercontrolled behavior that are viewed by boys in the United States, Germany, Chile, and Kenya, are also quite accessible to boys in Thailand. All this is to say that cultures are both complex and permeable; and given our mass communication capacity, it is fair to say that virtually any culture is a moving target. None of this should prevent us from studying developmental psychopathology cross-nationally. But the complexity of the task certainly justifies caution, and humility.

10. *Findings from different cross-national studies may not necessarily fit together to form a seamless fabric.*

Finally, we emphasize that cross-national research on developmental psychopathology is not a perfectly additive process, particularly if one adopts a strategy of methodological diversity. As methods and informants change, so may the findings. As one example, consider our recent multimethod study of Thai and American children's problem behavior in school classrooms (Weisz, Chaiyasit, Weiss, Eastman, & Jackson, 1995). As Figure 25.6 shows, data from our trained observers in the classrooms clearly showed rates of problem behavior that were twice as high among American children as among Thai children. However, teacher reports *on the same children* showed *precisely the opposite* cross-national difference, with problem scores twice as high for Thai children as for their American counterparts. To complicate matters further, both sets of findings differed notably from our parent-report epidemiologic surveys, which have shown *negligible* Thai–U.S. differences in total problems. Overall, these contrasting findings serve as one of several

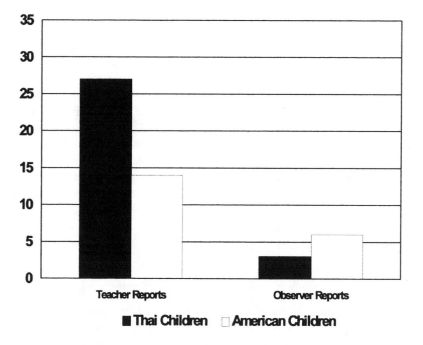

Figure 25.6. Total problem scores of Thai and American children, as reported by the children's teachers and by trained observers. *Source:* Weisz, J. R., Chaiyasit, W., Weiss, B., Eastman, K. L., & Jackson, E. W. (1995). A multimethod study of problem behavior among Thai and American children in school: teacher reports versus direct observations. *Child Development, 66,* 402–415. Copyright 1985 by the University of Chicago Press. Reprinted by permission.

reminders in our data that the study of child psychopathology is the study of both child behavior and the perspective from which that behavior is viewed by the individuals who report on it. Different individuals see the child, and the child's behavior, differently, and different groups of informants (e.g., observers vs. teachers vs. parents) observe different samples of child behavior occurring in different settings. Accordingly, it should not surprise us that groups as different as parents, teachers, and trained observers should present rather different pictures of the children on whom they report.

Concluding thoughts

Having considered ten rather specific lessons derived from our research, we would now like to address three rather global issues. One of these concerns the nature of "psychopathology"; the other two concern the relation between our findings and some basic themes of developmental psychopathology.

Psychopathology: A blend of behavior and lens

One general conclusion is that "psychopathology" is inevitably a convergence of actual behavior and the lens through which that behavior is viewed – by particular individuals, in particular societies, and at particular points in time. Because the lens is apt to be tinted by the cultural background, values, and standards of the viewer, the very same behavior may be viewed as deviant and/or seriously disturbed in one society, and as relatively normal in another. This fact is suggested rather directly by the findings of our vignette research (Weisz et al., 1988b; see Figure 25.3); but it is implicit within many of our other findings, and it needs to be factored into interpretation of those findings. For example, as noted in Lesson 9, the fact that Thai parents report the problem "unusually loud" more for their children than do American parents for their children may reflect the influence of both the actual child behavior they have observed and their own culturally shaped expectation regarding what is "usual" for children.

Ethnotypic consistency in child and adolescent behavior

A second general concept relates to the notion of *heterotypic continuity* (see Hinshaw, 1994; Kagan, 1969), the idea that an underlying trait may be expressed in different forms at different developmental levels. Perhaps it is also true that a common core problem, or type of dysfunction, may be manifest in different overt forms by youngsters from different societies. We call this concept *ethnotypic consistency.* As an example of the concept, "disobedience" in the United States may typically take such overt and direct forms as refusing to comply and/or saying no; such direct forms may be rare among Thai children, for whom "disobedience" may instead consist of looking uninterested, or hesitating (and thus signaling unwillingness) before complying. Calibrated according to the standards and expectations of the two societies, these overtly different behaviors may have similar underlying meaning – that is, they reflect disobedience as the respective societies construe that concept.

The notion of ethnotypic consistency highlights a methodological dilemma. Suppose it is true, for example, that concepts such as "disobedience," "unusually loud," "talks too much," and "swearing" are defined in terms of rather different specific child behaviors in one culture than in another. How then should one respond in designing cross-national research on such concepts? Should one aim for literal equivalence – for example, defining "disobedience" in terms of exactly the same child behaviors? Or should we aim for conceptual equivalence – for example, letting "disobedience" be defined differently across cultures, to fit prevailing societal concepts? Arguably, it is the culturally calibrated definitions of the various problem concepts (disobedience, talking too much, etc.) that we most need to tap in our assessments. On the other hand, interpreting group differences becomes difficult when standardization is violated by using different criteria for different cultures. Cross-cultural research may require us to make hard choices, pitting the rigor of literal equivalence against the cultural sensitivity of conceptual equivalence.

Correlational nature of cross-cultural research and the context of discovery

Cross-cultural research is inherently correlational, and cross-cultural differences are inevitably overdetermined. In such research, we compare groups of children who were – blessedly – not randomly assigned to a culture, and the cultures we compare differ along an infinite array of dimensions. These two truths will mean that "the true cause" of any specific cross-cultural difference is apt to remain elusive. What then is the purpose of cross-cultural research?

Zigler and Seitz (1982, p. 188) suggested that cross-cultural research may provide "natural experiments" concerning factors that may influence development; in the present context, this might mean, for example, factors related to the development of overcontrolled child problems, which appear to be more prevalent among Thai youth than their American counterparts. We have suggested, also, that cross-cultural research can broaden our understanding of the range of variation that is possible over the course of development, the robustness of theoretically important subgroup differences (e.g., gender differences in undercontrolled behavior), and differences in adult judgments about, and responses to, various child and adolescent problems.

More broadly, we think it is useful to view cross-cultural research in the light of the distinction between "context of discovery" and "context of confirmation," as proposed by philosophers of science (e.g., Popper, 1961) and applied to our field by developmental theorists (e.g., Achenbach, 1982). In the context of discovery, ideas are generated (e.g., via intuition, happenstance, naturalistic observation); in the context of confirmation, these ideas are subjected to systematic test. Cross-cultural research on developmental psychopathology may be best construed as part of the context of discovery – that is, as a means of generating ideas about causal processes that can later be tested more rigorously through those experimental means that are not feasible within a cross-national design.

How our findings relate to developmental psychopathology

Chapters throughout this volume have emphasized and illustrated several central themes of developmental psychopathology (some articulated in Cicchetti, 1984, 1989). In this spirit, we note here a few of these recurrent themes as they relate to the cross-national research we have reviewed.

Linking classical developmental issues, theory, and research to psychopathology: Cross-national similarities and differences and their implications for socializa-

tion. Many core developmental issues are addressable in part via cross-national research. As one example, a long-standing issue dating at least from the early work of Vygotsky (later summarized in Vygotsky, 1978) has been the degree to which behavior is subject to the influence of variations in socialization practices. Applied to the study of psychopathology, this issue takes the form of the following question: To what extent do various patterns of psychological dysfunction reflect general developmental influences of childhood and adolescence, and to what extent do they represent social-environmental factors? Cross-cultural research can help us address this question.

When such research reveals patterns that are highly similar across very *dissimilar* cultures, culture-general developmental and biological causal processes need to be seriously considered. In our findings, there were two examples: a striking Thai–U.S. similarity in the general population prevalence of most problems, and a distinct cross-national similarity in the relation between gender and problem behavior, with most of the individual problem gender effects showing higher levels of undercontrolled problems in boys than girls. Evidently, the marked Thai–U.S. differences in socialization of children have not had much impact on these two phenomena.

By contrast, when cross-cultural research reveals patterns that are quite different from one culture to the next, the search for causes needs to include social-environmental processes that may differ across the cultures. In our research, examples include the findings that, compared with their American counterparts, Thai youth showed more overcontrolled problems, Thai youth were more likely to be referred to clinics for overcontrolled problems, and Thai adults were less likely to regard child problems as serious or worrisome, more likely to attribute such problems to faulty child rearing, and more likely to favor psychodynamic or "talking" interventions. Here, then, are several areas where culture may well have a marked impact.

Using insights from atypical or rarely studied populations to enrich our understanding of normal developmental processes. Population groups that are already widely studied have thus been given multiple opportunities to be incorporated into the literature and theoretical models of our field. Stretching our data base to include such rarely studied cultures as Thailand may help broaden our thinking about "normal" or "typical" development. For example, the findings suggest hypotheses about the role of suppression-facilitation processes in normal socialization that may influence children's susceptibility to overcontrolled problems. Such hypotheses may, of course, be tested within our own culture by studying the prevalence of overcontrolled problems as a function of variations in American child-rearing practice.

Linking findings derived from psychological methods with ideas and evidence from other disciplines. We have relied heavily on ethnographic and clinical literature from Thailand to identify mainstream socialization practices there and to develop ideas about how these might influence the prevalence of particular types of child problems (see, e.g., Moore, 1974; Phillips, 1965; Sangsingkeo, 1969; Suvannathat, 1979; Suwanlert, 1974). The same body of literature has been helpful in generating possible interpretations of our findings, as reflected in the series of "lessons" we have detailed here. Beyond the written work of other disciplines, we have found it useful to consult with practitioners who have their own kinds of expertise in developmental psychopathology – that is, clinical psychologists, psychiatrists, and physicians who live and work within the culture being studied.

Contributing to social policy and the development of preventive interventions. Some research efforts in developmental psychopathology generate applications to social policy and prevention (see Cohler, Stott, & Musick, 1995, on why such applications require attention to culture). Proper timing of such applications is difficult to perfect; it is hard to know when the base of information is sufficiently reliable, and when the proper interpretation of findings is sufficiently clear, to warrant a move toward policy recommendations. At times, the pace of unfolding events requires that we address social issues based on the best available evidence or lose the opportunity to have an impact (see, e.g., Zigler, 1976, and Zigler & Anderson, 1978, on "Operation Babylift" at the end of the Vietnam War).

In our work in Thailand, we are not faced with such a fleeting opportunity, and this is fortunate, because our data do not lead directly to major policy recommendations. However, work like ours may well form the basis for longitudinal research, which could, in turn, inform early detection and prevention efforts. Indeed, mental health officials in the Thai government are already beginning to use our Thai Youth Checklist in this way. The TYC will be administered to large groups of young children in Thailand, and periodic follow-up assessments will be used to determine which early problems predict longer-term difficulties.

Implications for American youth

The old proverb, "The fish is the last to discover water," suggests that is it difficult to see one's own environment clearly while confined within it. One of the benefits of cross-national research may be that it affords us an opportunity to step outside our own culture and thus see it more clearly. Indeed, our Thai–U.S. comparisons suggest certain perspectives on development within American society. For example, our referability research (see Figures 25.1 and 25.2, and see Weisz & Weiss, 1991) indicates that, for Americans but not for Thais, undercontrolled problems have much greater power to stimulate clinic referral than overcontrolled problems, and problems occurring in girls have greater power to stimulate referral than problems occurring in boys. Future efforts to understand such differential differences may sharpen our insight into our own culture, its perspective on child problems, and its implicit views on gender vis-à-vis developmental psychopathology.

One of the broad notions emerging from our work is that the culture not only defines what is deviant but also what is normal, and that these definitions may shift for the same individual, depending on which of his or her "cultures" is referenced. This point has particularly important implications for societies, like our own, which are both multicultural and subject to large cross-generational "cultural" differences. Luthar's (e.g., 1995) research on inner-city, primarily minority group American youth illustrates this point. She finds that good peer relations and sociability are *positively* correlated with academic failure and disruptive behavior – both seemingly consistent with the prevailing values of "bucking the system" and disdain for academics in these peer groups. What seems to be true for these popular youth is that they display behavior that is normative for the immediate culture of their peer group but deviant from the perspective of the mainstream general population. We noted that deviance, "pathology," and "normality" must necessarily represent a combination of the individual's actual behavior and the lens through which that behavior is viewed by others in the culture. Luthar's findings underscore the fact that individuals often partake of multiple cultures, arrayed a bit like concentric circles, and that for some young people, the most immediate "culture" of the peer group may be much more powerful in its impact than the broad national culture within which that peer group is situated.

As this point suggests, studying the relation between culture and developmental psychopathology is a complex, multilayered enterprise – indeed, an enterprise that has just barely begun. The findings presented in this chapter illustrate some of the lessons that may be learned from the process; but, almost certainly, the most important lessons have yet to be identified. Our hope is that through continued study of child and adolescent behavior, culture, and the interplay of these factors, we may all come to understand development and dysfunction in ways that would not otherwise be possible.

References

Achenbach, T. M. (1982). *Developmental psychopathology*. New York: Wiley.

Achenbach, T. M. (1991a). *Manual for the Child Behavior Checklist and 1991 Profile*. Burlington: University of Vermont, Department of Psychiatry.

Achenbach, T. M. (1991b). *Manual for the Teacher's Report Form and 1991 Profile*. Burlington: University of Vermont, Department of Psychiatry.

Achenbach, T. M., & Edelbrock, C. S. (1978). The classification of child psychopathology: A review and analysis of empirical efforts. *Psychological Bulletin, 85,* 1275–1301.

Achenbach, T. M., & Edelbrock, C. S. (1981). Behavioral problems and competencies reported by parents of normal and disturbed children aged 4–16. *Monographs of the Society for Research in Child Development, 46,* No. 188.

Achenbach, T. M., Hensley, V. R., Phares, V., & Grayson, D. (1990). Problems and competencies reported by parents of Australian and American children. *Journal of Child Psychology and Psychiatry, 31,* 265–286.

Bernstein, G. A., & Borchardt, C. M. (1991). Anxiety disorders of childhood and adolescence: A critical review. *Journal of the American Academy of Child and Adolescent Psychiatry, 30,* 519–532.

Boesch, E. (1977). Authority and work attitudes of Thais. In K. Wenk & K. Rosenberg (Eds.), *Thai in German eyes* (pp. 176–231). Bangkok: Kledthai.

Cicchetti, D. (1984). The emergence of developmental psychopathology. *Child Development, 55,* 1–7.

Cicchetti, D. (Ed.). (1988). *The emergence of a discipline: Rochester symposium on developmental psychopathology* (Vol. 1). Hillsdale, NJ: Erlbaum.

Cohen, J. (1988). *Statistical power analysis for the behavioral sciences* (rev. ed.). San Diego, CA: Academic Press.

Cohler, B. J., Stott, F. M., & Musick, J. S. (1995). Adversity, vulnerability, and resilience: Cultural and developmental perspectives. In D. Cicchetti & D. J. Cohen (Eds.), *Developmental Psychopathology*, Vol. 2: *Risk, Disorder, and Adaptation* (pp. 753–800). New York: Wiley.

Draguns, J. G. (1973). Comparison of psychopathology across cultures: Issues, findings, directions. *Journal of Cross-Cultural Psychology, 4,* 9–47.

Draguns, J. G. (1982). Methodology in cross-cultural psychology. In I. Al-Issa (Ed.), *Culture and psychopathology* (pp. 33–70). Baltimore: University Park Press.

Gardiner, H. W. (1968). Expression of anger among Thais: Some preliminary findings. *Psychologia, 11,* 221–228.

Gardiner, H. W., & Suttipan, C. S. (1977). Parental tolerance of aggression: Perceptions of preadolescents in Thailand. *Psychologia, 20,* 28–32.

Gotlib, I. H., & Hammen, C. L. (1992). Child and adolescent depression: Features and correlates. In I. H. Gottlib & C. L. Hammen (Eds.), *Psychological aspects of depression: Toward a cognitive-interpersonal integration* (pp. 36–66). New York: Wiley.

Gray, J. A. (1982). *The neuropsychology of anxiety: An enquiry into the functions of the septo-hippocampal system.* Oxford: Oxford University Press.

Hetherington, E. M., & Martin, B. (1986). Family interaction. In H. C. Quay & J. S. Werry (Eds.), *Psychopathological disorders of childhood* (3rd ed., pp. 332–390). New York: Wiley.

Hinshaw, S. P. (1994). Conduct disorder in childhood: Conceptualization, diagnosis, comorbidity, and risk status for antisocial functioning in adulthood. In D. C. Fowles, P. Sutker, & S. H. Goodman (Eds.), *Progress in experimental personality and psychopathology research* (pp. 3–44). New York: Springer.

Kagan, J. (1969). The three faces of continuity in human development. In D. A. Goslin (Ed.), *Handbook of socialization theory and research* (pp. 983–1002). Chicago: Rand McNally.

Kagan, J. (1989). Temperamental contributions to social behavior. *American Psychologist, 44,* 668–674.

Kagan, J., Reznick, J. S., & Snidman, N. (1987). The physiology and psychology of behavioral inhibition in children. *Child Development, 58,* 1459–1473.

Kazdin, A. E. (1996). Conduct disorder across the life span. In S. S. Luthar, J. A. Burack, D. Cicchetti, & J. Weisz (eds.), *Developmental psychopathology: Perspectives on risk and disorder.* New York: Cambridge University Press.

Luthar, S. S. (1995). Social competence in the school setting: Prospective cross-domain associations among inner-city teens. *Child Development, 66,* 416–429.

Maccoby, E. E., & Jacklin, C. N. (1974). *The psychology of sex differences.* Stanford, CA: Stanford University Press.

Moore, F. J. (1974). *Thailand: Its people, its society, its culture.* New Haven, CT: HRAF Press.

National Identity Office (Kingdom of Thailand). (1984). *Thailand in the 80s.* Bangkok: Muang Boran Publishing House.

Phillips, H. P. (1965). *Thai peasant personality: The patterning of interpersonal behavior in the village of Bang Chan.* Berkeley: University of California Press.

Popper, K. R. (1961). *The logic of scientific discovery.* New York: Science Editions.

Rutter, M. & Garmezy, N. (1983). *Developmental psychopathology.* In P. Mussen & E. M. Hetherington (Eds.), *Handbook of child psychology* (Vol. 4, pp. 775–911). New York: Wiley.

Sangsingkeo, P. (1969). Buddhism and some effects on the rearing of children in Thailand. In W. Caudill & T. Y. Lin (Eds.), *Mental health research in Asia and the Pacific* (pp. 286–295). Honolulu: East-West Center Press.

Suvannathat, C. (1979). The inculcation of values in Thai children. *International Social Science Journal, 31,* 477–485.

Suwanlert, S. (1974). Some personality characteristics of Thai students. In W. P. Lebra (Ed.), *Youth, socialization, and mental health in Asia and the Pacific* (pp. 75–84). Honolulu: University Press of Hawaii.

Verhulst, F. C., & Achenbach, T. M. (1995). Empirically-based assessment and taxonomy of psycho-pathology: Cross-cultural applications. A review. *European Child and Adolescent Psychiatry, 4,* 61–76.

Vygotsky, L. S. (1978). *Mind and society.* Cambridge, MA: Harvard University Press.

Weisz, J. R. (1989). Culture and the development of child psychopathology: Lessons from Thailand. In D. Cicchetti (Ed.), *The emergence of a discipline: Rochester symposium on developmental psychopathology* (Vol. 1, pp. 89–117). Hillsdale, NJ: Erlbaum.

Weisz, J. R., Chaiyasit, W., Weiss, B., Eastman, K. L., & Jackson, E. W. (1995). A multimethod study of problem behavior among Thai and American children in school: Teacher reports versus Direct Observations. *Child Development, 66,* 402–415.

Weisz, J. R., & Eastman, K. L. (1995). Cross-national research on child and adolescent psychopathol-ogy. In F. C. Verhulst & H. M. Koot (Eds.), *The epidemiology of child and adolescent psycho-pathology* (pp. 42–65). Oxford: Oxford University Press.

Weisz, J. R., Suwanlert, S., Chaiyasit, W., & Walter, B. (1987a). Over- and Undercontrolled referral problems among children and adolescents from Thailand and the United States: The *Wat* and *Wai* of cultural differences. *Journal of Consulting and Clinical Psychology, 55,* 719–726.

Weisz, J. R., Suwanlert, S., Chaiyasit, W., Weiss, B., Achenbach, T. M., & Eastman, K. L. (1993). Epidemiology of behavioral and emotional problems among Thai and American adolescents: Parent reports for ages 12–16. *Journal of Abnormal Psychology, 102,* 395–403.

Weisz, J. R., Suwanlert, S., Chaiyasit, W., Weiss, B., Achenbach, T. M., & Trevathan, D. (1988a). Epidemiology of behavioral and emotional problems among Thai and American children: Teacher reports for ages 6–11. *Journal of Child Psychology and Psychiatry, 30,* 471–484.

Weisz, J. R., Suwanlert, S., Chaiyasit, W., Weiss, B., Achenbach, T. M., & Walter, B. (1987b). Epi-demiology of behavioral and emotional problems among Thai and American children: Parent re-ports for ages 6–11. *Journal of the American Academy of Child and Adolescent Psychiatry, 26,* 890–897.

Weisz, J. R., Suwanlert, S., Chaiyasit, W., Weiss, B., & Jackson, E. W. (1991). Adult attitudes toward over- and undercontrolled child problems: Urban and rural parents and teachers from Thailand the the United States. *Journal of Child Psychology and Psychiatry, 32,* 645–654.

Weisz, J. R., Suwanlert, S., Chaiyasit, W., Weiss, B., Walter, B., & Anderson, W. (1988b). Thai and American perspectives on over- and undercontrolled child behavior problems: Exploring the thresh-old model among parents, teachers, and psychologists. *Journal of Consulting and Clinical Psy-chology, 56,* 601–609.

Weisz, J. R., & Weiss, B. (1991). Studying the referability of child clinical problems. *Journal of Consulting and Clinical Psychology, 59,* 266–273.

Zigler, E. (1976). A developmental psychologist's view of operation babylift. *American Psychologist, 31,* 329–340.

Zigler, E., & Anderson, K. (1978, December). The last victims of Vietnam. *Psychology Today,* pp. 24, 30.

Zigler, E., & Child, I. L. (1969). Socialization. In G. Lindzey & E. Aronson (Eds.), *Handbook of social psychology* (2nd ed., pp. 450–589). Reading, MA: Addison-Wesley.

Zigler, E., Lamb, M. E., & Child, I. L. (1982). *Socialization and personality development* (2nd ed.). New York: Oxford University Press.

Zigler, E., & Seitz, V. (1982). Future research on socialization and personality development. In E. Zigler, M. E. Lamb, & I. L. Child (Eds.), *Socialization and personality development* (2nd ed., pp. 185–199). New York: Oxford University Press.

Subject index

593

Author index

Aber, J. L., 167, 178, 284, 320, 335, 340, 393, 400, 417, 419, 421, 470, 471, 472, 552
Abidin, R. R., 175
Aboud, F., 52, 56, 61
Abramson, L., 284, 295, 296
Achenbach, T. M., xviii, 17, 96, 97, 99, 100, 101, 103, 105, 109, 111, 189, 228, 234, 236, 238, 241, 250, 278, 291, 376, 427, 429, 570, 572, 573, 582, 587
Acunzo, M. A., 231
Adamse, M., 179
Ageton, S. S., 268
Ainsworth, M. D. S., 289, 329, 419, 423, 555, 556, 557, 558, 559
Akbari, H. M., 171
Akman, D., 390
Alafat, K. A., 42
Albee, G. W., 67, 529
Albersheim, L. J., 555
Albin, J. B., 549
Alessandri, S. M., 174
Alexander, J. F., 557
Alicke, M. D., 6, 468
Allen, J. P., 301, 335, 400, 417, 550, 551, 552, 553, 554, 555, 556, 557, 558, 563
Allen, L., 63, 472
Alloy, L., 296
Alpern, L., 291, 559
Altman, I., 144, 145, 146
Amaro, H., 168, 171, 176
Amato, P. R., 357, 360, 361, 362
Ames, C., 77, 78, 79, 84, 85, 86
Ames, R., 79
Ammerman, R. T., 390
Anand, P., 43
Anday, E. K., 173
Anderman, E. M., 36
Anderson, E. R., 121
Anderson, G., 209
Anderson, J., 251, 471, 510
Anderson, K., 589
Anderson, S. C., 441
Andreason, J. C., 276
Andrews, B., 393

Andrucci, G. L., 444
Angold, A., 275, 276
Anisfeld, E., 172
Anthony, E. J., 463
Anton, S. F., 178, 438, 40, 441, 444, 448
Antonovsky, A., 528
Arbisi, X., 301
Archer, J., 77, 85, 86
Archer, R. P., 444
Ardila, A., 179
Arendt, R., 172
Arkinson, J., 77
Armsden, G., 292, 429
Aronson, E., 43
Arroyo, C. G., 473, 474
Ashbrook, F., 200
Asher, S. R., 251
Asperger, H., 214, 218, 219
Astone, N. M., 476
Atkins, M. S., 402
Atkinson, J., 83
Atwood, A., 212
Ayers, W. A., 6
Ayoub, C., 333
Azmitia, E. C., 171
Azuma, S. D., 172

Babad, E., 80
Babigian, H., 528
Babor, T. F., 441
Bachman, J. G., 252
Baillargeon, R., 477
Baker, A. H., xvii
Baldwin, A. L., 317, 445, 471, 477, 520, 560
Baldwin, C., 317, 445, 471, 520, 560
Baldwin, D. V., 427
Balla, D., 3, 156, 157, 234, 237, 240, 335, 489
Ballenger, J., 276, 300
Ballou, M., 68
Baltes, P. B., 528
Bandura, A., 19, 419, 421, 422
Bank, L., 251
Barad, S., 427

602